THE CAMBRIDGE WO

*

VOLUME VI

The era from 1400 to 1800 saw intense biological, commercial, and cultural exchanges, and the creation of global connections on an unprecedented scale. Divided into two books, Volume VI of *The Cambridge World History* series considers these critical transformations. The first book examines the material and political foundations of the era, including global considerations of the environment, disease, technology, and cities, along with regional studies of empires in the eastern and western hemispheres, crossroads areas such as the Indian Ocean, Central Asia, and the Caribbean, and sites of competition and conflict, including Southeast Asia, Africa, and the Mediterranean. The second book focuses on patterns of change, examining the expansion of Christianity and Islam, migrations, warfare, and other topics on a global scale, and offering insightful detailed analyses of the Columbian Exchange, slavery, silver, trade, entrepreneurs, Asian religions, legal encounters, plantation economies, early industrialism, and the writing of history.

JERRY H. BENTLEY was Professor of History at the University of Hawaii at Manoa. He was the author of *Old World Encounters: Cross-Cultural Contact and Exchange in Pre-Modern Times* and *Traditions and Encounters*.

SANJAY SUBRAHMANYAM is Distinguished Professor of History, and the Irving and Jean Stone Endowed Chair in Social Sciences at the University of California, Los Angeles, and the Chair in Histoire Globale de la Première Modernité at the Collège de France. He is the author or editor of nearly thirty books, including *The Portuguese Empire in Asia, 1500–1700: A Political and Economic History*, *The Career and Legend of Vasco da Gama* (Cambridge, 1997), and *Indo-Persian Travels in the Age of Discoveries* (Cambridge, 2007).

MERRY E. WIESNER-HANKS is Distinguished Professor and Chair of the History Department at the University of Wisconsin-Milwaukee. She is the author or editor of twenty books, including *A Concise History of the World* (Cambridge, 2015), *Early Modern Europe 1450–1789* (Cambridge, 2nd edn., 2013), *Women and Gender in Early Modern Europe* (Cambridge, 3rd edn., 2008), *Christianity and Sexuality in the Early Modern World: Regulating Desire, Reforming Practice* and *Gender in History: Global Perspectives*.

The Cambridge World History is an authoritative new overview of the dynamic field of world history. It covers the whole of human history, not simply history since the development of written records, in an expanded time frame that represents the latest thinking in world and global history. With over two hundred essays, it is the most comprehensive account yet of the human past, and it draws on a broad international pool of leading academics from a wide range of scholarly disciplines. Reflecting the increasing awareness that world history can be examined through many different approaches and at varying geographic and chronological scales, each volume offers regional, topical, and comparative essays alongside case studies that provide depth of coverage to go with the breadth of vision that is the distinguishing characteristic of world history.

THE CAMBRIDGE WORLD HISTORY

*

VOLUME VI
The Construction of a Global World, 1400–1800 CE

Part 1: Foundations

*

Edited by
JERRY H. BENTLEY
University of Hawaii

SANJAY SUBRAHMANYAM
University of California, Los Angeles and Collège de France

MERRY E. WIESNER-HANKS
University of Wisconsin-Milwaukee

CAMBRIDGE
UNIVERSITY PRESS

CAMBRIDGE
UNIVERSITY PRESS

University Printing House, Cambridge CB2 8BS, United Kingdom

Cambridge University Press is part of the University of Cambridge.

It furthers the University's mission by disseminating knowledge in the pursuit of education, learning and research at the highest international levels of excellence.

www.cambridge.org
Information on this title: www.cambridge.org/9780521761628

© Cambridge University Press 2015

First published 2015
Paperback edition first published 2017

Printed in the United Kingdom by TJ International Ltd. Padstow Cornwall

A catalogue record for this publication is available from the British Library

ISBN 978-0-521-76162-8 Hardback
ISBN 978-1-108-40773-1 Paperback

In honor and memory of Jerry Bentley (1949–2012)

Contents

Contents

Contents

Figures

Maps

Tables

Contributors

THOMAS T. ALLSEN, University of Oregon
JERRY BENTLEY, University of Hawaii
FRANCESCA BRAY, University of Edinburgh
PETER BURKE, University of Cambridge
GIANCARLO CASALE, University of Minnesota
FILIPPO DE VIVO, University of London
JORGE FLORES, Brown University
JACK A. GOLDSTONE, George Mason University
JOS GOMMANS, Leiden University
LAURA HOSTETLER, University of Illinois at Chicago
ALAN L. KARRAS, University of California, Berkeley
RAY A. KEA, University of California, Riverside
MICHAEL LAFFAN, Princeton University
ROBERT B. MARKS, Whittier College
MATTHEW RESTALL, Penn State University
MORRIS ROSSABI, Columbia University
SANJAY SUBRAHMANYAM, University of California, Los Angeles, and Collège de France
JAMES L. A. WEBB, JR., Colby College
MERRY E. WIESNER-HANKS, University of Wisconsin-Milwaukee

Preface

The Cambridge Histories have long presented authoritative multi-volume overviews of historical topics, with chapters written by specialists. The first of these, the *Cambridge Modern History*, planned by Lord Acton and appearing after his death from 1902 to 1912, had fourteen volumes and served as the model for those that followed, which included the seven-volume *Cambridge Medieval History* (1911–1936), the twelve-volume *Cambridge Ancient History* (1924–1939), the thirteen-volume *Cambridge History of China* (1978–2009), and more specialized multi-volume works on countries, religions, regions, events, themes, and genres. These works are designed, as the *Cambridge History of China* puts it, to be the "largest and most comprehensive" history in the English language of their topic, and, as the *Cambridge History of Political Thought* asserts, to cover "every major theme."

The *Cambridge World History* both follows and breaks with the model set by its august predecessors. Presenting the "largest and most comprehensive" history of the world would take at least 300 volumes – and a hundred years – as would covering "every major theme." Instead the series provides an overview of the dynamic field of world history in seven volumes over nine books. It covers all of human history, not simply that since the development of written records, in an expanded time frame that represents the newest thinking in world history. This broad time frame blurs the line between archaeology and history, and presents both as complementary approaches to the human past. The volume editors include archaeologists as well as historians, and have positions at universities in the United States, Britain, France, Australia, and Israel. The essays similarly draw on a broad author pool of historians, art historians, anthropologists, classicists, archaeologists, economists, sociologists, and area studies specialists, who come from universities in Australia, Britain, Canada, China, France, Germany, India, Israel, Italy, Japan, the Netherlands, New Zealand, Sweden, Switzerland, Singapore, and the United States. They include very senior scholars whose works have helped to form the field, and also mid-career and younger scholars whose research will continue to shape it in the future. Some of the authors are closely associated with the rise of world history as a distinct research and teaching field, while others describe what they do primarily as global history, transnational history, international history, or comparative history. (Several of the essays in Volume I trace the development of these overlapping, entangled, and at times competing fields.) Many authors are simply specialists on their topic who the editors thought could best explain this to a broader audience or reach beyond their comfort zones into territory that was new.

Reflecting the increasing awareness that world history can be examined through many different approaches and at varying geographic and chronological scales, each volume

xvii

offers several types of essays, including regional, topical, and comparative ones, along with case studies that provide depth to go with the breadth of vision that is the distinguishing characteristic of world history. Volume I (*Introducing World History* [*to 10,000 BCE*]) introduces key frames of analysis that shape the making of world history across time periods, with essays on overarching approaches, methods, and themes. It then includes a group of essays on the Paleolithic, covering the 95 percent of human history up to 10,000 BCE. From that point on, each volume covers a shorter time period than its predecessor, with slightly overlapping chronologies volume to volume to reflect the complex periodization of a truly global history. The editors chose the overlapping chronologies, and stayed away from traditional period titles (e.g. "classical" or "early modern") intentionally to challenge standard periodization to some degree. The overlapping chronologies also allow each volume to highlight geographic disjunctures and imbalances, and the ways in which various areas influenced one another. Each of the volumes centers on a key theme or cluster of themes that the editors view as central to the period covered in the volume and also as essential to an understanding of world history as a whole.

Volume II (*A World with Agriculture, 12,000 BCE–500 CE*) begins with the Neolithic, but continues into later periods to explore the origins of agriculture and agricultural communities in various regions of the world, as well as to discuss issues associated with pastoralism and hunter-fisher-gatherer economies. It traces common developments in the more complex social structures and cultural forms that agriculture enabled, and then presents a series of regional overviews accompanied by detailed case studies from many different parts of the world.

Volume III (*Early Cities in Comparative Perspective, 4000 BCE–1200 CE*) focuses on early cities as motors of change in human society. Through case studies of cities and comparative chapters that address common issues, it traces the creation and transmission of administrative and information technologies, the performance of rituals, the distribution of power, and the relationship of cities with their hinterlands. It has a broad and flexible chronology to capture the development of cities in various regions of the world and the transformation of some cities into imperial capitals.

Volume IV (*A World with States, Empires, and Networks, 1200 BCE–900 CE*) continues the analysis of processes associated with the creation of larger-scale political entities and networks of exchange, including those generally featured in accounts of the rise of "classical civilizations," but with an expanded time frame that allows the inclusion of more areas of the world. It analyzes common social, economic, cultural, political, and technological developments, and includes chapters on slavery, religion, science, art, and gender. It then presents a series of regional overviews, each accompanied by a case study or two examining one smaller geographic area or topic within that region in greater depth.

Volume V (*Expanding Webs of Exchange and Conquest, 500 CE–1500 CE*) highlights the growing networks of trade and cross-cultural interaction that were a hallmark of the millennium covered in the volume, including the expansion of text-based religions and the transmission of science, philosophy, and technology. It explores social structures, cultural institutions, and significant themes such as the environment, warfare, education, the family, and courtly cultures on both a global and Eurasian scale, and continues the examination of state formation begun in Volume IV with chapters on polities and empires in Asia, Africa, Europe, and the Americas.

The first five volumes each appear in a single book, but the last two are double volumes covering the periods conventionally known as the early modern and modern, an organization signaling the increasing complexity of an ever more globalized world in the last half millennium, as well as the expanding base of source materials and existing historical analyses for these more recent eras. Volume VI (*The Construction of a Global World, 1400–1800 CE*) traces the increasing biological, commercial, and cultural exchanges of the period, and explores regional and transregional political, cultural, and intellectual developments. The first book within this volume, "Foundations," focuses on global matrices that allowed this increasingly interdependent world to be created, including the environment, technology, and disease; crossroads and macro-regions such as the Caribbean, the Indian Ocean, and Southeast Asia in which connections were especially intense; and large-scale political formations, particularly maritime and land-based empires such as Russia, the Islamic Empires, and the Iberian Empires that stretched across continents and seas. The second book within this volume, "Patterns of Change," examines global and regional migrations and encounters, and the economic, social, cultural, and institutional structures that both shaped and were shaped by these, including trade networks, law, commodity flows, production processes, and religious systems.

Volume VII (*Production, Destruction, and Connection, 1750–Present*) examines the uneven transition to a world with fossil fuels and an exploding human population that has grown ever more interactive through processes of globalization. The first book within this double volume, "Structures, Spaces, and Boundary Making," discusses the material situations within which our crowded world has developed, including the environment, agriculture, technology, energy, and disease; the political movements that have shaped it, such as nationalism, imperialism, decolonization, and communism; and some of its key regions. The second book, "Shared Transformations?", explores topics that have been considered in earlier volumes, including the family, urbanization, migration, religion, and science, along with some that only emerge as global phenomena in this era, such as sports, music, and the automobile, as well as specific moments of transition, including the Cold War and 1989.

Taken together, the volumes contain about 200 essays, which means the *Cambridge World History* is comprehensive, but certainly not exhaustive. Each volume editor has made difficult choices about what to include and what to leave out, a problem for all world histories since those of Herodotus and Sima Qian more than two millennia ago. Each volume is arranged in the way that the volume editor or editors have decided is most appropriate for the period, so that organizational schema differ slightly from volume to volume. Given the overlapping chronologies, certain topics are covered in several different volumes because they are important for understanding the historical processes at the heart of each of these, and because we as editors decided that viewing key developments from multiple perspectives is particularly appropriate for world history. As with other *Cambridge Histories*, the essays are relatively lightly footnoted, and include a short list of further readings, the first step for readers who want to delve deeper into the field. In contrast to other *Cambridge Histories*, all volumes are being published at the same time, for the leisurely pace of the print world that allowed publication over several decades does not fit with twenty-first-century digital demands.

In other ways as well, the *Cambridge World History* reflects the time in which it has been conceptualized and produced, just as the *Cambridge Modern History* did. Lord Acton envisioned his work, and Cambridge University Press described it, as "a history of the world," although in only a handful of chapters out of several hundred were the principal actors individuals, groups, or polities outside of Europe and North America. This is not surprising, although the identical self-description of the *New Cambridge Modern History* (1957–1979), with a similar balance of topics, might be a bit more so. The fact that in 1957 – and even in 1979 – Europe would be understood as "the world" and as the source of all that was modern highlights the power and longevity of the perspective we have since come to call "Eurocentric." (In other languages, there are perspectives on world history that are similarly centered on the regions in which they have been produced.) The continued focus on Europe in the mid-twentieth century also highlights the youth of the fields of world and global history, in which the conferences, professional societies, journals, and other markers of an up-and-coming field have primarily emerged since the 1980s, and some only within the last decade. The *Journal of World History*, for example, was first published in 1990, the *Journal of Global History* in 2005, and *New Global Studies* in 2007.

World and global history have developed in an era of intense self-reflection in all academic disciplines, when no term can be used unself-consciously and every category must be complicated. Worries about inclusion and exclusion, about diversity and multi-vocality are standard practice in sub-fields of history and related disciplines that have grown up in this atmosphere. Thus as we editors sought topics that would give us a balance between the traditional focus in world history on large-scale political and economic processes carried out by governments and commercial elites and newer concerns with cultural forms, representation, and meaning, we also sought to include topics that have been important in different national historiographies. We also attempted to find authors who would provide geographic balance along with a balance between older and younger voices. Although the author pool is decidedly broader geographically – and more balanced in terms of gender – than it was in either of the *Cambridge Modern Histories*, it is not as global as we had hoped. Contemporary world and global history is overwhelmingly Anglophone, and, given the scholarly diaspora, disproportionately insti-tutionally situated in the United States and the United Kingdom. Along with other disparities in our contemporary world, this disproportion is, of course, the result of the developments traced in this series, though the authors might disagree about which volume holds the key to its origins, or whether one should spend much time searching for origins at all.

My hopes for the series are not as sweeping as Lord Acton's were for his, but fit with those of Tapan Raychaudhuri and Irfan Habib, the editors of the two-volume *Cambridge Economic History of India* (1982). In the preface to their work, they comment: "We only dare to hope that our collaborative effort will stimulate discussion and help create new knowledge which may replace before many years the information and analysis offered in this volume." In a field as vibrant as world and global history, I have no doubts that such new transformative knowledge will emerge quickly, but hope this series will provide an entrée to the field, and a useful overview of its state in the early twenty-first century.

MERRY E. WIESNER-HANKS

Introduction

SANJAY SUBRAHMANYAM

Introduction

Although the practice of writing history on a large scale can be traced back many centuries – perhaps nearly as far back almost as the writing of history itself – each recent generation has refined and modified its habits in view of changes in method, as well as in perspective. Still, it is not a coincidence that the 'early modern' period has been the focus of a good deal of the exercise of writing 'world history' over the past half-century or so. Conventional dates of the Common Era such as 1453 – the fall of Constantinople to the Ottomans; 1492 – the year of the trans-Atlantic voyage of Columbus and of the expulsion of the Jews from Spain; 1498 – the voyage of Vasco da Gama to India; 1519 – when the Spanish *conquistadores* arrived in Mexico; or even 1522 – the return to Spain of Juan Sebastián Elcano from the voyage of circumnavigation begun by Ferdinand Magellan, have often been used since the nineteenth century to speak of an epochal shift, though usually in terms of what still remained a heavily Eurocentric history. More recent exercises have chosen other dates, based on different geographies. The death of the great Central Asian con-queror Amir Temür, or Tamerlane, at Otrar in February 1405 is sometimes taken to be one such moment, closing a cycle of universal empire-building that had begun with Chinggis Khan in the late twelfth and early thirteenth centuries.[1] The celebrated Ming maritime expeditions of the first third of the fifteenth century, which took Chinese fleets as far to the west as the East African coast, constitute another increasingly popular marker for world historians.

At the other end of the early modern period, as the eighteenth century drew to a close, and the world at large embarked on a distinctly industrial age based on the systematic harnessing of mechanical power, many writers

---

[1] John Darwin, *After Tamerlane: The Global History of Empire* (London: Allen Lane, 2007).

reflected on what the previous three or four centuries had wrought by way of change, and they often came to the conclusion that the period that was ending was momentous for the world in more ways than one. One of the most celebrated, not to say clichéd, evocations comes to us from the pen of the Scottish philosopher and political economist Adam Smith (1723 to 1790). In Book IV of his *An Inquiry into the Nature and Causes of the Wealth of Nations*, published in the fatal year of 1776, Smith thus stated:

> The discovery of America, and that of a passage to the East Indies by the Cape of Good Hope, are the two greatest and most important events recorded in the history of mankind. Their consequences have already been very great; but, in the short period of between two and three centuries which has elapsed since these discoveries were made, it is impossible that the whole extent of their consequences can have been seen. What benefits or what misfortunes to mankind may hereafter result from those great events, no human wisdom can foresee. By uniting, in some measure, the most distant parts of the world, by enabling them to relieve one another's wants, to increase one another's enjoyments, and to encourage one another's industry, their general tendency would seem to be beneficial.[2]

Smith's position here is typical of his thinking, but also somewhat more subtle than is sometimes suspected. He excludes from the comparison of the 'greatest and most important events' the human discovery of fire or the invention of the wheel, since these were not 'recorded' events in the history of mankind. As for 1492 and 1498, he highlights them precisely in terms of suggesting that contact and commerce are in general to be preferred to isolation and autarchy, since they increase the benefits to all participants through the division of labour and specialization. But he is also commendably cautious in distinguishing between ideal and reality.

> To the natives, however, both of the East and West Indies, all the commercial benefits which can have resulted from those events have been sunk and lost in the dreadful misfortunes which they have occasioned. These misfortunes, however, seem to have arisen rather from accident than from anything in the nature of those events themselves. At the particular time when these discoveries were made, the superiority of force happened to be so great on the side of the Europeans that they were enabled to commit with impunity every sort of injustice in those remote countries. Hereafter, perhaps, the natives of those countries may grow stronger, or those of

---

[2] Adam Smith, *An Inquiry into the Nature and Causes of the Wealth of Nations*, Edwin Cannan (ed.), 2 vols (London: Methuen, 1904), vol. 2, p. 125.

Europe may grow weaker, and the inhabitants of all the different quarters of the world may arrive at that equality of courage and force which, by inspiring mutual fear, can alone overawe the injustice of independent nations into some sort of respect for the rights of one another. But nothing seems more likely to establish this equality of force than that mutual communication of knowledge and of all sorts of improvements which an extensive commerce from all countries to all countries naturally, or rather necessarily, carries along with it.

In other words, Smith recognized that one of the characteristic features of the preceding three centuries had been the creation and consolidation of great colonial empires (typically centred in Europe), which had proceeded to commit 'every sort of injustice' rather than simply embarking on 'improvements'. Further, the Scottish savant did not simply lay such charges at the door of the benighted Catholic Iberians; as is well known, he reserves some of the most savage criticisms in his text for the behaviour of the East India Companies founded by the Dutch and English nations.[3] Still, his use of the term 'accident' to place in parenthesis many inconvenient and painful historical processes can only appear to us today to be inadequate. In turn, such a recourse to euphemism has to be explained, as we shall see below, by a particular form of teleology, wherein such 'accidents' could be juxtaposed to the very inherent 'nature' of the broad historical process, the direction of which was already largely determined.

Adam Smith is generally recognized as one of the key innovative figures of the later phase of the Western European Enlightenment, but he shared many ideas with other thinkers of that broad movement. In his case, a particular emphasis on political economy meant that he saw the immediately preceding centuries as a struggle between forces that were attempting to stifle or control exchanges of goods and ideas (what he and others summed up under the broad heading of 'mercantilist' thinking and action), and other, far more positive, tendencies which gave humanity the possibility to engage in its natural 'propensity to truck, barter, and exchange one thing for another'. For him, the normal or default tendency of human societies was towards 'the natural progress of opulence'. Further, he writes, 'had human institutions, therefore, never disturbed the natural course of things, the progressive wealth and increase of the towns would, in every political society, be consequential, and in proportion to the improvement and cultivation of the

---

[3] See the fine analysis by Sankar Muthu, *Enlightenment against Empire* (Princeton University Press, 2003).

territory or country'. Thus, despite some notable caveats and reservations, Smith saw human history as regulated by a powerful motor of progress, itself underpinned by strong characteristic features of human nature.

Could one have found such a view expressed in Europe three centuries earlier? In certain respects, Smith's position shares with a broad swathe of earlier thinkers a distinct faith in a history that has both a direction and an end, in short what the German philosopher Christian Wolff first defined in 1728 as 'teleology'. Wolff himself, while professing a deep and abiding interest in distant lands such as China, was however very much intellectually located in Christian theology, albeit in a rationalistic strain thereof.[4] Smith's rather materialistic understanding of the idea of progress would therefore not have found much of an echo with him, and even less in writers of the sixteenth century in Europe, or even the Mediterranean world. For such writers, the dominant paradigm for understanding large-scale history was an eschatological one, which sometimes shaded off into more constrained forms of providentialism with a reduction in scale. The sixteenth century saw an expansion and propagation of many such views for a variety of reasons. For most Europeans, and Iberians in particular, the opening of new routes for trade and spaces for conquest was a divine confirmation of their own status as agents in a process of eschatological revelation. Columbus, it was later recalled by his son Hernando Colón, was not merely an adept of Franciscan millenarianism, but also read much into Seneca's celebrated passage from *Medea* with its phrase *nec sit terris ultima Thule*. In the *Libro de las Profecías*, written in the early sixteenth century, Columbus offered his own loose translation of Seneca as follows.

> In the late years of the world shall come certain times when the Ocean Sea shall loosen the bonds of things; a great land shall open up and a new seaman like the one who was Jason's steersman and who was called Tiphys shall discover a new world, and then the island of Thule shall no longer be the outermost of lands.[5]

Later Iberian writers like Bartolomé de las Casas, López de Gómara and even José de Acosta would continue to find in the Senecan text, if not a holy prophecy, then at least something akin to the sibylline texts in which the ancients presciently saw what the moderns would come to achieve. Such forms of reasoning and historical emplotment went far beyond the Christian

---

[4] Charles A. Corr, 'The Existence of God, Natural Theology and Christian Wolff', *International Journal for Philosophy of Religion*, 4(2) (1973), 105–18.

[5] As cited in Sabine MacCormack, *On the Wings of Time: Rome, the Incas, Spain and Peru* (Princeton University Press, 2007), p. 248.

world, even if they were not always intended to analyse the same sequences
of events. For Muslims, the tenth century of their Hegiran calendar began in
1494 to 1495 of the Common Era, and ended in 1591 to 1592. As a consequence
of this brute calendric fact, there was both much popular expectation and
sophisticated theological speculation on what that century would bring in
terms of world-historical events. Several monarchs of the Muslim world,
from those of Morocco to the Ottoman Empire, to Mughal India, seized the
occasion to present their own claims as the central millenarian figures that
would 'renew' the Muslim community. Key amongst them were the Ottoman ruler Süleyman the Lawgiver (r. 1520 to 1566), and the Mughal emperor
Jalal-ud-Din Muhammad Akbar (r. 1556 to 1605).[6] While Süleyman's claims
were made in the context of a titanic struggle for control over both the
Mediterranean and Central Europe with the Habsburgs (and notably Charles V),
Akbar made his own later ambitions known in a context that included not
only Christians (both Armenians and Iberian Catholics), but also his many
and diverse 'Hindu' subjects. In each of these imperial projects, the claim
was that of introducing a form of universal peace (what the Mughal called
sulh-i kull), permitting diverse communities to coexist and prosper. Significantly, both these rulers promoted the writing of powerful ideological texts
that tried to sustain their arguments, drawing both on theology and on other
sources, including secular histories. The cultural confidence of the Mughals
is evident in letters, such as the following one written in 1581, on behalf of
Akbar, to the Habsburg ruler Philip II:

> It is not concealed and veiled from the minds of intelligent people, who have
> received the light of divine aid and are illuminated by the rays of wisdom
> and knowledge, that in this terrestrial world, which is the mirror of the
> celestial, there is nothing that excels love and no propensity so worthy of
> cultivation as philanthropy, because the peace of the world and the harmony
> of existence are based upon friendship and association, and in each heart
> illuminated by the rays of the sun of love, the world of the soul, or the
> faculties of the mind are by them purged of human darkness; and much
> more is this the case, when they subsist between monarchs, peace among
> whom implies the peace of the world and of the denizens thereof.

Composed by Akbar's chief ideologue of the time, the celebrated Shaikh
Abu'l Fazl ibn Mubarak, this opening passage is thus a call for peaceful

---

[6] Sanjay Subrahmanyam, 'Turning the Stones Over: Sixteenth-century Millenarianism
from the Tagus to the Ganges', *Indian Economic and Social History Review*, 40(3) (2003),
131–63.

exchange, at a great distance from the realities of Mughal–Habsburg relations, which consisted of an ongoing series of petty skirmishes both on land and on sea. The next passage then embarks on a still bolder gambit, relativizing the truth of various religions:

> As most men are fettered by the bonds of tradition, and by imitating the ways followed by their fathers, ancestors, relatives and acquaintances, every one continues, without investigating the arguments and reasons, to follow the religion in which he was born and educated, thus excluding himself from the possibility of ascertaining the truth, which is the noblest aim of the human intellect. Therefore we associate at convenient seasons with learned men of all religions, and thus derive profit from their exquisite discourses and exalted aspirations.[7]

The letter then goes on to ask that the Habsburgs send the Mughals an authentic version of the Christian scriptures, so that they might examine them in the context of wide-ranging discussions in their court. The implication here is that the Mughal ruler, as a millenarian and messianic figure, pretty much stands above religions and their petty differences. Rather than promoting a project for the worldwide spread of a single faith, the Mughals claim to stand here for a policy of balance, in which different communities and their beliefs can find a place.

This exchange between Mughals and Habsburgs allows us to consider at least one broad framework within which early modern world history could be conceived and written, namely that of inter-imperial competition. About a dozen significant empires of varying dimensions can be said to have existed between about 1400 and 1800. These would include the Russian state based at Moscow and expanding to the east and southeast, the Chinese state of the Ming and Qing dynasties, the Mughal Empire in South Asia, the Ottoman domains stretching from Basra and Baghdad in the east to the Maghreb in the west, and the Spanish, Portuguese, French, British and Dutch Empires. Other imperial projects of shorter duration can be found in Central Asia, Southeast Asia and also arguably in pre-Columbian Mesoamerica. These empires coexisted in turn with smaller states, sometimes by co-opting them into larger systems, but also by using them as ideological foils – as we can see in the relationship between Safavid Iran, on the one hand, and the Ottoman and Mughal Empires on the other. At the same time, it is one of the characteristics of the early modern period that no single empire from

---

[7] Edward Rehatsek, 'A letter of the Emperor Akbar asking for the Christian Scriptures', *Indian Antiquary*, 16 (April 1887), 135–39.

amongst these achieved a hegemonic status, even to the extent that the British Empire was able to do so in the nineteenth century. The greatest of the early modern imperial enterprises in terms of physical extent at least (if not of population) was the joint Hispano-Portuguese monarchy of the period 1580 to 1640. Although three Habsburg rulers of that time claimed that they ruled notionally over the 'four parts of the world' (in the sense of having possessions in the four continents – albeit not in Australia), they could never claim a real superiority or domination over some of the other empires of the time.[8]

From this simple political fact alone, we can deduce that early modern world history should not be written from a single centre, and that it must necessarily be thought of as polyphonic. It would be a signal error to see these centuries as just preparing the ground for the hegemonic systems that would emerge later, and we would thus ourselves succumb to a particularly simplistic form of teleological thinking. Processes leading towards unification and homogenization certainly existed, but they were also accompanied by other processes which led to political, economic and cultural division and fragmentation. This is one of the reasons why not every significant trend of this period can be summed up under the heading of a single characterizing scheme such as 'globalization'. It is precisely in order to have a better grasp of this complexity that we have chosen in these volumes to vary scales of analysis, as well as varying the points of perspective. Before turning to a consideration of these, however, some further macroscopic considerations may be in order.

Debates and differences

The two parts of Volume 6 of the *The Cambridge World History* essentially concern the 'early modern' centuries, those running from about 1400 to 1800. This is a period characterized by an intensification of long-distance contacts, best symbolized perhaps by Ferdinand Magellan's project of a voyage of global circumnavigation from west to east. Magellan (in Portuguese: Fernão de Magalhães) was born into a family of minor nobility in the north of Portugal in about 1480, and first made his way to the Indian Ocean when he was about 25 years of age. There, he participated in a number of naval combats, and came to acquire first-hand knowledge of Southeast Asia in the

---

[8] Serge Gruzinski, *Les Quatre Parties du Monde: Histoire d'une mondialisation* (Paris: La Martinière, 2004).

aftermath of the Portuguese conquest of the great port-city of Melaka in August 1511. On returning to Portugal, he was eventually disappointed with the rewards he received for his services, and therefore resolved to mount his project of circumnavigation from west to east with Spanish support, using his own cartographic knowledge as well as the networks of correspondents and informants he possessed in the larger Iberian world. Magellan misread the location of the anti-meridian defining the geographic partition between Spaniards and Portuguese, and claimed that a significant part of the Moluccas (or Spice Islands) could be seen as falling to the Spanish Crown. He was thus able to gather enough financial support to set out with a fleet of five vessels and some 230 men in late September 1519, and after numerous difficulties entered the Pacific Ocean over a year later, at the end of 1520. By March, Magellan found himself in the Philippines, and began a process there of trade and negotiation, amply mixed with threats of violence. A reaction inevitably ensued, and the Portuguese captain was eventually killed on the small island of Mactan (near Cebu) in April 1521. The feeble remnants of the fleet eventually limped home to Spain in early September 1522, just under three years from the day of their departure. Yet, when compared to the voyages of 1492 and 1498, there is a reason that this voyage of 1519 to 1522 stands out. Conceptually, in terms of the redefinition of space that it produced, and its implications for cosmography, it may be seen as more important in many ways than Gama's voyage a quarter of a century earlier. But it also remained orphaned, in the sense of having no rapid follow-up or consolidation. The expeditions of García Jofre de Loyasa and Álvaro de Saavedra in 1525 to 1527 were unable to return to their points of departure, and the same fate befell the Grijalva and Villalobos expeditions of the late 1530s and early 1540s. It was not until 1565, then, that Andrés de Urdaneta was able successfully to complete a return voyage from the Philippines to New Spain, making a trans-Pacific economic and cultural link a real possibility on an ongoing basis.[9]

From the last quarter of the sixteenth century onwards then, the idea of an integrated global history based on the existence of worldwide networks of trade, exchange, conquest and circulation can be thought to have at least partly become a reality. American plants, birds and even some animals now reached the Indian Ocean not only via the Atlantic and Europe, but directly through the Pacific. The so-called 'Manila Galleon', which linked together the Mexican port of Acapulco and the Philippines, was perhaps a fragile

---

[9] Avelino Teixeira da Mota (ed.), *A viagem de Fernão de Magalhães e a questão das Molucas* (Lisbon: Junta de Investigações Científicas do Ultramar, 1975).

thread, but it was nevertheless an important one. To some extent, Asian spices and other plants were also to have an impact on the Americas as a result. Not only administrators and powerful traders, but even more humble travellers with some degree of curiosity, could think of making a voyage around the world. An important early example is the Italian Francesco Carletti, who after trading slaves alongside his father in the Atlantic, then embarked on a voyage that took him from Mexico and Peru to the Philippines, to China and Japan, then to Goa, and eventually back to his native Italy, where he wrote his *Ragionamenti*, devoted to his circumnavigation between the years 1594 and 1602. His rough contemporary was the Breton Pierre-Olivier Malherbe, who claimed for his part to have made a leisurely voyage around the world from 1581 onwards, eventually returning to his native France only in 1608. Malherbe was to boast not only of having known the Mughal emperor Akbar, but of having 'gone by land from New Spain or Mexico, where he stayed a long time, to Peru and the extremity of the kingdom of Chile, making it a point to see all that was rare and singular by way of cities, inhabitants, countries, plants, animals, and ruins'. Not least of all, Malherbe claimed he had 'seen and descended [the mine] of Potosí, where he learned to be a great miner of metals, since the said [mine] is the richest in the world, and has no end to it'.[10]

This evocation of the iconic Bolivian mine of Potosí was to be very nearly an obligatory point of passage from the last third of the sixteenth century onwards. The mine came to stand not only for the unparalleled riches of America (also evoked in the celebrated myth of El-Dorado), but for the Spanish Empire that largely controlled them. But these were ambiguous riches, as we already see in the closing years of the sixteenth century, when the precious metals brought by the returning Spanish fleets to Europe were blamed for inflation and social instability in Iberia, as well as in the world beyond, even as far as the Ottoman Empire. A widespread 'decline' literature began to arise in this period, in which empire and its attendant novelties were portrayed as much as a curse as a blessing. However, it is now increasingly clear that a good part of Potosí's silver went not to Europe, but across the Pacific. In other words, the substantial Chinese demand for silver in the period was met in part through the ramifications of the

---

[10] See Grégoire Holtz, 'Pierre-Olivier Malherbe: The Journey of a Manuscript from India to France (First Half of the 17th Century)' in Vijaya Rao, (ed.), *Reaching the Great Moghul: Francophone Travel Writing on India of the 17th and 18th Centuries* (New Delhi: Yoda Press, 2012), pp. 20–39.

Acapulco–Manila link, as a complex trade-pattern grew up linking Manila, Melaka, the Portuguese settlement of Macau and the port of Nagasaki in southern Japan. It was also through this network that the first Tokugawa ambassadors appeared in Mexico in 1614, en route to Europe, attracting the attention of the Nahuatl-language chronicler Chimalpahín. Again, the first colonies of East Asians who appeared in American cities such as Lima and Mexico clearly traversed this passage, as did a good many of the more ambitious merchants of the time, whether *marranos* or Armenians.

Every history of the early modern period is thus at least partly a history of trade and merchants, who were the most conspicuous actors of the period alongside the usual warriors and conquerors who populate earlier epochs as well. Two of the most substantial attempts to write early modern world histories in the second half of the twentieth century demonstrate this fact well enough. The first is Fernand Braudel's three-volume work, *Civilisation matérielle, économie et capitalisme, XVe-XVIIIe siècle*, which first appeared in 1979, and was translated soon after into English and a host of other languages.[11] The second, more schematic and certainly more controversial, is the historical sociologist Immanuel Wallerstein's *The Modern World-System*, the first volume of which – largely devoted to the sixteenth century – appeared already in 1974, and of which subsequent volumes dealing with the periods from 1600 to 1750, from the 1730s to the 1840s, and from 1789 to 1914, have since been published.[12] Braudel in his volumes evoked the encounters between different 'world-economies' (*économies-mondes*) at a variety of levels, defining a 'world-economy' as 'a fragment of the universe, a part of the planet that is economically autonomous, and essentially capable of being self-sufficient, and whose connections and internal exchanges give it a certain organic unity'. From this perspective, quite large zones such as the Indian Ocean, pre-Columbian America or the Russian Empire could be thought of in the fifteenth or sixteenth centuries as 'world-economies', without a clear hierarchy between them. While each of these 'world-economies' might possess some degree of internal differentiation, their interactions might then produce further integration or frictional conflict, with no outcome being considered as historically inevitable. Braudel's world history, while largely focused on material life, nevertheless remained remarkably open-ended.

---

[11] Fernand Braudel, *Civilization and Capitalism*, Siân Reynolds, (trans.), 3 vols (London: Collins, 1981–4).

[12] Immanuel Wallerstein, *The Modern World-System*, re-edn, 4 vols (1974–2011) (Berkeley, CA: University of California Press, 2011).

In contrast, Wallerstein's vision can better be compared to a deterministic model, located in a clear if apparently unstated teleology. Here, the creation of a modern and capitalistic 'world-system' is essentially the work of European agents acting over ever wider spaces. It is the dynamism of the Western European economy, emerging from the demographic collapse of the latter half of the fourteenth century, that permits the progressive 'incorporation' of other parts of the world, which become subordinate to the powerful European core that is first located in the Iberian Peninsula, and then shifts to northern centres such as Amsterdam and London, as we move from the sixteenth into the seventeenth century. The building of the 'world-system' is thus coterminous with the traditional narrative of a succession of European empires, first constrained by their subordination to the remnants of 'feudal' institutions, and then increasingly liberated from them. Thus, first America, then the Indian Ocean, and eventually the Islamic World and Africa, are brought into the ambit of this unified system, as 'peripheries' in relation to a dynamic European core. Posed ostensibly in the language of 'dependency theory', and as a variant of the grand Marxist narrative, it has been claimed sometimes by critics that Wallerstein represents a 'neo-Smithian Marxism'.[13] But this may be giving a less than fair treatment to Adam Smith, who in fact had a rather sceptical view of the functioning of the key European mercantile institutions of the seventeenth and eighteenth centuries. Rather, Wallerstein's project represents the apogee of an unapologetically Eurocentric world history, which is dismissive of the dynamic potential of most non-European societies, whose fate seems to be to await more or less passively their formal conquest, or informal 'incorporation' by European agents. Societies like those of South and East Asia, or of the Middle East and Africa, are assimilated here into some variant of an 'Asiatic Mode of Production', a sort of historic slumber of homeostasis from which only contact with Europe will awaken them.

It was thus only natural that Wallerstein's construct would evoke sceptical reactions amongst historians of the non-European world, who had long struggled against hegemonic models such as those of 'Oriental Despotism' (revived by Karl Wittfogel in a controversial work of 1957), and the 'Asiatic Mode of Production', which had also known a number of late avatars. These reactions took a number of different forms, of which at least three principal ones can be enumerated. The first was the work of macro-historians and

---

[13] Robert Brenner, 'The Origins of Capitalist Development: A Critique of Neo-Smithian Marxism', *New Left Review*, 104 (1977), 25–92.

historical sociologists, who pointed to the inadequacy of core–periphery models in rendering a sufficiently subtle account of the variety of institutional arrangements that existed in the sixteenth or seventeenth centuries to organise trade and exchange. Thus, the trade between India and Central Asia, or India and East Africa, already involved a considerable degree of differentiation and specialization. Central Asian elites came to dominate some of the major political systems of South Asia, while at the same time powerful South Asian traders came to control some of the key Central Asian markets, to cite but one example. The complex relationship between the Mughal and Safavid domains is another thorny matter. Could one really talk of a north Indian 'core' in relationship to an Iranian 'periphery', to cite another example? Similar questions could be asked with regard to the relationship between coastal China, Korea and Japan.

A second set of concrete doubts emanated from the work of comparative historians, who set about asking whether systematic comparisons between European and non-European institutions always redounded in favour of the former. If this were indeed so, how did Armenian, Hokkienese or Gujarati traders not only survive, but even prosper in the face of stiff European competition until well into the eighteenth century? Similarly, historians of science and technology suggested that a triumphant European narrative, wherein the rest of the world was already subordinate to the hegemony of a purely home-grown European science and technology by 1700 or 1750, was something of a mirage. These comparative projects eventually gave rise to two broad debates by the end of the twentieth century. One, more focused on economic indicators, was that on the 'great divergence', and centred on when Western Europe effectively diverged in its economic trajectory from the rest of Eurasia; in recent years, the debate has largely dealt with the question as it is posed in the context of the Europe–China comparison by Kenneth Pomeranz.[14] The second debate, more concerned with political institutions and political culture, has developed around the wide-ranging synthesis proposed by Victor Lieberman through the paradigm of 'strange parallels'. Here, Lieberman argues that a number of distinct trajectories were possible in Eurasia over the long term (say 800 and 1800 CE), but that they do not correspond to the core-periphery geographies of older 'world-systems'

---

[14] Kenneth Pomeranz, *The Great Divergence: China, Europe and the Making of the Modern World Economy* (Princeton University Press, 2000); Jean-Laurent Rosenthal and R. Bin Wong, *Before and Beyond Divergence: The Politics of Economic Change in China and Europe* (Cambridge, MA: Harvard University Press, 2011).

theory.[15] On the one hand, the unifying factors in Eurasian history are brought out; and on the other hand, it is suggested that even a space like Southeast Asia or Western Europe should in fact be carefully separated into varying trends.

A third tendency that has been visible since the 1980s is one that challenges the Wallersteinian perspective on account of its empirical poverty and monophonic character. Here, the emphasis is much more on the richness and variety of source-materials that can be tapped with regard to the early modern period, which thus also have the effect of creating a far more nuanced vision of historical agency.[16] Wallerstein's view of the Portuguese in the Indian Ocean, to take one example, is made up of claims such as that 'Vasco da Gama came, saw, and conquered far more and far faster than Julius Caesar', and that as a result 'in a very few years, Portuguese ships completely dominated the extensive trade of the Indian Ocean'.[17] Such a stance simply cannot be sustained in view of a variety of source-materials now available to us in Arabic, Persian and Ottoman; and indeed, even a close reading of the Portuguese archives of the period show it to be unsustainable. The growing literature on 'encounters' now leads us away from such one-dimensional renditions to a closer reading of sources, which give us a sense of the fine grain of situations, and the tangled threads of actors' motivations. This then is partly a question of scale in history-writing. The shifting focal points the reader will find in various chapters of Volume 6 of the *Cambridge World History* therefore represent an attempt to capture some of the problems of grappling with a variety of source-materials in the writing of world history.

Demography and material life

It remains for us to deal with a few other important questions of a macro-scopic level in this Introduction, before setting out the structure and logic of the volumes themselves. One of these, which has also naturally concerned the editors of other volumes, is the question of demography posed on a worldwide scale. As we are generally aware, population statistics are both

---

[15] Victor B. Lieberman, *Strange Parallels*, 2 vols (New York: Cambridge University Press, 2003–9). Also see the responses, often rather critical, to Lieberman's ideas in Victor B. Lieberman (ed.), *Beyond Binary Histories: Re-imagining Eurasia to c.1830* (Ann Arbor, MI: University of Michigan Press, 1999).

[16] See e.g. Frank Perlin, *The Invisible City: Monetary, Administrative, and Popular Infrastruc-tures in Asia and Europe, 1500–1900* (Aldershot: Variorum-Ashgate, 1993); also Sugata Bose (ed.), *South Asia and World Capitalism* (Delhi: Oxford University Press, 1990).

[17] Wallerstein, *Modern World-System*, vol. 1, pp. 215–16.

Table 1.1 *Estimate of world population, 1400–1800 (millions)*

Year	Asia	Europe	Africa	America	Oceania	World
1400	203	63	68	39	2	375
1500	247	82	87	42	3	461
1600	341	108	113	13	3	578
1700	437	121	107	12	3	680
1750	505	141	104	18	3	771
1800	638	188	102	24	2	954

unreliable and uneven for the centuries before 1800. Any estimates are thus based on heroic assumptions and extrapolations, and are better treated therefore as 'guesstimates'. Here is one such broad view for the centuries under survey in these volumes.[18]

These figures provided by the Italian demographer Massimo Livi-Bacci, based on an earlier estimate by Jean-Noël Biraben, while necessarily subject to caution, are nevertheless a useful point of departure for a discussion of world population. He suggests that in about 1400, the world's population was somewhat lower than that in 1200, mainly on account of the intervention in the fourteenth century of massive waves of the Eurasian plague. He then sees population growth as continuing more or less uninterrupted over the next four centuries, with a marked acceleration after about 1750. However, this growth is also accompanied by some significant redistribution. Asia, which had accounted in 1400 for 54 per cent of world population, had increased its share in 1800 to as much as 67 per cent. Europe's share of population was 16 per cent in 1400, and over 19 per cent four centuries later. The most substantial transformation in the negative direction was caused by the American population collapse of the sixteenth century, with only a partial recovery being evident even as late as 1800, based in part on processes of migration – very largely from Africa and Europe.

The difficulties with these numbers can be seen by comparing them to an alternative projection, from the economic historian Angus Maddison. The two sets of numbers are not entirely dissimilar, but they do diverge in some interesting respects. Maddison's global figures for 1500, 1600 and 1700 are always below those of Biraben and Livi-Bacci, sometimes by a factor of over

---

[18] Massimo Livi-Bacci, *A Concise History of World Population*, 5th edn (Chichester: Wiley-Blackwell, 2012), p. 25; this is largely based on Jean-Noël Biraben, 'Essai sur l'évolution du nombre des hommes', *Population*, 34(1) (1979), 13–25.

Table 1.2 *An alternative estimate of world population, 1500–1820 (millions)*

Year	China	India	Europe	Africa	L. America	Total*
1500	103	110	71	47	17.5	438
1600	160	135	90	55	8.6	556
1700	138	165	100	61	12	603
1820	381	209	169	74	21.6	1,041

*Note: some areas have been omitted, so the totals shown here are not the sum of the five areas specified in the table.

10 per cent. It is only at the very end of the period, in the early nineteenth century, that their figures finally appear to converge.[19]

Further, Maddison's estimates have the advantage of pointing to a brute fact of early modern history, namely that India and China between the two of them appear to have accounted for half (or at times slightly over half) of the world's population. But we may also emphasize a significant difference in the two chronologies. Unlike Biraben and Livi-Bacci, who see a growth rate of around 18 per cent between 1600 and 1700, Maddison is quite reserved regarding population growth in the seventeenth century, which he perceives as barely attaining 8.5 per cent over the whole period. As we can see from Table 1.2, this is largely accounted for by a significant fall in the Chinese population according to his estimates for the period. This pessimistic view of world demography in the seventeenth century has recently been given further support by Geoffrey Parker, in an ambitious attempt at a total global history for the period. Parker argues that a combination of negative climatic events (the 'Little Ice Age') and other natural phenomena, taken together with incessant war-making and poor political management, created a situation wherein the global population actually fell in absolute numbers – much as it had in the fourteenth century. In his view, which is in fact more extreme than that of Maddison, 'with the exception of Japan, New England and New France, the demographic balance of the seventeenth century was negative'.[20] This would separately imply a fall in population not only for China, but also for Europe and India, trends that are not currently accepted in a universal manner by demographers of the latter two regions. It is thus worth noting

---

[19] Angus Maddison's estimates are widely available on a number of websites, such as www.ggdc.net/MADDISON/oriindex.htm. See also Angus Maddison, *The World Economy: A Millennial Perspective* (Paris: OECD, 2001).

[20] Geoffrey Parker, *Global Crisis: War, Climate Change and Catastrophe in the Seventeenth Century* (New Haven, CT: Yale University Press, 2013), p. 674.

that we are even today far from attaining a consensus with regard to all the basic trends in world demography for the early modern period.

If this is the case even with such a relatively simple matter as demography, the matter is immeasurably more complicated when one turns to questions such as the comparative study of production, revenues, standards of living and the like. The debate sparked off by the publication of Pomeranz's thesis on the 'great divergence' has already been mentioned above. To sum the matter up in broad terms, Pomeranz wished to challenge an older consensus which posited that by the seventeenth or early eighteenth centuries, many parts of Western Europe already enjoyed a far higher standard of living than even the most prosperous parts of the non-European world (and notably Asia and Africa). The significance of this claim had been twofold. The first was to suggest that Europe had enjoyed a long and unique cultural trajectory that had enabled it to produce unique and superior institutions that were in turn singularly well adapted to give birth to prosperous societies. The second aspect was the implication that European prosperity of the nineteenth and earlier twentieth centuries owed little or nothing to the building of colonial empires, but instead had far older roots going back into early modern times, if not earlier still. In contrast, Pomeranz wished to argue, first, that the alleged 'divergence' had begun rather late, and second, that it could not be divorced from the creation of European empires in the Atlantic which enabled certain crucial resources to be made available at cheap rates. While a part of the debate that has followed has been empirical – namely identifying appropriate data with which to refine the comparison, as well as extend it to other regions of the world like South Asia, much of it has undoubtedly been strongly motivated by rather elementary ideological considerations. These include the desire on the part of some historians to defend the 'exceptional-ism' of European values, a question not unrelated to the contemporary politics of migration in Europe. But they also touch upon a large and thorny question, namely attitudes towards colonialism and in particular the Euro-pean colonial empires. One can see why it may be necessary from certain ideological standpoints to divorce the question of European prosperity from the colonial question. For to argue that European industrialization and prosperity were in some way linked to unequal power relations with the rest of the world would not only sully the immaculate birth of European modernity, but might even lend itself to the language of 'reparations'.

At any rate, it would seem that the part of the Pomeranz Debate that has enabled a widening of the body of empirical materials from which compari-sons can be made has been somewhat fruitful. More technical debates on how comparisons should be made, and what should be compared, are also of some significance. But what is also glaringly evident is the extremely thin basis of the comparisons, even as they are made today. To take but one world region into account, namely South Asia, materials on standards of living are so thin, and so limited to a few coastal regions, that it is clear that we have no real sense today of variations within South Asia, let alone differences between South Asia taken as a whole, and China, East Africa or England. It thus appears that we are still very often better off with qualitative comparisons, with all their limitations, than with the illusory certitudes of quantitative comparisons, especially if these in reality reflect no more than the ideological prejudices of those making the comparisons. Whether these qualitative exercises are in turn of an extremely wide-ranging character, such as that of Lieberman mentioned above, or more limited examinations of two or more trajectories, is quite another matter. Certainly, issues such as the nature of political institutions or cultural complexes are far more amenable to this type of analysis.

In an exercise such as this in world history, we are thus obliged in one fashion or another to engage, whether explicitly or implicitly, with a certain number of debates regarding the appropriate conceptual categories to be deployed. Given the nature of the historical profession today, it is largely inevitable that no tight epistemological consensus underlies these chapters, even as a certain variety of viewpoints can be found in any academic institution devoted today to the study of history. While the problem of convergence-divergence animates some of the writings that follow, other authors have chosen quite different angles of attack. Some privilege ideas of connection rather than comparison, whether such connections are of a material nature – goods, monetary media, microbes, animal species and so on – or in terms of cultural flows. Within this tendency, there are also historians who maintain a greater or lesser distance from classic ideas of diffusion or 'transfer'. Again, the weight given to material and cultural phenomena often varies a great deal from chapter to chapter and from one historian to another. And yet, despite this diversity, there is little doubt that these volumes bear the unmistakable stamp of the time in which they are written, and can hardly be mistaken for exercises in world history from the early twentieth century, or even from 1950. To take but one obvious instance, even if the preoccupation is not entirely new, historians of the early twenty-first century are particularly mindful of problems linked to the environment, to the fragile nature of the ties between men and nature, as well as to the concerns caused by the non-renewability of many of the resources on which the prosperity of modern societies is based. Even if many of these limits were made evident in recent times, it is no coincidence that the Senecan prophecy regarding Thule, 'the last of the lands', played the part it did already in the imagination of the sixteenth century. Early modern experiences with 'island Edens' and the destruction of many 'exotic' species certainly had a part to play in the matter, as historians of the last generation have taken pains to underline.[21]

An overview

The architecture of these twin volumes requires some explanation, as do some of the choices that have been made for the inclusion and exclusion of themes. The first book in the volume, *Foundations*, opens with a section entitled 'Global matrices', consisting of five wide-ranging chapters that deal respectively with the relationship between environment and history, diseases, technologies and their transformation, patterns of urbanization on a world-scale, and gender and sexuality in the context of social history. These chapters of considerable scope, together with the present introduction, set the stage for later chapters that are often somewhat more limited in their geographical scope. These chapters naturally approach questions to a large extent from a materialist standpoint, though cultural questions are by no means absent here. They enable the reader to have a sense equally of the comparative and connective dimensions of practising world history today. Equally, they are interesting in that they represent the writings of historians across a significant generational spread.

A second set of chapters, entitled 'Macro-regions', then takes a somewhat different approach, breaking down the space of the world into significant clusters, which have in the recent past been the object of significant historiographical interest. The section begins with a chapter devoted to the heritage of the 'world-conquering' Mongols of the thirteenth century, which also serves as a connection into the preceding volume of the series, edited by Benjamin Kedar and Merry Wiesner-Hanks. As we are aware, several significant early modern dynasties bore the imprint of a Mongol heritage, some by way of direct descent (as with the Indian Timurids or Mughals), still others in

---

[21] Richard H. Grove, *Green Imperialism: Colonial Expansion, Tropical Island Edens and the Origins of Environmentalism, 1600–1860* (Cambridge University Press, 1995); John F. Richards, *The Unending Frontier: An Environmental History of the Early Modern World* (Berkeley, CA: University of California Press, 2003).

more indirect ways. Individual chapters in this section then deal with the Indian Ocean, which has been the object of a real historiographical renaissance in the past generation, the Americas before the European conquest and Africa. One of the purposes of this section is to provide a certain number of spatial building blocks in order to have a better-balanced world history. We note for example that Africa is often given short shrift in world-historical analyses, either because it did not fit the civilizational conceptual framework of earlier generations, or because it could only be treated through a reductive lens, such as that of the trans-Atlantic slave trade.

A third set of chapters deals with 'Large-scale political formations' such as the Iberian Empires, as well as Sino-Russian competition, before concluding with a broad-ranging discussion of the Islamic Empires of the period, which deliberately chooses to go beyond the classic triptych of Ottomans, Safavids and Mughals. These chapters are concerned to accomplish several objects: to consider imperial spaces as zones of analysis, and to look into the interactions between formations that are often kept apart in a somewhat artificial manner (such as the Dutch and English, or the Portuguese and Spanish Empires).

A fourth section then addresses the problem of space in a somewhat different manner, by using the idea of the 'crossroads' that has gained influence in the past few decades, particularly after the work of the French historian Denys Lombard, author of *Le Carrefour javanais* ('The Javanese Crossroads').[22] Chapters here treat classic regions such as the Mediterranean, but also more intriguing zones such as Southeast Asia and Central Asia, as well as the Caribbean. No doubt other instances could have been added to this section, such as the Baltic Sea or the South China Sea. These chapters also seek to build on the recent spurt of interest in 'thalassography', or the use of maritime zones as areas of analysis to go beyond conventional national or imperial histories.[23] The volume then concludes with an ambitious and wide-ranging comparative analysis of political trajectories, which seeks to understand both the gradual changes in state-forms worldwide, and the eventual emergence of Western Europe into a position of dominance – a process that we must note, however, was still incomplete as well as highly contested in 1800.

---

[22] Denys Lombard, *Le Carrefour javanais: Essai d'histoire globale*, 3 vols (Paris: Editions de l'EHESS, 1990).

[23] Peter N. Miller (ed.), *The Sea: Thalassography and Historiography* (Ann Arbor, MI: University of Michigan Press, 2013).

The first book in this volume can be considered therefore to be largely, though not exclusively, organized around spatial questions, as well as questions of how space should be divided and reconfigured for the purposes of historical analysis. We have deliberately eschewed for the most part the use of 'civilizations' as building blocks, a strategy that would in the early twentieth century have appealed variously to the Weberians, as much as to Arnold Toynbee or Oswald Spengler. While the analysis of comparative civilizations continues to have a hold on the popular imagination, in particular in the genres of the 'West and the Rest' or the 'Clash of Civilizations', it appeared to us that it had largely run its course as a heuristic tool.

Indeed, rather than simply assuming the existence of civilizations based on stable religious identities, as Weberians might once have done, the second book, *Patterns of Change* (Part II of Volume VI), here attempts at one and the same time to address large questions of circulation and interaction, and the issues raised by some categories that were treated as self-evident or natural by earlier generations. Its opening section, entitled 'Migrations and encounters', is made up of individual chapters that treat migration as a worldwide phenomenon, as well as warfare, a crucial theme that has been a staple of debates since at least the 1980s, in the aftermath of controversies concerning the concept of the 'military revolution' in the early modern period. There are also considerations in the following chapters of various types of encounters and inter-cultural exchanges, as well as the legal forms and structures that mediated such exchanges. This is followed by an extended set of chapters organized under the rubric of 'Trade, exchange and production'. These chapters address important questions that have preoccupied early modern world historians of the past several generations: the so-called 'Columbian Exchange' of flora and fauna between the New and Old Worlds, the emergence and consolidation of the African slave trade in much the same period, the circulation of precious metals and the emergence of a global monetary system, as well as a consideration of the trading and entrepreneurial systems that made such exchanges feasible. Indeed, one of the advantages of organizing a volume on the early modern period is the plethora of debates that have abounded in the historiography in the past half-century. Some of these have concerned various sorts of material 'revolutions': military, monetary, scientific, commercial and so on. But there have also been significant debates concerning what one might term 'mental revolutions'. One of the most important of these calls into question a central category through which world history was once organized, namely religion. It thus appeared to us entirely justified to devote a section to the problem of 'Religion and religious change', beginning with a chapter devoted to the 'invention' and generalization of the idea as a conceptual category, followed by a series of case studies devoted to Christianity, Islam and the East Asian religions. Since the ambition of these volumes is not to be encyclopedic, there are certainly exclusions here, which are of course partly made up through discussions in other chapters. We have thus often used the case study or a series of case studies to illustrate a large point, rather than claiming to treat an issue comprehensively.

The second book closes two complementary reflections on the very practice of world history, in terms of tracing its intellectual genealogies into the early modern period. While this might appear to some to be an unusual choice, it seemed to us important, also in order to recognize the emergence into prominence of a new intellectual history, or history of ideas, in the past few decades. These chapters of a somewhat more reflexive nature also are intended to redress the balance in regard to the often highly materialist emphasis of world histories as they are practised in the English-speaking world. They also address questions regarding the various ways in which different trends and tendencies in historiography – such as 'microhistory' and 'world history' – can be reconciled, or treated as productive of a set of fecund and productive tensions.[24]

Concluding remarks

Writing world history, like writing any history on any scale, is indeed a matter of choices. Our intention was certainly not that of the imaginary seventeenth-century empire where first 'the Art of Cartography attained such Perfection that the map of a single Province occupied the entirety of a City, and the map of the Empire, the entirety of a Province', before subsequently attaining an even higher level, namely 'a Map of the Empire whose size was that of the Empire, and which coincided point for point with it'.[25] In the at-times artificial debate that has in recent decades opposed 'national' historians and 'world' historians, a criticism that is sometimes heard is that the

---

[24] For earlier reflections, see Carlo Ginzburg, 'Latitude, Slaves, and the Bible: An Experiment in Microhistory', *Critical Inquiry*, 31(3) (2005), 665–83; and Sanjay Subrahmanyam, 'On World Historians in the Sixteenth Century', *Representations*, 91 (Fall 2005), 26–57.

[25] Jorge Luis Borges, 'Of Exactitude in Science', in Borges, *A Universal History of Infamy*, Norman Thomas di Giovanni (trans.) (London: Penguin, 1972), p. 141. Borges attributes the story to the fictional Suárez Miranda, *Viajes de varones prudentes* (1658).

spatial ambitions of world history render it impossible.[26] Yet, as Borges's story cited above makes clear, we are all pretty much in the same boat here. No one would reasonably expect a 'national' historian of Thailand or France to provide coverage of every town and province, every social category and cultural manifestation, or every political tendency, within his or her space of predilection.

At the same time, it is clear that world history – whether in its present-day incarnations or those of the past – places certain types of demands on the historian that histories on a smaller scale may not. What is called for is a grasp of a wider and more disparate literature, as well as in many cases a mastery of a great number of sources and archives. But there is also a balance to be struck between monographic research and the synthesis, each of which require distinct skills and approaches. It should be clear that these two volumes, like the others in the series of the *Cambridge World History*, are tilted towards the genre of the synthesis. Yet, it should also be evident to the reader that the thirty and more contributors to these two volumes are without exception also perfectly familiar with primary materials, often in more than one archive, and thus have spent their professional careers navigating between the genres of monograph and synthesis. This is worth emphasizing, even if we have deliberately chosen to keep citations to primary and archival materials limited in the pages that follow. There is little doubt that, in other circumstances, these volumes might have turned out differently. Some chapters that were originally in our plan could not be brought to fruition, because authors had other conflicting commitments, or because of situations of *force majeure*. It is also very likely that these volumes would have turned out rather differently if their authors had written from a different set of locations, rather than their current positioning, which is – with some notable exceptions – largely Euro-American. But the fact is that the interest in world history remains uneven in the early twenty-first century: if it is now often accepted in the academic worlds of the United States, Canada, Australia, the United Kingdom and Germany, it is still seen as relatively marginal in many other parts of Europe, and subject to often violent critiques, sometimes based on deep misunderstandings regarding its nature. Equally, in most parts of Asia, world history has been slow to emerge side by side with national or regional histories, although there are again some

---

[26] For an attempt to caricature world history, and its alleged poverty, from the perspective of national history, see Krzysztof Pomian, 'World History: Histoire mondiale, histoire universelle', *Le Débat*, 154 (2009), 14–40.

important exceptions to this rule.[27] This is partly due to the hold of nationalism on the teaching of history, although there are undoubtedly other reasons which also account for it. At any rate, it is very likely that a generation or two from now, if such an exercise were attempted once again, many new themes would have emerged, while others would have been discarded or reduced to a small place. Let us not forget that in the end, world history too is a form of provisional history.

---

[27] See the interesting reflection in Dominic Sachsenmaier, *Global Perspectives on Global History: Theories and Approaches in a Connected World* (Cambridge University Press, 2011).

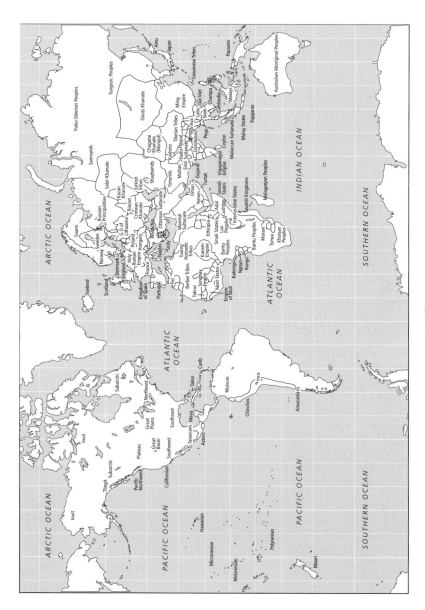

1.1 World map 1500

ARCTIC OCEAN

Inuit

Tlingit
Subarctic
Pacific
Northwest
Californian
Plateau
Great
Basin
Southwest
Great
Plains
Northeast
Southeast
Subarctic

ATLANTIC
OCEAN

Tarascans Maya
Aztecs
Taino
Carib

Muiscas

Chinchas
Inca

Araucanians

PACIFIC OCEAN

Hawaiian

Micronesian

Melanesian

Polynesian

Maori

SOUTHERN OCEAN

PACIFIC OCEAN

ARCTIC OCEAN

Paleo-Siberian Peoples

Tungusic Peoples

Oirats Khanate

Ainu

Japan

Ming
Empire

Tlawamee Tribes

Champa
Dai Viet
Laos
Cambodia
Pegu Siam
Java
Gondwana
Ceylon

Papuans

Malay States

Australian Aboriginal Peoples

Samoyeds

Sabir Khanate

Chagatai
Khanate
(Mongol)

Kashmir

Tibetan Tribes

Multan Delhi Sultanate
Sind
Gujarat

Vijayanagari
Empire

Malaccan Sultanate

Pajajaran

INDIAN OCEAN

Russian
Principalities
Saami

Sweden
Norway

Kazan
Khanate

Rázan

Crimean
Khanate

Turkish
Tribes

Shaybanids

Timurids

Ottoman Sultanate

Oman

Yemen

Fartak

Somali
States

Malagasyan Peoples

Swahili Kingdoms

SOUTHERN OCEAN

Iceland

Scotland
England
Denmark
Ireland
G D of
Lithuania
Poland
Holy
Roman
Empire Hungary
France
Naples
Sicily
Walachia

Mamluk
Sultanate

Ethiopia
Adal
Luo
Peoples Cushans
Shetolasine States

Small States

Marawi
Torwa
Khoisan
Peoples

Bantu Peoples

Kingdom
of Spain
Portugal

Fez

Berber Tribes

Tuareg
Nomadic
Tribes

Kanem
Empire

Bantu Peoples

Takrur

Songhay
Empire

Akon States

Empire
of Mali

Kakongo
Ngoyo
Kongo

ATLANTIC
OCEAN

24

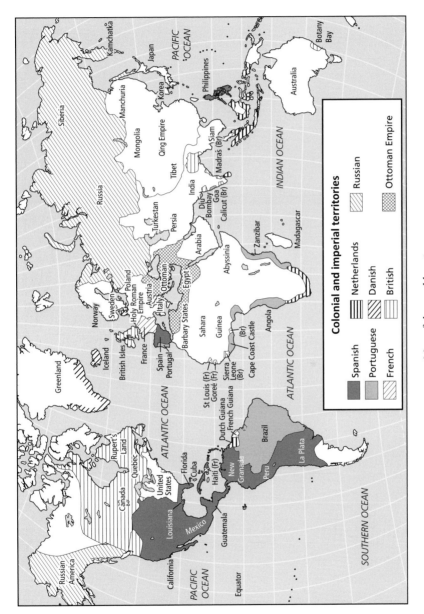

1.2 Map of the world c. 1800

Colonial and imperial territories

Spanish
Portuguese
French
Netherlands
Danish
British
Russian
Ottoman Empire

PACIFIC OCEAN

Kamchatka
Botany Bay
Japan
Siberia
Manchuria
Korea
Philippines
Australia
Mongolia
Qing Empire
Tibet
INDIAN OCEAN
Russia
Siam
Madras (Br)
Turkestan
India
Persia
Goa
Bombay
Diu
Calicut (Br)
Arabia
Zanzibar
Madagascar
Poland
Austria
Ottoman
Holy Roman Empire
Italy
Egypt
Abyssinia
Sweden
Norway
France
Barbary States
Sahara
Guinea
Angola
Iceland
British Isles
Spain
Portugal
Sierra Leone (Br)
Cape Coast Castle
Greenland
St Louis (Fr)
Gorée (Fr)
Dutch Guiana
French Guiana
ATLANTIC OCEAN
Rupert's Land
Quebec
Canada (Br)
United States
Florida
Cuba
Haiti (Fr)
New Granada
Brazil
Peru
La Plata
Louisiana
Mexico
Guatemala
California
Russian America
PACIFIC OCEAN
Equator
SOUTHERN OCEAN
ATLANTIC OCEAN

25

PART ONE

*

GLOBAL MATRICES

2

"Exhausting the Earth": environment and history in the early modern world

ROBERT B. MARKS

Exhausting the Earth and *The Unending Frontier* are the titles of two books that capture different but related aspects of the environmental history of the early modern world. In *Exhausting the Earth*, Peter Perdue examines how the interests of the central Chinese state in growing its tax base intersected with peasant farmers' desires to grow more food for themselves and for export, thereby increasing the population, intensifying the use of land for agricultural purposes, and putting pressure on natural hydrological systems and upland forests.[1] In *The Unending Frontier*, John F. Richards argues that from 1500 to 1800, worldwide processes had significant environmental effects. Newly empowered and enriched European central states with land and sea power engaged in a relentless global pursuit for seemingly endless frontier resources following the Columbian voyage of 1492.[2] In Richards's view, much early modern environmental change was driven by the exploitation of frontiers. Taking these two books together, the emerging theme of the environmental history of the early modern world combines the intensive exploitation of resources in densely populated core regions of the Earth with the creation and exploitation of new frontiers, both globally and within states.

But of course the idea of "the unending frontier" was ironic, for although the New World appeared to offer unlimited abundance well into the nineteenth century, resource shortages and environmental challenges cropped up around the world towards the end of the early modern period. "Conservation, minimal consumption, and eventually, population restraints," Richards observed, "became a necessity in societies across Eurasia in the eighteenth century."[3] Indeed, those constraints may well have continued to

---

[1] Peter Purdue, *Exhausting the Earth: State and Peasant in Hunan, 1500–1850* (Cambridge, MA: Harvard University Council on East Asian Studies, 1987).

[2] John F. Richards, *The Unending Frontier: An Environmental History of the Early Modern World* (Berkeley, CA: University of California Press, 2003).

[3] Richards, *Unending Frontier*, p. 622.

get ever-more severe as early modern societies more intensively used and exhausted the resources available to them. The world began to escape from those constraints in the nineteenth century with the emergence of modern fossil-fueled economic growth. Whether that breakthrough was necessary, accidental, or inevitable remains hotly debated and beyond the scope of this chapter.[4] But I do hope that a better understanding of the environmental history of the early modern world not only sheds light on the modern era, but also can inform assessments of it.

The early modern world as an "advanced organic" or "biological old" regime

Environmental history examines the mutual relations and interactions between humans and nature over time. Humans have always been part of nature, and like all other animals depend upon it for survival. But unlike other species, we have developed the increasingly powerful ability to alter the environment, sometimes intentionally and sometimes not, mostly locally where we have lived, but increasingly on a global scale.

The environmental history of the early modern world, defined in this volume as the period from 1400 to 1800, is bounded by several important historical developments. During those four centuries, the world's human population more than doubled from about 380 to 950 million. In terms of global epidemic disease, the early modern world falls after the disasters of the Black Death in the mid-fourteenth century, but before the eighteenth- and nineteenth-century slowing of smallpox epidemics and the last bubonic plague outbreak. Climatically, the early modern world unfolded at a time of global cooling so severe at times, especially in the mid-seventeenth century, that climatologists label the period of the fourteenth through the nineteenth centuries the "Little Ice Age." Politically, the fourteenth-century collapse of the Mongol empire opened space for new states and empires to arise throughout Eurasia, while in the Americas two large empires – the Aztec and the Inca – arose. Propelled by military confrontation among themselves, Eurasian states increased their grasp over their subjects and extended their rule into frontiers, setting off as well an era of seafaring and empire building across the globe. Markets came to organize more and more

---

[4] Kenneth Pomeranz rekindled the debate with *The Great Divergence: China, Europe, and the Making of the Modern World* (Princeton University Press, 2000).

of the world's economy, and natural products gathered from around the globe satisfied a fast-growing consumer demand.

Perhaps most importantly for the purposes of this chapter, the early modern world was "organic" in the sense that humans got energy mostly by tapping and concentrating solar flows to grow food for themselves and their animals, and to heat their homes and to make other industrial products;[5] farms and forests thus constituted the most important sources of energy to support human populations. To the extent that nearly all work (with the exception of some use of wind and water) was done by the exercise of human or animal muscle, the early modern world was, in J. R. McNeill's terms, "a somatic society." It was, in Fernand Braudel's estimation, a world of biological limits, obstacles, and restrictions – the *biological old regime*.[6] This was the world before the release of vast amounts of energy from fossil fuels propelled industrialization in the nineteenth and twentieth centuries and dramatically changed nearly everything about the world, including the number of humans living on Planet Earth and the very nature of the relationship of humans with the natural environment.[7]

The world in 1400 consisted of a biosphere that contained life on Earth, humans included, extracting sufficient energy from their environment not just to sustain their species, but if possible to increase their numbers. In the twentieth century, biologists came to understand the differences among the various environments which sustain life in terms of ecological principles that differentiated among terrestrial and marine "biomes" or "eco zones," such as broadleaf forests, grass savannah, arid desert, or freshwater lakes, with the number of biomes varying depending on the taxonomical scheme. Those biomes in turn include over a thousand ecoregions, each with specific kinds of ecosystems. Living things adapt to those varying environments, extract energy from them, and alter them in various ways. By 1400, humans had come to inhabit nearly all terrestrial biomes (except Antarctica and some of the world's driest deserts), and had developed ways of extracting food and energy from a vast number of the world's ecosystems, ranging from forests and grasslands to semi-arid deserts, and to transform a portion of those

---

[5] Peat was used in some places, such as the Netherlands, and coal had been used in China for centuries, while in England coal was increasingly used for heating the homes of London as sources of wood disappeared with forests.

[6] Fernand Braudel, *The Structures of Everyday Life*, Sian Reynolds (trans.) (New York: Harper & Row, 1981), p. 70.

[7] J. R. McNeill, *Something New under the Sun: An Environmental History of the Twentieth Century* (New York: W. W. Norton & Company, 2000).

ecosystems into farms where favored grains, such as maize in the Americas, wheat in Europe, and rice in East and South Asia, and other plants and animals were raised for human consumption.

Long-term environmental changes

The human population was not distributed evenly over the Earth, but concentrated in some fifteen more densely populated regions that some have called "civilizations." The total dry land area of the world is about 150 million square kilometers (today as in the early modern period), of which forests and grasslands in 1400 comprised approximately equal amounts of about 65 million square kilometers each (see Table 2.1); arid deserts and mountain ranges covered perhaps 10 million square kilometers; and about 16 million, or about 10 percent of the Earth's dry land surface at the beginning of the early modern period, was farmed at varying levels of intensity.[8]

Table 2.1 documents the long-term transformation of forests and grasslands into farmland – a rough gauge of global deforestation, if you will. Excepting deserts, what these data show is that in 1400 at the beginning of the

Table 2.1 *Global land use (millions of ha) and world population (millions), 1400–1850*

	Year			Change	
	1400	1700	1850	Amount	Percent
Forests and woodlands	6,554	6,363	5,965	−589	−9%
Grassland and pasture	6,860	6,159	5,987	−873	−13%
Croplands	180	296	540	360	200%
Temperate world	95	137	375	280	295%
Tropical world	75	128	180	105	140%
World population (est.)	390	679	1,260	870	223%

Sources: Land use based on John F. Richards, "Land Use" in B. L. Turner *et al.* (eds.), *The Earth as Transformed by Human Action: Global and Regional Changes in the Biosphere over the Past 300 Years* (New York: Cambridge University Press, 1990), p. 164. Cropland breakdown into temperate and tropical world based on Michael Williams, *Deforesting the Earth: From Prehistory to Global Crisis* (University of Chicago Press, 2003), pp. 277 and 335. World population based on Paul Demeny, "Population" in B. L. Turner *et al.* (eds.), *The Earth as Transformed by Human Action: Global and Regional Changes in the Biosphere over the Past 300 Years* (New York: Cambridge University Press, 1990), p. 42.

[8] Braudel, *Structures of Everyday Life*, p. 56.

early modern period nearly all of the world's forests and grasslands were intact; just 1 percent of the world's land surface was given over to cropland. In 1400, China, South Asia, and Europe accounted for 60 percent of the world's cropland, most of which was in the temperate parts of the world. By 1850, those areas accounted for 70 percent of the world's cropland, indicating that agricultural expansion in the early modern world occurred mostly in regions controlled by existing central states, expanding the sown area by 360 million hectares, or about 300 percent more than what there was in 1400 (see Table 2.1). As we will see, some climatologists think that that increase in farmland at the expense of forest and grassland released sufficient amounts of carbon dioxide and methane into the atmosphere to have an effect on the global climate system.

Not all humans in 1400 gained their livelihood by farming. Some gathered, hunted, and foraged in forests or fished in lakes and along coastlines. Others were nomadic pastoralists who had learned to exploit the vast Eurasian steppe or African savanna to sustain their herds of cattle, horses, sheep, goats, or camels. Still others combined some form of simple farming using hoes or sticks with husbandry and hunting and gathering, sometimes as upland specialists exploiting ecosystems abandoned or overlooked by low-land farmers. But as a portion of the total human population the numbers of non-farmers were relatively small – maybe 5 percent. Settled farming pro-duced the most food and hence sustained the largest and most dense concen-trations of people on Earth.

Dynamics of the biological old regime

Epidemic disease, famine, war, and other disasters kept human life expectancy much shorter than it is today.[9] In many of the richest and most advanced parts of the pre-modern world, from China and Japan in East Asia to England and Holland in Europe, life expectancies at birth were 30 to 40 years, or half of what they are today for most of the developed world. Of course, those life spans were short largely because infant and childhood mortality were high: women bore many children and were lucky if half survived to the age of 15. Once through the dangers of death from childhood disease, many people could expect to live into their 60s—under good agricultural conditions, that is.

[9] Note: this section is adapted with some changes from Robert B. Marks, *The Origins of the Modern World: A Global and Environmental Narrative from the Fifteenth to the Twenty-first Century* (Lanham, MD: Rowman & Littlefield, 2007), pp. 28 and 30–2.

Famine

Food shortages, dearth, and famine were an all too real part of life (and death) for most of the people living in 1400. It is of course easy to blame such disasters on "natural causes" alone. But the fact of the matter is that 80 to 90 percent of the world was composed of one vast farming peasantry, rural people who produced food and industrial raw materials and who were obligated to give up a certain amount of their harvest each and every year to agents of the state in the form of taxes and, unless they were in the small minority lucky enough to own their land free and clear, in the form of rent and labor services to the landowner. Throughout much of the most densely populated part of Eurasia (that is, in China, Europe, and India), peasant families gave up as much as half of their harvest to the state and landlords. In the pre-Columbian Americas, the Aztecs extracted tribute from subject peoples in central Mexico, and in Peru the Incas organized a mountainous "vertical" empire to bring resources to Cuzco high in the Andes. In Africa, states were more interested in controlling people and their labor as a source of wealth than in "owning" the much more plentiful land.

In good or improving times, farming families might be able to make ends meet, providing for their own subsistence needs and also meeting their obligations to the tax man and rent collector, and to produce a surplus that might be sold in the market. But what about those times when the harvest fell short? A "good" government or a "good" landowner might recognize that to take their regular share would push the peasant family below subsistence levels, and thus would lower or cancel taxes and rents for that year. But if the government or landowners either could not or would not be lenient—if they had debts to pay others, for instance—then the squeeze would be on. Indeed, Japanese landowners in the eighteenth century said of peasants that they were like sesame seeds: the more you squeezed, the more you got. So, famine was not so much a "natural" as a "social" phenomenon. The supply of food thus was a constraint on human population growth.

Epidemic disease

The 80 to 90 percent of the world that was this vast farming peasantry—whether in China, India, the various parts of Europe, or Mesoamerica—supported the elites, who governed, warred, ministered, and traded. The peasantry, in the words of one historian, thus made it possible for various forms of human "macro-parasites" to live off them. Additionally, the entire human population was subject to epidemic disease carried by micro-parasites—for

34

example, the plague bacteria of the Black Death, the smallpox or influenza viruses, the bacteria causing dengue fever or dysentery—and all the other germs and pathogens that caused diseases we now cannot identify because they have since mutated or died away.[10]

To be sure, the wealthy in both town and countryside had more ways of avoiding death from epidemic disease than the peasants or the poor of the towns and villages, but epidemics could—and did—affect entire populations. Epidemic diseases also traveled the world, slowly at first because of the slowness of trade and contacts between the centers of civilization, as in the period just after the collapse of the Roman and Han Chinese Empires, when smallpox and the measles spread from their point of origin in Europe to China. As the world became even more linked together in the thirteenth century by long-distance trade, a single epidemic disease could—and did—move much more rapidly from one end of the Eurasian continent to the other: the Black Death spread from China to Europe in a matter of years, and once in Europe it engulfed nearly the entire region within three years from late 1347 to 1350. And as we will see below, wave after wave of epidemic disease carried off vast numbers of Amerindian peoples after 1492.

The balancing act of people fending off or dying from both macro- and micro-parasites—elites living off farmers, civilizations fighting off or losing to horse-riding invaders, and germs multiplying inside of and then killing pastoralists or foragers and city dwellers alike—is key to what Braudel meant by the "biological old regime." Human populations were limited in size and environmental impact by these very material constraints. In this world—the world not just of 1400, but the world for millennia before and then afterwards until well into the nineteenth century—the human population lived very much in the environment and had to be very mindful of the opportunities and limits it placed on human activity.

Farming

Agriculture not only provided the food for the entire society, but most of the raw materials for whatever industry there was, especially textiles for clothing. In China, silk and cotton reigned supreme; in India, cotton and silk; and in northwestern Europe, wool. The raw materials for these all came from farms. Fuel for processing these materials, as well as for keeping warm, also came from forests. To this extent, the biological *ancien regime* was

---

[10] William McNeill, *Plagues and Peoples* (New York: Anchor, 1976).

organic, that is, it depended on solar energy to grow crops for food and the stored biomass in trees for fuel. The biological old regime thus limited the range of possibilities for people and their history because virtually all human activity drew upon renewable sources of energy supplied on an annual basis by the sun.

All living things need food for energy to live, and increasing amounts of both to sustain larger populations. What agriculture allowed people to do, in effect, was to capture natural processes and to channel that energy into the human population. In the biological old regime, agriculture was the primary means by which humans altered their environment, transforming one kind of ecosystem (say, forest or prairie) into another (say, rye or wheat farms, rice paddies, fish ponds, or eel weirs) that more efficiently channeled food energy to people. The size of human populations thus was limited by the amount of land available and the ability of people to use the energy from that land for their purposes. The most productive agricultural systems supported the densest human populations, and those were the Aztec's *milpas*, and in parts of China, Japan, India, and Southeast Asia, wet-rice paddies.

In effect, farmers selected a favored few of the plants and animals from their ecosystem, and lavished time, energy, and nutrients on their propagation. To be sure, some of the plants and animals that flourished were unintended—weeds and vermin came along with planted crops. Other unfavored species, though, declined or disappeared. Humans and their farms simplified nature into fewer and fewer ecosystems.

As the human population more than doubled from about 380 to 950 million during the early modern era, something had to change in terms of the relationship of people with the availability of land and their efficiency in working it. On the one hand, Europeans encountered a whole new world, the Americas. While this New World was already quite populated in 1400 and the land already used by native Amerindians, a massive biological exchange radically altered those relationships, making the Americas a relatively depopulated world by the year 1600, but providing new crops to greatly increase the food supply across Afro-Eurasia and increase the human populations there. In addition, truly global trading relationships were established, allowing a considerable increase in overall production and productivity as specialization allowed people in one part of a regional trading network to produce goods that their environment was especially suited to, and to trade via markets with countless others who were doing the same thing. Market specialization spread, thereby allowing economies throughout the world to produce more than they ever had in the past, yet without escaping the limits of the biological old regime.

Wildlife

As in other historical periods, including the modern and ancient worlds, in the early modern world there was an inverse relationship between the population size and density of humans and the population size and density of other animals. We cannot possibly survey the entire wild animal population of the early modern world in this chapter, although we will encounter numerous species as they were hunted or displaced. Animals inhabit ecological niches and relate with one another in trophic chains where energy moves up to larger and more dominant species as others are consumed. The idea of ecosystems of plants and animals cycling and recycling energy is more complex than a system of "prey and predator," although it is in part that. But ecologists recognize that ecosystems do have "star species" such as tigers, elephants, wolves, and lions that can serve as indicators of entire functioning ecosystems down to the soil bacteria and earthworms that break down organic material so it can be taken up again in the roots of other plants, as well as "keystone species" like beavers that hold ecosystems together.

In the early modern world, the 16 million square kilometers of terrestrial land taken by human farming populations still left more than 130 million square kilometers for all kinds of other animals to flourish, not to mention the vast aquatic life of the oceans. But even in their densely populated early modern civilizations, humans were not walled off from contact with "nature" or from the rather fierce creatures we can now call "star species." There was indeed a human–"wild" animal interface that struck fear into human minds.

Even though most of the weight of the world's population lived in just a few highly developed islands of human civilization, the intervening expanses were inhabited by people, differently organized people to be sure, but people nonetheless. Indeed, by 1400 humans had migrated through or to virtually every place on the globe: if not full, the Earth was known, at least to those who lived there. Of course, the foragers and pastoralists who lived in the vast spaces outside the densely populated farming civilizations were very few and far between, leaving much room for wildlife of all kinds.

Wolves roamed throughout most of Eurasia and the Americas, as can be attested by *Grimm's Fairy Tales*.[11] Tigers at one time inhabited most of China, and periodically attacked Chinese villages and cities, carrying away piglets and babies alike when humans disrupted their ecosystem by cutting away the forests that provided them with their favored game, deer or wild

---

[11] Braudel, *Structures of Everyday Life*, pp. 66–7.

boar.[12] Grassland wolves constituted a "keystone species" in the Mongolian grasslands, keeping down populations of gazelle, marmots, and mice, as well as the Mongols' own horses. The greatest natural bounty, though, was in the New World, particularly North America, where the first European visitors described "unbelievable" numbers and sizes of fish, birds, deer, bear, and trees (the surprising historical reasons for that abundance will be discussed below).[13] In Africa, large animals from elephants to rhinos, giraffes, and lions had evolved with humans, and learned to keep their distance. So did Africans know the dangers of those large animals, as well as the diseases that came with the tsetse fly that infected humans and livestock alike with sleeping sickness, thereby keeping humans out of the fly's extensive bush environment. Like the Americas but for different reasons, Africa in the early modern era supported vast animal populations.

Thus, from 1400 to 1800, when the human population of the world increased from 380 to 950 million, there was still plenty of room for wildlife of all kinds. Nonetheless, the relationship between the two populations clearly was inverse: the more people, the less wildlife, especially as those in the "civilizations" developed a taste for wearing furs (in China, Europe, and North America), or eating exotic fish and fowl. Great hunting expeditions to kill whales, tigers, bison, beavers, homing pigeons, sharks, fox ... the list goes on ... for their hides, their meat, their various other body parts, started then and continue to this day, except for those species already extinct or, in some parts of the world, protected.

The Columbian Exchange and its environmental consequences

The "Columbian Exchange" refers to the exchange of plants, animals, and pathogens between the Americas and Afro-Eurasia following Christopher Columbus's voyage to the Americas in 1492 (see Chapter 5, "The Columbian Exchange," volume VI, part 2). The importance of the Columbian Exchange cannot be overstated. Over the course of world history, the Neolithic agricultural revolution and the Industrial Revolution wrought the most significant changes in the ways in which humans related to the natural world. But the Columbian Exchange, around which much of early modern world history turned, runs a close third in significance.

---

[12] See Robert B. Marks, *Tigers, Rice, Silk, and Silt: Environment and Economy in Late Imperial South China* (Cambridge University Press, 1998), ch. 10.

[13] William Cronon, *Changes in the Land: Indians, Colonists, and the Ecology of New England* (New York: Hill and Wang, 1983).

The Columbia Exchange is often portrayed as interactions between the "Old World" of Eurasia and the "New World" of the Americas. But as Shawn Miller perceptively points out, the "New World" was already quite "old" when encountered by Europeans. Humans had migrated into the Americas perhaps as early as 40,000 BCE, probably wiping out large mammal populations by 10,000 BCE, thus even before a wide range of agricultural practices (albeit without draft animals) sent human populations soaring to perhaps 70 to 100 million by 1491. Then when Europeans and Amerindians came into contact, wave after wave of communicable diseases that had incubated among Europeans—especially smallpox, measles, and influenza—raged among the native peoples of the Americas who had never experienced these diseases, killing 90 percent by 1600.[14]

The removal of nearly the entire Amerindian population had dramatic environmental consequences. Without human hands to maintain the cultured landscapes, forests returned, as did resurgent wildlife populations of all kinds. For Europeans who came to the Americas in the century after conquest, the "New" world appeared to be a cornucopia, stocked with nature's bounty there for the taking—"immeasurable forests, abundant wildlife, and few people."[15]

Where there may have been 70 to 100 million people in the Americas in 1491, as late as 1750, there were only 12 million humans in the Americas, and most of those were enslaved black Africans because they tended to survive malaria and yellow fever—environmental diseases unwittingly imported from Europe and Africa that became embedded in the Americas as part of the Columbian Exchange.[16] The "Great Dying" had removed a source of labor for European colonizers who then turned to the African slave trade for labor to work sugar plantations in Brazil and the Caribbean. The sugar plantation complex ecologically transformed forested islands into deforested plantations, starting with Barbados and then moving on to Montserrat, Martinique, St. Vincent, Antigua, and St. Kitts. Once wood needed to boil their sugar had been removed by the eighteenth century, English planters began to import coal from England.[17] This deforestation of islands for sugar

---

[14] David Noble Cook, *Born to Die: Disease and New World Conquest, 1492–1650* (New York: Cambridge University Press, 1998), pp. 13 and 206.

[15] Shawn Miller, *An Environmental History of Latin America* (Cambridge University Press, 2007), p. 57.

[16] Miller, *Environmental History of Latin America*, pp. 50–5.

[17] J. R. McNeill, *Mosquito Empires: Ecology and War in the Greater Caribbean, 1620–1914* (New York: Cambridge University Press, 2010), pp. 25–8.

plantations (and later coffee in Brazil) contributed to massive erosion, most spectacularly and enduringly in Haiti. It also apparently had local climatic effects, in particular by decreasing rainfall in some locations.[18] But on balance, the depopulating of the Americas resulted in the regrowth of a great amount of forest. Some climatologists have argued, in fact, that this removed so much carbon dioxide (which we now see as a "global warming gas") from the atmosphere that it contributed to the onset of the "Little Ice Age," an early modern climatic change to be discussed in the next section.[19]

Beside sugar plantations and enslaved Africans, Iberians brought horses, cattle, and sheep to the Americas, and the populations of these animals exploded in Latin America. In part, those ungulates had the grasslands created by the Amerindians on which to graze (the Argentine pampas, etc.), and no competition from other large mammals—those had been eliminated thousands of years earlier. As Miller summarizes the outcome: "The biological conquest of America is more accurately seen as the replacement of Indians not with Europeans [or Africans] or microbes, but with cows, sheep, pigs, chicken, and hundreds of other new nonhuman species, in addition to the resurgence of native wildlife."[20]

The effect of the Columbian Exchange on New World human populations and ecologies certainly was dramatic. But in the view of the scholar who developed the idea of the Columbian Exchange in the first place, Alfred Crosby, more significant was the explosive growth of human numbers in the Old World, fueled by the spread of New World food crops, "which is the most impressive single biological development of this millennium." By and large, New World foods (in particular maize, white and sweet potatoes, yams, and manioc) produce more calories per sown area than wheat, barley, or oats; only rice rivals maize and potatoes. According to Crosby:

> The great advantage of the American food plants is that they make different demands of soils, weather and cultivation than Old World crops, and are different in the growing seasons in which they make these demands. In many cases the American crops do not compete with Old World crops but complement them. The American plants enable the farmer to produce food

---

[18] Richard Grove, *Green Imperialism: Colonial Expansion, Tropical Island Edens and the Origins of Environmentalism, 1600–1860* (Cambridge University Press, 1995), pp. 184–99.

[19] Robert A. Dull et al., "The Columbian Encounter and the Little Ice Age: Abrupt Land Use Change, Fire, and Greenhouse Forcing," *Annals of the American Association of Geographers* 100 (2010), 755–71. For a readable overview, see Charles C. Mann, *1493: Uncovering the New World Columbus Created* (New York: Alfred A. Knopf, 2011), pp. 25–35.

[20] Miller, *Environmental History of Latin America*, p. 58.

from soils that prior to 1492, were rated as useless because of their sandiness, altitude, aridity, and other factors.

Not surprisingly, farmers throughout Afro-Eurasia added New World foods into their cropping patterns as soon as they got their hands on them, and that was very quickly. Europeans especially adopted potatoes and beans, but also maize (mostly as animal fodder); manioc became the food staple of many African peoples, who also raised maize, beans, and peanuts; and in China, which was perhaps the fastest adopter of New World foods, by the early sixteenth century farmers were planting peanuts and sweet potatoes in otherwise marginally used land.[21] Farmland throughout the temperate world expanded rapidly at the expense of forests, and human populations surged.

Farming and global climate change in the early modern world

During the early modern era, the natural environment both provided resources that allowed humans to increase their numbers, but constrained that growth within limits set by the dynamics of the biological old regime. Nonetheless, people had dramatic impacts on the environment, mostly through activities necessary for farming, starting with the removal of forests to make way for farms. But besides simplifying complex natural ecosystems into agro-ecosystems and removing habitats for many animal species, some scholars now think that humans were affecting the global climate system through farming.

The very act of removing forests through girdling, felling, and burning released carbon dioxide (CO_2) into the atmosphere, while the subsequent farming (especially of wet-rice paddy) and animal husbandry released large amounts of methane (CH_4) into the atmosphere. Both carbon dioxide and methane are among the most significant greenhouse gases. Several scholars, led by William Ruddiman, think that farming itself released sufficient greenhouse gases into the atmosphere prior to the modern era (with its release of those gases from burning fossil fuel) to have had an impact on the Earth's climate system. Ruddiman thinks that impact began with the first emergence of farming some 8,000 years ago,[22] while John L. Brooke thinks that the

---

[21] Alfred Crosby, *The Columbian Exchange: Biological and Cultural Consequences of 1492* (Westport, CT: Praeger Publishers, 2003), pp. 165, 175, 177–85, and 198–201.

[22] William F. Ruddiman, *Plows, Plagues, and Petroleum: How Humans Took Control of Climate*, Princeton Science Library edn. (Princeton University Press, 2010), chs. 9–10. Ruddiman thinks the emission of CO_2 and CH_4 probably was sufficient to prevent the Earth from slipping into a cold climate. In his view, the warm period over the past 8,000 years is a result of human activity.

tripling of farmland during the early modern era itself was sufficient to affect global climate.[23]

Interestingly, the likelihood that humans affected global climate through farming is confirmed by the conjuncture of the demographic disaster that befell the native American populations following the European arrival with a natural cycle of slight climatic cooling. The "Little Ice Age," variously dated from 1400 or 1550 to 1750 or 1850, started with natural perturbations that may have made life difficult enough for native American populations. But the massive die-off caused mostly by diseases spread from Europeans to native Americans by 1600 had removed the tens of millions of people who had tended their farms and gardens. Ruddiman argues that the regrowth of American forests, resulting in the sequestering of massive amounts of carbon dioxide, is what was responsible for the drop in atmospheric CO_2 levels that caused the climatic cooling of the Little Ice Age.[24] And that early modern climate shift had dramatic consequences for human populations.

Without delving into the potential anthropogenic contributions to the Little Ice Age, historian Geoffrey Parker has detailed its impact on human societies in *Global Crisis: War, Climate Change & Catastrophe in the Seventeenth Century*. This very large book looks at what he calls the "fatal synergy" between climate change and state breakdowns around the world in the seventeenth century, and the disasters that befell entire populations that resulted in mass deaths and global population declines of as much as one-third. Although some places on Earth apparently escaped the worst effects of the cooling climate, or—more interestingly—had states that took actions to mitigate the impact of cooler temperatures on farming and harvest yields, most notably in Japan and India— most other states in the world had short-sighted rulers who chose not just to continue their local or regional wars (the worst being the Thirty Years War in Europe, 1618 to 1648), but to increase taxes at the same moment that harvest yields fell because of the cold, piling misery upon misery. In a hopeful note to what otherwise is a horrifying chapter in human history, Parker shows how people and states around the world did learn some lessons from their near-death experiences, and began in the eighteenth century the processes of rebuilding more compassionate and climatically resilient states and societies even while the cooling climate continued for another century or more.[25]

---

[23] John L. Brooke, *Climate Change and the Course of Global History: A Rough Journey* (New York: Cambridge University Press, 2014), pp. 476–9.

[24] Ruddiman, *Plows, Plagues, and Petroleum*, pp. 121–4; Brooke, *Climate Change*, pp. 438–41.

[25] Geoffrey Parker, *Global Crisis: War, Climate Change & Catastrophe in the Seventeenth Century* (New Haven, CT: Yale University Press, 2013).

Processes of early modern environmental change

Besides population growth and the spread of farms, other human forces driving environmental change included the growing ability of states to extend their power beyond their territorial borders, the closer knitting together of the world by sailing vessels, and the growth of global markets for all kinds of natural products, including animals and their skins obtained through a "world hunt." The early modern period also saw the extension throughout the world of a particular kind of legal framework for human interaction with nature, built on the idea of private ownership of property.[26]

Private property and environmental change in a global perspective

Processes transforming land previously held collectively or by customary use into private property unfolded across the early modern world, especially when and where taxable farming marched across the landscape. This happened across Eurasia and throughout the Americas, and in some cases (in Africa) has endured to the present day. For instance, in colonial New England, as William Cronon has argued, such transformations underlay the European land grabs from Indians. Private property did not exist among people who followed the seasons and their game: "English colonists could use Indian hunting and gathering as a justification for expropriating Indian land" because they did not use the land "properly ... This was, of course, little more than an ideology of conquest conveniently available to justify the occupation of another people's lands."[27]

In an important essay, "Toward a Global System of Property Rights in Land," John F. Richards sketched out these processes. Richards argued that "every human society has moved toward a similar regime of rights in landed property. Bewilderingly complex, particularized, local systems of property rights in land have been altered, transformed, or replaced by simplified, more unified sets of rules in a remarkably similar fashion across all world regions." Since the fifteenth century, processes involving centralizing states, population growth, and technological change "have imparted economic value to a

---

[26] These driving forces are adapted from Jerry H. Bentley, "Early Modern Europe and the Early Modern World" in Jerry H. Bentley and Charles. H. Parker (eds.), *Between the Middle Ages and Modernity: Individual and Community in the Early Modern World* (Lanham, MD: Rowman & Littlefield, 2007), pp. 13–31; and John Richards, "Toward a Global System of Property Rights in Land" in Edmund Burke III and Kenneth Pomeranz (eds.), *The Environment and World History* (Los Angeles, CA: University of California Press, 2009), pp. 54–80.

[27] Cronon, *Changes in the Land*, pp. 53–7.

greater and greater share of the earth's land surface. In spite of the vicissitudes of political struggles and shifting ideologies, the long-term trend is toward more transparent, accessible markets in private property rights in land. In these markets, land use shifts rapidly and suddenly to meet economic incentives," setting up struggles over land and land use, particularly over the rights to exploit or use natural resources.[28]

This fixedness of private property gives the appearance that farming was settled and that hunting and gathering peoples were nomadic wanderers. But Hugh Brody suggests that the opposite was true:

> A look at how ways of life take shape across many generations reveals that it is the agriculturalists, with their commitment to specific farms and large numbers of children who are forced to keep moving, resettling, colonizing new lands. Hunter-gatherers, with their reliance on a single area, are profoundly settled. As a system, over time, it is farming, not hunting, that generates "nomadism" ... In the history of ... agricultural cultures, the combination of settlement, large families, and movement has resulted in a more or less relentless colonial frontier. An agricultural people can never rest—as farming families, as a lineage—in one place.[29]

From this perspective, as farming populations in central states throughout Afro-Eurasia produced more people than could be supported by the available land, pioneers set out for frontiers inhabited by others, but with their states' power at their backs, imposed settled farming techniques and ideas of private property on these others who had had rather different ideas about the land and its proper uses.

Exhausting the Earth

Certainly, there is compelling evidence that early modern states across Eurasia and in the pre-Columbian Americas depleted natural resources in their core areas as farmland replaced forests. Throughout much of Northern Europe, the combination of interstate competition, economic growth, and population growth put a strain on natural resources. For instance, as the population of France increased from 14 to 25 million from 1550 to 1789, the amount of forest shrank from 18 to 9 million hectares.[30] Most of this

[28] John F. Richards, "Toward a Global System of Property Rights in Land" in Burke and Pomeranz, *Environment and World History*, pp. 14–15, 70, and 73.
[29] Hugh Brody, *The Other Side of Eden: Hunters, Farmers, and the Shaping of the World* (New York: North Point Press, 2000), p. 86.
[30] Tamara L. Whited *et al.*, *Northern Europe: An Environmental History* (Santa Barbara, CA: ABC-CLIO, 2005), p. 80.

deforestation was for farming, but manufacturing needed charcoal, and navies (not just the French, but also other European states) consumed 3,500 mature trees for one ship. According to Whited et al.: "Overexploitation of the land was one sign of environmental stress in northern Europe in the eighteenth century." Erosion of farmland led to the build up of sandy plains and dunes from Denmark to the Netherlands, England, Sweden, Central Europe, and the Atlantic coast of France.[31] "[B]y the end of the eighteenth century ... the people in northern Europe lived, from an environmental perspective, in an impoverished world. In comparison to the Middle Ages, Europe was home to less wildlife and fewer forests. Climatic conditions had become unfavorable. The landscape showed severe signs of erosion."[32]

In China, New World food crops, especially maize, sweet potatoes, peanuts, and tobacco, enabled farmers to exploit land that previously had been marginal at best. Throughout East and South China, erosion of hills and mountains bedeviled lowland farmers and officials alike. "Economic growth based on highland reclamation was clearly unsustainable."[33] On the other hand, India's Mughal emperors transformed much of swampy Bengal into rice paddies that produced so much food that much of the subcontinent's forests remained standing into the nineteenth century.[34]

Among all the most advanced parts of the early modern world, Japan was among the first to begin to experience shortages of natural resources, to fear the consequences, and to begin to take actions to avoid going over an ecological cliff from which there might have been no recovery. By the end of the seventeenth century, forests in Japan's three major islands had been depleted. Cultivatable land probably reached its limit by 1720. Rice yields stagnated, even as some cash crops such as sugar and sericulture displaced paddies. Famines in the eighteenth century, although brought on by cold snaps that shortened the growing season, heightened awareness that Japan may have been getting close to the edge of sustainability and going down into a vicious cycle, depleting more and more resources to support their society until nature's storehouse was emptied.

In these circumstances, individuals, families, daimyo lords, and the central Tokugawa state began to take a number of measures that reduced human demand on the natural environment. Sumptuary laws limiting the size and

---

[31] Whited et al., Northern Europe, p. 89.   [32] Whited et al., Northern Europe, p. 101.

[33] Anne Osborne, "Barren Mountains, Raging Rivers: The Ecological and Social Effects of Changing Landuse on the Lower Yangzi Periphery in Late Imperial China," unpublished PhD dissertation, Columbia University (1989), p. 229.

[34] Richards, Unending Frontier, pp. 36–8.

construction of houses and feasting at weddings and funerals were aimed at the elite; timber shortages prompted changes in building styles; diets incorporated more seafood, including whale meat and blubber, freeing land for plants that had supported farm animals; and perhaps most significantly, families chose to reduce family size, and their progeny followed similar birth strategies, giving Japan a virtual zero population growth from the eighteenth into the nineteenth century.

Perhaps most remarkably of all, Japan began conscious policies of reforestation and then the protection of those forests. First, the central government and the daimyo lords issued numerous edicts protecting existing stands of forest and controlling the use of forest resources. But that was insufficient. Foresters developed the abilities to select, plant, and raise seedlings; daimyo lords requisitioned labor each spring to plant seedlings and then to care for them. "Widely accepted and applied, protective and regenerative forestry halted deforestation in Tokugawa Japan. Afforestation replaced exploitative overcutting."[35] Using the title of Conrad Totman's seminal book on this transformation, Japan became "the green archipelago."[36]

Japan may have been exceptional in the early modern world in terms of conscious conservation and active reforestation, but forests and their wildlife communities elsewhere also survived the early modern world, albeit for varying reasons. In India, the transformation of the Bengali "swamp" into productive rice paddies saved the Deccan forests. In the Americas, as we have already seen, the dying off of 90 percent of the Amerindians—itself the result of a combination of historical acts and accidents—led to the vast reforestation of North and South America. And in Africa, the tsetse fly, elephants, and lions helped preserve both forest and savannah, while malaria kept European slave traders to a few outposts on the West African Atlantic coast.

The world hunt

European sailing ships not only knit the Atlantic world together in increasingly tighter relations and extensive biological exchanges, but they also carried with them the lust for wealth that had driven Diaz, Columbus, da Gama, Cortez, and Pizarro, among others. Gold and silver were not the only

---

[35] Richards, *Unending Frontier*, pp. 186–7.
[36] Conrad Totman, *The Green Archipelago: Forestry in Preindustrial Japan* (Berkeley, CA: University of California Press, 1989).

New World natural products that scratched that itch; increasingly the bounty available in the forests, rivers, and oceans—furs and pelts from fur-bearing animals and oils and bone from whales—did as well. The first wave of wealth building in the Americas (following the plundering of silver and gold stocks) centered on the sugar plantation complex and all the environmental changes around the world that this spawned, with especially horrific consequences for the native peoples of the Americas. As Beinart and Hughes note, "[t]he indigenous population ... had no place in this system and was largely destroyed or its remnants absorbed."[37] But in what John Richards has called "the world hunt,"[38] in contrast to the experience in the Caribbean, "Native Americans had a major role in supplying imperial markets."[39] This was especially true for extracting the furs and pelts from North America and Siberia.

Fur-bearing animals

Throughout North America, the native peoples had hunted animals for their own uses and sometimes for barter with other tribes, in particular fur-bearing animals such as beaver, fox, and marten, and deer for their pelts and horns. European demand changed that relationship of Indians with their environment. Pushing into North America up the St. Lawrence seaway and overland into Pennsylvania, European traders brought iron and other metal tools, woolen blankets, as well as alcohol and tobacco, to trade for the furs and pelts. As a consequence, Indian hunting and killing of the wildlife of North America became linked to European demand, which was already large and growing. There were 60 to 100 million beavers in North America prior to the arrival of Europeans, but their populations were severely depleted already by the mid-seventeenth century. Because the beaver was an ecological "keystone" species, its removal led to the decay and drying of their ponds and to declining biological diversity. The marten was hunted to extinction in the nineteenth century, and wolves and wolverines were pushed to the brink. According to Richards, "the cumulative record of the fur trades in North America is clear and unambiguous. Once Indians were touched by the stimulus of market demand, any restraints they had previously maintained eroded rapidly."[40]

---

[37] William Beinart and Lotte Hughes, *Environment and Empire* (Oxford University Press, 2007), p. 40.
[38] Richards, *Unending Frontier*, p. 461.
[39] Beinart and Hughes, *Environment and Empire*, p. 40.
[40] Richards, *Unending Frontier*, p. 507.

The outcome was similar in Siberia, although the main animal hunted was the sable, and the extraction of the furs was organized differently. Whereas the North America fur trade was based on trade and mostly cordial relations with Indians, in Siberia the expanding Russian state in the seventeenth century imposed quotas called *iasak*—a requirement that each adult pay tribute of a sable pelt each year (as well as vow loyalty to the Russian tsar)—on the peoples they conquered. The result was predictable: sable populations declined and sable were locally extirpated.[41]

Another result of contact between Europeans and the native peoples of the cold northern climates was the introduction of epidemic disease. Smallpox brought by the French swept through Algonkian territory in the St. Lawrence region in 1639 to 1640; epidemics laid low the Hurons between 1634 and 1640; the English brought smallpox to the Connecticut valley in 1633 to 1634; Chinese-borne smallpox threatened Mongols and Manchurians; and Russians spread smallpox to native Siberians, who, "when they are stricken with smallpox . . . die like flies."[42]

In East Asia, after capturing Beijing and settling in to the Ming imperial palace, China's Manchu rulers relied on Manchuria to supply them and the imperial household with all kinds of foods and furs. Indeed, David Bello argues that although the Manchu state was initially dependent "on the region's biodiversity for its very existence,"[43] over the first half century or more of its rule, it developed hunting and gathering policies for Manchuria that were linked with Manchu identity, policies that Bello calls "imperial foraging." The Manchus established an entire bureaucracy to oversee the procurement of game and supplies from specially designated enclaves throughout Manchuria, as well as licensing foragers and imposing tribute quotas on them. Tigers, bears, leopards, fish, feathers, storks, and pine nuts, among other forest products, were foraged from Manchurian forests and sent to Beijing.

By the early 1700s, "elite demand approached mass consumption," and shortages began appearing, raising concern among China's Manchu rulers. "[T]here are indications that intensification of hunting and gathering [to meet that demand] . . . as well as illicit poaching and environmental degradation related to [illegal] Han migration, seem to have contributed to the depletion

---

[41] Richards, *Unending Frontier*, pp. 517–37.
[42] Richards, *Unending Frontier*, pp. 474–5, 479, 502, and 539.
[43] David Bello, "The Cultured Nature of Imperial Foraging in Manchuria," *Late Imperial China* 31 (2010), 3.

of resources." But rather than seeing these "shortages" as possibly indicating that the wildlife populations were being ravaged to the point of collapse, the rulers "interpreted shortfalls in anthropogenic terms that were centered on human idleness, incompetence, or greed," and so intensified the foraging. Where pine nuts earlier had been easily gathered, as low-hanging fruit, as it were, by the late eighteenth century, "the only way to obtain pine nuts and pinecones was to cut down trees." Bello concludes that although the Manchu imperial foraging, intensified by Han in-migration, did not permanently exhaust the most valuable resources of the northeast, the "extractions proved unsupportable by the early nineteenth century."[44]

China's ecological shadow reached across the Pacific to the American northwest. American and British traders newly arrived at the Columbia River and the access that it gave to the vast natural wealth of what is now the states of Washington and Oregon in the United States were so taken with the idea of the "China market" in the 1820s that they launched several ships loaded with furs from the northwest directly to China's port of Guangzhou. The problem was that the sellers found no market for furs in subtropical south China, and by 1828 the beaver pelt trade failed. What emerged instead was a much more complex system by which American ships traded north-western furs, timber, and fish among the Pacific islands, including Hawaii, ultimately winding up in Guangzhou with items acquired along the way, including sandalwood, the demand for which deforested many Pacific islands.[45]

Sea animals

But a fur that did meet a significant Chinese demand was the pelt of the sea otter, obtained from animals whose habitat stretched 4,000 miles along the American west coast from Alaska to Baja California. Whereas the sea otter's sleek black coat brought a high price of 40 Spanish dollars in Guangzhou near the end of the eighteenth century, 30 years later they were selling for two. The reason for the drop in price wasn't a drop in Chinese demand, but an explosion in the supply. "Killing sea otters ... was a very specialized skill

---

[44] Bello, "The Cultured Nature of Imperial Foraging in Manchuria," 12 and 20–4.

[45] John R. McNeill, "Of Rats and Men: A Synoptic Environmental History of the Island Pacific," *Journal of World History* 5 (1994), 299–349. See also Richard Mackie, *Trading beyond the Mountains: The British Fur Trade on the Pacific 1793–1843* (Vancouver: UBC Press, 1997), pp. 51–5. See also James R. Gibson, *Otter Skins, Boston Ships, and China Goods: The Maritime Fur Trade of the Northwest Coast, 1785–1841* (Seattle, WA: University of Washington Press, 1992).

and demanded the labor of native hunters," in particular the Aleut and Kodiaks from Alaska. In a very nasty business, Russian procurers held these natives' women and children hostage to force the men to work up and down the American west coast for British and American traders. "The entire coastline soon became an extended killing field [and] ... the region's sea otter population soon faced extinction ..."[46]

Exploiting the oceans did not require indigenes (except for a brief time when the Dutch traded with Inuits in Greenland), but the vast cod fishing and whaling fleets did require lots of capital, technological expertise, and skilled labor to build, sail, and operate increasingly sophisticated equipment. Cod is high in protein, and the stocks in north Atlantic and Arctic waters were prodigious. So much cod was taken and its price was so low that it was a staple food for African slaves laboring in American sugar plantations as well as ordinary urban laborers in Europe.[47] Hundreds of European ships took nearly 200,000 metric tons of cod annually for sale in Europe. The take appeared to be sustainable during the early modern period, although there are indications that the size of the fish and of the catches had declined by the mid-eighteenth century. Nonetheless, "[s]o numerous were codfish and so resilient ... that it took five hundred years for human fishing to cause stocks to crash—as they did in the 1980s."[48]

Whales were not so fortunate. Taken for their oil that had both domestic and industrial uses, and their plastic-like whalebone that also had industrial uses, in the eighteenth century Basque, Dutch, German, and Danish whalers hunted, killed, and processed several tens of thousands of bowhead and right whales. By the mid-nineteenth century, when state-subsidized British whaling had pushed aside competitors and the bow whale went extinct, over 160,000 whales had been taken to meet European and North American demand.[49]

Conclusion

The dynamics of the early modern world were not necessarily leading to the modern world, but just as likely to the depletion of natural resources, the culturing of nature, vast environmental change, and an increasingly intensive

[46] David Iger, "Diseased Goods: Global Exchanges in the Eastern Pacific Basin, 1770–1850," *American Historical Review* 109 (2004), 714–15.
[47] Richards, *Unending Frontier*, pp. 546 and 564.   [48] Richards, *Unending Frontier*, p. 573.
[49] Richards, *Unending Frontier*, pp. 574–613.

use of the land. Joachim Radkau concludes that by the eighteenth century, the world "entered into a new era . . . in the history . . . [of] the environment" as resources became scarce and limits were reached. In his view, "the urge to exploit the last reserves possesses an epochal character in environmental history. It led to a fundamental shift in strategies of sustainability. Until then, the sustainability of agriculture was in many cases guaranteed not only by fertilizer and fallow, but also by the fact that one could make use, as needed, of semi-wild outlying areas: commons, forests, heaths, moors, and swamps." The Columbian Exchange of New World crops throughout Afro-Eurasia, especially of maize, manioc, and the potato, "promoted population densities that led to overuse of forests and pastures."[50]

Continuous farming of the same land required the development of strategies to maintain the fertility of the land, from laying fallow part of it in Europe, to massive fertilizing using animal and human manure in China and Japan. Even then, evidence suggests a declining fertility of all of these lands, especially a decline in critical nutrients such as nitrogen, by the later early modern period. Further indicators of declining fertility of early modern farms are found in the growing global demand for guano and nitrates,[51] and the push into frontier areas where new farms could—for a while—tap the land's natural fertility.

To be sure, the Americas continued to hold a vast treasure trove of natural resources as late as 1800 (or as early as, from an American perspective). But as we have seen in this chapter about other places on Earth, a Jeffersonian vision of an America of smallholding farmers armed with iron axes and plows would have rapidly mowed down the North American forest to make way for farms. And although repeating rifles may well have been an artifact of the nineteenth-century industrial era, the massive bison herds approaching 30 million animals roaming the North American Great Plains in 1800 were cut down to a few thousand by 1900.[52] The frontier everywhere on Earth was ending as the modern world was emerging, and that process was more than well on its way in the early modern world. Climate change and the human

---

[50] Joachim Radkau, *Nature and Power: A Global History of the Environment* (New York: Cambridge University Press; Washington DC: German Historical Institute, 2008), pp. 195–8.

[51] Gregory T. Cushman, *Guano and the Opening of the Pacific World: A Global Ecological History* (New York: Cambridge University Press, 2013), ch. 1. Although this book is mostly about the nineteenth century, the introduction usefully locates the global search for guano in an early modern context.

[52] Andrew C. Isenberg, *The Destruction of the Bison: An Environmental History, 1750–1920* (New York: Cambridge University Press, 2002), p. 23.

and environmental responses to it also constitute an important chapter of the early modern era.

Finally, it is apparent that the dynamics of the early modern world did not originate in Europe and emanate around the world. States, markets, productive agriculture, and rising populations moved environmental change in the Americas before 1492, in East and South Asia, and in Africa. Those apparently independent developments around the world eerily recall the simultaneity of the Neolithic agricultural revolution, for which we also lack a unified explanation.[53] So future generations of historians will have to tackle the questions of what connections there are between the early modern and modern worlds, and why there were so many "strange parallels" across the early modern world.[54]

FURTHER READING

Beinhart, William and Lotte Hughes, *Environment and Empire: Oxford History of the British Empire Companion Series* (Oxford University Press, 2009).

Braudel, Fernand, *The Structures of Everyday Life*, Sian Reynolds (trans.) (New York: Harper & Row, 1981).

Cook, David Noble, *Born to Die: Disease and New World Conquest, 1492–1650* (New York: Cambridge University Press, 1998).

Cronon, William, *Changes in the Land: Indians, Colonists, and the Ecology of New England* (New York: Hill and Wang, 1983).

Crosby, Alfred W., Jr., *The Columbian Exchange: Biological and Cultural Consequences of 1492* (Westport, CT: Praeger Publishers, 2003).

   Ecological Imperialism: The Biological Expansion of Europe, 900–1900 (Cambridge University Press, 2004).

Elvin, Mark, *Retreat of the Elephants: An Environmental History of China* (New Haven, CT: Yale University Press, 2004).

Grove, Jean, *The Little Ice Age* (London: Methuen, 1988).

Grove, Richard, *Green Imperialism: Colonial Expansion, Tropical Island Edens and the Origins of Environmentalism, 1600–1860* (Cambridge University Press, 1995).

Hill, Christopher V., *South Asia: An Environmental History* (Santa Barbara, CA: ABC-CLIO, 2008).

Maddox, Gregory H., *Sub-Saharan Africa: An Environmental History* (Santa Barbara, CA: ABC-CLIO, 2006).

Mann, Charles C., *1491: New Revelations of the Americas before Columbus*, 2nd edn. (New York: Vintage Books, 2011).

---

[53] J. R. McNeill, "Global Environmental History: The First 150,000 Years" in J. R. McNeill and Erin Stewart Mauldin (eds.), *A Companion to Global Environmental History* (Oxford: Blackwell Publishing, 2012), p. 7.

[54] Victor Lieberman, *Strange Parallels: Southeast Asia in a Global Context* (Cambridge University Press, 2009), vols. 1–2.

Marks, Robert B., *China: Its Environment and History* (Lanham, MD: Rowman & Littlefield, 2012).

  Tigers, Rice, Silk, and Silt: Environment and Economy in Late Imperial South China (Cambridge University Press, 1998).

McNeill, J. R., *Mosquito Empires: Ecology and War in the Greater Caribbean, 1620–1914* (New York: Cambridge University Press, 2010).

  "The State of the Field of Environmental History," *Annual Review of Environment and Resource* 35 (2010), 345–74.

McNeill, William, *Plagues and Peoples* (New York: Anchor, 1976).

Melville, Elinor G. K., *A Plague of Sheep: Environmental Consequences of the Conquest of Mexico* (Cambridge University Press, 1997).

Miller, Shawn William, *An Environmental History of Latin America* (Cambridge University Press, 2007).

Perdue, Peter C., *China Marches West: The Qing Conquest of Central Eurasia* (Cambridge, MA: Harvard University Press, 2005).

  Exhausting the Earth: State and Peasant in Hunan, 1500–1850 (Cambridge, MA: Harvard University Council on East Asian Studies, 1987).

Pomeranz, Kenneth, *The Great Divergence: China, Europe, and the Making of the Modern World* (Princeton University Press, 2000).

Ponting, Clive, *A Green History of the World: The Environment and the Collapse of Great Civilizations* (New York: Penguin Books, 1991).

Radkau, Joachim, *Nature and Power: A Global History of the Environment* (New York: Cambridge University Press; Washington DC: German Historical Institute, 2008).

Rangarajan, Mahesh, *India's Wildlife History: An Introduction* (New Delhi: Ranthambhore Foundation, 2001).

Reader, John, *Africa: The Biography of a Continent* (New York: Vintage Books, 1999).

Richards, John F., *The Unending Frontier: An Environmental History of the Early Modern World* (Berkeley, CA: University of California Press, 2003).

Thornton, John, *Africa and Africans in the Making of the Atlantic World, 1400–1800* (New York: Cambridge University Press, 1998).

Totman, Conrad, *The Green Archipelago: Forestry in Preindustrial Japan* (Berkeley, CA: University of California Press, 1989).

Turner, B. L., W. C. Clark, R. W. Kates, J. F. Richards, J. T. Mathews and W. B. Meyer (eds.), *The Earth as Transformed by Human Action: Global and Regional Changes in the Biosphere over the Past 300 Years* (New York: Cambridge University Press, 1993).

Webb, James L. A., Jr., *Desert Frontier: Ecological and Economic Change along the Western Sahel, 1600–1850* (Madison, WI: University of Wisconsin Press, 1995).

  Humanity's Burden: A Global History of Malaria (Cambridge and New York: Cambridge University Press, 2009).

Whited, Tamara L., Jens I. Engels, Richard C. Hoffmann, Hilde Ibsen and Wybren Verstegen, *Northern Europe: An Environmental History* (Santa Barbara, CA: ABC-CLIO, 2005).

Williams, Michael, *Deforesting the Earth: From Prehistory to Global Crisis* (University of Chicago Press, 2003).

Wrigley, E. A., *Continuity, Change, and Chance* (Cambridge University Press, 1990).

3

Globalization of disease, 1300 to 1900

JAMES L. A. WEBB, JR.

During the long era from the fourteenth century through the nineteenth century, the global webs of human commercial and social interactions extended and thickened. Some disease pathogens reached new populations, and the disease environments of humankind were more fully integrated than ever before. This was an extremely destructive process. Some of the upheavals, such as the Eurasian outbreak of Black Death of the fourteenth century and the introduction of Old World diseases to the Americas in the sixteenth and seventeenth centuries, had such broad historical consequences that they seem to stand categorically outside of earlier human experience. Yet, even the major catastrophes had ecological limitations, and they took place within discrete macro-disease environments that had evolved more or less independently over many millennia. For this reason, the historical epidemiological processes of the era 1300 to 1900 can best be grasped by a consideration of the earliest and most foundational human experiences with infectious disease.

The deep contexts of human disease history

Human beings have never lived free from disease. Our earliest human ancestors were subject to a broad range of bacterial, helminthic, viral and protozoan infections in tropical Africa. These infections could inflict severe suffering or death. Yet, from an epidemiological point of view, they were episodic and transient, because early human groupings were too small to circulate the infections on an ongoing basis and there were only intermittent contacts between them. The dynamics of infectious disease transmission could not change until human groups grew in size, and this could only happen as a result of technological innovation that helped them to extract more resources from their environments.

As early as 87,000 BCE, groups congregated seasonally along tropical African riverbanks to use new fishing technologies. In these seasonal settlements, vivax malarial infections became endemic, and eventually the malaria pressure selected for a genetic mutation to protect against vivax infection, marking the first chapter in the history of human disease.[1] Many tens of thousands of years later, small bands of *Homo sapiens* who had migrated out of Africa began to undertake major, gradual transitions in their lifestyles, from gathering, hunting, foraging, and fishing to settled agriculture. In the process, they accomplished the genetic selection of food plants with desirable characteristics that would repay the effort of intentional cultivation. These transitions, known as the 'agricultural revolutions', blossomed in a variety of settings, including the vegeculture of the wet tropics as well as the seed agriculture of the riverine floodplain societies along the southern rim of Eurasia.

The vegeculturalists who planted tubers and the agriculturalists who sowed grain increased their numbers with difficulty. They harvested calories sufficient to sustain slow growth in population, yet their increasing population densities and the ecological transformations that these denser populations provoked created new vulnerabilities to disease.

The nature of these vulnerabilities varied. In tropical Africa, human beings had long had to contend with diseases transferred from wild animal populations by insect vectors. There were a plethora of such infections, including the trypanosome that causes sleeping sickness, the virus that causes yellow fever, and the plasmodia that cause different kinds of malaria (including vivax). The initial disease burden of the African tropics was probably higher than elsewhere in the world, and over time, as populations grew, this disease burden increased.[2] The vulnerability to malaria intensified when vegeculturalists expanded into the forest zones and inadvertently opened up breeding habitat for the anopheline mosquitoes that transmitted malaria. At least by the first millennium BCE, the intensity of malaria transmission in the villages had created a basic epidemiological divide. Those who lived in villages encountered malaria in their early childhood years. The mortality costs were high, but the survivors developed a partial (and sometimes even a full) immunity to malarial infection. The non-immunes who encountered the villages had no such protection. The historical result was an epidemiological juggernaut that allowed for the 'Bantu'-speaking agriculturalists to expand throughout tropical Africa, at the expense of those who gathered, fished, foraged and hunted.

---

[1] James L. A. Webb, Jr, *Humanity's Burden: A Global History of Malaria* (Cambridge and New York: Cambridge University Press, 2009), pp. 18–41.

[2] William H. McNeill, *Plagues and Peoples* (New York: Anchor, 1976), pp. 35–53.

The expansion of the disease-experienced populations, at the expense of the non-disease-experienced populations, was not confined to tropical Africa. It was repeated elsewhere in the river basin societies of southern Eurasia and northern Africa. Yet, there the mix of pathogens was considerably different. In southern Eurasia and Northern Africa, there was neither sleeping sickness nor yellow fever. The intensity of malaria transmission was lower, and the mix of malarial parasites caused fewer deaths. Yet, by approximately the fifth millennium BCE, the Eurasian and Northern African disease environment had begun to take on entirely new properties. As early agriculturalists began to domesticate animals, some of their pathogens leaped across species to infect human beings. These zoonoses – diseases that pass from animals to humans – were virulent and wreaked havoc on the settled communities.

The zoonoses were varied, and the survivors of measles, mumps, chickenpox, and several other major zoonotic killing diseases acquired lifetime immunity. This produced a paradox, similar to that in tropical Africa. The settled communities were the most unhealthy and epidemiologically dangerous places in the world, yet the survivors were disease-hardened. And when they encountered non-disease-experienced populations, they transmitted their diseases to them. Thus, the immunologically-naïve populations, rather than encountering the pathogens exclusively during their childhood years, met them across the entire age spectrum, with devastating results. The expansion of the river basin societies into their hinterlands had a powerful epidemiological dimension. It was one of the principal forces of cultural expansion both in tropical Africa and Northern Africa and Eurasia.

The disease environments of tropical Africa and those of Northern Africa and Eurasia were profoundly different from that of the Americas. Human beings had entered the Americas well before the era of the domestication of animals and agricultural revolutions. They entered an environment profoundly altered by glacialization, and insect-borne disease was a far smaller burden in northern climes. Small human groupings, even when they first turned to agriculture in what is today central Mexico, developed sedentary societies without large working animals, because with the exception of the llama and alpaca of the high Andes, there were no large animals in the Americas that were amenable to domestication.[3]

---

[3] For an overview of the domestication of animals, see Jared Diamond, *Guns, Germs, and Steel: The Fate of Human Societies* (New York: W. W. Norton & Company, 1997), pp. 157–75.

The result was not a disease-free paradise. Intestinal diseases were rife, and syphilis and tuberculosis were among the important infectious diseases. In the American tropics, there were also indigenous vector-borne diseases, such as jiggers and Chagas disease, which could be fatal. Yet, the New World disease environment was less deadly than those in the Old World. Human populations in the Americas did not have to deal with the major vector-borne diseases of tropical Africa or the zoonoses of Eurasia and Northern Africa.

Major disease environments of the world, *c.* 1300

Over millennia, the major civilizational areas of the world achieved epidemiological distinctiveness within the three disease meta-regions described above – tropical Africa, Northern Africa and Eurasia, and the Americas. Their differences were in part a function of the environments in which they were centred, because the soil endowments, growing seasons, and regional flora and fauna shaped in fundamental ways the systems of agriculture and vegeculture, upon whose success all else rested.

The practice of agriculture and vegeculture entailed the refashioning of landscapes to make them productive. This meant extensive environmental change – particularly deforestation to produce arable fields for grains and tubers. This involved extensive habitat change for the local faunal populations. It tended to drive out the large mammals from the sedentary communities, opening up lands for the tending of small stock animals, and it transformed the environments for insects and small mammals that found stable food sources in the sedentary communities.

Some of this environmental transformation of the microfauna had profound implications for human disease. One of the most clear-cut examples, from the world of insects, is that of human malaria. Across the arable lands of the Old World, malaria became established among the sedentary communities. Malaria is a parasitical disease, borne by mosquitoes of the genus Anopheles. There are scores of anopheline species with different capabilities for transmitting malaria, and these species breed in a wide variety of habitats. For this reason, malaria became an endemic disease across virtually the entire expanse of the temperate and tropical Old World, and in the core areas of human settlement it became an intensely transmitted infection. Malaria can debilitate and kill, and in the face of this selection pressure human beings who had inherited genetic mutations that reduced the possibility of lethal complications from malarial infections had better chances for survival. Some mutations, such as sickle-cell trait, were haemoglobinopathies that produced incorrectly functioning globins. Others, known as thalassemias, produced too few globins. Across the Old World, these haemoglobin mutations became one of the most important and widely expressed genetic conditions, lessening the bearers' susceptibility to death from malaria, but also rendering them vulnerable to anaemia and other conditions that could severely compromise health.

Other risks to health blossomed within the farming systems. Seed crops in particular were at risk from wind-blown fungal blights that could reproduce easily in mono-cropped fields, where the host plants were clustered. The rice blasts, wheat rusts and other pathogens that preyed upon domesticated cultigens were a scourge of agricultural communities. Outbreaks of plant disease could in turn compromise the nutritional status and thus the health of the agriculturalists whose lives depended directly upon the success of their harvests.

Nor was famine the only major risk. Nutritional diseases were the consequence of a deep dependence upon a staple crop. In the maize-producing regions of the Americas, this staple was frequently eaten in combination with beans to produce a diet with a full complement of essential amino acids. When beans went missing from the diet, agriculturalists fell prey to pellagra, a nutritional deficiency disease. In the rice-farming systems of Southeast Asia, the husking of the rice harvest removed vitamins, and there were outbreaks of beriberi, a disease caused by a deficiency of the vitamin B12. In the Mediterranean world, the cultivation of fava beans produced valuable vegetable protein, but for those who carried a genetic mutation known as G6PD eating fava beans could result in severe anaemia. Forest and dry-land gatherers and hunters had far less exposure to these diseases, because their diets were more varied.

In 1300, the infectious disease environments of the three macro-regions were not static. This was particularly the case in Eurasia. Across the temperate expanses of Eurasia where domesticated animals became a critical component of the regional ways of life, diseases circulated. The pathogens were not continuously shared among the peoples living in densely settled regions, and thus there was always the ongoing threat of a pilgrim or travelling merchant introducing a 'new' disease into a settled community.

This threat was multiplied by the development of long distance trade across the grasslands and borderlands of Afro-Eurasia. This was, in part, a function of the caravan rest stops that made long distance trade more feasible. The caravanserai provisioned the travellers and their animals and thereby helped the caravans to cover great distances in relatively short periods of time. This meant that settled population densities no longer were the most important constraint on the transmission of infectious disease. The archipelago of caravanserai meant that it was possible to transfer human disease, and insect vectors that attached themselves to the caravanning animals, across great distances. In this sense, long distance trade facilitated the most catastrophic outbreaks of epidemic disease in world history.

The early outstanding example of this long-range transmission of insect vectors and human disease was the transportation of the rat flea (*Xenophylla cheopis*) that carried the plague bacillus (*Yersina pestis*) to western Eurasia from another region of that continental land mass. The species of black rat that carried the plague bacillus appears to have lived originally in India, and it may have made its way from India to the Mediterranean with the opening of sea communications.[4] The first major catastrophic outbreak of bubonic plague across the Eurasian steppes took place in the sixth century CE. Many historians consider it to be an historic marker of the integration of eastern and western Eurasia. It had broad consequences. It accelerated the decline of Roman cultural synthesis in the Mediterranean basin, and it likely had far-reaching effects elsewhere in Eurasia. It is possible that its influence was transmitted into the Nilotic Sudan, although the expanse of the Sahara Desert and the difficulty of overland travel within humid regions to the south may have acted as a barrier to the extensive transmission of the plague into sub-Saharan Africa.

The convulsions of Afro-Eurasian reintegration in the fourteenth century

During the first half of the fourteenth century, an even more catastrophic epidemic struck many of the peoples of Eurasia. The epidemic may have been the result of the expansion of Mongol hegemony across eastern and central Eurasia. In several respects, it seems to have been a replay of the disaster of the sixth century CE, when bubonic plague broke out across much of the Afro-Eurasian land mass north of the Sahara. It was, however, a broader disaster because the agricultural regions of Eurasia had become more extensive, reaching into more northern latitudes, and it was more destructive in terms of the number of lives lost. Moreover, the epidemic struck repeatedly over succeeding decades and centuries. Serial convulsions shattered the affected Eurasian communities repeatedly.

---

[4] McNeill, *Plagues and Peoples*, pp. 137–40.

There is much that is not known about the black plague of the fourteenth century. Medical historians are not agreed that the disaster can be solely attributed to *Yersina pestis*; it is possible that other pathogens were involved, and that the extent of the population loss was a result of multiple infections or the synergy of co-infections. It is impossible to determine its precise origins. The imaginative reconstruction of William H. McNeill, who located the origins of the epidemic in China in 1331 and its subsequent spread along the trade routes between China and southwest Asia during the rule of the Mongol Empire (1206 to 1368 CE), is broadly accepted. In McNeill's view, horsemen within the Mongol domains likely acquired the infection some- where on the northern or southern reaches of China (Manchuria or Yunnan); fleas infected with the plague bacillus (*Yersina pestis*) burrowed into their animals and at length made their way across central Eurasia, reaching the edges of the Mediterranean world.

Microbiological evidence also supports the thesis that the epidemic ini- tially arced across Eurasia, from east to west.[5] The historical evidence, however, is scant for the bubonic plague epidemic in China and central Eurasia, and more is known about the progress of the pandemic on the western steppes. There, in the 1340s, Mongol armies attacked the Black Sea port of Caffa in the Crimean region, and from that point on the infection spread into the Mediterranean, and then north into Europe, reaching Scandi- navia within two years, and east and south into the Muslim societies of the eastern Mediterranean and North Africa. The spread of the plague in Europe is best documented; and on the basis of the microbiological evidence, it is now understood that two distinct bubonic plague infections entered Europe via Mediterranean ports. The infections spread through the bites of fleas that lived as a parasite on the common black rat throughout the Mediterranean. The flea vector was highly mobile, because the black rat was a common feature of farm, town and ship.

The initial wave of mortality in the affected areas of Europe killed approximately one-third of the population. Historians have estimated com- parable mortality in the Muslim world of the eastern Mediterranean and North Africa. Thereafter, successive waves of the plague, beginning in the 1360s and continuing into the late seventeenth century, killed large numbers, but never as high a percentage as in the initial wave. European populations

[5] Mark Achtman, Raffaela Bianucci, Barbara Bramanti *et al.*, 'Distinct Clones of *Yersinia pestis* Caused the Black Death', *PLoS Pathogens* 6 (2010), e1001134, doi:10.1371/journal. ppat.1001134.

may not have regained their pre-plague size until the eighteenth century, and Muslim populations may not have done so until much later, if at all.

What was the extent of the spread of the black plague elsewhere in Eurasia? It seems likely to have been a broad demographic disaster, but the documentary evidence outside of the Mediterranean world is scant. It seems likely that the population of China was hard hit; and it is possible that the population of China decreased by as much as 50 per cent, although the Mongol invasions may have also been a major contributor to the decline. A major lacuna in our knowledge is the extent of the population loss in other major densely populated areas such as Persia and India. Some historians have advanced estimates of the loss of population at 30 per cent or so, but the evidentiary basis of these estimates is not robust. On the basis of an absence of confirmatory documentary evidence from the Arabic language texts of the western Sahel, it appears that the plague was not transmitted extensively across the Sahara.

The Christian and Muslim societies of Eurasia took the arrival of the black plague as a sign of God's judgment upon them. The literatures of the Christian and Muslim world are replete with references to this divine judgment, and in the Christian world, visual images of human suffering illuminate these cultural perspectives. As yet, little is known about the cultural responses to bubonic plague in South Asian, Southeast Asian and East Asian civilizations.

Within the Christian and Muslim civilizations of western Eurasia, the long-term impacts of bubonic plague differed greatly. In Muslim societies, the plague did not engender any fundamental reordering of social, economic or political institutions. In Europe, by contrast, the devastations of the bubonic plague remade basic institutions. In the aftermath of the first waves of the plague, with the dying off of clerics who were masters of the Latin script, vernacular languages – French, Italian, German, English, Dutch – emerged as languages of written communication. The population losses of European peasants unbalanced the fundamental relations between land and labour. With fewer hands to labour in the fields, landowners gave over their arable lands to livestock herding, which had lower demands for labour. The loss of manpower stimulated a burst of experimentation with wind, water and mechanical sources of power.

The upshot was that although European Christian societies had suffered demographic losses at least as great as those of the Muslim societies of the greater Mediterranean, the black plague shifted the balance of power in the Mediterranean region. Before the mid-fourteenth century, historians

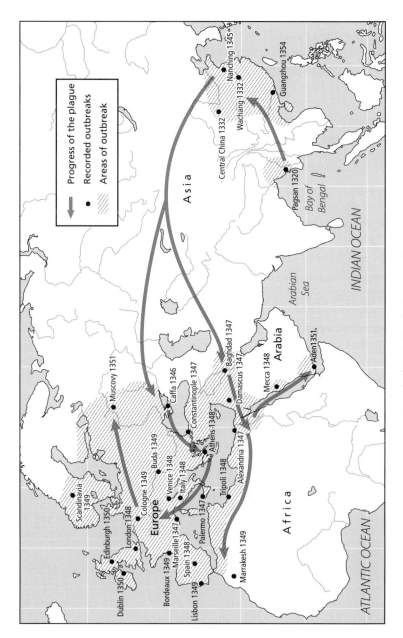

3.1 Spread of Black Death through Afro-eurasia

Progress of the plague
Recorded outbreaks
Areas of outbreak

Asia

Nanching 1345
Wuchang 1332
Guangzhou 1354
Central China 1332
Pagsan 1320

Bay of Bengal

INDIAN OCEAN

Arabian Sea

Baghdad 1347
Mecca 1348
Damascus 1347
Aden 1351

Arabia

Muscovy 1351
Caffa 1346
Constantinople 1347
Athens 1348
Alexandria 1347
Tripoli 1348

Buda 1349
Cologne 1349
Venice 1348
Italy 1348
Palermo 1347
Marrakesh 1349

Scandinavia 1349
Europe
Edinburgh 1350
London 1348
Marseille 1347
Dublin 1350
Bordeaux 1349
Spain 1348
Lisbon 1349

Africa

ATLANTIC OCEAN

are agreed that the more powerful and dynamic societies in the region were Muslim. Historians disagree on when the definitive shift in the balance of power took place, with some arguing for 1400, 1500 or 1600, but most are agreed that by the later date a basic transformation in power relations had taken place. The Christian West had emerged as the more dynamic and inventive Mediterranean cultural zone. The sources of the transformation were, of course, complex and numerous. Yet, one of the most important factors – indeed, perhaps the prime force behind these profound shifts – was the plague pandemic.

Other power balances on the Eurasian continent shifted as well. This was most noticeable on the steppes of central Eurasia, where the power of the nomadic confederations was fractured and would never be integrally restored. Mongol hegemony collapsed, and the horse-riding successors to the great Khanate could not project their power beyond their regional domains. Neither the Ming Dynasty (1368 to 1644) nor its successor the Qing Dynasty (1644 to 1911) had to contend with serious challenges to authority from pastoral nomads from central Eurasia.

The great epidemiological disaster left in its wake European societies that set about processes of internal transformation. Economic competition became more extensive, and the exercise of political power became more dependent upon alliances with merchants. Merchants who sought personal enrichment made common cause with nobles who sought to improve their positions through trade. The net result was not only an increase in regional commerce. Some merchant visionaries and their political backers were emboldened to make direct contact with distant Asian and African societies with whom they had previously been linked by long distance overland caravan trade via intermediaries. The political disorder on the Eurasian steppes and in much of Northern Africa made the prospects of maritime trade more attractive. By the early fifteenth century, Portuguese vessels had begun to venture progressively down the Atlantic coast of Africa. Some European adventurers began to look across the Atlantic in search of a passage to the East. These initiatives would inadvertently trigger even larger epidemiological disasters in the western hemisphere.

The first wave of global integration, c. 1500 to 1650

Following the first landfalls of European ships in the Americas, the crews began to spread Old World diseases among New World peoples whom they encountered, and the epidemiological integration of Afro-Eurasian

disease into the Americas began. The introductions were limited initially
to those diseases that could remain infectious or dormant during the long
ocean passage across the Atlantic. Some of the first introductions were
relatively minor. The common cold was almost certainly among the first of
the Old World viruses to infect individuals in the Caribbean, and among the
first bacilli was almost certainly gonorrhea, a sexually transmitted infection.

The transfer of some of the other common infectious Old World pathogens, including measles, rubella, mumps, smallpox and chickenpox, was
hampered by the fact that most of the crew members had been exposed
to the diseases in childhood and had thereby gained immunity to them.
The number of non-immunes on board the first ships to make the Atlantic
crossing was likely very small or perhaps zero. Indeed, it is striking that the
first recorded transfer of disease in the 'Columbian Exchange', a phrase
coined by Alfred Crosby to refer to a broad range of biological exchanges
between the eastern and western hemispheres, was from the Americas
eastward across the Atlantic. In 1495, an outbreak of syphilis, apparently
previously unknown in Europe, erupted in Naples and was quickly disseminated to France and the rest of Europe. Thereafter, the 'French pox', as it was
widely known, continued to infect, disfigure and kill widely.[6]

Syphilis quickly spread beyond Europe. It travelled overland via long-
distance trade caravans and through religious pilgrimage throughout Eurasia
and from North Africa across the Sahara into tropical Africa. It was disseminated from every caravanserai and commercial node across the overland
routes that criss-crossed the Old World. And syphilis became a quintessen-
tially mobile pathogen as the Portuguese and Spaniards established their
imperial networks of maritime trade. Syphilis rode the high seas of oceanic
commerce and imperial colonization from the late fifteenth century onward.
It was disseminated in every oceanic and inland sea port of call, and it
became one of the first truly globalized infectious diseases.

The linking of the eastern and western hemispheres involved the
biological exchange of animals from the Old World to the New World,
and some of these faunal transfers brought disease. Eurasian sheep introduced new pathogens to the Americas that wreaked havoc on the llamas and
alpacas. In some regions, the die-off was so extensive that the sheep replaced

---

[6] Recent examination of skeletal evidence allows for the identification of the New World
origin of syphilis. See Bruce M. Rothschild, 'History of Syphilis', *Clinical Infectious
Diseases* 40 (2005), 1454–63. For the history of syphilis, see Claude Quétel, *History of
Syphilis*, Judith Braddock and Brian Pike (trans.) (Baltimore, MD: Johns Hopkins
University Press, 1992).

them. And yet other pathogens could not successfully be transferred across the Atlantic Ocean. This was the case with rinderpest, the classic viral disease of cattle and other cloven-hoofed animal populations in Eurasia and Africa. The virus, transmitted rapidly between the animals on board ocean-going ships, left the survivors with immunity. No cattle, sheep or goats infected with rinderpest sank their hooves in the soils of the New World. Rinderpest never established itself in the Americas.

The Columbian Exchange also involved the transfer of cultural practices, some of which left in their wake profound morbidity. Consider, for example, the habit of tobacco use. Tobacco was native to the Americas, and yet the addictive quality of nicotine in the tobacco plant ensured that populations introduced to the leaf as chewing or smoking tobacco or as snuff would crave more, and in the centuries following the early European voyages to the Americas, an international demand developed. Tobacco became a staple of exchange along the coast of Western Africa during the era of the Atlantic slave trade and a passion among those who frequented the early coffee salons of Europe. It took root in the soils of Africa and Eurasia. The early transfers of tobacco smouldered and eventually ignited a global conflagration of morbidity and mortality.[7]

The most immediate and profound chapter in the globalization of disease in the first 150 years of the Columbian Exchange was the transfer of infectious disease from Europe to the Americas. Within the first decade or two after 1492, infectious disease began to take a deep toll on the Carib, Arawak and Taino peoples who inhabited the Caribbean islands. The surviving documentation does not allow identification of the pathogens, and it is likely that death arrived in a swirl of infections. The diseases took hold while the Spanish conquistadores enforced a brutal labour regime on the indigenous peoples, and overwork and physical abuse undoubtedly accelerated the destruction. Within a few generations, virtually all of the indigenous peoples in the Caribbean Basin had died. This disaster was a harbinger of what would occur in the aftermath of the Spaniards' mainland conquests of Mexico and Peru.

Beginning in 1519, the Spanish conquest of Mexico introduced Eurasian killing diseases to the mainland. As in the Caribbean, a number of virulent diseases including measles, typhus, mumps and rubella, must have wreaked

---

[7] Tobacco use is projected to be the single largest contributor to excess global mortality in the twenty-first century. See Allen M. Brandt, *The Cigarette Century: The Rise, Fall, and Deadly Persistence of the Product that Defined America* (New York: Basic Books, 2009).

their havoc, but in Mexico the evidence for the centrality of smallpox as the disease that was the most destructive of the Aztecs and other peoples of Central America is unambiguous. Smallpox produced a case fatality rate of about 30 per cent and terrible suffering and disfigurement in survivors. The catastrophe was compounded by the fact that smallpox is highly contagious. It can be spread through tiny droplets in breath, and in the densely settled urban areas of Central America it was communicated broadly. Moreover, those infected by smallpox are able to infect others for several days before they themselves become symptomatic. Thus, many who fled the epidemics, warfare and terror in the conquered towns inadvertently visited the suffering on the communities in which they sought refuge. This expanding catastrophe was felt throughout the densely populated regions of Central America and probably far beyond. It undoubtedly played a significant role in the collapse of Aztec power.

The epidemiological assault was not confined to Central America. The Eurasian pathogens reached the Andean world at least by the 1530s, when a population crash comparable to that in Central America took place. As in the Aztec areas, the Spaniards established political control. In areas with lower population densities, it was more difficult to sustain and transmit the pathogens, but even so, populations collapsed throughout most regions in the Americas. The general estimate is for population decline of around 90 to 95 per cent by the end of the first century of contact. The psychological impacts of the onslaught must have also been overwhelming. All of the Eurasian infections were previously unknown, and they must have sown terror. None of the indigenous therapeutics was efficacious. A profound spiritual and cultural crisis engulfed the survivors of the American holocaust.[8]

In the aftermath of the demographic collapse, Europeans sought ways to wring profit from the widowed lands. A new era of more focused biological transfers began, and some of these transfers established new disease processes. The cultivation of sugar cane on New World plantations, for example, involved brutal work regimes that visited early death on workers in the prime of life. In the early decades of plantation agriculture, indigenous peoples from Brazil made up most of the enslaved labour force. But by the middle of the seventeenth century, the work forces on the burgeoning plantations had become increasingly Africanized. This transformation was

---

[8] The demographic impact of the introduction of Eurasian infections has generated considerable debate. See David Henige, *Numbers from Nowhere: The American Indian Contact Population Debate* (Norman, OK: University of Oklahoma Press, 1998).

accompanied by a new racial ideology that held that Africans had a lower moral and intellectual potential than did Europeans, and justified the brutality of the labour system. This racist ideology was one of the foundations of new disease patterns in the South Atlantic in the post-1500 era: it underwrote suffering, torture and early death for millions of Africans held in the New World systems of racial slavery.

The second wave of global integration, c. 1650 to 1850

Beginning in the middle of the seventeenth century, a second wave of infections from the Old World crossed the Atlantic and opened a new chapter in the global integration of infectious disease. The wave inundated the American tropics and sub-tropics, the regions in which Portuguese colonizers in Brazil and the principally British, Dutch and French colonizers in the Caribbean Basin focused on export-oriented plantation agriculture. By the mid-seventeenth century, the centre of plantation activity had moved from northeastern Brazil to the islands of the Caribbean, with peripheral extensions along the northern coast of South America and the eastern coast of North America.

This second wave of infections originated from the coastal regions of Western Africa. It was a direct result of the depopulation of the Americas. The trade in African captives constituted the largest transoceanic movement of people in the pre-industrial era, and an epidemiological process drove its exponential growth. African captives introduced the principal killing diseases of tropical Africa to tropical America. Two major infections – falciparum malaria, caused by a single-celled parasite, and yellow fever, caused by a virus – made the journey, and once established in the Americas, these pathogens brought about dramatic change in the demographic make-up of the South Atlantic populations.

The two pathogens were exceptional in that most of the vector-borne tropical African diseases could not be transmitted across the Atlantic, either because the New World ecologies were unsuited to the African vectors or because the vectors could not survive the oceanic passage. For example, the biting flies of the genus *Glossina* – and the parasites that they can host – which cause trypanosomiasis (sleeping sickness) never found an ecological niche in tropical America.

Falciparum malaria did. The advantage that falciparum malaria held was that the parasites could travel across the Atlantic in human bodies.

Falciparum parasites were present in the Mediterranean Basin, as well as in sub-Saharan Africa, but around the Mediterranean Basin, they competed with other malaria parasites for their ecological niche. The Mediterranean mosquitoes were also far less capable of transmitting malaria than were the sub-Saharan African mosquitoes, and thus the levels of parasitization were lower. In sub-Saharan Africa, falciparum constituted the lion's share of more than 90 per cent of all malaria infections and the parasites were transmitted by the most efficient vectors in the world. For these reasons, the arrival of African captives in large numbers provided the critical element – a densely parasitized human population – in the transformation of the malarial environments in the New World tropics and sub-tropics. In a stroke of bad luck, the anopheline mosquitoes of the South Atlantic proved highly capable as vectors; the transfer of an African mosquito was unnecessary to establish malaria in the New World.[9]

The arrival of the yellow fever virus in the South Atlantic added to the makings of the highly dangerous disease environment. In tropical Africa, yellow fever was an endemic infection. Many Africans got sick with yellow fever in childhood, and some evidence suggests that childhood infections may have been less virulent than infections acquired later in life. The virus made its way across the Atlantic via both infected humans brought as captives and infected monkeys brought as pets and curiosities. But unlike malaria infections, the establishment of yellow fever transmission in the South Atlantic basin depended upon the biological transfer of an African mosquito, *Aedes aegypti*, across the Atlantic and its successful colonization in the New World.[10] The date of the transfer can be inferred by what appears to be the first outbreak of a yellow fever epidemic in the mid-seventeenth-century Caribbean. Thereafter, yellow fever, which conveyed lifelong immunity to those who survived an initial bout, became a notorious scourge of the South Atlantic. Its presence tended to support the Spanish hold on its New World Empire, because when the British, French and Dutch sought to gain control of Spanish territories, they generally had ferocious encounters with yellow fever (and malaria), and few non-immunes were left standing.[11]

<hr/>

[9] Webb, Jr, *Humanity's Burden,* pp. 66–91.

[10] Following the successful yellow fever eradication campaigns of the early twentieth century, scientists discovered a reservoir of yellow fever virus in the primates that live in the canopies of the South American tropical rainforests. There, the mosquito vectors for yellow fever transmission belong to the genus *Haemagogus.*

[11] John R. McNeill, *Mosquito Empires: Ecology and War in the Greater Caribbean, 1620–1914* (New York: Cambridge University Press, 2010).

The transformations in this period extended far beyond the Americas. The development of new global networks of oceanic commerce, pioneered by the British, French and Dutch commercial joint stock companies that supplemented and in some regions replaced the earlier Portuguese and Spanish global maritime networks, were integrated with older regional trade webs of exchange around the globe. They increasingly drew larger populations into the webs of exchange.

These networks facilitated the transfer of infectious disease, as had taken place during the first era of the Columbian Exchange. Some were extensions of established diseases that reached new populations. This was true, for example, of the spread of tuberculosis from European immigrants who crossed the Atlantic and settled in the urban centres of the New World, syphilis that reached Native American populations in the trans-Appalachian west, and a new round of smallpox that travelled north from Mexico and devastated Native American populations on the Great Plains.

Other transfers of infectious disease, however, were entirely new and unprecedented. This was the case for cholera, a bacillus transmitted by a faecal-oral route of contamination. It burst forth from Bengal in 1817, eventually striking down populations far beyond the subcontinent of South Asia, and reaching the Americas in the 1830s in the first of seven cholera pandemics that continue to the present day.[12] The destructiveness of cholera (and the terror that it provoked) was the principal impetus to the establishment of the first international agreements to impose quarantine to limit the spread of disease. These first efforts at the control of infectious disease were the precursors to the League of Nations and United Nations in the twentieth century.

The thickening webs of exchange also introduced new populations around the world to new drugs and addictive recreational habits. They spawned new sets of disease consequences that have profoundly influenced global health up to the present. The two principal drugs were distilled alcoholic spirits and tobacco. The availability of distilled alcohol increased alcoholism among all populations in which it found purchase. Among observant Muslim communities, the damage from alcohol was largely foregone through religious proscription. Elsewhere, particularly among European Christian populations, alcoholism became a familiar and entrenched curse. In Russia it reached epidemic proportions, in part because of the inexpensiveness and easy

---

[12] Myron Echenberg, *Africa in the Time of Cholera: A History of Pandemics from 1817 to the Present* (New York: Cambridge University Press, 2011).

availability of distilled spirits made from potatoes or grain. Perhaps the worst consequences of all were among some non-European populations with a genetic predisposition to alcohol addiction. Cheap gin and grain alcohol accelerated the abject decline of some indigenous peoples that European settlers plied with hard drink. Such was the fate of the Khoi of South Africa, aboriginal peoples in Australia and some of the Native Americans in the United States and Canada.

Tobacco had a wider if less immediately deleterious impact. During the era 1650 to 1850, it moved far beyond its initial aficionados in the Americas, Europe, the Muslim Mediterranean and the western coasts of Africa. It spread globally through the new European maritime commercial networks, and in short order tobacco dug footholds outside the Americas. Tobacco began to be cultivated in sub-Saharan Africa and in the moderate climes of Eurasia. Populations took enthusiastically to smoking, chewing and using snuff, and thereby laid the groundwork for new patterns of lung, mouth, tongue, throat and nose cancers. Yet, because these cancers typically emerge only after long-term use, and because life expectancies had yet to dramatically lengthen, these conditions lurked in the backgrounds and would emerge fully only in the twentieth century.

The third wave of global integration, *c.* 1850 to 1900

From the seventeenth century into the middle of the nineteenth century, the networks of international exchange continued to thicken and reached into previously unaffected regions. This growth was facilitated by new maritime technologies that allowed for larger ships and lower per-unit shipping costs. During the period 1650 to 1850, it remained quite expensive to move an array of common goods, such as grain or meat, over great distances. All this began to change during the transport revolution of the mid-nineteenth century: overland transport costs dropped precipitously, as railroads began to spread over the hinterlands; and on the high seas, new steamships and larger sailing ships brought about steep declines in shipping costs. The result was the ability to move new classes of goods longer distances. Lower shipping costs also meant that, after the illegalization of the transoceanic trade in human captives by the European states that had pioneered it, poor, mostly male, individuals in their millions began to traverse long distances looking for work. The epidemiological consequences were to accelerate the global mixing of genetic inheritances and more rapidly to globalize disease than ever before.

One of the outstanding examples is that of bubonic plague. It had been confined for centuries to the expanses of Eurasia, breaking out periodically. After the disastrous fourteenth-century pandemic, the outbreaks had been regionally contained, in part through the practice of quarantine. But with larger and faster ships, it became possible to transport larger numbers of people, greater quantities of bulk foodstuffs and larger populations of attendant vermin over greater distances more rapidly. This superseded the biological constraints that had previously limited the transmission of plague across the oceans. Instead of burning themselves out during the long ocean voyages, plague infections now could continue to circulate on board ship even as they arrived at distant ports of call. During the early years of the third plague pandemic, from 1894 to 1901, plague called at ports around the globe, and bubonic plague became a global disease.[13]

Everywhere, infectious diseases found new homes, as European, African and Asian labourers sought out new opportunities or were coerced into new working environments. Millions of workers migrated overseas and across land.[14] The rigours of long distance travel took a sizeable toll in mortality and morbidity. Many who survived these rigours encountered new disease environments. Tuberculosis became entrenched in the squalid, overcrowded urban neighbourhoods peopled by recent immigrants around the Atlantic, Pacific and Indian Ocean basins. Other increases in infectious disease were the direct result of development and infrastructure projects. In the massive irrigation projects in the Punjab region of British India, for example, new environments were created for vector mosquito breeding. Malaria infections soared, and malaria deaths reached epidemic levels.

In the second half of the nineteenth century, other disease processes followed in the wake of the European colonial conquests that accomplished the 'second great expansion of Europe' that brought nearly all of the Old World tropics under European colonial administration. Some processes were linked directly to colonial warfare and imperial troop movements. Meningitis was largely confined to some European populations before it was inadvertently introduced to Egypt during the Napoleonic Wars, and to Northern Nigeria in the early twentieth century. Thereafter, it became endemic in the Sahelian regions. Many scholars believe that the 'childhood diseases' of

---

[13] Myron Echenberg, *Plague Ports: The Global Urban Impact of Bubonic Plague, 1894–1901* (New York University Press, 2007).
[14] Adam McKeown, "Global Migration: 1846–1940", *Journal of World History* 15 (2004), 155–89.

Eurasia, such as measles, mumps and rubella, were introduced into Western Africa during the era of the slave trade and that an increase in infectious disease, as a result of new introductions of pathogens and the destruction and dislocation of warfare, took place during the 'Scramble for Africa' in the late nineteenth century.

Other disease processes were epizootic – limited to animals – yet still produced disastrous consequences for human populations. An outstanding example is the inadvertent Italian introduction of rinderpest, the great scourge of Eurasian cattle and other cloven-hoofed animals, into Eritrea in 1881 during a campaign of imperial expansion. From northeast Africa, rinderpest travelled south through Eastern Africa, from Eritrea to South Africa. It killed about 90 per cent of the cattle populations on which East African pastoral peoples depended for their livelihood. During the last two decades of the nineteenth century, the disease produced famine, impoverishment and death.

The more rapid movement of peoples and new commodities also opened up possibilities for the transmission of plant diseases, and these diseases in turn had health consequences for those dependent upon the cultivation of susceptible plants. In 1869, one of the world's premier coffee economies in the highlands of colonial Ceylon (modern Sri Lanka) was struck by an epidemic of a fungal blight known as coffee rust that sickened the coffee plant, rendering it unproductive. This drove plantation labourers out of the highlands, either to return to even greater poverty in south India or to search elsewhere for agricultural work. In short order, coffee planters and coffee plantation workers inadvertently transmitted the coffee blight throughout the coffee plantations of the Indian and Pacific Oceans. This was the beginning of the first global plant disease pandemic. It had the effect of increasing the importance of the slave-produced coffee in Brazil and in driving the extension of coffee production elsewhere in the Americas.[15]

The nineteenth century also saw the development of international efforts to block the expansion in epidemiological processes. One major thrust was in the extension of quarantine, long practised to prevent the spread of contagious disease from shipboard to land and across national boundaries. Beginning with the first International Sanitary Conference in Paris in 1851,

[15] Stuart McCook is currently writing a book on the global history of coffee rust. On the outbreak in colonial Ceylon (Sri Lanka), see James L. A. Webb, Jr, *Tropical Pioneers: Human Agency and Ecological Change in the Highlands of Sri Lanka, 1800–1900* (Athens, OH: Ohio University Press, 2002), pp. 108–16.

new international regimes of quarantine linked signatory nations in joint efforts to coordinate their policies. The regimes were difficult to enforce, however, and did not enjoy broad success.

A substantial advance in military health was accomplished with the establishment of routine medical practices. In the 1850s, the use of cinchona bark to treat malaria became standardized on British ships sailing in malarial regions. Also in the 1850s, modern epidemiology made a major advance with the researches of the physician John Snow, who determined that a contaminated water supply was the cause of cholera in London. New understandings of the efficacy of sanitation to reduce or eliminate the contamination of water supplies with faecal matter eventually helped to drive down the number of deaths and illnesses from this source in the developing nations that made these investments. These were the most successful investments in public health that have ever been made.

Sanitation could also be practised in the colonial field. When new public health practices were adopted by European armies in the colonies, deaths of European troops and native troops under European command in these areas dropped accordingly. Covering and liming latrines and rudimentary water filtration systems paid large dividends in improving the health of the troops.[16]

The second half of the nineteenth century also saw a paradigm shift in thinking about disease processes that had substantial consequences for human health. The gradual acceptance of the germ theory of disease and the practice of pasteurization reduced the incidence of tuberculosis from cow's milk in the late nineteenth century in France, which presaged a broader revolution that would make significant gains in reducing the transmission of pathogens from contaminated food supplies. These practices began in the industrialized nations in the late nineteenth century and only gradually made their way to the rest of the world.

Conclusion

The major chapters in the globalization of disease processes in the period 1300 to 1900 can best be appreciated through a comparative, macro-contextual approach. In tropical Africa, populations had long suffered from a broad range of bacterial, helminthic, viral and protozoan infections. In Northern Africa and Eurasia, the disease burden was substantially different,

---

[16] Philip D. Curtin, *Death by Migration: Europe's Encounter with the Tropical World in the Nineteenth Century* (New York: Cambridge University Press, 1989).

because many of the tropical diseases could not be transmitted in other ecological zones and because the domestication of animals and dense human settlement brought about the transfer of animal diseases to humans. In the Americas, human populations carried a different and generally lighter burden of disease.

In the year 1300, no human populations enjoyed robust health. Human populations were subject to a wide variety of diseases of which many were endemic and others had been introduced from beyond their immediate ecosystems. Food was frequently in short supply, and accidents often opened the door to bacterial infections that proved fatal. These, in addition to the killing diseases of the densely settled areas, were the main reasons that life expectancies across the globe were brutally short by the standards of the twentieth or twenty-first centuries. Human beings suffered from nutritional disease, vitamin deficiencies and genetic disorders.

Before the early trans-Atlantic voyages that linked the eastern and western hemispheres, major disease processes were regional and, only occasionally, as in the case of the bubonic plague, continental in extent. Beginning in 1492, the European trans-Atlantic voyages carried Eurasian diseases to the Americas and initiated the most extensive human demographic disaster on record. In the aftermath, a massive slave trade from Africa to the Americas took place for centuries that changed the disease environment of tropical America.

Since 1492, there have been complex and ongoing global ecological exchanges that have affected human health around the globe. These exchanges have involved the transfer of plants, animals, drugs and cultural practices, as well as infectious pathogens. The extent of this globalization was limited by the time, risk and cost of transport, and by ecological factors, such as the disease barrier that prevented Europeans and other non-natives from entering the interior of Africa. In the late nineteenth century, some of these ecological impediments were surmounted, through the use of quinine to reduce the malaria burden and sanitation measures. These advances, in conjunction with new military technologies that reduced the costs of conquest to industrialized nations, underwrote the epidemiological changes of the second half of the nineteenth century.

FURTHER READING

Carpenter, Kenneth J., *The History of Scurvy and Vitamin C* (New York: Cambridge University Press, 1986).
Courtwright, David T., *Forces of Habit: Drugs and the Making of the Modern World* (Cambridge, MA: Harvard University Press, 2001).

Crosby, Alfred W., Jr, *The Columbian Exchange: Biological and Cultural Consequences of 1492* (Westport, CT: Greenwood Press, 1972).

Curtin, Philip D., *Death by Migration: Europe's Encounter with the Tropical World in the Nineteenth Century* (New York: Cambridge University Press, 1989).

Echenberg, Myron, *Africa in the Time of Cholera: A History of Pandemics from 1817 to the Present* (New York: Cambridge University Press, 2011).

Plague Ports: The Global Urban Impact of Bubonic Plague, 1894–1901 (New York University Press, 2005).

Fenn, Elizabeth A., *Pox Americana: The Great Smallpox Epidemic of 1775–1882* (New York: Hill and Wang, 2001).

Gottfried, Robert S., *The Black Death: Natural and Human Disaster in Medieval Europe* (New York: The Free Press, 1983).

Kiple, Kenneth A. (ed.), *The Cambridge World History of Human Disease* (New York: Cambridge University Press, 1993).

McNeill, John R., *Mosquito Empires: Ecology and War in the Greater Caribbean, 1620–1914* (New York: Cambridge University Press, 2010).

McNeill, William H., *Plagues and Peoples* (New York: Anchor, 1976).

Riley, James C., *Rising Life Expectancy: A Global History* (New York: Cambridge University Press, 2001).

Stannard, David E., *American Holocaust: The Conquest of the New World* (New York: Oxford University Press, 1993).

Webb, James L. A., Jr, *Humanity's Burden: A Global History of Malaria* (Cambridge and New York: Cambridge University Press, 2009).

4

Technological transitions

FRANCESCA BRAY

The history of the early modern era is often told as a story about how technology drove the rise of the West. This is a Europe-centred history of key inventions and great inventors; of the emergence of distinctively Western attitudes to 'useful knowledge'; of the professionalisation of technical expertise; of steady improvement in investigating, understanding and applying the scientific principles that govern the material world; of accelerating innovation and of increasingly efficient and profitable manufacturing, culminating in the Industrial Revolution and the birth of a modern, machine-made world.

Although inherently Europe-centred, the narrative of progress no longer excludes other regions of the world. The flowering of world history as a discipline since the 1990s coincided with a heightened interest among historians of technology in how social context shapes technological systems. From the perspective of world history, the story of Europe's rise to supremacy is no longer presented as largely autonomous, an inevitable outcome of superior European brains or culture, but rather as the outcome of continually shifting global and regional flows, exchanges, networks, encounters and competition, accommodation and appropriation, adoption and rejection. Recent studies address the stimulus and challenge of differentials in technical knowledge across the world, examining imitations, improvements and borrowings in every direction.

In an increasingly close-knit world of trade and conquest, local technological exchanges or encounters frequently had repercussions much further afield. It is not surprising that some of the earliest and most influential world histories took weapons and warfare as their theme, nor that these technologies continue to stimulate fertile research and debate. Sources for many regions of the world are rich enough to address broad comparative questions about the relation between war and imperialism, or how military technologies travel;[1] and such detailed questions as how guns contributed to the birth of the Comanche Nation, or who borrowed which gunpowder technology from whom during the wars along the Vietnam–China border in the fifteenth century.[2]

Few other domains of technology are as well documented. On building, food and clothing, hygiene, ceramics, metal-working, mechanics or hydraulics, sources for different parts of the world vary greatly, and most are very patchy. Some societies did not have writing: what we know about technology in pre-conquest Peru, for example, has to be pieced together from Spanish documents, archaeology and ethno-history. The literate classes of Indian society had little interest in crafts or technology; even in the case of the textile industry, early-modern India's foremost economic sector, we rely almost exclusively on foreign observers for information. Chinese records of technological practices are as rich as European sources, but Chinese accounts by policy makers, administrators, encylopaedists, craftsmen and connoisseurs provide views of which technologies mattered, to whom and why, which are very different from the European corpus of documents left by monarchs, prelates, craftsmen, patent officers, French *Encyclopédistes*, entrepreneurs and engineers.[3]

Despite the historiographical challenges, following a 'global commodity', whether it be indigo dye, porcelain, raw cotton, muslin or muskets, proves a fruitful method for investigating technologies, the social and cultural systems in which they are embedded, and patterns of change. Through the early-modern era new tastes and desires, as well as the lust for power, drove history: we see the first traits of consumer society emerge in Ming China, Edo Japan and the Dutch Republic. The historians of commodities rightly insist that production and consumption cannot be treated separately: a commodity has meaning as well as utility, a machine produces goods whose value is not always best calculated in terms of labour efficiency or profit margins.

The concern for meaning brings recent global histories of commodities like textiles or porcelain closer to anthropological approaches. Societies have

---

[1] Daniel R. Headrick, *Power over Peoples: Technology, Environments, and Western Imperialism, 1400 to the Present* (Princeton University Press, 2010); and Peter A. Lorge, *The Asian Military Revolution: From Gunpowder to the Bomb* (Cambridge University Press, 2008).

[2] Pekka Hämäläinen, 'The Politics of Grass: European Expansion, Ecological Change, and Indigenous Power in the Southwest Borderlands', *William & Mary Quarterly* 67 (2010), 173–208; and Sun Laichen, 'Military Technology Transfers from Ming China and the Emergence of Northern Mainland Southeast Asia (c. 1390–1527)', *Journal of Southeast Asian Studies* 34 (2003), 495–517.

[3] Dagmar Schäfer (ed.), *Cultures of Knowledge: Technology in Chinese History* (Leiden: Brill, 2012).

characteristic technological cultures: ideas about which technologies are important and why; about their significance, nature and impact; about the forces they mobilise and the sources of technical skills. The artefacts that technical action produces have different meanings in different societies, and so do the actions themselves. The value attributed to a certain kind of work, or skill, or product, will usually combine a sense of economic worth with beliefs about its symbolic, political or social value. In rural India, the humble female task of butter-churning constitutes a daily renewal of the cosmic order; the Incas' dazzling palanquin was made of an alloy of precious metals that symbolised political unification; designing software is more prestigious than gutting chickens, and thus contemporary governments do more to keep software designers than chicken-gutters within their borders. In tracing the impact of technological change, whether indigenous or triggered by external encounters, and how it was construed and experienced, it is important for world historians to ask not only how technologies performed materially, but also how they contributed to building a political, social and symbolic order.

Several of the grand themes in the world history of technology are addressed elsewhere in this volume, so this chapter proposes a linked sequence of vignettes, chosen to highlight some typical early-modern forms of encounter and transition, while suggesting the diversity of responses. Silver provides the link. All along the emerging world circuit of commerce, in mines and mints, banks, dockyards, arsenals, state factories and humble farmyards, silver quickened the pace of life and heightened the levels of financial risk, bringing now prosperity, now ruin. The silver circuit brought all the regions of the world into contact, confronting societies and their material worlds, and ushering in an age of true world-systems (see Chapter 9, 'Silver in global context, 1400–1800', volume VI, part 2). This chapter asks how the rise of the early-modern silver trade affected technological practices and meanings at different points along the global network it helped to create. It begins with the great silver mine of Potosí in Peru, untouched by the Incas, but opened by the Spanish in 1545. What did silver-mining mean to the vanquished and to the conquerors, and what was the impact of this clash of technological cultures?

Second, we turn to China, the country that absorbed so much of the early-modern world's silver supply, to consider transitions in its biggest industry, textiles and the impact of China's own 'cotton revolution', which began around 1300. Technological developments supported a huge expansion and diversification of the whole textile industry, and transformed the gendered division of labour. Imperial China was hardly unique in this respect, but official reactions were unusual, largely because of the moral and cosmic significance attributed to work and technical skills.

The next link in the silver chain is Europe, where economic historians have identified 'import substitution' as a key motive for the transformations of European production technologies that culminated in the Industrial Revolution. World historians argue that in fact a tangle of motives and strategies were involved. The third section contrasts two cases of import substitution, where European technicians learned to imitate Asian technologies that were draining silver from national coffers. Porcelain was reinvented *de novo* in eighteenth-century Europe, without any direct transfer or even understanding of the Chinese technology. Calico-printing, in contrast, involved a slow infusion of Asian skills, materials and experts into Europe. But advances in chemistry and mechanical science triggered technical improvements that by 1800 had so transformed the industry, that it was now seen by contemporaries as a thoroughly European creation, owing much to the scientific method and nothing to Asian craft roots.

The concluding section asks how successfully world-history approaches challenge master-narratives of Western exceptionalism, pointing to some troublesome limitations.

Purity and lightning: technological cultures of silver-mining in the Andes

In 1545, the Spanish discovered a mountain of silver, Cerro Rico, at Potosí in the Viceroyalty of Peru.[4] The new silver mine proved to be the richest ever known, supplying as much as two-thirds of world output between 1570 and 1610. On a hitherto deserted and barren mountainside sprang up a town that rivalled Paris in size and wealth, dominated by the magnificent stone façade of the Casa de la Moneda, the mint where the silver ingots and coinage were cast that bought Spain an empire.

---

[4] Note: this section is based on Enrique Tandeter, 'The Mining Industry' in Victor Bulmer-Thomas, John Coatsworth and Roberto Cortes-Conde (eds), *The Cambridge Economic History of Latin America* (Cambridge University Press, 2006), vol. I, pp. 315–56; Barbara H. Mills and Mary Van Buren, 'Huayrachinas and Tocochimbos: Traditional Smelting Technology of the Southern Andes', *Latin American Antiquity* 16 (2005), 3–25; Thérèse Bouysse-Cassagne, 'Las minas del centro-sur andino, los cultos prehispánicos y los cultos cristianos', *Bulletin de l'IFEA* 34 (2005), 443–62; and Thérèse Bouysse-Cassagne, 'Le palanquin d'argent de l'Inca: petite enquête d'ethnohistoire à propos d'un objet absent', *Techniques et cultures* 29 (1997), 69–111.

Silver was a key symbolic and material resource for imperial rule under both the Incas and the Spanish. Andean technologies and organisation of silver production were transformed under Spanish rule, as were the meaning and powers of the precious metal. Splicing Spanish accounts and Inca codices, archaeological finds and ethnography, we can piece together an account of pre-conquest and colonial silver-mining practices that reveals the social and symbolic impact of technological change under Spanish rule. The Spanish exploitation of mineral treasures in the Americas transformed the material and social landscape, but while new technologies threatened indigenous cosmologies and identities, some Andean technological traditions survived alongside imported practices, expressing indigenous identity in ways that were invisible, or appeared trivial, to the colonial conquerors.

In the 1530s, the conquistadores had taken over the biggest silver mine of the Inca empire, Porco, dividing it up into huge estates, *encomiendas*. Ignorant themselves of mining techniques and metallurgy, the Spanish initially relied on the expertise of local Caranga Indians whom they set to work as tied *encomienda* labourers, prospecting and mining the ore using traditional tools and techniques, but smelting in Castilian-type ovens. When the Spanish opened Cerro Rico, the first workers were *yanaconas*, Indians with indigenous mining expertise but free of *encomienda* obligations, who leased galleries of silver ore quite profitably from the Spanish owners. The *yanaconas* used traditional tools and techniques for prospecting and extracting the ore, but, unlike the Porco workers, they also used indigenous ovens for smelting. *Guayras* (or *huayrachinas*) were cylindrical single-chamber furnaces of rock and mortar less than 1 metre high, pierced with holes to channel the draught. Unlike Castilian ovens, they reached temperatures high enough to smelt Potosí ores. No bellows were needed: the *guayras* were lit at dusk when the night breezes rose and burned untended until morning. In 1585, a Spanish mill-owner reported over 6,000 *guayras* lighting up the night sky over Potosí. The ore was ground and mixed with galena (lead sulphide), then fired using charcoal. The resulting alloy, more lead than silver, was then separated using an Andean cupellation hearth, a small, dome-shaped muffle-furnace called a *tocochimbo*.

For the first few decades of operation, then, the huge wealth of Potosí was produced using indigenous technologies, under indigenous control. But by the 1570s wood supplies were running out and the proportion of high-grade ore suitable for smelting with *guayras* was declining. Many *yanaconas* left. Meanwhile, flooding was hampering work at Porco, and the Porco mine-owners looked to Potosí for new opportunities.

A technology that successfully extracted silver from low-grade ores reanimated the Potosí industry: mercury amalgamation, the 'patio process' (probably developed in Saxony), was introduced from Mexico in 1572. It consisted of grinding the ore, mixed with water, to a fine paste using a stamping mill (Figure 4.1). The paste was spread out on a large patio, sprinkled with mercury and trodden for hours or even weeks until the silver was thoroughly mixed, after which the amalgam was rinsed, squeezed and heated to extract pure silver. In Mexico, mules turned the wheels and often trod the amalgam. In barren Potosí it was difficult to keep livestock, so on the order of the Viceroy, Francisco de Toledo, a hydraulic system of lakes and channels sufficient to run 300 mills was built (no doubt mobilising the fabled Andean hydraulic skills)[5] and completed in 1575. Treading out the amalgam was done by human workers, as was the extraction of mercury, supplied by the Peruvian mine of Huancavelica.

When processing at Potosí shifted to these ingenios – large-scale milling refineries which only Spaniards could afford to build and run – the *yanaconas* lost the advantage of their technical and managerial skills. Some continued to work as miners extracting ore, but the bulk of the new workforce was coerced labour. Viceroy Toledo established a system of compulsory labour-service, the *mita*, loosely based on Inca practice, which every year brought in around 13,000 workers and their families, drawn from across the Andes, to work in the mines. It is not surprising that few people voluntarily engaged in work involving mercury, which could prove lethal after only a few weeks or months. The *mita* was a continual point of friction between the colonial government, the local headmen responsible for selecting *mita* workers and their communities; many men fled their homes to avoid the *mita*, regional populations were decimated and legislative changes to guarantee *mita* numbers often provoked revolts.

Between the 1580s and the 1750s, no technical improvements occurred in the silver mines of Peru. Capital became scarce after the collapse of silver prices in China in the 1630s, when the Ming state began to crumble, and incentives to invest in improvement were few until the early 1700s, when renewed demand from China (now stabilised under Qing rule) coincided with a gold boom in Brazil to restore the world value of silver. In 1703, production in Potosí began a period of slow recovery, peaking in 1805 at around half the output of 1600. No technical improvements were

---

[5] Katharina Schreiber and Josué Lancho Rojas, *Irrigation and Society in the Peruvian Desert: The Puquios of Nasca* (Lanham, MD: Lexington Books, 2003).

Figure 4.1 Overshot water wheel turning the cam-shaft of a stamping mill being used to turn the crush ore to begin the process of extracting metal from the ore won from a mine. From *De re metallica* by Agricola, pseudonym of Georg Bauer (Basle, 1556), woodcut (Universal History Archive / UIG / Bridgeman Images).

involved: any increases in production or in profits were the outcome of processing more ore, using the hated system of *mita* labour.

The Incas had also used forced labour to mine precious metals and to build vast imperial projects including temples, palaces, roads and irrigation systems. Nobody would argue that the Incas were considerate employers. Yet, in drawing together workers of many ethnic groups from across a vast territory that they had conquered in a matter of decades, the Incas intended *mita* to build a sense of common purpose among their subjects. Most Inca

state-building projects mobilised pan-Andean religious beliefs or cosmo-
logical symbols as vehicles of political assimilation. In the case of mining,
Andean peoples shared the belief that the hills containing precious metals,
and the mines within them, belonged to – or rather were – *huaca* (deities).
They could be opened for human use only if the deity gave permission.
In that case a shrine (also *huaca*) had to be set up and consecrated before
mining began. The *huaca* of Porco had given permission to mine for silver,
but the Incas refrained from opening up Cerro Rico because when a dedica-
tion ritual was attempted the deity spoke in a thunderous voice, declaring
that the mine was reserved for himself. The whole process of extraction
was sacralised: miners drank, danced and offered coca to the *huaca* guarding
the entrance to the mine and to the *huacas* inside the galleries that they were
working, smelters prayed and offered coca before lighting the *guayra*. When
Inca workers migrated to fulfil their *mita* duties in the mines, not only were
they fulfilling a compulsory duty, they were also performing sacred work
for the common good.

Silver and gold played a key role in Inca government, not as inert
metals, but as living forces creating wealth and strength. The ruler of the
Inca Empire, also known as the Inca, was carried through the streets on a
palanquin made of silver alloyed with gold, glittering like the sun. Alloys
were more highly prized than pure metals, for they symbolised the blending
of peoples under Inca rule. Ritual exchanges of objects in precious metals
between the living Inca and his feudatories mirrored and fed an underworld
network of exchange. Just as lightning struck the mountains, fertilising germs
of metal beneath the soil so that they grew into rich deposits of metal and
ore, so precious objects buried with members of the ruling class germinated
in the tombs, bringing fertility to their lands and victory to their armies. The
Incas valued the silver of the Porco mine especially highly for its 'extremely
white' colour. But this should not be taken as a measure of metallic purity
such as the Spanish would have valued. The 'white' Porco silver was
especially precious because whiteness betokened lightning, the weapon of
the supreme deity who bestowed fertility, wealth and military success.

The Spanish saw nothing as the Andean peoples did. They considered
that burying objects of precious metal in tombs was a scandalous waste, a
perversion of Christian values. They equated value with purity and weight:
the worth of the Inca regalia was assessed by melting it down, weighing it
and assaying the metal, in the process ostentatiously destroying the most
powerful symbols of Inca rule and cosmology. Fearless of the wrath of pagan
spirits, the Spanish ripped open the silver lodes of Potosí. Catholic priests

banned the mining rituals of drinking and dancing and demolished the *huacas* that had crowned the silver-mountains, replacing them with shrines to the Virgin. Andean miners duly paid homage at the new shrines, a transfer of loyalty doubtless eased by a fortunate ambiguity: the Quechua name given to the Virgin, Coya (Queen), coincided with that of the Andean deities of the mine galleries (*koya*). Ostensibly Catholic though the miners now were, it seems that numerous *huacas*, especially those located safely out of sight underground, continued in use well into the seventeenth century. Moreover, recent ethnographic studies record that in modern Andean villages where traditional metal-working survives, offerings of coca or animals are still made before entering the mines or firing the *guayra*. Metallurgy is just one example of a craft-skill that served to keep Andean cosmology and identity alive through centuries of European rule.[6]

To the Spanish, the silver of Potosí was money, pure wealth. The Spanish crown levied a 20 per cent tax on the silver produced in Peru and used it to build an empire. The treasure that flowed from the American silver mines into the coffers of Madrid had no aura, nor (unlike gold) was it specially valued as a material. Economic historians observe that the Spanish, unlike the Dutch or the Japanese, did not spend their silver wealth wisely. They did not invest in technical or institutional innovations, nor did they finance improvements in agriculture or industry. Instead of using capital to generate wealth by developing the means of production, the Spanish monarchs of the Golden Age fostered what Thomas Misa calls 'technologies of the court',[7] technologies that consumed rather than generated wealth. American silver paid for Spanish palaces, cathedrals and roads, for bureaucratic salaries, patronage of the arts and royal regalia, but above all for soldiers and sailors, ships and guns. The Spanish monarchs thirsted for glory: their mission was to stamp out the Reformation and to rule as the foremost power in Europe. To this end they went deeply into debt for wars that they lost. High silver prices in Ming China, where the exchange rate with gold was twice the level in Europe, kept Spain afloat until the 1630s, but thereafter, when the collapse of the Ming state led to a short-term but serious drop in silver values, 'Spain vanished as a serious Western power'.[8]

---

[6] See 'Further reading'.

[7] Thomas J. Misa, *Leonardo to the Internet: Technology and Culture from the Renaissance to the Present* (Baltimore, MD: Johns Hopkins University Press, 2004), pp. 1–32.

[8] Dennis O. Flynn and Arturo Giráldez, 'Born with a "Silver Spoon": The Origin of World Trade in 1571', *Journal of World History* 6 (1995), 212. Flynn and Giráldez argue that silver brought the fall of the Ming dynasty, but pay less attention to the role of silver in the rapid rise of the Qing.

China's 'cotton revolution': work, gender and cosmic order

In China, by contrast, silver wealth brought substantial long-term gains. Ming China lacked silver of its own, but purchased it with manufactured goods.[9] The imported silver fuelled technical improvements, economic growth and a rise in consumption.[10] The Ming cotton industry in particular was a silver-driven engine of growth, and its technical development catalysed significant changes in gender roles. The responses of the ruling class highlight the political and cosmic significance attributed to technological practices.

By the late 1500s, cotton merchants were among the wealthiest and most powerful people in China, treated like princes wherever they went. The merchants bought raw cotton in the north, shipped it south for processing, then re-exported the cloth across China and East or Southeast Asia, supplying the government as well as selling on open markets. Since they controlled the whole chain of production, setting local prices for raw cotton, yarn or cloth, their profits were immense, and so too was their need for liquid capital. Cotton merchants embodied early-modern China's insatiable thirst for silver, carrying thousands of ounces with them as they went about their business.

The Chinese cotton revolution had begun under Mongol rule, in the 1270s. Until then, cotton was an exotic luxury. Hemp was the coarse fibre worn by commoners in the north; ramie was everyday wear in the south. Rich people wore silks, ranging in quality from simple under-and-over tabby-weaves to elaborate damasks or brocades. Every household had to pay taxes in cloth, and all women wove. Peasant women raised silkworms or processed the hemp that their husbands grew, weaving cloth on cheap and simple looms small enough to fit in a cottage. In richer families, women might use drawlooms to weave patterned fabrics. In urban or imperial workshops, where the very finest silks were woven, some workers were men. But generally speaking, textiles were women's work: women were responsible for every stage of cloth processing, from hatching silkworm eggs and splicing ramie fibres to weaving the cloth and making the clothes. All this was to change dramatically.

---

[9] Note: this section is based on Francesca Bray, *Technology and Gender: Fabrics of Power in Late Imperial China* (Berkeley, CA: University of California Press, 1997).

[10] See Robert Marks, *Tigers, Rice, Silk, and Silt: Environment and Economy in Late Imperial South China* (Cambridge University Press, 1998).

The Mongol rulers introduced cotton to North China from Central Asia. Long wars had devastated the silk industry, but the state still needed vast quantities of tax-cloth to pay civil servants, clothe the army and bestow upon neighbouring rulers. Qubilai himself commissioned technical instruction manuals and established Cotton Bureaus around the country to teach people how to grow and process the new crop; as a further incentive, taxes on cotton cloth were set at favourable rates compared to other textiles. The Ming government, which used 15 to 20 million bolts of cotton a year, initially continued the cotton tax. Even without these fiscal pressures, the rapid success of cotton would have been assured. Cotton cloth was light and fine, softer than hemp and cheaper than silk, warm in winter and cool in summer, and a bolt could be woven in a single day on a simple loom. It could also be used for fancy weaves, dyed in rich colours and calendered (pressed with a heavy stone roller) to a shine that approached the gloss of silk.

The new crop grew well almost everywhere in China. In the northeast, cotton could be interplanted with wheat; it throve in the subtropical south; in the Shanghai area it replaced rice in many higher fields. It did especially well in the dry and sunny north, provided it was watered from a river or well. But processing was more tricky. All traditional Chinese textiles were made from long fibres, and in order to process short-stapled cotton the Chinese had to become familiar with a whole new technological kit. Local historians of Songjiang district, near Shanghai, claimed that the cotton kit was first introduced to China in the 1290s, by a woman, a certain Auntie Huang. After spending her girlhood years in the remote southern island of Hainan, where cotton had long been grown and processed using technology that was presumably Indian in origin, Auntie Huang moved to Songjiang and taught the locals to make and use the cotton-processing tools. Male writers sang her praises as the woman who had single-handedly transformed a rural backwater into one of the most prosperous districts in China.

The new equipment included the cotton gin, which eliminated the seeds; the technique of bowing, which untangled and fluffed up the fibre ready for spinning; and the multiple-spindle, treadle-operated spinning-wheel, which allowed one woman to spin several threads simultaneously (Figure 4.2). All this equipment was illustrated, and its construction and function explained, in a comprehensive treatise on agriculture composed by a Yuan official, Wang Zhen, in 1313. It was small and cheap enough to be used in peasant households; with a treadle-wheel one could spin 4 to 6 Chinese ounces of cotton in a day, so it took only two days to spin the pound of thread needed

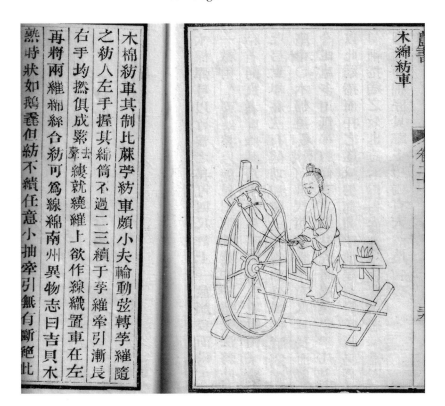

木棉紡車其制比麻苧紡車頗小夫輪動弦轉苧繀隨之紡八左手握其綿筒不過二三繀于莩繀牽引漸長右手均撚俱成緊去縷就繞繀上欲作線織置車在左再將兩繀抽絲合紡可為線綿南州異物志曰吉貝木熟時狀如鵝毳但紡不繢任意小抽牽引無有斷絕比

木綿紡車

Figure 4.2 Triple-spindle wheel for processing cotton from the *Nongshu* (1783 edition) (courtesy of the Needham Research Institute).

to weave a bolt of cloth.[11] Wang Zhen wrote that these tools were still little known, despite state efforts to propagate them, and he expressed the hope that their use would spread rapidly.

The use of the new technology was, however, circumscribed by climatic factors. The north was so dry that thread came out brittle and uneven, whereas the humid summers of Jiangnan (the lower Yangzi region) were ideal for spinning cotton. A regional division of labour quickly emerged. Merchants bought raw cotton in the north and exported it to Jiangnan, which grew less cotton than it could process. The merchants distributed the cotton

---

[11] Over time, the Chinese ounce varied between about 30 and 40 grams; there were 10 ounces in the Chinese pound or catty. A bolt for tax payment measured 2.2 by 40 Chinese feet, roughly 50 cm by 10 m.

to peasant households to spin and weave, then carried the cloth north and sold it in the same markets where they bought the raw cotton. Songjiang, the Jiangnan district blessed by the legacy of Auntie Huang, became the centre of a national trade. Jiangnan peasant families wove not only plain cottons, but also patterned cloth and twills, and special sizes of cloth for export to Yunnan and the northwest.

'Raw cotton is cheap in the north and cloth is dear, while in the south the contrary is true', wrote Xu Guangqi, a high official and expert on cotton production, in the 1620s. By setting relative prices in their favour, cotton merchants became extremely wealthy. Their power was further enhanced by the Ming state's shift towards commuting household taxes from grain and cloth to payments in silver. By the 1580s, all taxes in kind were abolished. The state now relied on the market for its textile needs, providing merchants with a further opportunity for profit. Canton began to rival Jiangnan as a centre of commercial production. These southern districts were the hubs of the internal and overseas trade in fine cotton cloth. They imported raw cotton from north China, inland provinces and even India. They also imported rice, as growing numbers of farming households switched entirely to textile production. In Jiangnan, for instance, it was not uncommon for the husband to sit at the loom while his wife and daughters worked frantically to spin the thread and reel it onto bobbins fast enough to keep him supplied.

As in Europe some centuries later, the advent of cotton in China triggered dramatic growth and also fundamental technical and social changes through the whole textile industry. Cotton almost eliminated hemp textiles, now used only for mourning garments, and largely replaced ramie, which was more complicated to process. Simple silks also lost out in competition with high-quality cottons, especially after the 1580s when they no longer served as tax payments. Yet, the demand for fine silks continued to grow, for both internal and export markets. As with cotton, silk output was increased by a combination of technical innovations and organisational changes. The net effect was to marginalise women's status as the primary producers of silk textiles.

A series of improvements in silk technology through the later Song, Ming and Qing dynasties (around 1200 to 1800) had the cumulative effect of shifting most silk reeling and weaving to specialist households, or to commercial or state workshops. The most important innovations were in yarn production. Some new machines improved the quality of thread; others increased output; others broke down yarn production into a series of separate stages, further facilitating specialisation. Some reeling-machines were a boon to sericultural households in a region like Huzhou, famous for the quality of its cocoons and its yarn: the machines were relatively slow, but they incorporated processes of rolling and twisting, allowing skilled workers to produce yarn of excellent quality for highly competitive markets. In contrast, the elaborate and expensive 'complete silk-reeling frame', which became standard in urban workshops between about 1600 and 1800, was a treadle-operated machine that enabled one worker to reel between 600 and 1,000 grams of thread a day (see Figure 4.3). Its sophisticated design automated the adjustment of rollers, guiding-eyes, etc., so the operator had only to concentrate on the reels. This machine greatly increased efficiency and facilitated mass-production; indeed, it was easily converted to steam power in the nineteenth century.[12]

While the breeding of silkworms and some reeling and winding of silk continued to be carried out in specialist rural households, silk weaving disappeared from the countryside. Even in regions like Huzhou, where the quality of silk yarn was superb, once taxes in kind were abolished the incentives for household weaving of simple silks declined drastically. The draw-looms used for patterned silks had always been beyond the resources of ordinary households. Up to 6 metres long and 5 metres high, draw-looms were very expensive to make and required specialist skills to dress, operate and maintain them (Figure 4.4). Satins, gauzes or brocades each required special looms and skills. From the early 1600s, most quality silk weaving and finishing was concentrated in southern cities like Hangzhou, Suzhou, Nanjing and Canton. The imperial manufactures that had initially relied on state service from specialised artisans of both sexes to produce the most splendid silks gradually lost out in expertise and flexibility to the private sector. As the silk trade became more competitive and equipment more costly, the advantages of owning capital increased, exploitation intensified and skilled artisans who would once have run their own small family workshop were reduced to hired hands. Since respectable women did not work outside the home, much silk reeling and weaving became a male preserve.

The textile industry was a powerful engine of economic growth and market integration, contributing to monetisation, occupational specialisation and rising living standards. Affordable and attractive cotton cloth allowed even modest families to indulge in occasional fashionable splurges, like the pretty kerchiefs in which one cluster of Jiangnan villages specialised. But specialisation and economic interdependence also brought risk and vulnerability. By the late Ming there were always more skilled workers than day-jobs in the urban silk

[12] Dieter Kuhn, *Science and Civilisation in China* (Cambridge University Press, 1986), vol. 5, pt 9, p. 390.

治絲二

皇子頭

法絲子

不

Figure 4.3 Complete silk-reeling frame as illustrated in the *Tiangong kaiwu* of 1637 (1929 edition) (courtesy of the Needham Research Institute).

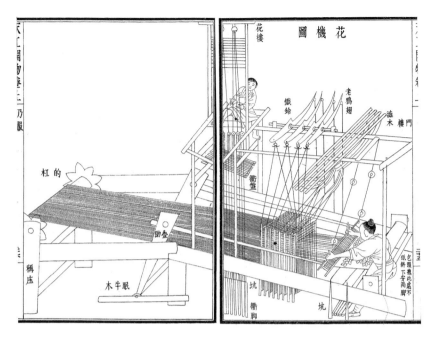

Figure 4.4 Chinese draw-loom with pattern tower as illustrated in the *Tiangong kaiwu* of 1637 (1929 edition) (courtesy of the Needham Research Institute).

industry. If the silk-weaving shops ran out of orders, then a whole class of quillers, reelers and weavers went hungry. Writing during the period of the Wanli emperor (1573 to 1620), a gazetteer of Songjiang district deplored its excessive dependence on cotton weaving, which 'pays for [the villagers'] taxes, their food and clothing, their equipment, their entertainments and ceremonies, all the costs of living and dying'.

Officials and statesmen were worried by the risks and the social tensions that accompanied growth and rising prosperity. While admitting that the clock could not be turned back to an innocent and idyllic past when peasants supposedly were really peasants, they worried about the dangers of shifting from cereal farming to commercial crops and crafts. They fretted whether enough rice was being grown to feed the army and protect the frontiers; they feared that by turning to crafts and trade the common people were betraying their proper roles as subjects of the state, and as men and women. In the Confucian ideal, farming and weaving were the most honourable occupations after ruling. The classic fiscal system of taxes in grain and cloth had symbolised a direct interdependence between peasant families and the state, unmediated by merchants. Many officials, while admitting the practical aspect of paying taxes in silver, felt this shift from use-value to exchange-value threatened the moral and cosmic coherence of the polity.

One point of special concern was the masculinisation of the textile industry. The classic gender division of labour in China was encapsulated in the for-mula 'men till, women weave'. Right through the imperial era China's ruling elite considered women's productive labour as just as fundamental to social welfare and to the political and moral order as men's. For centuries, household taxes were levied in kind, and men and women contributed equally. Husbands and sons paid taxes from the grain they grew, wives and daughters from the cloth they wove, contributing directly to the cohesion and prosperity of a state that, just like a family, needed both food and cloth.

By the late Ming, taxes in kind had vanished and women were no longer weavers. Most silk cloth and almost all the cotton cloth that entered the market was woven by men. In the new division of labour, raising silkworms, reeling the cocoons and spinning cotton were still performed by women, but many women did no textile work at all. Moreover, the essential transform-ation of yarn into cloth, its transformation into a saleable commodity with a value expressed in a monetary price, was now in the hands of men. This was a radical transformation of women's work.

The official Hu Juren (1434 to 1484) was among the first to lament that commercialisation and the spread of artisanal activities had turned weaving into a man's job. When men and women no longer performed their proper work, the cosmic balance of *yin* and *yang* was upset and the very fabric of society, its fruitfulness and its natural hierarchies were threatened. Through-out history, when the Chinese state conquered new territory it taught the inhabitants Chinese methods of farming, not just to increase output (sometimes the new methods proved unsuited to local conditions), but as a potent method of acculturation. Since spinning and weaving inculcated proper feminine virtues, teaching women in far-flung border regions to weave on Chinese looms was also considered an effective method of indoc-trination. By learning this work and the bodily and mental habits which went with it, barbarian women would abandon their loose ways, learn proper family values and help their families pay their taxes. In China proper, we find many cases of late imperial magistrates or provincial governors complaining that the women in their district 'had no occupation' or 'did not work'. Often, these women were contributing significantly to family income by curing tea, brewing, raising livestock or making handicrafts. But this work was invisible to officials: only weaving counted in their eyes as true womanly work.

When Lü Kun (1536 to 1618), the author of a famous work on womanly virtue, was governor of Shanxi he ordered all female adults 'without occupation' to be taught silk spinning and weaving. Shanxi had been famous for its silk tabbies in earlier times, but by the mid-Ming the industry had been abandoned, since there was no market for what were now seen as mediocre textiles. After Lü was transferred, the Shanxi women sensibly let the weaving drop. But officials and emperors continued throughout the Ming and Qing to invest in costly and often fruitless projects of this kind, intended to bring both economic and moral benefit to impoverished rural districts by restoring women to their proper productive roles. Not coincidentally, all the officially commissioned or approved treatises and handbooks that illustrate textile technology through the early-modern period show women operating the equipment, even though many were produced long after these tasks had shifted to men. One single maverick study of crafts, published by a disgruntled and very minor official at his own expense in 1637, accurately portrays textile machinery operated by men.

Porcelain and calico prints: Asian technologies remade in Europe

The cotton industry was an engine of growth and prosperity in early-modern China, stimulating economic activity within and beyond the frontiers and absorbing, investing and circulating vast amounts of the world's silver. But most Chinese cottons were consumed within China and were thus not seen by Europeans as a drain on their national wealth. Chinese porcelains and fine Indian cottons were quite a different matter. By the eighteenth century, porcelains, printed calicoes and muslins, tea, silks and other Asian luxuries were pouring into Europe. They drove fashions and created crazes. Monarchs, ministers, moralists and pamphleteers all agreed that something must be done to stem the inflow of Asian goods and the outflow of European wealth. Many ineffectual attempts were made to ban imports. More effective, certainly in the longer term, were various projects to copy, adapt or reinvent Asian luxury manufactures in Europe.

The perspective of global history has stimulated enlightening new research on these complex processes of import substitution and the extent to which they involved technology transfer, whether direct or 'remote'. Recent scholarship on 'global commodities', for instance, raises some interesting challenges to assumptions about European exceptionalism and the goals and defining technologies of the Industrial Revolution. Porcelain and calico prints, two high-value global commodities that were successfully recreated as manufactures in Europe in the eighteenth century, offer an instructive contrast: porcelain was effectively reinvented from scratch in Europe, while the development of calico printing involved successive phases of knowledge transfer and appropriation between Asia and Europe.

The alchemy of 'white gold'

Chinese potters began producing high-temperature ceramics (ci) in the Neolithic period. By Tang times (618 to 907), the elegant forms and beautiful glazes of these Chinese proto-porcelains were prized throughout Asia and the Islamic world.[13] By the early Song dynasty (960 to 1279), local experiments with different combinations of china clay (kaolin) and china stone (petuntse), different kiln forms and glazes allowed connoisseurs to choose between a range of local porcelains, each famous for particular qualities and colours (Figure 4.5). Subtle green celadons were especially appreciated. The Song kilns at Jingdezhen in South China specialised in a lustrous pure-white porcelain. During the Yuan period (1279 to 1368), Jingdezhen potters began to apply blue decoration to their wares. The cobalt oxide they used may have been introduced from Persia by the Muslim merchants from the nearby port of Quanzhou, who handled the already substantial porcelain trade to the Middle East. The new Chinese blue-and-white ware took the world by storm, and was coveted, collected and imitated from Damascus to Delft.

The first Chinese porcelains to reach Europe, in the fourteenth and fifteenth centuries, came as gifts from Asian or Islamic rulers to kings or popes, who set off these treasured gifts, like religious relics, in mounts of gilt or enamel. The material itself aroused considerable curiosity. Some believed that porcelain was a precious stone, others that it was made of ground eggs or seashells. Spanish missionaries to Southern China had written one or two quite accurate accounts of porcelain production in the 1580s, yet in the *Novum Organum* of 1620 Francis Bacon still described it as made of a 'magic mixture' buried underground for decades to mature. European rulers – Lorenzo de Medici, the kings of Portugal, England's Queen Elizabeth, the tsars – all caught the fatal passion. By the seventeenth century, kings and dukes were spending fortunes on their porcelain collections, and commoners too had

---

[13] Note: this section is based on Rose Kerr and Nigel Wood, *Science and Civilisation in China* (Cambridge University Press, 2004), vol. 5, pt 12; Robert Finlay, 'The Pilgrim Art: The Culture of Porcelain in World History', *Journal of World History* 9 (1998), 141–87; and Lothar Ledderose, *Ten Thousand Things: Module and Mass Production in Chinese Art* (Princeton University Press, 2000).

Figure 4.5 China-stone was pulverised by water-driven trip-hammers before being made into bricks and transported to the potteries for processing. This painting is one of a set of twenty-four depicting the porcelain industry in China. Produced between 1770 and 1790 by an unknown artist, these images were typical of a genre depicting Chinese crafts or industries, produced specifically for a European clientele (Trustees of the Victoria and Albert Museum).

acquired an expensive taste for 'china-ware'. In 1600, the East India Companies, first the Dutch then the English, French, Danish and Swedish, began importing hundreds of thousands of pieces of porcelain every year, commissioning Chinese merchants in Canton to organise mass production and individual orders of novel wares like dinner services, tureens or coffee sets. Almost all the imports were blue-and-white wares from the kilns of Jingdezhen.

How were the Jingdezhen manufacturers able to respond so efficiently to the explosion of European orders? One key factor was the Chinese system of 'modular production'; another was Jingdezhen's centuries-long experience of innovation in response to imperial and foreign demand.

Modular production significantly shaped Chinese material culture and technological problem-solving. The system was already used in Neolithic China for the high-temperature ceramics that were the ancestors of porcelain. Thereafter, it was applied to the manufacture of both precious and utilitarian objects: Shang-dynasty ritual bronzes, the terracotta army of the

First Emperor, cast-iron ploughshares and cooking pots, casings for shells and mines, fine lacquer-wares and imperial porcelains. Modular production involves breaking down the production of complex artefacts into multiple components and processes. A typical teapot, for instance, consists of a body made in two moulded halves, spout, handle and lid, each produced by a series of specialised workers; the components are then assembled and trimmed, the pot is dipped in glaze, decorated, fired and polished. From pounding the clay to polishing, the manufacture of a typical Jingdezhen pot involved 72 separate steps.

Modular production requires centralised management, design and coordination, and the standardisation of components; it facilitates quality control and mass-production; variations are easily produced through different combinations of components or scalar variation to produce matching sets in different sizes. While modular skills and procedures discourage creativity or innovation at an individual level, the system can quickly operationalise the results of successful experiments.

Jingdezhen had supplied imperial orders since the eleventh century. In the 1370s, it was designated an imperial factory, but 'popular kilns' also flourished, with workers moving back and forth between the two. The world's largest industrial operation, sixteenth-century Jingdezhen had over 1,000 kilns and 70,000 workers, supplying orders of up to 100,000 pieces to the court, and responding rapidly to new fashions and tastes.

> Technicians at the factory were subjected to repeated demands for innovatory products, many of them stimulated by receipt of tributary artefacts from beyond the borders of China. New shapes were potted, often with immense difficulty and high failure rate. Glaze recipes were improved, while trials were conducted [in coordination with the imperial workshops of Beijing] with a palette of overglaze enamel colours ... The massive support that central government procurement of ceramics guaranteed gave technological superiority to the whole Chinese ceramics industry.[14]

New designs and technical improvements circulated freely between the 'official kilns' at Jingdezhen, which depended on court commissions, and the 'popular kilns', which supplied other Chinese consumers and – from 1600 – met the huge surge in European orders.

The earliest European attempts to recreate porcelain were the projects of royal collectors. The desire to produce the miraculous translucent substance

---

[14] Kerr and Wood, *Science and Civilisation*, p. xlvii.

in their own court was partly motivated by economy, but also by the typical wish of sovereigns – in China as well as Europe, as we have just seen – to have nature at their command, to patronise ingenious skills and lavish displays.

Since porcelain was still regarded as a mysterious or even magical material, it is not surprising that alchemists were often tasked with recreating the 'white gold'. The first known attempt was by a Venetian alchemist, Maestro Antonio, in the late fifteenth century; the first success was at Meissen in 1708. In 1705, Augustus of Saxony, a fanatical collector, set two people to work on his porcelain project: Johann Friedrich Böttger, an alchemist, and Ehrenfied Walther von Tschirnhaus, a mathematician and physicist who had spent some time surveying the soils and minerals of Saxony. Adding alabaster and quartz to local china-clay, and firing at 1,350°C, together they succeeded in producing a translucent, tough porcelain which equalled Chinese porcelains in quality, although it was made quite without knowledge of Chinese techniques.

In 1712, the French missionary Père d'Entrecolles sent a detailed description of Jingdezhen production, along with a sample, to the chemist René Réaumur. Réaumur successfully analysed its composition, but his results were not taken up by French manufacturers who chose to substitute soft pastes in their recreations of porcelain designs. In Britain, however, several experimenters pored over d'Entrecolles's descriptions. The invention of bone-china, an extremely successful porcelain look-alike that combines clay with calcined animal bones, may be the product of a misreading of d'Entrecolles's remark that the Chinese distinguished between kaolin and china-stone as the 'bone and flesh' of porcelain. One experimenter who followed d'Entrecolles attentively was the pharmacist William Cookworthy, who successfully located china-clay and china-stone deposits in Cornwall and developed reduction-firing kilns and Jingdezhen-type glazes in the 1760s. By the early nineteenth century, European and especially British factories were producing on an industrial scale a range of porcelain-style wares, which completely displaced Chinese porcelains for everyday use in Europe.

Although European manufacturers successfully harnessed new technological and scientific knowledge to reinvent china-wares, this entailed no disparagement of Chinese achievements in porcelain production. Indeed, from the mid-nineteenth century to the 1920s, government scientists in France, Germany and Britain continued research on Chinese porcelain samples in the hope of reproducing their special qualities.

Coping with the 'calico craze'[15]

The case of Indian printed textiles offers a striking contrast. In the seventeenth century, European travellers and craftsmen alike expressed admiration for Indian dyeing skills, acknowledging their superiority to European techniques. Between 1670 and 1740, the transmission of methods originating in India played a key role in the advancement of cotton-printing in Europe. Yet, by the 1770s, 'the very idea that ... India possessed – or had possessed in the past – skills and knowledge unknown to Europeans on how to produce printed cotton textiles was ... considered blatantly false'.[16] From admiration, Europeans had moved to disdain. Indian printers were disparaged for their ignorance of science, lack of creativity and slavish adherence to tradition: progress in calico-printing was held up as an irrefutable demonstration of the superiority of European civilisation and the scientific method.

As early as 1500, the delicate patterns, glowing colours and lasting brilliance of cottons from Gujarat, Coromandel and Bengal, their 'finenes and cunning workmanship', made them 'better esteemed than silke', a fitting exchange for precious spices along Asian trade routes.[17] With the influx of Japanese and American silver from the 1580s, demand rose, the industry expanded, and new credit and joint-capital institutions emerged to handle increased flows of raw materials and finished products. With the rise of the East India Companies in the 1600s, Indian calico-prints (along with other fine Indian cottons like muslins, and Chinese silks) made their way to Europe (Figure 4.6). Unrivalled for quality by local wools and linens, the exotic textiles became wildly popular, stimulating new fashions and novel forms of consumerism (Figure 4.7). Expenditure on these luxury goods (the so-called 'calico craze') rose to such alarming levels that by around 1700 most European governments had banned imports.

European attempts to develop textile-printing techniques to compete with Indian imports began in the 1620s, but local knowledge of mordants (fixatives) and dyes was still too primitive for success. Producers were reduced to painting linens in imitation of Indian cottons. Although several European observers provided quite detailed accounts of sophisticated Indian

---

[15] This section is based on Giorgio Riello, 'Asian Knowledge and the Development of Calico Printing in Europe in the Seventeenth and Eighteenth Centuries', *Journal of Global History* 5 (2010), 1–28; and Giorgio Riello and Tirthankar Roy, *How India Clothed the World: The World of South Asian Textiles, 1500–1850* (Leiden: Brill, 2009).

[16] Riello, 'Asian Knowledge', 2.

[17] John Huygen van Linschoten, *Voyage to the East Indies* (1598), quoted in Riello and Roy, 'Introduction' in Riello and Roy, *How India Clothed the World*, p. 1.

Figure 4.6 Early eighteenth-century Indian chintz (dyed cotton) fabric from the Coromandel Coast, part of a set of bed-hangings made for export (Trustees of the Victoria and Albert Museum).

printing and dyeing techniques, they had no impact on their home industries. One likely reason is that Europeans were still ignorant of many key principles involved, and thus unable to apply the information properly. Another is that alum, the main mordant in Indian processes, was scarce in Europe. One further obstacle, since dyeing recipes and processes involve great precision, was that Indian craftsmen neither wrote down what they did, nor provided quantitative descriptions of their techniques.

Instead of any direct transfer of Indian dyeing and printing expertise, the necessary knowledge filtered in via the Middle East. Indian cottons were extremely popular in the Ottoman Empire. Armenian craftsmen based in Anatolia had become expert reproducers of the prized textiles, which Armenian merchants sold throughout Asia and imported to Europe through depots in port-cities like Marseilles, Genoa and Amsterdam. During the 1670s, Armenian entrepreneurs established calico-printing workshops in several European cities, in partnership with local craftsmen, and the Anatolian techniques spread like wildfire through the continent. Because of problems

Figure 4.7 English bed-hangings, crewel-work embroidery, 1680 to 1700. European dyers were not yet able to produce prints with the vivid colours and sharp patterns of Indian chintzes, but embroidery could be used to produce similar effects (Trustees of the Victoria and Albert Museum).

with procuring suitable dye-stuffs and mordants, however, the quality remained crude, uncompetitive with Asian imports, and European manufacturers still sent cloth to Turkey for dyeing.

By the 1760s, however, a new, truly distinctive European cotton-printing technology was emerging, based on experiments with mordants and the development of new dye-mixtures, in particular for the two key colours, indigo blue and Turkey red. In the early eighteenth century, Europeans experimented with processes unknown in Asia, such as the use of cold vats (*cuves à froid*) that dissolved indigo using iron sulphate. Perfected in England in 1734, this rapidly replaced the more wasteful procedure of hot fermentation. Numerous types of blue and red dye were concocted, using different mineral additives and application techniques. In the late eighteenth century, Claude Flachat, a French chemist and dyer, analysed the composition of alum and developed an industrial process for synthesising it. Perhaps the most dramatic transformation came with the application to cotton-printing of contemporary innovations in printing and engraving on paper. The use of copper-plate, pioneered by Francis Nixon of Dublin in 1754, permitted a level of detail and precision that matched engravings on paper. The new *toiles* transformed consumer tastes. Gone was the passion for Asian patterns: now customers clamoured for life-like depictions of Waterloo or French shepherdesses (Figure 4.8). The final transformation of cotton-printing into a thoroughly Western, modern mass-industry came in 1783, when Thomas Bell of Preston in England developed a rotary printing machine with engraved cylinders that produced 200 to 500 pieces of six-colour prints a day.

The late-eighteenth-century European cotton-printing industry was a true hybrid, a complex weave of Asian craft-knowledge and European mechanical and chemical innovation; of dye-stuffs, fibres and minerals from colonies and trading-partners around the globe; and of dense international networks of financial, entrepreneurial and technological expertise. Skills were diffused by a cosmopolitan array of experts. Between 1650 and 1750, Armenian craftsmen and entrepreneurs played a key role, mediating between Asian and European skills. By the 1730s, however, the informal nature of the common knowledge base was changing, as professional chemists, technicians and colour-makers built up a public, scientific domain of analysis, experimental results and precise measurements and designs. The term 'experimental researches' features in a number of publications on dyeing and printing by the 1790s; chemistry, moreover, had now advanced sufficiently to explain the processes in terms of scientific laws. Since the Indian dyers never recorded their efforts at improvement, nor did foreign observers attempt to investigate changes in

Figure 4.8 Toile de Jouy depicting manufacture work at the factory, after designs by Jean Baptiste Houet, 1784 (De Agostini Picture Library / G. Dagli Orti / Bridgeman Images).

the industry as opposed to its routines, it is hardly surprising that European textile-experts could no longer conceive of any debt, past or present, that their industry might owe to India. Charles O'Brien, in his *Treatise on Calico Printing, Theoretical and Practical* (1792), was typical in attributing Indian accomplishments to 'accidental discoveries'.

Beyond 'European exceptionalism'?

Cotton-printing is an excellent example of how Europeans 'invented invention'.[18] Even in 1800, many of its processes still owed as much to craft-skills as to scientific research, but it was well on the way to becoming a modern, research-driven industrial process, where skills and knowledge were (at least in principle) standardised and transferred from the human operator into machines and procedures that (again, in principle) would work as efficiently in Potosí as in Preston. Cotton-printing was already regarded as a European creation, the product of a characteristically European propensity for scientific method. Indians slavishly imitated, Europeans innovated: although the Industrial Revolution was still just unfolding, competence in the 'mechanical arts and sciences' already signified the superiority of Western civilisation.

The development of cotton-printing embodied the spirit of what Joel Mokyr calls 'Industrial Enlightenment', the conviction that social progress is furthered by applying scientific understanding to the processes of production – and that innovation should be encouraged, for the public good, by protecting inventors' intellectual property rights through patents and scientific publications. It is often argued that the first stages of industrialisation were geared towards the mass-production of cheap, poor-quality goods. But world-history approaches usefully emphasise that many early industrial innovations were initially designed to improve quality rather than increase output. The case is clear for luxury goods like printed cottons and porcelain. But what of ordinary cotton-yarn? Here, too, world historians have shown that European inventors initially sought to improve quality, not quantity, with Asia setting the standards. Crompton's mule, patented in 1779, was considered to have matched Indian quality for the first time, thus opening the way for British manufacturers to compete against Indian producers.[19]

---

[18] David S. Landes, *The Wealth and Poverty of Nations: Why Some Are So Rich and Some So Poor* (New York: W. W. Norton & Company, 1999), pp. 45–59.
[19] Maxine Berg, 'Quality, Cotton and the Global Luxury Trade' in Riello and Roy, *How India Clothed the World*, p. 405.

As we see, world history brings useful correctives to grand historical narratives about technology. Instead of accepting that Europe was unique and its rise to world precedence inevitable, world historians document the high levels of technological efficacy elsewhere around the globe that built an early-modern ecumene of manufactures, commerce and ferocious competition. They trace the travels of technological skills that created wealth in other civilisations like India, Persia and China, and show how they were first inserted into a European repertory of craft-skills, then reworked and transmuted into science, the miracle ingredient of modern Western technological culture.

World historians have successfully challenged standard eurocentric accounts of phenomena like the 'rise of the West' and the Industrial Revolution, and persuaded us that we need to rethink not only the contributions of non-Western technological cultures to modernity, but also the nature and processes of technological change in Western societies. Yet, current approaches do not resolve all the problems of eurocentrism and teleology in the history of technology. Periodisation, for example, is a knotty problem. World history still largely depends on Western historical landmarks to structure its accounts. Yet, the very definition of an 'early-modern era' that begins and ends with vital changes in Europe imposes chronological cut-off points, comparisons and teleologies likely to distract us from vital features of the technological cultures and historical trajectories of other societies. Some of the most interesting arguments about technology in the Andes depend on tracing evolving traditions back (through archaeology) to the pre-Christian era and forward to the ethnographic present. The same is true of African metallurgy. The rise of the Indian Ocean trade and of the porcelain and calico industries long pre-dates 1400 and the Iberian voyages of discovery. The history of the 'traditional' textile sectors in China and India did not grind to a halt with industrialisation: they persisted in parallel, adapting technically, socially and symbolically to the new environment.

Another weakness in the world-history approach is its emphasis on circulation and encounters, on interfaces between societies rather than the matrices within which local technological cultures took shape. Encounters or flows directly involving Europe typically attract more attention than those involving only non-Western actors, although this is beginning to change. But we also need more studies that focus on technological landscapes, the circulation of knowledge and historical changes *within* specific non-European societies or regions, if we are to account satisfactorily for patterns of transmission or adaptation between societies, or to compare how technology was construed at different points around the world.

Finally, world historians of technology have tended (understandably) to organise their arguments around the domains of activity like textile production, warfare or transportation, which helped to knit the modern world together. But a broader, more anthropological approach towards which technologies mattered in other societies, and why, enriches our understanding both of local matrices and of the encounters, flows and disruptions placed in the foreground by world historians. Fortunately, as this chapter has suggested, an emerging corpus of richly detailed and thought-provoking studies of local technological cultures suggests that the time is now ripe for creatively rethinking the place of technology in world history.

FURTHER READING

Berg, Maxine, 'Quality, Cotton and the Global Luxury Trade' in Giorgio Riello and Tirthankar Roy, *How India Clothed the World: The World of South Asian Textiles, 1500–1850* (Leiden: Brill, 2009), pp. 391–415.

Bouysse-Cassagne, Thérèse, 'Las minas del centro-sur andino, los cultos prehispánicos y los cultos cristianos', *Bulletin de l'IFEA* 34 (2005), 443–62.

'Le palanquin d'argent de l'Inca: petite enquête d'ethnohistoire à propos d'un objet absent', *Techniques et cultures* 29 (1997), 69–111.

Bray, Francesca, *Technology and Gender: Fabrics of Power in Late Imperial China* (Berkeley, CA: University of California Press, 1997).

Buren, Mary Van and Barbara H. Mills, 'Huayrachinas and Tocochimbos: Traditional Smelting Technology of the Southern Andes', *Latin American Antiquity* 16 (2005), 3–25.

Chao, Kang, *The Development of Cotton Textile Production in China* (Cambridge, MA: Harvard University Press, 1977).

Finlay, Robert, 'The Pilgrim Art: The Culture of Porcelain in World History', *Journal of World History* 9 (1998), 141–87.

Flynn, Dennis O. and Arturo Giráldez, 'Born with a "Silver Spoon": The Origin of World Trade in 1571', *Journal of World History* 6 (1995), 201–21.

Hämäläinen, Pekka, 'The Politics of Grass: European Expansion, Ecological Change, and Indigenous Power in the Southwest Borderlands', *William & Mary Quarterly* 67 (2010), 173–208.

Headrick, Daniel R., *Power over Peoples: Technology, Environments, and Western Imperialism, 1400 to the Present* (Princeton University Press, 2010).

Kerr, Rose and Nigel Wood, *Science and Civilisation in China* (Cambridge University Press, 2004).

Kuhn, Dieter, *Science and Civilisation in China* (Cambridge University Press, 1986).

Laichen, Sun, 'Military Technology Transfers from Ming China and the Emergence of Northern Mainland Southeast Asia (c. 1390–1527)', *Journal of Southeast Asian Studies* 34 (2003), 495–517.

Landes, David S., *The Wealth and Poverty of Nations: Why Some Are So Rich and Some So Poor* (New York: W. W. Norton & Company, 1999).

Ledderose, Lothar, *Ten Thousand Things: Module and Mass Production in Chinese Art* (Princeton University Press, 2000).

Lorge, Peter A., *The Asian Military Revolution: From Gunpowder to the Bomb* (Cambridge University Press, 2008).

Marks, Robert, *Tigers, Rice, Silk, and Silt: Environment and Economy in Late Imperial South China* (Cambridge University Press, 1998).

Misa, Thomas J., *Leonardo to the Internet: Technology and Culture from the Renaissance to the Present* (Baltimore, MD: Johns Hopkins University Press, 2004).

Nagahara, Keiji and Kozo Yamamura, 'Shaping the Process of Unification: Technological Progress in Sixteenth- and Seventeenth-Century Japan', *Journal of Japanese Studies* 14 (1988), 77–109.

Riello, Giorgio, 'Asian Knowledge and the Development of Calico Printing in Europe in the Seventeenth and Eighteenth Centuries', *Journal of Global History* 5 (2010), 1–28.

Riello, Giorgio and Tirthankar Roy, *How India Clothed the World: The World of South Asian Textiles, 1500–1850* (Leiden: Brill, 2009).

Schäfer, Dagmar (ed.), *Cultures of Knowledge: Technology in Chinese History* (Leiden: Brill, 2012).

Schreiber, Katharina and Josué Lancho Rojas, *Irrigation and Society in the Peruvian Desert: The Puquios of Nasca* (Lanham, MD: Lexington Books, 2003).

Tandeter, Enrique, 'The Mining Industry' in Victor Bulmer-Thomas, John Coatsworth and Roberto Cortes-Conde (eds), *The Cambridge Economic History of Latin America* (Cambridge University Press, 2006), vol. 1, pp. 315–56.

5

Patterns of urbanization, 1400 to 1800

PETER BURKE

This chapter is concerned not so much with cities as with the process of urbanization.[1] In other words, it deals not only with the growth of cities, but also with the rise in the proportion of the population that lived in cities (the Netherlands, for instance, was 37 per cent urban in 1815); with the reorganization of cities that followed their growth; and with the spread of urban attitudes and values. It will also be concerned with the forces that drove this process, whether the cities themselves were the motors of change or whether they simply reveal change more clearly than other parts of society.

As so often happens in the case of global history, the dates chosen in this volume, the beginning and end of the so-called 'early modern' world, are more appropriate to some parts of that world than others. There are no 'natural' dates for this chapter. Paul Bairoch, for instance, treated the period 400 to 1700 as a unit, presenting it as a long trough between the end of one urban civilization and the rise of another.[2] Historians of China generally treat the Ming dynasty (1368 to 1644) and the Qing dynasty (1644 to 1912) as units, while the Japanese think in terms of the Ashikaga and Tokugawa periods (1336 to 1573 and 1603 to 1868).

However, the period 1400 to 1800 has some kind of unity. The years around 1400 mark a moment of recovery from the great plague of 1348–9, which affected Western Asia as well as Europe, as well as a recovery from the destruction of cities by the Mongols, from China to Eastern Europe. As for the years around 1800, they mark not only the rise of new major cities, from New York to Shanghai or Kolkata (Calcutta), but also the beginning of

---

[1] Philip M. Hauser and Leo F. Schnore, *The Study of Urbanization* (New York: Wiley, 1965); Jan de Vries, *European Urbanization, 1500–1800* (Cambridge, MA: Harvard University Press, 1984); and Ad van de Woude, Akira Hayami and Jan de Vries (eds), *Urbanization in History* (Oxford University Press, 1990).

[2] Paul Bairoch, *De Jericho à Mexico: villes et économie dans l'histoire* (Paris: Gallimard, 1985).

new patterns of urbanization in an age of industrialization in a world economy that was dominated for the first time by the West.[3]

By the standards of the period 1800 to 2000, let alone the megacities of the twenty-first century, urbanization in the four centuries between 1400 and 1800 was a rather modest process. Cities were islands in a rural sea. In the year 1800, the world population was around 900 million, but less than 2 per cent of that number was housed in cities of 100,000 people or more.[4] All the same, a few cities reached a size that is substantial even by our standards. Early modern population figures are often uncertain, indeed controversial, but it is likely that at least three cities had a million inhabitants or more apiece at some point in our period: Beijing, Edō (later known as Tokyo) and London. In 1400, the largest city in the world was probably Nanjing, by 1500 it was Beijing, by 1700 Edō and by 1800 it was London.

The population of another nine cities reached figures somewhere between half a million and a million: Nanjing, Guangzhou (formerly known in the West as Canton), Cairo, Isfahan, Istanbul, Agra, Delhi, Lahore and Paris. Urban growth was sometimes rapid. Amsterdam had about 30,000 inhabitants in 1550, 90,000 in 1620 and 200,000 in 1680; London, 200,000 in 1600 rising to 400,000 in 1650; and St Petersburg, 100,000 in 1750 but 220,000 in 1790.[5]

However, a study of the process of urbanization should not confine itself to individual cities, no matter how spectacular their growth. It is more illuminating to consider urban systems, networks of cities, large, medium and small, that rise or decline together. These urban networks, especially dense in some regions, cannot be considered in isolation either, since they depended on rural areas not only for food, but also for the immigrants that allowed them to grow. This hinterland was usually near, but might be further away if there was a good system of communication in place. Beijing, for instance, depended on grain that came from the Yangzi valley via the Grand Canal. Istanbul depended on food supplies from Thrace. London was fuelled by what are now known as the 'home counties', including Essex, Hertfordshire and Kent.

Urbanization was described above as 'a process', but this begs an important question. Was there one process or many? Were the urban histories of different regions separate or connected? Did different cities, or cities in

---

[3] Rhoads Murphey, 'Traditionalism and Colonialism: Changing Urban Roles in Asia', *Journal of Asian Studies* 29 (1969), 67–84.

[4] Hauser and Schnore, *Study of Urbanization*, p. 7.

[5] Tertius Chandler, *Four Thousand Years of Urban Growth* (Lewiston, NY: E. Mellen Press, 1987).

different parts of the world, grow for the same reasons? It is obviously necessary to distinguish between different kinds of city, such as the port (Guangzhou, Ōsaka, Amsterdam), the capital (Beijing, Edō, Isfahan), the sacred city (Rome, Mecca), the craft centre (Florence, Suzhou) and so on. It may also be necessary to distinguish patterns of growth in different regions.

What follows will concentrate on Japan, China and Western Europe before turning to the colonial city and finally to some general conclusions about the causes and consequences of early modern urbanization.

The Japanese model

It is convenient to begin with Japan because this group of islands was relatively isolated from the rest of the world, especially from the early seventeenth century onwards, the time when urban growth was accelerating. Foreign trade was strictly controlled and confined to one city, Nagasaki (indeed, the personnel of the Dutch East India Company were confined to Deshima, a small island just outside the city). Hence, urbanization in early modern Japan was essentially stimulated from within the country.

The process of urbanization began from a low base. The political climate of the later Ashikaga period, *c.* 1450 to 1600, known as the period of 'warring states' (*Sengoku*), was unfavourable to the growth of cities, although regional warlords established what became known as 'castle towns' (*jokamachi*) as centres of administration.[6] However, under the successive rule of three leaders, Oda Nobunaga, Toyotomi Hideyoshi and Tokugawa Ieyasu (the founder of a dynasty of *shoguns*, or commanders, which remained in power until 1868), Japan was gradually unified and pacified.

Unity and peace were important preconditions for the growth of population and hence the growth of cities. The population of Japan was about 8 million in 1400 and about the same a century later. However, by 1600 it had increased to 12 million; by 1700 it had more than doubled, to 28 million, increasing slowly thereafter to about 30 million in the year 1800. In the case of the period 1650 to 1700 in particular, it seems no exaggeration to speak of a population explosion. This explosion would have been impossible without an agricultural revolution that included irrigation and land reclamation.

---

[6] John W. Hall, 'The Castle Town and Japan's Modern Urbanization', *Far Eastern Quarterly* 15 (1955–6), 37–56; Susan B. Hanley and Haruko Wakita, 'Dimensions of Development: Cities in Fifteenth- and Sixteenth-century Japan' in J. W. Hall *et al.*, (eds), *Japan before Tokugawa* (Princeton University Press, 1981), pp. 295–326.

Between 1550 and 1650, the amount of rice paddy doubled. The productivity of agriculture was increased by the use of fertilizers such as grasses, rapeseed and sardine meal.[7]

Thanks to this revolution, it was possible to feed the inhabitants of Japan's growing cities. Under the Tokugawa regime, the peasants were taxed heavily, paying in rice. Much of this rice went to the samurai and their lords the *daimyō*, who were paid stipends in kind rather than money. The samurai, who had previously lived in villages, were encouraged to move into castle towns or larger cities, bringing their servants with them. By 1700, more than 5 per cent of Japanese lived in cities of 100,000 people or more, compared to 2 per cent in Europe.[8]

Three cities were particularly large. The first was Kyōto, which had been the capital of Japan since 794, but had suffered considerable damage during the Sengoku period, especially during the Onin war of 1467 to 1477. It was extensively rebuilt by Hideyoshi. With a population of 150,000 to 180,000 people in 1500, Kyōto grew to about 350,000 in 1600 and then remained more or less stable for the rest of the period. Hideyoshi built a castle in the second major city, Ōsaka, which developed into a major port and commercial centre from the early seventeenth century onwards, partly at the expense of its neighbour Sakai, which had become virtually self-governing during the wars of the sixteenth century, but declined thereafter. Ōsaka by contrast was subservient to the central government, the *Bakufu*, although there was a council of merchants for everyday administration.[9]

By 1600, Ōsaka was home to about 400,000 people, many of them migrants from the Kinai region (the names of certain quarters of the city, such as Ise and Awaji, suggest that they originally housed people from those parts of the region). Reading space as evidence of process, we may conclude that 'chain migration' was common, in other words that (as still happens today) new migrants encourage relatives and neighbours to join them in the city, working in the same occupation and living in the same district. The government encouraged the migration of merchants to Ōsaka by means of tax exemptions. However, the most spectacular growth was that of the third

---

[7] Toshio Furushima, 'The Village and Agriculture during the Edō Period' in John W. Hall (ed.), *Early Modern Japan, Cambridge History of Japan* (Cambridge University Press, 1991), vol. 4.

[8] James L. McClain and Nobuhiko Nakai, 'Commercial Change and Urban Growth in Early Modern Japan' in Hall, *Early Modern Japan*, pp. 519–95.

[9] James L. McClain and Osamu Wakita (eds), *Ōsaka: The Merchants' Capital of Early Modern Japan* (Ithaca, NY: Cornell University Press, 1999).

major city, Edō, which, like Ōsaka, was no more than a village in 1400 or even 1590, but expanded rapidly after Tokugawa Ieyasu chose it to be the capital, dominated by a huge castle, built where the imperial palace now stands. With a population of about 350,000 people in 1600, Edō continued to grow, more rapidly than its rivals, and probably contained over 1 million people by the early eighteenth century.[10] All three cities depended on a flow of migrants from the countryside, mainly of young men who found employment as labourers, apprentices, pedlars or servants.

These three cities were the three major nodes in an urban system or network that included the new castle town of Nagoya and also Kanazawa, the capital of the domain of one of Tokugawa Ieyasu's leading allies in his struggle for power.[11] Trade flourished, and with it the merchants, the *chōnin*. Japan, like parts of Europe in this period, was becoming a commercial society, with commercial values memorably expressed in the *Nihon eitaigura* or *Everlasting Storehouse of Japan* (1688) by Ihara Saikaku, a collection of stories of enterprising tradesmen who went from rags to riches.

There was a kind of division of labour, or division of function, between the three major cities. Ōsaka, originally the headquarters of the shogun in western Japan, became the 'merchant's capital', the economic centre of what was becoming a national market. Edō was the political centre of the new regime, while Kyōto, still the place of residence of the prestigious if powerless emperor, remained the cultural centre, with large numbers of skilled artisans who made fans, porcelain and paper, and who also wove silk. It should be added that while politics, trade and culture made the three cities distinctive, all three of them were full of shops and shopkeepers.

Ōsaka, conveniently located at the junction of the coast and the Yodo and Yamato Rivers, became the centre for the distribution of food, which led to its being nicknamed 'Japan's kitchen'. There was a rice market with hundreds of brokers, who converted the stipends of the *daimyō* and samurai, which were paid in kind, into cash, and also offered them loans. There were also fish and vegetable markets. New canals, financed by merchants, were constructed in the early seventeenth century, in order to improve the distribution system and so encourage trade. A number of industries also developed in Ōsaka, among them ship-building, copper refining and sake brewing. The growth of

---

[10] Gilbert Rozman, 'Edō's Importance', *Journal of Japanese Studies* 1 (1974), 91–112; Ugawa Kaoru, James McClain and John M. Merriman (eds), *Edō and Paris: Urban Life and the State in the Early Modern Era* (Ithaca, NY: Cornell University Press, 1994).

[11] Gilbert Rozman, *Urban Networks in Ch'ing China and Tokugawa Japan* (Princeton University Press, 1973).

5.1 Early modern Japan

the city encouraged the commercialization of agriculture in the area around Ōsaka, including the production of cotton for sale in the city. Cotton goods and sake were exported to Edō.

Edō was not only a centre of administration, but also a centre of consumption, assisted by the fact that the Tokugawa shoguns insisted that not only their own retainers move to the city but also that the *daimyō* who ruled the provinces build houses in Edō and live there for at least part of the time (the obligation to live in the capital and send relatives to live there during one's absence was known as the system of 'alternate attendance', or *sankin kotai*). As Edō grew, the food, clothing and building trades all flourished. Artisans, shopkeepers and merchants naturally followed their potential customers to the city. Rivalry between *daimyō* led to increasingly conspicuous consumption, paid for by the mobilization of local resources and placing more pressure on the peasants (which probably encouraged some of them to migrate to cities).

This conspicuous consumption was imitated by the new rich, such as the lumber merchants who profited from the boom in construction. It is obviously too simple to reduce the process of urbanization to the rise of the *chōnin* (as in the case of the rise of the middle class in the West), since the shoguns, *daimyō* and samurai are all part of the story, but the *chōnin* certainly played a major role in the story of urbanization in early modern Japan. By the eighteenth century, even Edō had become a city dominated, in numbers at least, by this middle class, while Ōsaka had always been a *chōnin* city.[12]

The centralization of wealth, both old and new, in cities had important cultural consequences that may be summed up in a phrase originally coined to refer to eighteenth-century London, but applicable much more widely: the commercialization of leisure. In Japan this meant the rise of tea-houses, sumo wrestling, puppet shows and so on. Among the most visible of these consequences was the rise of the pleasure quarters in the three great cities: the Yoshiwara quarter in Edō, the Shimabara in Kyōto and the Shinmachi in Ōsaka. In these quarters, separated from the rest of the city so that they could be controlled more easily, could be found courtesans of different ranks and also actors in the *kabuki* theatre, another art form that originated at this time. These pleasure quarters were known as *ukiyo*, 'floating world'. Originally a Buddhist term for the transience of all worldly things, the phrase acquired hedonist overtones in the seventeenth century and came to mean 'living for the moment', particularly if that kind of living took place in the pleasure quarters of the three great cities. The 'floating trade' was prostitution.[13]

The Genroku period (1688 to 1704) was considered, at least retrospectively, to have been the golden age of the new urban culture, expressing the values of the *chōnin*, although the coloured woodblock prints that evoke that world (especially the floating world) so vividly were mainly produced later in the

[12] Charles D. Sheldon, *The Rise of the Merchant Class in Tokugawa Japan* (Locust Valley, NY: Augustin, 1958); contrast E. S. Crawcour, 'The Tokugawa Period and Japan's Preparation for Economic Growth', *Journal of Japanese Studies* 1 (1974), 113–25.
[13] Howard Hibbett, *The Floating World in Japanese Fiction* (London: Oxford University Press, 1959); Teruoka Yasutaka, 'Pleasure Quarters and Tokugawa Culture' in C. Andrew Gerstle, *Eighteenth-Century-Japan: Culture and Society* (Sydney: Allen & Unwin, 1989), pp. 3–32.

eighteenth century. Ōsaka played a key role in the creation of new forms of culture: the playwright Chikamatsu Monzaemon and the storyteller Ihara Saikaku both came from that city. On the other hand, the *chōnin* of Edō, known as the *Eddoko*, helped to accommodate these new cultural forms to older, more aristocratic traditions. The women of this class, who imitated aristocratic forms of speech, helped to standardize the language.[14] One might therefore speak of the urbanization of language in early modern Japan, as in Europe at this time.

The urban culture of both work and leisure was described and sometimes celebrated not only in the fiction of Saikaku and his colleagues, but also in a new genre: the urban guidebook. Some of them were written for visitors and concentrated on the sights of the city, while others listed the shops to be found in every street together with the goods that they sold.[15] As the rise of this genre suggests, in some respects early modern Japan was becoming a commercial society, offering high rewards to entrepreneurs. This was in spite of the country being ruled by an authoritarian regime that is sometimes described as 'feudal', thanks to the dominance of the military class, the samurai and the decentralization of government that left the *daimyō* as masters of their own houses in the provinces. At times, there were conflicts between the commercial and feudal parts of the system. In 1705, for instance, the *Bakufu* confiscated the wealth of a leading merchant family in Ōsaka, the Yodoya, in order to remind merchants to know their place (which was officially below that of peasants in the status hierarchy) and also to cancel the debts of some *daimyō* to that family. On the other hand, many merchants flourished, together with an urban culture that attracted samurai as well as merchants and artisans.

The Chinese model

The story of urbanization in early modern China is not as simple as in the case of Japan. First, China was less isolated, despite attempts to close the country to foreign trade in the early sixteenth century.[16] Second, it has been argued that China had not one urban system, but several, each based on a

[14] Matsunosuke Nishiyama, *Edō Culture: Daily Life and Diversions in Urban Japan, 1600–1868* (Honolulu: University of Hawaii Press, 1997), p. 45.
[15] Mary Elizabeth Berry, *Japan in Print: Information and Nation in the Early Modern Period* (Berkeley, CA: University of California Press, 2006).
[16] Timothy Brook, *The Confusions of Pleasure: Commerce and Culture in Ming China* (Berkeley, CA: University of California Press, 1998), pp. 123–4.

different region, the most densely urbanized region being the Lower Yangzi. Third, the narrative focuses on recovery rather than irresistible rise, and a limited recovery at that. One leading scholar in the field places this period between 'two great macrocycles' of urban growth, the thirteenth and the nineteenth centuries.[17]

It is the period of the Song dynasty (960 to 1276) that witnessed an urban revolution. In the twelfth century, Kaifeng, the capital, was home to about 1 million people, while Hangzhou may have reached 1.2 million, making it the largest city in the world at that time. No wonder Marco Polo was impressed by the size of Chinese cities. This urban revolution was made possible by a rising population, which in turn depended on an agricultural revolution, spread over the centuries 900 to 1200, of which the central feature was the expansion of rice production thanks to irrigation and new strains of rice that ripened more quickly, allowing several crops a year.[18] The agriculture of the Yangzi delta was probably the most productive in the world, and an efficient system of water transport via the Yangzi and Yellow Rivers and the Grand Canal brought food to the growing cities. As a result, the population of China rose to about 120 million. The invasion of the Mongols brought these developments to a halt. Indeed, the population probably fell to half what it had been at its height, recovering slowly to reach around 80 million by the year 1400.

By 1400, a new dynasty, the Ming, was in power and a limited urban revival was in progress, assisted by the rise in the country's population. From around 80 million in 1400, it had doubled to around 160 million by 1600 and then more than doubled again, to around 350 million in 1800.[19] This increase suggests that the productivity of Chinese agriculture continued to increase, thanks in part to the European discovery of the New World: maize was introduced to China by the Portuguese in the sixteenth century, while the sweet potato made its way there via the Spanish colony of the Philippines.

The government encouraged the growth of some cities. At the beginning of Ming rule in 1368, Nanjing became the capital and so the administrative

---

[17] G. William Skinner (ed.), *The City in Late Imperial China* (Stanford University Press, 1977), introduction, and Rozman, *Urban Networks*.

[18] Mark Elvin, *The Pattern of the Chinese Past* (London: Eyre Methuen, 1973); and Mark Elvin, 'Chinese Cities since the Sung Dynasty' in Philip Abrams and E. Anthony Wrigley (eds), *Towns in Societies* (Cambridge University Press, 1978), pp. 79–89.

[19] Patricia Ebrey, *The Cambridge Illustrated History of China* (Cambridge University Press, 1996), p. 197.

centre of China. There followed an influx of soldiers (200,000 of them, according to a contemporary source), civil servants (about 15,000) and students (8,000 to 9,000 by the end of the fourteenth century), who hoped that good results in the public examinations would launch their careers as officials. By 1400, the population of Nanjing was a little short of half a million by one estimate and around 1 million by another, which would have made it the largest city in the world at that time.[20] In 1421, however, Nanjing lost its status as the capital and gradually declined in numbers, although it remained an important city. It recovered to some extent in the sixteenth century and became a centre of silk weaving under the Qing dynasty. In 1600, it housed more than 300,000 people, in 1800 about 220,000.

In 1421, the government moved the capital to Beijing, and the soldiers, officials and students followed, together with increasing numbers of merchants, shopkeepers and artisans to meet the needs of the upper classes. The imperial household (including the politically influential eunuchs) was already established there. Some industries also flourished in the capital, from ironwork to printing. When the Qing dynasty replaced the Ming in 1644, Beijing remained the capital, and there was a new influx of military men organized under the 'banner' system, some 300,000 of them in the 1640s, a number that had doubled by the 1720s.[21] With a population of about 320,000 in 1400, Beijing grew to about 700,000 in 1600 and 1,100,000 in 1800, making it the largest city in the world at that time, even if it was soon to be surpassed by London. The topography of Beijing resembled an onion, with an Outer City, an Inner City and an Imperial City within which the Forbidden City or imperial palace was to be found.

The capital city, whichever it was, was far from being the only important city in China. If the growth of Nanjing and Beijing was driven by politics, the expansion of other cities was driven by trade in an age of commercialization – not only trade in necessities, but also in luxuries and luxury substitutes. Hangzhou, for instance, remained important and continued to grow throughout the period, from 250,000 or 325,000 in 1400 to half a million in 1800, on the eve of the second great period of urban expansion. It was famous for the tea trade, but also for the market in rice, salt and cotton and the luxury trade in textiles. Thanks to the water transport system,

---

[20] Frederick W. Mote, 'The Transformation of Nanking, 1350–1400' in Skinner, *The City*, pp. 31 and 101–53. The lower figure comes from Chandler, *Four Thousand Years*.
[21] Susan Naquin, *Peking: Temples and City Life 1400–1900* (Berkeley, CA: University of California Press, 2000), pp. 293 and 376.

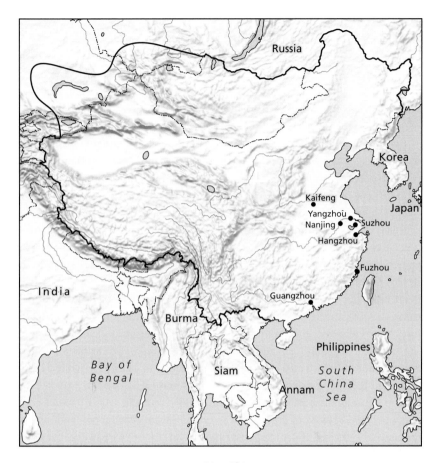

5.2 Qing China

by 1800 Hangzhou was turning into a kind of Ōsaka – in other words, a centre for the distribution of goods throughout what was becoming a national market.[22]

Again, Suzhou was one of the great cities of the pre-industrial world, which 'continued to outclass Hangzhou in the late Ming as a production and consumption centre'.[23] Its population, between 120,000 and 250,000 in 1400,

[22] William T. Rowe, *Hankow: Commerce and Society in a Chinese City, 1796–1889*, 2 vols (Stanford University Press, 1984–9).
[23] Michael Marmé, *Suzhou: Where the Goods of All the Provinces Converge* (Stanford University Press, 2005).

increased to at least 240,000 and possibly much more by 1800, supported by the production of silk and cotton.[24] Its canals reminded the Italian Jesuit missionary Matteo Ricci in the late sixteenth century of Venice. Yangzhou, a former capital, was another important city, a centre for trade in salt, rice and silk. So was Guangzhou, on the Pearl River, close to the South China Sea, with about 350,000 people in 1600, but 800,000 by 1800, when it had become a major international port.

Even minor Chinese cities were large by European standards. Nanchang, for instance, was 'twice Florence', as Ricci commented with admiration. His remark is corroborated by the census of 1587, in which Nanchang figured with 167,000 people.[25] There was a rise of small towns, especially in the Yangzi delta, making the region more highly urbanized than ever before.

Relatively little is known about the process of immigration, which was crucial to the growth of cities in China as elsewhere in the world. It was sometimes compulsory, as in the case of Nanjing in 1368 and Beijing in 1644. It was sometimes extensive: half the population of Hangzhou in 1813 had been born outside the city. Many immigrants were 'sojourners', men who came to work in the city but left their families behind. A number of urban institutions allowed immigrants to maintain their regional identities, including temples, meeting halls and lodging-clubs (*huiguan*). Some cities became multi-ethnic. Nanjing had a sizeable community of Muslims, while Hangzhou had foreign quarters for Muslims, Jews and Christians.[26]

The consequences of urbanization are more palpable. As in Japan, large cities became centres of conspicuous consumption. After 1600, landowners increasingly moved from the countryside to the city. Rivalry between members of the elite, or between newly rich merchants and the elite, led to an escalation in the consumption of luxuries; grander banquets, more expensive clothes, larger houses. Some of the salt merchants of Yangzhou employed their own opera troupes. Commercial publishing expanded in the sixteenth century, and many more printed books went into circulation. Leisure districts developed, such as Suzhou's Tiger Hill and Hangzhou's West Lake. In Nanjing, there were 'amusement areas' populated by jugglers, acrobats, storytellers and prostitutes, a kind of Chinese floating world. Booksellers had their own quarters, such as Chang Gate in Suzhou,

[24] Marmé, *Suzhou*; the lower figure, once again, comes from Chandler, *Four Thousand Years*.
[25] Quoted in R. Po-Chia Hsia, *A Jesuit in the Forbidden City* (Oxford University Press, 2010), p. 148.
[26] Jacques Gernet, *A History of Chinese Civilization* (Cambridge University Press, 1986).

or Three Mountains Street in Nanjing, conveniently sited between the examination hall and the pleasure quarter.[27] In Beijing in 1800, there were twenty-one theatres in the outer city, for men only, as well as theatre-restaurants that allowed women to watch the spectacle from the balcony. The new commercial urban culture may well have acted as a safety valve, since urban revolts happened rarely, if at all, although even the large cities lacked autonomy.

The European model

In some ways, the pattern of European urbanization resembles that of China. For one thing, it is probably more illuminating to think in terms of several urban systems than of one alone – indeed, given the political fragmentation of the continent, polycentrism is still more obvious in the case of Europe. Again, as in China, the largest cities were smaller in 1400 than they had been in 1300. In Europe, the decline was a result of the bubonic plague, known as the 'Black Death', in which a third of the population had died in 1348 to 1349. Between 1400 and 1500, the population of some major cities declined still further. Paris went from 275,000 to 225,000; Bruges, which was losing trade to Antwerp, from 125,000 to 90,000; Granada, following the expulsion of Muslims and Jews, from 100,000 to 70,000. In 1500, there were only three or four European cities with a population over 100,000: Paris, Venice, Naples and possibly Milan (leaving aside Istanbul and Edirne, which will be discussed in the following section).[28]

However, the three or four cities of 100,000 people in 1500 had become twelve 100 years later, with the addition (among others) of Lisbon, Seville, London, Rome and Moscow. This number remained more or less constant in the seventeenth century, when the population of Europe was fairly stable, but between 1700 and 1800 it rose from twelve to twenty-two cities, led by London and followed by Paris, Naples, Moscow, Lisbon, Vienna, St Petersburg and Amsterdam. This growth was made possible by a revolution in farming that made agriculture more productive. Conversely, the urban demand for food stimulated the development of commercial agriculture, especially in regions surrounding cities. Cities of 100,000 or more were

---

[27] Lucille Chia, *Printing for Profit: The Commercial Publishers of Jianyang, Fukien* (Cambridge, MA: Harvard University Press, 2003).

[28] Christopher R. Friedrichs, *The Early Modern City, 1450–1750* (London: Longman, 1995); Alex F. Cowan, *Urban Europe, 1500–1700* (London: Arnold, 1998); and Jean-Luc Pinol (ed.), *Histoire de l'Europe urbaine*, 2 vols (Paris: Seuil, 2003).

becoming more important in the sense of accounting for an increasing percentage of the urban population, from 16 per cent in 1600 to 22.5 per cent in 1800. The bigger fish were eating up the smaller ones.

The rapid rise of a few European cities is reminiscent of the Japanese model, especially the rise of Edō. Madrid, for instance, was a small town in 1561, when King Philip II moved the court there. It doubled in size in the twenty years from 1597 to 1617, and by 1700 it was home to some 110,000 people, slowly increasing to 123,000 by 1750 and 169,000 in 1800.[29] London (which might be described as an Edō, Ōsaka and Kyōto rolled into one, far larger than its provincial rivals) doubled in size between 1600 and 1650, rising from 200,000 to 400,000 inhabitants. St Petersburg more than doubled between 1750 and 1800, from 100,000 to 238,000 people.

Like Madrid, Paris, Naples, London, Vienna and St Petersburg all grew because they were the capitals of states, Peter the Great having transferred the capital from Moscow to St Petersburg just as Philip had transferred his capital from Valladolid to Madrid. The social structure of the population of these capital cities is what might have been expected from their political functions. In 1789, a quarter of the population of St Petersburg was military. As for civil servants, there were some 3,000 of them, excluding clerks, in Vienna in 1782, while in St Petersburg numbers had climbed by 1833 to 10,000 officials and 23,000 clerks.[30]

As in the case of Edō and Beijing, European capitals were centres of conspicuous consumption by an elite that was increasingly drawn to the court. The population of these cities therefore included unusually high proportions of servants and tailors. In Rome in 1526, 'tailor' was the most common single occupation and accounted for 8 per cent of the work force, a proportion matched by Valladolid before the court moved to Madrid. Lawyers too made up a surprising large proportion of the population of capitals. The contemporary estimate that 30,000 people made their living from the law in seventeenth-century Naples must be an exaggeration, but there is hard evidence that lawyers accounted for over 7 per cent of the active population of Valladolid in 1570.[31]

Other European cities grew for economic reasons. Seville, for instance, was a boom town in the sixteenth century because it was the port through

[29] David R. Ringrose, *Madrid and the Spanish Economy 1560–1850* (Berkeley, CA: University of California Press, 1983).
[30] Peter Clark and Bernard Lepetit (eds), *Capital Cities and Their Hinterlands in Early Modern Europe* (Aldershot: Scolar, 1996).
[31] Bartolomé Bennassar, *Valladolid au siècle d'or* (Paris, The Hague: Mouton, 1967).

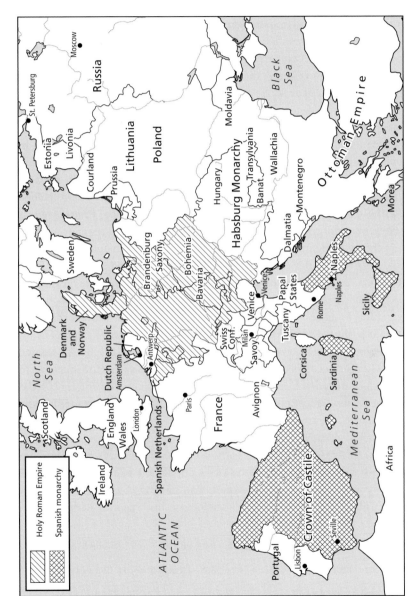

5.3 Europe in 1700

which the silver mined in Mexico and Peru reached Spain. By 1600, its population was about 144,000, declining together with the Spanish economy in the seventeenth century.[32] Amsterdam was another success story, growing in part at the expense of Antwerp, which had itself grown at the expense of Bruges. It prospered first on the basis of trade with the Baltic region, and later with the East and West Indies. Amsterdam was fourth in the sequence of early modern cities identified by Fernand Braudel as the centres of world economies, following Venice, Antwerp and Genoa. Its great age of expansion was the seventeenth century: the city had about 90,000 inhabitants in 1620, but 200,000 in 1680. It was no larger in 1800, since the Dutch Republic had gone into economic decline and it was now the turn of London to be a centre of trade.[33]

Industry, in the sense of the crafts, was less important than trade as an engine of urban growth. Leading craft-industrial or proto-industrial cities such as Florence, Segovia, Leiden and Amiens, all centres of cloth making; Lyon, a centre of silk weaving; and Leipzig, a centre of printing, all remained below the 100,000 level for most of the period before 1800. Printing was a relatively important industry in Venice in the sixteenth century, in Amsterdam in the seventeenth century and in London in the eighteenth century, as it was in seventeenth-century Ōsaka, but it contributed much less than international trade to the growth of these cities. As far as size was concerned, the producer city lagged behind the consumer city.

Migration to cities is better documented in the case of Europe than that of East Asia, but it appears to have followed the usual pattern of chains. In sixteenth-century Venice, the Greeks tended to live in the parish known as 'San Giorgio dei Greci' and the Slavs along the Riva degli Schiavoni. In eighteenth-century Paris, certain streets were dominated by migrants from particular regions, the Rue Mouffetard by Auvergnats, for instance. In the case of Paris, contracts of apprenticeship reveal cases of immigrants with relatives already established in the city who guaranteed their good behaviour. In Amsterdam in the early seventeenth century, 73 per cent of newly-weds and 33 per cent of the city's population were immigrants. As usual, migrants were more often young than old and more often male than female. Unlike anthropologists or sociologists, historians of early modern

---

[32] Jean Sentaurens, 'Seville dans la seconde moitié du 16me siècle', *Bulletin Hispanique* 77 (1975), 321–50.

[33] Herman Diederiks, 'Amsterdam 1600–1800. Demographische Entwicklung und Migration' in Roelof van Gelder and Renée Kistemaker (eds), *Amsterdam, 1275–1795* (Amsterdam: Meulenhoff, 1983).

Europe cannot ask immigrants what brought them to the city, but there is some evidence to illustrate both rural 'push' and urban 'pull'. That hunger was an important push factor becomes clear when we consider the chronology and the geography of migration, which was most intense in times of famine and from the relatively infertile areas of heath and mountain.

As for urban pull, it may be summed up in the famous German phrase 'Town air makes you free' (*Stadtluft macht frei*). The phrase originally referred to freedom from serfdom, but it may be expanded to include freedom from parental control and, following the Reformation, religious freedom as well, especially in Venice, Antwerp and Amsterdam. As in China, certain institutions helped immigrants to adjust to the alien environment of the city and to maintain connections with their region of origin. In Rome, for example, the French immigrants attended the church of San Luigi dei Francesi, the Spaniards that of San Giacomo degli Spagnuoli, and the Florentines that of San Giovanni dei Fiorentini.

The city was also the promised land of social mobility. That it was perceived as such is shown by the story of Dick Whittington, the poor country boy who became Lord Mayor of London, a story that circulated widely in seventeenth-century England and ended in one version with this verse: 'And you poor country boys/Though born of low degree/See by Gods Providence/What you in time may be.' Hence cities such as Rome, Paris, Amsterdam and London attracted talented people, provided spaces in which they could meet and thus became centres of innovation. The concentration of institutions such as libraries, universities and learned academies in a few cities turned them into centres of knowledge.

As in the case of both Japan and China, the growth of cities led to the commercialization of leisure – the rise of the theatres for instance. Plays had long been performed by travelling actors, but as cities grew, it was possible for actors to remain in the same place and still perform for a different audience every night, whether in the courtyard of inns, as in Madrid, or in purpose-built theatres such as Shakespeare's Globe in London. The new genre of opera moved from the court to the city: the first opera house, catering to anyone who could buy a ticket, opened in Venice in 1637. Something like the Japanese 'floating world' developed in European cities, even if the pleasure quarters were not formally segregated. Actors and courtesans shared the same spaces in the city, such as Drury Lane and Covent Garden in London. As in China, booksellers had their own quarters, such as St Paul's Churchyard in London or the Rue Saint-Jacques in Paris. The growth of cities also encouraged the development of an art market (as opposed to the patronage system), first in Bruges and Antwerp and later in Amsterdam, Venice, Rome, Paris and London.

Just as Chinese and Japanese cities had their tea-houses, so European cities such as Venice, Vienna, Paris and London had their coffee-houses from the late seventeenth century onwards, which functioned as so many centres of sociability, conversation and the exchange of information. Urbanization, including regular encounters between individuals from different regions, encouraged the standardization of languages, spoken as well as written. As in ancient Greece and Rome, early modern European cities were often represented as the sites of 'civilization', 'urbanity' and 'politeness', words derived from classical terms for 'city'. Immigration helped cities to spread their values more widely: it has been calculated that one-sixth of the population of seventeenth-century England had direct experience of London life.[34]

The Middle East and India

A number of major cities could be found in other parts of the world at this time, especially in the Middle East and India. In 1400, the largest of these was probably Cairo, with a population that reached at least 150,000 and might have been as high as 450,000.[35] The population of Vijayanagara, the capital of an empire in south India, might have been as high as 350,000, followed by Tabriz with about 200,000 people and Damascus and Baghdad with about 100,000 each.

Constantinople, still the capital of the Byzantine Empire, was declining in numbers at this time as the Ottoman Turks advanced towards it. In 1453, when the sultan Mehmed I conquered the city, Istanbul, as it would be known henceforth, was probably home to 50,000 people. Then the city rose again, thanks in part to emigration by order of the sultan, from the Caucasus, Syria, Serbia and elsewhere. New quarters of the city were given the names of regions such as Aksaray and Balat, suggesting that, once again, chain migration took place. By 1500, Istanbul had a population of 200,000 and by 1700, 700,000, a number which then gradually declined.[36]

[34] E. Anthony Wrigley, 'A Simple Model of London's Importance, 1650–1750', Past and Present 37 (1967), 44–70.
[35] André Raymond, 'Cairo's Area and Population in the Early Fifteenth Century', Muqarnas 2 (1984), 21–31; André Raymond, The Great Arab Cities (New York University Press, 1984); and Clifford E. Bosworth (ed.), Historic Cities of the Islamic World (Leiden: Brill, 2007).
[36] Ebru Boyar and Kate Fleet, A Social History of Ottoman Istanbul (Cambridge University Press, 2010).

The rise of cities in the Middle East and India in the early modern period seems to have happened for political rather than economic reasons. This is not to say that commerce and crafts were unimportant: Cairo, for instance, was a centre of the international trade in pepper and coffee, as well as crafts such as weaving (cotton and silk) and leather-working. Istanbul was home to more than a thousand guilds, as well as to groups of foreign merchants, Italians and Greeks in particular. Surat, the population of which may have reached 200,000 by 1700, was a major port.

However, the cities that grew most in these parts of the world were the capitals of states: not only Istanbul, but also Isfahan, capital of the empire of the Safavids (said to have reached the 600,000 mark in 1700) and Agra, periodically the capital of the Mughal Empire (500,000 in 1600). When Shah Jahan transferred his capital in 1648 from Agra to Shahjahanabad (better known as Delhi), the former city declined and the latter rose, to reach around 500,000 people by 1700. In 1757, the English soldier Robert Clive called the capital of Bengal, Murshidabad, 'as extensive, populous and rich as the City of London'.[37]

The Frenchman François Bernier, who lived in Delhi in the 1660s, remarked on the absence of merchants ('the middle state') and considered the place a collection of villages rather than a true city. He could hardly have said the same thing about Istanbul or Isfahan, with their huge bazaars in the centre of the city. In Isfahan, the royal square or *Maidan* impressed a traveller from Rome, Pietro della Valle, as being grander than the Piazza Navona. Tea-houses, coffee-houses, taverns and brothels were to be found in this area, together with jugglers and acrobats – in other words, a kind of floating world (in Istanbul, this world was located in the district of Galata).[38]

Cities with a population of 100,000 or more could also be found in other parts of the early modern world, though relatively little is known about them. In 1400, for instance, Samarqand, Angkor and Seoul had around 100,000 people each. In the New World, when Hernán Cortés reached the Aztec capital, Tenochtitlán, in 1519, it was home to 300,000 or even half a million people. It may have been the greatest city in the world at that time,

---

[37] Ebba Koch, 'Mughal Agra' in Salma K. Jayyusi *et al.* (eds), *The City in the Islamic World*, 2 vols (Leiden: Brill, 2008), pp. 555–88; and Philip B. Calkins, 'The Role of Murshidabad in Bengal' in Richard L. Park (ed.), *Urban Bengal* (East Lansing, MI: Michigan State University, 1969), pp. 19–28.

[38] Wilfrid Blunt, *Isfahan: Pearl of Persia* (London: Elek Books, 1966).

though it was probably surpassed by Beijing. Cuzco, the Inca capital, was a city of about 100,000 people when Pizarro arrived. In North America, the largest cities in 1800 were New York, with 60,000 inhabitants, and Boston, with 25,000.[39]

In Africa south of the Sahara, although the tradition of Yoruba urban culture goes back to this period, cities tended to be small. Among the largest were Elmina, a port on the Gold Coast (15,000 to 20,000 in the 1620s), Great Accra (20,000 in 1700) and the slave-trading city of Abomey (24,000 in 1800). An African 'urban revolution' did not occur until the nineteenth century.[40]

The colonial city

The economic and political expansion of Europe into other parts of the world in the early modern period led to the rise of another type of city: the colonial city, established either to control the region or to manage the unequal trade between colony and metropolis.[41] Hence colonial cities have sometimes been viewed as outposts of the metropolis that were alien to the local environments. However, it is surely more realistic to regard them as hybrid cities, facing both ways, outwards towards the distant metropolis and inwards towards their own hinterland. The physical structure of these cities revealed their dual function. Manila, for instance, was divided into a section for the Spaniards and another section for the Chinese. Madras (Chennai) and Calcutta (Kolkata) were divided into the so-called 'white' towns, inhabited by Europeans, and the 'black' towns inhabited by every-one else.[42] In Mexico City, the Spaniards and their descendants generally lived in the centre and the Indians on the periphery. Despite these attempts at segregation, however, these cities revealed both cultural and social mixing.

[39] Jorge Hardoy, Nora Scott Kinzer and Richard Schaedel (eds), *Urbanization in the Americas from Its Beginnings to the Present Day* (The Hague: Aldine de Gruyter, 1978).

[40] Catherine Coquery-Vidrovitch, *History of African Cities South of the Sahara* (Princeton, NJ: Markus Wiener, 2005).

[41] Robert Ross and Gerard J. Telkamp (eds), *Colonial Cities* (Dordrecht: Martinus Nijhoff, 1984).

[42] Robert R. Reed, *Colonial Manila* (Berkeley, CA: University of California Press, 1978); Peter J. Marshall, 'Eighteenth-Century Calcutta' in Ross and Telkamp, *Colonial Cities*, pp. 87–104; Sanjay Subrahmanyam, 'Madras, Chennai and São Tomé' in Clara García Ayluardo and Manuel Ramos Medina (eds), *Ciudades mestizas* (Mexico, DF: Condumex, 2001), pp. 221–39.

Most colonial cities were ports.[43] In order of size they were led by Madras, a former fishing village that had grown to a city of 300,000 people by 1800. Then came Bombay (Mumbai), another former fishing village, and also Calcutta, with 200,000 people apiece by the end of the eighteenth century. There followed Havana and Batavia, with almost 100,000 each at this time, and Manila, with 75,000. Earlier in the early modern period, leading Asian ports that might be described as 'semi-colonial cities' (in which European merchants were present but not yet dominant) included Goa, with 75,000 inhabitants in 1630 and Macao, with the same number in 1700; still more complex was the case of Surat, a multicultural city under Mughal rule until about 1760 with a prosperous merchant community, the *banias*, who acted as brokers for the Portuguese, Dutch, French and British, as well as pursuing their own interests.[44]

Two major colonial cities were not ports. One was Mexico City, the capital of the viceroyalty of New Spain, built on the ruins of Tenochtitlán. It was home to 110,000 people in 1750, in a region undergoing a slow recovery after the demographic disaster that followed the arrival of the Spaniards and the consequent transmission of the diseases of the Old World to the New. The other was Potosí in the viceroyalty of Peru, which has been described as 'boom town supreme', based on the extraction of silver from the nearby mountain. The city reached a peak of 160,000 people around the year 1650, making it by far the largest city in early modern South America, followed by Salvador (50,000 or more in 1800), Rio de Janeiro (43,000 in 1800) and Lima (30,000 in 1650).[45]

Conditions in colonial cities varied with the colonial power (Portuguese, Spanish, Dutch, French or British), the presence or absence of an urban tradition, the proportion of resident Europeans and so on. What these cities had in common, and what made them different from other cities, was the

---

[43] Frank Broeze, *Brides of the Sea: Port Cities of Asia from the Sixteenth to the Twentieth Century* (Honolulu: University of Hawaii Press, 1989); Franklin W. Knight and Peggy K. Liss (eds), *Atlantic Port Cities: Economy, Culture, and Society in the Atlantic world, 1650–1850* (Knoxville, TN: University of Tennessee Press, 1990); and Michael N. Pearson, *Port Cities and Intruders: The Swahili Coast, India and Portugal in the Early Modern Era* (Baltimore, MD: Johns Hopkins University Press, 1996).

[44] Balkrishna G. Gokhale, *Surat in the Seventeenth Century* (London; Curzon Press, 1979); and Leonard Blussé, 'Batavia 1619–1740: The Rise and Fall of a Chinese Colonial Town' in Leonard Blussé, *Strange Company: Chinese Settlers, Mestizo Women, and the Dutch in VOC Batavia* (Dordrecht: Foris, 1986), pp. 73–96.

[45] David Brading, 'The Colonial City' in John P. King and Linda Newson (eds), *Mexico City through History and Culture* (Oxford University Press, 2009), pp. 39–54; and Lewis Hanke, *The Imperial City of Potosí* (The Hague: Mouton, 1965).

importance of race. Some European cities were also home to different ethnic groups, as we have seen, but the cultural and physical contrasts between the Chinese, Javanese, Gujaratis, Tamils, Amerindians and West Africans who lived together in some colonial cities were much greater. Intermarriage, or more often interbreeding, took place, producing *mestizos* and *mulattos* who occupied the middle places in a social hierarchy based on colour, sometimes described as a 'pigmentocracy'.

The concern with colour on the part of the inhabitants of colonial cities is revealed, in the case of Spanish America, by the so-called *casta* paintings, representing the offspring of a Spaniard with an Amerindian, Spaniard with an African, Amerindian with African and so on and by the elaborate vocabulary that developed to describe differences in colour or descent (*pardos, zambos* and so on). The same preoccupation is revealed by insults traded in the street and recorded in judicial archives, such as this from Mexico: 'Look out you dog, you are a mulatto and I am very much Spanish [*Mira perro que eres un mulato y yo soy muy español*].'[46]

Comparisons and conclusions

Let us begin with common features. In all regions, cities were both 'agents' and 'patients'; in other words, they were affected by change, but they contributed to further change in their turn. Cities have often been described as engines of change, but the engine needed fuel. The city needed immigrants, but they could only come if the productivity of rural labour increased, thus freeing some people to migrate. In any case, the increasing numbers of city dwellers needed to be fed. Hence an agricultural revolution, most visible in China and Europe, was a precondition for an urban revolution. Conversely, the rise of cities encouraged the commercialization of agriculture in their hinterlands, and also rural 'proto-industrialization' – in other words, the rise of rural crafts such as spinning and weaving for an urban market.[47]

In all regions, some cities were 'market-oriented', growing for essentially economic reasons, while others, the capitals in particular, were 'coercion-oriented' or 'state-oriented' and grew for essentially political reasons, such as the unification of the country (Japan, India, Spain) or the centralization of power (France). The rise of cities was associated with the rise of the

[46] Cheryl E. Martin, 'Popular Speech and Social Order in Northern Mexico, 1650–1830', *Comparative Studies in Society and History* 32 (1990), 305–24.

[47] Richard Graham, *Feeding the City* (Austin, TX: University of Texas Press, 2010).

bourgeoisie (including the *chōnin* and the *banias*). The concept of the rise of the middle class has often been criticized. All the same, it remains virtually indispensable, and is particularly useful when distinctions are drawn between kinds of bourgeoisie (officials and lawyers as well as merchants) and also between kinds of rise (in numbers, for instance, or in wealth and power).

These rises were part of the commercialization of society and especially of leisure, increasingly visible in various parts of the early modern world in the period. As cities grew, they became more effective as centres of information, communication, calculation and innovation. Commercialization went hand in hand with occupational specialization, which was at once possible, because of the concentration of people, and necessary, to survive in a competitive world. In Amsterdam, for instance, painters distinguished themselves from their rivals by specializing in a single genre such as townscapes, group portraits or flower pieces.

Moving to differences, distinctions between economic centres or producer cities and political capitals or consumer cities are obviously necessary.[48] So are distinctions between macro-regions, more or less unified (Japan more, Europe less). There were also some differences in the way in which growth occurred. In China, the Ottoman Empire and also in colonial cities that depended on slavery, there was compulsory immigration. In Europe, by contrast, governments (in Britain, France, Spain and Piedmont) intervened to forbid immigration to some cities, though without success. The major exception to the rule was Louis XIV's Versailles, where the leading nobles were expected to make their appearance – an informal version of the *sankin kotai* system in force at Edō, with similar consequences for conspicuous consumption.

A final comparison and contrast concerns periodization. Compared with the years before 1400, there was a dramatic increase in the flows of people, goods and information in the early modern period, with major cities as nodes in communication networks: European cities such as Venice and Amsterdam, and colonial cities such as Mexico and Goa.[49]

---

[48]   Robert Redfield and M. Singer, 'The Cultural Role of Cities', *Economic Development and Cultural Change* 3 (1954–5), 53–73; and Bert F. Hoselitz, 'Generative and Parasitic Cities', *Cultural Change* 3 (1954–5), 278–94.

[49]   Alan Pred, *Urban Growth and the Circulation of Information: The United States System of Cities, 1790–1840* (Cambridge, MA; Harvard University Press, 1973); Manuel Castells, *The Informational City* (Oxford: Blackwell, 1989); and Peter Burke, 'Early Modern Venice as a Center of Information and Communication' in John Martin and Dennis Romano (eds), *Venice Reconsidered: The History and Civilization of an Italian City-State 1297–1997* (Baltimore, MD: Johns Hopkins University Press, 2000), pp. 389–419.

As for comparisons and contrasts between the early modern and late modern periods, they are sometimes expressed as one of two extremes. One extreme view sees cities that developed after 1800 – the industrial city, the late colonial city, the 'global city' and the 'informational city' – as completely different from their predecessors. The opposite extreme argues that the changes that took place after 1800 were not really important, and that cities that developed after 1800 were largely the same as those that grew up earlier.

A better view would avoid these extremes. Modern cities have indeed come to depend on a series of new forms of communication: the railways, the steamship, the telegraph, the telephone, the airplane, the radio, the Internet . . . All the same, as we have seen, certain cities already performed important functions, both economic and political, in the early modern 'world system'.

FURTHER READING

Ayluardo, Clara García and Manuel Ramos Medina (eds), *Ciudades mestizas* (Mexico, DF: Condumex, 2001).
Bairoch, Paul, *De Jericho à Mexico: villes et économie dans l'histoire* (Paris: Gallimard, 1985).
Berry, Mary Elizabeth, *Japan in Print: Information and Nation in the Early Modern Period* (Berkeley, CA: University of California Press, 2006).
Blunt, Wilfrid, *Isfahan: Pearl of Persia* (London: Elek Books, 1966).
Blussé, Leonard, 'Batavia 1619–1740: The Rise and Fall of a Chinese Colonial Town' in Leonard Blussé, *Strange Company: Chinese Settlers, Mestizo Women, and the Dutch in VOC Batavia* (Dordrecht: Foris, 1986), pp. 73–96.
Bosworth, Clifford E. (ed.), *Historic Cities of the Islamic World* (Leiden: Brill, 2007).
Boyar, Ebru and Kate Fleet, *A Social History of Ottoman Istanbul* (Cambridge University Press, 2010).
Brading, David, 'The Colonial City' in John P. King and Linda Newson (eds), *Mexico City through Culture and History* (Oxford University Press, 2009), pp. 39–54.
Broeze, Frank (ed.), *Brides of the Sea: Port Cities of Asia from the Sixteenth to the Twentieth Century* (Honolulu: University of Hawaii Press, 1989).
Brook, Timothy, *The Confusions of Pleasure: Commerce and Culture in Ming China* (Berkeley, CA: University of California Press, 1998).
Burke, Peter, 'Early Modern Venice as a Center of Information and Communication' in John Martin and Dennis Romano (eds), *Venice Reconsidered: The History and Civilization of an Italian City-State 1297–1997* (Baltimore, MD: Johns Hopkins University Press, 2000), pp. 389–419.
Calkins, Philip B., 'The Role of Murshidabad in Bengal' in Richard L. Park (ed.), *Urban Bengal* (East Lansing, MI: Michigan State University, 1969), pp. 19–28.
Castells, Manuel, *The Informational City* (Oxford: Blackwell, 1989).
Chandler, Tertius, *Four Thousand Years of Urban Growth* (Lewiston, NY: E. Mellen Press, 1987).

Chia, Lucille, *Printing for Profit: The Commercial Publishers of Jianyang, Fukien* (Cambridge, MA: Harvard University Press, 2003).

Clark, Peter and Bernard Lepetit (eds), *Capital Cities and Their Hinterlands in Early Modern Europe* (Aldershot: Scolar, 1996).

Coquery-Vidrovitch, Catherine, *History of African Cities South of the Sahara* (Princeton, NJ: Markus Wiener, 2005).

Cowan, Alex F., *Urban Europe, 1500–1700* (London: Arnold, 1998).

Diederiks, Herman, 'Amsterdam 1600–1800. Demographische Entwicklung und Migration' in Roelof van Gelder and Renée Kistemaker (eds), *Amsterdam, 1275–1795* (Amsterdam: Meulenhoff, 1983).

Ebrey, Patricia, *The Cambridge Illustrated History of China* (Cambridge University Press, 1996).

Elvin, Mark, 'Chinese Cities since the Sung Dynasty' in Philip Abrams and E. Anthony Wrigley (eds), *Towns in Societies* (Cambridge University Press, 1978), pp. 79–89.
  The Pattern of the Chinese Past (London: Eyre Methuen, 1973).

Friedrichs, Christopher R., *The Early Modern City, 1450–1750* (London: Longman, 1995).

Gernet, Jacques, *A History of Chinese Civilization* (Cambridge University Press, 1986).

Gokhale, Balkrishna G., *Surat in the Seventeenth Century* (London: Curzon Press, 1979).

Graham, Richard, *Feeding the City* (Austin, TX: University of Texas Press, 2010).

Hall, John W., 'The Castle Town and Japan's Modern Urbanization', *Far Eastern Quarterly* 15 (1955–6), 37–56.

Hanke, Lewis, *The Imperial City of Potosí* (The Hague: Mouton, 1965).

Hanley, Susan B. and Haruko Wakita, 'Dimensions of Development: Cities in Fifteenth- and Sixteenth-Century Japan' in J. W. Hall, Nagahara Keiji and Kozo Yamamura (eds), *Japan before Tokugawa: Consolidation and Economic Growth, 1500–1650* (Princeton University Press, 1981), pp. 295–326.

Hardoy, Jorge, Nora Scott Kinzer and Richard Schaedel (eds), *Urbanization in the Americas from Its Beginnings to the Present Day* (The Hague: Aldine de Gruyter, 1978).

Hauser, Philip M. and Leo F. Schnore, *The Study of Urbanization* (New York: Wiley, 1965).

Hibbett, Howard, *The Floating World in Japanese Fiction* (London: Oxford University Press, 1959).

Hoselitz, Bert F., 'Generative and Parasitic Cities', *Economic Development and Cultural Change* 3 (1954–5), 278–94.

Hsia, R. Po-Chia, *A Jesuit in the Forbidden City* (Oxford University Press, 2010).

Kaoru, Ugawa, James L. McClain and John M. Merriman (eds), *Edo and Paris: Urban Life and the State in the Early Modern Era* (Ithaca, NY: Cornell University Press, 1994).

Knight, Franklin W. and Peggy K. Liss (eds), *Atlantic Port Cities: Economy, Culture, and Society in the Atlantic World, 1650–1850* (Knoxville, TN: University of Tennessee Press, 1990).

Koch, Ebba, 'Mughal Agra' in Salma K. Jayyusi, Renata Holod, Attilio Petruccioli and André Raymond (eds), *The City in the Islamic World*, 2 vols (Leiden: Brill, 2008), pp. 555–88.

Marmé, Michael, *Suzhou: Where the Goods of All the Provinces Converge* (Stanford University Press, 2005).

McClain, James L. and Nobuhiko Nakai, 'Commercial Change and Urban Growth in Early Modern Japan' in John W. Hall (ed.), *Early Modern Japan* (Cambridge University Press, 1991), pp. 519–95.

McClain, James L. and Osamu Wakita (eds), *Osaka: The Merchants' Capital of Early Modern Japan* (Ithaca, NY: Cornell University Press, 1999).

Mote, Frederick W., 'The Transformation of Nanking, 1350–1400' in G. William Skinner (ed.), *The City in Late Imperial China* (Stanford University Press, 1977), pp. 101–53.

Murphey, Rhoads, 'Traditionalism and Colonialism: Changing Urban Roles in Asia', *Journal of Asian Studies* 29 (1969), 67–84.

Naquin, Susan, *Peking: Temples and City Life 1400–1900* (Berkeley, CA: University of California Press, 2000).

Nishiyama, Matsunosuke, *Edo Culture: Daily Life and Diversions in Urban Japan, 1600–1868* (Honolulu: University of Hawaii Press, 1997).

Pearson, Michael N., *Port Cities and Intruders: The Swahili Coast, India and Portugal in the Early Modern Era* (Baltimore, MD: Johns Hopkins University Press, 1996).

Pred, Alan, *Urban Growth and the Circulation of Information: The United States System of Cities, 1790–1840* (Cambridge, MA: Harvard University Press, 1973).

Raymond, André, 'Cairo's Area and Population in the Early Fifteenth Century', *Muqarnas* 2 (1984), 21–31.

The Great Arab Cities (New York University Press, 1984).

Redfield, Robert and Milton Singer, 'The Cultural Role of Cities', *Economic Development and Cultural Change* 3 (1954–5), 53–73.

Ringrose, David R., *Madrid and the Spanish Economy 1560–1850* (Berkeley, CA: University of California Press, 1983).

Ross, Robert and Gerard J. Telkamp (eds), *Colonial Cities* (Dordrecht: Martinus Nijhoff, 1984).

Rowe, William T., *Hankow: Commerce and Society in a Chinese City, 1796–1889*, 2 vols (Stanford University Press, 1984–9).

Rozman, Gilbert, 'Edo's Importance', *Journal of Japanese Studies* 1 (1974), 91–112.

Urban Networks in Ch'ing China and Tokugawa Japan (Princeton University Press, 1973).

Sentaurens, Jean, 'Seville dans la seconde moitié du seizième siècle', *Bulletin Hispanique* 77 (1975), 321–50.

Skinner, G. William (ed.), *The City in Late Imperial China* (Stanford University Press, 1977).

Vries, Jan de, *European Urbanization, 1500–1800* (Cambridge, MA: Harvard University Press, 1984).

Woude, Ad van de, Akira Hayami and Jan de Vries (eds), *Urbanization in History* (Oxford University Press, 1990).

Wrigley, E. Anthony, 'A Simple Model of London's Importance, 1650–1750', *Past and Present* 37 (1967), 44–70.

Yasutaka, Teruoka, 'Pleasure Quarters and Tokugawa Culture' in C. Andrew Gerstle (ed.), *Eighteenth-Century Japan: Culture and Society* (Sydney: Allen & Unwin, 1989), pp. 3–32.

6

Gender and sexuality

MERRY E. WIESNER-HANKS

Gender is a very old conceptual category, but a relatively new framework for historical analysis. All human societies had (and have) gender systems, in which there were two primary genders defined in relation to one another into which most people were categorized at birth, along with additional gender categories in many societies. These additional categories were sometimes based on ambiguous genitalia, castration or other physical circumstances, but more commonly they were based on social or cultural roles that individuals adopted as they matured, and could change across the lifespan. Thus, gender is a culturally constructed system of differences based to some degree on physical, morphological and anatomical features—what are often called "biological differences"—but the relationship between biology and culture is not unidirectional. Children born with ambiguous external sexual and reproductive anatomy—now generally termed "intersexed"—have generally not been assigned to a third gender, but categorized "male" or "female" at birth, and assigned to the sex they most closely resembled, an assignment sometimes reinforced by surgical procedures. Dichotomous cultural norms about gender (that everyone *should* be a man or a woman) could thus determine "biological" sex, as well as the other way around.

Despite the presence of additional gender categories, and other factors that suggest gender is fluid and malleable, the dualistic male/female gender system has been extremely powerful. It has been associated with other dichotomies, such as body/spirit, public/private, nature/culture, light/dark, up/down, outside/inside and sun/moon. Some of these dichotomies are naturally occurring and in many places viewed as divinely created, which has enabled people to view the male/female dichotomy also as natural or divinely ordained. Most of these dichotomies, including gender, have been viewed as a hierarchy, with the male linked with the stronger and more positive element in other pairs (public, culture, light, sun, etc.) and the female with the weaker and more negative one (private, nature, dark, moon, etc.). This gender hierarchy is highly variable in its intensity and manifest-ations, but it is found in every human group that left written records, and most that did not. Hierarchies in other realms of life were often expressed in terms of gender, with dominant individuals or groups described in masculine terms and dependent ones in feminine. These ideas in turn affected the way people acted, though explicit and symbolic ideas of gender could also conflict with the way people chose or were forced to operate in the world.

Because of this hierarchy, the vast majority of people who obtained a formal education or held positions as official recorders and transmitters of history and tradition until the middle of the twentieth century were men. Those men often commented about women, and engaged in what we would now term "gender analysis," which generally meant explaining why women were inferior. But the histories that they wrote, that is, narratives about what happened and why, focused on men's actions and viewed the male experi-ence as universal; when women appeared in their histories, they were exceptions that usually brought disaster. That emphasis on men's actions was further enhanced in the nineteenth century, when the male scholars at universities first in Germany and then elsewhere who were creating the professional discipline of history decided that the proper focus of all real history was political and military, that the proper unit of study was the nation-state, and that only men had the rational capacity to do professional history.

The women's rights movements, along with other factors, changed this situation. The first wave of feminism in the nineteenth and early twentieth centuries created improved opportunities for women to obtain higher edu-cation and to write histories, some of which focused on women. The second-wave feminist movement of the 1960s and 1970s resulted in an explosive growth in women's history, as advocates of women's rights in the present turned their attention to the past, discovered rich sources that had been lost or neglected, and mined familiar sources in new ways, finding women everywhere. Historians familiar with studying women increasingly began to discuss the ways in which systems of sexual differentiation affected both women and men, and by the early 1980s to use the word "gender" to describe these culturally constructed, historically changing and often unstable systems of difference. They asserted that gender is an appropriate category of analysis when looking at all historical developments, not simply those involving women or the family. Gender is a lens through which all of history can be examined, they argued, as well as a topic of inquiry. It should be analyzed in conjunction with other categories of identity, including economic status, nationality, religion and so on, a method for which the legal scholar Kimberlé Crenshaw coined the term "intersectional."[1]

Sexuality is also a relatively new category of historical study, inspired in part by the gay liberation movement that began in the 1970s. Historians and scholars in other disciplines debated the extent to which sexual desire and sexual relations were "biological" or were socially constructed, and how that construction had changed over time. They asked, for example, whether sexual relations in most societies were simply acts that people engaged in, or whether people might have had some sort of "sexual identity" even before that concept was articulated in the nineteenth century. Beginning in the 1990s, queer theory challenged the assumption that certain sexual attitudes and practices are "natural" and unchanging, and viewed the entire idea of an identity—sexual, gender, racial or other—as oppressive. One should go beyond intersectionality, argued queer theorists, and celebrate hybridity, performance and boundary crossing, for which they found examples in the past from both new and familiar sources, just as women's historians had found women's actions and ideas.

Scholars of the period from 1400 to 1800 have been at the forefront of all of these developments: women's history, gender history, the history of sexuality and queer theory. Women's history of this period, as of most periods, began by asking what women contributed to the developments traditionally viewed as central, in a search for what Natalie Zemon Davis termed "women worthies."[2] The earliest history of sexuality was also somewhat hagiographic, what later historians sarcastically labeled the search for "great gays of the past." Most research focused initially on Western Europe: How were women involved in the Renaissance, the Protestant and Catholic Reformations, the Scientific Revolution, the Enlightenment? Who were the great women artists/musicians/scientists/rulers? Which great male artists/musicians/scientists/rulers were gay? What was women's role in political movements and economic transformations, and how did these affect women? How did intellectual and cultural changes shape attitudes towards homosexuality and the treatment of those who engaged in same-sex relationships? Studies that addressed these questions were generally narrative, and may now seem

---

[1] Kimberlé Crenshaw, "Demarginalizing the Intersection of Race and Sex: A Black Feminist Critique of Antidiscrimination Doctrine, Feminist Theory and Antiracist Politics," *University of Chicago Legal Forum* (1989), 139–66.

[2] Natalie Davis's survey of the writing of European women's history and suggestions for future research directions is still useful and thought-provoking: "Women's History in Transition: The European Case," *Feminist Studies* 3 (Winter 1975/76), 83–103.

to be under-theorized and either overly celebratory or overly pessimistic because they often highlighted agency or oppression. It is important to remember, however, that in the 1970s and 1980s, the simple statements that women *did* preach, paint, work, compose, protest and engage in other forms of public activity, or that some of the men who engaged in these actions were sexually attracted to other men, were quite novel and sometimes threatening to those who had a more traditional view of what history was.

The Renaissance historian Joan Kelly's straightforward yet provocative question "Did women have a Renaissance?" led to broader questioning of historical periodization, as well as decades of intensive historical and literary research on the Renaissance itself, as people attempted to confirm, refute, modify or nuance her answer that no, women did not, or at least not during the Renaissance.[3] Various golden ages, dark ages, high points and declines in many places and eras were reassessed, as historians challenged periodization for women's history drawn rather unreflectively from men's, just as world historians challenged periodization drawn solely from European history. Such questioning has extended to the term "early modern," which was first widely adopted by economic and social historians of Europe in the 1970s.[4] As Sanjay Subrahmanyam notes in the "Introduction" to this volume, and as many other historians of places outside of Europe have also commented, both "modern" and "early modern" are problematic. Reflecting sentiments that are widely shared, the historians of Southeast Asia Leonard and Barbara Andaya comment, "especially in light of subaltern writings that reject the notion of modernity as a universal . . . the very invocation of the word implicitly sets a 'modern Europe' against a 'yet-to-be modernized' non-Europe."[5] From the perspective of women's history, the historian of medieval Europe Judith Bennett has also questioned the validity of a medieval/modern divide, challenging, in Bennett's words, "the assumption of a dramatic change in women's lives between 1300 and 1700."[6]

---

[3] First published in R. Bridenthal and C. Koonz (eds.), *Becoming Visible: Women in European History* (Boston, MA: Houghton Mifflin, 1978) and widely reprinted.

[4] For a history of the term "early modern," see Randolph Starn, "The Early Modern Muddle," *Journal of Early Modern History* 6 (2002), 296–307.

[5] Leonard Y. Andaya and Barbara Watson Andaya, "Southeast Asia in the Early Modern Period: Twenty Five Years On," *Journal of Southeast Asian Studies* 26 (1995), 92–8; See also Jack A. Goldstone, "The Problem of the 'Early Modern World,'" *Journal of the Economic and Social History of the Orient* 41 (1998), 249–84, with replies by Peter van der Veer and David Washbrook.

[6] J. Bennett, "Medieval Women, Modern Women: Across the Great Divide" in A.-L. Shapiro (ed.), *Feminists Revision History* (New Brunswick, NJ: Rutgers University Press, 1994), pp. 47–72.

She has recently broadened her focus and called for an emphasis on continuities in all of women's history, and on what she terms the "patriarchal equilibrium" across all periods, not simply across "the great divide" of 1500.[7]

Bennett's advice not to forget continuities is well taken, as the hierarchical gender system has survived every change, from the Neolithic to now: every revolution, whether French, Haitian, Russian, Scientific or Industrial, every war, religious transformation, technological development and cultural encounter. Notions about the proper roles for men and women created in Confucian thought, Buddhism, Christianity, Islam and other religious traditions and discussed in previous volumes of this *Cambridge World History* continued throughout the period covered in this volume. Institutions of higher learning continued to be for boys and men only. Gender divisions of labor that began with the development of agriculture continued, with tasks normally assigned to women generally not valued as highly as tasks normally assigned to men, and if they were paid, not paid as much. Women continued to have less access to land, cash, trade goods or other types of wealth than did the men of their family or social group. Most states of the world continued to be under the authority of hereditary rulers; women inherited the crown in some states when male heirs were lacking, and in others held great power because of their position as mother or wife to a male ruler, but the preference was always for a male ruler. But gender was also a dynamic category in this period. Every development discussed in the other chapters in this volume, including warfare, trade, migration, the slave trade and industrialization, brought change to people's lives as women and as men, and was itself shaped by gender.[8] Among the gender structures that changed were many that related to sexuality, such as marriage, divorce and illegitimacy. This chapter will focus on three topics that each involved both gender and sexuality: migration, intermarriage and the cross-cultural blending that resulted from these; third- and transgenders; and religious transformations.

---

[7] Judith Bennett, "Confronting Continuities," *Journal of Women's History* 9 (1997), 73–94, with responses by Sandra E. Greene, Karen Offen and Gerda Lerner, pp. 95–118; and Judith Bennett, *History Matters: Patriarchy and the Challenge of Feminism* (Philadelphia, PA: University of Pennsylvania Press, 2006), ch. 4, pp. 54–81.

[8] On the role of male and female family members, and larger kin groups, in mercantile activities, see the chapters by Charles H. Parker and Francesca Trivellato in this volume.

Migration, intermarriage and cross-cultural blending

The contacts between cultures before 1400 that changed gender structures had often been carried out through the transmission of ideas and construction of institutions by individuals or small groups of people; the spread of Buddhism and Islam are both examples of this. Beginning in the late fifteenth century, however, contacts often involved the movement of large numbers of people over vast distances. These brought groups that were different from one another in language, religion, ethnicity, culture and traditions together, which despite widely held norms prescribing group endogamy, resulted in sexual relationships, particularly because the gender balance between men and women among migrants was never equal. In settings of conquest and colonization, sexual relations between members of different groups frequently involved violence or coercion, but relationships sanctioned by authorities or by community norms were also common, as they were in port-cities and others centers of trade. These included marriage, concubinage, long-term unions in which a couple and their children formed a household but did not officially marry, temporary marriages in which it was understood that the man would at some point return home and various other sorts of unions. All marriages and marriage-like relationships involved issues of power and authority, both within the relationship and in relations beyond it, but those that brought these into sharpest relief were those that crossed some sort of boundary between groups, and in many parts of the world these became a matter of political and sometimes religious policy.

The Manchu Qing emperors who conquered China in the seventeenth century initially encouraged marriage between Manchu men and Han Chinese women as a way of blending the two cultures, but in 1655 reversed course and forbade these unions. They enforced this by requiring Manchu soldiers, known as bannermen, to live in separate walled quarters of Chinese cities. There were very few marriages, although Manchu bannermen did buy Han Chinese women as concubines and servants.

In the Americas, the Spanish and Portuguese crowns first hoped to avoid such relationships by keeping groups—Europeans, Africans and indigenous peoples—apart. The fact that the vast majority of European and African immigrants were men made this impossible, however, and authorities quickly gave up. A *mestizo* culture emerged in which not only ethnicity, but religions, family patterns, cultural traditions and languages blended. French authorities, and those of the Dutch and British East India Companies, initially encouraged sexual relations and even marriage between European men and indigenous women as a means of making alliances, cementing their power and spreading Christianity. In the Dutch East Indies, soldiers, merchants and minor officials married local women, as did fur-traders in French North America. Women acted as intermediaries between local and foreign cultures, sometimes gaining great advantages for themselves and their children through their contact with dominant foreigners, though also sometimes suffering greatly as their contact with foreigners began when they were sold or given as gifts by their families, or taken forcibly.[9] Attitudes towards mixed marriages began to change as more European women moved to the colonies, however, and as it became clear that cultural transformation often went in the direction opposite to that favored by missionaries and officials, with European men "going native" instead of local women becoming French or Dutch.

In settler colonies such as those in British North America, immigrants often came in family groups, and there were many more women; this plus a high birth rate meant the main story of native–immigrant relations was one of European appropriation of native lands, not the formation of blended families. In the southern colonies of North America, increasing numbers of immigrants were enslaved Africans. Laws were passed in all the southern colonies and some of the northern ones prohibiting marriage or other sexual relationships between whites and "negroes, mullatoes, or Indians," and also decreeing that all children born from enslaved women would be slaves. Only in New England were marriages between slaves legally recognized, and family groups were routinely broken up through sales. Laws regarding intermarriage were usually framed in gender-neutral language, but what lawmakers were most worried about was, as the preamble to a Virginia law of 1691 states: "negroes, mulattoes, and Indians intermarrying with English, or other white women" and the resultant "abominable mixture and spurious issue."[10] The concern about "issue"—that is, children—was picked up by Thomas Jefferson, who commented: "Were our state a pure

---

[9] See the essays by Verena Stolcke on the Atlantic World, Barbara Andaya on Southeast Asia, and Marcia Wright on Africa in Teresa A. Meade and Merry E. Wiesner-Hanks (eds.), *A Companion to Gender History* (Malden, MA: Blackwell, 2004). For North America, see Susan Sleeper-Smith, *Indian Women and French Men: Rethinking Cultural Encounter in the Western Great Lakes* (Amherst, MA: University of Massachusetts, 2001); and Gunlög Fur, *A Nation of Women: Gender and Colonial Encounters among the Delaware Indians* (Philadelphia, PA: University of Pennsylvania Press, 2009).

[10] William Waller Hening (ed.), *The Statutes at Large; Being a Collection of All the Laws of Virginia, from the First Session of the Legislature* (1823; facsimile reprint Charlottesville, VA: University of Virginia Press, 1969), vol. 3, p. 86.

democracy ... there would still be excluded from our deliberations ... women, who to prevent deprivation of morals and ambiguity of issue, should not mix promiscuously in the public meetings of men."[11]

In the colonial world, attitudes towards sexual relations between certain types of individuals, and the policies and practices that resulted from those attitudes, were shaped by notions of difference that were increasingly described as "race," a category that came to be regarded as inherited through the blood, so that the children of parents from different cultures were regarded as "mixed-blood." As many studies (and the quotations above) make clear, race is a gendered category, and so is mixed-blood.[12] In eighteenth-century Saint Domingue, for example, mixed-race men were thought to be foppish and beardless, while mixed-race women, according to one European visitor, "combine the explosiveness of saltpeter with an exuberance of desire, which, scorning all, drives them to pursue, acquire and devour pleasure."[13] Critiques of the masculinity of men in other parts of the world were common features in European colonial discourse, but this visitor's view was also shaped by the fact that the mixed-race men of Saint Domingue were generally half French. In the eighteenth century, men in other parts of Europe, especially Britain, worried about the effects of French culture on the masculinity of their own area, particularly among well-to-do gentlemen. In Britain, such concerns led to the creation of a distinctly British version of the gentleman, who dressed in a more subdued way, rarely showed his emotions, and spoke little.[14] Such constructions of national masculinities were accompanied by a disparagement of the masculinity of other nations, which was generally seen as praiseworthy only if it was similar to one's own.

---

[11] Thomas Jefferson, Letter to Samuel Kerchival (1816), in Paul Leicester Ford (ed.), *The Works of Thomas Jefferson* (New York: G. P. Putnam's Sons, 1904), vol. 10, p. 46.

[12] Intersectional studies of race and gender have become increasingly common in early modern English literature. See, e.g., Ania Loomba, *Shakespeare, Race, and Colonialism* (Oxford University Press, 2002); Joyce Green MacDonald, *Women and Race in Early Modern Texts* (Cambridge University Press, 2002); and Sujata Iyengar, *Shades of Difference: Mythologies of Skin Color in Early Modern England* (Philadelphia, PA: University of Pennsylvania Press, 2005).

[13] Baron de Wimpffen, quoted and translated in John D. Garrigus, "Tropical Temptress to Republican Wife: Gender, Virtue, and Haitian Independence, 1763–1803," unpublished paper.

[14] See, among many, David Kuchta, *The Three-Piece Suit and Modern Masculinity: England, 1550–1850* (Berkeley, CA: University of California Press, 2002); and Alexandra Shepard, *Meanings of Manhood in Early Modern England* (Oxford University Press, 2003). For a later period, see Mrinalini Sinha, *Colonial Masculinity: The "Manly Englishman" and the "Effeminate Bengali" in the Late Nineteenth Century* (Manchester University Press, 1995).

The migration of large numbers of men had an influence on gender structures in the areas that they left as well as those to which they went. Two-thirds of the slaves carried across the Atlantic from Africa were male, with female slaves more likely to become part of the trans-Saharan trade or stay in West Africa. This reinforced polygyny, because enslaved women could join households as secondary wives, thus increasing the wealth and power of their owner/husbands through their work and children.[15] They were often favored as wives over free women as they were far from their birth families who could thus not interfere in a husband's decisions. In parts of Europe, male migration also contributed to a gender imbalance among certain social groups. Because Christianity and Judaism did not allow polygyny, solutions were more difficult than in Africa. Male migration may have contributed to the entry of more women into convents in Catholic areas, or to dowries reaching the stratospheric heights they did for wealthy families in Italian cities, which itself led to more women being sent to convents. In Protestant areas, male migration reinforced an existing pattern of late marriage and large numbers of women who remained single and had to support themselves through their own work. How they did this can be seen in the English word that in the seventeenth century came to describe both a woman's marital status and her occupation: spinster.

Marriage with immigrants in the early modern period often built on earlier patterns. In West Africa, for example, Mandinka traders from the Mali Empire had moved into the area of Upper Guinea south of the Gambia River beginning in the thirteenth century; they married local women, particularly among the Kassanké lineage who lived along the Casamance River, and the two groups accommodated to one another. The Kassanké adopted the Mandinka language, ritual practices and agricultural techniques, while the Mandinka often adopted Kassanké matrilineality and practices of lineage formation.[16] Thus, when Portuguese traders arrived in the area in the fifteenth century, they encountered people who were already used to forming marriage alliances with outside traders. Many of those Portuguese traders were New Christians—converts from Judaism—who were themselves already familiar with adopting new practices to fit in with a dominant culture, because that is just what they had done in Portugal. The pattern of

---

[15] Jennifer Morgan, *Laboring Women: Reproduction and Gender in New World Slavery* (Philadelphia, PA: University of Pennsylvania Press, 2004).

[16] Toby Green, *The Rise of the Trans-Atlantic Slave Trade in Western Africa, 1300–1589* (Cambridge University Press, 2012).

intermarriage and cultural accommodation continued, eventually creating *Crioulo*, the mixture of Portuguese and African languages that became common in the South Atlantic, and a broader "creolized" culture of mixture and syncretism that included the creation of new religions.

In the patrilineal societies of West Africa, such as the Wolof, Portuguese men and their mixed-race children were not allowed to marry local people of free standing, as this could give them claims to land use; their children could not inherit or join the kin and age-grade associations that shaped political power structures. Mixed-race sons generally continued in the trading occupation of their fathers, and in some places women became the major traders, with large households, extensive networks of trade, and many servants and slaves. Because these wealthy female traders—termed *nharas* in Crioulo and *signares* in French—had connections with both the African and European worlds, they were valued as both trade and marriage partners by the French and English traders who moved into this area in the eighteenth century. "Some of these women were married in church," reported one French commentator, "others in the style of the land, which in general consists of the consent of both parties and the relatives."[17] In the latter form of marriage, the women's European husbands paid bridewealth to their new in-laws (instead of receiving a dowry as was the custom in Europe), provided a large feast and were expected to be sexually faithful. If the husband returned to Europe, the *signare* was free to marry again.

Short-distance migration and religious conversion also led to marriages between spouses from different groups. In Europe, religious leaders uniformly opposed marriage across religious lines, but such mixed marriages occurred regularly after the Reformation, particularly in areas where Catholics and different types of Protestants lived in close proximity to one another, such as the territories within the Holy Roman Empire that were officially bi-confessional, or cities in Germany, Switzerland, the Netherlands and Eastern Europe that saw a great deal of trade and immigration.[18]

---

[17] Quoted in George E. Brooks, *Eurafricans in Western Africa: Commerce, Social Status, Gender, and Religious Observance from the Sixteenth to the Eighteenth Century* (Athens, OH: Ohio University Press, 2003), p. 214. Other studies that also examine gender in the early modern Afro-Portuguese Atlantic include: James Sweet, *Recreating Africa: Culture, Kinship and Religion in the African-Portuguese World, 1441–1770* (Chapel Hill, NC: University of North Carolina Press, 2003); and J. Lorand Matory, *Black Atlantic Religion: Tradition, Transnationalism, and Matriarchy in the Afro-Brazilian Candomblé* (Princeton University Press, 2005).

[18] See Dagmar Friest, "Crossing Religious Borders: The Experience of Religious Difference and Its Impact on Mixed Marriages in Eighteenth-century Germany" and Bertrand Forclaz, "The Emergence of Confessional Identities: Family Relationships and Religious Coexistence in Seventeenth-century Utrecht" in Simon Dixon, Dagmar Friest and Mark Greengrass (eds.), *Living with Religious Diversity in Early-Modern Europe* (Aldershot: Ashgate, 2009), pp. 203–66.

In Wilno (Vilnius), for example, the second capital of the Polish-Lithuanian Commonwealth, there were five kinds of Christians—Catholics, Lutherans, Calvinists, Orthodox and Uniates—among its 20,000 inhabitants, plus Jews and Tatar Muslims. Marriages in which a Christian spouse married a Jewish or Muslim one were very rare, and always involved the conversion of the non-Christian, but those involving various types of Christians were common enough to occasion little comment. They occurred especially among the city's mercantile and governing elite, who also interacted in their neighborhoods and business networks, finding co-existence and toleration preferable to confessional rigidity.[19] Quantifying mixed marriages is difficult, but in a few parts of Europe as much as 10 percent of marriages may have been religiously mixed. Clergy of all denominations denounced such marriages, and yet they still performed mixed weddings, reasoning that the risk to their church by not doing so was greater than that posed by performing the wedding, for spouses wed in their own confession were less likely to convert later.

In the Muslim world, members of Sufi *tariqa* brotherhoods, who were or claimed to be blood descendents of the Prophet Muhammad's family, intermarried with local women as they spread Islam from West Africa to the Philippines. Their heirs and successors (who could be very numerous given Islam's acceptance of multiple marriages) established lineages that blended Muslim and local claims to power and authority, which were further expanded when the descendent of an important Sufi traveled to a new area, gained further converts and patrons, and himself married local women.[20]

Whether they brought together French men and Native American women in North America, Portuguese men and Wolof women in West Africa, Catholic men and Calvinist women in Poland-Lithuania, or Arab Sufis and Uyghur women in Central Asia, mixed marriages opened possibilities for cultural exchange and mixture, just as they created children who embodied that very mixture. They facilitated cultural hybridity in many parts of the increasingly interconnected early modern world.[21]

---

[19] David Frick, *Kith, Kin, and Neighbors: Communities and Confessions in Seventeenth-Century Wilno* (Ithaca, NY: Cornell University Press, 2013), p. 211.

[20] For more on this, see the chapter in this volume by Nile Green on Islam in the early modern world.

[21] See many of the essays in Tony Ballantyne and Antoinette Burton (eds.), *Bodies in Contact: Rethinking Colonial Encounters in World History* (Durham, NC: Duke University Press, 2005) and *Moving Subjects: Gender, Mobility, and Intimacy in an Age of Global Empire* (Urbana: University of Illinois, 2008); and also Kirsten Fischer, *Suspect Relations: Sex,*

Third- and transgenders

Migration not only brought men and women from different groups together, but also introduced explorers, soldiers, settlers and officials to individuals who were understood in their own societies to be a third or fourth gender. The best known of these were found among several Native American peoples, and the Europeans who first encountered them regarded them as homosexuals and called them "berdaches," from an Arabic word for male prostitute. Today, many Native Americans regard the word "berdache" as derogatory, and use either the word for this gender category from their own language, or "two-spirit people," a phrase coined by Native queer activists in the 1990s. They note that although Europeans focused on their sexuality, two-spirit people were generally distinguished from others by their work or religious roles, as well as their sexual activities. They often had special ceremonial roles because they were regarded as having both a male and female spirit rather than the one spirit that most people had, and could mediate between both the male and female world and the divine and human world. The difference was thus one of gender rather than sexuality. Some of these individuals may have been intersexed, but more commonly they were morphologically male or female but understood to be something else—a third and fourth gender, or transcending gender completely. Male-bodied two-spirits were found among more groups than female-bodied two-spirits. Spanish conquistadors and missionaries encountered them in Mesoamerica, Florida, and the Andes, and French traders and missionaries in the western Great Lakes.

Race, and Resistance in Colonial North Carolina (Ithaca, NY: Cornell University Press, 2001); Magal M. Carrera, *Imagining Identity in New Spain: Race, Lineage, and the Colonial Body in Portraiture and Casta Paintings* (Austin, TX: University of Texas Press, 2003); Nancy Shoemaker, *A Strange Likeness: Becoming Red and White in Eighteenth-century North America* (Oxford University Press, 2004); Thomas N. Ingersoll, *To Intermix with our White Brothers: Indian Mixed Bloods in the United States from Earliest Times to the Indian Removal* (Albuquerque, NM: University of New Mexico Press, 2005); Barbara Watson Andaya, *The Flaming Womb: Repositioning Women in Early Modern Southeast Asia* (Honolulu: University of Hawaii Press, 2006); Juliana Barr, *Peace Came in the Form of a Woman: Indians and Spaniards in the Texas Borderlands* (Chapel Hill, NC: University of North Carolina Press, 2007); Jean Gelman Taylor, *The Social World of Batavia: European and Eurasian in Dutch Asia*, 2nd edn. (Madison, WI: University of Wisconsin Press, 2009); Jennifer M. Spear, *Race, Sex, and Social Order in Early New Orleans* (Baltimore, MD: Johns Hopkins University Press, 2009); Sophie White, *Wild Frenchmen and Frenchified Indians: Material Culture and Race in Colonial Louisiana* (Philadelphia, PA: University of Pennsylvania Press, 2012); Saliha Belmessous, *Assimilation and Empire: Uniformity in French and British Colonies, 1541–1954* (New York: Oxford University Press, 2013).

There is sharp disagreement about how to understand two-spirit people. Some scholars have asserted that most Native American groups valued femininity, so did not disparage men or boys who dressed as women or took the female role (i.e. passive and penetrated) in actual or ritualized same-sex relations.[22] Others have argued that this is wishful thinking, and stress that sex was linked to conquest in both the pre-colonial and colonial period; wearing women's clothes or doing women's work was a form of social failure for a male-bodied person, they argue, and the passive partner was mocked and vilified.[23] One's position in this debate shapes how one views the impact of European conquest, that is, whether the Spanish and Portuguese, and later other European powers, introduced new attitudes and punishments, or whether they reinforced existing ones.[24]

Most scholarship on two-spirit people has, unsurprisingly, contextualized them within understandings of gender and sexuality, but Mark Rifkin considers them within the framework of state-building and the cultural interaction that is central to the global history of this era. He examines the ways in which European Americans sought to "insert American Indians into the ideological system of heterosexuality," especially in an emphasis on the monogamous conjugal couple, which denied "the possibility of interpreting countervailing cultural patterns," including polygamous households, same-sex attachments, two-spirit people and kin groups "as principles of geopolitical organization."[25]

[22] Walter L. Williams, *The Spirit and the Flesh: Sexual Diversity in American Indian Culture* (Boston, MA: Beacon Press, 1986); Will Roscoe, *Changing Ones: Third and Fourth Genders in Native North America* (London: Macmillan Press, 1998); and Michael J. Horswell, *Decolonizing the Sodomite: Queer Tropes of Sexuality in Colonial Andean Culture* (Austin, TX: University of Texas Press, 2005).

[23] Richard C. Trexler, "Making the American Berdache: Choice or Constraint?" *Journal of Social History* 35(3) (2002), 613–36; Ramón Gutiérrez, "Warfare, Homosexuality, and Gender Status among American Indian Men in the Southwest" in Thomas A. Foster (ed.), *Long before Stonewall: Histories of Same-sex Sexuality in Early America* (New York University Press, 2007), pp. 19–31; and Sabine Lang, *Men as Women, Women as Men: Changing Gender in Native American Cultures* (Austin, TX: University of Texas Press, 1998). See also the essays in Sue-Ellen Jacobs, Wesley Thomas and Sabine Lang (eds.), *Two-Spirit People: Native American Gender Identity, Sexuality, and Spirituality* (Urbana, IL: University of Illinois Press, 1997).

[24] Martin Nesvig, "The Complicated Terrain of Latin American Homosexuality," *Hispanic American Historical Review* 81(3, 4) (2001), 689–729, presents a good overview of this debate, as well as other issues. For other studies of sexuality and colonization in Latin America, see: Federico Garza Carvajal, *Butterflies will Burn: Prosecuting Sodomites in Early Modern Spain and Mexico* (Austin, TX: University of Texas Press, 2003); "Sexual Encounters/Sexual Collisions: Alternative Sexualities in Colonial Mesoamerica," special issue of *Ethnohistory* 54(1) (2007), 3–194; and Pete Sigal, *Infamous Desire: Male Homosexuality in Colonial Latin America* (University of Chicago Press, 2003).

[25] Mark Rifkin, *When did Indians Become Straight?: Kinship, the History of Sexuality, and Native Sovereignty* (New York: Oxford University Press, 2011), p. 7.

The Americas were not the only area of the world in which there were individuals regarded as neither men nor women, or both men and women, or in some other way transcending dichotomous gender classifications in this era. In some cases these individuals appear to have been physically intersex, either from birth or as the result of castration, though in others their distinctiveness or androgyny was purely cultural, and was either permanent or temporary. In some cultures such individuals engaged in sexual activities or had permanent or temporary sexual relationships, while in others they did not.[26]

The gender and sexuality of such individuals is thus complex and highly variable, but in many cultures where they were found, they had special ceremonial or religious roles. In the Philippines, religious leaders termed *baylans* or *catalonans* were generally married older women, regarded as to some degree androgynous because they were no longer able to have children. They were thought to be able to communicate with both male and female spirits, and this, in addition to their lack of fertility, gave them greater freedom of movement than younger women had. When men performed rituals as *baylans* or *catalonans*, they wore women's clothing or a mixture of men's and women's clothes.[27]

The Bugis people of South Sulawesi (today part of Indonesia) had five genders: men, women, *calabai* (male-bodied individuals who wear female clothing and carry out certain female-identified tasks), *calalai* (female-bodied individuals who wear male clothing and present themselves as men) and *bissu*, who combined gendered clothing, behaviors, and actions in a way that is now often labeled "gender transcendent." The *bissu* could be intersexed or female-bodied, but were more often male-bodied. They were linked to the androgynous creator deity, acted as shamans and entered into divinatory trances.[28] In the early modern period, *bissu* carried out special rituals thought

[26] Collections of articles from many parts of the world include: Gilbert Herdt (ed.), *Third Sex, Third Gender: Beyond Sexual Dimorphism in Culture and History* (New York: Zone Books, 1994); and Saskia E. Wieringa and Evelyn Blackwood (eds.), *Female Desires: Same-Sex Relations and Transgender Practices across Cultures* (New York: Columbia University Press, 1999).
[27] Carolyn Brewer, *Shamanism, Catholicism, and Gender Relations in Colonial Philippines, 1521–1685* (Aldershot: Ashgate, 2004).
[28] Leonard Y. Andaya, "The Bissu: Study of a Third Gender in Indonesia" in Barbara Watson Andaya (ed.), *Other Pasts: Women, Gender, and History in Early Modern Southeast Asia* (Honolulu: Center for Southeast Asian Studies, University of Hawaii at Manoa, 2000), pp. 27–46; Sharyn Graham Davies, *Challenging Gender Norms: Five Genders among the Bugis in Indonesia* (London: Wadsworth, 2006); and Michael Peletz, *Gender Pluralism: Southeast Asia since Early Modern Times* (London: Routledge, 2009).

to enhance and preserve the power and fertility of the rulers, which was conceptualized as "white blood," a supernatural fluid that flowed in royal bodies.

In Northern India, divine androgyny was replicated in the human world by religious ascetics termed *hijra*, impotent or castrated men dedicated to the goddess Bahuchara Mata; they were regarded as having the power to grant fertility and so performed blessings at marriages and the births of male children.[29] In Polynesian societies, *mahus* had certain ceremonial roles and generally performed women's work, though apparently they were morphologically male.[30]

Some of these third- and transgender categories have continued to today, and studies of them are based on ethnographic research and interviews, with relatively little concern for change over time. Others have largely disappeared, a process that often began in the early modern period. The erosion of gender variation resulted to some degree from the spread of Christianity and Islam, but also resulted from changes in indigenous traditions and local circumstances. In Central and South America, because third gender individuals were understood by Spanish and Portuguese authorities within a framework of aberrant sexuality, they were described as "sodomites" and treated as such. This included a notorious slaughter of men dressed as women by the conquistador Vasco de Balboa in his march across Panama in 1513, and questioning, accusations and occasional mass trials in church courts, much like the waves of persecution that characterized the handling of sodomy in Europe at the time. If third-gender individuals had ritual power, as in Chile and the Phillipines, their actions were prohibited by Catholic authorities as part of the suppression of indigenous religions.[31] In South Sulawesi, the initial conversion of local rulers to Islam in the seventeenth century led to a brief

---

[29] Serena Nanda, *Neither Man nor Woman: The Hijras of India* (Belmont: Wadsworth Publishing Co., 1990); and Gayatri Reddy, *With Respect to Sex: Negotiating Hijra Identity in South India* (University of Chicago Press, 2005).
[30] Robert J. Morris, "Aikane: Accounts of Hawaiian Same-sex Relationships in the Journals of Captain Cook's Third Voyage (1776–80)," *Journal of Homosexuality* 19(4) (1990), 21–54; and Stephen O. Murray, *Homosexualities* (University of Chicago Press, 2000), pp. 291–2.
[31] For Chile, see: Ana Mariella Bacigalupo, "The Struggle for Mapuche Shamans' Masculinity: Colonial Politics of Gender, Sexuality, and Power in Southern Chile," *Ethnohistory* 51(3) (Summer 2004), 490 and *Shamans of the Foye Tree: Gender, Power, and Healing among the Chilean Mapuche* (Austin, TX: University of Texas Press, 2007). For the Philippines, see Brewer, *Shamanism, Catholicism*, and her "From Animist 'Priestess' to Catholic Priest: The Re/gendering of Religious Roles in the Philippines, 1521–1685" in Andaya, *Other Pasts*, pp. 69–86.

period when the *bissu* were banned from the palace, but they soon returned and regained much of their influence. In the early nineteenth century, they were targeted by rulers influenced by scholars recently returning from the Arabian holy places with puritanical versions of Islam, but did not fully lose their advisory role until the Indonesian governments banned the local princely courts in 1957.[32]

Gender and sexuality in religious transformations

Religious authorities had far broader aims in terms of gender and sexuality in this era than simply disciplining individuals who did not fit in the standard two gender categories. They sought to discipline men and women as well, transforming them into moral individuals whose actions reflected a purer piety. The sixteenth century in particular was a period of religious reform, in which individuals and groups decided that practices or institutions had grown stale or corrupt, and sought to focus on what they viewed as the core or developed new spiritual practices and sometimes new institutions they believed fit better with divine will. These new or reformed religious traditions were begun by individuals with a powerful sense of spiritual calling, and ultimately gained many adherents because large numbers of people found their message persuasive, or because they saw social, economic or political benefits in converting (or all three). Converts included rulers, who often demanded their subjects adhere to the same religion. Once they were established, these new religions became part of inherited traditions, as children followed the faith of their parents. Both reformers and those who supported older religious traditions set out certain duties as incumbent on a believer, often with distinctions between men and women. They viewed everyday activities and family life as opportunities for people to display religious and moral values, though at the same time criticized religious practices if they were done without the proper inward belief or faith.

Among these transformations, the simultaneous splintering of Christianity in Europe with the Protestant Reformation and spread of Catholic Christianity around the globe were the most dramatic. (Missionaries gained some converts to Protestant Christianity among people who were not European or

---

[32] William G. Clarence-Smith, "Same-sex Relations and Transgender Identities in Islamic Southeast Asia from the Fifteenth Century" in Raquel A. G. Reyes and William G. Clarence-Smith (eds.), *Sexual Diversity in Asia, c. 600–1950* (London: Taylor & Francis, 2012), pp. 67–85.

European background before 1800, but not many.) Both brought new ideas about the relationship between sexuality and holiness to those who were their adherents. Protestant reformers rejected practices for which they did not see a Biblical basis, including clerical celibacy, which Martin Luther (1483 to 1546) and other reformers thought was a fruitless attempt to control a natural human drive and brought no spiritual benefits. Protestants proclaimed family life in which men were serious, responsible husbands and fathers and women loving, obedient wives and mothers as the ideal for all men and women, and regarded unmarried people of both sexes as suspect. Most Protestant areas came to allow divorce and remarriage for a limited range of reasons, although the actual divorce rate remained very low, as marriage created a social and economic unit that could not easily be broken apart. The ideas of John Calvin (1509 to 1564) and others inspired a second wave of Protestant reform in the 1550s, in which order, piety and discipline were viewed as marks of divine favor.

An emphasis on morality and social discipline emerged in Catholic areas as well, however, and Protestant and Catholic religious authorities both worked with rulers and other secular political officials to make people's behaviour more orderly and "moral." This process, generally termed "social discipline" or "the reform of popular culture," has been studied intensively over the last several decades in many parts of Europe and the European colonies. Scholarship on social discipline recognizes the medieval roots of such processes as the restriction of sexuality to marriage, the encouragement of moral discipline and sexual decorum, the glorification of heterosexual married love, and the establishing of institutions for regulating and regularizing behaviour, but it also emphasizes that all of these processes were strengthened in the sixteenth and seventeenth centuries.[33] Sexual practices that did not fit the

---

[33] The scholarship on social discipline and the Protestant and Catholic Reformations is huge. For a global analysis, see my *Christianity and Sexuality in the Early Modern World: Regulating Desire, Reforming Practice*, 2nd edn (London: Routledge, 2010). For a theoretical discussion, see the "Focal Point: Confessionalization and Social Discipline in France, Italy, and Spain," with articles by James R. Farr, Wietse de Boer and Allyson Poska, *Archiv für Reformationsgeschichte* 94 (2003), 276–319. Representative monographs include: Martin Ingram, *Church Courts, Sex and Marriage in England 1570–1640* (Cambridge University Press, 1987); Jeffrey R. Watt, *The Making of Modern Marriage: Matrimonial Control and the Rise of Sentiment in Neuchâtel, 1550–1800* (Ithaca, NY: Cornell University Press, 1992); Michael F. Graham, *The Uses of Reform: "Godly Discipline" and Popular Behavior in Scotland and Beyond 1560–1610* (Leiden: Brill, 1996); Allyson Poska, *Regulating the People: The Catholic Reformation in Seventeenth-Century Spain* (Leiden: E. J. Brill, 1998); and Ann Marie Plane, *Colonial Intimacies: Indian Marriage in Early New England* (Ithaca, NY: Cornell University Press, 2000).

norm, including prostitution, pregnancy out of wedlock and sodomy, were increasingly subject to punishment, in what some historians have termed the "criminalization of sin."[34]

The intensification of social discipline brought changes in men's lives as men in Christian areas. For craft masters, merchants and other middle-class men, the qualities of an ideal man increasingly centered on their role as heads of household: permanence, honesty, thrift, control of family members and servants. Manhood was linked to marriage, a connection that in Protestant parts of Europe and British and Dutch colonies even included the clergy. This notion of masculinity became increasingly hegemonic, and was enforced by law as well as custom. Men whose class and age would normally have conferred political power but who remained unmarried did not participate to the same level as their married brothers; in some cities they were barred from being members of city councils. Unmarried men were viewed as increasingly suspect, for they were also not living up to what society viewed as their proper place in a gendered social order.[35]

The enforcement of social discipline had an even greater impact on women's lives. Laws regarding such issues as adultery, divorce, "lascivious carriage" (flirting), enclosure of members of religious orders or inter-denominational marriages were rarely gender neutral. The enforcement of such laws was even more discriminatory, of course, for though undisciplined sexuality and immoral behaviour of both women and men were portrayed from the pulpit or press as a threat to Christian order, it was women's lack of discipline that was most often punished, by both secular and religious courts.[36]

European colonizers took these ideas, laws and institutions with them. Along with explaining concepts central to Christianity, missionaries also attempted to persuade—or force—possible converts to adopt Christian

[34] Kent Gerard and Gert Hekma (eds.), *The Pursuit of Sodomy: Male Homosexuality in Renaissance and Enlightenment Europe* (New York: Harrington Park Press, 1989); Thomas Betteridge (ed.), *Sodomy in Early Modern Europe* (New York: Manchester University Press, 2002); Helmut Puff, *Sodomy in Reformation Germany and Switzerland, 1400–1600* (University of Chicago Press, 2003); and Joanne M. Ferraro, *Nefarious Crimes, Contested Justice: Illicit Sex and Infanticide in the Republic of Venice, 1557–1789* (Baltimore, MD: Johns Hopkins University Press, 2008).
[35] See Scott Hendrix and Susan Karant-Nunn (eds.), *Masculinity in the Reformation Era* (Kirksville, MO: Truman State University Press, 2008); and Thomas A. Foster, *Sex and the Eighteenth-Century Man: Massachusetts and the History of Sexuality* (Boston, MA: Beacon, 2006).
[36] Ulinka Rublack, *The Crimes of Women in Early Modern Germany* (Oxford University Press, 1999); Georgina Dopico Black, *Perfect Wives, Other Women: Adultery and Inquisition in Early Modern Spain* (Durham, NC: Duke University Press, 2001); and Daniela Hacke, *Women, Sex, and Marriage in Early Modern Venice* (Aldershot: Ashgate, 2003).

practices of marriage, sexual morality and day-to-day behavior.[37] A religious play written in Nahuatl, the language of the Aztec Empire, and performed in the 1530s, for example, centers on the fate of Lucia, an indigenous woman who did not marry in a Christian ceremony. The play ends with demons beating her and hauling her off to hell, as she screams that the "frightening fire serpent" that "signifies how I used to enjoy myself on earth" is winding around her neck.[38]

Many people resisted Christian teachings and continued to follow their original spiritual practices. In some areas, such as the Andes of South America and the Philippines, women had been important leaders in animistic religions, and they were stronger opponents of conversion than were men; this pattern was enhanced by male missionaries' focus on boys and young men in their initial conversion efforts. Far more people became Christian, however, including women, who sometimes became fervent in their devotions or used priests and church courts to oppose their husbands or other male family members on matters of inheritance or the marriage of children.

The process of conversion used to be described by scholars as a "spiritual conquest," in which indigenous beliefs and practices were largely wiped out through force and persuasion. The spread of Catholic Christianity is now viewed very differently, not simply as conquest and resistance—though it was that—but as a process of cultural negotiation and synthesis, during which Christian ideas and practices were selectively adopted, mixed with existing practices and openly, unknowingly or surreptitiously rejected in a process of creolization. Creolization included the creation of new gender patterns; although officials tried to impose European Catholic patterns— monogamous marriage, male-headed households, limited (or no) divorce— where these conflicted with existing patterns they were often modified and what emerged was a mixture of local and imported practices.[39] The prominent

[37] Irene Silverblatt, *Moon, Sun and Witches: Gender Ideologies and Class in Inca and Colonial Peru* (Princeton University Press, 1987); Ramón A. Gutiérrez, *When Jesus Came, the Corn Mothers Went Away: Marriage, Sexuality, and Power in New Mexico 1500–1846* (Stanford University Press, 1991); Martha Few, *Women Who Live Evil Lives: Gender, Religion, and the Politics of Power in Colonial Guatemala* (Austin, TX: University of Texas Press, 2002); and Nora E. Jaffary (ed.), *Gender, Race, and Religion in the Colonization of the Americas* (Burlington, VT: Ashgate, 2007).
[38] Barry D. Sell and Louise M. Burkhart (eds.), *Nahuatl Theater*, vol. 1: *Death and Life in Colonial Nahua Mexico* (Norman, OK: University of Oklahoma Press, 2004), p. 207.
[39] James Lockhart, *The Nahuas after the Conquest: A Social and Cultural History of the Indians of Central Mexico: Sixteenth through Eighteenth Century* (Stanford University Press, 1992); and Pete Sigal, *From Moon Goddesses to Virgins: The Colonization of Yucatecan Maya Sexual Desire* (Austin, TX: University of Texas Press, 2000).

men whom missionaries most hoped to convert often had multiple wives and concubines, and missionaries argued about whether they had to give up all but one before Christian baptism, or whether Christian practice would (they hoped) follow baptism.

Protestant Christianity was not the only new religious tradition to emerge in this period. At about the same time the Protestant reformers were first breaking with the Catholic Church, Nanak (1469 to 1538), a spiritual teacher living in the Punjab area of what is now the India–Pakistan border added his own insights to elements of Hinduism, Islam and other traditions to found what was later called Sikhism, a word taken from the Sanskrit word for "learner" or "disciple." Nanak taught that people can come to know God by looking inward and recognizing their complete dependency on God. Worldly values such as money or fame are not evil in and of themselves, but they are unreality (*maya*), an illusion or deception that keeps people separate from God. Turning away from *maya* to God is difficult for humans to do alone, and in this they need a teacher, or *guru*, a word that came to be applied to Nanak and the line of successors who spread his teachings. The succession of *gurus* transformed his followers into a community, developing rituals and ceremonies for major life changes (including marriage), building temples, creating systems for gathering donations and compiling sacred writings. The Sikh community was initially too small to be viewed with much concern by the Muslim Mughals who ruled the Punjab, but by the early seventeenth century this changed, and later Sikh gurus were military as well as spiritual leaders.

In terms of gender, Sikh ideas included both egalitarian and hierarchical elements.[40] Guru Nanak maintained that women (and members of lower castes) were able to obtain full enlightenment, and emphasized that proper devotional discipline could be done by people living in families and involved with the ordinary things of the world. In fact, service to others was an important part of spiritual life and living in the world with a family was spiritually superior to renouncing family ties, a position very different from that of most Hindu teachers of Nanak's time. But he also held that giving birth to sons was essential for women to fulfill their divine purpose, and described attachment to women as part of the *maya* that keeps a true believer

---

[40] Most of the published work on gender in Sikh history has been done by one scholar, Doris Jakobsh, including *Relocating Gender in Sikh History: Transformation, Meaning and Identity* (New Delhi: Oxford University Press, 2003) and an edited collection, *Sikhism and Women: History, Texts, and Experience* (Oxford University Press, 2010).

from God. As Sikh practices became more institutionalized, formal positions of authority were limited to men (a common development in all types of groups, religious and otherwise). In 1699, the tenth and final guru, Gobind Rai, established the military brotherhood of the Khalsa, calling on all initiates to adopt the name "Singh," wear five articles, including a sword, and be prepared to fight. Members of the Khalsa, all male, were increasingly regarded as the true Sikhs, and those who were not, including all women, had secondary status. Even God was militarized and masculinized, increasingly referred to as *Sarab Loh*, "All Steel," rather than as *Akal Purakh*, "Timeless Being," the most common descriptor of the early guru period.

Other religious transformations in the early modern period also had implications for ideas and practices of gender and sexuality. In Korea, the promotion of Confucianism by the Choson dynasty that took over power in 1392 led to a gradual restructuring of the kinship system from a relatively egalitarian one to one that emphasized patrilineal primogeniture; increasingly only the eldest son of the primary wife could carry out the proper rituals of ancestor worship. Women often responded by becoming supporters of Buddhist monasteries and convents, and, as widows, nuns themselves.[41] In Japan, women were also important as patrons and leaders of Buddhist convents, and some became vocal and active proponents of Christianity.[42] In Mesoamerica, leaders in the Aztec Empire increasingly encouraged the worship of the warrior god Huitzilopochtli in the fifteenth century, who demanded many sacrificial victims, preferably warriors; this led to special wars aimed at capture, and a growing emphasis on militarized masculinity in Aztec culture.[43] In Bengal, the Hindu thinker who later took the name Krishna Chaitanya (1486 to 1534) developed new spiritual insights and devotional practices to worship the great god Krishna; his most fervent followers believed that he became the goddess Radha and, like her, glowed golden in his passionate longing for Krishna. Among Jews, thinkers such as Isaac Luria (1534 to 1572) advocated stricter ethical principles based on the teachings of the Kabbalah, a group of mystical texts that originated in Spain and Southern France in the thirteenth century but looked back to much older

[41] For more on these developments, see the chapter on religious change in East Asia by Eugenio Menegon and Gina Cogan in this volume.
[42] Haruko Nawata Ward, *Women Religious Leaders in Japan's Christian Century* (Aldershot: Ashgate, 2009).
[43] Miguel León-Portilla, *Mexica Thought and Culture: A Study of the Ancient Nahuatl Mind*, Jack Emory David (trans.) (Norman, OK: University of Oklahoma Press, 1963); and Rosemary A. Joyce, *Gender and Power in Prehispanic Mesoamerica* (Austin, TX: University of Texas, 2001).

traditions. The Kabbalah offered (and continues to offer) ways of approaching God through intense prayer, study, rituals, mystical ceremonies, interior individual piety and moral behavior, and was practiced by both women and men in many Jewish communities in the Ottoman Empire and in Europe.[44]

Conclusions

The idea that gender and sexuality are socially constructed seemed radical when it was first articulated in the 1970s, but now seems patently obvious, with the global diversity of gender ideals and sexual norms evident in all media, gender-bending performers popular on television and YouTube channels, and transsexual and transgender individuals asserting their rights around the world. Examples of the fluid and performative nature of gender and sexuality were widely evident in the early modern era as well, as on stage, in religious rituals and in daily life individuals conformed to or challenged societal expectations, developing new notions of gender as they did so. The idea that gender is not part of the natural or divinely ordained world, but a human creation, seems to be especially threatening, however. Even those willing to envision revolutionary change in other institutions and areas of life could not envision this for gender and, in fact, sometimes called for a strengthening of gender hierarchies and a narrowing of sexual possibilities, perhaps to compensate for the breaks with established ideas and practices they were advocating elsewhere. Such reassertions of "tradition" were never just that, however, but were themselves changes, and the traditions were sometimes invented rather than remembered. The global world of the early modern era was built on the foundation of existing structures of gender and sexuality, and every development brought change to people's lives as women, men or neither.

FURTHER READING

"AHR Forum: Transnational Sexualities," *American Historical Review* 114(5) (2009), 1250–354.

Amussen, Susan D. and Allyson M. Poska, "Restoring Miranda: Gender and the Limits of European Patriarchy in the Early Modern Atlantic World," *Journal of Global History* 7 (3) (November 2012), 342–63.

---

[44] Lawrence Fine, *Physician of the Soul, Healer of the Cosmos: Isaac Luria and His Kabbalistic Fellowship* (Stanford University Press, 2003).

Andaya, Barbara Watson, *The Flaming Womb: Repositioning Women in Early Modern Southeast Asia* (Honolulu: University of Hawaii Press, 2006).

(ed.), *Other Pasts: Women, Gender, and History in Early Modern Southeast Asia* (Honolulu: Center for Southeast Asian Studies, University of Hawaii at Manoa, 2000).

Ballantyne, Tony and Antoinette Burton (eds.), *Bodies in Contact: Rethinking Colonial Encounters in World History* (Durham, NC: Duke University Press, 2005).

Moving Subjects: Gender, Mobility, and Intimacy in an Age of Global Empire (Urbana, IL: University of Illinois, 2008).

Barr, Juliana, *Peace Came in the Form of a Woman: Indians and Spaniards in the Texas Borderlands* (Chapel Hill, NC: University of North Carolina Press, 2007).

Brooks, George E., *Eurafricans in Western Africa: Commerce, Social Status, Gender, and Religious Observance from the Sixteenth to the Eighteenth Century* (Athens, OH: Ohio University Press, 2003).

Crawford, Katherine, *European Sexualities, 1400–1800* (Cambridge University Press, 2007).

Foster, Thomas A. (ed.), *Long before Stonewall: Histories of Same-Sex Sexuality in Early America* (New York University Press, 2007).

Gerard, Kent and Gert Hekma (eds.), *The Pursuit of Sodomy: Male Homosexuality in Renaissance and Enlightenment Europe* (New York: Harrington Park Press, 1989).

Herdt, Gilbert (ed.), *Third Sex, Third Gender: Beyond Sexual Dimorphism in Culture and History* (New York: Zone Books, 1994).

Jacobs, Sue-Ellen, Wesley Thomas and Sabine Lang (eds.), *Two-Spirit People: Native American Gender Identity, Sexuality, and Spirituality* (Urbana, IL: University of Illinois Press, 1997).

Jaffary, Nora E. (ed.), *Gender, Race, and Religion in the Colonization of the Americas* (Burlington, VT: Ashgate, 2007).

Jakobsh, Doris, *Relocating Gender in Sikh History: Transformation, Meaning and Identity* (New Delhi: Oxford University Press, 2003).

Joyce, Rosemary A., *Gender and Power in Prehispanic Mesoamerica* (Austin, TX: University of Texas, 2001).

Ko, Dorothy, JaHyun Kim Haboush and Joan R. Piggott (eds.), *Women and Confucian Cultures in Premodern China, Korea, and Japan* (Berkeley, CA: University of California Press, 2003).

Masterson, Lenore and Margaret Jolly (eds.), *Sites of Desire, Economies of Pleasure: Sexualities in Asia and the Pacific* (University of Chicago Press, 1997).

Morgan, Jennifer, *Laboring Women: Reproduction and Gender in New World Slavery* (Philadelphia, PA: University of Pennsylvania Press, 2004).

Rifkin, Mark, *When Did Indians Become Straight?: Kinship, the History of Sexuality, and Native Sovereignty* (New York: Oxford University Press, 2011).

Ruch, Barbara (ed.), *Engendering Faith: Women and Buddhism in Premodern Japan* (Ann Arbor, MI: Center for Japanese Studies at the University of Michigan, 2002).

Sigal, Pete, *From Moon Goddesses to Virgins: The Colonization of Yucatecan Maya Sexual Desire* (Austin, TX: University of Texas Press, 2000).

Sleeper-Smith, Susan, *Indian Women and French Men: Rethinking Cultural Encounter in the Western Great Lakes* (Amherst, MA: University of Massachusetts, 2001).

Smith, Merril D., *Sex and Sexuality in Early America* (New York University Press, 1998).

Taylor, Jean Gelman, *The Social World of Batavia: European and Eurasian in Dutch Asia*, 2nd edn. (Madison, WI: University of Wisconsin Press, 2009).

Traub, Valerie, *Making Sexual Knowledge: Thinking Sex with the Early Moderns* (Philadelphia, PA: University of Pennsylvania Press, 2015).

Ward, Haruko Nawata, *Women Religious Leaders in Japan's Christian Century* (Aldershot: Ashgate, 2009).

Wiesner-Hanks, Merry E., *Christianity and Sexuality in the Early Modern World: Regulating Desire, Reforming Practice*, 2nd edn. (London: Routledge, 2010).

Women and Gender in Early Modern Europe, 3rd edn. (Cambridge University Press, 2008).

Za'evi, Dror, *Producing Desire: Changing Sexual Discourse in the Ottoman Middle East, 1500–1900* (Berkeley, CA: University of California Press, 2005).

PART TWO

★

MACRO-REGIONS

7

Eurasia after the Mongols

THOMAS T. ALLSEN

Reverberations from the Mongols' explosive expansion were felt across the entire continent. In England there was a fad for Tartar clothing and in Japan the thwarted Mongol invasions spawned the notion of kamikaze, the divine protective wind. These reverberations were also communicated across time. In the sixteenth century, states headed by Chinggisids were still in power throughout Inner Asia, one of which, the Tümed Mongols, forced Ming China to cede advantageous trade privileges in 1570, and another, the Crimean Tatars, attacked and burned Moscow in 1571.

Yet, these dramatic events did not presage the reassertion of nomadic military power or the revival of the Chinggisid idea of steppe unity and universal empire. On the contrary, by the seventeenth century European observers were predicting the decline of the nomads and their subjugation by neighbouring sedentary states. And, in the eighteenth century, this came to pass. What follows is an attempt to explain how this happened and why.

Political devolution

In the middle of the thirteenth century, the high point of its unity and extent, the Empire of the Great Mongols held sway over the vast Eurasian steppe that stretched from the Black Sea to Siberia, Korea, Manchuria, North China, Tibet, South Siberia, East and West Turkestan, Iran, Iraq, Asia Minor, Caucasia, Crimea, Volga Bulgharia and Russia. Thereafter, expansion slowed as Chinggisid princes turned their energies inward in divisive civil wars. The result was the formation of four autonomous successor states in the decade following 1259, three of which, the Il-khans in Iran, the Chaghadai Khanate in Turkestan and the Yuan Dynasty in China, controlled extensive agricultural lands south of the steppe, while the fourth, the Golden Horde on the lower Volga, had its major holdings in the forest zone north of the steppe.

In each, direct descendants of Chinggis Khan continued to rule and continued their struggles with one another. These conflicts, which lasted into the fourteenth century, were not, however, the only sources of their decline. The Il-khans collapsed in 1335 and the Yuan in 1368 largely as a consequence of court factionalism and the mismanagement of their agricultural populations. The Chaghadai Khanate fell in 1370 and a few decades later the Golden Horde entered an extended period of disintegration. In their case, growing internal discord was accelerated by external blows administered by Temür (also spelled Timur, and historically known as Tamerlane, d. 1405), whose devastating campaigns gave him control over most of the Chaghadai and Il-khan realms and fatally weakened the Golden Horde.

In the aftermath, integrated states, the Ming Dynasty (1368 to 1644) and the Timurids (also spelled Temürids, 1370 to 1506), came to power south of the steppe and in Moscovy to the north; but in the nomadic world the political situation was different, a kaleidoscope of 'minimal states' perennially in conflict. The fragmentation is fully apparent in the fifteenth century, which witnessed the emergence of many new polities and ethnicities in the steppe: the Crimean Khanate in the west, the Great Horde/Astrakhan Khanate on the lower Volga, the Kazan Khanate on the Kama, the Noghais on the Ural River, the Siberian Khanate on the Tobol, the three Kazakh Hordes in the central steppe and the Kirghiz in the southern Altai. The eastern steppe was similarly divided among shifting coalitions of northern (Khalkha), southern (Tümed and Chahar) and western (Oirat/Junghar/Kalmyk) Mongols. The decentralization, however, did not end there; even during periods of ascendency, rulers' authority was limited and power over local populations was commonly in the hands of nominally subordinate leaders.

One source of this devolution, noticed by seventeenth-century Russian envoys, was the large number of claimants for leadership roles and the incessant succession struggles among them.[1] The line of Batu Möngke, most powerful Mongol ruler of the day, well exemplifies the problem; throughout much of his reign (c. 1482 to c. 1532), his authority was contested and ultimately curtailed by Chinggisid rivals, and following his death these struggles intensified as he produced nine sons surviving into adulthood who in six generations begat 300 male offspring, all potentially legitimate rulers!

---

[1] N. P. Shastina, *Russko-Mongol'skie otnosheniia XVII veka* (Moscow: Izdatel'stvo vostochnoi literatury, 1958), pp. 80 and 100.

The legacy in steppe and sown

Although the empire fell and the steppe fragmented, the Chinggisid idea survived. Great empires live on as models for successors, an 'after-life' that constitutes an integral part of their history. The phenomenon of *translatio imperii*, the transfer of power from one dynasty or people to another, is a regular feature of the political history of Eurasia. The Mongols in this regard were quite typical; they appropriated the ideology and sacral territory of their Turkic predecessors, and those who followed laid claim to the Chinggisid legacy.

This legacy is best thought of as an attractive package of institutions, ideological precepts, symbols, ceremonies and territorial claims that could be adapted to local needs and circumstances. In the Mongol case, its attractiveness is closely related to the size of their empire, which was approximately four times larger than any predecessor, a quantum leap in scale that contemporaries could only account for in terms of special cosmic or heavenly dispensations. And, given the diversity of their subjects and vastness of their holdings, they developed a wide array of governing techniques for successors to consider. The choices made were, of course, always selective and subject to reinterpretation.

The Mongols, naturally, made extensive use of this inheritance. When ousted from China, the Mongol court retreated into the steppe where descendants of Khubilai (r. 1260 to 1296) established the Later Yuan. In subsequent centuries, other Chinggisids, including Batu Möngke and his progeny, dominated the chaotic political life of Eastern and Southern Mongolia. In Moghulistan and later in Kashgar, a similar monopoly prevailed; here lineal descendants of Chaghadai (r. 1227 to 1242) ruled, sometimes as figureheads, for nearly 500 years.

In such environments, non-Chinggisids had to fashion new political strategies. The solutions they developed, while acknowledging the Chinggisid principle in theory, undermined it in practice. The history of the Temürids illustrates the process. Reared in the Mongol tradition, Temür felt compelled to rule through puppets and manufacture Chinggisid descent through his maternal line, all the while proclaiming himself a dutiful imperial son-in-law (*küregen*) restoring the Mongol Empire on behalf of its rightful rulers. But even Temür, ruling over settled Muslim populations, had recourse to Islamic forms of legitimation. His heirs gave these forms greater emphasis; they abandoned Chinggisid figureheads, relying instead on their founding father's charisma, derived from his spectacular conquests in Central and West Asia. In these parts, the Temürid principle came to rival the Chinggisid for about a century.

The erosion is noticeable, too, in the western steppe. Among the successors of the Golden Horde some ruling houses could boast Chinggisid lineages, but others could not. Lacking these credentials, both the Noghai Tatars and the Taybughid Dynasty, founders of the Siberian Khanate, made heavy use of Islam in their search for legitimacy, ignoring and in some cases openly challenging the Chinggisid principle.[2] The same lack confronted the rulers of the last great power in steppe history, the Junghars of Western Mongolia, who turned to Buddhism for ideological support. Their most powerful khan, Galdan (r. 1676 to 1697), was confirmed in office by the Fifth Dalai Lama as a promoter and defender of the faith.

Ideologies from the sedentary world of sown agriculture had greatly altered the forms of legitimacy in the steppe, which, by the eighteenth century, was divided between Mongolian-speaking Buddhists in the east and Turkic-speaking Muslims in the west. The transformation, a slow, incremental process, can be explained by the interplay of a number of forces set in motion during the empire: the Mongols' exposure to the beliefs of subject populations; their general tolerance in religious matters, which allowed princely lines to follow their personal preferences; their patronage of religious institutions and grants of immunity to clerical classes, which attracted missionaries to their courts; their close involvement with long-distance merchants who were normally adherents of world religions; and their forcible transfer of entire communities, mainly Muslim, into eastern Inner Asia.

The resulting changes in the religious landscape of the steppe were profound, strikingly different from the conditions that obtained on the eve of the Mongol unification. Then, all nomads from Manchuria to the Black Sea shared a common repertoire of religious-ideological concepts – heavenly mandates, universal empire and special good fortune that ensured leaders' success. Now, however, these ideas were increasingly challenged, diluted or displaced by world religions that were exclusive and hostile to one another.

There were many sources of antagonism: differences in doctrine, such as Buddhist notions of reincarnation and Muslim abhorrence of idolatry, as well as in daily practice, including matters of ritual cleanliness and food preparation. The growing tension is reflected in Muslim historiography of the sixteenth to nineteenth centuries, which portrays the Junghars (called Kalmyks) as alien

---

[2] Vadim V. Trepavlov, 'The Formation and Early History of the Manghit Yurt', *Papers on Inner Asia* 35 (2001), 21 and 46; and Allen Frank, 'The Siberian Chronicles and the Taybughid Biys of Sibir', *Papers on Inner Asia* 27 (1994), 23 and 26.

and threatening, perennial enemies to be defeated and converted. Similar sentiments are expressed in the oral epics of Kazakhs and Kirghiz, which took their present form in the seventeenth and eighteenth centuries, the period of their wars with the Junghar; in these, Kalmyks are castigated for their cruelty and treachery and ridiculed for their ugliness and incomprehensible language.

This is not to argue that religion was the major cause of conflict in the steppe. There were still rivalries generated by raiding and competition over pasture, booty and markets; these, however, took on a distinct religious colouration in the course of the endless clashes between Buddhist and Muslim nomads. As a result, communal identities hardened and became an additional ethnic marker for both Turks and Mongols.

The growing religious divide undercut prospects for nomadic unity in yet another way. In the steppe, the process of state formation always involved the reworking of shared mythologies of origins and descent. In the post-Mongol era, however, alternative political myths and models gained currency.[3] Tibetan spiritual advisers transformed Chinggis Khan and his successors into *Chakravartins*, 'Universal Emperors', making them heirs of ancient Indian-Buddhist or Chinese royal lines, while Muslim scholars situated Turkic dynasties within the Biblical and Iranian traditions and provided them with genealogical ties to Muslim royal lines. A common historical memory, so useful in welding together multi-ethnic, multi-lingual steppe armies and polities, was no more.

Although more selective, the Mongols' sedentary successors also mined this legacy. The Ming Dynasty, whose emergence is usually understood as a nativistic reaction to nomadic rule, embraced elements of this inheritance. In the first place, the Ming court authorized an official history of the Yuan, thereby formally acknowledging the Mongols' place in the orthodox line (*zhengtong*) of Chinese dynasties. Further, their engagement with their Yuan predecessor was widely felt in art, personnel policies, military institutions and court culture. And their successors, the Manchu-Qing dynasty (1644 to 1911), who were much more attuned to Inner Asian traditions, appropriated many Mongol institutions, symbols, titles and political-ideological concepts and made extensive use of co-opted Chinggisids in their relations with Inner Asian peoples.

---

[3] On these themes, see Mihály Dobrovits, 'The Turko-Mongolian Tradition of Common Origin and the Historiography in Fifteenth-Century Central Asia', *Acta Orientalia Academiae Scientiarum Hungaricae* 47 (1994), 269–77; and Ágnes Birtalan, 'A Oirat Ethnogenetic Myth in Written and Oral Tradition', *Acta Orientalia Academiae Scientiarum Hungaricae* 55 (2002), 70–85.

More consequentially, the Yuan, by its conquests and unification of the multi-state system then prevailing in East Asia, helped fashion the modern notion of the 'proper' territorial configuration of the Chinese state. This conception of China, reinforced by the Manchu-Qing conquests, was embraced by modern nationalists and, with the exception of Outer Mongolia, was fully realized.[4]

The use of Chinggisid precedents to justify territorial expansion is common to all successor states. The Jalayirids (1336 to 1432), who supplanted the Mongols in Azerbaijan, used their control of Tabriz, the Il-khan capital, to affirm their legitimacy and to counter claims of rivals. And for the princes of Muscovy, the seizure of Golden Horde territories along the Volga in the 1550s signalled their elevation from principality to empire, one headed by a tsar, a title heretofore reserved for Chinggisids; this is why Ivan IV (r. 1533 to 1584) always insisted that European rulers include 'Tsar of Kazan and Astrakhan' in his titles.

The Moscovite embrace of the Mongol legacy, like that of others, was fraught with contradiction. While the Moscovite princes justified their authority over Christian subjects in purely Christian terms, they played by Chinggisid rules in the steppe. In the fourteenth century, Moscovite court chronicles excoriate Temür and others for attempting to usurp power from legitimate Chinggisid rulers of the Golden Horde, their sovereigns and benefactors.[5] A century later, when Muscovy achieved a measure of independence, the rulers maintained a large stable of 'tame' Chinggisid princes in the satellite Kasimov Khanate (c. 1450 to 1681), whom they used to influence and divide Tatar rivals.[6] And on one famous occasion, they even played a Chinggisid card in their own domain. In 1575, Ivan IV suddenly 'abdicated' and temporarily ruled through a Chinggisid puppet, the Kasimov prince Simeon Bekbulatovich, a practice that had clear precedent in the Golden Horde. While such policies perplexed European contemporaries, they played well in the steppe, where Moscovite (and later Romanov) rulers were regularly styled Chaghan Khans, 'White or Western Khans', and accepted as legitimate successors of the Golden Horde.

---

[4] Hidehira Okada, 'China as a Successor State to the Mongol Empire' in Reuven Amitai-Preiss and David O. Morgan (eds), *The Mongol Empire and Its Legacy* (Leiden: Brill, 1999), pp. 260–71.

[5] Charles J. Halperin, 'Russia and the "Mongol Yoke": Conceptions of Conquest, Liberation and the Chinggisid Idea', *Archivum Eurasiae Medii Aevi* 2 (1982), 99–107.

[6] Janet Martin, 'Moscovite Frontier Policy: The Case of the Khanate of Kasimov', *Russian History/Histoire russe* 19 (1992), 169–79; and Chantel Lemercier-Quelquejay, 'Cooptation of the Elites of Karbarda and Daghestan in the Sixteenth Century' in Marie Bennigsen Broxup (ed.), *The North Causasus Barrier* (London: Hurst & Co., 1992), pp. 20–1.

The Moscovites' familiarity with nomadic tradition was a consequence of their deep involvement in steppe politics dating back to 1327, when Ivan I became the Horde's chief fiscal agent in the Russian principalities. Exploiting this office, their rulers achieved predominance over rivals and began 'gathering up the Russian lands', a task which entailed conflict with states on their western frontier. But once this was in hand, they turned their attention to Tatar polities in the east.

Geopolitical realignment

Kazan, conquered in 1552, is significant because it was Muscovy's first major acquisition of Golden Horde territory. But the Muscovite annexation of the Astrakhan Khanate in 1556, usually mentioned as a sidelight, is equally consequential because the 'conquest of the Volga' meant that for the first time a sedentary power had a permanent presence in the political heartland of the western steppe. While Moscow's line of communication with Astrakhan was sometimes precarious, Russian rulers nonetheless transformed it into a formidable outpost able to withstand major assaults.

Their control of the Volga, and later the Terek, enabled the Russians to exert considerable influence over the nomads, first the Noghais and later the Kalmyks, a disgruntled segment of the Oirat/Junghars who migrated west in the 1620s. From these riverine outposts, the Russians kept careful watch on the nomads and by means of diplomacy, coercion, economic aid and bribery tried to control their migratory movements and political associations. Their success in doing so was facilitated by the divisions among the nomads and by the Russian policy of allowing allies and clients internal autonomy, a measure that made it easier to co-opt steppe elites.

The motives behind Moscow's forward policy in the steppe are not hard to discern – the quest for territory, resources, markets and security. Among the latter were serious concerns about population loss. With the spread of Islam in the western steppe, the slave trade in the Black Sea region shifted attention from the nomads to the peoples of the forest. From the late fourteenth to the early eighteenth centuries, Russia was a major target, losing tens of thousands of subjects to the Crimean Tatars. Their raids, the largest slaving operation prior to the Atlantic trade, constituted a continuous demographic drain on the Russian state.

The response was twofold: freeing Christians from Tatar captivity became government policy and extensive new defensive works were prepared. These included the fortification of major cities and lengthy defensive lines (*cherty*) along the frontier composed of watchtowers, forts, abatis and ditches to slow down and give early warning of Tatar attacks. Starting in the sixteenth century, new lines were built, pushing the Russian frontier southward out of the forest zone into the steppe, which they penetrated along the major rivers and their tributaries, gradually enclosing and transforming rich pasture land into productive cropland.[7]

It was this intensified competition with successors of the Golden Horde that led to Russia's renewed interest in Siberia. The drive beyond the Urals was initiated by private interests and Cossack irregulars, but once the Siberian Khanate was vanquished in the 1580s, Moscovite officials arrived on the scene and henceforth new conquests were conducted in the name of the tsar. Driven by the allure of furs and prospects of trade, the Russian advance was rapid. Using the river systems and portages, secured with fortified trading posts (*ostrog*), the Russians reached the Pacific in 1639. Their primary axis of advance was the taiga, the belt of coniferous forests between the tundra and the steppe, an environment to which the Russian system of extensive woodland agriculture, which combined readily with cattle raising, hunting and fishing, was well adapted. The relative ease of conquest is attributable to their technological and organizational superiority, the lack of coordinated resistance among the Siberian natives and their susceptibility to introduced diseases, which so reduced their numbers that by 1700 Slavic-speaking colonists were in the majority. On the whole, the acquisition of this vast territory was accomplished rapidly and cheaply, a very profitable venture requiring limited investment from the centre.

When, however, the Russians reached East Asia in the early seventeenth century, they encountered an opponent they could not overpower or intimidate, the Ming Dynasty. Even though weakened and in the final decades of its existence, the Ming easily kept the Russians at arm's length. Their approach to interstate relations had not always been so defensive. During its early years, the Ming pursued more aggressive policies towards its northern neighbours, launching several major campaigns into Mongolia. While these blunted the nomad threat, they did not eliminate it and the costs proved prohibitive. The result was the building of the Great Wall and the use of attractive trade and tributary privileges to buy off Mongol rulers. By these means, the Ming managed to fend off the nomads but never subdue them.

[7] D. B. J. Shaw, 'Southern Frontiers of Moscovy, 1500–1700' in James A. Bater and R. A. French (eds), *Studies in Russian Historical Geography* (London: Academic Press, 1983), pp. 118–42.

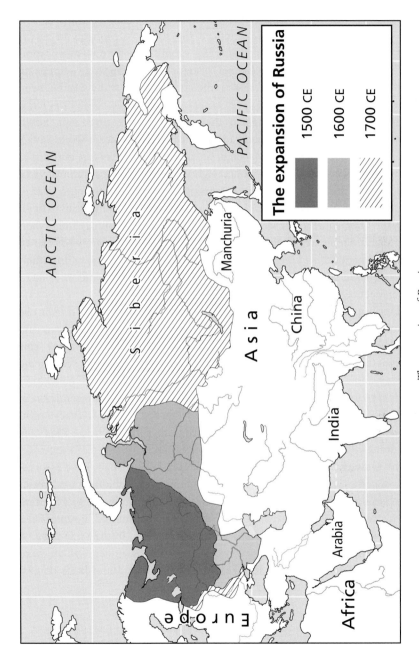

The expansion of Russia

1500 CE
1600 CE
1700 CE

7.1 The expansion of Russia

167

But where the Ming failed, the Manchus succeeded, becoming the first sedentary power to subjugate, reorganize and administer the eastern steppe. Their efforts began a decade before their conquest of China. Seeking additional manpower, the Manchus induced the southern Mongols to accept their suzerainty in 1634 to 1636. Following submission, they were incorporated into the Manchu military banner system, which effectively segregated them from their northern kin, creating the current political division between Inner and Outer Mongolia.

The northern Mongols retained their independence until 1691, when growing fear of the Junghars persuaded their leaders to accept Qing protection. Once in command, the Manchus isolated the Khalkhas and introduced the banner system; in all, they formed eighty-six such military-administrative units, each with a defined territory and assigned population, and each headed by a hereditary princely line, eighty-two of which were Chinggisids. Thereafter, the Qing court took care to monitor their succession and maintain their loyalty and obedience. In their use of ritualized gift exchange, royal hunts, imperial banquets and progresses to periodically renew and affirm their personal ties to the emperor, the Manchus followed age-old patterns of Inner Asian statecraft.[8]

Manchu policy in the north did not neglect the forest peoples. In their rise to power, the Manchus first subjugated the populations of southern and central Manchuria and later extended their control into the Amur basin. This brought them in direct contact with the advancing Russians, producing tensions and clashes that were resolved in 1689 by the Treaty of Nerchinsk. By its provisions, Russia, in return for trade relations and representation in Beijing, vacated the Amur watershed and recognized Mongolia as a Manchu sphere of interest. This allowed the Manchus to concentrate on their one remaining rival in Inner Asia, the Junghar Khanate.

The western Mongols, who formed the core of this state, have a somewhat shadowy history. Under the name Oirat, they fashioned a powerful confederation in the early fifteenth century, which soon broke apart due to internal fissures. Thereafter, although nominally reconstituted, it remained a very loose confederation into the seventeenth century. In the view of some scholars, the Junghar Empire only comes into being under Galdan, who successfully warred with the Kazakhs, seized the agricultural lands of East Turkestan in 1678 and defeated the Khalkhas in 1688.

[8] Ning Chia, 'The Lifan Yuan and Inner Asian Rituals in the Early Qing', *Late Imperial China* 14 (1993), 64.

The Manchu response was measured, if not hesitant; in the end, it took several campaigns into Mongolia and civil war among the Junghars before they vanquished Galdan's forces in 1696. Despite the setback, the Khanate survived under Galdan's nephew and rival, Tsewang Rabdan (r. 1697 to 1727). Although still regarded as a great power, their reputation proved illusory. The ethnic composition of their state was one underlying weaknesses. Individual Muslims served the Junghars as court merchants, diplomats and local officials, but the agricultural population of East Turkestan became increasingly restive under their authority, expressing their discontent in open rebellion and flight into Qing territory. Furthermore, there were no Muslim nomads in their armies; true, they defeated Kazakhs and Kirghiz and occasionally formed alliances with them, but never managed to integrate non-Buddhist steppe peoples into their state. Even more telling, however, is their failure to incorporate other western Mongols, the Volga Kalmyks and Qinghai Oirats, into their empire.

Until the 1740s, the Qing court held a monolithic view of the Junghars, but in the next decade began to realize the extent of their divisions from the steady stream of defectors asking for asylum. Renewed military pressure, it was now thought, could bring about their dissolution into four separate and subservient khanates. But their weaknesses were greater than estimated and Junghar resistance collapsed under the massive Manchu assault. Even the revolt of the Khalkhas, reacting to heavy Qing demands for military service, corvée and taxes, could not save the situation and in 1757 the Junghar forces went down in defeat. Following victory, the Qing armies instituted an extermination campaign in the conquered land; contemporaries estimated that these organized massacres, in combination with flight and epidemic disease, reduced the population of Jungharia by 90 per cent.

The Junghar wars were a pivotal event in the subjugation of the steppe peoples. The threat they posed induced the Khalkhas to submit to the Manchus in 1691 and the Kazakhs to seek closer relations with the Russians after 1730. While both powers made good use of these opportunities, their goals and tactics in the steppe differed appreciably.

The Manchus pursued a policy of divide and direct rule; they reconfigured and registered their nomadic subjects, restricted their movements and intervened in their legal disputes. The Russians, with more modest objectives, pursued a policy of influence and indirect rule, using policies first developed west of the Urals. Under their system of protectorates, the tsars exacted an oath of allegiance (*shert'*) from Kazakh khans, confirmed them in office, co-opted them for limited service to the Empire, but otherwise permitted them

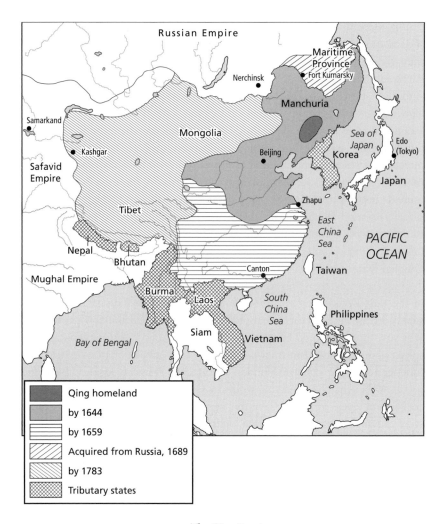

7.2 The Qing Empire

wide latitude in the conduct of internal affairs. And, although they encouraged the formation of a fourth, Inner Kazakh Horde in 1801, the Russians were generally content to maintain pre-existing political divisions in the central and western steppe.

The military policies of the two also differed. The Manchus subdued the Mongols by force and threat of force and occupied the eastern steppe, thereby rendering the Great Wall obsolete. The Russians, in contrast, continued to invest in fortifications, establishing a defensive line (*liniia*) of watchtowers and pickets along the steppe frontier to screen Siberia from the nomads. By the early eighteenth century, the line extended from the Ural River into the central steppe and, following the Treaty of Kiakhta, 1727, across the entire Russian–Mongol frontier. Like the earlier *cherty*, the *liniia* provided intelligence, advanced warning of attacks, raised the cost of raiding and slowly encroached upon the steppe.

But however different their policies, the end result was the same: 'free nomads' of the open steppe, who negotiated access to seasonal pastures and migratory routes with other nomads, were progressively transformed into 'enclosed nomads', forced to negotiate such rights with sedentary states.

Military balance

New developments in weapons technology and the conduct of war also hastened the end of nomadic dominance. Their long-standing advantage over the sedentary peoples of sown agriculture was based on a number of factors. Most fundamentally, nomads had much lower military costs; their equipment and mounts played a productive role in their herder-hunter mode of resource extraction and they could mobilize most of the adult male population without serious harm to their pastoral economy. In combination this made raiding and warfare a sound and attractive investment.[9] And, once in the field, they enjoyed another set of advantages: mobility, tactical flexibility, skill in horsemanship and weaponry, a sense of solidarity rooted in beliefs about common ancestry and the ability to concentrate forces.

To counter this threat, sedentary peoples recruited nomads as march wardens and trained their own troops in steppe methods of warfare. Russia did both; they acquired effective and loyal Tatar auxiliaries and developed an army on their southern frontier, mainly cavalry that specialized in fending off nomadic incursions. On their western borderlands, however, they faced a different kind of enemy, one that increasingly relied on firearms and infantry. The Russians therefore endeavoured to keep apace of Europe's ongoing military revolution and in the process gained a measure of self-sufficiency and equality. Thus, while Russia was a borrower, not an innovator, she did obtain a technological edge over her nomadic rivals.

---

[9] Kenneth Chase, *Firearms: A Global History until 1700* (Cambridge University Press, 2003), pp. 21–2.

Although the new weapons were not decisive in steppe warfare, they enabled the Russians to better defend their cities and frontier fortifications and allowed them to overwhelm the hunter-gatherers of Siberia. As a result of these experiences, the Russians came to believe that their firearms and artillery were far superior to those of actual and potential enemies in Inner Asia. That their perception was correct is affirmed by the attitude of steppe rulers they encountered: all, without exception, held Russian weaponry in high regard, repeatedly requesting gunpowder, weapons and gunsmiths from the tsarist government.[10] The Russians occasionally responded with limited diplomatic gifts to favoured rulers, but otherwise placed strict controls on the sale of firearms, powder and lead to the nomads.

The nomads knew how to make gunpowder and some, the Junghars, founded their own cannon, utilizing captured European technicians. But even with these measures they could not keep up and the weapons gap, both qualitatively and quantitatively, continued to widen. And they fared no better further east, where the Manchus sent large military forces into the steppe. They were victorious in their campaigns against the Junghars because they had larger armies, better balanced and integrated forces of infantry, artillery and cavalry, and more abundant European-style firearms.

In the view of some scholars, as long as the nomads' weaponry was equivalent to that of their sedentary opponents, their mobility and tactics gave them a decided advantage that lasted for several millennia, an advantage that came to an end with the development and spread of firearms.[11] Their argument is persuasive but incomplete; there was another, less noticed change underway. The balance of horse power that long favoured the nomads also eroded in the seventeenth and eighteenth centuries. By means of improved domestic production and trade arrangements, the Manchus and Russians secured military mounts in sufficient numbers to successfully challenge the nomads on their home ground.[12]

The chronology of this shift can be formulated as follows: the Qing victory over Galdan in 1696 marks the beginning of the end, their crushing defeat of

---

[10] See, e.g., Henry Serruys, 'Three Mongol Documents from 1635 in the Russian Archives', *Central Asiatic Journal* 7 (1962), 3 and 21.

[11] L. S. Stavrianos, *Lifelines from Our Past: A New World History* (Armonk, NY: M. and E. Sharpe, 1992), pp. 84–6; and William H. McNeill, *The Pursuit of Power: Technology, Armed Force, and Society since A.D. 1000* (University of Chicago Press, 1982), p. 60.

[12] S. A. M. Adshead, 'Horse Administration under the Ch'ing', *Papers on Far Eastern History* 17 (1978), 71–9; and Jos Gommans, 'Warhorse and Post-Nomadic Empire in Asia, c. 1000–1800', *Journal of Global History* 2 (2007), 1–21.

the Junghars in 1757 constitutes the climactic test of arms and two events in its aftermath provide final proof that the nomads were a spent force.

The first occurred in 1771, when some 150,000 Volga Kalmyks, fearful of further Russian encroachment on their pastures and interference in their internal affairs, set out for their depopulated Jungharian homeland. The Qing court accepted the 50,000 who survived the trek and the Kazakh depredations, assigned them territories and formed them into banners. What is most striking about this event is its west-to-east direction, reversing the predominant east-to-west pattern of migration of previous centuries. The last time this occurred was the early thirteenth century, when the Chinggisids dispatched nomads from the western steppe to China for military service. The difference, of course, is that nomads were now at the beck and call of sedentary empires.

The second was the Russians' defeat of the Crimean Tatars in 1783. These long-time clients of the Ottomans were the last hold-outs, and once the brief campaign ended, the Russians were in control of the entire western steppe. It is noteworthy, too, that immediately after victory the Russians rounded up 6,000 Noghais in the Crimea, had them swear allegiance to Catherine II and then celebrated the occasion with a great feast at which the new subjects of the crown consumed 100 oxen, 800 sheep and 500 buckets of vodka, a fitting demonstration of the Russians' command of the steppe and its political culture.[13]

In hindsight, this certainly marks the end, but when was this realized by the sedentary powers? Russia's reorganization of its military in the early eighteenth century to fight European-style armies tells us that in their calculations the age-old nomadic threat had been reduced to a police problem. For the Qing, the realization came later; it took Manchu and Chinese statesmen nearly a century to adjust to the new realities and to come to terms with the threat posed by European maritime power.

Economic containment

The occupation of the taiga by the Russians and Manchus dramatically transformed the geopolitical environment of Inner Asia. How this affected the balance of power between nomadic and settled peoples requires a brief examination of Siberia's place in steppe history.

[13] B. B. Kochekaev, *Nogaisko-russkie otnosheniia v XV–XVII vv* (Alma-Ata: Izdatel'stvo 'Nauka' Kazakhskoi SSR, 1988), pp. 230–1.

All major nomadic empires, Xiongnu, Türk, Uighur and Mongol, took an active interest in Siberia; indeed, one of the initial and crucial steps in the rise of each was the subjugation of the forest zone. Imperial founders, even mythical ones in epic traditions, follow the same policy: they first dispose of rivals in the steppe, then campaign in the north and lastly turn attention to agricultural lands in the south. There were sound reasons for this strategy.

The territories to the north of the steppe, unlike those to the south, were generally stateless, offering soft frontiers and political space for successful nomadic rulers as well as a refugium for the unsuccessful. Once, however, the Russians and Manchus came to terms at Nerchinsk and Kiakhta, this formerly open frontier was closed, with dire consequences for the nomads. For one thing, close attention was now paid to the movement of runaways and refugees crossing demarcated and policed borders, an issue that came up frequently in Russian-Manchu diplomacy. For another, the southern portions of the taiga, though not densely populated, offered productive recruiting grounds, which the Chinggisids eagerly and systematically exploited in search of military manpower. By the seventeenth century, however, the Russians and Manchus were recruiting these same populations as auxiliaries and border guards, measures that enabled them to contest the nomads' access to the abundant economic resources of the taiga.

From the military perspective, the most important of these was iron. Not only was Siberia rich in ores, it also contained early centres of iron-working. For the nomads, this was a primary source of war matériel, made all the more vital by the policy of southern rivals to prohibit the export of iron into the steppe. The Russians, too, adopted similar policies and from the beginning of their eastward expansion took over existing mines and opened up new ones. While their development was slow and inefficient, this nonetheless had the effect of denying the nomads a vital strategic commodity.

The Russian advance similarly limited the nomads' access to luxury and prestige goods so profitable in long-distance trade and so necessary for state formation. Of these, furs, collected forcibly from the forest peoples, were the most desirable. The Russians therefore strove to monopolize the tribute (iasak) formerly paid to the nomads. Such control was a major objective in their conflict with the Siberian Khanate; and, as they moved eastward, there was continuing competition with other steppe peoples over the right to impose iasak in the taiga, competitions the Russians eventually won.

The emergence of new tributary relationships and markets in Inner Asia raises the much debated question of the impact of European maritime expansion and seaborne trade on the inland caravan system. The nomads, to be sure, patronized and benefited from long-distance trade. Their returns, both luxuries and necessities, were then redistributed among their nomadic subjects. Without external resources, nascent steppe states lacked the ability to attract substantial followings or create permanent political institutions. Thus, the political economy of the steppe was sensitive to changes in transcontinental exchange networks. In light of these considerations, there is a certain appeal to the theory that Ottoman expansion in the Black Sea in the late fifteenth century followed by European maritime expansion into the Indian Ocean in the early sixteenth combined to divert trade from the overland routes, turning Inner Asia into a commercial and political backwater.

But while plausible, this line of argument is open to a number of criticisms. First of all, the spice/drug trade that first attracted the Portuguese eastward was mainly seaborne, and had been for centuries, so it is hard to see how Europe's arrival in the Indian Ocean could have diverted traffic from overland routes. This conclusion is reinforced by recent research on the timing of European impact on Asian maritime trade; many now believe its influence was not felt until the early eighteenth century and that its range was restricted to the southern littoral of Asia. Further, since there is little concrete data on the volume and profitability of overland trade during the Mongol era, the presumed golden age, there is no statistical basis for establishing and measuring its later 'decline'. And, when we finally have such data, from the sixteenth to eighteenth centuries, the presumed 'age of decadence', it reveals lively and extensive commercial exchange throughout Inner Asia. Finally, the caravan merchants' rapid response to the emerging opium market in China strongly suggests that the overland routes remained viable and competitive into the early nineteenth century.

It is true, of course, that there were periodic downturns in commercial activity, usually tied to political-military disturbances. But such disturbances were a recurrent feature of steppe history, including the Mongol period. Caution is therefore required in handling this kind of data, since what often passes as evidence for systemic decline may only be the downside of shorter-term economic cycles.[14]

Still, a case can be made that in the post-Mongol era the nomads' share in overland trade declined, not as a consequence of the rise of European maritime powers, but of the commercial interests and practices of neighbouring

---

[14] R. J. Barendse, 'Trade and State in the Arabian Seas: A Survey from the Fifteenth to the Eighteenth Centuries', *Journal of World History* 11 (2000), 224.

land powers. Their encroachment, which disrupted older patterns of commercial traffic in the steppe, begins in the mid-sixteenth century, with Moscow's conquest of the lower Volga, long the nexus of north–south and east–west exchange in western Eurasia. In Russian hands, Astrakhan became a major entrepôt, attracting nomads as well as international traders from Transcaucasia, Persia, Central Asia and India. Like their nomadic predecessors, the Russian authorities encouraged these merchants to form permanent settlements which they then monitored, licensed and taxed.

In time, this growth in trade stimulated Russian interest in more distant markets and their own merchants came to play an active role in Central Asian trade in direct competition with those of the nomads. This becomes apparent once the Russians crossed the Urals and revived an older east–west route through southern Siberia that had flourished under the Mongols.[15] The way, of course, was long and arduous but nonetheless a viable alternative, since the Russian Government provided authorized merchants, Christian and Muslim, with protection and absorbed some of their transportation costs.

In accessing the extent of this transformation, there is a major perceptual problem to overcome, the 'silk road syndrome', our fixation on east–west exchange. Before, during and after the Mongol Empire there was an active north–south exchange, one that the Russians exploited early on and ultimately came to dominate with the growth of Orenburg and other frontier markets in Siberia. It is therefore arguable that the most profound change in the commercial life of Inner Asia during the post-Mongol period was not a decline in volume, but a reorientation in direction.

Control over these routes and markets, both old and new, gave the Russians added leverage in inter-regional and transcontinental trade. So, too, did their imposition of state monopolies on commodities from Siberian furs to Chinese rhubarb, monopolies that were partially replaced in the eighteenth century by state-backed charter companies enjoying exclusive commercial rights in Central Asia and China. The combined effect of these policies was to reduce the nomads' share in the proceeds of long-distance trade. But it did more than this: over several centuries, the nomads became dependent on Russian products and markets, a trend first noticeable in their relations with the Noghais around Astrakhan. In the central steppe, Russian frontier posts became magnets for the Kazakhs and Kirghiz; here, they traded livestock and hides for agricultural and manufacturing goods.

---

[15] For a description, see Robert J. Kerner, *The Urge to the Sea: The Course of Russian History* (Berkeley, CA: University of California Press, 1946), pp. 165–72.

This represents a complete reversal of traditional exchange between the steppe and Siberia; the nomads no longer enjoyed an asymmetrical relationship with the forest peoples, one based on coerced extraction of tribute, and now had to barter goods in Russian markets, an arena in which they were the disadvantaged party. The great disparity between the size and productivity of the Russian economy and those of the steppe polities institutionalized this dependency. By the eighteenth century, the Russians had the ability, which they regularly used, to squeeze or reward the nomads and thus the ability to exert substantial influence, and a measure of control, over the political life of the steppe.

Something similar happened in Mongolia, the unplanned consequence of two Manchu policies. First, they effectively isolated the Khalkhas from Russian influence, and then during the Junghar wars brought many Chinese merchants into Mongolia for logistical support. Once in residence, and without outside competition, they soon dominated exchange throughout the region. They sold goods to Mongol princes and herders on time and the usurious rates charged kept the buyers perpetually in debt. Again, this represents a dramatic reversal. For most of steppe history merchants were the allies and partners of the nomads, helping them extract wealth from the sedentary world through trade, tribute and tax-farming arrangements; now most merchants operating in and around the steppe were agents of sedentary powers helping them control and exploit exchange within the nomadic world.[16]

Global contexts

The foregoing analysis does not mean that the demise of the nomads was solely a product of forces originating in the territories of the former Mongol Empire; external forces produced by fundamental shifts in global political and economic history were also in play. In the most general terms, the nomads were victims of sedentary competitors better positioned to benefit from emerging world exchange networks. Even land-locked Moscovy was connected. In 1478, Ivan III seized Novgorod and established beneficial commercial relations with Europe through the Hanse, and in 1553, just before Ivan IV seized Astrakhan, these ties were reinforced by the arrival of the English and Dutch in Arkhangelsk.

---

[16] On this issue, see G. L. Penrose, 'Inner Asian Influences on the Earliest Russo-Chinese Trade and Diplomatic Contacts', *Russian History/Histoire russe* 19 (1992), 361–92.

But wider commercial reach was not their only advantage. Sedentary states had greater opportunity to tap into global information networks and greater capacity to exploit new knowledge and technology. Their impersonal, bureaucratic systems of government, in contrast to the more volatile personal, patrimonial regimes in the steppe, gave them better administrative control over resources and their improved logistical and financial skills allowed them to maintain and direct larger, more complex military machines using gunpowder weaponry. They had a staying power and a measure of continuity in policy that nomad polities could not match.[17]

The extent to which global environmental forces were felt in the steppe is unknown. Purely natural phenomena, such as the disturbed climatic conditions found in many regions of the world during the fifteenth to seventeenth centuries, have yet to be scientifically documented for Inner Asia.[18] We are somewhat better informed on human-induced environmental change. For the peoples of the steppe, the balance sheet of the 'Columbian Exchange' was singularly negative. There were no new animal species to increase productivity of their herds, while the new plant species served to increase agricultural productivity and sustain rapid demographic growth in the settled zones of Eurasia, most spectacularly in Qing China, whose population doubled during the eighteenth century.

The only part of the exchange in which the nomads participated was the spread of tobacco-smoking and new diseases, principally syphilis and smallpox. While it seems evident that the introduction of smallpox into the steppe in the sixteenth century added to the general instability and frequency of succession disputes since it targeted elites in contact with sedentary peoples, we do not know what role it played in the often hypothesized demographic decline of the Mongols over the last several centuries.[19] In any event, it can hardly be doubted that in the post-Columbian era the population of the sown was growing at a far faster rate than that of the steppe.

Only after we have far more data on the environmental history of Inner Asia will we be able to adequately gauge the balance of internal and external

[17] To my knowledge, this perspective was first suggested by Andrew Hess, 'The Ottoman Conquest of Egypt (1517) and the Beginning of the Sixteenth Century World War', *International Journal of Middle East Studies* 4 (1973), 58. Recently, more comprehensive frameworks for the comparative study of Eurasian history have been developed by Victor Lieberman and Peter Perdue – see Further Reading.
[18] Such studies are now underway. See Mara Hvistendahl, 'Roots of Empire', *Science* 337 (2012), 1596–9.
[19] Henry Serruys, 'Smallpox in Mongolia during the Ming and Ch'ing Dynasties', *Zentralasiatische Studien* 14 (1980), 41–63.

forces that quelled the nomads. In the present state of our knowledge all that can be can said is that while global influences were present, the immediate agents of the nomads' demise were two land-based empires with closer ties to the continental heartland than to the maritime rimland.

Conclusions

The political fragmentation of the nomads in the post-Mongol era was the norm in steppe history. The Chinggisid unification was the exception, so exceptional that it created a lasting legacy in both steppe and sown. This unparalleled success invested their line with a special charisma and a widely acknowledged claim on legitimacy, qualities that also made the empire's institutions and political culture attractive to successors.

At the same time, the legacy contributed to the nomads' later division and weakness. The displacement of indigenous political doctrines by imported ideologies from the sown and the attenuation of the principle of Chinggisid descent by the proliferation of claimants in the steppe can be traced back to Mongol imperial policies and practices. These divisions, found across the steppe, proved fatal in the long-term competition with politically integrated sedentary rivals.

Their growing vulnerability was exposed by Russia's advance eastward and her takeover of Tatar–Mongol tributary relations with Siberian peoples, which in turn provoked the Manchu occupation of the Amur basin. While there was no master plan or strategic vision underlying the Russians' actions, their demarcation and control of the forest zone transformed the geopolitical environment of Inner Asia and brought about a discontinuity in steppe history.

For the first time, the steppe faced major powers along its forest frontier, powers possessing new weapons technology that enhanced their defensive capability and reduced the return on nomadic military ventures. This, too, was part of the Chinggisid legacy, for it was the Mongols who initially diffused and demonstrated gunpowder, a Chinese invention, throughout Eurasia; and when, following successful attempts at replication in other parts of the continent, it returned to Inner Asia, it did so in new, improved forms and in the hands of the Russians and Manchus.

The loss of their military supremacy together with the commercial policies of the Russians and Manchus also ended the nomads' dominance of overland trade; by their joint closure of the forest frontier, they limited the nomads' access to external resources so crucial to their political economy. Steppe resources alone cannot sustain steppe polities.

The emergence of a global system of exchange, fashioned by the maritime powers of the Far West, served to extend and consolidate the growing disparity between the power potential of the sown and the steppe, since the nomads, unlike their principal sedentary protagonists, were only indirectly and intermittently connected to these networks.

To sum up, in the thirteenth century, the Mongols mobilized resources from steppe and sown to subjugate most of Eurasia. In the eighteenth century, the Russians and Manchus used the same formula to subjugate the nomads.

FURTHER READING

Basin, V. IA., *Rossiia i kazakhskie khanstva v XVI–XVIII vv* (Alma-Ata: Nauka, 1971).
Bergholz, Fred W., *The Partition of the Steppe: The Struggle of the Russians, Manchus, and the Zunghar Mongols for Empire in Central Asia, 1619–1758* (New York: Peter Lang, 1993).
Dale, Stephen F., *Indian Merchants and Eurasian Trade, 1600–1750* (Cambridge University Press, 1994).
DeWeese, Devin, *Islamization and Native Religion in the Golden Horde* (University Park, PA: Pennsylvania State University Press, 1994).
Di Cosmo, Nicola, Allen J. Frank and Peter B. Golden (eds), *The Cambridge History of Inner Asia: The Chinggisid Age* (Cambridge University Press, 2009).
Dmytryshyn, Basil, E. A. P. Crownhart-Vaughan and Thomas Vaughan (eds and trans.), *The Russian Conquest of Siberia, 1558–1700, A Documentary Record* (Portland, OR: The Press of the Oregon Historical Society, 1985), vol. 1.
Khazanov, Anatoly M., *Nomads and the Outside World*, 2nd edn (Madison, WI: University of Wisconsin Press, 1994).
Khodarkovsky, Michael, *Russia's Steppe Frontier: The Making of a Colonial Empire, 1500–1800* (Bloomington, IN: Indiana University Press, 2002).
Levi, Scott, *The Indian Diaspora in Central Asia and its Trade, 1550–1900* (Leiden: Brill, 2002).
Lieberman, Victor, *Strange Parallels: Southeast Asia in Global Context* (Cambridge University Press, 2009), vol. 2.
Mancall, Mark, *Russia and China: Their Diplomatic Relations to 1728* (Cambridge MA: Harvard University Press, 1971).
Manz, Beatrice Forbes, *Power, Politics and Religion in Timurid Iran* (Cambridge University Press, 2007).
Pelenski, Jaroslaw, *Russia and Kazan: Conquest and Imperial Ideology (1438–1560s)* (Paris: Mouton, 1974).
Perdue, Peter C., *China Marches West: The Qing Conquest of Central Eurasia* (Cambridge, MA: Harvard University Press, 2005).
Serruys, Henry, *Sino-Mongol Relations during the Ming* (Brussels: Institut belge des hautes études chinoises, 1967), vol. 2.
Stevens, Carol Belkin, *Soldiers of the Steppe: Army Reform and Social Change in Early Modern Russia* (DeKalb, IL: Northern Illinois Press, 1995).

Struve, Lynn A. (ed.), *The Qing Transformation in World Historical Time* (Cambridge, MA: Harvard University Asia Center, 2004).

Subtelny, Maria E., *Timurids in Transition* (Leiden: Brill, 2007).

Sunderland, Willard, *Taming the Wild Field: Colonization and Empire on the Russian Steppe* (Ithaca, NY: Cornell University Press, 2004).

Ziiaev, Kh. Z., *Ekonomicheskie sviazi Srednei Azii s Sibir'iu v XVI-XIX vv.* (Tashkent: Fan, 1983).

Zlatkin, I. IA., *Istoriia dzhungarskogo khanstva, 1635–1758*, 2nd edn (Moscow: Nauka, 1983).

8

Continuity and change in the Indian Ocean basin

JOS GOMMANS

Geographic categories like 'Europe' or 'Asia' hardly qualify as a canvas on which to paint an adequate picture of the historical developments in the early modern period. Even though we can still discuss the revolutionary process of European expansion in the area that is now called Asia, it was only after our period that a sharp dichotomy began to develop between the two. Besides leading into the trap of anachronism, the categories of Europe and Asia are too general and fail to do justice to either the diversity within or the continuity between both areas. Vasco da Gama's arrival in South India in 1498 was not so much a dramatic 'first contact' between two completely separate civilizations as it was a return to a world long familiar to traders, in which it did not take long to make oneself understood even in Italian or Castilian. Vasco da Gama's revolution was not like that of Christopher Columbus, the discovery of a new world, but rather the discovery of a new *route* leading back into the old world.

What image should we conceive of the latter? It was certainly a world of which Europe was a part, albeit on its outermost western periphery. In many ways, it was an 'unbroken landscape', a huge Afro-Eurasian continuum that owed its unity to two binding geographical elements: the seas in the south and the savannahs in the north.[1] Chiefly due to the work of the French historian Fernand Braudel, historians have grown very much aware of the linking characteristic of seas and oceans, and because of this we can perceive not only a highly connected Mediterranean, but also an Atlantic, a Baltic and

I would like to thank Thomas Allsen for some incisive comments on an earlier draft.
[1] Cf. Marshall G. S. Hodgson, *The Venture of Islam: Conscience and History in a World Civilization*, vol. 2: *The Expansion of Islam in the Middle Period* (University of Chicago Press, 1994), pp. 68–91. For an interesting institutional analysis of this unbroken landscape in the early-modern period, see Frank Perlin, *Unbroken Landscape: Commodity, Category, Sign and Identity: Their Production as Myth and Knowledge from 1500* (Ashgate: Variorum, 1994) and *The Invisible City: Monetary, Administrative and Popular Infrastructures in Asia and Europe 1500–1900* (Ashgate: Variorum, 1993).

indeed, in our case, an Indian Ocean world. Logistic advantages transformed these seas into extremely important connecting arteries for transport and trade.[2] Already since at least the first century BC, extensive commercial and cultural contacts existed between the Mediterranean Sea and the western Indian Ocean, both through the Persian Gulf and the Red Sea. This is illustrated in the old Roman complaint about the permanent stream of precious metals flowing in the direction of India. Already during the early centuries CE, the Roman court experienced recurrent waves of fascination with the 'East' and even a sort of Indomania.

Although much remained the same during the so-called Vasco da Gama era, there were indeed two major innovations brought by Europeans: the development of the Cape route and the European (re)discovery of America. However, initially these two factors heralded nothing more than a quantitative change in the ancient trading relations between the Mediterranean Sea and the Indian Ocean, with an ever-growing stream of precious metals flowing eastward against mainly spices and textiles flowing westward. Of course, this is just part of the story, and therefore we must not commit the mistake made by some historians who refused to detect structural change in pre-colonial 'Asia'. To avoid the Asia–Europe dichotomy, let us first determine the proper geographical categories by sketching what Braudel labelled *la longue durée*: the relatively unaltered climatological and geographical characteristics of the Indian Ocean region.

Indian Ocean and Arid Zone

The idea of a single world economy that connects all regions surrounding the Indian Ocean basin derives from one of Braudel's disciples, the Indian historian K. N. Chaudhuri. Taking the prevailing monsoon pattern as a starting point, he distinguished three large maritime trading circuits: (1) the Arabian Sea; (2) the Bay of Bengal; and (3) the Chinese Seas. These overlapping commercial zones resulted naturally from the annual rhythm of the monsoons: southwesterly winds from April to August; northeasterly winds

---

[2] Apart from numerous surveys, the most pioneering and comprehensive Indian Ocean works are by K. N. Chaudhuri, *Trade and Civilization in the Indian Ocean: An Economic History from the Rise of Islam to 1750* (Cambridge University Press, 1985) and *Asia before Europe: Economy and Civilisation of the Indian Ocean from the Rise of Islam to 1750* (Cambridge University Press, 1990). For the earlier period, see André Wink's three-volume *Al-Hind: The Making of the Indo-Islamic World* (Leiden and Boston: Brill, 1990–2004). For Southeast Asia only, see Anthony Reid's two-volume *Southeast Asia in the Age of Commerce 1450–1680* (New Haven and London: Yale University Press, 1988–93).

from December to March. These winds dictated the rhythm of maritime and to a large extent also that of continental traffic. The optimal annual radius of action of shipping under these circumstances resulted in the coastal areas situated around these three seas being in closer contact with each other than any of them were with the world outside. Not surprisingly, the most important staple ports were located in the areas where these circuits overlapped. These ports, such as Khambayat or Cambay (and later Surat, both in Gujarat), Calicut, Goa and Melaka, were the natural transhipment harbours which connected two of these maritime zones. Hence, in the early sixteenth century, the Portuguese traveller Tomé Pires could speak of the 'two arms' of Cambay: one extending westwards to Aden; the other eastwards to Melaka. What makes the case of Cambay exceptional, though, was that there was not only the sea and its immediate hinterlands, but actually a third and a fourth arm, the first stretching eastward towards South and Central India, the second northward into Hindustan and beyond to Iran and Central Asia. The combination of its relatively fertile agrarian conditions with so many sea and land routes explains the extraordinary position of the Gujarat ports as perhaps the most important trade emporia in the Indian Ocean.

Although this chapter focuses on the maritime world of the Indian Ocean and, in particular, its western and middle sections, the concept automatically evokes the importance of its continental counterpart: the great desert, savannah and steppe area which stretches from Morocco in the farthest west to the Great Wall of China in the farthest east. As with the ocean, this area, known as the Arid Zone, was an important trading artery between the continents of Africa, Europe and Asia and its logistic possibilities made it splendidly suitable for long-distance trade. Since ancient times, these relatively dry areas had been the home of stock-breeding and trading nomads who owned vast herds of dromedaries, Bactrian camels and, most important of all, the world's best war-horses. In addition, the warlike traditions of many of these people, whose skill as mounted archers aroused both admiration and fear, meant that the Arid Zone harboured an enormous potential in both commercial logistics and military might. Just as the coastal areas of the Mediterranean Sea and the Indian Ocean, it was principally the transitional areas between these dry nomadic zones and the wetter agricultural areas which distinguished themselves as centres of economic and political vitality and dynamism.

It is no accident that the centres of the most successful large realms in Eurasia were situated either on the sea coasts – for example, Lisbon, Amsterdam, London and Istanbul – or on the fringes of the Arid Zone – for example,

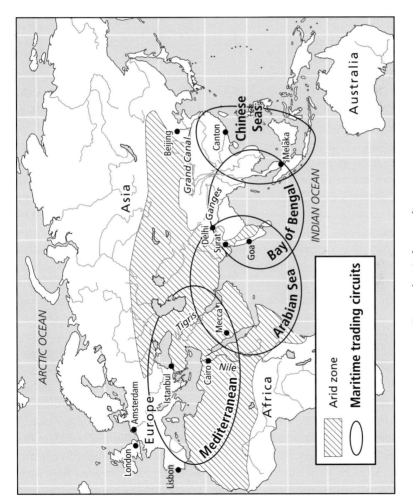

8.1 Eastern hemisphere trading zones

Delhi and Beijing. Moreover, the most powerful *anciens régimes* – such as the Ottomans in the Eastern Mediterranean, the Safavids in Iran, the Mughals in India and the Manchus (Qing) in China – were those that were able to link the agrarian exploitation of their realm with the dynamism of both the maritime and arid frontiers. Unquestionably, their initial existence and later continuity were dependent on their ability to link these two huge commercial arteries and spheres of mobile resources with each other. The Mughals in India, for instance, managed their connections with the sea trade via Surat and their links with the arid grazing areas and caravan trade via Kabul, a logistic split between the Indian Ocean and Central Asia that reveals the crucial importance of permanent control of the road network in this empire. Hence, none of these empires should be regarded as huge, closed geographical blocks, but instead as far-flung, open networks of military and commercial routes. By dint of the services provided by military-fiscal elites, backed up by agents and bankers, it was possible to exploit the surrounding area and keep it under control. The administrative corps of these empires was anything but an 'Oriental Despotism' characterized by a rigid, closed hierarchical structure, as earlier generations of Western observers asserted. Its overriding character far more resembled an infinitely expandable, diffuse structure composed of overlapping political and fiscal rights, which was controlled to the best of its ability by an often itinerant court employing whatever fairly makeshift means came to hand. In the Indian case, this open configuration offered European and other outside powers every opportunity to enter and exploit it as active co-sharers of the realm.

Despite the continuity of ocean and savannah, within this Afro-Eurasian continuum there were certainly parts that were less integrated than others. One such area roughly corresponds to the geographical boundaries of modern Europe, which from about AD 1000 was very little or not at all influenced by the powers in the Arid Zone. From the military point of view, state-formation in this northwesternmost corner of Eurasia, what Paul Valery has called an eccentric *Cap d'Asie*, was dominated not by the highly manoeuvrable warfare on horseback of nomads that predominated in the Arid Zone, but by a combination of the continual evolution of artillery and an infantry armed with firearms. This separation was not complete: Russia as well as the Ottoman Empire, both of which were increasingly taking shape as 'European' powers, continued to keep one foot in the nomadic world. In the rest of Europe, however, beyond the natural reach of nomadic forces, the coastal areas had a relatively free hand to develop; for centuries they were also increasingly capable of severing their bonds with the continental powers.

In this context, the successful Portuguese, Dutch and English resistance against the Habsburg dynasty marked a decisive victory for the sea over the land, although this was not necessarily a foregone outcome, as the violent history of the 'maritime' Huguenots in France – ultimately defeated by the land-based forces of the French monarchy under Louis XIV – reveals.[3] Interestingly, this success story of coastal emancipation repeated itself in the least arid, most tropical and most maritime areas of the Indian Ocean region: Ceylon (or Sri Lanka), the Indonesian archipelago and mainland Southeast Asia.

A similar autonomy was far more difficult to establish in the coastal areas of Iran, India and China, since most of these lay within the reach of the imperial cavalries and thus were less suitable to autonomous maritime developments, whether or not they were stimulated by the commercial activities of the Europeans. As a result, these areas remained at least until the eighteenth century relatively well integrated in the great continental empires. The possibility for Europeans to establish themselves as coastal powers is therefore explained by the geo-political situation in Eurasia. In the case of the empires connected to the Arid Zone, such as the Safavids, Mughals and Manchus, the European powers virtually without exception had to restrict themselves to setting up commercial offices. Here, their role was in the main restricted to that of merchant and pirate, profiting equally from the sale of spices and from the splendidly equipped politico-economic infrastructure of these empires which integrated coast with hinterland. From the outset, in these places the Europeans remained heavily dependent on the cooperation of the local authorities and above all on that of an influential group of indigenous middlemen of merchants and bankers. At the same time, the European sea-powers experienced little difficulty in carving out their niches in the Indonesian archipelago, the Malabar Coast and Ceylon. These just happened to be the production areas of the most profitable commodities on the European markets: pepper, cloves, nutmeg, mace and cinnamon. Finally, those coastal areas that were poorly or only moderately well integrated into their hinterlands, such as East Africa or the mainland of Southeast Asia, were far less interesting for the Europeans and were only of temporary or marginal importance to their trade. Overall, the process of European expansion in this period must be seen as part of a much wider Afro-Eurasian *Age of Commerce* which in the context of booming maritime commerce, witnesses,

---

[3] Edward Whiting Fox, *History in Geographic Perspective: The Other France* (New York: Norton, 1971).

on the one hand, a pattern of rising maritime frontiers, and on the other hand, impressive imperial state-formation along the southern fringes of the Arid Zone.[4] For the imperial authorities of the seventeenth and eighteenth centuries, the main challenge was to integrate the booming coasts with the political heartlands of the interior.[5]

Rivers, canals and coasts

Rivers played a key role in connecting the political capitals near the Arid Zone to the commercial hubs along the coast. Empires could not dispense with rivers as economic lifelines, providing both transport and irrigation. The best example of this is the importance of the Ganges River, which connected the ever-expanding Bengal economy to the political centres of the Mughal emperors and their Rajput generals in the arid northwest of the subcontinent. If there was no river to connect the political and economic centres, one had to construct one, such as the Chinese Grand Canal that linked the economic powerhouse of the lower Yangzi River valley to the peripheral northern capital of Beijing.

In the case of the Ottomans, their Grand Canal, across Suez to connect the Mediterranean to the Red Sea, never materialized, despite several plans to build it in the sixteenth century. This was compensated for by the caravan routes that connected Egypt and the Levant to Mecca and on to the port of Aden in Yemen. Despite an ongoing silting process, in the north the rivers Tigris and Euphrates complemented and further facilitated the caravan routes to the Persian Gulf. Indeed, the sixteenth-century rapid expansion of the Ottoman Empire at the very crossroads of the Mediterranean and Indian Ocean, and with this the creation of a monetary union of the silver *akçe*, raises the question of whether we should really perceive the two oceans as distinct zones. At that time, the Mediterranean and Arabian Sea were definitively closer to each other than the latter to the Chinese Sea. All this is confirmed by what is now perceived as a sixteenth-century Ottoman 'Age of Exploration' in which the Turks consciously turned east to forge an anti-Portuguese alliance of Indian Ocean states that more or less acknowledged the suzerainty of the Ottoman sultan, including Mombasa on the African

---

[4] The term is Anthony Reid's, although he only uses it for Southeast Asia.

[5] For an impressive *longue durée* survey of this integration process, see Victor Lieberman's two-volume *Strange Parallels: Southeast Asia in Global Context, c. 800–1830* (Cambridge University Press, 2009).

Coast and Aceh in the Far East. Within this alliance, Gujarat was at the forefront of Ottoman attention. Between 1538 and 1573, the port-city of Surat was governed by an uninterrupted series of Ottoman (Rumi) commanders, one of whom was Hoja Safar, *alias* Khudavend Khan, the leader of the Rumi community in Gujarat, who was actually from Otranto in southern Italy.[6]

In Southeast Asia, rivers were as relevant to the process of state-formation as they were in West, South and East Asia. In mainland Southeast Asia, and to a lesser extent in Java as well, the principal political and agrarian centres at the end of the first millennium AD were not established in the deltas, which were forever subject to floods and changes in the course of the waterways, but further upstream in the interior in often semi-arid areas that were easier to reclaim. This included the ancient capitals of Pagan in Burma, Sukhothai in Siam and Angkor in Cambodia. Under ideal circumstances, the rulers stimulated agricultural expansion in the interior and maintained control of the deltas and the coastal areas downstream via the rivers. The economic centre of gravity was intensive rice cultivation, and trade was of only secondary importance. One consequence of this pattern was that very large areas, usually far from the navigable rivers, did not actually fall under the authority of the ruler. The result was a settlement pattern of relatively small, widely scattered, densely populated cultivated nuclear areas in the midst of enormous jungles, some of which were extensively exploited, others not at all. In those regions where the interior was not conducive to intensive rice cultivation, such as in Sumatra and the Malay Peninsula, the situation was entirely different. Here, coastal port-cities without much hinterland but with crucial transregional functions could emerge, especially at the transshipment zone between the Bay of Bengal and the Chinese Sea, where there was a long-term continuity of important entrepots: Srivijaya before our period, Melaka-Johor during it, and Singapore in the modern era.

From the fifteenth century onwards, so just before the arrival of Vasco da Gama, this pattern began to change, and the relative weight of interregional trade as a source of income for the rulers showed a marked increase. At precisely this time, as a consequence of drier climatic conditions and of the introduction of new crops and agricultural techniques, it became easier to reclaim the swampy river deltas and settle people on the land. These developments probably played an important role in the growing orientation of states towards their southern coastal areas: in Burma, Pegu became more

---

[6] Giancarlo Casale, *The Ottoman Age of Exploration* (Oxford University Press, 2010).

important (until 1634), in Siam – Ayutthaya, in Cambodia – Phnom Penh, in Vietnam (albeit somewhat later) – Champa. On Java and Ceylon, this coastal efflorescence and integration with the interior was nipped in the bud by the early seventeenth-century agression of the Dutch East India Company (VOC), which left Mataram and Kandy relatively isolated states in the interior. Some other kingdoms, most important among them Burma and Japan, tried to withdraw from this new maritime dynamism by opting for rigid mercantilist control or even downright isolation. However, by the eighteenth century, exponentially growing Chinese participation in the economies of the South China Sea stimulated the rise of the Southeast Asian littorals even further.

Empires

From the fifteenth century onward, arid and maritime frontier-zone empires emerged. The first is exemplified by the vast Central Asian conquests of Temür, to be followed one century later by the emergence of the great Islamic empires of Ottomans, Safavids and Mughals. The seventeenth-century rise of the Manchus in China is another example of an expanding Central Asian frontier-empire. Although conquest was relatively easy, the ability of these empires to continue depended on their capacity to link nomadic military power to the resources of the sedentary economy and to the bustling commercial outlets at the coast. In an optimal scenario, the new conquerors were able to build on the achievements of their immediate predecessors. In India, the consolidation of the sultanates in the North and even Hindu Vijayanagara in the South were very much the result of the increased power of Turkish-style cavalry armies and their techniques, but experienced great difficulties in exploiting the rich agricultural lands along the rivers and the coasts. At one of the driest areas of the subcontinent, but also along the life-giving Tungabhadra River, Vijayanagara emerged as an empire that connected India's west and east coast, partly by coercion, but chiefly through the building and patronage of huge temple-complexes in the affluent coastal regions of the Coromandel Coast. Threatened by their northern neighbours in the Deccan, the rulers of Vijayanagara were always keen to use the Portuguese merchants at Goa and other settlements on the west coast to procure war-horses in return for local commodities such as precious stones, spices and textiles. Similarly, the sultans of the Deccan could only survive when they were able to link their capitals in the dry interior to the coast. This pattern led to the emergence of new coastal emporia catering to the interior capitals: Cambay / Surat catering to Delhi, Chaul to Ahmadnagar, Dabhol to Bijapur, Masulipatam to Golkonda and, indeed, Goa to Vijayanagara.

Meanwhile, in China, the Ming emperors (1368 to 1644) decided to turn their back on the nomadic world. By reconstructing the Great Canal they fully exploited the southern rice economy – the north produced mainly millet, wheat and sorghum – and with the expeditions of the Muslim admiral Zheng He (1371 to 1433), they decided to plunge into the deep sea to seriously explore the opportunities of maritime trade. Hence, in the period from 1405 to 1433, huge Chinese fleets visited the entire stretch of the Indian Ocean, from the Indonesian archipelago to Mogadishu. Apart from exploration and trade, the main aim of these expeditions was propagandistic: to claim power and demand tribute by demonstrating China's superiority. Although this active maritime engagement came to an early close in part due to some ongoing worries about traders turning into pirates, in the sixteenth century Ming China developed into a highly commercialized and outward-oriented society. Trade with the outside world was not forbidden, but regulated at earmarked outlets such as Macau, which the Portuguese were allowed to lease in 1557. China's sixteenth-century turn to the coast was further enhanced by the opening up of the Pacific Ocean following the Spanish conquest of the Philippines, which brought huge amounts of South American silver, but also new crops like maize, tobacco and sweet potatoes. Together with imports from Japan, these stimulated the Chinese economy, in particular along the southeast coast in the previously unsettled hill areas of Fujian. The demographic upsurge that followed made possible the migration of many Chinese from this region to Southeast Asia. Here, under Spanish and Dutch supervision, they created an informal Chinese empire, developing places like Manila (from 1571), Batavia (from 1621) and Taiwan (from 1624), but still remaining connected to their homeland.

In the seventeenth century, even stronger and larger empires developed in much of Eurasia. The explanation for this has been sought in the introduction of new gunpowder technology, but the military mainstay of all these powers remained the war-horse, albeit less so for the Ottomans. Especially in the case of the two wealthiest empires, those of the Mughals and the Manchus, their unprecedented capacity to combine Central Eurasian military recruitment, agrarian exploitation and maritime trade was more important than simple military superiority. Although it was helped by the favourable infrastructure of the Ganges River and the Great Canal, their expansion could only be implemented by the importation of massive amounts of gold and particular silver from the New World. Of course, the Indian sultans – including the ruler of Vijayanagara, known as the 'sultan among hindu kings' – and the Ming emperors had shown the way, but they had struggled to pay for their huge armies by taking recourse to tinkering policies like issuing paper money or sheer plunder. By contrast, the Mughals and the Manchus were now able to raise more cash to pay for a more professional administrative and military apparatus to oversee increasing agricultural exploitation. One of the major consequences of this process was political integration, as illustrated in the rise of the imperial port-cities of Surat and Canton (Guangzhou) as the two major maritime outlets and trading hubs of the Indian Ocean.

Companies

The rise of the European powers in the Indian Ocean is part of the wider process of emerging littoral societies which embraced the entire Eurasian continent. Whereas in the areas surrounding the Arid Zone empires were able to retake control of the new maritime dynamic, in peripheries like Western Europe and Southeast Asia, the mercantile elites of the coastal states were in a position to take their fate into their own hands. Before Vasco da Gama's trip around the Cape, the lion's share of the European trade with the Indian Ocean was in the hands of the Italian city-states, Venice in particular, which had already used their extensive Mediterranean network to the Levant to keep the Holy Roman Empire and France at a safe distance. The trading world of the Mediterranean was conveniently linked to that of the Indian Ocean by the so-called *funduq* (Arabic) or *fondaco* (Italian), an extraterritorial enclave consisting of an inn or warehouse that catered to foreign merchants and protected their merchandise. *Funduqs* greatly facilitated the further spread of European merchant communities into the Indian Ocean.[7]

The Italian city-states developed business procedures that have been described as early capitalism, although this was already business as usual in Asian port-cities such as Cambay, Calicut and Zayton. Ongoing commercial competition among the Italian cities, combined with their dependence on the Ottoman Empire for gaining access to the East, made these urban republics eager to explore alternative routes further south- and westward. As early as

[7] Olivia Remie Constable, *Housing the Stranger in the Mediterranean World: Lodging, Trade, and Travel in Late Antiquity and the Middle Ages* (Cambridge University Press, 2003).

the thirteenth century, Genoa had dreamed of a direct route to the Indies, and Genoese merchants and mariners were active in many maritime ventures. Among these were those sponsored first by Portugal and then by Spain.

Situated at the crossroads of the Mediterranean and the Atlantic, the Portuguese kings embraced the opportunities provided by their geographic position to carve out what seemed to be a truly global empire on the coastal rim of the Atlantic and Indian Oceans. Although very much a Portuguese achievement, this would hardly have been possible without the considerable contributions of Italian, German and Dutch investors; indeed, Lisbon's Age was also the Age of Antwerp and Genoa, the latter maintaining the connection with American silver gained through Spanish *asientos*.[8]

More than was the case with the great empires of the Indian Ocean, those of Europe were increasingly dominated by the financial elites of the port-towns on the coast. Nonetheless, even the most sea-oriented of them, the Portuguese Empire, was not run by merchants, but by admirals and officials. Its kings contented themselves with taxing and farming out the routes and sales they could control through the threat or actual deliverance of violence. Sea trade had often involved violence, but the sheer effectiveness of more cannon on stronger ships was unprecedented and gave the Portuguese *Estado da Índia* the edge on the high seas of the Indian Ocean. The bulk of the intra-Asian trade, however, was left to their mostly Asian competitors and also increasingly to private Portuguese settlers (*casados*), many of whom were converted Jews known as 'New Christians', who often intermarried with local women. They were based at their own port-cities in the Arabian Seas such as Diu, Goa, Colombo and Cochin, but also in areas beyond the reach of the *Estado*, such as in the swampy borderlands between Pegu and Bengal. Two of them – Filipe de Brito and Sebastião Gonçalves Tibau – emerged as powerful warlords who even managed to carve out their own principalities. Despite the decline of official Portuguese trade in the first decades of the seventeenth century, private intra-Asian trade continued to support the largely flourishing Luso-Asian communities in India and China deep into the eighteenth century.[9]

---

[8] Fernand Braudel, *Civilization and Capitalism, 15th–18th Century*, vol. 3: *The Perspective of the World* (London: Fontana Press, 1985), p. 168.

[9] Sanjay Subrahmanyam, *The Portuguese Empire in Asia, 1500–1700: A Political and Economic History* (London and New York: Longman, 1993) and James Boyajian, *Portuguese Trade in Asia under the Habsburgs, 1580–1640* (Baltimore, MD: Johns Hopkins University Press, 2007).

The best way to achieve coastal autonomy was the formation of a mercantile organization that could operate independently from the dynastic and territorial concerns of the polity in which the coast was located, with the exclusive aim of making profit elsewhere and distributing it to the investors back home. The establishment of the English (1600) and Dutch (1602) joint-stock East India Companies confirmed the rising power of the mercantile elites of the northwestern European littoral and gave them a highly effective instrument to expand that power even further along the coastal rim of the Indian Ocean. During the seventeenth century, the Dutch were by far the most successful in this respect, but only conquered those coastal and island territories which produced commodities that could easily be monopolized – hence the VOC's early aggression against the spice islands in the eastern Indonesian archipelago (cloves, nutmegs and mace) and Ceylon (cinnamon). At the same time, both the English and the Dutch tried to wipe out Iberian competition as quickly as possible, and turned their eyes to the main Portuguese strongholds. The English conquered Bandar-e Abbas in 1622 (with the help of the Safavids) and the Dutch conquered Melaka in 1641 (with the help of Johor). At this stage, the English lacked the capital to keep pace with the Dutch. The latter more or less forced the English to focus their investments on the Indian subcontinent, which at that time was not at all the most desired prize. Here the European companies were faced with the military superiority of the Mughals and, as had the Venetians earlier in the Ottoman Empire, they were quite happy to use the protection and the sophisticated trading and credit facilities – *funduqs*, markets, banks, mints, roads, insurance, bills of exchange, etc. – provided, often through contract, by the Mughal Empire.

The company as an institution was a highly successful phenomenon in the Indian Ocean: after the Dutch and English had shown the way, most other European countries followed suit. What was new was the pooling and securing of large amounts of capital for the long term as business risk was spread through shareholders. As a result, the company could build and maintain elaborate infrastructures from a great distance, predict and 'internalize' protection costs, and impose monopolies or design other more effective market policies.[10] Although they were certainly innovative, companies could only survive because at crucial moments they were backed up by their states, which were often ruled by the very same families that managed the

[10] Niels Steensgaard, *The Asian Trade Revolution in the Seventeenth Century: The East India Company and the Decline of the Caravan Trade* (University of Chicago Press, 1974).

companies. Much more than was the case with the other trading networks of the Indian Ocean, European states frequently intervened in company affairs, providing additional protection and reducing overheads. The company as an institution was a wonderful instrument to operate against great risks and at a great distance. It worked particularly well for the richest merchants in Amsterdam and London in already sophisticated market economies such as those of the Indian Ocean.

In the second half of the seventeenth century, due to the conquests of the main production and trading centres, the VOC managed to impose a monopoly on cloves, nutmeg and mace which also virtually excluded the traditional trading circuits from access to the Spice Islands. This important shift in the trade with and within the Indonesian archipelago brought an early end to its Age of Commerce and actually precluded the political integration of coast and hinterland as experienced in the Middle East, Iran, India and China. For most areas west and north of the archipelago, however – with the exception of the islands of Ceylon and Taiwan – relatively few visible changes came from any 'innovative' behaviour or institutions of the European companies.

Like the Portuguese before them, the companies had to adapt themselves to the existing trading pattern in the Indian Ocean, although in trading their monopoly products, they managed to circumvent these to some degree. For example, after 1611, Dutch ships were able to skirt around the whole system by sailing with the prevailing westerly winds around 40 degrees South Latitude after leaving the Cape and then using the southeast trade winds to reach the Sunda Strait. The Dutch thus built up their own interregional circuit parallel to the existing routes. In the seventeenth century, Batavia emerged as a new Southeast Asian rendezvous, offering an alternative port to such existing regional centres as Malacca and Bantam. From Batavia, a new trade system of bilateral long-distance relations developed, which infringed on important sections of the existing pattern. Japanese copper was brought to the market in Surat and fine spices were sold in Persia via Batavia. At the same time, though, the existing Asian trading pattern was hardly subjected to change; the VOC was simply making use of the existing intra-Asian market relations. The difference it brought to the Indian Ocean was that there was now this one sole trading organization that was willing and able to undertake transportation over the whole route from production centre to market, covering more than two circuits. Nevertheless, it would be too much to claim that this was an absolute innovation because, prior to 1600, this practice had already been prevalent among the Portuguese and even among the

Armenian and Indian trading communities scattered throughout the region, albeit on a much more limited scale and with far less bureaucracy involved.

One long-neglected contribution of the VOC to the Indian Ocean trading world was the creation of a new southern zone of forced migration which actually connected the already existing slave-trading networks of the East African Swahili coast with those of South and Southeast Asia. Although the volume of the slave trade in the Indian Ocean never reached the scale of the Atlantic – approximately half a million people as opposed to 12 million – about half the population in the VOC port-cities consisted of resident slaves, arriving at a total figure of 66,350 slaves for the years 1687 to 1688. Although the VOC itself traded a considerable number of slaves, most were purchased through existing trading networks. In contrast to the more agrarian slavery of the Atlantic, most slaves in Dutch Asia were used in smaller numbers per household for mostly domestic services in an urban context. In the second half of the eighteenth century, this southern slave trade expanded massively as a result of the new plantation economies of the French Mascarene Islands, where the slave population more than tripled from c. 40,000 in 1766 to 133,000 in 1808.[11] Parallel to the slave trade, another much smaller south–south circuit of forced migration emerged under VOC control, consisting of convicts and exiles, mostly from the Indonesian archipelago, who ended up in Ceylon and the Cape.[12]

Although this is sometimes over-emphasized, the Dutch colonial establishments in the Indian Ocean seem to have been more segmented than the Portuguese ones. Rather than the broad Lusitanian middle-ground consisting primarily of Eurasian *casados*, the Dutch engineered a more layered society that in theory ranged from European Christians to Eurasians, Christian client communities and freed slaves (for example, the so-called Mardijkers, Topasses and Free Blacks), non-Christian but free 'foreign' groups (for example, Chinese), slaves and finally the local people. However, because Dutch law was not imposed on local communities, but was rather constantly renegotiated with them, actual colonial practice often looked very different.[13]

[11] Markus Vink, '"The World's Oldest Trade": Dutch Slavery and Slave Trade in the Indian Ocean in the Seventeenth Century', *Journal of World History* 14(2) (2003), 131–77; and Richard B. Allen, 'Satisfying the "Want for Labouring People": European Slave Trading in the Indian Ocean, 1500–1850', *Journal of World History* 21(1) (2010), 45–73.
[12] Kerry Ward, *Networks of Empire: Forced Migration in the Dutch East India Company* (Cambridge University Press, 2009).
[13] Ulbe Bosma and Remco Raben, *Being 'Dutch' in the Indies: A History of Creolization and Empire, 1500–1920* (Athens, OH: Ohio University Press, 2008).

During the mid-eighteenth century, the great days of the companies gave way to the British country trader who by now, like his Asian counterpart, could operate more flexibly and with lower costs. At the same time, he could still count on the protection and infrastructure provided by the East India Company. The latter had gradually developed from a maritime trading institution into a devastating war machine on land; it was paid not by profit, but by the spoils of war. At the same time, the Dutch spice monopoly was maintained, but spices had lost much of their appeal as luxury goods. Far more attractive now were Indian commodities, particularly textiles and opium, as these could be used more profitably to exploit the Chinese – in particular in exchange for tea and porcelain – and various other markets in the Indian Ocean and even beyond, in the slave trade along the West African coast.

Meanwhile, on the Indian mainland, the military balance started to change. From the middle of the eighteenth century onward, larger and better drilled and equipped British and French *sepoy* armies proved able to withstand the cavalry-based armies of the Mughals and their successors. As in the earlier cases of Dutch Java and Ceylon, this first engendered the coasts' breaking away, soon followed by further integration from coasts that were now completely dominated by the new colonial headquarters of Calcutta, Madras and Bombay. Nevertheless, in many other parts of the Indian Ocean, the Europeans were still playing second fiddle; tried and tested trading networks like those of various Arab, Indian, Chinese, Jewish or Armenian groups, but also relatively new ones like that of the Buginese in the Indonesian archipelago, held sway deep into the eighteenth century, and in some places long after.

Asian trade networks

The Asian merchants were not organized in companies, but mostly in family firms. Some of these firms participated in transregional trade networks that were based on the mutual trust of partners with a common ethnic, religious or caste background and which made them stand out from the majority of the population of the regions where they traded. Like the European companies, some of these 'trade diasporas' could count on the support of their political patrons. For example, the Armenian trade network started as a local enterprise along the Ottoman–Safavid border that profited from increasing European demand for Iranian silk. After 1605, when the Safavid ruler Shah Abbas relocated the Armenians to New Julfa at the outskirts of his new capital of Isfahan, they started to develop a huge trading network spanning the Mediterranean, the entire Indian Ocean and even beyond to Russia, the Baltic Sea and the Atlantic Ocean. It seems that through various formal and informal means, all the nodes in the network were connected and subordinated to the centre in New Julfa. At the very basis of the network stood the *commenda* partnership, in which a settled 'capitalist' provided the capital or commodities to his agent who would supply his labour by travelling on his master's behalf to distant markets and putting the entrusted capital or goods to use by investing it on behalf of the partnership. The profit coming out of the joint venture was divided between the master and his agent. Although the *commenda* was open-ended in principle, in the Armenian case the inner circle of partners were all part of an extended family of sons, brothers and cousins under the direction of a senior family member residing in New Julfa. Beyond this inner circle, there was a 'coalition' of other Armenian agents whose conduct was monitored and enforced, since they were also linked to other Armenian families in New Julfa.

Although most of the other Asian trading networks in the Indian Ocean were not based on a single nodal centre, all of them functioned on the basis of the family firm, using *commenda* or some other flexible form of partnership such as the commission agency, which tended to be a short-term, less personal contract that included partners beyond the inner circle of kin or even the ethnic-religious denomination.[14] Many of these Asian trade networks were entangled with the political authorities that patronized them or were supported by them as much as the European companies were. The courts of Southeast Asia, including that of the VOC High government in Batavia, were highly mercantilist and deeply involved in trade activities; many of these rulers were the country's prime merchants themselves, often imposing monopolies on the foremost commodities in their realms. For the various coastal city-states of the Malay world, which lacked substantial hinterlands, interregional trade was the *sine qua non* of state-formation. Although some Southeast Asian states supported indigenous mercantile groups (*orang kaya*), the bulk of the external trade was in the hands of minorities who lived in separate quarters with their own chiefs but appointed by the state. Some of them were allowed to gain major political responsibilities such as harbour master (*shahbandar*) or financial minister (*phraklang* in Siam). Obviously, their minority status was supposed to prevent these

---

[14] Sebouh David Aslanian, *From the Indian Ocean to the Mediterranean: The Global Trade Networks of Armenian Merchants from New Julfa* (Berkeley, CA: University of California Press, 2011), pp. 215–34.

groups from taking power, but this did not always happen. Apart from the well-known Dutch case, the eighteenth-century expansion of the Buginese serves as another example of what could happen if trade networks were allowed too much leeway. Although the Dutch had imposed their spice monopoly on them and threatened their home-base in Celebes, the Buginese managed to expand over the Malay waters and to establish themselves as the ruling power in Kelang, Lingga, Selangor and Johor.

In the smaller principalities of South India, the situation was not really different, as long-distance maritime trade was dominated by ethnic or religious minorities such as Jews, Armenians, Mappila or Maraikkayar Muslims, or specific caste-groups such as Chetties and Chulias. Especially the latter two groups were perfectly situated to connect the ports of the Indian Ocean to the temples and markets of the interior. All of these groups operated beyond the grip of the main empires. They behaved very much like 'portfolio-capitalists' for whom the boundaries between trading, agricultural exploitation and politics were extremely porous.[15] However, with only a few exceptions – such as the Ali Rajas of Cannanore, the Zheng 'pirates' of Amoy and indeed the Buginese – maritime traders hardly ever became full-fledged territorial rulers.

Although they may have taken a rather aloof public attitude towards trade, the rulers of the big Asian empires were pretty much aware that, through the cash-nexus, trade affected the ability to collect land revenue and to pay salaries. While the Ottomans exploited Christian and Jewish trading minorities through their *millet* system, the Safavids forcefully settled the Armenian trading community in New Julfa. In the late sixteenth century, Iranian merchants played a vital role in connecting Iran to the Bay of Bengal through Masulipatam, the newly emerging maritime outlet of the Golconda sultanate.[16] From the mid-seventeenth century, however, connections beyond the Arabian Sea became increasingly dominated by Arab and South Indian merchants. The Mughal Empire was well served by various trading communities consisting of both foreign – mainly Europeans, Armenians and Turks – as well as indigenous groups – mainly Indian Muslims, Banias, Parsis and Jains.

---

[15] Sanjay Subrahmanyam and C. A. Bayly, 'Portfolio Capitalists and the Political Economy of Early Modern India', *Indian Economic and Social History Review* 25 (1988), 401–24.

[16] For the Iranian connections across the Indian Ocean World, see Sanjay Subrahmanyam, 'Persians, Pilgrims and Portuguese: The Travails of Masulipatam Shipping in the Western Indian Ocean 1590–1665', *Modern Asian Studies* 22 (1988), 503–30 and 'Iranians Abroad: Intra-Asian Elite Migration and the Early Modern State Formation', *Journal of Asian Studies* 51 (1992), 340–62.

The emperors often preferred a laissez-faire approach towards Indian Ocean trade, not because they were less interested, but because they could afford such a policy. Thanks to the structural trade surplus of India, they simply had to tax in- and outgoing trade flows at the main imperial gateways in Gujarat and Bengal.

By far the most important commercial hub that connected Mughal India to the outside world was the port-city of Cambay, during the sixteenth century, to be followed by Surat during the seventeenth and eighteenth centuries. Although Gujarati traders had dominated the Indian trade to Southeast Asia, due to Dutch aggression in the archipelago their role substantially diminished after the mid-seventeenth century. However, in the eighteenth century, Gujarati traders became increasingly prominent in the western Indian Ocean, in particular in the Red Sea and along the African coast. Meanwhile, the connections of the Arabian Sea with the archipelago were taken over by mercantile groups from the Hadhramaut and South India. Through the Siamese ports of Mergui-Tenasserim and Junk Ceylon (Ujang Selang/ Phuket), they could skip the Dutch ports to trade with Aceh and the newly assertive sultanates of eastern Sumatra, including Palembang, Siak and Indragiri. Moreover, many mercantile communities from the Minangkabau proliferated along the east coast of Sumatra, but also in Naning, Rembau and Sungai Ujong on the Malay Peninsula. From these strongholds, they increasingly mingled into the politics of neighbouring polities such as Perak, Kedah and Johore. As indicated already, here they found themselves in the midst of tremendously expanding Buginese and Chinese trading networks.

In contrast to the Indian empires, the Chinese ones upheld a long tradition in which merchants were distrusted and trade was closely supervised. As we have seen already, their involvement with the Indian Ocean was rather ambivalent. In the sixteenth century, the Chinese themselves referred to the *Nanyang*, a Chinese 'Southern Ocean', which at that time was encircled by an eastern and a western trading route. The western route (*Hsi Yang*) ran to Java via Champa, Cambodia, Siam, the Malay Peninsula and Sumatra; its eastern counterpart (*Tung Yang*) went through the Philippines, the Sulu Archipelago and Celebes to the Moluccas. Japan does not feature on the list because trade to this island empire was banned by the Chinese Government for most of the sixteenth century.

In this period, the Spaniards – who had managed to ensconce themselves in the Philippines and the Moluccas – were the predominant European power along the eastern route, whereas the Portuguese succeeded in making themselves masters of a number of key positions along the western route, such as Melaka and Macau. In the course of the seventeenth century, the Portuguese share in the lucrative China trade was gradually taken over by the Dutch and the English. Nevertheless, in contrast to the situation in those areas where the VOC could actually exercise political control, in most of the western *Nanyang* Dutch undertakings were completely overshadowed by the Chinese economy, particularly when that economy embarked on yet another exceptional growth spurt at the end of the seventeenth century. Purely and simply on account of its size, the Chinese economy tended to dominate Southeast Asia. In the era of the Company, Southeast Asia, including the Indonesian archipelago, was home to an estimated 20 to 30 million inhabitants, about the same as Japan, but China had roughly ten times that number of inhabitants! Thus, the orientation towards China throughout this region as a whole reflected contemporary demographic realities. In the eighteenth century, especially, the effect of this Chinese world economy increased exponentially. Because the Malay Peninsula and the islands of the East Indies were both being drawn increasingly into the orbit of the VOC, mainland Southeast Asia in particular felt the effects of this growth.

However attractive participation in the burgeoning China trade might have been for the surrounding kingdoms, it always held the ever-present threat of being overwhelmed by an influx of Chinese immigrants, eventually causing the loss of domestic political control. In Japan, matters were complicated by the shogunate which was constantly assailed by fears that the growing trade with China could lead to an unstaunchable draining away of the domestic supplies of precious metals. In colonial trade centres such as Batavia and Manila, the waxing economic power of China was viewed by the authorities as less of a threat, and throughout the eighteenth century Chinese traders continued to be largely welcome to offer their goods and services locally. As with the other political regimes of Southeast Asia, colonial centres could hardly dispense with Chinese expertise and manpower to work the expanding new plantations and mines of the region. However, as pogroms in various cities in which many Chinese were killed bear witness (six in Manila, one in Batavia), Sinophobia could also suddenly rear its ugly head. This was actually a sign that in those areas, too, the economy had gradually become dependent on the swelling group of Chinese immigrants. Although the Chinese were increasingly running the economies of Southeast Asia, they were neither directed by the Qing authorities nor did they organize themselves effectively beyond the region of their settlement.

To end this section on political and commercial networks, let us briefly recap the impact of the European operations in the Indian Ocean as a whole.

Although the Asian trading networks in the Indian Ocean were negatively affected by the European presence in the Indonesian archipelago in particular, they were able to adjust themselves quite well, even to a point where they were able to exploit the new conditions. For example, Gujarati and Sindi traders left the eastern Indian Ocean in the seventeenth century, to make room for Dutch, British, Arab and South Indian competitors, only to become increasingly prominent in the western Indian Ocean in the eighteenth century. In a way, this reconfirmed the old triple segmentation of the Indian Ocean in which Arab merchants, from both the Hadhramaut and the southern Persian Gulf, increasingly dominated the western, South Indians the middle, and the Chinese the eastern section of the Indian Ocean. At the same time, the European companies and private traders penetrated all three zones, but focused in particular on the easily colonized southern, tropical fringes which included the plantations of the French Mascarene Islands, Ceylon and the Indonesian archipelago. In the end, the British proved most successful as they were best situated to use the Indian subcontinent as a bridgehead to open direct trade with China.

More important than the phenomenon of European expansion was the expansion of the great Islamic empires which through networks of rivers and roads connected the already flourishing coasts to ever deeper and better-cultivated hinterlands. All this was achieved thanks to the service of various transregional trading communities which, apart from their core business of trade and transport, operated the imperial cash-nexus through a sophisticated system of mints, banks and other credit facilities. Hence, the financial support of these same communities, many of them ethnic or religious minorities, often became the key to shifting power relationships, as is famously demonstrated by the support provided by the Jagath Seth banking family of the British conquest of Bengal. The aftermath of this conquest in the nineteenth century shows how the Indian Ocean littoral became so economically and demographically heavy that it could no longer be controlled from the interior. With the help of new and more sophisticated techniques of military and economic exploitation, the Europeans were now able to turn the tables to start dominating the interior from their rapidly expanding coastal urban enclaves.

Cosmopolis

The political and trading networks of the Indian Ocean provided the basic infrastructure for the circulation of ideas in the region. Obviously these ideas were communicated through human agents: traders, sailors, soldiers, pilgrims, artists and many other travellers who, attracted by various financial and spiritual incentives, frequented the various ports, camps and courts of the Indian Ocean. Recently, though, scholars are beginning to pay more attention to written texts as equally important transmitters of ideas. Still, before printing technology started to have an impact on the societies of the Indian Ocean, texts were written, read out, compiled, copied, translated and, crucially, often considerably adjusted to meet the imagination of an audience with different cultural and linguistic backgrounds. These same scholars have detected what they have called a Sanskrit and an Arabic *cosmopolis*, the latter following the first, but both of them connecting the linguistic environments of South and Southeast Asia.[17] Both Sanskrit and Arabic represent a highly cosmopolitan language, a 'metamode of discourse' in which well-known stories are shared by the various local communities that actively participate in the making of the discourse by constantly creating their own vernacular versions of it. An earlier generation of scholars would have analysed this phenomenon under the heading of civilization, religion or great tradition, and hence would have used terms like indianization, islami(ci)zation or 'little tradition' to study their dissemination and adaptation. More recently, social scientists would have described the process with the two container concepts of globalization and glocalization, the latter a word that emerged first in business jargon to describe adapting a global product for local conditions or culture. The term 'cosmopolis' has an advantage over these, however, in that it is open-ended and does not posit a clear centre from which influences are diffused. Hence, it does not privilege authenticity, but recognizes an ongoing, multi-centric dynamic of diffusion and regional acculturation affecting both form and contents. As this meta-discourse involves shared values and ideas, a cosmopolis is much more than just a linguistic sphere, but also includes literature, religion, ethics and knowledge. Obviously, Arabic, considered to be God's own perfect tongue, possessed a unique status among languages. Although clearly linked to Islam, the Arabic cosmopolis spread much beyond the community of Muslim believers. Actually, Arabic texts spanned the literary worlds of Islamic and non-Islamic West, South and Southeast Asia, with deep effects on the contents and language of Tamil, Malay and Javanese discourse.

[17] Sheldon Pollock, *The Language of the Gods in the World of Men: Sanskrit, Culture, and Power in Premodern India* (Berkeley and Los Angeles, CA: University of California Press, 2006); and Ronit Ricci, *Islam Translated: Literature, Conversion and the Arabic Cosmopolis of South and Southeast Asia* (Chicago and London: University of Chicago Press, 2011).

At the end of our period, this literary 'Arabicized' cosmopolis stretched from Morocco to the Philippines. It overshadowed not only the old Sanskrit cosmopolis, but also the encroaching but still very much secluded Chinese and European cosmopolises. In the Indian Ocean, it had spread mostly along the more southern littorals of South and Southeast Asia. From there, it often followed the plough into the freshly cultivated and islamicized interiors of eastern Bengal, Java and Sumatra.[18] Its agents were often cosmopolitan figures who combined an identity of trader, religious scholar and Sufi. An increasing number of them followed the Shafi'i school of law, were connected to Hadhrami or other Arabic Sufi brotherhoods (tarīqa), and considered Mecca the heart of their world, to which they should at least once go on pilgrimage. During our period, this southern, sea-oriented cosmopolis flourished in the interstices of the encroaching European powers. It actually gained status by a pronounced discourse of resistance (in Arabic, jihād) which became particularly prominent during moments of intense conflict such as among the Mappilas against the Portuguese in the mid-sixteenth century and among the Javanese against the Dutch at the end of the seventeenth century.

Due to the spread and further intensification of the Arabic cosmopolis in Southeast Asia, Persian as the classical language of the Islamic courtly society lost some of its ground. Of course, Arabic considerably overlapped with a sphere that we may call the Turko-Persian ecumene, or indeed cosmopolis, which dominated the continental courts of West, Central and South Asia ruled by Sufi-oriented Turkish warrior elites. Not being the prime language of religious discourse, Persian was the language par excellence of political wisdom and good manners (adab; akhlāq). Its non-sectarian and liberal features matched the vision of universal empire and made it an ideal forum through which 'foreign' conquerors like the Mughals could effectively negotiate the enormous diversity of Indian society.

The Arabic and Turko-Persian cosmopolises overlapped almost everywhere but converged most fruitfully away from their imagined epicentres in Arabia and Iran, on the Indian subcontinent where both had started to participate in the ongoing production of the old Sanskrit cosmopolis. From the mid-sixteenth century until the end of the eighteenth century, it was this tripartite confrontation of Sanskrit, Turko-Persian and Arabic cosmopolises which created a unique South Asian engagement with other cultures as well

---

[18] Richard Eaton, The Rise of Islam and the Bengal Frontier, 1204–1760 (Berkeley, CA: University of California Press, 1993); and Denys Lombard, Le carrefour javanais, 3 vols (Paris: EHESS, 1990).

as concern for one's own agency and identity. As a result, more than others, Indian religious scholars were involved in fierce theological debates about the monism (*waḥdat al wujūd*) of the Ibero-Arab scholar Ibn Arabī (1165 to 1240), in which they discussed to what extent observation could be accommodated by Islamic episteme. Increasingly so, the works of North Indian *'ulamā* and Sufis were at the heart of the theological discourse that raged both in the Arabic world, including Mecca, and, through Hadhramauti and other Arabic channels, in the Indonesian archipelago.

Apart from being at the front of cultural dialogues, the increasingly prominent place of Indians in the Arabic cosmopolis can also be explained by pointing towards India's growing political and economic clout during Mughal rule. For example, from Emperor Akbar (r. 1556 to 1605) onwards, influence at Mecca was bought by distributing enormous quantities of money and sumptuous gifts for both the dignitaries and the poor. At the same time, increasing numbers of Arab Sufi brotherhoods set up their hospices on the Indian subcontinent, as this would enable them to channel profits from the India trade into various *waqf* foundations back home; one example is provided by the Aydarus family from the Hadhramaut.[19] In many of these cases, commercial and religious networks conveniently sustained each other and both point towards an expanding and highly dynamic Arabic cosmopolis characterized by increasing mobility, interaction and dialogue, within and beyond the cosmopolis. Although direct Persian and North Indian contacts with Southeast Asia declined during the seventeenth century, Persian and, in particular, Indian voices continued to have a major impact on the region, albeit now mainly through Arabic channels and mainly on theological issues. Meanwhile, as it was spreading, the Arabic cosmopolis itself became less Arabic as it was heavily vernacularized in all the local languages that it touched, from Swahili on the African coast to Javanese in the Indonesian archipelago.

Although the Arabic cosmopolis was the most prominent one in the western and central sections of the Indian Ocean, it was certainly not the only one, and some areas were hardly affected by it at all. Obviously, on its western fringe, the Ottoman Empire was very much a participant. Especially during the sixteenth century when the Ottomans increasingly looked East

---

[19] Esther Peskes, *Al-'Aidarūs und seine Erben: Eine Untersuchung zu Geschichte und Sufismus einer Ḥaḍramitischen Sada-gruppe vom fünfzehnten bis zum achtzehnten Jahrhundert* (Stuttgart: Franz Steiner Verlag, 2005). See also Engseng Ho, *The Graves of Tarim: Genealogy and Mobility across the Indian Ocean* (Berkeley, CA: University of California Press, 2006).

and many rulers of the Indian Ocean acknowledged their suzerainty, there was an upsurge of writings which assimilated Turkish exploration with already existing Arabic knowledge of the Indian Ocean. Later, during the late sixteenth and seventeenth century, the Turkish cosmopolis remained closely associated with Arabic as it continued to patronize and control the Hajj. At the same time, however, Persian and Indian influences declined as the Ottomans increasingly turned West.

At this early stage, the Western – or should we say Latin – cosmopolis itself hardly had an impact on the Indian Ocean, although it affected the world views of some elites, including artists and intellectuals at the various courts, and a little sometimes trickled down to other parts of the society. Actually, the Western cosmopolis was much more strongly affected by the cosmopolises of the Indian Ocean than vice versa, which, similar to the Indian case, gave rise to deep epistemological rethinking and fierce theological debates. Obviously, in scarcely populated areas that were colonized early, there was, indeed, a deep colonial impact through slavery, forced migration and conversion. In the Portuguese establishments and French slave colonies, widespread creolization occurred in which the indigenous population and migrants quickly shed their mother tongues for European languages and various Creole speeches, and, by doing so, constructed new identities for themselves.[20] At the same time, Portuguese retained its position as the lingua franca of the Indian Ocean port-towns.

More or less parallel to the north–south Arabo-Indian networks of the Arabian Sea and as such crossing the east–west Arabo-Indonesian networks linking the Bay of Bengal, we may detect a still vibrant Pali cosmopolis or *imaginair*. This encompassed Sri Lanka and much of mainland Southeast Asia where, from the early second millennium onward, it also became widely disseminated among the peasantry. Taking Pali as the prestige language for textual embodiments of ideology meant that people privileged Sinhalese monastic lineages and a relatively unchanging canon of Pali texts and Theravada-Buddhist thoughts.[21] It remains to be seen, though, to what extent the various centres of this cosmopolis were able to communicate with each other and with the other cosmopolises. We know, for example, that during the eighteenth century Dutch ships transported monks from Arakan and

[20] Pier M. Larson, *Ocean of Letters: Language and Creolization in an Indian Oceanic Diaspora* (Cambridge University Press, 2009).
[21] Steven Collins, *Nirvana and Other Buddhist Felicities* (Cambridge University Press, 1998), pp. 71–2.

Siam in order to let them revive the Sinhalese Sangha. Somewhat earlier, there were still a substantial number of Iranian and other Muslim traders on the mainland who gained a great deal of influence at the Siamese court and even gave rise to the short-lived mid-seventeenth-century sultanates of Champa and Cambodia. But it was only at the court of Arakan that we may perceive in the works of the Bengali poet Alaol something of a true dialogue between the Sanskrit, the Turko-Persian and perhaps even the Buddhist cosmopolis of his patron.[22] Even more than the Buddhist cosmopolis, the Neo-Confucian (or Chinese) cosmopolis of the most eastern section of the Indian Ocean was hardly influenced by the Arabic cosmopolis, partly because it was seen as an officially approved canon of scholarly and literary works. More than the others of the Indian Ocean, this cosmopolis was supervised closely by the state and, as such, was reproduced by the courtly literati of the Chinese Empire and the states which shared its Confucian tradition: Korea, Japan and Vietnam. If Islamic voices penetrated their world, it was like Buddhism earlier, more through Central Asia than through the South China Sea.

Epilogue

During the fifteenth to eighteenth centuries, the people of the countries surrounding the Indian Ocean witnessed unprecedented interaction. More than ever before, new Asian empires, European companies and Asian trade networks generated a new Age of Commerce, very much facilitated by the bullion of the New World arriving through the Levant, the Cape and the Pacific. During this period, the triple segmentation of the Indian Ocean was strengthened as the north–south connections within the Arabian Sea, the Bay of Bengal and the South China Sea began to supersede the east–west ones via the Indian subcontinent. At the same time, European traders and companies were the first to exploit the two most lucrative direct linkages: first, from the Indian Ocean to Europe and, second, from India to China. So, despite ongoing segmentation, both European companies and Asian trade networks continued to span the entire Indian Ocean. In fact, the arrival of the Europeans widened the reach of the Indian Ocean world to further integrate

---

[22] Thibaut d'Hubert and Jacques Leider, 'Traders and Poets in Mrauk-U: On Commerce and Cultural Links in Seventeen Century Arakan' in Rila Mukherjee (ed.), *Pelagic Passageways: Dynamic Flows in the Northern Bay of Bengal World before the Appearance of Nation States* (New Delhi: Ratna Sagar, 2008), pp. 345–79.

an already connected world that now not only encompassed the Mediterranean, but also the Atlantic. This further expansion of the Indian Ocean into Europe was visible in many ways as it had a huge impact on consumer behaviour, production processes and, most importantly, world views. Although the latter can be seen as a side-product of growing commercial interaction, it was also the outcome of increasing cultural interaction which sparked a phase of enormous creativity in which people began to rethink their own origins and identities in the light of an endless stream of new knowledge. Although we may label this process with familiar terms like Renaissance or Enlightenment, we should bear in mind that it was a global phenomenon, most prominently so in those regions and times where people experienced rapid convergence of great cultural diversity, be it through migration, conquest or trade. In other words, globalization always and everywhere engendered glocalization, a process that was mediated through the various cosmopolises of the Indian Ocean and was at its most creative along the various inner and outer boundaries of these cosmopolises.

FURTHER READING

Allen, Richard B., 'Satisfying the "Want for Labouring People": European Slave Trading in the Indian Ocean, 1500–1850', *Journal of World History* 21(1) (2010), 45–73.

Aslanian, Sebouh David, *From the Indian Ocean to the Mediterranean: The Global Trade Networks of Armenian Merchants from New Julfa* (Berkeley, CA: University of California Press, 2011).

Bosma, Ulbe and Remco Raben, *Being 'Dutch' in the Indies: A History of Creolization and Empire, 1500–1920* (Athens, OH: Ohio University Press, 2008).

Boyajian, James, *Portuguese Trade in Asia under the Habsburgs, 1580–1640* (Baltimore, MD: Johns Hopkins University Press, 2007).

Casale, Giancarlo, *The Ottoman Age of Exploration* (Oxford University Press, 2010).

Chaudhuri, K. N., *Asia before Europe: Economy and Civilisation of the Indian Ocean from the Rise of Islam to 1750* (Cambridge University Press, 1990).

  Trade and Civilization in the Indian Ocean: An Economic History from the Rise of Islam to 1750 (Cambridge University Press, 1985).

Eaton, Richard, *The Rise of Islam and the Bengal Frontier, 1204–1760* (Berkeley, CA: University of California Press, 1993).

Ho, Engseng, *The Graves of Tarim: Genealogy and Mobility across the Indian Ocean* (Berkeley, CA: University of California Press, 2006).

Hodgson, Marshall G. S., *The Venture of Islam: Conscience and History in a World Civilization*, vol. 2: *The Expansion of Islam in the Middle Period* (University of Chicago Press, 1994).

Larson, Pier M., *Ocean of Letters: Language and Creolization in an Indian Oceanic Diaspora* (Cambridge University Press, 2009).

Lieberman, Victor, *Strange Parallels: Southeast Asia in Global Context, c. 800–1830* (Cambridge University Press, 2009).

Lombard, Denys, *Le carrefour javanais*, 3 vols (Paris: EHESS, 1990).

Perlin, Frank, *The Invisible City: Monetary, Administrative and Popular Infrastructures in Asia and Europe 1500–1900* (Ashgate: Variorum, 1993).

    Unbroken Landscape: Commodity, Category, Sign and Identity: Their Production as Myth and Knowledge from 1500 (Ashgate: Variorum, 1994).

Peskes, Esther, *Al-'Aidarūs und seine Erben: Eine Untersuchung zu Geschichte und Sufismus einer Ḥaḍramitischen Sada-gruppe vom fünfzehnten bis zum achtzehnten Jahrhundert* (Stuttgart: Franz Steiner Verlag, 2005).

Pollock, Sheldon, *The Language of the Gods in the World of Men: Sanskrit, Culture, and Power in Premodern India* (Berkeley and Los Angeles, CA: University of California Press, 2006).

Reid, Anthony, *Southeast Asia in the Age of Commerce 1450–1680* (New Haven, CT and London: Yale University Press, 1988–93).

Ricci, Ronit, *Islam Translated: Literature, Conversion and the Arabic Cosmopolis of South and Southeast Asia* (Chicago and London: University of Chicago Press, 2011).

Steensgaard, Niels, *The Asian Trade Revolution in the Seventeenth Century: The East India Company and the Decline of the Caravan Trade* (University of Chicago Press, 1974).

Subrahmanyam, Sanjay, 'Iranians Abroad: Intra-Asian Elite Migration and the Early Modern State Formation', *Journal of Asian Studies* 51 (1992), 340–62.

    'Persians, Pilgrims and Portuguese: The Travails of Masulipatam Shipping in the Western Indian Ocean 1590–1665', *Modern Asian Studies* 22 (1988), 503–30.

    The Portuguese Empire in Asia, 1500–1700: A Political and Economic History (London and New York: Longman, 1993).

Subrahmanyam, Sanjay and C. A. Bayly, 'Portfolio Capitalists and the Political Economy of Early Modern India', *Indian Economic and Social History Review* 25 (1988), 401–24.

Vink, Markus, '"The World's Oldest Trade": Dutch Slavery and Slave Trade in the Indian Ocean in the Seventeenth Century', *Journal of World History* 14(2) (2003), 131–77.

Ward, Kerry, *Networks of Empire: Forced Migration in the Dutch East India Company* (Cambridge University Press, 2009).

Wink, André, *Al-Hind: The Making of the Indo-Islamic World* (Leiden and Boston: Brill, 1990–2004).

9

The Americas in the age of indigenous empires

MATTHEW RESTALL

On November 8, 1519, the history of the Americas was forever changed. For a quarter-century, three empires had been aggressively expanding in the hemisphere, and on that day two of them met. The meeting took the form of a diplomatic encounter between Moctezuma, the emperor of the Aztecs, and Fernando Cortés, the dominant captain of a Spanish expedition of invasion.

As told by some of the Spaniards who were there—most notably Cortés himself—the Aztec ruler came with a vast entourage to the edge of his capital city of Mexico-Tenochtitlán to welcome the foreign visitors, who for several months had been working their way across the empire from the coast. Upon first meeting, the two leaders exchanged greetings and necklaces, before the Spaniards were led to their guest quarters in the palace of Moctezuma's late father. There, the emperor delivered a speech to Cortés, who a year later repeated it in a letter to the king of Spain, styled as a statement of surrender. Cortés's strategic interpretation of the speech found a ready audience; it was echoed in subsequent Spanish and indigenous accounts of the conquest years, working its way into chronicles, histories and paintings, becoming an elemental part of the traditional narrative of the conquest that survives to this day.[1]

In my view, the meeting of November 8 was defined not by Moctezuma's alleged surrender, but by misunderstanding. A symbolic moment came when

---

[1] There are numerous primary sources, textual and visual, on this meeting (they underpin a book project of mine with the working title of *The Meeting*), but good starting points are: Anthony Pagden, *Hernán Cortés: Letters from Mexico* (New Haven, CT: Yale University Press, 1986), pp. 83–7; and James Lockhart, *We People Here: Nahuatl Accounts of the Conquest of Mexico* (Berkeley, CA: University of California Press, 1993), pp. 114–19. Starting points in secondary sources are Hugh Thomas, *Conquest: Montezuma, Cortés, and the Fall of Old Mexico* (New York: Touchstone, 1995), pp. 277–85; and Matthew Restall, *Seven Myths of the Spanish Conquest* (New York: Oxford University Press, 2003), pp. 77–82.

Cortés attempted to put his arms around the emperor. In the conquistador's own words, "when we met, I dismounted and went to embrace him alone, but those two lords who had come with him stopped me with their hands, so that I could not touch him."[2] In other words, the meeting was replete with miscommunication. As a diplomatic encounter, it was doomed to fail, with conflict bound to follow.

Inevitable conflict has tended to be a common theme in the history of the Americas in the age of indigenous empires. The historiography of the Aztec and Spanish Empires is heavy with assumptions not only regarding the predictability of events, but also the contributing attitude of contemporary actors. For example, Moctezuma surrenders only because he sees Spanish victory as predetermined; and Cortés's bold vision is driven by his belief that God is on his side. But from 1492 through the 1510s, the European discovery and knowledge of the Americas was limited to Caribbean islands and portions of the circum-Caribbean; likewise, the vast majority of Amerindians had not yet discovered Europeans or been impacted by their existence. The parallel, completely separate development of three empires in the Americas during that quarter-century reflected the limited nature of Spanish colonialism prior to 1519 (see Map 9.1). Eventual contact between two or more of these empires may have been inevitable, but nobody knew that at the time, nor was the post-1519 sequence of events preordained. The "real discovery of America" was thus arguably not the day in 1492 when Christopher Columbus saw land; it was the day Moctezuma met Cortés on the causeway leading into Tenochtitlán.[3]

This chapter explores imperial history in the Americas from the early fifteenth to late sixteenth centuries, with particular attention paid to the 1492 to 1519 years. Although contextual attention is paid to earlier periods and other indigenous groups, such as the Maya, the chapter's focus is on the parallel lives of the three empires—the Aztec, Inca and Spanish—each developing unbeknownst to the others. The period of the early fifteenth to late sixteenth centuries was an era of intense conflict and change, albeit with the (sometimes surprising) persistence of certain patterns. It began with the rise of the Aztec and Inca Empires in the 1420s to 1430s; it spanned the rapid

---

[2] My translation of the original passage on f. 44 of the 1522 Seville edition of the letter; but see Pagden's translation in *Hernán Cortés*, p. 84.

[3] As Hugh Thomas put it at the time of the Columbus quincentennial: Hugh Thomas, *The Real Discovery of America: Mexico, November 8, 1519* (Mount Kisco, NY: Moyer Bell, 1992), p. 19.

expansion of those mainland empires in the 1490s to 1510s, while Spaniards were forging a fledgling empire in the Caribbean; and it concluded with the Spanish-initiated partial transformation and partial destruction of the Aztec and Inca Empires from the 1510s to 1570s. The story after 1519 is not a simple one of sudden conquest, of one empire destroying another; but nor is it one solely of cooperation and collaboration. It is all of the above—a muddled, messy, mix of misunderstandings.

Categorizing Native Americans

> The conquerors of the New World were mostly illiterate adventurers, destitute of all the ideas which should have directed them in contemplating objects, so extremely different from those with which they were acquainted. Surrounded continually with danger, or struggling with hardships, they had little leisure, and less capacity, for speculative inquiry. Eager to take possession of a country of such vast extent and opulence, and happy in finding it occupied by inhabitants so incapable to defend it, they hastily pronounced them to be a wretched order of men, formed merely for servitude.

Thus did William Robertson, the eighteenth-century Scotsman who wrote the first modern English-language history of the Americas, characterize that thwarted embrace of Spaniards and native peoples in the age of discovery, invasion, conquest and resistance.[4] In fact, Robertson realized that not all Spanish newcomers were so destitute of ideas, and he himself tended to dismiss many indigenous peoples as culturally wretched. That is, he was the heir to a European tradition that struggled to understand Native American civilizations, a complex engagement with the indigenous past and present that—paradoxically—denigrated native cultures, admired their achievements, and simplified or ignored the post-conquest processes of their survival and transformation.

The first generations of European travelers to the Americas, from Columbus in the 1490s to Sir Walter Raleigh a century later, carried with them preconceived ideas about indigenous peoples and their cultures. Columbus reported to the Castilian queen that one Caribbean island was inhabited by cannibals, another by people with tails and a third by Amazons—women warriors who lived in communities entirely without men. The Governor of Cuba instructed Cortés to find out if there were men with heads of dogs in

---

[4] William Robertson, *The History of America* (London: Thoemmes Press, 1777), vol. 1, p. 285.

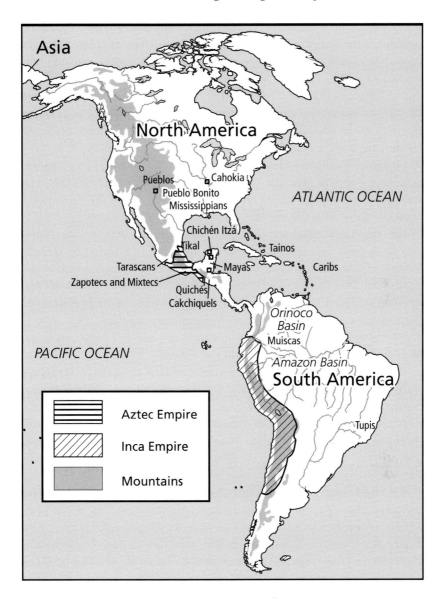

9.1 Map of Native America before 1492

Yucatan or Mexico. Raleigh looked in vain in South America for acephali, or headless people, described to him by Spaniards and Amerindians as having "their eyes in their shoulders, and their mouths in the middle of their breasts."

We may no longer hunt for such monsters, yet arguably Native Americans continue to be viewed primarily through the prism of the non-native imagination; the Mexica, for example, have repeatedly been invented and reinvented as the "Aztecs" (as we shall call them here), alternately derided as cannibalistic savages and celebrated as symbols of Mexican national glory. Despite the immense amount of knowledge that archaeologists, ethnohistorians and other scholars have compiled on the native peoples of central Mexico, the popular and common image of them still centers on so-called Aztec human sacrifices—as did the prejudiced first impression by conquistadors such as Bernal Díaz del Castillo. Díaz's account of the Spanish-Aztec war, first published in 1632, has remained until today one of the foundational cornerstones of how that war and its protagonists are perceived.[5]

The reluctance of sixteenth-century Spaniards to believe that Native Americans built their own civilizations is thus part of a thread of Western thought that survives to this day. In the decades after Columbus, it was argued that Amerindians were descended from one of the lost tribes of Israel or refugees from Atlantis, or they were "taught" civilization by Egyptians and Carthaginians. We may not take such theories seriously, but they were as popular in their day as were late-twentieth-century notions of alien assistance or a lost ten-thousand-year-old global civilization.

Some sixteenth-century Europeans were willing to credit Amerindians with the civilizational developments that were very much still visible after the Spanish Conquest. One of these was the Franciscan friar Diego de Landa, who asserted that the pyramids and other buildings he saw in the Yucatan Peninsula "were not made by any peoples other than these Indians."[6] Landa was right. He was referring to the Mayas, but he would have been equally correct making the same observation anywhere in the Americas.

We might forgive early modern observers for failing to grasp the deep temporal roots of settlement and civilization in the Americas; it has taken scholars many decades to construct an understanding of what preceded the Aztecs and Incas, an understanding that continues to evolve. As detailed elsewhere in these volumes, some Native American populations began to

[5] Among many editions of Díaz's book, a fine recent one is Bernal Díaz del Castillo, *The History of the Conquest of New Spain*, Davíd Carrasco (ed.) (Albuquerque, NM: University of New Mexico Press, 2009); for an argument that Cortés was the real author of Díaz's *True History*, see Christian Duverger, *Crónica de la Eternidad: Quien escribió la Historia verdadera de la conquista de la Nueva España?* (Mexico City: Taurus, 2013).

[6] Diego de Landa, *Relación de las cosas de Yucatán*, ch. 5. My translation from the manuscript in the Royal Academy of History, Madrid.

abandon nomadic hunting in favor of a more settled and permanent exist-ence some 8,000 to 10,000 years ago. The earliest evidence of this transition is found in the Andes region of South America and in Mesoamerica; there, beginning about 3000 BC, native peoples developed more sophisticated societies and distinctive styles of art and architecture. Andeans developed the great Chavín civilization in the northern Andes, while Mesoamericans produced the great Olmec civilization of Mexico's Gulf Coast. Between 200 BC and AD 1300, a number of distinct civilizations rose and fell in the Andes and Mesoamerica, some of them reaching imperial status and all of them building on and borrowing from their predecessors. Before the period of the Incas, the Moche and the Sicán civilizations stand out in northern Peru, while to the south there rose the Nazca, Huari and Tiahuanaco. The two greatest civilizations to develop in Mesoamerica before the fifteenth century were those of Teotihuacán in central Mexico and, to the south, the Classic Maya. All of these civilizations centered on large, ceremonial cities with substantial stone temple complexes.[7]

The Aztecs and Incas evolved from deep cultural roots in Mesoamerica and the Andes. So too did the Mayas, yet the Mayas (as we think of them) were part of neither empire, nor had they ever forged their own. Neither had the Taíno and indigenous peoples of the Caribbean, whose society was different in crucial ways from those of the Mesoamericans. Native American societies were complex and varied, but can be divided into four categories: "concentrated sedentary," "segmented sedentary," "semi-sedentary" and "non-sedentary."[8]

The first two categories refer to permanently settled societies whose members lived in built communities, typically in the valleys or plateaus of the tropical Americas, rather than in densely forested areas. Sedentary societies relied on permanent, intensive agriculture for their survival. This required irrigation and other complex and labor-intensive water control systems, but it also allowed populations to swell; the Aztec capital of Tenochtitlán, with perhaps as many as 100,000 people, was one of the largest cities in the world. Intensive agriculture also fostered social stratification;

---

[7] See chapters by Gerardo Gutiérrez, *Cambridge World History*, vol. v, and Michael Smith, *Cambridge World History*, vol. vi, and also William T. Sanders, Alba Guadalupe Mastache and Robert H. Cobean (eds.), *Urbanism in Mesoamerica* (Mexico City: Instituto Nacional de Antropología e Historia; University Park, PA: Pennsylvania State University Press, 2003).

[8] This passage is based in part on Matthew Restall and Kris Lane, *Latin America in Colonial Times* (Cambridge University Press, 2011), pp. 12–16. I am grateful to Kris for permitting me to draw freely from our book here and elsewhere in this chapter.

while the majority of subjects in sedentary Native American societies farmed, a minority lived and worked as merchants, artisans, warriors, nobles and royalty. Sedentary societies are built to expand. This was true in the Andes and Mesoamerica, the two most densely populated regions of the Americas and the location of concentrated sedentary societies; expanding polities or empires of some kind rose and fell in concentrated sedentary societies for centuries prior to the European invasion.

Other sedentary peoples—segmented societies—occupied lands where there were no empires or large polities. Key examples of segmented sedentary societies could be found to the north of the Inca Empire and in southern Mesoamerica. In northern Colombia, the Tairona and the Muisca built stone temples and palaces in their city centers; they traded in gold, emeralds and cotton textiles with each other and their neighbors. Segmented Mesoamerican societies included the Zapotecs, Mixtecs and other smaller groups to the south of the Aztec Empire, as well as the Mayas of the Yucatan Peninsula and smaller Maya polities in Guatemala. These peoples were all fully sedentary, and many had in previous centuries been part of larger regional polities, some of which had developed into incipient empires of sorts, centered on such cities as Tikal (at the Yucatan's southern end) and Chichén Itzá (to its north). But at the time of the Spanish invasion, the Mayas were at the segmented stage of a cycle marked by periods of expansion and centralization followed by eras of political and demographic collapse.

For example, as recently as the early fifteenth century, much of the Yucatan Peninsula had been organized into a mini empire centered on the city of Mayapan; had their invasion of the peninsula been delayed by a century or so, the Spaniards might have encountered a similar such polity instead of the two dozen loosely delineated city-states (i.e. segmented societies) they in fact found in the sixteenth century (see Map 9.2). Not that segmentation facilitated invasion and conquest from outside. Some Mayan kingdoms, due to their size and location, escaped violent invasion, but were gradually absorbed into New Spain (such as the Chontal kingdom of Acalan); others fought off repeated invasions, but eventually accommodated Spanish colonization (such as the Xiu, Pech and other polities in northern Yucatan, whose conquest took almost two decades; and the rival kingdoms of highland Guatemala, the Cakchiquel and Quiché, whose conquest took a bloody decade); others successfully prevented Spanish settlement, accepting Christianity on their own terms and even without non-Mayan priests, but suffered massive population decline and gradually faded away as viable polities (such as those in what is now western Belize); and, finally, others persisted, even

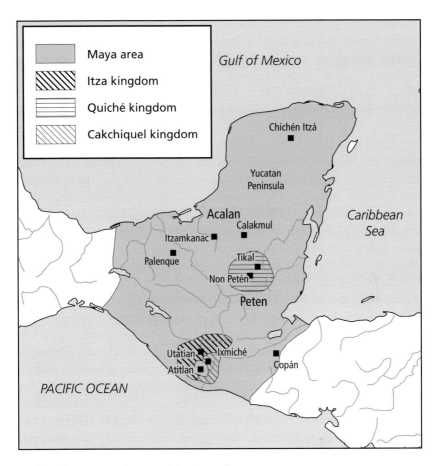

9.2 The Maya area at the turn of the sixteenth century

expanded, for generations (such as the Itzá Mayan kingdom in the Petén region of northern Guatemala, not destroyed by Spaniards until 1697).[9]

In terms of total population, the vast majority of Native Americans living at the time of European contact were sedentary agriculturalists, yet it was

---

[9] On the varied Spanish conquests in the Maya region, see the sources cited in Matthew Restall, *Maya Conquistador* (Boston, MA: Beacon Press, 1998); Matthew Restall and Florine Asselbergs, *Invading Guatemala: Spanish, Nahua, and Maya Accounts of the Conquest Wars* (University Park, PA: Pennsylvania State University Press, 2007); and Matthew Restall, "Invasion: The Maya at War, 1520s–1540s" in Andrew K. Scherer and John W. Verano (eds.), *Embattled Bodies, Embattled Places: Conflict, Conquest, and the Performance of War in Pre-Columbian America* (Washington, DC: Dumbarton Oaks, 2013), pp. 93–117.

semi-sedentary peoples, the third category, who occupied the most territory. Semi-sedentary societies relied only partially on agriculture, requiring them to hunt and forage to meet the remainder of their dietary needs. Semi-sedentary peoples were not nomads, but their subsistence needs and sometimes cultural or religious factors caused them to move to new areas for fresh land. Periodic movement, sometimes over great distances, prevented semi-sedentary peoples from developing dense populations and, since they had to carry their belongings with them, it also reduced the complexity of material culture and craft specialization. Semi-sedentary groups could and did expand. The Tupi, for example, were still moving north along the coast of Brazil when Europeans reached them around 1500. The Tupi planted crops as they moved, and mostly fought with each other, but many other semi-sedentary peoples expanded at the expense of sedentary neighbors, acting partly as parasitical raiders. This seems to have been true of the Caribs, who had expanded from the northern coasts of South America into the southern Caribbean, displacing the Taíno from some islands—a process halted by the arrival of Spaniards and the diseases they brought.[10]

A great number of semi-sedentary peoples occupied two vast portions of the Americas. In the south, groups such as the Lucayans, Taíno, Caribs and Tupi inhabited the Caribbean islands plus eastern and central South America. The Taíno and Lucayans (both an Arawak people) are particularly relevant here, because while the Aztec and Inca Empires expanded and thrived for two to three decades after 1492, the Arawaks suffered invasion, enslavement, epidemic disease and catastrophic demographic decline. Their semi-sedentary character exacerbated the negative impact of the European invasion. Spread across the Greater Antilles, or larger Caribbean islands, the Taíno seem to have been influenced by Mesoamerican civilization; their towns were centered on plazas, featured large ball courts, and housed up to several thousand residents. But such communities lacked the social stratification, political centralization and material complexity of Mesoamerican societies.[11] (For more on the Caribbean, see the chapter by Alan Karras in this volume.)

---

[10] Although note that the long-held view, based on early European observations, that the indigenous peoples of the Caribbean were bifurcated into Taíno or Arawaks and Caribs, has been overturned in recent decades; scholars now believe there were many ethnic groups, "nearly all of them" speakers of "mutually unintelligible" Arawakan languages; Samuel M. Wilson, *The Indigenous People of the Caribbean* (Gainesville, FL: University Press of Florida, 1997), p. 7.

[11] See Wilson, *Indigenous People*; Samuel M. Wilson, *Hispaniola: Caribbean Chiefdoms in the Age of Columbus* (Tuscaloosa, AL: University of Alabama Press, 1990); William F.

To the north, at least half of North America was inhabited by semi-sedentary peoples, with the densest settlements around the Great Lakes, Mississippi basin, Eastern Woodlands and Pacific Northwest. Some semi-sedentary peoples there came close to forming fully sedentary societies. The Ancestral Pueblo of northern New Mexico built substantial adobe and stone dwellings and ritual complexes sustained by maize agriculture, and the Mississippian culture centered on the Cahokia ceremonial site boasted populations in the tens of thousands. Both the Ancestral Pueblo and Mississippian cultures traded with Mesoamericans, but for reasons that remain disputed, their population densities dropped before the arrival of Europeans.

In the Amazon and neighboring Orinoco basins, semi-sedentary and non-sedentary, or nomadic, peoples (the last of the four categories used here) often competed with one another for access to waterways and forests, and some groups went back and forth between the two life ways. Truly non-sedentary peoples were most prevalent in the non-tropical Southern Cone of South America. The same was true in the vast deserts, plains and arctic regions of North America. Although their numbers were small and their material goods relatively modest and portable, the Americas' non-sedentary peoples were everywhere masters of adaptation to demanding environments. Such societies, including the Tehuelche of southern Argentina, were highly mobile, and often followed the seasonal movements of game. Compact, itinerant, hunting bands were typical, and many non-sedentary peoples preyed on sedentary neighbors in times of stress. Nomadic or non-sedentary societies had few material possessions, yet nearly all passed down elaborate oral histories and complex spiritual beliefs. Their medicinal practices, which often drew from long experience with plants, insects and animals, were sometimes sought out by sedentary peoples as well.

Native American settlement patterns and categories might be imagined as concentric circles emanating from two centers. The centers constituted the two core regions of sedentary population—the Andes, with some 15 million people, most within the Inca Empire, and Mesoamerica, with about 30 million people at the time of European contact, most of them in central Mexico. The first circles around them encompassed semi-sedentary peoples, surrounding

Keegan, *Taino Indian Myth and Practice: The Arrival of the Stranger King* (Gainesville, FL: University Press of Florida, 2007); José R. Oliver, *Caciques and Cemí Idols: The Web Spun by Taíno Rulers between Hispaniola and Puerto Rico* (Tuscaloosa, AL: University of Alabama Press, 2009); and Scott M. Fitzpatrick and Ann H. Ross (eds.), *Island Shores, Distant Pasts: Archaeological and Biological Approaches to the Pre-Columbian Settlement of the Caribbean* (Gainesville, FL: University Press of Florida, 2010).

Mesoamerica to the north (North America), to the east (the Caribbean) and to the south (the lower half of Central America), and adjacent to the Andes, to the north and the east. Beyond these were larger circles encompassing non-sedentary peoples, those who dwelt mostly in interior regions of South America and at the most southern and northern edges of the Americas. These circles made up roughly another 20 million people. Thus, the total Native American population at European contact was approximately 65 million, similar to that of Western and Central Europe at that time, and probably not so different from that of Atlantic Africa. The analogy of concentric circles should not be taken to suggest that civilization emanated out from the Inca and Aztec Empires. Nor should the circles be thought of as some sort of judgmental scale, with the core superior and civilized and the outer limits inferior and savage. Instead, it is more useful to think of differences among indigenous groups (and between them and Europeans or Africans) in terms of geographical constraints and opportunities. In short, as elsewhere in the world, Native Americans built the kinds of societies that their environments best sustained.

The Aztecs: a Mesoamerican empire

The broad and deep roots of civilization in the Americas meant that a culture such as that of the Aztecs was merely the latest in a sequence of empires, and the heir to a great regional cultural tradition. This tradition had certain characteristics or defining features, set out below as a list of ten. (For more on Mesomerica in the period 500 to 1500, see the chapter by Michael Smith in Volume V of this book.)

Many Mesoamericans lived in (1) cities that featured monumental urban architecture, in particular pyramidal structures and other impressive buildings facing large, open plazas. The Aztec capital city of Tenochtitlán was a striking example of this phenomenon, and one of the greatest urban achievements in human history. As Gerardo Gutiérrez notes in Volume III of this book, the lacustrine metropolis embodied "the spirit of the Aztecs" and was "the most refined expression of Mesoamerican urbanism."[12] Mesoamerican

[12] Gutiérrez, *Cambridge World History*, vol. v, p. 2; Sanders *et al.*, *Urbanism in Mesoamerica*; Pedro Carrasco, *The Tenochca Empire of Ancient Mexico: The Triple Alliance of Tenochtitlán, Tetzcoco, and Tlacopan* (Norman, OK: University of Oklahoma Press, 1999); Leonardo López Luján, *The Offerings of the Templo Mayor of Tenochtitlan* (Albuquerque, NM: University of New Mexico Press, 2005); Michael S. Smith, *Aztec City-State Capitals* (Gainesville, FL: University Press of Florida, 2008); and a forthcoming book on Tenochtitlán by Barbara Mundy.

cities also tended to contain (2) ball courts and (3) specialized markets, which operated both at local and regional levels. Such markets featured consumer products and material goods of numerous kinds, but (4) included items of particular cultural and economic importance—most notably, jade (used decoratively), obsidian (used decoratively and to create blades for tools and weapons) and cacao (the chocolate seed used sometimes as currency, in bean form, but more widely as a highly prized beverage, in liquid form). More commonly available in markets were the everyday items that formed the basis of the Mesoamerican diet: (5) maize (corn), squash and beans. Of these, maize was the most important, both nutritionally and culturally.

The Mesoamerican world-view (6) was oriented towards two principles, that of the cardinal directions and that of duality (whereby everything in the universe formed part of a pair, such as day and night, life and death, supernatural and natural, and male and female). These principles were also part of (7) Mesoamerica's complex pantheistic religion, which included such features as nature deities, deified royal ancestors, and a multi-tiered heaven and underworld. Not all gods were equal. Among the many deities of the Aztec variant on Mesoamerican pantheism, two were of primary importance, acting as patron deities of the empire: Huitzilopochtli and Tlaloc, the gods of war and water. Atop the Templo Mayor, the great pyramid on Tenochtitlán's plaza, were twin temples to this pair of gods. The Aztecs had probably migrated into Central Mexico in the eleventh or twelfth centuries, and according to Aztec political mythology, Huitzilopochtli had guided the ancestors from northern Lake Aztlán south to Lake Texcoco, where the site of an eagle with a snake in its mouth alighting on a prickly-pear cactus was the divine sign of arrival. On that spot in 1325, according to Aztec tradition, Tenochtitlán was founded.

At times, human communication with the gods involved (8) sacrificial rituals, ranging from the offering of animals to self-sacrificial bloodletting and the ritualized execution of human captives through decapitation or heart removal. The latter has been especially associated with the Aztecs, since Spanish conquistadors witnessed it. It is possible that the Aztecs did indeed develop a more violent, bloody and macabre culture than did their predecessors in Mexico, as many have argued.[13] Or perhaps the exaggerations and value judgments of Spaniards and other Europeans have distorted our view

---

[13] See studies ranging from George C. Vaillant, *Aztecs of Mexico: Origin, Rise and Fall of the Aztec Nation* (Garden City, NY: Doubleday, 1941) to Inga Clendinnen, *Aztecs: An Interpretation* (Cambridge University Press, 1991).

of Aztec human "sacrifice," and that in reality the Aztecs practiced forms and
levels of ritual execution on a scale similar to that of the cultures from which
they inherited such traditions (or, for that matter, on a scale no greater than
that of Europeans at the time). Either way, it seems clear that while
Mesoamericans had ritually executed war captives and other select victims
for millennia, only with the rise of the Aztecs did such executions become
central to imperial expansion and maintenance. Huitzilopochtli was typically
offered the hearts of war captives, whose heads were placed on the skull rack
in the plaza of Tenochtitlán. Much more rarely, Aztec children were sacrificed to the water god Tlaloc, a ritual intended to provoke much sadness and
offerings of tears.

The Aztecs may have believed themselves responsible for carrying out all
these sacrificial rituals in order to maintain cosmic harmony by paying debts
to the gods. If that was true, they were not the only polity to pay such a debt;
the same culture of ritualized violence was shared by other Nahuas (Nahuatl-
speaking peoples of Central Mexico). Aztec neighbors and enemies such as
the Tlaxcalans, for example, also tore the hearts from prisoners of war
atop temple-pyramids. It even appears that such enemies as Tlaxcala and
Tenochtitlán shared larger ritual dramas. According to some sources, conventional warfare between the Aztecs and enemies such as the Tlaxcalans
was sometimes replaced, sometimes supplemented, by the "flowery wars"
(*xochiyaoyotl*), in which scattered red blossoms represented the blood of
warriors and selected warriors were traded as captives to be sacrificed;
casualties in flowery wars died a *xochimiquiztli*, a "flowery death" or "fortunate death" (because it was an honorable way to sacrifice one's life). Tlaxcala
was never conquered, but its inhabitants lived on constant alert, their daily
existence hemmed in and overshadowed by the looming Aztec tributary
apparatus that surrounded them. In the end, Tlaxcalan resentment of Aztec
aggression greatly enabled the Spanish invasion.[14]

Related to religious beliefs, but also to Mesoamerican understandings of
agricultural cycles, was (9) a sophisticated knowledge of the celestial bodies
and their movements. This formed the basis of a complex permutation
calendar that featured a 365-day solar year (like our year), and an additional
cycle of 260 days; the Mayas of the Classic period maintained a long count
(rather like our years, centuries and millennia), but a fifty-two-year cycle was

[14] See Carrasco, *Tenochca Empire*; and Ross Hassig, *Aztec Warfare: Imperial Expansion and
Political Control* (Norman, OK: University of Oklahoma Press, 1988), pp. 7–10, 130,
213 and 256.

the longest calendar tracked by the Aztecs. Calendrical knowledge, religious beliefs and—above all—political and historical records were all carved or written down on materials ranging from fig-bark paper to bone and stone; for Mesoamericans had developed (10) a complex writing system. The system actually comprised three related systems, named (by us) after the three cultures that were maintaining them when the Spaniards invaded: the Aztecs, Mixtecs and Mayas. These systems were partly pictographic and partly syllabic. The most complete system, and the only one that was a fully developed hieroglyphic script, was that of the Mayas, which meant that the literate Maya minority could express anything they wanted in writing. The sophistication and cultural significance of writing also meant that, in the sixteenth century, Nahuas, Mixtecs, Mayas and some other Mesoamerican groups would easily make the transition to the alphabetic writing brought by the Spanish.

One vivid example of Aztec writing and calendrical recording is the extraordinary monolith known to us as the Calendar Stone (Figure 9.1).

Figure 9.1 Aztec Calendar, known as Stone of the Sun, from Tenochtitlán, now in the National Museum of Anthropology and History, Mexico City (De Agostini Picture Library / G. Dagli Orti / Bridgeman Images).

The stone was carved and placed in Tenochtitlán's central plaza, probably during the reign of Moctezuma in the early years of the sixteenth century, although some scholars have suggested it might have been created late in the previous century. In the violent collapse of the city in 1521, the stone was buried, and not discovered again until street-paving workers uncovered it in 1790. At its center is a deity, most likely the monstrous Earth deity, Tlaltecuhtli, representing the Aztec capital's own position as the fearsome, sacred center of the world. Tlaltecuhtli's tongue is carved as a flint knife, the symbol for war in the Aztec writing system. The concentric circles of the image depict the five creations of the world, the twenty day signs that constituted an Aztec month, and a series of icons representing the movement of the sun, indirectly evoking the fifty-two-year calendar. The stone was a political and religious statement about Tenochtitlán's centrality in time and space—and the sacrificial warfare it would take to ensure the sacred role of the city and its rulers.[15]

That role went back almost a century, to 1428, when Itzcoatl, the fourth Aztec king and the first we might reasonably call an emperor, forged an alliance with the lakeside cities of Texcoco and Tlacopan. The city-state that had previously been dominant, Azcapotzalco, was defeated, and the empire was born. That same year, Itzcoatl and his chief minister and general, a nephew named Tlacaelel, collected and burned all hieroglyphic books that recorded the history of the region. That history was then rewritten with the Aztecs at its center, as the heirs to the legacy of the Toltecs (whose city of Tula had dominated the valley four centuries earlier) and as the divinely sanctioned rulers of the known world. The power that emperors would exercise for 100 years over the Aztecs themselves and their neighbors was justified by the claim of privileged access both to the regional great tradition of the Toltecs and to the will of the gods, especially Huitzilopochtli and Tlaloc.

Although a few city-states were able to avoid defeat by the Aztecs and incorporation into their tribute-paying imperial network—most notably Tlaxcala, and the small Tarascan Empire to the west—the Aztecs rapidly came to dominate highland Mexico. Moctezuma Ilhuicamina succeeded his uncle Itzcoatl in 1440, followed by three sons: Axayácatl, Tizoc and Ahuitzotl. At Ahuitzotl's 1486 coronation, visiting rulers from many of the empire's tributary cities (according to an early colonial account) "saw that the Aztecs

[15] See Khristaan D. Villela and Mary Ellen Miller (eds.), *The Aztec Calendar Stone* (Los Angeles, CA: Getty Research Institute, 2010).

were masters of the world, their empire so wide and abundant that they had conquered all the nations and that all were their vassals. The guests, seeing such wealth and opulence and such authority and power, were filled with terror."[16]

The last independent Aztec emperor, an aggressive and able ruler, was the namesake grandson of the first Moctezuma, Moctezuma Xocoyotl. This second Moctezuma consolidated and extended the empire from 1502 until 1520, when he was murdered by Spanish invaders or (according to most Spanish accounts) by his own people. Despite his numerous successes as a ruler, Moctezuma Xocoyotl would be blamed by both Spaniards and Nahuas for his empire's demise. The emperor became a scapegoat, and his alleged speech of surrender became an accepted fact. History's Moctezuma thus became a myth, a caricature of ineptitude.

The Incas: an Andean empire

Are there coincidences in history? At the same time that the Aztecs were forging their empire in Central Mexico, the Incas were developing theirs in Peru. Yet, there is no evidence that Mesoamericans and Andeans knew of each other's existence, just as empires in other parts of the world developed in isolation from one another.

In 1438, a secondary Inca prince named Cusi Yupanqui repelled an attempt by his neighbors, the Chancas, to seize control of the Inca capital of Cuzco and surrounding territory. Exultant, Cusi Yupanqui forced his father to retire and took the Inca crown, with its distinctive fringe, from the designated heir. The first true Inca emperor, Yupanqui renamed himself Pachacuti, which means "world-changer" or "time-turner." The new emperor quickly established a mythological history that seemed to predict his arrival and also justified his aggressive vision of the future. Pachacuti reorganized the Inca system of rule from one centered on stability and reproduction to one that sought to encompass as much territory and as many subjects as possible. The justification for Inca expansion was ethnocentric but not unusual: Pachacuti claimed he wanted to "civilize" all Andean peoples after the Inca fashion.[17]

---

[16] See Carrasco, *Tenochca Empire*; Hassig, *Aztec Warfare*; and Susan D. Gillespie, *The Aztec Kings: The Construction of Rulership in Mexico's History* (Tucson, AZ: University of Arizona Press, 1989).

[17] See Catherine Julien, *Reading Inca History* (Iowa City, IA: University of Iowa Press, 2000); and Alan L. Kolata, *Ancient Inca* (Cambridge University Press, 2013), pp. 28–48.

(For more on the Inca state, see the chapter by Sabine MacCormack in Volume V of this book.)

In fact, the Incas were heirs to the great tradition of civilization in the central Andes. They were not outside invaders, but a Cuzco-based, Quechua-speaking people who conquered and administered what they called Tawantinsuyu, or the Union of the Four Quarters. ("Inca" was the emperor's title, a term we now use for the whole empire.) By the 1520s, the Inca Empire was far larger than the Aztec one had been – perhaps four times as large (see Map 9.3).[18] Its capital of Cuzco was smaller than Tenochtitlán, however, although its role as a sacred center to the empire (and the world) was similar.[19]

The Incas may be compared with the Aztecs on the ten points noted above. Like Mesoamerican urban centers, Andean cities (1) were also carefully planned and oriented, and they contained similarly oriented stone or adobe temples of great size, some of them pyramidal, but more often U-shaped. As in Mesoamerica (and unlike ancient Egypt), the enormous monuments served as stages for religious-political drama rather than personal sepulchers for elites. There were (2) no ball courts to compare to those in Mesoamerica. But Andean cities were (3) places of material exchange and craft specialization. Items traded over great distances included (4) *Spondylus* and other marine shells, salt, fine textiles, and a variety of utilitarian and decorative metal items.[20] Andean metallurgy was in fact far more advanced and widespread than that of Mesoamerica; long before the rise of the Incas one finds arsenical bronze tools, copper currency, and even platinum jewelry.[21]

It is worth noting here one important difference between Inca and Aztec Empires: the migration of peoples within the empire and the role played by such movements in the empire's creation and maintenance. The Incas were like the Aztecs in quickly growing their empire by using threats and strategic alliances to augment violent military conquests. But once subject peoples

---

[18] See Brian S. Bauer, *The Development of the Inca State* (Austin, TX: University of Texas Press, 1992); Michael A. Malpass, *Daily Life in the Inca Empire* (Westport, CT: Greenwood Press, 1996); Terence N. D'Altroy, *The Incas* (Malden, MA: Blackwell, 2002); Gordon F. McEwan, *The Incas: New Perspectives* (Santa Barbara, CA: ABC-CLIO, 2006); and Kolata, *Ancient Inca*.

[19] On Cuzco, see Brian S. Bauer, *Ancient Cuzco: Heartland of the Inca* (Austin, TX: University of Texas Press, 2004); Craig Morris and Adriana Von Hagen, *The Incas: Lord of the Four Quarters* (London: Thames & Hudson, Ltd., 2011), pp. 102–32; and Kolata, *Ancient Inca*, pp. 45–8 and 58–71.

[20] Kolata, *Ancient Inca*, p. 226.

[21] McEwan, *The Incas*, pp. 161–78; and Morris and Von Hagen, *The Incas*, pp. 48–64.

were conquered, the Incas favored centralized control over the indirect rule and tribute-collecting mechanism used by the Aztecs. Inca rule was distinct from that of the Aztecs in at least four ways. The Incas exacted tribute, but more in the form of labor rather than goods. The imperial labor system, or *mita* (in Quechuan, *mit'a*—literally "turn," a system revived under Spanish colonial rule), required local farmers to work lands taken over by the Inca state as well as their own plots. Male subjects also had to rotate into the Inca army and serve in various construction levies.[22] Rotational labor systems existed in Central Mexico, such as the *coatequitl* draft (literally "snake-work," because the labor draft circled in turn to each of a town's neighborhoods, symbolized by a snake curled up in a circle). But these were not run by imperial officials or formalized for long-term purposes.[23]

Mita workers supplied labor for the empire's extensive, 14,000-mile network of royal roads (a system that had no Aztec equivalent) (see Map 9.3). The Inca road, or *capac ñan*, included everything from broad desert avenues to grass-fiber suspension bridges spanning mountain gorges. The bridges had to be strong enough to sustain relay messengers, llama herds, streams of tribute-bearing porters and even armies. The road system also included a series of carefully located inns and warehouses. Stored goods were used to feed mita workers, supply troops and keep luxury goods flowing to the wealthy Inca elite. The road system also facilitated the forced migration of entire communities—a technique of imperial and labor control used increasingly by the Incas to build public works projects or defend frontiers. The Incas officially required migrant communities to keep their original identities, but they also demanded that all subjects use the Quechua language for exchanges and imperial affairs. All this had an impact on the look and function of urban spaces. Inca cities and towns tended to be more polyglot and multiethnic than those within the Aztec empire. But unlike the Aztecs, with their large marketplaces dominated by regional traders, the Incas managed most exchanges at the state level in a redistributive way, suppressing free market activity.[24]

Continuing with the ten-point comparison: (5) the Andean diet varied considerably, but generally consisted of potatoes and other high-altitude tubers, maize, beans, squash and capsicum peppers. At lower altitudes,

---

[22] Kolata, *Ancient Inca*, pp. 104–21.
[23] The *coatequitl* did become more formalized, however, in the Spanish colonial period; see, e.g., Rebecca Horn, *Postconquest Coyoacan: Nahua-Spanish Relations in Central Mexico, 1519–1650* (Stanford University Press, 1997), pp. 39–42, 91, 101–7 and 230.
[24] Kolata, *Ancient Inca*, pp. 139–45.

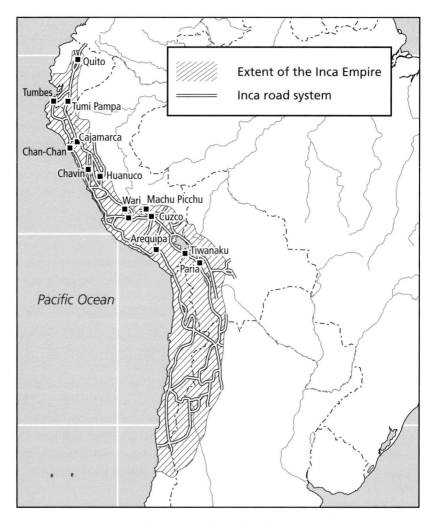

Quito

Tumbes
Tumi Pampa

Cajamarca
Chan-Chan

Chavin   Huanuco

Wari Machu Picchu
          Cuzco

Arequipa
              Tiwanaku
        Paria

Pacific Ocean

	Extent of the Inca Empire
	Inca road system

9.3 The Inca Empire and road system

manioc, seafood and freshwater fish were equally important. Guinea pigs, or
cuyes, and llamas, the only domesticated animal of any size in the Americas,
were eaten on special occasions. Tobacco was sometimes employed in ritual
healing ceremonies, but from Colombia to Chile, mildly stimulating coca
leaves and maize beer were the preferred stimulants. Intensive agriculture
entailed complex terraces, long aqueducts and extensive raised fields. These
human-constructed features in the landscape, along with many natural ones,

were—like the ubiquitous ancestor mummies of the Andes, a cultural phenomenon inherited and maintained by the Incas—regarded as deeply sacred.

Unlike that of Mesoamerica, the Andean world-view tended to conceive of the landscape in (6) radial rather than strictly cardinal terms. Surviving temples contain sculptures of fierce, semi-human feline and reptilian creatures, suggesting (7) religious themes still evident in lowland South American shamanism. Religion and politics were not separate concerns, however, as Andean temples from the earliest to latest times were clearly sites of (8) ritualized human execution (like their counterparts in Mesoamerica). Some Inca sacrificial practices have inevitably drawn modern attention—most notably the depositing of children to die of exposure in high altitude locations, such as Aconcagua, the hemisphere's tallest mountain. Nonetheless, human sacrifice was practiced on a relatively small scale, both generally speaking in Andean societies and specifically by the Incas.[25]

Like Mesoamericans, Andeans gave considerable attention—and mythic weight—to (9) astronomical phenomena. However, Andean peoples appear not to have developed writing systems of the traditional kind, instead employing (10) knotted strings, called quipus (khipus), which they used to record numbers, lineages and possibly some historical events. Runners, carrying quipus, used the road system to relay information across thousands of miles with amazing speed.[26]

The net effect of the structural development of Inca imperialism was a kingdom that stretched from what is today northern Chile to Ecuador. It was on Tawantinsuyu's northern frontier, near the modern Ecuador–Colombia border, where the Inca Huayna Capac was told of an epidemic sweeping through the empire. The year was 1525, and the emperor was told that the new illness was already ravaging the capital of Cuzco. Within a few years, possibly in 1527, the disease seems to have killed the Inca himself. Although descriptions of the symptoms are hazy, and were only related to the Spanish after the conquest, this was probably the first wave of smallpox to penetrate South America. It had most likely begun with the arrival of Europeans in the region of what is now Buenos Aires. The disease also appears to have killed Huayna Capac's preferred heir—all this before a single Spaniard set foot in Tawantinsuyu. The deaths produced a succession crisis between two brothers, Atawallpa and Huascar, sons of Huayna Capac by different mothers. Their feud soon grew into a full-blown civil war, splitting the Inca Empire in

[25] McEwan, The Incas, pp. 137–59; and Morris and Von Hagen, The Incas, pp. 230–3.
[26] Kolata, Ancient Inca, pp. 89–93.

half. When Francisco Pizarro sought to conquer the Incas in 1532, he had epidemic disease and internal division on his side.

More danger than profit: the Spanish Caribbean

"This Empire consisted not so much in any Thing real, as in the Hopes they had conceived from several Discoveries and Inroads made by some of our Captains with various Success, but more Danger than Profit."[27] Thus did Antonio de Solís sum up the Spanish possessions in the Caribbean prior to the Spanish discovery of the Aztecs and Incas. Writing almost two centuries later, as the official chronicler of the conquests, Solís captured the perception by Spaniards—which had deepened with hindsight—of the chasm between expectations and the reality of colonization in the early Caribbean.

What were those expectations, and how did they shape the Spanish Empire in the Americas before the meeting between Moctezuma and Cortés? European and indigenous societies are generally compared on different terms, but they may also be compared on the same terms, within the framework of the ten characteristics used above. I use the shorthand term "Spaniards," but my broad frame of reference is Iberian civilization in the fifteenth and sixteenth centuries, and my narrower subject is the experience of Spaniards (and small numbers of Portuguese and Italians) in the Caribbean from the 1490s to the 1510s.

We begin again with cities. Spaniards prized (1) monumental urban architecture as much as Aztecs, Mayas and Incas did. It was equally essential to their sense of political and religious ritual and the ordering of society. Although Spanish cities did not have stone ball courts (2), the use of stone for other buildings was symbolically important, and stone buildings tended to face and define ceremonial plazas.[28]

However, the kinds of cities Spaniards were to find on the mainland—with urban spaces like Tenochtitlán and Cuzco not just meeting but surpassing their expectations—were not to be found among the Taíno. Nor did the early decades of the colonial Caribbean economy support the construction of more

[27] Here I have used Thomas Townsend's 1724 English translation of Solís: Thomas Townsend (trans.), *History of the Conquest of Mexico by the Spaniards* (London: Printed for T. Woodward, J. Hooke and J. Peele, 1724), pp. 11–12 (copy in John Carter Brown Library).
[28] Spanish urbanism has been broadly studied, but a good starting point, especially as it emphasizes Spanish American cities, is Richard L. Kagan, *Urban Images of the Hispanic World, 1493–1793* (New Haven, CT: Yale University Press, 2000).

than the palest, small-scale imitations of a Spanish city. Indeed, the first European "city" created in the Americas lasted less than five years; founded by Columbus in 1493 and named La Isabela, after the queen of Castile, it was located on the coast of Hispaniola adjacent to a Taíno village.[29]

Bartolomé de las Casas wrote later of the Spaniards' gratitude to God for giving them a "very fertile and beautiful" place to plant their city.[30] Columbus saw it as a base for regional expansion and trade with Asia (which he believed was close by), and a capital city for the governorship that he would pass on to his descendants. But rather than transform a Taíno village into a regional capital city, La Isabela merely destroyed the village. By 1500, its handful of brick buildings were abandoned and Columbus was under arrest and shipped back to Spain. A new capital, Santo Domingo, fared better, but in its early decades came nowhere close to the Spanish urban ideal. When, in 1518, Judge Alonso de Zuazo reported to the king on the modest nature of the Hispaniola colony, there was a stone church and some stone houses in Santo Domingo, but otherwise in the city and throughout the island, "there are only houses of straw . . . like a poor village in Spain."[31]

Within their cities, Spaniards, like Aztecs and Incas, expected to see (3) the flourishing of specialized markets, in which a wide variety of goods were exchanged. That meant not just local products and foodstuffs, but also (4) items whose cultural significance imbued them with particular value. While the Aztecs and other Mesoamericans prized jade, obsidian and cacao, and Andean peoples fine textiles and worked metal objects, rare and high-value goods sought by Spaniards included fine textiles, precious stones and spices, but above all—and in the earliest stages of exploration and conquest almost exclusively—precious metals. Gold and silver were non-perishable, easily transported and divided, and underpinned the European-Mediterranean economy. By the turn of the sixteenth century, Iberians were already accustomed to finding West African merchants willing to trade gold, ivory, pepper and slaves for textiles, horses, ironware and other goods. However, the Spaniards in the Caribbean found no merchants or markets to compare with those of

[29] See Kathleen Deagan and José María Cruxent, *Columbus's Outpost among the Taínos: Spain and America at La Isabela, 1493–1498* (New Haven, CT: Yale University Press, 2002).

[30] From Las Casas, *History of the Indies*, quoted in Restall and Lane, *Latin America in Colonial Times*, p. 58.

[31] Zuazo's letter of January 1518 is reproduced in Joaquín Francisco Pacheco, Francisco de Cárdenas y Espejo and Luis Torres de Mendoza (eds.), *Colección de documentos inéditos relativos al descubrimiento, conquista y colonización de las posesiones españoles en América y Oceania* (Madrid: Madrid Imprenta de Manuel B. de Quirós, 1864), vol. i, p. 311.

West Africa or the sedentary societies of the American mainland. The Taíno did not trade in luxury commodities or in slaves. They did possess some gold, but they used wood and stone tools, and were local-minded subsistence farmers and fishing folk, not habitual consumers or producers of exports. Frustrated by their failure to mold the Taíno on Hispaniola into cooperative colonial subjects, the Spaniards resorting to slave raiding and plundering as they moved from island to island—to Puerto Rico in 1508, Jamaica in 1509 and Cuba in 1511 (see Map 9.4). Efforts to impose Spanish systems of rule and economic exploitation foundered or met with open resistance; massacres occurred, and local agriculture was disrupted or destroyed.[32]

The first generations of Europeans in the Americas were amazed by (5) the variety of unfamiliar foods, plants and herbs. But despite that amazement, and the early appreciation of some indigenous foods by some Spaniards, the newcomers were generally slow to value or adopt local staples such as manioc and maize—generally derided as "Indian food." Latin America's new regional cuisines took many generations to develop. Spaniards in the early Caribbean took what food they needed or wanted from the Taíno, but they also initiated, beginning in the 1490s, the process of importing whatever domestic animals and food crops they could. Cattle were especially important to Spaniards—for dairy products, meat and leather goods—and cattle ranching was already fairly well developed on Hispaniola and Cuba by 1519. Cortés was, in fact, a cattle rancher in Cuba in the 1510s. Pigs flourished too; Cuba's conqueror and first governor, Diego de Velázquez, told the king in 1514 that the swine brought to the island in the conquest campaign of a few years earlier already numbered some 30,000.[33]

In terms of their (6) world-view and (7) religion, Spaniards in the early Caribbean brought with them a deep-rooted sense of ethnic and cultural superiority, bolstered by an aggressively exclusionist monotheistic faith. Their god, Dios, was the only God, albeit manifested in the Holy Trinity and the cult of saints in ways that would strike Native Americans as familiarly pantheistic. Following the model of recent conquest and colonization in Granada and the Canary Islands, Spaniards believed that God had guided them to settle and rule the New World; the papal grant of 1493, whereby Pope Alexander VI "donated" the Americas to the Iberians, confirmed that

---

[32] Wilson, *Hispaniola*, pp. 74–142.
[33] Hugh Thomas, *Conquest: Montezuma, Cortés, and the Fall of Old Mexico* (New York: Touchstone, 1995), pp. 68 and 133; and the chapter by Alan Karras, "The Caribbean region: crucible for modern world history" in this volume.

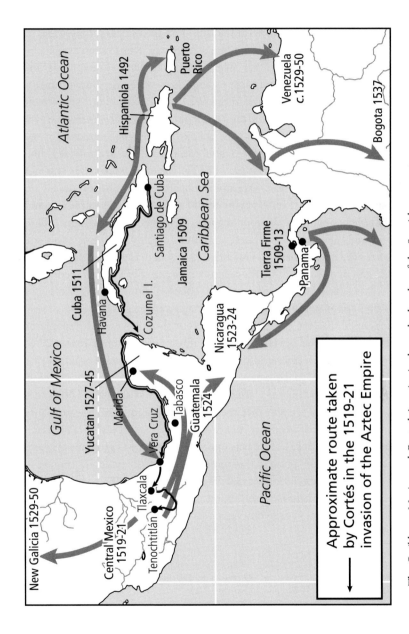

Atlantic Ocean

Hispaniola 1492

Puerto Rico

Venezuela c.1529-50

Bogota 1537

Cuba 1511

Santiago de Cuba

Caribbean Sea

Jamaica 1509

Tierra Firme 1509-13

Havana

Panama

Gulf of Mexico

Cozumel I.

Nicaragua 1523-24

Yucatan 1527-45

Mérida

Tabasco

Guatemala 1524

Vera Cruz

Pacific Ocean

New Galicia 1529-50

Tlaxcala

Central Mexico 1519-21

Tenochtitlán

Approximate route taken by Cortés in the 1519-21 invasion of the Aztec Empire

9.4 The Caribbean, Mexico and Central America in the early decades of the Spanish conquests

233

conviction. Each new province discovered and conquered was to be part of a new kingdom, making the Spanish Empire the sum of all its kingdoms; the Caribbean islands were eventually part of the viceroyalty or kingdom of New Spain, the first new kingdom in the Americas.

Spaniards expected that the conquered local peoples would be converted to Christianity, allocated to work on the land or in the mines, and required to pay tribute (a basic head tax) to the Spanish crown. This system was to be administered by Spanish settlers, who were as crucial to the imagined colonies as converted local subjects. As Francisco López de Gómara put it in his history of the early empire in Spanish America, "without settlement there is no good conquest, and if the land is not conquered, the people will not be converted."[34] This essentially medieval European model for an American empire failed in the early Caribbean even more dramatically than La Isabela had foundered in the 1490s, and for the same reasons: it was not well suited to the region and its native peoples. The Taíno produced no significant surpluses for tribute payment, did not use gold as currency, and had no experience with harsh labor regimes or religious persecution. These gaping cultural differences frustrated ambitious, wealth-seeking Spanish settlers to no end, leading them to violently enslave native peoples throughout the Caribbean in order to force them into a recognizably Western economic system. Mass enslavement soon proved counterproductive. World-views clashed. The Taíno population collapsed.

Demographic disaster in the Caribbean was shocking even to Spaniards at the time. Bartolomé de las Casas, the most vocal Spanish defender of indigenous peoples in the era of contact and conquest, estimated that Hispaniola was home to between 1 and 4 million Taíno when Columbus first reached the island in 1492. The real number was probably close to 1 million, but Las Casas's claim that the Taíno population had fallen 90 percent by the mid-sixteenth century is more or less accepted today. The friar's claim, however, that this decline was entirely due to the "egregious wickedness" of the Spaniards ignored the massive impact of epidemic disease—a factor not fully grasped by Spaniards at the time. Most likely, most Taíno deaths were from smallpox, measles or influenza. Nonetheless, conquest violence, displacement, enslavement, overwork and other brutal colonial

---

[34] From López de Gómara, *Historia General de las Indias* (Madrid: Impr. de la Real academia de la historia, 1852), p. 181 (first published in 1553) in J. H. Elliott (trans.), *Spain, Europe, and the Wider World, 1500–1800* (New Haven, CT: Yale University Press, 2009).

impositions certainly played a central role in devastating the Caribbean's native populations.[35] The Spaniards did not consider themselves to practice anything like the (8) ritual executions or human sacrifices of the Aztecs and other native groups. Yet, their violent efforts to impose their world-view in the Caribbean—not to mention the ritual executions later carried out in the mainland colonies by the Spanish Inquisition—must have struck indigenous people as horrifyingly brutal in the way that Aztec heart-sacrifice stunned conquistador witnesses.

The final two points of civilizational comparison—(9) planetary and calendrical knowledge and (10) writing systems—do not need explanation, but it is worth making the following observation: The European understanding of the night skies and resulting navigational technology of the fifteenth century, combined with alphabetic writing and the recently developed technology of printing, allowed the Spaniards to reach the Caribbean islands and communicate what they learned about its natural and human environment. In other words, they made the Spanish presence possible. It is highly debatable, however, whether they made conquest and colonization possible. Claims that literacy gave Spaniards a decisive advantage are not, in my view, persuasive.[36]

Imperial afterlives

Imagining the three empires of the Americas as they stood in the 1510s, and casting a comparative eye from one to the other, a conundrum emerges. The Aztec and Inca Empires appear as impressive examples of expansionist imperialism, driven by powerful political-religious ideologies and institutions of central control, supported by adaptable and deeply rooted organizational systems, arguably yet to reach their apex, let alone their decline. In contrast, the Spanish Empire in the Caribbean seems to be in a constant struggle, undermined from the very onset by the contradictions between colonial expectations and the realities of the natural and human environment on the islands. Paradoxically, the early Spanish Caribbean both lacked a center (despite a series of small capitals, no imperial metropolis emerged in the

---

[35] Bartolomé de Las Casas, *An Account, Much Abbreviated, of the Destruction of the Indies*, Franklin Knight (ed.), Andrew Hurley (trans.) (Indianapolis, IN: Hackett, 2003); and Noble David Cook, *Born to Die: Disease and the New World Conquest, 1492–1650* (New York: Cambridge University Press, 1998). For an argument against the assumption that the indigenous population on Puerto Rico collapsed completely, see Tony Castanha, *The Myth of Indigenous Caribbean Extinction: Continuity and Reclamation in Borikén (Puerto Rico)* (New York: Palgrave Macmillan, 2011).
[36] For a brief discussion of these claims, see Restall, *Seven Myths*, pp. 90–3 and 137–9.

islands as a large and dynamic controlling hub) and simultaneously suffered from too much of a center (Spain itself dominated, and yet was so distant). So, therefore, why was it the marginalized failure-of-an-empire that expanded to destroy the two aggressively successful ones?

This, of course, is a version of the question that has been raised and answered—usually in simplistic and misleading ways—for the past five centuries (how was the Spanish Conquest possible?). Let us dispense with the traditional explanations (the Spaniards had God on their side; European civilization was more sophisticated than that of native peoples; European technology was superior),[37] and focus on a nexus of explanations tied to the themes of this chapter.

First, the paradox of the absent yet distant center meant that Spanish colonialism in the Caribbean had either to collapse completely or find itself a local center capable of supporting regional empire. That it found that center in 1519—on November 8, the day of Cortés's thwarted embrace of Moctezuma—was not as inevitable as is usually assumed. Had the Spanish presence in the Caribbean been truly dynamic, well funded and driven hard from Spain, that center—and the subsequent imperial center in South America— would have been found years, even decades, earlier. But it was not dynamic, and it would not have been surprising had the Spanish Caribbean limped on for another decade or so, unaware of the Aztecs and Incas—with Spain increasingly distracted by territorial and religious conflict in Europe, Cortés and his generation leading mediocre lives on the colonial margins, while the Aztecs expanded into Mayan kingdoms and the Incas consolidated their hold on the Andes. However, once imperial centers in the Americas were found, the existence of Spain as a distant but dominant center became crucial. The mechanisms of imperial control were fully activated. The three separate spheres of the 1510s disappeared. The trunk lines that carried administrators, migrants, African slaves, fungible goods and merchandise and precious metals, ideas and beliefs, quickly developed to link the three centers: Madrid and Seville; Tenochtitlán-Mexico; Cuzco and Lima. The Caribbean ceased to be merely the margins and gave up its weak attempt to be a center, instead becoming an all-important link in the imperial chain—a position cemented by its geographical location and the wind systems of the Atlantic Ocean.

---

[37] Such explanations can be found both proposed and criticized, in historical literature stretching from conquistador reports up to the very present; one might begin with the summaries in Restall, *Seven Myths*, pp. 131–40; Matthew Restall and Felipe Fernández-Armesto, *The Conquistadors: A Very Brief Introduction* (Oxford University Press, 2011); and Restall and Lane, *Latin America in Colonial Times*, pp. 88–9 and 102–5.

Second, the very failure of the early Spanish Caribbean led to continued Spanish exploration of the circum-Caribbean. This point is closely related to the one just made, but here I mean failure in terms more specifically of the Spanish relationship to the region's native peoples. A "good conquest," as López de Gómara put it, was understood by Spaniards to mean pacification, settlement, and conversion—a peaceful transition to a colonial life that required both indigenous subjects and Spanish settlers.[38] It is true that, almost from the start, the colonial model allowed for the interpolation of black African slaves and their descendants into its middle, and that African slaves would come to replace the indigenous population of the islands. But the early sixteenth century was too soon for that pattern to be clearly seen by contemporaries, nor would it have necessarily been perceived as a solution. In short, Spaniards needed people, local people, sedentary people; they needed Mesoamericans and Andeans.

As mentioned earlier, a primary—arguably *the* primary—cause of native demographic collapse was disease, the lethal epidemiological side to the Columbian Exchange. This, the third explanatory factor, led to the extinction of indigenous populations on most Caribbean islands, with disease spreading to the mainland faster than Europeans did. While fatal illnesses cannot alone explain the Spanish conquests, there is no doubt that the outbreak of epidemics shortly before or during Spanish invasions had a negative effect on indigenous abilities to resist—and motivated elites to seek to accommodate the newcomers sooner than they otherwise might have.

Fourth, and finally, the impression that I have given above of the Spaniards of the Caribbean moving on to destroy the Aztec and Inca Empires is misleading. Certainly, the Caribbean and circum-Caribbean was a staging ground for mainland conquests, central to the chain or stepping-stone system of conquest. The years that Cortés spent in Hispaniola and Cuba before going to Mexico, like those spent by Francisco Pizarro in Panama before going to Peru, made them more typical than the minority of conquistadors who came directly from Spain (like Gonzalo Jiménez de Quesada). However, every Spanish encounter with indigenous groups and kingdoms expanded the conquest cast of characters, permitting the complex participation of some native elites and polities in the process of expansion and colonization.

---

[38] For what is arguably a book-length discussion of how López de Gómara and his compatriots viewed "good conquest," see Cristián A. Roa-de-la-Carrera, *Histories of Infamy: Francisco López de Gómara and the Ethics of Spanish Imperialism* (Boulder, CO: University Press of Colorado, 2005).

The workings and implications of the phenomenon are complex—their analysis arguably underpins the recent wave of scholarship sometimes called the New Conquest History[39]—but for our purposes three factors can be identified.

Factor one: most of the people directly involved in the conquest wars were indigenous. The majority of conquest fighting was done by indigenous warriors, and the support personnel—spies, porters, cooks and so on—were also native. As is now well known, Spanish conquistadors were outnumbered not just by enemy forces, but by their own, invaluable, indigenous allies.[40]

Factor two: Spaniards did not so much destroy the Aztec and Inca Empires as appropriate them. In 1521, for example, while Tenochtitlán was in ruins and the Aztec leadership was mostly dead or captive, the empire's framework of trade routes, tribute lists and diplomatic relations between ruling families remained in place. In the 1520s and 1530s, Spaniards, accompanied by Aztec and other native warriors, used the same chain of conquest that the Aztecs had developed in previous decades. The Aztec Empire was turned into New Spain, often through the non-violent negotiation and confirmation of prior political and tribute arrangements; in some cases, Spaniards were not even present when these initial confirmations were made. In addition to reconfirming the Aztec Empire, the Spanish and indigenous creators of New Spain also expanded it. They began by invading regions that the Aztecs had already attempted to subdue, or had planned to, and likely would have attacked according to a similar timetable had the Spaniards not yet arrived—most notably, the Tarascans and the Mayas of highland Guatemala and northern Yucatan.[41] A slightly different, but similar, pattern emerged in Peru in the wake of Pizarro's capture of the Inca capital of Cuzco in 1534. The Inca Empire was in disarray, but its structure was intact, and an incumbent emperor, the Inca Manco Capac, was recognized by the conquistadors. Again, the Spaniards were only able to create a colony in Peru and the Andes by appropriating, not destroying, what the Incas had built. The complex imperial networks of the

---

[39] Matthew Restall, "The New Conquest History," *History Compass* 10 (2012), 151–60, http://history-compass.com/caribbean-latin-america.

[40] Laura E. Matthew and Michel R. Oudijk (eds.), *Indian Conquistadors: Indigenous Allies in the Conquest of Mesoamerica* (Norman, OK: University of Oklahoma Press, 2007).

[41] Michel R. Oudijk and Matthew Restall, "Mesoamerican Conquistadors in the Sixteenth Century" in Matthew and Oudijk, *Indian Conquistadors*, pp. 28–64; and Michel R. Oudijk and Matthew Restall, *Conquista de Buenas Palabras y de Guerra: una visión indígena de la conquista* (Mexico City: UNAM, 2014).

Figure 9.2 The execution of the Inca Tupac Amaru in 1571, by order of the Spanish
Viceroy of Peru, lamented by watching Andean nobles. Facsimile of a drawing by
Felipe Guaman Poma from his *El Primer Nueva Coronica y Buen Gobierno* (Universal
Images Group / photograph by Werner Forman / Getty Images).

Aztecs and Incas were exactly the kind of thing the Spaniards had sought and needed, but not found, in the Caribbean.

Manco Capac takes us to the third factor constituting the process whereby native protagonists played active, Complex roles in the conquest: Manco symbolized the simple fact that the Spanish Conquest did not end as suddenly and completely as Spaniards claimed. Elsewhere, I have characterized this theme as "the myth of completion" and "the incomplete conquest," and articulated various elements and manifestations.[42] Here, let us take the example of the Incas, and use it to conclude the chapter.

Manco Inca was later derided by Spaniards as a puppet of Pizarro. But Andeans saw him as the legitimate ruler, and his son Titu Cusi Yupanqui— who succeeded him as Inca—insisted that Manco had been the legitimate emperor since before Spaniards reached the Andes.[43] Manco almost succeeded in expelling the Spanish interlopers in 1536. He failed and was driven south down the Urubamba River. But in the wet lowlands at Vilcabamba, he was able to maintain a modest version of the Inca state, where he and his sons ruled until 1572, when the Inca Túpac Amaru was captured and executed (see Figure 9.2). Nonetheless, large portions of the Andes remained outside Spanish control for centuries, while the Inca nobility maintained status and privilege within the Viceroyalty of Peru.[44]

Long gone, then, was that brief era of unwitting, parallel imperial lives— the age of indigenous empires in the Americas, when, for a quarter-century, a foreign empire was born and struggled to survive in the hemisphere. But the two indigenous empires that were partially destroyed and profoundly transformed after the 1520s and 1530s had afterlives. Aztec and Inca imperial stories of triumph and tragedy persisted within the forms of New Spain and Spanish Peru.

FURTHER READING

Bauer, Brian S., *Ancient Cuzco: Heartland of the Inca* (Austin, TX: University of Texas Press, 2004).
Carrasco, Pedro, *The Tenochca Empire of Ancient Mexico: The Triple Alliance of Tenochtitlán, Tetzcoco, and Tlacopan* (Norman, OK: University of Oklahoma Press, 1999).

[42] Restall, *Seven Myths*, pp. 64–76; and Restall and Lane, *Latin America in Colonial Times*, pp. 109–28.
[43] Julien, *Reading Inca History*, pp. 41–6; Restall and Fernández-Armesto, *Conquistadors*, pp. 33–6; and Kolata, *Ancient Inca*, pp. 260–3.
[44] Julien, *Reading Inca History*; and David T. Garrett, *Shadows of Empire: The Indian Nobility of Cusco, 1750–1825* (Cambridge University Press, 2005).

Clendinnen, Inga, *Aztecs: An Interpretation* (Cambridge University Press, 1991).

Cook, Noble David, *Born to Die: Disease and the New World Conquest, 1492–1650* (New York: Cambridge University Press, 1998).

D'Altroy, Terence N., *The Incas* (Malden, MA: Blackwell, 2002).

Deagan, Kathleen and José María Cruxent, *Columbus's Outpost among the Taínos: Spain and America at La Isabela, 1493–1498* (New Haven, CT: Yale University Press, 2002).

Díaz del Castillo, Bernal, *The History of the Conquest of New Spain*, Davíd Carrasco (ed.) (Albuquerque, NM: University of New Mexico Press, 2009).

Fitzpatrick, Scott M. and Ann H. Ross (eds.), *Island Shores, Distant Pasts: Archaeological and Biological Approaches to the Pre-Columbian Settlement of the Caribbean* (Gainesville, FL: University Press of Florida, 2010).

Gillespie, Susan D., *The Aztec Kings: The Construction of Rulership in Mexico's History* (Tucson, AZ: University of Arizona Press, 1989).

Hassig, Ross, *Aztec Warfare: Imperial Expansion and Political Control* (Norman, OK: University of Oklahoma Press, 1988).

Julien, Catherine, *Reading Inca History* (Iowa City, IA: University of Iowa Press, 2000).

Keegan, William F., *Taíno Indian Myth and Practice: The Arrival of the Stranger King* (Gainesville, FL: University Press of Florida, 2007).

Kolata, Alan L., *Ancient Inca* (Cambridge University Press, 2013).

Las Casas, Bartolomé de, *An Account, Much Abbreviated, of the Destruction of the Indies*, Franklin Knight (ed.), Andrew Hurley (trans.) (Indianapolis, IN: Hackett, 2003).

López Luján, Leonardo, *The Offerings of the Templo Mayor of Tenochtitlan* (Albuquerque, NM: University of New Mexico Press, 2005).

Matthew, Laura E. and Michel R. Oudijk (eds.), *Indian Conquistadors: Indigenous Allies in the Conquest of Mesoamerica* (Norman, OK: University of Oklahoma Press, 2007).

McEwan, Gordon F., *The Incas: New Perspectives* (Santa Barbara, CA: ABC-CLIO, 2006).

Morris, Craig and Adriana Von Hagen, *The Incas: Lord of the Four Quarters* (London: Thames & Hudson, Ltd., 2011).

Oliver, José R., *Caciques and Cemí Idols: The Web Spun by Taíno Rulers between Hispaniola and Puerto Rico* (Tuscaloosa, AL: University of Alabama Press, 2009).

Oudijk, Michel R. and Matthew Restall, *Conquista de Buenas Palabras y de Guerra: una visión indígena de la conquista* (Mexico City: UNAM, 2014).

Pagden, Anthony, *Hernán Cortés: Letters from Mexico* (New Haven, CT: Yale University Press, 1986).

Restall, Matthew, *Maya Conquistador* (Boston, MA: Beacon Press, 1998).

"The New Conquest History," *History Compass* 10 (2012), 151–60, http://history-compass.com/caribbean-latin-america.

Seven Myths of the Spanish Conquest (New York: Oxford University Press, 2003).

Restall, Matthew and Florine Asselbergs, *Invading Guatemala: Spanish, Nahua, and Maya Accounts of the Conquest Wars* (University Park, PA: Pennsylvania State University Press, 2007).

Restall, Matthew and Felipe Fernández-Armesto, *The Conquistadors: A Very Brief Introduction* (Oxford University Press, 2011).

Restall, Matthew and Kris Lane, *Latin America in Colonial Times* (Cambridge University Press, 2011).

Sanders, William T., Alba Guadalupe Mastache and Robert H. Cobean (eds.), *Urbanism in Mesoamerica* (Mexico City: Instituto Nacional de Antropología e Historia; University Park, PA: Pennsylvania State University Press, 2003).

Smith, Michael S., *Aztec City-State Capitals* (Gainesville, FL: University Press of Florida, 2008).

Wilson, Samuel M. (ed.), *The Indigenous People of the Caribbean* (Gainesville, FL: University Press of Florida, 1997).

10

Africa in world history, 1400 to 1800

RAY A. KEA

Multi-disciplinary perspectives, an expanding and more diversified corpus of source materials, and wide-ranging research projects have enlarged and deepened historical knowledge about early modern Africa (1400 to 1800): its multi-layered phases of material and social development, its roles in the Afro-Eurasian *oikumene* and its position in world history historiography. Even though Africanist historical research has emphasized the sovereignty of Africa—Africans are the acting subjects of their own histories—it has been selective, not comprehensive, in its coverage of the continent, both spatially and temporally. Time periods before the twentieth century have been largely ignored, many territories are *terra incognito*, a wide range of primary sources, textual and non-textual, remain unexamined, and a number of themes and topics are studiously avoided. This chapter offers a synthesis of Africa's early modern history with particular reference to phases of historical change and social development and their intersections with the rest of the world as well as the local interplay of structure, culture and historically determined forms of social production.

For heuristic purposes, the chapter divides Africa into two geo-regions: the greater Sahara, north of the equator, and greater Zambezia, south of the equator. In contrast to conventional world history meta-narratives which construct the Sahara as an ahistorical wasteland and an impenetrable barrier, the following discussion sees the desert as a crossroads, a space of culture and cross-cultural ventures, and a resource base for salt, copper, dromedaries and semi-precious gemstones which supported different ways of rural and urban life in the bordering steppes and grasslands. Adjoining areas of the desert include the Nile valley, the Lake Chad basin, and the basins of the Middle Niger and Senegal Rivers. Greater Zambezia, comprising northern and southern Zambezia, is defined as the lands drained by the Zambezi and Limpopo Rivers and the headwaters of the Congo River. It was an immense resource-rich space and a multi-centric *locus* of interacting and fluctuating patterns of human activity and cross-craft interaction.

Thanks to its geographical location, Africa was an area of intersection for three world spaces—the Mediterranean basin and the Indian and Atlantic Oceans. The area of intersection was a site of exchanges—biological, commercial and cultural. The ports (entrepôts, emporia or gateway cities) of Mediterranean Africa, Indian Ocean Africa and Atlantic Africa were directly connected to the interaction spheres and networks of the greater Sahara interior. The interaction spheres and networks of the greater Zambezia interior were directly linked to Indian Ocean Africa and Atlantic Africa and indirectly to Mediterranean Africa. The commercial integration of the Mediterranean and Indian Ocean basins dates from ancient times; the commercial integration of the Atlantic basin dates from the sixteenth century. While local structures and factors contributed to broad cultural and social developments, extensive trans-local contacts between groups and communities were manifested in the regular exchange of ideas, artifacts, materials and techniques.

For example, a culture of travel was important to the Muslim Jakhanke clerical community of the Middle Niger basin. The Jakhanke *ulama* (scholars) proclaimed that there was blessing in travel. One travelled for many reasons that were not mutually exclusive. One performed the pilgrimage to Mecca and one also travelled in search of knowledge, to trade, to experience a sense of adventure and to satisfy one's curiosity about the wonders of the world.

In a thoughtful and informative essay, historian Sanjay Subrahmanyam offers an extended definition of early modernity within a comparative world history frame. He argues that concurrent developments and changes (or "synchronicities") across the Afro-Eurasian *oikumene* between *c.* 1350 and *c.* 1750 were foundational in the emergence of early modernity. The specific elements that were constitutive of early modern conditions were necessarily heterogeneous—cultural, commercial, discursive, intellectual, ideological, social and political: (1) the emergence of new ideas pertaining to travel and "discovery" and the related appearance of travel literature as a literary genre; (2) heightened systemic conflict between settled urban societies and nomadic groups of pastoralists and foragers; (3) intensification of global commodity and bullion flows and the enhanced circulation of ideas, goods and people in ways not known earlier due to new modes of communication and transportation; (4) a new political theology concerning the Universal Empire, millenarian visions of empire, empire-building projects, and revolution in military organization and methods of warfare; (5) and new ideas concerning universalism that were expressed as new and intensified forms of hierarchy, domination and exclusion, and a humanism that formulated conceptual and empirical links between medical knowledge, religion and novel conceptions of the individual.[1] The discussion that follows tracks the interconnected relationship of Africa's historical experiences with these key early modern elements: travel, trade, "political theology" and "historical anthropology."

For analytical and descriptive purposes, Africa's history in the 1400 to 1800 period can be viewed in terms of cultural-political paradigms with specific and very different social contents; each can be used as a prism that illuminates conjunctural changes and trajectories of development. With regard to greater Saharan history, three cultural-political paradigms are invoked: the city (as a central place in structural opposition to the rural); the *zawiya* (a Sufi educational-religious community); and the world port or entrepôt (a site of global commerce and contact). In greater Zambezia history, four cultural-political paradigms are recognized: the *dzimbabwe* (pl. *madzimbabwe*, royal settlement); the stone fort (associated with warlordism); the palace (linked to military-mercantile functions and interests); and the territorial cult (emblematic of a public sphere and associational life). Each cultural-political paradigm incorporated different ideologies and perspectives and in different conjunctures represented a social force and/or functioned as an agent of authority and control. In this respect, it represented a socio-political order in which the interests of both dominant and subordinate classes were served. The social vitality and structural consequences of the paradigms are apparent in a range of processes, relationships and practices.

Greater Sahara

The (fortified) city

The historical landscape of the greater Sahara in the early modern period was dominated by dense urban networks and city-oriented economies. Across the southern steppes and grasslands, from the Atlantic seaboard to the Lake Chad basin, a distance of over 3,000 kilometers, archaeological surveys have brought to light the ruins of 10,000 walled towns and cities and an unspecified number of unwalled cities and towns. East of Lake Chad, archaeologists

---

[1] Sanjay Subrahmanyam, "Connected Histories: Notes towards a Reconfiguration of Early Modern Eurasia" in Victor Lieberman (ed.), *Beyond Binary Histories. Re-Imagining Eurasia to 1830* (Ann Arbor, MI: University of Michigan Press, 1999), pp. 289–316.

have located a broad zone of fortresses, caravanserai, craft workshops, strongholds of different kinds, and walled and unwalled settlements up to the banks of the Nile River, which from Egypt to Nubia was lined with cities, towns and fortresses.

Urban morphology varied. There were double towns, separated from each other by a few kilometers. One half functioned as a political-military center and the other half as a commercial, craft and (Islamic) clerical center. Triple towns had, in addition to spatially distinct political-military and commercial-craft components, a clerical space with mosques, schools and *madrasas*. A founding principle of these divisions was that the political-military group had a right to rule and the clerical-merchant group had a right to autonomous jurisdiction over their own affairs.

The wider context for an understanding of urbanization and urbanism must include the operations of the Mediterranean gold and silver bullion market. The latter depended solely on West African gold production, one source estimating that, until the late sixteenth century, 20 to 30 tons of gold were exported annually to Mediterranean emporia. The gold trade was integral to long-established continental traffic and substantial inter-regional exchanges between producing areas and complementary zones of consumption. Urban networks set the logic and rules of discourse and patterns of mobility, sociality and settlement, and they functioned as seats for different kinds of political and surplus accumulation regimes, ranging from city-states and principalities to expansive imperial formations.

The urban–rural division of labor was fundamental in the history of the greater Sahara. The view of urban-based Oyo nobles regarding rural folk is instructive: "The rights of the *talaka* ['peasant'; 'commoner'] do not matter; they can be trampled upon"; "the poor man's mouth is a cutlass. We shall use it to clear the forest." The upper classes of the Borno sultanate also had a contemptuous view of peasant life on the Borno plains: "The peasant is grass, fodder for the horses. To your fields peasant that we may eat!" The peasant was summarily excluded from the urban world of the Borno ruling classes. The historical identity and unity of Borno's upper classes were realized, in part, in their cities, which were described in the early nineteenth century as large and well-built with walls 12 to 14 meters high and 6 meters wide. Borno's cities, whose commercial and diplomatic links were transcontinental, were built and maintained by conscripted rural labor.

State power was strongest in the cities. In a treatise on rulership, Muhammad Bello (1775 to 1837), a prominent jihad leader, states that a ruler "must see to the construction of walled towns and bridges and the maintenance of markets and roads and the realization of the public welfare, so that the harmony of this world may be maintained." Elsewhere, he valorizes the urban at the expense of the rural. He writes that it is better to dwell in towns than in villages and to dwell in villages is better than to dwell in the desert, and he theorizes that "human perfection is not reached save through urbanization and [its] civilization."[2] The ideological and conceptual juxtaposition of city and village within their historical context illustrates a systemic tension and opposition between urban and rural divisions of labor. This structured polarity generated from the late fifteenth to the late eighteenth century waves of anti-urban movements, from Tichitt (Mauretania) to Gazargamu (the Borno capital), of peasants, pastoralists, artisan castes and slaves, often led by intellectual elites who generated a large body of material in Arabic and Ajami (i.e. West African languages written in a modified Arabic script) concerning political, theological, polemical, historical and social matters. The movements called for economic and social equality, an end to the amassing of riches and the overthrow of hereditary dynasties. These protests articulated a particular "political theology," one that propounded an end to inequality, kings and dynasties, and affirmed a "historical anthropology" that advocated the liberation of the poor and the downtrodden.

Critical Muslim clerics poured scorn on urban-dwelling political and merchant elites who were corrupt, despised the poor and lived in luxury. A Borno scholar named Muhammad ibn al-hajj 'Abd al-Rahman al-Khatib ibn Bint al-hajj al-Barnawi (d. 1746), for example, wrote a lengthy and scathing criticism of the Borno political establishment. Rulers of Borno, he wrote, were tyrannical and corrupt, the rich withheld food at famine time in the hope of making a profit, usury was concealed in the renting of land, judges accepted bribes as did governors of provinces and gambling (for example, horse-racing) was common among the upper classes.[3] In the seventeenth and eighteenth centuries, clerics who shared al-Barnawi's sentiments tended to withdraw from the cities and retire to the countryside and teach in a peasant village or join a *zawiya*, a clerical town or a Sufi order, or establish a clerical community. A further option was to perform the pilgrimage to Mecca. A last

---

[2] B. G. Martin, "A Muslim Tract from Northern Nigeria: Muhammad Bello's Usul al-Siyasa" in D. F. McCall and N. R. Bennet (eds.), *Aspects of West African Islam* (Boston, MA: African Studies Center, Boston University, B. G. 1971), pp. 63–86.

[3] A. D. H. Bivar and M. Hiskett, *The Arabic Literature of Nigeria to 1804: A Provisional Account* (London: School of Oriental and African Studies, 1961).

resort was to remain in the city and assume an administrative position and try to uphold religious standards by example.

The earliest known clerical town dates from the thirteenth century, but from the fifteenth century onwards clerical towns and communities appear in increasing numbers in different places in the southern Sahara, Senegambia, the Upper and Middle Niger basins and the Lake Chad basin. Self-governing and politically independent, the clerical town (*bilad al-fuqaha'*; *morikunde*) of scholars, teachers, students, mosques, schools and libraries was an instrument of Islamization in rural areas. It functioned too as a sanctuary and haven for escaped slaves, political exiles, social outcasts, debtors and the like. Even if a man had killed the son of a king, he could find safety and refuge in the inviolable space of a clerical town. A common social practice was for Muslim as well as non-Muslim rulers to grant holy men (s. *shaykh* or *wali*) or scholars (s. *'alim*, pl. *'ulama*), together with their students, disciples and followers, a landed estate, usually comprising a number of villages and/or groups of pastoralists, and privileges, such as immunity from taxes and military conscription. In return for the endowment, the holy men or scholars were expected to offer counsel and to place their skills, including knowledge of the *shari'a*, literacy, divination and magic, at the disposal of ruling dynasties. The estate and privileges were guaranteed by a royal charter. Students not only studied the Islamic sciences, including the philological and religious sciences and jurisprudence, but they were also obliged to learn a craft, such as rope-making, weaving and sandal-making. Students were sent by their shaykhs into the countryside to non-Muslim villages, hamlets and encampments where they would preach, set up schools and mosques, teach, convert and practice their crafts. The clerical town bridged the material and social divide between city and village. It introduced elements of urban life such as schools and libraries into the countryside and created a new institutional focus for rural identity. At the same time, rural areas became a social basis of the clerics' position vis-à-vis ruling political authorities. With regard to the politics of royal courts, the clerical towns generally remained aloof, but with regard to proselytization and education, they pursued a vigorous activist program.

In the course of the seventeenth and eighteenth centuries, another form of urbanism emerged in Senegambia and the Upper and Middle Niger basins. This was the large, fortified market center of merchants, with their armed retainers and entourages, and clerics, with their students and followers, and artisan castes. In the hinterland were plantations worked by enslaved labor and village farms cultivated by indebted peasants. The market center was the proprietor of the land and owner of the slaves' and peasants' conditions of production. It promoted the commodification of agricultural production and reduced indebted peasants to the status of tenants, thus furthering the process of de-peasantization which was a defining feature of the early modern period in the greater Sahara and greater Zambezia (see below). The commercial town, a place of trans-shipment, price-fixing mechanisms and partnerships, was a domain of commodity exchanges and credit. The logic of the clerical town included proselytizing in the countryside and the maintenance of a network of rural schools—developed in opposition to the market town.

The spread of clerical towns coincided with the decline of imperial Mali and the rise of the Songhay Empire (1460 to 1591). The market center with a dependent hinterland of enslaved labor and peasants in debt bondage was a consequence of the fall of Songhay following its conquest by Morocco in 1591. Cities were instrumental in these developments. When wealthy merchants decided to transfer their capital and commercial operations from Malian cities (such as Niani, Dia and Walata) to Middle Niger and southern Saharan cities (for example, Jenne, Timbuktu, Takedda and Agades), Mali declined. Merchants' support of Songhay ruling dynasties resulted in the establishment of a centralized bureaucratic hegemony in the Middle Niger basin. Sultan Ahmad al-Mansur (1578 to 1603), the Moroccan conqueror of Songhay, justified his invasion by contrasting the poverty of Morocco and the wealth of Songhay, with its "many cities, running rivers, forested fields, trade routes, numerous *zawiyas*, and salt and gold mines." Songhay's cities, trade routes, *zawiyas* and mines were supported by specialized slave groups (blacksmiths, leather workers, boat-builders, boatmen, masons, herders, cultivators, horse trainers, messengers, armed retainers, hunters, fishermen and so on) who provided services in kind, taxes and labor designated for the needs of the royal court, the central administration and the army.

The material and moral foundations of Songhay rested on three elements, according to the *'ulama'* of Timbuktu and Jenne: urbanism (*'amara*), long-distance trade (*mu'amalat*) and Islam (*diyanat*). Trade and Islam, in its dominant Sunni Maliki expression, flourished in cities like Jenne, Timbuktu, Diakha-Masina, Tadmakka, Takkeda, Kano, Katsina and Agadez. Sunni Malikism was a general conception of life for urban commoners, but for intellectuals it was a scholastic program or a set of principles. Islam was pluralistic and multi-faceted. Two figures, Muhammad ibn 'Abd al-Karim ibn Muhannad al-Maghili of Tlemcen (*c.* 1440 to 1504/05) and Jalal al-Din 'Abd al-Rahman al-Suyuti of Cairo (d. 1504/05), introduced several ideas to Songhay clerics—the role of the sultan as guardian of Islam, the idea of asceticism (*zuhd*) and the millenarian doctrines of the *mujaddid* and the *mahdi*, the messiah. At the same time, Sufism, in the form of different orders (*turuq*; s. *tariqa*) became an important subject of study in places like Timbuktu, but with the fall of Songhay Sufism became an important current of belief and action for reformers and a political project for jihadists.

A geographical description of the world published by the cosmographer Giovanni d'Anania (1545 to 1607) in 1582 includes accounts of three premier cities in Africa: Cairo in Ottoman Egypt, Fez in the Saadi sultanate (Morocco) and Kano—capital of the Kano sultanate and a Songhay tributary. This urban triangle defined the geography of a vast interaction sphere in the interior of the greater Sahara in which Songhay was the dominant political and socio-economic power. Songhay's collapse was followed by the rapid dispersion of *zawiyas* and Sufi orders within this urban triangle and the dissemination of clerical towns across the southern reaches of the greater Sahara, from the Atlantic to Darfur.

The fall of Songhay contributed to the continued economic, cultural and political development and territorial expansion of polities in the Lake Chad basin, particularly the Borno Empire, whose sway extended from the Hausa sultanates to Darfur and northwards to the Fazzan. The city of Katsina, capital of the Katsina sultanate and a Borno tributary, replaced its rival Kano, emerging as one of the principal commercial centers in the greater Sahara in the seventeenth and eighteenth centuries. Its growth and prosperity was due to expanded trade with the Ottoman Empire, the Volta River basin in the Gold Coast hinterland and the Lower Guinea Coast.

Borno rulers actively promoted trans-Saharan commerce, sending numerous commercial and diplomatic missions to Istanbul, Cairo and Tripoli. North African, Egyptian, Ottoman and Italian merchants traveled to the Borno capital importing large quantities of manufactured goods. The growth of the clerical class in Borno and Hausa cities was significant. They were guardians of learning, scholarship and education. They were surveyors and town builders. With the support of rich merchants and artisans, they laid out new towns or rebuilt old ones, all of which were oriented towards Mecca. The nouveau riche of merchants, artisans and clerics sent their sons and daughters to local and regional schools and centers of learning, to North Africa and Egypt and to Baghdad. They also encouraged them to perform the pilgrimage to Mecca. The significant expansion of educational facilities for higher education and the production of learned and popular works led to the growing political influence of the scholarly classes in the cities and the countryside.

Itineraries and lines of communication stretched across considerable distances. The travels of two men—a Katsina scholar and a Borno royal—were typical. Muhammad ibn Muhammad al-Fullani al-Kashnawi (d. 1741/42), from the Katsina sultanate, a man learned in many branches of knowledge especially mathematics, numerology, magic squares and other esoteric sciences, traveled extensively in search of knowledge and wrote a now lost *Rihla* ("Travel") describing his travel experiences. He performed the pilgrimage to Mecca in 1730 and in 1733/34 settled in Cairo, where he died. In the 1760s or 1770s, an unnamed Borno prince from the walled city of Gazargamu, the capital of Borno, traveled to Italy with his family and servants and spent six months there touring the country. Travelers, not all of whom were merchants, journeyed from the emporia on the Mediterranean African coastline to ports on the Gold Coast seaboard.

The experience of a Franciscan friar named Peter Farde (1651 to 1691) illustrates an unexpected line of communication. Farde, an enslaved Franciscan friar in the southern Saharan city of Agadez, was guaranteed his freedom as soon as his owner, a rich merchant named Sura Bellin, received the ransom. From 1686 to 1688, Farde corresponded with his superiors in Amsterdam. Farde's letters were carried by camel caravan across the Sahara to a North African port and from there to Amsterdam. The replies of his superiors went by Dutch ships to the Gold Coast port of Elmina, the commercial headquarters of the Dutch West Indies Company in Atlantic Africa, and from there, merchant caravans en route to interior markets conveyed the letters to Agadez, over 1,000 kilometers from Elmina. When the ransom was delivered, Farde was released from bondage. Epistolary intercourse across such distances sheds light on the integrity of lines of communication between cities in the greater Sahara and Europe.

The zawiya

In the seventeenth and eighteenth centuries, the *zawiya* was a leading educational, scholarly and religious institution throughout the central and western Sahara, Senegambia, the Upper and Middle Niger basins and the Lake Chad basin. It was seminal in the spread of Sufi orders, including the Qadiriyya, Shadhaliyya, Khalwatiyya, Mahmudiyya and Fadeliyya, the creation of Sufi networks that crossed the desert and the ruralization of Islam. The *zawiya* existed before the sixteenth century, but its instrumental role in the evolution of movements of reform and armed resistance can be attributed to a shift of institutional resources and merchant capital away from cities like Timbuktu, Tadmakka and Jenne to the southern Sahara, the

Upper Niger basin and Senegambia. Those responsible for setting up *zawiyas*, known as marabouts or *mubashshirun* ("those who propagate the Faith"), sometimes served as royal advisors to Muslim and non-Muslim rulers. High scholarship flourished in *zawiyas*.

One of the most prominent figures in the history of West and North African Sufism was Sidi al-Mukhtar al-Kunti (1729 to 1811) of Azawad (north of Timbuktu). A prolific writer with more than 200 works to his credit, he founded a new Sufi order, al-Qadiriyya al-Mukhtariyya. A strong proponent of asceticism and austerity, he realized that God called upon him to enter the world and to engage in its pursuits. Over the years he amassed great wealth from the trans-Saharan trade and raising livestock, but "the world and its possessions and pleasures meant nothing to him."[4] His desire was to spend on the poor and needy, and on guests, refugees and neighbors.

Sidi al-Mukhtar believed he was the *mujaddid* of the thirteenth century of the Hijra (the eighteenth century in the Christian calendar), the person called by God at the beginning of every century to renovate Islam and to restore the *umma* to its glorious past throughout the entire Muslim world. To him, West Africa was at the heart of Islamic culture, a place where outstanding scholastic standards were reached. North Africa was under the rule of despotic princes, the East was falling under the influence of the Wahhabis, and pure Islam was to be found only within the precincts of the *zawiya*. His reputation came to extend from northern and central Sahara to Senegambia and the Lake Chad basin and southwards to the forest zones of present-day Côte d'Ivoire and Guinea: "all along this area one finds disciples and followers of Sidi al-Mukhtar who are among the notables and celebrities of their respective localities."[5] His eminence encompassed the largest area ever to come under the authority of an African Muslim without military conquest. The geographical sphere of his prestige and authority corresponded to the area of jurisdiction and alliances of imperial Songhay in the sixteenth century. He belongs to the Timbuktu tradition of scholarship and spirituality. In one of his works ("The Gift of the Followers of the Path of Muhammad"), he examines the history of Songhay and discusses important questions of Islamic law that arose in the empire, including the status and rights of women and children in a Muslim society.

[4] Aziz A. Batran, "The Qadiriyya-Mukhtaryya Brotherhood in West Africa: The Concept of Tasawwuf in the Writings of Sidi al-Mukhtar al-Kunti (1729–1811)," *Transafrican Journal of History* 4(1–2) (1974), 41–70.
[5] Batran, "The Qadiriyya-Mukhtaryya Brotherhood."

The world of Sufis and Sufism spread in a time when in Upper Guinea there was a strengthening of military regimes and in Lower Guinea a militarization of political institutions and culture. Military regimes were strengthened in two ways. Dynastic states either depended on armies of mounted slave-warriors (*cheddos*) or they relied on free professional soldiers (*nyanchos*) and mercenaries as cavalry troops. In this environment, the construction of fortified cities, towns, castles and forts was vigorously carried out. The demands of the military, the costs of building fortifications and strongholds, and the expense of siege warfare required that dynastic regimes increase their revenues so that dynasties could acquire money, horses, weapons, armor, produce, livestock and siege equipment. Their needs were met by merchants and artisan castes and by the development of scale economies in metal-working and mining. New systems of taxation, including military conscription and corvée labor, were imposed on peasant and pastoralist communities, and state industries were developed, including arsenals for weapons, boat-building, metal-working and mining. Slave-warriors put down peasant and pastoralist rebellions and the defeated were sold into Atlantic slavery or were settled in urban hinterlands as slave cultivators. In seventeenth- and eighteenth-century Upper Guinea, the urban centers declared war on the countryside, a phenomenon that can be assigned to the long process of de-peasantization.

Four major movements emerged in the Senegambian region between the mid-seventeenth and the late eighteenth century. The movements' leadership, which consisted of scholars, teachers and shaykhs, responded to the crises in the countryside. They included the War of the Marabouts (1647 to 1677), the Futa Bundu jihad (1680s to 1690s), the Futa Jalon jihad (1725 to 1750) and the Futa Toro jihad (1776 to 1783). In each case, a new kind of Islamic state was created—the *imamiyya* or imamate—which in theory and practice was opposed to any form of hereditary rule.

The victors, the clerical class and its adherents, emerged politically with disposal over larger concentrations of power and wealth than the previous dynastic regimes, and sold the vanquished into the Atlantic slave trade.

The guiding principles of these movements constituted what one writer has called the radical tradition in the literature of Muslim West Africa.[6] In summarizing these principles, he relates that the tradition: (1) emphasized true rights of common people against the claims of their rulers; (2) took an

[6] A. G. Hopkins, "Changing Theories of Political Economy in Africa" in Christopher Fyfe (ed.), *African Studies since 1945: A Tribute to Basil Davidson* (London: Longman, 1976).

egalitarian attitude to differences of status, rank, wealth, gender and ethnic origin, and any privileges based upon these; (3) was concerned with changing institutions as a precondition of changing human beings, and opening up new possibilities for their development; (4) attached importance to the widest possible diffusion of knowledge and education; (5) stressed the principle that men and women belong to an international community (*dar al-islam*; *jamaa'at al-sudaniyya*), whose claims surpassed those of a particular state, region, cultural or linguistic group; and (6) emphasized the urgency of social change and reform, regarding as justified the use of revolutionary (violent) methods to achieve it.

In the struggle against royalism and mercantilism, Malik ibn Nabir, a participant in the Futa Toro jihad, emphasized agency and the role of individuals/people making their own history. He wrote: "Verily God does not change the conditions of a people until they change themselves inwardly" and "every revolution creates new social values, and these are capable of transforming men and women."[7]

The world port

Along the Atlantic seaboard, from Senegambia to Kongo-Angola, was a succession of world ports or entrepôts, many with fortified trading stations belonging to European chartered companies. In the seventeenth and eighteenth centuries, the ports provided the economic, social, technical and organizational arrangements required for Atlantic maritime exchanges. Specifically, they accommodated the export of an estimated 12 million captive bodies (mainly males) to American plantations and mines and facilitated the annual import of tens of thousands of tons of merchandise. The bulk of imported trade goods, in the range of 60 to 90 per cent, was destined for consumption in inland cities. In addition, the ports were responsible for organizing the sale and exchange of provisions and other products necessary for the maintenance of the slaving ships as they crossed the Atlantic.

Between the sixteenth and eighteenth centuries, Upper and Lower Guinea ruling classes created a cultural landscape of palaces and royal courts, public gardens, multilingual literate cultures and libraries, marketplaces and commercial districts, as well as mosques and prayer grounds, Koranic schools and *madrasas*, shrines and temples, and, in some places, churches and schools for

---

[7] Boubacar Barry, *Senegambia and the Atlantic Slave Trade*, Kwei Armah (trans.) (Cambridge University Press, 1998).

Christian converts. In this period, about two dozen West African languages began to be written in modified Arabic script, and eighteenth-century Gold Coast ports used Portuguese Creole as a lingua franca in their written communications. This landscape, with its normative structures, epitomized an upper class social imaginary of order, efficiency, predictability, prosperity and reason, and the achievement of personal capacity and spiritual agency. From the point of view of the countryside, this landscape was realized at great social cost.

Archaeological fieldwork has identified an early modern urban zone from 10 to 100 kilometers from the Lower Guinea coastline, from the Ivory Coast to the Lower Niger basin, consisting of walled and unwalled cities and towns and belonging to different kinds of political formations—city-states, federations, kingdoms and empires. This included Fante and Asante in the Gold Coast region, and Allada, Savi, Benin, Dahomey, Oyo and Benin in the Slave Coast region (Figure 10.1). At the eastern end of this zone, in the lands of Aja-, Edo- and Yoruba-speaking populations, there were urban assemblages of great extent and complexity. Massive earthwork structures, up to several thousand kilometers in total length, and monumental fortifications, some with walls up to 25 meters in height and over 100 kilometers in length, were major collective and public works projects.

Slave Coast polities like Ardra, Savi, Dahomey and Oyo were palace-centered in the sense that the palace reinforced the sacralizing persona of the ruler and his court and the palace functioned as the locus of the central apparatus of the state. For the urban-based upper classes of the Yoruba-Aja Commonwealth, the cultural climate of the region was characterized by a dialogic ethos and a constant effort to exchange ideas, experience and material culture. One of the doctrines at work was *Asuwada*, a corpus of ideas concerning the making or creating of human society, emphasizing principles of association and sociality. Society brings into being various potentials and constructs: it creates, it destroys and it modifies. Created society consists of two contending modalities: the civil or political domain and the religious or spiritual domain and the possibility of political or religious emancipation. Society-making created the "free citizen" and the non-citizen, "a thing belonging in cords and deprived of liberty" in contexts of stormy and bloody conflicts, hierarchical order of authority and a quest for social and spatial mobility. *Asuwada* and other doctrines were codified in the meta-languages of *Ifa* and *Vodun*.

On the Gold Coast, a contingent condition of a life of luxury consumption and high culture was the cultural-historical "gap" between the ports

Figure 10.1 View of city of Benin with royal palace, Nigeria, engraving from *Description of Africa*, by Olfert Dapper (*c.* 1635–1689), 1686. (De Agostini Picture Library / A. Dagli Orti / Bridgeman Images).

inhabited by affluent traders and brokers and hinterland plantations worked by servile labor. The bonded laborers lived a secluded life, hardly ever visiting the ports; hence they were ignorant of the rules and manners of the more extended spheres of urban cultural and social life. They were not citizens of the ports. In contrast, the owners of the plantations who were also citizens—political officials, brokers and merchants—enjoyed a life of prosperity and wealth. Their culture of high consumption included a tradition of travel. Prominent port residents traveled abroad as teachers, students, tourists, apprentices, envoys and merchants to Europe and occasionally to the Americas. A 1787 report, for example, relates that fifty boys and girls, from wealthy West African households, were studying in schools in and around Liverpool. Gold Coast youths, in particular, studied in Denmark, the Netherlands, England, Ireland and France. The earliest known travel journals from the Gold Coast were written (in German) by a Gold Coast Christian named Christian J. Protten (1715 to 1769), who studied at the

University of Copenhagen (1732 to 1735) and traveled to the Danish West Indies (1744 to 1745) and Europe (1750s and 1760s).

Upper class ideology codified and theorized distinctions of class, lifestyle and status as grounded in the nature of the universe (Fate), the nature of nature (disorder/order), the nature of human nature (rational/irrational) and the essence of society (independence/dependence). Key concepts included the idea of "crossroad," a concept with multiple and antithetical significations (opportunity, achievement, prosperity and health; loss, sickness, disgrace, poverty), the culture–nature binary (or the opposition between rationality and irrationality) and the freedom–necessity binary (or the opposition between wealth and poverty). "Freedom" connoted self-actualization and the ability and right to participate in the public debates and politics of the town, as well as the town's holidays, festivities and celebrations. "Necessity" defined the world of commoners and slaves and a life devoted to acquiring the means of subsistence.

To lower the risk of social unrest among commoners, debtors and slaves and to alleviate their conditions of material need, the upper classes and European factors distributed, through the agency of the ports' local priests and priestesses, gold, produce, trade goods, small livestock and salt. This practice flourished in the seventeenth century. In addition, communities of priests and priestesses served as places of refuge and sanctuary for escaped slaves, social outcasts, outlaws, debtors, thieves, the poverty-stricken and exiles. These communities were inviolable. Whoever found refuge in them could not be apprehended by any political authority. For the excluded, the priesthood created a sense of belonging and social connectedness in a time from the fifteenth to the eighteenth centuries of intense urbanization and mercantile accumulation on a large scale.

Greater Zambezia

The dzimbabwe

The Indian Ocean commercial system extended from the Red Sea and the Eastern Mediterranean to Eastern Africa and to the Straits of Malacca and the Indonesian Archipelago. From Mogadishu (Somalia) to Chibuene (Mozambique), a distance of more than 3,000 kilometers, the Swahili urban maritime culture and its Indian Ocean trade reached its peak between 1300 and 1500. The largest towns, like Kilwa, Pate, Lamu, Malindi, Mombasa, Mogadishu and Merca, maintained merchant fleets and conducted long-distance exchanges in a wide range of goods with the Arabian Peninsula,

India, Southeast Asia and China, as well as with the coastal countryside, which supplied agricultural and other necessities and provided labor and markets for the cities (Figure 10.2). The Swahili economy was monetized: Kilwa and Mogadishu minted gold and silver coins. The cities established trading partnerships with interior states, particularly in southern Zambezia, where in the early sixteenth century there were an estimated 10,000 Swahili merchants settled in commercial and political centers. Swahili merchants had well-established trade routes along major navigable rivers. The gold trade was at its peak in the fifteenth century. Estimates of annual gold export from southern Zambezia range from 1 ton in the fifteenth century to several thousand tons from the thirteenth to the sixteenth centuries. Whatever the actual volume, research has shown that Zambezian gold was the most important component of the financial basis of Indian Ocean trade until the arrival of Brazilian and West African gold in the course of the sixteenth and seventeenth centuries.

From the Horn of Africa, Christian and Muslim Ethiopians traded along the Swahili coast and sailed to India. Ethiopian churchmen, envoys and diplomatic missions traveled to the Holy Land, Rome and different European courts and cities, as well as in the Islamic world throughout the early modern

Figure 10.2 Husuni Kubwa, a palace and market built in the fourteenth century for the Sultan of Kilwa, on Kilwa Kisiwani, an island in present-day Nigeria. (Ulrich Doering / Alamy).

period. In 1488, Lucas Marcus, an Ethiopian priest, was sent from Rome to Lisbon and, together with an Ethiopian monk called Jacob, traveled to West Africa on board a Portuguese ship in search of the legendary Prester John. In the early sixteenth century, Ethiopian monks named Antonio and Thomas, having traveled to India, sailed from there to Portugal. The Ethiopian monk Abba Tesfa Sion, Abbot of St. Stefano and the leader of the Ethiopian scholars in Rome, published in 1549 the New Testament in Geez, an Ethiopian language. In the preface he wrote: "I am an Ethiopian pilgrim [traveling] from place to place, from province to province, from the land of the infidels [i.e., Muslims] to the land of the faithful [i.e., Christians], through sea and land. At Rome I found rest for my soul through the right faith."[8] Published itineraries indicate that fifteenth- and sixteenth-century Ethiopian churchmen, envoys and merchants were well acquainted with the Mediterranean, Indian Ocean and Atlantic Ocean routes.

International commerce and external relations were the culmination of processes generated within local and regional economies and political structures that were able to exploit long-distance trade as a component of hierarchical functions already supervising regional resources on a large scale. Archaeological fieldwork in southern Zambezia provides details about settlement patterns, different aspects of material and cultural life, and local and long-distance interconnections. Comparable fieldwork has not been carried out in northern Zambezia. Hundreds of thousands of stone wall structures throughout southern Africa testify to the density of rural and urban habitation sites. Some places were major political centers, like Great Zimbabwe and Khami. A number of towns, built along lines of mineral deposits, were associated with scale economies in mining and metal-working operations. Such sites show extensive evidence of high temperature metallurgical technologies, extensive mining and metal extraction technologies, and the mass production of pottery. Still others were seats of "cattle barons," who combined livestock breeding on a grand scale with copper mining and ivory production. Near the Limpopo River, the stratified community of Thulamela, dated between the thirteenth and late seventeenth centuries, had elites residing in a large *dzimbabwe* on the hilltop and the rest of the population of craftsmen, herders and peasants in the valley below. The town exported copper, gold, iron and tin into the Indian Ocean trading system and imported glass beads and other luxury goods, thus demonstrating

---

[8] Hans Debrunner, *Presence and Prestige: Africans in Europe. A History of Africans in Europe before 1918* (Basel: Basler Afrika Bibliographien, 1979).

commercial contact with North Africa and Egypt, western Asia, India and China. Mining and metallurgy were salient factors in urbanization, social structuring and state formation.

State structures evolved to protect populations involved in commerce, animal husbandry, crafts and mining. New social and cultural identities were created as producers were incorporated into expanding political structures and into circuits of mercantile accumulation. Foreign imports were socialized at the level of the state and its public structures, a development that ensured the circulation of luxury goods in ruling class circles. Archaeological evidence indicates that throughout southern Zambezia, there was a general homogeneity of ruling class material culture through the importation of foreign luxury goods such as Chinese porcelain, Persian glassware, Indian textiles and Egyptian ceramics. Ruling classes shared legal prescriptions, festivals, territorial cults, healing associations, and ritual actions and formulae.

The period from the mid-thirteenth to the early sixteenth centuries was a time of political aggregation. Large centralizing political hegemonies—the Zimbabwe imperium (1250 to 1450) and the Mwene Mutapa Empire (1450 to 1630) which emerged out of the Zimbabwe polity—and the centralization of surplus extraction in a context of expanding agro-pastoral and artisan-mining frontiers were dominant processes. In the Zimbabwe polity, 150 provincial towns functioned as administrative-political centers over the lowland lands between the eastern Kalahari desert and Indian Ocean and the high plateau between the Zambezi and Limpopo Rivers. They specialized in craft industries and trade in gold, ivory, textiles, glass beads, cattle and produce. An estimated 500 smaller *madzimbabwe*, in the hands of powerful descent groups, were responsible for agricultural production and the management of royal cattle herds and trade routes. At the base of the Zimbabwe settlement hierarchy were several thousand villages in which kinship systems were based on a collective ethic and collective ownership of land.

Great Zimbabwe, capital of the Zimbabwe state (1290 to 1450), was a metropolis with many quarters: palace and royal court, elite residences of state officials, merchants, and priests and priestesses, ritual centers, public ceremonial courts, public forums, markets, and houses for commoners and artisans. The principal buildings were constructed in dressed stone with regular coursing. Estimates of the city's population range between 11,000 and 50,000 for the fourteenth and early fifteenth centuries.

The Zimbabwe ruling class was sustained by an economy based on mineral wealth, especially copper and gold, trade with the Indian Ocean commercial system and herds of cattle. Backed by a large army, the ruler appropriated surplus in the form of state taxes from village communities (rural social commons) in the form of labor services, agricultural produce, craft goods, livestock and raw materials. The gold trade was supported by vast herds of cattle that were used to pay the miners and to subsidize the subsistence of residents in the major urban centers. The upper classes of Great Zimbabwe were buried with gifts of gold jewelry, jeweled iron work, large copper ingots and Chinese porcelain. Peasants, on the other hand, were buried with few or no grave goods—after lives spent growing millet and sorghum.

The rulers of the Mwene Mutapa inherited the Zimbabwe administrative-political and economic systems with some modifications. They abandoned Great Zimbabwe as a political center and established their capital near the Zambezi River as well as more than sixty new towns, including centers of metal-working and new ports on the Zambezi River. The structure of the new towns was similar to that of Great Zimbabwe, which became a religious and pilgrimage center after 1450. The Mutapa rulers now exercised control over all branches of production, including agriculture, mining, craft indus-tries and livestock, and these sectors paid a tribute-rent in labor and kind. In the 1480s, ports on the Mozambique coast were re-built—Angoche, Nyashawa and Nyembani—so that the ruling dynasty would have direct access to the Indian Ocean commercial world. This project failed to materi-alize, however, as a result of civil wars following rebellions of provincial governors in the 1490s and through the sixteenth century. These struggles led to dismemberment of the Mwene Mutapa polity and widespread political fragmentation or disaggregation in southern Zambezia. Sub-imperial polities like the Khami kingdom under the Rozwi-Chagamire dynasties (1450 to 1800) emerged and expanded as they conquered and incorporated vassal territories. Warlords and principalities ("chiefdoms") with mercenary and slave armies appeared on the political scene in the sixteenth century, together with stone forts. There were constant struggles over the control of gold and copper mines, markets like Ingombe Ilede on the Zambezi and trade routes. With shifts in the distribution of military and political power, the social commons of rural villages were appropriated by new political classes who established themselves as proprietors of the land.

An archaeological interpretation of the monumental architecture of Great Zimbabwe contends that the ruling class viewed it as an extension of the natural environment; that is, the architecture of royal constructions was to represent assimilation of and not the domination of nature. Monu-mental architecture of Khami's *madzimbabwe*, by contrast, represented royal domination of nature; that is, natural geographical features were enclosed in a built environment of monumentality in the form of terraces and massive platforms over 8 meters high and up to a kilometer or more in length. This was a time when the communal organization of peasant village communities was breaking up in particular areas of the high plateau and the Zambezi basin, a time of expanding and contracting commercial and political networks, and a time of contested hierarchies with the growing presence of enslaved labor, mercenary soldiers and displaced peasants.

The breakdown of imperial authority and the processes of de-peasantization and enslavement were concurrent with the arrival on the Eastern African coast of Portuguese ships. The dynamics of contact in southern Zambezia created an intersection of networks and hierarchies organized around three interacting entities: Zambezian polities with resources and labor, Swahili merchants with trading capital and Portuguese entrepreneurs (and their African allies) with firearms (see below).

In northern Zambezia, the situation was different. There, political aggregation or centralization prevailed in the sixteenth through the eighteenth centuries. The cultural-economic complexes of the Luba and Lunda formations, which were based in the headwaters of the Congo River, gave rise to imperial political systems and associated satellite polities, such as Kazembe and the Marave confederation, in the 1600s and 1700s. The seventeenth- and eighteenth-century Lunda Empire established a trans-continental network that linked southern Swahili ports and southern Angolan ports. The empire was a principle supplier of captive labor to the Americas, especially in the eighteenth century.

The stone fort and the palace

The stone fort and the palace became prominent landscape features in southern Zambezia from the sixteenth to the eighteenth centuries in the context of an expanding mercantile frontier, political de-centralization on a regional scale and militarism. The stone fort, signaling the spread of military architecture and firearms, attests to heightened armed conflicts among several different political actors: local warlords, the declining Mwene Mutapa state, Portuguese and Afro-Portuguese entrepreneurs, and military predatory states. For the first time, armies of slaves and mercenaries appeared on battlefields as decisive military combatants. The contending forces fought over trade routes and gold-mining areas, creating in the process armed commercial networks dotted with garrisoned soldiers in stone forts. Portuguese and Afro-Portuguese traders established markets along the Zambezi River and in the gold-producing districts. They promoted Christianization in their sphere of influence, unlike their Muslim Swahili competitors who did not attempt to convert Zambezian populations to Islam.

The royal palace, with its courtiers, sacralizing functions and practices of governance, belonged to an earlier era. The seventeenth-century palace had two primary functions: as a citadel with a garrison of armed retainers—usually mercenaries, but also armed slaves; or as a site of merchant activities. In a few instances, it combined the two functions. Throughout the northern high plateau, Mwene Mutapa rulers no longer had large *madzimbabwe* as their political capitals, but ruled through palaces as citadels and palaces as markets. Both functions were associated with the expansion of the mercantile frontier from Portuguese-dominated Indian Ocean emporia to Zambezi River-based entrepôts and the gold fields of the central and northern high plateau. Portuguese missionaries were active evangelizing in and around Portuguese and Afro-Portuguese market centers, where they also built churches and chapels.

In the late seventeenth century, rulers of the Khami kingdom, which dominated the southern high plateau, destroyed the markets of the Portuguese and Afro-Portuguese and drove the Portuguese and their African allies out of the middle Zambezi valley and the northern high plateau and closed the gold mines. Henceforth, southern Zambezia's exports to the wider Indian Ocean world were primarily ivory and copper. Khami rulers, who continued to receive luxury goods from Indian Ocean commerce, symbolized the shift from the primacy of gold to the primacy of ivory by lining the walls and steps of their palaces with ivory panels.

In the lower Zambezi valley, the Portuguese and Afro-Portuguese managed to consolidate their positions as estate-holders (*prazeros*) in their fortified landed estates (*prazos*) of peasants and slave cultivators with the help of their armies of slaves and mercenaries (*Chikunda*). Estate-holders militarized trade routes leading to the gold fields by setting up garrisoned forts along them; but their purpose, to gain access to gold-mining areas, was ultimately unsuccessful.

The territorial cult

Historical studies have shown that the Luba-Lunda heartland, situated in the headwaters of the Congo and Zambezi Rivers, was the source of a range of institutions, practices, beliefs and ideas that became over a period of centuries hegemonic throughout much of greater Zambezia. They included: (1) political ideas and institutions; (2) medical-religious systems concerning the medico-empirical (common physical ailments) and the medico-religious (witchcraft); (3) religious shrines and territorial cults; (4) music and musical instruments; and (5) specialized vocabularies relating to political, religious and medical matters.

The territorial cult was associated with mental and physical health, medical knowledge and practices, and mercantile wealth. Its principal concern was the material and moral well-being of the population of a territory, both rulers and ruled. It could cut across major political, cultural and linguistic boundaries, embracing an area of several thousand square kilometers. As public institutions and definers of a public sphere and civil society, territorial cults stood for the mediation of social conflict and the socialization of individuals, groups and communities. They had multiple functions with regard to rituals, ceremonial protocols, symbolisms of different kinds, cosmology and medical-religious systems, and numerous organizational expressions—commercial, magical, spiritual, judicial, associational and textual. They exercised control over norms of discourse and cultural representations.

Each cult center had its specialists (priests and priestesses), some of whom served more than one cult. Each cult had its congregation of worshippers and its shrine and oracles, with the latter serving as pilgrimage sites for individual supplicants from a very wide area. The territorial cult had its code of practice and rules, but at the same time it was open, dynamic and action-filled. In the eighteenth century, Christian *prazeros* assimilated elements of certain territorial cults, creating in the Lower Zambezi valley a hybrid Christian-territorial cult system of belief.

Archaeological research has revealed that a territorial cult could sustain trans-oceanic links. For example, certain mining and metal-working towns in southern Zambezia—"healing towns"—were also important ritual sites and places of healing. The metal tools and glass objects that were used in rituals associated with medical practices and healing ceremonies are similar in form to metal artifacts and glass jewelry found in south Indian "healing temple" iconography and ritualized medicinal practices. Indian technical specialists traveled to southern Zambezia and African technical specialists traveled to south India. Southern Zambezian "healing towns" maintained trans-oceanic ties with southern Indian "healing temples" from ancient times up until the seventeenth century and possibly later. Alongside long-distance trade routes crossing the Indian Ocean, there was also a long-distance cultural-informational route that linked local politics of medical knowledge and public health to distant sources of knowledge.

With a rise of ivory exports from greater Zambezia in the seventeenth century, the network of professional hunters' guilds expanded. The guilds were linked to one or another territorial cult and shrine, such as cults of the land. With intensification of the Atlantic slave trade in the seventeenth and eighteenth centuries, a new territorial cult, the Lemba association, emerged in the Lower Congo basin. It was linked to the rise of merchant-warriors who were engaged in buying and selling slaves for the Atlantic trade and established themselves in market towns with their armed retainers of slaves and mercenaries. Most of the enslaved were captives from Lunda imperial expansion. To alleviate social and political conflicts in the areas and along the routes where the slave trade transactions occurred, militarized market towns were turned into centers of negotiation, adjudication and cooperation presided over by merchant-warriors who served as judges. The ideological and institutional basis for the merchant-warriors' authoritative role as judges was the Lemba association. This was a healing association and an organization engaged in long-distance commerce, which had ritual networks associated with medical healers and public health. Dominated by rich merchant-warriors, its membership also included skilled orators, reputable healers, priests, officials and their wives, and it maintained social alliances with key landed families. It kept the markets "calm," and it "calmed" towns and villages by cementing alliances and "healing" controversies and violent conflicts. It represents another organizational side of the interplay between the expanding frontier of Atlantic mercantile transactions and the continuity and stability of rural and urban life in the Lower Congo basin.

Conclusion

Sanjay Subrahmanyam characterizes early modernity in terms of travel, global trade, urban-rural dynamics, political theology and historical anthropology. These features were salient across the Afro-Eurasian *oikumene*. The present study examines the historical specificity of early modernity in greater Sahara and greater Zambesia through particular prisms—the city, the zawiya, the world port, the *dzimbabwe*, the stone fort and palace, and the territorial cult. The prisms anchor socio-political and cultural phenomena, illuminate local and trans-local levels of activity, mediate social conditions in which Africans are the historical subjects, and register the contexts in which early modern features emerged within the transactional spaces of the greater Saharan and greater Zambezian interaction spheres. Furthermore, they indicate that particular African experiences and conditions were, in varied ways, congruent with developments in other parts of the Afro-Eurasian *oikumene* and, simultaneously, reveal that certain situations, events and relationships were specific to the internal dynamics of the two interaction spheres. As "texts" or fields of signification, the prisms enable local and global ways of reading Africa in the early modern era. The study shows how generations of early modern Africans imagined and organized societal order and societal relationships in local- and world-historical contexts of change, struggle, rupture and transformation.

FURTHER READING

Ajaye, J. F. Ade and Michael Crowder (eds.), *History of West Africa*, 3rd edn. (Harlow: Longman Group Ltd., 1985).

Austen, Ralph A., *Trans-Saharan Africa in World History* (Oxford University Press, 2010).

Bassani, Ezio, "Additional Notes on the Afro-Portuguese Ivories," *African Arts* 27(3) (1994), 34–45, 100–1.

Batran, 'Abdu-'Aziz 'Abdullah, "The Qadiriyya-Kukhtaryya Brotherhood in West Africa: The Concept of Tasawwuf in the Writings of Sidi al-Mukhtar al-Kunti (1729–1811)," *Transafrican Journal of History* 4(1–2) (1974), 41–70.

Birmingham, David and Phyllis Martin (eds.), *History of Central Africa* (London and New York: Longman Group Ltd., 1983), vol. 1.

Boston, Thomas D., "On the Transition to Feudalism in Mozambique," *Journal of African Studies* 8(4) (1981), 182–7.

Brett, Michael, *Approaching African History* (Woodbridge: James Curry, 2013).

Chami, Felix and Gilbert Pwiti (eds.), *Southern Africa and the Swahili World* (Dar es Salaam: Dar es Salaam University Press Ltd., 2002).

Connah, Graham, *African Civilizations. An Archaeological Perspective* (Cambridge University Press, 2006).

Crawford, O. G. S. (ed.), *Ethiopians' Itineraries circa 1400–1524* (Cambridge: The Hakluyt Society, 1958).

Debrunner, Hans, *Presence and Prestige: Africans in Europe. A History of Africans in Europe before 1918* (Basel: Basler Afrika Bibliographien, 1979).

Ehret, Christopher, *The Civilizations of Africa. A History to 1800* (Charlottesville, VA: University Press of Virginia, 2002).

Garlake, Peter S., *Great Zimbabwe* (New York: Stein and Day, 1973).

Gijanto, Liza and Rachel L. Horlings, "Connecting African Diaspora and West African Historical Archaeology," *Historical Archaeology* 46(2) (2012), 134–56.

Gray, Richard and David Birmingham (eds.), *Pre-Colonial Africa Trade: Essays on Trade in Central and Eastern Africa before 1900* (London: Oxford University Press, 1970).

Hall, Martin, *Farmers, Kings, and Traders. The People of Southern Africa 200–1860* (University of Chicago Press, 1990).

Haour, Anne, *Rulers, Warriors, Traders, Clerics. The Central Sahel and the North Sea 800–1500* (Oxford University Press, 2007).

Hunwick, John, *Timbuktu and the Songhay Empire. Al-Sa'di's Ta'rikh al-sudan down to 1613 and Other Contemporary Documents* (Leiden: Brill, 1999).

Inikori, Joseph E., "Africa and the Globalization Process: Western Africa, 1450–1850," *Journal of Global History* 2 (2007), 63–86.

Kea, Ray A., *A Cultural and Social History of Ghana from the Seventeenth to the Nineteenth Century. The Gold Coast in the Age of Trans-Atlantic Slave Trade*, 2 vols. (Lewiston, NY: The Edwin Mellen Press, 2012).

Settlements, Trade, and Polities in the Seventeenth-Century Gold Coast (Baltimore, MD: Johns Hopkins University Press, 1982).

Kusimba, Chapurukha M., *The Rise and Fall of Swahili States* (Walnut Creek, CA: Altamira Press, 1999).

LaViolette, Adria, "Swahili Cosmopolitanism in Africa and the Indian Ocean World, A.D. 600–1500," *Archaeologies: Journal of the World Archaeological Congress* 4(1) (2008), 24–49.

Lawuyi, Olatunde Bayo, "Studies on Traditional Religion" in Toyin Falola (ed.),*Yoruba Historiography* (Madison, WI: African Studies Program, University of Wisconsin, 1991), pp. 43–9.

Lowe, Kate, "'Representing' Africa: Ambassadors and Princes from Christian Africa to Renaissance Italy and Portugal, 1402–1608," *Transactions of the Royal Historical Society* 17 (2007), 101–28.

MacDonald, Kevin C., "'The Least of Their Inhabited Villages are Fortified': The Walled Settlements of Segou," *Azania: Archaeological Research in Africa* 47(3) (2012), 343–64.

McDougall, James and Judith Scheele (eds.), *Saharan Frontiers: Space and Mobility in Northwest Africa* (Bloomington, IN: Indiana University Press, 2012).

Meillassoux, Claude (ed.), *The Development of Indigenous Trade and Markets in West Africa* (Oxford University Press, 1971).

Mitchell, Peter, *African Connections. Archaeological Perspectives on Africa and the Wider World* (Walnut Creek, CA: Altamira Press, 2005).

Monroe, J. Cameron, "Power and Agency in Precolonial African States," *Annual Review of Anthropology* 42 (2013), 17–35.

"Urbanism on West Africa's Slave Coast," *American Scientist* 99 (2011), 400–9.

Monroe, J. Cameron and Akinwumi Ogundiran (eds.), *Power and Landscape in Atlantic West Africa. Archaeological Perspectives* (Cambridge University Press, 2012).

Mouser, Bruce, "Rebellion. Marronage, and *Jihad*: Strategies of Resistance to Slavery on the Sierra Leone Coast, c. 1783–1796," *Journal of African History* 48 (2007), 27–44.

Niani, D. T. (ed.), *General History of Africa IV. Africa from the Twelfth to the Sixteenth Century* (Berkeley, CA: University of California Press, 1984).

Northrup, David, *Africa's Discovery of Europe 1450–1850*, 3rd edn. (Oxford University Press, 2014).

Ogot, B. A. (ed.), *General History of Africa V. Africa from the Sixteenth to the Eighteenth Century* (Berkeley, CA: University of California Press, 1992).

Pikirayi, Innocent, "Stone Architecture and the Development of Power in the Zimbabwe Tradition AD 1270–1830," *Azania: Archaeological Research in Africa* 48(2) (2013), 282–300.

The Zimbabwe Culture. Origins and Decline of Southern Zambezian States (Walnut Creek, CA: Altamira Press, 2001).

Reese, Scott S. (ed.), *The Transmission of Learning in Islamic Africa* (Leiden: Brill, 2004).

Salvadore, Matteo, "The Ethiopian Age of Exploration: Prester John's Discovery of Europe, 1306–1458," *Journal of World History* 21(4) (2011), 593–627.

Wise, Christopher (ed.), *Ta'rikh al fattash. The Timbuktu Chronicles 1493–1599*, Christopher Wise and Hala Abu Taleb (trans.) (Trenton, NJ: Africa World Press, 2011).

PART THREE

★

LARGE-SCALE POLITICAL FORMATIONS

The Iberian empires, 1400 to 1800

JORGE FLORES

In his *Comédia de Dio*, a Portuguese play from 1601 that is framed around the first siege of Diu in 1538, Simão Machado (1557 to 1634) adopted a striking device: for the Portuguese characters, the poet allowed them to speak in their own language, whereas, with the Hindu and Muslim characters – especially the Italian-turned-Turk 'Cojosofar' (Hoja Safar) – he had them uniformly speak in Spanish.[1] Machado was not the only Portuguese author to use this sort of linguistic ploy, loaded with symbolism, to accentuate differences and draw boundaries, but there were other authors from the same time period for whom the Portuguese and the Spanish were, to use the words of the chronicler Diogo do Couto (1542 to 1616), 'from the same law, and so conjoined by nature and related that they were almost one'.[2] To complicate matters even further, Sir Anthony Sherley (*c.* 1565 to 1636), an unpredictable English adventurer who served Philip III (r. 1598 to 1621) and Philip IV (r. 1621 to 1665) and was never favoured by the Portuguese, wrote in 1622 that 'Portugal is opposed to and fights against the Castillian government, and, as they are distinct in their language, they distinguish themselves as much as possible in their dress and in their customs; they are an old enemy and an uncertain vassal, and their faith is quick to change, as they cannot, even if they are vassals, hide their extreme hatred'.[3]

The positions taken by Machado, Couto and Sherley show how complex the relationship between Portugal and Spain (and, as this chapter will address, between their overseas empires) in the early modern period was. There are identities and differences to explore as far as the Iberian empires

---

[1] Simão Machado, *Comédia de Dio*, Paul Teyssier (ed.) (Rome: Edizione dell'Ateneo, 1969).

[2] Diogo do Couto, *Ásia. Dos feitos que os Portugueses fizeram no descobrimento dos mares, e conquistas das terras do Oriente*, Década IV, 2nd part, book 6, ch 11 (Lisbon: Livraria Sam Carlos, 1973), p. 106.

[3] Sir Anthony Sherley, *Peso de todo el mundo (1622); Discurso sobre el aumento de esta monarquía (1625)*, Ángel Alloza et al. (eds) (Madrid: Polifemo, 2010), p. 90.

are concerned, especially since, during the sixty years of the Iberian Union (1580 to 1640), the two empires found themselves under the same crown. Were they rival empires that were considerably distinct from one another, or were they rather interrelated and similar? Were they empires that ignored or antagonized each other, or did they 'contaminate' or even admire one another? These and other questions cannot be studied through the flattening, often essentializing lenses of national histories, as has predominated for decades, but rather should be analysed in a context characterized by a prevalence of 'composite' and 'polycentric' monarchies, conglomerates of diverse political entities, as was the case, in fact, with the Hispanic Monarchy.[4] In this context, and given the 'transnational' and pluricontinental quality of both empires, it is legitimate to consider them as a kind of 'composite empire', playing a tangible role in the emergence of a global world in which many other empires, not all of them European, existed and interacted.[5]

The early modern Iberian empires: an overview

In Portugal's case, the empire allowed it to compensate for its marginal geographic position and its diminutive territorial size, where the Iberian and European contexts are concerned; considering the smallness of the country and its geographic closing off by Castile, it was inevitable to look at the sea as a gateway, something that chroniclers such as Gomes Eanes de Zurara (1410 to 1474) and João de Barros (1496 to 1570) did not fail to emphasize in their own time. From a geopolitical perspective, Portugal sought to safeguard the autonomy of its Atlantic coast and, simultaneously, provide the country with a sort of 'maritime backyard'. This intrinsic relationship with the sea – highlighted by sixteenth-century authors such as Dom João de Castro (1500 to 1548), who praises the Portuguese who 'plow' the ocean – resulted, however, in a certain estrangement of Portugal from general European concerns, ones in which, indeed, the country carried very little weight.

Domestically, overseas expansion turned out to be a socially indispensable project. It became an effective way to occupy a nobility that, prevented from

---

[4] John Elliot, 'A Europe of Composite Monarchies', *Past and Present* 137 (1992), 48–71; Pedro Cardim *et al.* (eds), *Polycentric Monarchies. How Did Early Modern Spain and Portugal Achieve and Maintain Global Hegemony?* (Eastbourne: Sussex Academic Press, 2012).

[5] The concept of 'composite empire' was put forward by Sanjay Subrahmanyam, 'Holding the World in Balance: The Connected Histories of the Iberian Overseas Empires, 1500–1640', *American Historical Review* 112(5) (2007), 1359–85.

waging war in the Iberian Peninsula after the signing of a peace treaty with Castile in 1411, and (unlike the Castilian nobility) with scarce natural resources at hand, was forced to find alternatives outside the kingdom. The empire became a true social valve that channelled the turbulent nature of certain groups and individuals to various overseas territories. With regard to demographic stability, however, this represented an enormous risk. In the mid-sixteenth century, when the Portuguese Empire had subjects on every continent, the country itself never had more than 1.5 million inhabitants. The scarcity of people in the kingdom was a chronic problem, and it worried prominent intellectuals like Francisco Sá de Miranda (1481 to 1558) and Manuel Severim de Faria (1584 to 1655). Other lesser-known figures, such as the *arbitrista* Francisco Rodrigues Silveira (1558 to c. 1634), even questioned the point of the whole ordeal a century after Portugal's arrival in India: 'From where did we find the number of people that were needed to navigate, to fight, to populate, to trade and to die . . .? What grander contradiction could there be than losing what is ours in order to conquer what belongs to others? To dissipate forces by expanding boundaries. Lose our own blood in order to take it from others.'[6]

On the other hand, Castile, which corresponded to the largest and best section of the Iberian Peninsula after the *reconquista*, possessed a more robust economy and, despite prior demographic crises, had almost 4 million inhabitants in about 1530. Compared to its main Iberian neighbour, Portugal, its maritime empire was a less pressing concern. The rise of Castile as a centrifugal force for the peninsula happened decisively in the final third of the fifteenth century through its union with the Aragonese Crown (itself a major gateway to the Mediterranean) and the conquest of the Muslim kingdom of Granada. With the voyages of Christopher Columbus (c. 1451 to 1506), an Atlantic pathway opened up, which until then had been improbable for the Catholic monarchs to establish. On the other hand, with the Emperor Charles V (r. 1519 to 1558; also ruling as King Charles I of Spain, r. 1516 to 1556) and the Habsburgs, the Hispanic monarchy also became a truly European empire.

The Portuguese Empire which was, in contrast, never quite European in character, began to take shape with the conquest of Ceuta in 1415. However, the capture of this North African city had more to do with the need to contro the Straits of Gibraltar and the connections between the Mediterranean and

---

[6] Francisco Rodrigues Silveira, *Reformação da milícia e governo do Estado da Índia Oriental*, Benjamin N. Teensma *et al.* (eds) (Lisbon: Fundação Oriente, 1996), pp. 226–7.

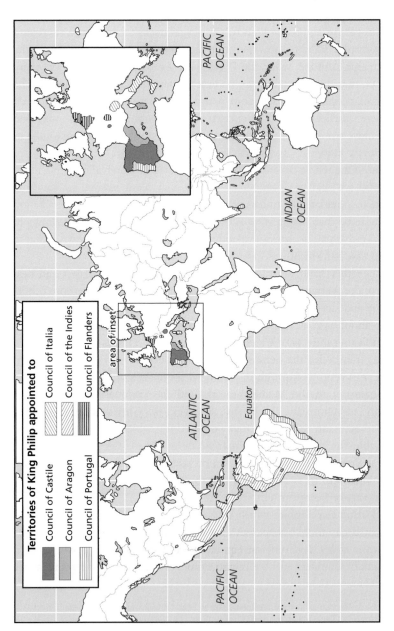

Territories of King Philip appointed to

Council of Castile	Council of Italia
Council of Aragon	Council of the Indies
Council of Portugal	Council of Flanders

area of inset

PACIFIC OCEAN

ATLANTIC OCEAN

Equator

PACIFIC OCEAN

INDIAN OCEAN

11.1 Iberian empires, 1598

the North Atlantic than the desire to explore the then-unknown South Atlantic. Morocco represented, in a certain way, an extension of the *reconquista* and, as a result, became an imperial project highly shaped by war and ideological conflict between Christians and Muslims. Still, it constituted an important space for important socio-cultural interactions at the hands of the Jews, captives, renegades and other go-betweens. A Portuguese-controlled North Africa – a project that held great social prestige for the nobility, while also representing a considerable political deployment by the House of Aviz – continued to be the goal to attain for more than another century and a half, getting snuffed out definitively with the Battle of al-Qasr al-Kebir in 1578. As for Spanish North Africa, that endeavour was considerably more tenuous. There were those, certainly, who dreamed of a Mediterranean Morocco as a sphere of influence for the Catholic monarchs after the conquest of Granada in 1492. There were no more than a limited number of Spanish enclaves, notably Oran (1509), but the project was to be taken up anew by Charles V with the conquest of Tunis (1535) and its strong European impact.

The Portuguese exploration of the South Atlantic began with the discovery and population of the archipelagos – both those closer to Europe, such as Madeira and the Azores, as well as those further away near the African coast, like Cape Verde and São Tomé – between 1420 and 1480. The islands in the Atlantic – including the Canary Islands, reclaimed and colonized by Castile during the same century – came to serve as indispensable points of support for oceanic navigation and important platforms for the circulation of people, plants, animals and technologies in the Atlantic Ocean and beyond. The archipelagos also assumed the function of imperial laboratories for the Iberian kingdoms. There, for the first time (though anchored in peninsular precedents), royal land grant systems were experimented with. That is the case of the *capitania-donatária* (donatory captaincy) – a solution later put into practice in Brazil and Angola, and one that was even sought to be implemented in Portuguese Asia – and, more importantly, of the *encomienda*, its Spanish equivalent, which was developed in America after a first trial in the Canaries. On these Atlantic islands, the first plantation economies were established based on slave labour and involving the production of sugar and other commodities. And it was equally there that relationships with indigenous people who were neither Christians nor Muslims, such as the Guanches in the Canary Islands, were experimented with for the first time.

This first 'ethnographic shock' was likely rather great for the Portuguese, thanks to their systematic contact with the human landscape of sub-Saharan

Africa. This corresponds to a geographical and chronological arc that extends from their arrival at Cape Bojador (1434) to the passage through the Cape of Good Hope (1487 to 1488). In this period, the initial military character of the Portuguese became diluted in order to accommodate a more commercially minded project which became principally concerned with the establishment of *feitorias* (factories, or Crown trading posts) and with the creation of access to cash crops—for example, Malagueta pepper. The gold found in Ghana, sucked away to Lisbon via the fortress at São Jorge da Mina since 1482, allowed the Portuguese Empire more robustness and consistency at a moment in which, under John II (r. 1481 to 1495), a heavy emphasis was being placed on the South Atlantic and the Indian Ocean. At the same time, the kingdom of Congo – through the conversion of its king and some of its political elite – provided Portugal with the first of many overseas experiences that came to centre around ideas of 'spiritual kinship' and political vassalage.

This 'factory-fortress model' was transplanted to Asia where, throughout the sixteenth and seventeenth centuries, the Portuguese Empire consisted of a vast maritime network that stretched from the eastern coast of Africa to the South China Sea. Created in 1505 and establishing its capital city in Goa in 1510 (a choice formalized in 1530), the *Estado da Índia* was essentially a sort of floating domain. The Portuguese Asian Empire was linked to Lisbon through the *Carreira da Índia* and the intercontinental spice trade, but it aimed at having a strong hand in intra-Asian commerce through the mastery of the major Indian Ocean trading routes. In some instances, the *Estado* corresponded to a project of sovereignty, while, in other situations, it merely represented a commercial enterprise. It was a loose network, very much dependent on the control of a set of relevant port-cities like Hormuz, Goa, Malacca and Macau, rather than a cohesive space – a political body 'written on water', as Sanjay Subrahmanyam put it.[7]

The successive loss of many key geographical positions – imposed on the Portuguese by the principal European commercial companies as by various Asian states – which occurred between the 1610s and 1660s, eventually led to the gradual degradation of the network and the transformation of the Portuguese Empire in Asia into a handful of disjointed and disperse territorial holdings: East Africa, western India (Goa, Daman and Diu), Timor and Macau. Even though a certain *Ásia portuguesa* survived, and even became

[7] Sanjay Subrahmanyam, 'Written on Water: Designs and Dynamics in the Portuguese *Estado da Índia*' in Susan E. Alcock *et al.* (eds), *Empires: Perspectives from Archaeology and History* (New York: Cambridge University Press, 2001), pp. 42–69.

reconfigured in the middle of the eighteenth century, what is certain is that by that time thinking in Lisbon had long since focused on the Atlantic. The late sixteenth century saw the emergence of Brazil, which had, until then, been considered as a 'dormant' colony, as a colonizing space based on the production of sugar and on the generation of a colonial society that was composed of a few hundred *senhores de engenho* (master sugar planters) and thousands of slaves, which the sociologist Gilberto Freyre consecrated as a society crafted in the relationship between the *Casa Grande* and the *Senzala*.[8] A Portuguese South Atlantic was built up which depended heavily on the slave markets of West Africa and which consequently led to the colonial valorization of the colony of Angola, especially after the foundation of the city of Luanda in 1576. Just over a century later, the sugar cycle in Brazil gave way to the gold cycle, but the need for slaves remained constant.

This was a late start for Brazil when compared to the might of contemporary Spanish America. When the so-called 'Atlantic (and terrestrial) turning' of the Portuguese Empire was undertaken in around 1570, Mexico and Peru were already firm colonial realities, with the Crown taking control of business after an initial period in which the agendas of the *conquistadores* had prevailed. The first phase, whose onset was marked by Columbus's expeditions, corresponded to the conquest and settlement of the Caribbean and to the centrality of Hispaniola and the city of Santo Domingo. Interest in the continent came a few years later, culminating in the conquests of Mexico in 1519 to 1521 by Hernán Cortés (1485 to 1547) and of Peru in 1531 to 1533 by Francisco Pizarro (1475 to 1541), as well as in the decline of the Aztec and Mayan Empires and in a demographic and human catastrophe. The first viceroys were put in place (for New Spain in 1535 and for Peru in 1542) and the first Spanish cities were founded (Veracruz, Mexico City, Puebla de Los Angeles and Lima), while indigenous cities were either razed (Tenochtitlán), looted (Cuzco) or preserved (Tlaxcala). Spanish colonization was shaped by the possession of large tracts of land by the *encomenderos*, in their intensive exploitation and in their extraction of tribute. Any early agriculture and raising of livestock was obscured by a focus on mining precious metals, especially silver from Potosí and Zacatecas, a practice which yielded around 17,000 tonnes of silver in the sixteenth century alone. Like in the case of

---

[8] Gilberto Freyre, *Casa Grande e Senzala. Formação da família brasileira sob o regime da economia patriarcal* (Rio de Janeiro: Maia e Schmidt, 1933), Eng. trans. Samuel Putnam, *The Masters and the Slaves: A Study in the Development of Brazilian Civilization* (New York: Alfred A. Knopf, 1946).

Brazilian sugar, this economic model hinged largely on the manual labour undertaken by African slaves, but also on corvée taken from indigenous populations.

The gap between Spanish America and Portuguese America closed in the eighteenth century, and both ceased to exist as such at the beginning of the next century, as all of the former colonies became independent nation-states. The ideology of colonial governance that characterized the Bourbon reforms in Spanish America beginning in the 1750s was guided by the principles of enlightened government and came to resemble the colonial programme implemented in Brazil following the policies of the Marquis of Pombal (1750 to 1777). It fell on the state to direct the economy and manage resources, regulate society and impose a legal order, affirm sovereignty over the land and encourage settlement, know the territory and define borders, and organize urban space and classify the natural world. The state also aimed at 'taming' the Church; the Jesuits were expelled and for a time disbanded, and state officials replaced clergy in the management of American Indians, now considered to be royal vassals.

Under this new order, focus in both the Americas was placed on agriculture, the monopoly trading companies, population increase and the colonization of the 'imperial peripheries'. Science, natural history and cartography soon came to be seen as pillars of the empire, and investments were made in organizing large scientific expeditions (scientific-philosophical journeys) on the American continent such as those by Alejandro Malaspina (1754 to 1809) and Alexandre Rodrigues Ferreira (1756 to 1815). In the Portuguese case, and on a smaller scale, the imperial programme that was developed in Brazil in the second half of the eighteenth century paralleled the project for a 'polished government' in Angola,[9] the reforms introduced in Mozambique, the plan of the *Novas Conquistas* ('New Conquests') in Goa, as well as the attempt to assert sovereignty in Macau.

'Contradictions and differences', likenesses and entanglements

The *Treatise in which some contradictions and differences of customs between the people of Europe and of this territory of Japan are recounted very briefly and*

---

[9] Catarina Madeira Santos, 'Um governo "polido" para Angola: Reconfigurar dispositivos de domínio (1750–c.1800)', unpublished PhD thesis, Lisbon and Paris, Universidade Nova de Lisboa and École des Hautes Études en Sciences Sociales (2005).

succinctly, written by the Portuguese Jesuit Luís Fróis in 1585, serves as a good starting point to discuss the relationship between the two Iberian empires.[10] The text unfolds as a sharp contrast between 'us', the Europeans, and 'them', the Japanese, a systematic and radically definitive differentiation that can easily be applied to the way in which the overseas empire developed by the Portuguese has, for a long time, been compared to that of the Spanish. Alongside the 'contradictions and differences' that clearly exist between both, however, one should also consider similarities and connections; it is instructive to analyse moments of 'contagion' and of mutual fascination, together with manifestations of distrust and disavowal, something that recent historiographical work has begun to address.

The period *c*. 1430 to 1530 is notable for the friction that emerged between the two empires. Portugal attempted and failed to claim the Canary Islands, while the Catholic monarchs of Spain sought to establish a position in West Africa and in the Atlantic beyond Cape Bojador. These conflicts were resolved through papal mediation and through the signing of the treaties of Toledo (1480) and Tordesillas (1494), which drew boundaries for the spheres of influence of Portugal and Castile through certain lines of latitude and longitude, respectively. More than a quarter-century later, the Spanish interest in the Moluccas and the question of how to define the so-called Tordesillas antimeridian was resolved through the Treaty of Zaragoza (1529), although the Spanish settlement in the Philippines and the founding of Manila in 1571 prolonged the tension between the two countries, this time with the South China Sea as the stage. Following the end of the 'Union of the Crowns' in 1640, the imperial conflicts between Portugal and Spain solidified in the Americas in a period initiated by the dispute over the colonies of Sacramento and Río de la Plata (1680), and concluded with the establishment of borders in the Amazon between Spanish America and Portuguese America (Treaty of Madrid, 1750; Treaty of San Ildefonso, 1777).

This is the most readily apparent side to the relationship between the two empires; this side, however, places the centres of power at the heart of the discourse, and privileges the political and institutional elements that were shaped by the outbreak of conflicts and subsequent solutions. An exercise that might end up being more interesting – equally departing from the Iberian (and European) politicization of non-European spaces in the early

---

[10] Luís Fróis, *Tratado em que se contêm muito sucinta e abreviadamente algumas contradições e diferenças de costumes entre a gente de Europa e a desta província do Japão*, Joseph F. Schütte, S. J. (ed.) (Tokyo: Sophia University, 1955).

modern era – is to replace the study of 'collision' with one of 'comparison' and 'connection', all the while weighing the two imperial models' rigidity or permeability through an analysis of their figurative DNA. It is clear that the Spanish Empire was mainly terrestrial and geographically rather coherent, and almost became synonymous with colonization of a sizeable chunk of the American continent; it was characterized by the possession of land, extraction of resources and extensive use forced labour.

This same pattern is obviously prevalent in colonial Brazil, but it is evident that the Portuguese Empire, being present on every continent and, by the very nature of its project, dispersed and fragmented, favoured maritime trade and was oriented towards holding control over the sea. *Ásia portuguesa*, confronted with 'dense and resilient populations and states with preexistent fiscal practices based on taxation rather than the exploitation of unfree labor', and dealing with societies in which the practice of slavery was far from the Atlantic model, was naturally distinct from Spanish America.[11] Even so, the Portuguese Empire did not lack either reflection or practice regarding property rights.[12] In the *Estado da Índia*, the most prevalent experiences with terrestrial colonization came with the concession of *prazos* (leased Crown estates) and took place in the *Província do Norte* (the 'Northern Province') in western India, and in the *Rios de Sena*, or the Zambezi river valley. But there was no lack of plans and actions surrounding the imperial control of Sri Lanka after the end of the sixteenth century, something that paralleled (and, to some extent, is comparable to) the interest in Angola's interior, where silver was believed at the time to be rather abundant. Albeit very different in nature, these cases should be coupled with a set of contemporary utopian projects for territorial conquest in continental Southeast Asia and in China.

There is no doubt that the first ideas about the territorialization of the Portuguese Empire came well before the Iberian Union, but it is also certain that the continental dimension of the Spanish Empire inspired more fascination in Portugal after 1580. Such fascination is obviously reflected in colonial Brazil, where even the ecclesiastical organization sought to follow the Peruvian model. It is worth recalling Frei Vicente do Salvador lamenting in his *História do Brasil* (1629) that the Portuguese had only weakly penetrated inland and, like crabs, were limited to merely scratching the land along the shore. Along the same lines, Ambrósio Fernandes Brandão opens the discussion about

---

[11] Subrahmanyam, 'Holding the World in Balance', 1383.
[12] See the research project 'Lands Over Seas: Property Rights in the Early Modern Portuguese Empire': http://landsoverseas.wordpress.com/english-2/.

the qualities of the Portuguese as conquerors in his *Diálogos das Grandezas do Brasil* (c. 1618). Having just arrived from the metropolis or *Reino*, Alviano (one of the two protagonists undertaking this fictional dialogue) recalls that the Portuguese had not 'spread out into the back country' and that they merely occupied themselves with 'making sugar'. An inhabitant of Brazil and a *senhor de engenho* himself, Brandão responds through Brandônio, the other character participating in the dialogue: he strongly prefers the practices of the Portuguese *conquistadores* over the Spanish, and even goes so far as to point out that the master sugar planters of the colony dress better than the courtiers in Madrid.[13]

These tense exchanges between Iberian experiences in America – between the Spanish disposition towards 'conquest' in the *Indias Occidentales* and the Portuguese concession to 'greedy interests and exploitations' in Brazil (as Sherley caricatured it)[14] – are also worth exploring in relation to Asia. What emerges is the allure of the Philippines for the Portuguese, well represented by the levels of praise Francisco Rodrigues Silveira and Jorge Pinto de Azevedo gave the successful missions on the islands under Spanish control, which contrasted with the meagre results of the 'spiritual conquest' of the lands overseen by the *Estado da Índia*.[15] Furthermore – in the Atlantic and in the Indian Oceans, much like on the Iberian Peninsula – the military capabilities of the Spaniards and Portuguese were often compared, and they often got ranked in relation to one another as well as to the hardship of the wars they waged overseas.[16]

In contrast, it is uncertain whether the Spanish Empire ontologically differed entirely from the Portuguese commercial maritime model. The Spanish Atlantic World ultimately was made up of a web of port-cities, merchants, products and businessmen, which used the Caribbean as a sort of 'Trans-Oceanic Mediterranean'.[17] On the other side of the world, the Philippines – even though they fell under the jurisdiction of the viceroy in New Spain, and, as such, were considered a somewhat eccentric geographical extension of the New World whose connections were cemented by

[13] Ambrósio Fernandes Brandão, *Dialogues of the Great Things of Brazil*, Frederick Holden Hall *et al.* (eds and trans.) (Albuquerque, NM: University of New Mexico Press, 1987), pp. 19, 146.
[14] Sherley, *Peso de todo el mundo*, pp. 90–1.
[15] Silveira, *Reformação*, pp. 146–7; Artur Teodoro de Matos, 'Advertências e Queixumes de Jorge Pinto de Azevedo a D. João IV, em 1646, sobre a Decadência do Estado da Índia e o Proveito de Macau na sua Restauração', *Povos e Culturas* 5 (1996), 474.
[16] Telling examples discussed in Paulo Pinto, 'No *Extremo da Esfera Redonda*: Relações luso-castelhanas na Ásia, 1565–1640. Um Ensaio sobre os impérios ibéricos', unpublished PhD thesis, Lisbon, Universidade Católica Portuguesa (2010), pp. 53–63.
[17] David Abulafia, 'Mediterraneans' in H. V. Harris (ed.), *Rethinking the Mediterranean* (Oxford and New York: Oxford University Press, 2005), pp. 64–93.

the Manila Galleon – were not slow to integrate themselves into the networks of trade and influence that formed the core of the 'Southeast Asian Mediterranean'.[18] Returning the focus to the Spanish presence on the land, it is well known that even by the end of the eighteenth century, 'independent, unsubjugated Indians effectively controlled at least half of the territory of continental Spanish America'.[19] Bearing this in mind, Frei Vicente do Salvador's 1629 crab metaphor about Brazil turns out not to seem at all inappropriate or inaccurate vis-à-vis Spanish America.

Understandably, the Iberian Empires shared many characteristics and, very much like in the capitals of their metropoles, the overseas territories served as a stage for a considerable intersection of methods and institutions, ideas and practices, people and businesses, languages and readers. The two entities grew out of the same stem and reflect how Iberian societies had permeated each other since the Middle Ages. The Iberian Union, with the Catholic monarchy at the helm as a 'planetary hat' and as instigators of an early form of globalization, created and intensified much of the intermixing that happened between the two empires.[20] But some of these phenomena had already existed before 1580, just as others lasted past 1640.

The Iberian empires emerged from societies that were rather interconnected through familial ties, social group affinities and shared economic interests. They were empires that, just like in their metropoles, often 'shared' subjects; for instance, the number of Spaniards who lived in the Portuguese-controlled areas of India was far from insignificant, and a similar statistic can be established regarding the numbers of Portuguese that circulated through spaces within the Spanish Empire, from Seville to Lima and Río de la Plata. This circulation was intense and involved not only merchants and businessmen, but also soldiers, adventurers and missionaries who moved at will between the two *Indias* and undoubtedly possessed an intimate and 'total' knowledge of both Iberian empires.

Among many well-known cases, it is important to consider that of Miguel de Jaque de los Ríos de Manzanedo, who authored *Viaje de las Indias Orientales y Occidentales* (1606). Born in Ciudad Rodrigo, Miguel de Jaque

---

[18] Denys Lombard, 'Une autre "Méditerranée" dans le Sud-Est asiatique', *Hérodote* 88 (1998), 184–93. Abulafia ('Mediterraneans', pp. 85–90) alternatively explores the idea of a 'Japanese Mediterranean'.

[19] Gabriel B. Paquette, *Enlightenment, Governance, and Reform in Spain and Its Empire, 1759–1808* (London: Palgrave Macmillan, 2011), p. 98.

[20] See Serge Gruzinski, *Les quatre parties du monde. Histoire d'une mondialization* (Paris: Éditions de La Martinière, 2004), who prefers 'mondialization' to 'globalization'.

spent fourteen years 'seeing all that can be found there, from East to West and West to East' and did not hesitate to designate Vasco da Gama (1469 to 1524) and Afonso de Albuquerque (1453 to 1515), together with Columbus and Cortés, as 'such brave men from our Spanish nation' who had made quite a name for themselves in the past century.[21] Another individual who proves perhaps even more interesting here is Alonso Ramírez, a carpenter who was native to Puerto Rico and who was taken captive by the English off of the coast of the Philippine Islands in 1687 as he travelled between Acapulco and Manila. Ramírez later crossed the Indian Ocean aiming to yet again round the Cape of Good Hope and head towards the Americas and towards Mexico City, where he saw the account of his turbulent life published in 1690.[22] This story contains some elements that, while certainly not unique to the Iberian empires, shaped them and relate them together: an individual adventurer and his autobiographical account, as well as the different experiences of the captured and the shipwrecked.[23] In this sense, the Portuguese who read the story of Ramírez's life at the end of the seventeenth century would not fail to connect it to the *Peregrinação* (1614), penned by the celebrated Fernão Mendes Pinto (*c.* 1509 to 1583). Conversely, a Spaniard who had one of the five seventeenth-century Spanish translations of *Peregrinação* in hand would be impelled to compare it to *Discurso de mi Vida* by Alonso de Contreras (1582 to 1641), an adventurer captain whom Lope de Vega (1562 to 1635) praised in a preface to a comedy, suggestively titled *El Rey sin Reino*.[24]

Imperial economies, universal monarchies and global religion

The economies of the Iberian empires were dependent on a set of maritime networks that put the two metropoles in contact with their several overseas markets and that also put these markets in contact with one another. The major arteries for this commercial body were the *Carreira da Índia*, which connected Portugal to Asia, and the *Carrera de Indias*, which linked Spain

---

[21] Miguel de Jaque de los Ríos de Manzanedo, *Viaje de las Indias Orientales y Occidentales (año 1606)*, Ramón Clavijo Provencio *et al.* (eds) (Seville: Espuela de Plata, 2008), pp. 49, 225.

[22] Fabio López Lázaro (ed.), *The Misfortunes of Alonso Ramírez. The True Adventures of a Spanish American with 17th Century Pirates* (Austin, TX: University of Texas Press, 2011).

[23] Lisa Voigt, 'Naufrágio, cativeiro, e relações ibéricas: A *História trágico-marítima* num contexto comparativo', *Varia Historia* 24(39) (2008), 201–26.

[24] Rebecca Catz (ed. and trans.), *The Travels of Fernão Mendes Pinto* (Chicago and London: University of Chicago Press, 1989); and Philip Dallas (ed. and trans.), *The Adventures of Captain Alonso de Contreras: A 17th Century Journey* (New York: Paragon House, 1989).

with the Americas. Lisbon and Seville (Cadiz after *c.* 1640), cities which the Portuguese humanist Damião de Góis (1502 to 1574) considered to be the 'queens of the Oceans', were the central nodes of these two commercial systems. Unsurprisingly, they hosted the institutions which regulated overseas Iberian trade: the *Casa da Índia*, the successor to the *Casa de Ceuta* and the *Casa da Guiné*, represented the Portuguese Crown's monopolistic interests in Lisbon. A monopoly was in force for the *Carreira da Índia*, whose ships always departed the capital under the king's eye, and in the Indian Ocean proper, where, for some routes, a system of concession voyages was adopted. In the Atlantic Ocean, with opportunities for profit that involved other ports beyond Lisbon (such as Oporto and Viana), the *Casa da Índia* became the core for private business and, consequently, for a growing number of participants, including sugar planters, merchants and transport agents. The *Casa de la Contratación* – created in Seville as early as 1503 with the Portuguese precedent in mind – organized the navigation of the *Carrera de Indias* and oversaw its economic activity, safeguarding royal interests (the prevention of smuggling, tax collection and migration control) in a system fundamentally dominated by private trade.

To these two principal routes, one should add a number of additional transcontinental, regional and local routes that the Portuguese and the Spanish either created or, as happened often in the Indian Ocean, merely integrated or participated in. Among the most noteworthy ones 'invented' by the Iberians are the Brazilian sugar and gold fleets, which structured the navigation and commerce of the South Atlantic. These are somewhat paralleled in the Indian Ocean by the 'great ship from Amacon'. Coming from Goa and stopping in Melaka, it linked the port-cities of Macau and Nagasaki (exchanging silk for silver) and made a considerable visual impact for the Japanese, as the so-called *nanban* screens produced by Japanese artists document. Equally important was the Manila Galleon, which, sailing out of Acapulco and crossing the Pacific since the 1560s to 1570s, delivered the silver from Potosí to the Philippines. Flynn and Giráldez argue that it was in the establishment of this latter route that the beginning of globalization might be identified. For these historians, the direct commercial connection between America and Asia (and the Afro-Eurasian world) represents the birth of the global silver market which, in turn, signals the entrance of the world into a truly global age.[25]

[25] Dennis O. Flynn and Arturo Giráldez, *China and the Birth of Globalization in the 16th Century* (Aldershot: Ashgate Variorum, 2010). See the chapter by Dennis Flynn in part 2 of this volume.

However, taking the Manila Galleon as an example, there are other dimensions to overseas trade that ought to be considered, ones that bring socio-cultural aspects of the first globalization into clearer focus. It is interesting, for instance, to reflect on the 'social life' of the 'imperial' products (especially textiles, chocolate, tobacco, precious stones and porcelain) and analyse the means through which these commodities relate to early modern consumption. Just as it brought silver to Asia, thus contributing to the 'silverization' of the global economy, the Manila Galleon unloaded massive quantities of silk and porcelain in Acapulco that must have transformed the daily lives of many people in New Spain and Andalusia alike.[26]

Despite the apparent compartmentalization of the two Iberian empires' economies along geographic lines (Atlantic Ocean and Indian Ocean) or 'national' lines (Spanish America and Portuguese America), the truth is that these spaces were permeable and that these historical actors were interconnected. The trade and social influence networks were transversal, making certain commercial activities acquire a dimension that often exceeded the limits of the empires themselves. The merchants on the Atlantic routes frequently maintained an economic interest in the *Estado da Índia* and vice versa. A strong Portuguese community existed in Seville, while many of the *asientistas* (or contractors) who regularly supplied African slaves to the New World were Portuguese in origin. It is known that Portuguese merchants in Buenos Aires commonly lived integrated into Spanish families, enjoying connections simultaneously to São Paulo, Rio de Janeiro, Madrid, Lisbon and Amsterdam. In turn, the ties that bound those who lived in Macau and Manila were always stronger than the trade embargos that proliferated between the two empires.

Meanwhile, the Jews and the New Christians who formed the so-called 'Portuguese Nation' moved freely between Amsterdam and Istanbul, between Cochin and Macau, between the *Rios da Guiné* and Buenos Aires, and between Livorno and Goa. These were men like Manuel Bautista Perez, a prominent resident of Lima in the seventeenth century whose library held books about Portugal, Spain and both the empires.[27] Couple this with the

---

[26] José Luis Gasch Tomás, 'Asian Silk, Porcelain and Material Culture in the Definition of Mexican and Andalusian Elites, c. 1565–1630' in Bartolomé Yun Casalilla and Bethany Aram (eds), *American Products in the Spanish Empire: Globalization and Diversity, 1492–1824* (London: Palgrave Macmillan, forthcoming).

[27] Daviken Studnicki-Gizbert, *A Nation upon the Ocean Sea: Portugal's Atlantic Diaspora and the Crisis of the Spanish Empire, 1492–1640* (Oxford and New York: Oxford University Press, 2007); Francesca Trivellato, *The Familiarity of Strangers: The Sephardic Diaspora, Livorno, and Cross-Cultural Trade in the Early Modern Period* (New Haven, CT and London: Yale University Press, 2009).

roles played by Italians, Germans and other Europeans in overseas Iberian trade, and one can easily imagine a situation in which business and culture, pepper and printed books, cinnamon and Persian rugs, and sugar and religious paintings could mix with ease.

The global web of Iberian business was matched by equally global administrative and institutional structures. The distance between the Spanish and Portuguese capital cities and their overseas domains, which proved incompatible with fast processes of political communication, led to the creation of viceroyalties, in which the viceroys and their respective courts sought to recreate the political worlds of Lisbon and Madrid. Spanish America saw many viceroyalties, thus adding an imperial dimension to an institution that the monarchy had already put into place in its European kingdoms. Portugal, in turn, created the viceroyalty of the *Estado da Índia* early on (1505), but it delayed applying the same model to Brazil for almost a century and a half (1640). The 'tyranny of distance' conditioned information-gathering, decision-making, the consulting process and the administration of justice. In order to negotiate distance, it was necessary not only to 'duplicate' the king on the ground, but also to multiply the number of councils and tribunals both in the metropole and in the overseas territories.

The Iberian colonial cities, which were frequently drawn and painted by artists in the period, constituted a key component of the two empires. In the Spanish case, this meant both inland and coastal urban spaces presenting a somewhat rigid layout. Where the Portuguese Empire is concerned, one mainly encounters port-cities with a more spontaneous urban grid, as the planned inland city did not make its way into existence before the second half of the eighteenth century in colonial Brazil. The bodies which governed colonial Portuguese and Spanish cities – the *câmara municipal* and the *cabildo*, respectively – corresponded to powerful centres and networks of political, social and economic influence. For the Portuguese, the municipal council was coupled with a charitable institution that made up another significant site of power: the *Santa Casa da Misericórdia* (Holy House of Mercy).

Thinking politically about the world at large was often practised in the Iberian Peninsula during the sixteenth and seventeenth centuries. *Arbitrismo*, a phenomenon that shaped the political life of Spain at the time and was considerably more prevalent in Portugal during the 'Union of the Crowns', makes up a central element of this trend. Many of the *arbitristas* who inundated Madrid with 'remedies' for various real and imagined problems during these years envisioned political and economic solutions for the empire on a global scale. This is the case with the *Instrución* by the Portuguese

Manoel de Andrada Castel Blanco (c. 1590) or, in a more sophisticated way, with the texts that Anthony Sherley wrote in the 1620s (*Peso de todo el mundo* and *Discurso sobre el aumento de esta monarquía*).[28]

Certainly, the Iberian Empires were sustained by an ideological infrastructure that was conceived to cover the globe, taking on various forms and showing different guises over time. Not being at all exclusive to either Western Europe or that time frame, the universally minded imperial ideologies that germinated there were shaped by their Roman heritage and by specific developments in the late Middle Ages, be it the tension between temporal power and spiritual authority, or the conflict opposing the *Respublica Christiana* to Islam. The concept of universality for the Iberian empires is central to this discussion and the Spanish case shows it *ad nauseam*, all the way from Charles V – who did everything to project himself as a universal ruler – to Philip II's famous *non sufficit orbis* and to the writings of Tommaso Campanella. Significantly, the concept of a universal monarchy led by a 'universal lord' rapidly spread to Mexico and Peru, mixing with indigenous ideas of power.

In Portugal, the origins of such a phenomenon can be traced back to the Crusades and to the concept of 'just war', which largely shaped the conquest of Ceuta. A discourse centred in the idea of a global empire began taking shape with the overseas project of John II and came to fruition under King Manuel I (r. 1495 to 1521), the 'king of the sea'. The Manueline imperial ideology propped itself up using mechanisms such as the royal title and regal iconography, and it adopted strong prophetic and messianic components, which can be more easily understood when viewed in the light of a global millenarian trend that marked the early modern world. The imperial Portuguese rhetoric also went by the rule of 'Christian faith' and took advantage of the establishment of political alliances with non-European kings which centred around their conversion and in the forging of a spiritual kinship. This created an imagined political and religious brotherhood and a Catholic political community on a global scale which stretched from Congo to the Moluccas, by integrating monarchs, royal families and elites. Charles V did something similar upon receiving members of the Mexica nobility into his court.

The issue of a world empire in the Iberian context leads us inevitably, more than a century later, to the universally flavoured providentialism of

---

[28] *Instrución que a V. Magestad se da para mandar fortificar el mar Oceano* . . ., ed. and trans. P. E. H. Hair, *To Defend Your Empire and the Faith. Advice offered c. 1590 to Philip, King of Spain and Portugal, by Manoel de Andrada Castel Blanco* (Liverpool University Press, 1990); and Sherley, *Peso de todo el mundo*.

the Jesuit missionary António Vieira (1608 to 1697) and of his 'Fifth Empire'. In turn, Vieira's universalism ended up projecting itself onto rather unexpected characters, like the king Dom Afonso VI (r. 1656 to 1683) and a fellow Jesuit named Valentin Stancel. In a work that the Moravian missionary dedicated to this Portuguese sovereign, titled *Orbe Affonsino ou Horoscopo Universal* (1658), he describes a world-clock that is able to show in the 'Eastern & Western Orb what the time is for all those who are vassals of such a great Monarch'.[29] On the Spanish end, and instead of an equivalent device to Stancel's 'time machine', one could alternatively contemplate a map produced a century later in Manila, also by a Jesuit. The map, drawn by Vicente de Memije in 1761, was named *Aspecto Symbólico del Mundo Hispánico* and represented Spain as the Virgin Queen. Its image filled the entire space of the Hispanic World – 'a unified body politic crowned with the kingdoms of Spain itself, draped with the Indies and the Pacific, and shod with islands that Memije called home'.[30]

Iberian monarchical universalism in turn stimulated political-juridical thought and theological reflection, as well as the production of a collective memory concerning concepts and themes such as sovereignty and suzerainty, conquest and dominion, commercial monopolies and the ownership of the sea, just wars and reprisal, tribute and vassalage, and language and empire. The Iberian empires also framed the debate about freedom (of Indians, of slaves) and property rights, and it was in the attempted resolution of these central issues that the most erudite among the detractors of the Iberian empires eventually based their criticisms and objections. The ways in which these empires juridically designed their power relations with an extraordinary diversity of societies represents a central point of contention. In the Iberian Peninsula, the legal regime had to respond to the challenges posed by global-scale empires, classifying differences, codifying human diversity, ranking societies, defining communities, assigning identities, and deciding who was a vassal and who could qualify as a citizen. It was a dynamic, tense and volatile process, with results that were not always predictable, as demonstrated by Tamar Herzog for early modern Spain and Spanish America: 'While Indians who were judged sufficiently Christian and

[29] Pedro Cardim and Gaetano Sabatini, 'António Vieira e o universalismo dos séculos XVI e XVII' in P. Cardim and G. Sabatini (eds), *António Vieira, Roma e o universalismo das monarquias portuguesa e espanhola* (Lisbon: CHAM, 2011), pp. 21–3.

[30] Ricardo Padrón, *The Spacious Word: Cartography, Literature, and Empire in Early Modern Spain* (Chicago and London: University of Chicago Press, 2004), pp. 232–4.

sufficiently civilized could be considered Spanish, Spaniards who were considered insufficiently Christian and insufficiently civilized could be treated as Indians'.[31]

Professing the 'right' religion – to be Christian, and Catholic – was a fundamental condition of the Portuguese and Spanish Empires, as the bond between the Church of Rome and the monarchies of the Iberian Peninsula – shown by the creation and longevity of the *Padroado* and the *Patronato* – shaped the two imperial experiences (and, indeed, the relationship between these two experiences) from the very first moment. The Iberian empires can be portrayed, in addition, as extensive and complex Catholic structures, made up of convents and churches, priests and nuns, and bishops and inquisitors. An enormous ecclesiastical and religious machine, it controlled the 'spiritual health' of those who were believers as intensely as it waged 'spiritual conquest' on those who were not. The conversion of the 'natives', and their successful integration into a new religious and political community, depended on the action of many religious orders and their agents. Created in 1534, the Society of Jesus excelled in defining the key contours of what missionary work meant in the context of the Iberian empires, be it through the international profile (and ethnically diverse nature) of its members and their extreme mobility, the transcontinental character of the society's structure and of its information-exchange mechanisms, or the comprehensiveness of its knowledge framework and practices. Overall, though, it was the society's ideas about total evangelization and of global mission which guided both its strategists in Rome and its missionaries in the field. 'Salvation' and 'globalization' went hand-in-hand in this period, and the Iberian empires contributed enormously to these ends.[32]

Even so, the perception that the missionaries (be they Jesuit or not) had about the conversion process did not always coincide with the vision of those who were converted. Where Rome, Lisbon and Madrid invariably saw (or wanted to see) 'perfect' conversions, Goa, Bahia and Puebla offered numerous and rich cases in which the Christian faith became indigenously appropriated or manipulated. Where one might expect the emergence of native Catholics who were as Portuguese as the Portuguese themselves, dissonant voices emerged, such as that of the Goan Catholic Brahmin

---

[31] Tamar Herzog, 'Can You Tell a Spaniard When You See One? "Us" and "Them" in the Early Modern Iberian Atlantic' in Cardim *et al.* (eds), *Polycentric Monarchies*, p. 149.

[32] Luke Clossey, *Salvation and Globalization in the Early Jesuit Missions* (Cambridge University Press, 2008).

Mateus de Castro (1594 to 1677). Written in Portuguese, his *Espelho dos Brâmanes* (1653) is an instructive text that not only reflects precise knowledge about what a 'composite monarchy' was ('the King of Spain and other Princes possess many kingdoms of various nations, and each of them enjoys all the goods from their motherland'), but it also mirrors a certain global perception of the era's politics, natural for someone like Castro, who travelled frequently between South Asia and Europe. The *Espelho* is a virulent anti-Jesuit manifesto that does not spare the King of Portugal, who controlled lands on which it was to be hoped that 'the natives were treated as vassals, and not as slaves'.[33]

Finally, one should not neglect the day-to-day practice of religion in the context of the Iberian missions as well as in the broader framework of an early modern global Catholic world. We refer specifically to relevant phenomena of spiritual circulation and transformation, anchored in the cult – often spontaneous and 'heretical', with results not always appreciated in Rome – devoted to 'global', 'colonial' and 'mestizo' saints, from St Anthony to St Benedetto. A good example is Catarina de San Juan (*c.* 1606 to 1688), a mystic from the Puebla de Los Angeles whom we know about through the thoroughness of her polemical biographer, the Jesuit Alonso Ramos, and to whom the power of bilocation is attributed. Catarina believed she had the capacity to fly throughout the entirety of the Spanish Empire and, thus, look after the Catholic subjects of Philip IV, concerning herself simultaneously with the defence of the empire and its ideological foundations.[34] We might also consider the appropriation and manipulation of Christian symbols and rites in Brazil, Africa and Asia by indigenous converts to suit their own agendas. The tragic figure of Dona Beatriz Kimpa Vita (1684 to 1706), from Congo, is a good case in point. At the turn of the eighteenth century, Beatriz believed herself to be the resurrected incarnation of Saint Anthony. She was ultimately executed, but meanwhile founded an influential prophetic movement that subverted the political, social and religious landscape of that African kingdom.[35]

---

[33] See Giuseppe Sorge, *Matteo de Castro (1594–1677). Profilo di una figura emblematica del conflitto giurisdizionale tra Goa e Roma nel secolo XVII* (Bologna: Clueb, 1986), which includes the *Espelho dos Brâmanes* in the Portuguese original as well as in the Italian translation (pp. 73–81).

[34] Alonso Ramos, S. J., *Primera [Segunda, Tercera] Parte de los Prodigios de la Omnipotencia, y Milagros de la Gracia en la Vida de la Venerable Sierva de Dios Catharina de S. Joan, natural del Gran Mogor, difunta en esta imperial ciudad de la Puebla de Los Angeles en la Nueva España*, 3 vols, (Puebla: Diego Fernández de León, 1689, 1690, 1692).

[35] John K. Thornton, *The Kongolese Saint Anthony: Dona Beatriz Kimpa Vita and the Antonian Movement, 1684–1706* (Cambridge University Press, 1998).

The socio-cultural world of the Iberian Empires

The examples of Catarina and Beatriz show how the Iberian empires served as a stage for unusual women. These were women with agency and who often moved about, like Catalina de Erauso (1585 to *c*. 1650), a nun from San Sebastian who escaped from convent life in Spain and travelled to America in 1603. She wandered between Peru and Chile, living disguised as a man and fighting with a sword in her hand. There was also Isabel Reigota, a Portuguese-Japanese resident of Macau from the same century and a businesswoman of that city who was rather influential in the sandalwood trade.[36]

The social world of the Iberian empires is, indeed, extraordinarily rich for the modern-day historian, though it perhaps was more disturbing than compelling to those observing it from Lisbon or Madrid at the time. Understandably, those in Portugal and Spain, who, over the centuries, conceptualized and managed the two empires, wanted to imagine that the social fabric in such faraway places was as ordered and contained as the society at 'home' was supposed to be. They dreamed of a regulated and hierarchical colonial society, similar to how the metropole already was in their ideal perspective. Observed from this angle, Spanish America should be handed over to an aristocracy of warriors and landowners, as well as to a plethora of bureaucrats shaped by the *merced* economy, which impelled them to prove their *méritos y servicios* in order to reach offices and privileges. Similarly, the Portuguese Empire was ideally made up of captains and soldiers, overseers and clerks, judges and inquisitors, and priests and missionaries, all the way from Brazil to Macau. In either instance, the 'barbarians' and the 'heathens' were to be converted, the 'Moors' were to be fought, and the Jews and the *Moriscos* were to be expelled. All the while, the chroniclers crafted the historical memory of both the empires, sometimes interlacing – as António Galvão (*c*. 1490 to 1557) did in his *Tratado dos Descobrimentos* (1563) – the two imperial experiences. These chronicles, along with many other works, could be read and indeed were read overseas, but there were also many prohibited books whose circulation and reading the Inquisition and the *Casa de Contratación* sought to prevent.

This exported Iberian society was still afforded the opportunity for some mobility. Merchants could become nobles due to the overseas trade, as

---

[36] *Lieutenant Nun. Memoir of a Basque Transvestite in the New World. Catalina de Erauso*, Michele Stepto *et al.* (trans.) (Boston: Beacon Press, 1996); and Elsa Penalva, *Mulheres em Macau. Donas honradas, mulheres livres e escravas (séculos XVI e XVII)* (Lisbon: CHAM and CCCM, 2011), pp. 115–42.

happened early in the fifteenth century with the Lisbon merchant Fernão Gomes, or with many of the inhabitants of Minas Gerais, Brazil, who attained noble status through the mining and trade of gold. But the temptation to engage in processes of social engineering and demographic manipulation held a considerable presence at the centre of both empires. This included casting away undesirables from the kingdom, transporting them to locations that lacked manpower; sending orphans to marry Portuguese soldiers in parts of the empire in which, as was the case in Mozambique in the seventeenth and eighteenth centuries, state settlement and colonization schemes were in the works; forcing Indians in the Amazon in the eighteenth century to live as vassals (that is, as vassals were imagined in Lisbon) in cities inspired by those in Portugal; and normalizing the result of mixed marriages in Spanish America, by imposing classifications that the so-called 'casta paintings' make clear graphically.[37]

It came to pass, however, that the world quickly became far more complex than how it appeared from the docks in Lisbon and Seville, particularly as the ethnic and social landscapes of these metropolitan cities also began to mirror the same imperial 'disorder'. One merely needs to think about the number of Asians, mestizos and especially Africans who lived in both of these cities, transforming them visually into true 'games of chess' (as people used to comment at the time). The capital of the Portuguese Empire was the 'mother of the black race' (Villalba y Estaña), as an anonymous painting c. 1570 to 1580 known as the *Chafariz d'El Rey* shows. The African population of Lisbon did not stop growing in the early modern period, sometimes emulating Portuguese and Catholic examples of social and spiritual organization (such as brotherhoods) and sometimes resisting this phenomenon through the practice of African cults and rituals (such as the use of the *bolsa de mandinga*).[38] And even in Iberian communities in which the ethnic landscape did not shift, as was the case with Oiartzun Valley in the Basque country, there is little doubt that the impact of the empire could be as economically beneficial as it was socially disruptive.[39]

---

[37] Ilona Katzew, *Casta Painting: Images of Race in Eighteenth-century Mexico* (New Haven, CT and London: Yale University Press, 2005).

[38] Jorge Fonseca, *Escravos e Senhores na Lisboa Quinhentista* (Lisbon: Edições Colibri, 2010), pp. 79–109; and Daniela Buono Calainho, *Metrópole das Mandingas. Religiosidade negra e Inquisição portuguesa no Antigo Regime* (Rio de Janeiro: Garamond, 2008).

[39] Juan Javier Pescador, *The New World inside a Basque Village. The Oiartzun Valley and Its Atlantic Emigrants, 1550–1800* (Reno, NV: University of Nevada Press, 2003).

Not uncommonly, the world desired by the imperial capitals was turned inside out. Those who were forcefully sent to São Tomé archipelago in the Atlantic managed to escape to Brazil, whereas those that were cast out from Mexico to the Philippines often created problems in Manila. The Jews and the *Moriscos* who were expelled from the Peninsula rooted themselves in the overseas holdings of the two empires. The Portuguese soldiers at the *Rios de Sena* did not want to marry the orphans that arrived from Lisbon. The *casados* (married settlers) of the *Estado da Índia*, agents of mixed marriages fostered by Governor Afonso de Albuquerque (1509 to 1515) in Goa, became known throughout the Indian Ocean as private traders who took on concubines. In Mexico and Peru, many Spanish stopped dressing, eating and behaving like those back in Spain, and consequently, as we have underlined above, stopped being treated as Spanish by their 'truer' countrymen. And even faithful vassals of Philip IV, like Don Guillén Lombardo Guzmán – a Spanish-styled name of an Irishman who had been a protégé of the Count-Duke of Olivares in Madrid – could undergo radical changes once they crossed the Atlantic: Guzman was arrested by the Mexican Inquisition in 1642 for leading a revolt and claiming for himself the title of 'King of New Spain'.[40]

Certainly, the Iberian empires constituted channels of circulation for people, instruments of social mobility and mechanisms for new identities. On the one hand, they allowed the creation and sedimentation of regional and 'proto-national' identities that, in Spanish America and in Portuguese America, eventually transformed Creoles into patriots. On the other hand, they strengthened the rise of individuals and groups that exhibited multiple and rather complex identities which depended on their agency, the place where they were located and also how others saw them. Jews and New Christians represent one of the most interesting and well-studied examples. But we can just as easily mention the Portuguese who became *lançados* ('expelled') in West Africa, embracing African cultures and cutting ties with Portugal; or those that became rebels (*alevantados*) or renegades in the Indian Ocean, far from Goa's sight, for whom many Asian societies were quick to assign a collective identity – a 'Portuguese tribe'.[41] The African slaves and the 'Atlantic Creoles', whose identities were constructed somewhere between

---

[40] Ryan Dominic Crewe, 'Brave New Spain: An Irishman's Independence Plot in Seventeenth-Century Mexico', *Past and Present* 207(1) (2010), 53–87.
[41] Stefan Halikowski Smith, *Creolisation and Diaspora in the Portuguese Indies. The Social World of Ayutthaya, 1640–1720* (Leiden and Boston: Brill, 2011).

Africa, America, and Europe, constitute another case in point. One sees them reflected in people like Domingos Álvares, who moved between West Africa, Brazil and Portugal in the mid-eighteenth century with a baggage of different identities; or in communities like the Luso-Africans, who transported their social dynamics to Cartagena de Indias and Havana.[42]

Finally, this world of composite identities is also constructed at the intersection of different intellectual contexts and of various processes of writing and visual representation, linking Iberian cultural paradigms to a plurality of models and practices that are somewhat alien to European and Christian models. This is often the domain of writers, interpreters, and bilingual and culturally ambivalent scribes who moved with ease between languages and intellectual traditions. There are well-known 'mestizo' authors, such as the Peruvian Felipe Guáman Poma de Ayala (c. 1535 to 1615) and the Portuguese-Malay Manuel Godinho de Erédia (c. 1558 to 1623). These names should be joined by others, such as the Cape Verdean André Álvares de Almada, the Mexican Domingo Chimalpahin or even the Sinhala poet Alagiyavanna Mukaveti (1552 to after 1622) who, following his conversion to Christianity and his adoption of the name Jerónimo, learned how to reconcile the imperial Portuguese bureaucracy with the writing of Buddhist poetry.[43]

A step below these individuals, we find – though considerably less visibly and thus with much more difficulty – the indigenous cartographers who drew up the 'Spanish' maps of New Spain, just like the indigenous writers who wrote the annals of Puebla in accordance with Nahua traditions while mainly observing the colonial society.[44] We can also find the black slaves and the *indios ladinos* from Lima, the *cabras* from Goa and the native scribes in Bahia. None of them would, certainly, have been able to read Cervantes or Camões, but, in service to the Iberian empires, each of them copied many documents and books written in Spanish or Portuguese.

[42] James H. Sweet, *Domingos Álvares, African Healing and the Intellectual History of the Atlantic World* (Chapel Hill, NC: University of North Carolina Press, 2011); Linda M. Heywood and John K. Thornton, *Central Africans, Atlantic Creoles, and the Foundation of the Americas, 1585–1660* (Cambridge University Press, 2007); and David Wheat, 'The Afro-Portuguese Maritime World and the Foundations of Spanish Caribbean Society, 1570–1640', unpublished PhD thesis, Nashville, TN, Vanderbilt University (2009).

[43] Stephen C. Berkwitz, *Buddhist Poetry and Colonialism. Alagiyavanna and the Portuguese in Sri Lanka* (Oxford and New York: Oxford University Press, 2013). On mestizo writers under the Catholic monarchy, see Gruzinski, *Les quatre parties du monde*.

[44] Barbara Mundy, *The Mapping of New Spain: Indigenous Cartography and the Maps of the Relaciones Geograficas* (Chicago and London: University of Chicago Press, 2000); and Camilla Townsend (ed.), *Here in this Year. Seventeenth-Century Nahuatl Annals of the Tlaxcala-Puebla Valley* (Stanford University Press, 2010).

Conclusion

Between 1400 and 1800, the Iberian empires shared many characteristics, but, at the same time, carved out distinctions between them. This mixture of proximity and distance reflects itself in the processes of mutual observation and emulation as well as in situations of opposition and conflict that were found among the two empires. We must consider, first of all, the identities and differences between the two kingdoms that drove Iberian oceanic expansion. Beyond that, it is necessary to bear in mind the chronology and the circumstances of the moment, as well as the geography and the specific context of each overseas space. The India that Vasco da Gama came across was different from Cortés's Mexico, and it was different still from Pombal's India. The Iberian empires were not set in stone, remaining rigid and unchanging over four centuries. Quite to the contrary, they oscillated and wavered, were transformed and became more complex, intertwined or distanced themselves, always at the mercy of time, space and the experiences of the neighbouring kingdom as well as of other more distant states. There is a considerable advantage, as has been stressed in the present chapter, in studying the integrated construction and evolution of the Iberian empires. However, placing the sole emphasis on a joint history of both conceived together also carries some risks. The outcome may well be the replacement of two national(ist) narratives by a single Iberian one (perhaps equally essentialist) which tends to exclude the histories of other, similar European enterprises, and limits the benefits that the comparative and connective exercise undertaken here obviously grants. By their nature and extent, the Iberian empires undeniably constituted global actors of the early modern era, but they were on a par with other, comparable European organisms. As such, they also need to be put in the global imperial context that includes various other empires, from the Ottoman world to Ming-Qing China.

FURTHER READING

Bethell, Leslie (ed.), *Colonial Brazil* (Cambridge and New York: Cambridge University Press, 1987).

Cardim, Pedro, Tamar Herzog, José Javier Ruiz Ibáñez and Gaetano Sabatini (eds), *Polycentric Monarchies. How Did Early Modern Spain and Portugal Achieve and Maintain Global Hegemony?* (Eastbourne: Sussex Academic Press, 2012).

Costa, Leonor Freire, *Império e grupos mercantis. Entre o Oriente e o Atlântico (século XVII)* (Lisbon: Livros Horizonte, 2002).

Delgado Ribas, Josep Maria, *Dinámicas imperiales (1650–1796). España, América y Europa en el cambio institucional del sistema colonial español* (Barcelona: Bellaterra, 2007).

Disney, A. R., *A History of Portugal and the Portuguese Empire* (Cambridge and New York: Cambridge University Press, 2009), vol. 2.

Elliott, John H., *Empires of the Atlantic World: Britain and Spain in America, 1492–1830* (New Haven, CT and London: Yale University Press, 2007).

Gruzinski, Serge, *Les quatre parties du monde. Histoire d'une mondialization* (Paris: Éditions de La Martinière, 2004).

Herzog, Tamar, *Defining Nations. Immigrants and Citizens in Early Modern Spain and Spanish America* (New Haven, CT and London: Yale University Press, 2003).

Kamen, Henri, *How Spain Became a World Power, 1492–1763* (New York: Harper Perennial, 2004).

Marcocci, Giuseppe, *A consciência de um império. Portugal e o seu mundo (sécs. XV-XVII)* (Imprensa da Universidade de Coimbra, 2012).

Pagden, Anthony, *Lords of All the World: Ideologies of Empire in Spain, Britain and France, c. 1500–c. 1800* (New Haven, CT and London: Yale University Press, 1998).

Paquette, Gabriel B., *Enlightenment, Governance, and Reform in Spain and Its Empire, 1759–1808* (London: Palgrave Macmillan, 2011 (1st edn 2008)).

Studnicki-Gizbert, Daviken, *A Nation upon the Ocean Sea. Portugal's Atlantic Diaspora and the Crisis of the Spanish Empire, 1492–1640* (Oxford and New York: Oxford University Press, 2008).

Subrahmanyam, Sanjay, 'Holding the World in Balance: The Connected Histories of the Iberian Overseas Empires, 1500–1640', *American Historical Review* 112(5) (2007), 1359–85.

    The Portuguese Empire in Asia 1500–1700. A Political and Economic History (West Sussex: Wiley-Blackwell, 2012 (1st edn 1993)).

Thomaz, Luís Filipe, *De Ceuta a Timor* (Lisbon: Difel, 1995).

Yun, Bartolomé, *Marte contra Minerva. El precio del imperio español, c. 1450–1600* (Barcelona: Crítica, 2004).

12

Imperial competition in Eurasia: Russia and China

LAURA HOSTETLER

Imperial Russia under the Romanovs and Imperial China during the Qing dynasty (1636/44 to 1911) competed with each other in contests for land, control over frontier peoples and for imperial status. They also engaged in important diplomatic initiatives. Each empire recognized that creating alliances with the other would strengthen its own position in various ways. For China, the main concern was avoiding any possible collaboration between Russia and the Zunghar Mongols. For Russia, an alliance promised not only peace, but also the possibility of a trade outlet for Siberian furs.

During the early modern period, both of these growing empires faced and came to terms with many of the same challenges in building their respective empires. These included: developing relationships with frontier peoples; imposing control on newly conquered territories; mapping their domains; documenting their diverse inhabitants; and representing their imperial formations both at home and abroad through the sponsorship of literary and artistic production. In short, these two empires were able to compete because they were playing the same game. Considering the competition between these two expanding empires in a world-historical context allows us to trace how the rules of that game were gradually established over the course of the early modern period, and how each of these empires positioned itself vis-à-vis the rest of the early modern world more generally from about 1600 until the late eighteenth century.

Growth of the empires

The Qing dynasty was first proclaimed in 1636 by Hong Taiji in the region of Northeast Asia that we now know as Manchuria. The early groundwork for the empire was, however, established by his father, Nurhaci. Nurhaci was a Jürchen tribesman who achieved a large measure of success in uniting different clans under his leadership. Initially recognized as a vassal by Ming

China, he challenged that dynasty's authority in 1610, proclaimed the founding of a rival Jin dynasty in 1616, and from that time until his death in 1626 continued to build up his own power base. His farsightedness and imperial ambitions can be seen in his commissioning of a written script for the Jürchen language and his development of the system of eight banners, or military ensigns, under which the military alliances he created were grouped, and which, with some revisions, would be a hallmark of the dynasty until its demise in 1911.

Nurhaci's eighth son, Hong Taiji, built on the advances made by his father. In competing against his brothers and consolidating his own position, he relied on Chinese advisors from the border areas and adopted Chinese-style bureaucratic structures. His renaming of the Jin dynasty established by his father to Qing in 1636 signaled a broader ambition and some distancing of himself from the Jürchen tribal origins of the Jin in order to broaden the ethnic composition of his base. Hong Taiji's followers were now to be called Manchus, a newly coined term meaning "great good fortune," which would have broader appeal. Within less than a decade, the Qing would move in to fill the power vacuum left in China by the fall of the Ming to internal rebels in 1644. The relationships established by Hong Taiji with (bilingual and bicultural) Chinese advisors from Liaodong enabled his imperial successors to be well positioned to implement the transition to a new dynastic house in China.

Following the establishment of Qing power in the former Ming territories, the scope of the empire was gradually expanded to include Taiwan (1681), southwest China (1683) and the Khalka Mongols (1691). In 1721, Qing armies would enter Tibet, where the empire's influence would continue to be felt until the end of the dynasty in 1911. Finally, in 1759, a series of wars against the Zunghar Mongols was brought to an end and Xinjiang was also incorporated into the Qing dynasty. Thus, within slightly more than a century the Qing doubled the territorial expanse controlled by the previous Ming dynasty. Many of the newly incorporated lands were populated by people who were not ethnically or culturally Chinese. In this process of growth and expansion, the Qing would also butt up against the Russian Empire, which was simultaneously expanding on its own eastern and southern frontiers with its colonization of Siberia.

The Russian Empire grew out of a power base in Muscovy. After the demise of the Golden Horde, to which Muscovy was a tributary until 1480, the principality continued to gain power and accrue additional territory under its dominion. By 1503, Ivan III had begun occasionally using the title of tsar, enhancing the profile of the region along with his own position. Officially, the first Muscovite monarch to be crowned as tsar and to use the title consistently was Ivan IV (the Terrible). Fueled at least in part by the desire to profit from its wealth in furs, Russian exploration of Siberia began by the 1580s. Imperial expansion continued under the leadership of the Romanovs, who gained power in 1613, and by 1639 Russian explorers reached the Pacific. It was in the Amur River valley during the 1640s that Russian explorers first came into conflict with the Qing. Several skirmishes followed in the next few decades, but neither the Qing nor the Russians had any real sense that these altercations involved the colonial reach of another major power until the 1670s.

Frontier management in both empires functioned according to a kind of tribute system in which gift exchange played a major role. The beauty, or at least durability, of the arrangement lay in its flexibility and the latitude it allowed for both parties not only to benefit, but also to interpret the relationship according to their own best interests. For the large empires, tributary relationship assured (bought) peace in the form of forging alliances that were ostensibly of a paternalistic and hierarchical nature. At times, these relationships were extractive—with demands for furs on the part of the Russian Empire and various local products on the part of the Qing. But at times they functioned in practice more as a pay-off in exchange for peace, with the balance of payments going in favor of the nominally subservient frontier groups.

In the Russian case, the requirements of tributary frontier tribes included *shert'*, *yasak* and *amanat*, all of which derived from the legacy of the steppe politics of the late Golden Horde. *Shert'* can be described as an oath of allegiance to the empire, the specifics of which were always cast in local terms. *Yasak* was a tax, paid in kind—usually in furs in Siberia. *Amanat*, usually translated as "hostage," was a practice that served to guarantee loyalty. Hostages would usually be selected from the extended family of a chief, often a son or nephew, as a kind of surety of allegiance. In return for allegiance, Muscovy provided various rewards and encouraged governors to feast and give gifts to local chieftains. In practice, these agreements were not exclusive; tribes could and did often conclude such agreements with multiple powers, although this was not Moscow's preference.

Over time, the hostage system began to be viewed as a kind of civilizing mission. In a statement reminiscent of Chinese attitudes regarding the desirability of transforming their own frontier peoples, a 1775 report from the governor of Astrakhan opined that: "By teaching the hostages the

Russian language, civilizing them and discouraging their barbaric customs, in a short time there would no longer be any need for hostages, and they would convert to Christianity."[1] Although made in a different context and at a later date, we can nonetheless see in the remark a pervasive attitude of imperial superiority and evidence of confidence in its civilizing mission. Even in the first decade of the eighteenth century, when what it meant to be civilized was changing from the standards of the old Muscovite tsardom into an imperial model built on a somewhat different notion of statehood, Peter the Great had a vision for including the sons of frontier nobility in his educational mission, wanting them trained in both a variety of languages and the emergent scientific methods so important to state building. In the late eighteenth century, male children of the frontier Khans were educated in St. Petersburg, where they lived at the court, received an education and were bestowed military rank. It was not uncommon for them to make their way into the Russian nobility. The offspring of lesser frontier nobles could at this time attend schools in Orenburg, where they were socialized into mainstream Russian ways.[2]

The Qing tribute system functioned in a similar, although not identical, way. Its primary requirements included the submission of tribute, normally transmitted in person to the emperor via a tribute mission. Tribute ceremonies included an extensive set of rituals with the exchange of gifts and often the conferral of titles by the emperor on the tributary. The tribute gifts were expected to consist of representative local products, which functioned much like the Russian *yasak*. The return gifts from the emperor were, in effect, a reward bestowed for loyalty.

Tulišen, the Manchu Qing ambassador to the Torghuts, describes a specific instance on the Russian frontier that sounds in practice much like the Russian arrangement of rewards and annuities. In his account he wrote: "Our Emperor ... readily received *O-la-pu-tchu-eur*, created him a prince of the empire (*Pei-tse*) and gave him an establishment ... Every year the Emperor makes him a present of silks and cattle, besides a pension in money, so that he is already become very rich and comfortable in his new situation."[3]

[1] Quoted in Michael Khodarkovsky, *Russia's Steppe Frontier: The Making of a Colonial Empire, 1500–1800* (Bloomington, IN: Indiana University Press, 2002), p. 56.
[2] For an overview of how the Russian imperial enterprise changed over the course of several centuries, see Willard Sunderland, *Taming the Wild Field: Colonization and Empire on the Russian Steppe* (Ithaca, NY: Cornell University Press, 2006).
[3] Tulišen, *Narrative of the Chinese Embassy to the Khan of the Tourgouth Tartars, in the Years 1712, 13, 14, & 15* (Arlington, VA: University Publications of America, 1976), pp. 99–100.

It may be that Russian and Qing frontier practices influenced each other as frontier groups played one power against the other in their negotiations, or rather even more likely, that both may have been derived from the earlier steppe, especially Mongol, practices.

We also see instances of sending hostages to court under the Qing Empire. In the course of the Qing conquests of the Zunghar Mongols in 1759, a variety of Central Asian peoples pledged loyalty to the Qing court. Afterwards, as described in the *Qing Imperial Illustrations of Tributary Peoples*, some sent sons and nephews to court. While not a formalized system, the presence of the sons and nephews in Beijing undoubtedly served as an informal guarantee of the loyalty of the far-away vassal. Reciprocally, the sons and nephews in the capital often benefited through quick promotion in the imperial ranks. Thus, the arrangement could work well for both parties as long as trust was not broken.

In time, as each empire grew in strength vis-à-vis its frontier peoples, tributaries were no longer able to exact the same kinds of gifts as rewards. By the nineteenth century, they were also unable to resist changes imposed by the imperial powers that would come to incorporate them in new ways, as the early modern period gave way to the modern era.

Mutual knowledge

In 1650, the Russian and Qing empires knew very little of each other, although presumably Russia had received word of the 1644 Manchu conquest of China. Motivated by a need for additional revenues that it hoped to attain by finding eastern markets for its furs, and the related desire for knowledge about its neighbor, the Russian court sent an ambassador to China in 1654. Beset by failures in communication and hung up on matters of ceremonial protocol, the embassy was a complete disaster, at least diplomatically speaking. The ambassador, Fedor Isakovich Baikov, was dismissed from Beijing without having his gifts or letters accepted. He was, however, able to record observations about the city of Beijing and its inhabitants as well as the kinds of goods available in the city's markets. Baikov's relatively unsuccessful diplomatic mission was followed by several trade missions that met with a somewhat more favorable reception.

Despite the 1654 mission, it was only in 1670 when Russian explorers in eastern Siberia came up against Qing subjects that they discovered that the various terms they used to refer to peoples in the Far East actually all referred to the same political entity in the form of the Qing dynasty.[4] This became clear in light of an international incident when the Qing objected that a Tungus chieftain by the name of Gantimur, who had for a time recognized Qing suzerainty, defected with his people.[5] Events surrounding the incident provoked the governor of Tobolsk to send an envoy to Beijing to discuss the issue. The envoy, Ignatii Milovanov, carried a letter that invited the Qing emperor to recognize the tsar's suzerainty and become a tributary! It was perhaps fortunate for all that the letter was unable to be translated at the time. Through this mission, however, Beijing came to realize that the settlements on the Amur where there had been skirmishes were functioning under the protection of the Russians. The conflict could no longer be interpreted as simply the product of unruly frontier settlers; it would need to be taken more seriously. Increased contact and negotiations between the two powers became necessary.[6]

Now with a better sense of whom they might be negotiating with, Moscow sent another mission to Beijing in 1674 led by Nikolai Milescu (also sometimes called Spafarii).[7] Trade issues dominated the Russian agenda for the mission. However, for the Qing the return of the renegade Gantimur and Russian evacuation of the Amur River area were prerequisites for any agreements. Russian refusal to negotiate on these questions and conflict over ceremonial protocol led to Milescu's expulsion from Beijing without any agreements having been reached.[8] The ambassador was, however, able to engage in several conversations with Ferdinand Verbiest, a Jesuit employed by the court, and through these conversations gain useful information.

Even though neither the Milovanov nor the Milescu mission achieved the goals of either empire, they did make it clear that the Russians were, at least nominally, in charge of the raiding parties of Cossacks on the borders. The Qing consequently stepped up its military presence in the area. In 1685 and again in 1686, the Manchus attacked Albazin, a settlement established on the

---

[4] Eric Widmer, "Kitai and the Ch'ing Empire in the 17th Century Russian Documents on China," *Ch'ing-shih Wen-t'i* 4 (1970), 26–35.

[5] Unlike most of the Tungusic clans in Siberia, Gantimur was the head of "horse-mounted Tungus," who were likely historically connected to Mongols.

[6] For a translation into English of instructions to the Russian ambassadors, and Russian documents concerning expansion into Siberia, see Basil Dmytryshyn, E. A. P. Crown-hart-Vaughan and Thomas Vaughan (eds.), *Russia's Conquest of Siberia 1558–1700: A Documentary Record* (Portland, OR: Oregon Historical Society, 1985), vol. 1.

[7] Spafarii was a Phanariot Greek, from the Greek elite of Romanian principalities under Ottoman control.

[8] It is also possible that his ignominious departure may have been due to the Qing discovery of Milovanov's original instructions. See Michel N. Pavlovsky, *Chinese-Russian Relations* (New York: Philosophical Library, 1949), pp. 141–4.

Amur River in the 1640s, which had sometimes served as a place of refuge for those who fled the Muscovite governors in Ilimsk or Nerchinsk, forcing its evacuation. Once it had become clear that the skirmishes in the Amur basin did indeed involve the tributaries of two competing empires, however recalcitrant, it was in the interest of both empires to establish a firm border so as to more easily regulate the movements and fix the loyalties of the frontier region's inhabitants.

In 1689, with the assistance of Jesuit translators and negotiators, a formal agreement on border, trade and sovereignty issues was reached in the form of the Treaty of Nerchinsk. Delimiting the frontier allowed both empires to begin to establish a firm boundary between them, which would limit, if not eliminate, the ability of frontier residents to play one power off against the other. Instead, the tributary and service obligations of frontier peoples would be fixed according to the empire in which they resided. Furthermore, their mobility across the newly established borders would also be limited under the new agreements. On the Russian side, peace was desirable in order to establish what they hoped would be profitable trade relationships. For the Qing, a major incentive in reaching an accord was to inhibit any kind of alliance between Russia and Mongol groups with whom they themselves had not formed alliances or with whom they were in active conflict, namely their formidable foe Galdan. These agreements would be refined and extended in 1727 in the Treaty of Kiakhta.[9]

Additional Russian embassies would travel to the Qing court after the Treaty of Nerchinsk was signed, but embassies not only traveled from Russia to China, but also in the other direction. As alluded to above and discussed further below, a Manchu envoy by the name of Tulišen left China in 1712 to visit the Torghuts (known in Russia as the Kalmyks), a Mongol tribe pushed by strife with the Zunghars into the Volga region of Russia. The Kangxi emperor was keenly aware that Tulišen might have the opportunity to have an audience with Peter the Great, and provided him with detailed instructions on what to say and how to behave in the case of such an eventuality. The Yongzheng emperor also sent two embassies to Russia in 1729 and 1730, prompted by his desire to ensure Russian neutrality in the Qing war with the Zunghar Mongols. Yongzheng was also interested in promoting the return of the Torghuts to Qing territory, which would finally happen in 1771 during the reign of the Qianlong emperor.

---

[9] Translations of the texts of the treaties can be found in Ting Tsz Kao, *The Chinese Frontiers* (Palatine, IL: Chinese Scholarly Publishing Company, 1980).

As Peter Perdue has pointed out, while the Qing and Russian Empires certainly competed with each other during the early modern period, they also practiced mutual accommodation in ways that allowed sedentary agriculturalists to thrive while undermining the power of nomadic peoples. For both the Qing and the Russian Empires, ending the raiding activity on which the steppe societies relied was crucial to imperial stability and prosperity. The treaties of Nerchinsk and Kiakhta were key in facilitating this transition of power.

Mapping the frontier

At the time of the Treaty of Nerchinsk, the frontier had not been systematically mapped, but that situation changed rapidly as both empires realized that it would be to their advantage to have a more precise picture of the region. A look into cartographies of exploration and expansion within each empire is quite instructional. Briefly, we can document that similar changes happened more or less simultaneously in both Imperial Russia and Qing China with regard to cartographic practices employed at the court. Formal border delineation began in the late seventeenth century, when the need to claim and defend frontier regions spurred mapping of the lands in question. Court officials first relied on indigenous cartographies, which would soon be supplemented by the latest in early modern mapping technology as both courts turned to the international language of early modern to-scale mapping to stake out their claims internationally. Simply put, we see overall a move towards imperial sponsorship of to-scale surveys that supplement but do not immediately supplant indigenous forms of cartography.

An overview of four carefully selected maps illustrates the kinds of activity occurring with regard to the mapping of the frontier between the Qing and Romanov Empires. The earliest surviving map of Siberia was made by Semon Remezov. Remezov's *Atlas of Siberia*, which contains twenty-four sheets, is largely organized around river systems (see Figure 12.1). Although the date of Remezov's earliest maps of Siberia is uncertain, they were probably made shortly after 1677 when the tsar ordered Peter Ivanovich Godunov, governor of Siberia, to have the region mapped. Remezov's completed atlas appeared in 1701. The first map in the atlas consists of an overview of the whole region. This map, which is oriented to the south, shows Beijing located behind the Great Wall in the upper left-hand corner. Major river systems and cities are labeled, as are the names of tribal peoples dwelling along the southern frontiers. Other maps in the atlas include both

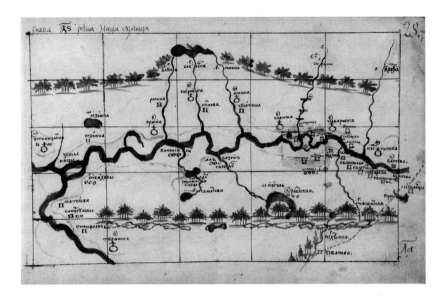

Figure 12.1 Overview map of Siberia from *Atlas of Siberia* by Semyon U. Remezov (MS Russ 72 (6), Houghton Library, Harvard University).

larger-scale maps of regions within Siberia, and a map of all of China, oriented to the north, that reaches as far south as Hainan Island and includes a full view of the southeast China coast. Korea is also clearly labeled on this map. While Remezov must have been relying on local surveys for the maps of Siberia, he clearly had access to additional information for the maps of China and other regions beyond his own ken. This map demonstrates Russian interest in Siberia and knowledge of the Great Wall of China beyond. It locates important towns and centers in Siberia, but leaves much ground uncharted.

"La Carte de Tartarie," published in 1706 by Guillaume Delisle, geographer to Louis XIV, dates not much later, but is done in a significantly different style. In contrast to the overview map of Siberia by Remezov, Delisle uses a northern orientation and relies on latitude and longitude as an overall guide for situating specific locations. Rivers are indicated but do not have the same prominence as on the Remezov map. It is likely that Guillaume Delisle gained some of his information from the map in Nicolaas Witsen's 1692 *Noorden Oost Tartaryen*. Witsen was a Dutch magistrate who visited Moscow twice and had extensive contacts with Russians who traveled in Siberia. Delisle's map demonstrates the latest in early modern techniques of scaled representation that would later be patronized by both Peter the Great (r. 1689 to 1725), who would later arrange for Guillaume's brother Joseph Nicholas to serve at his court,[10] and by the Kangxi emperor (r. 1661 to 1722) through the presence of European Jesuits at his court.

A third map of Russia entitled "Etats du Tsar" ("The Lands of the Tsar") grew out of a 1692 to 1694 embassy from Russia to Peking. According to information found on the cartouche, the map was based on Adam Brand's account of Evert Ides's 1692 embassy to Peking, and on observations made by Witsen and a certain Père Avril. Dating from 1722, this map in many ways serves as an amalgam of the Remezov and Delisle maps. Although oriented towards the north, the nature of the depiction of Beijing beyond the great wall recalls the Remezov map. And while later than the Delisle map, lines of latitude and longitude are not displayed, although they undoubtedly came into play in the making of the map. The emphasis here is specifically on travel routes from Moscow to Beijing. Not only is the actual route followed by the Ides embassy indicated on the map by means of a double line, but the names of localities along the route through which the embassy passed are also listed sequentially in a box appearing to the right-hand side of the map, forming a kind of textual route map of their own. The reference to trade in the heading of this list clearly indicates Russian incentives for the embassy, and for continued relationships with Beijing. In its enumeration of the coordinates of latitude and longitude for Constantinople, Moscow and Beijing, the cartouche additionally underscores the international standing of Moscow and Beijing as important imperial centers. Similarly, enumeration of scale in units of measure used in Moscow, Poland and Ukraine, and in estimated time between distances, also highlights both the expected international audience for the map and its intended utility for traders.

A desire to map the frontier was also very much present on the southern side of the Sino-Russian border. In the 1710s, Tulisen's embassy which traveled to Russia to meet with the Torghuts was instructed to give due attention to "the inhabitants of the Russian Territory, its natural and artificial productions," as well as "its geography and general appearance."[11] In fact, Tulinsen's entire narrative is carefully tuned in to the geographical situation of places visited with descriptions of particular settlements, noting carefully their size in

---

[10] Their half-brother, Louis Delisle, also sometimes referred to as Louis De L'isle de la Croyère, would also find employment in Russia. He participated in and lost his life during the second Kamchatka expedition.

[11] Tulišen, *Narrative of the Chinese Embassy*, p. 20.

terms of population, situation in relation to waterways, whether or not they were wooded, how many church buildings there were, whether they were garrisoned and, if so, with how many soldiers. The final summary of the trip could easily be plotted on a map and, in fact, the ambassador did "subjoin a sketch of the hills and rivers passed" en route to his textual description of the trip.[12] This trip was made a few years prior to the surveys for the Kangxi Atlas, and would have exceeded the northern bounds of its scope.

Jesuit missionaries, who had been present in China and served at the court in small numbers since the late Ming, introduced coordinate mapping to China. The Kangxi emperor (r. 1662 to 1722) was quick to see its merits. In the 1710s, he commissioned scaled maps of the entire Qing Empire. The Kangxi surveys were unprecedented in their scope and ambition. Drawing on the services of several teams of Jesuit surveyors and administered through institutions of the Qing court, surveys of every province of the empire (and as far as possible in Tibet and Korea) were carried out. The results appeared in various forms, including several Chinese atlas editions as well as versions published in France by Jean Baptiste D'Anville, and by J. B. Du Halde as part of his multivolume *Description ... de la Chine*, which was translated into a number of European languages, including Russian.[13] Truly an innovative early modern endeavor, the complete atlas of China, Chinese Tartary and Tibet appeared prior to the national surveys of both France and Russia. A sheet reproduced from a 1721 Chinese edition of the Kangxi Atlas shows the use of scaled mapping based on latitude and longitude for precise maps of the Chinese frontier (Figure 12.2).

This flurry of map-making activity and the technological advances it represented, which has been described as the "global integration of space,"[14] was due in large part to the patronage of monarchs such as the Kangxi emperor, Peter the Great and Louis XIV (r. 1643 to 1715), who recognized the utility—indeed necessity—of recording more precise geographic knowledge of their own realms and beyond. In fact, both Peter the Great and the Kangxi emperor were exceptional in the degree to which they displayed a personal interest in practical learning and scientific method, namely observation and

---

[12] Tulišen, *Narrative of the Chinese Embassy*, pp. 209–10.
[13] Only the first volume was translated into Russian. It appeared in two parts, in 1774 and 1777, and the overview and provincial maps were not reproduced. For additional details on this translation, see Boris Szczesniak, "A Russian Translation of J. B. Du Halde's Description De l'Empire De La Chine," *Monumenta Serica* 17 (1958), 373–6.
[14] Charles H. Parker, *Global Interactions in the Early Modern Age, 1400–1800* (Cambridge University Press, 2010).

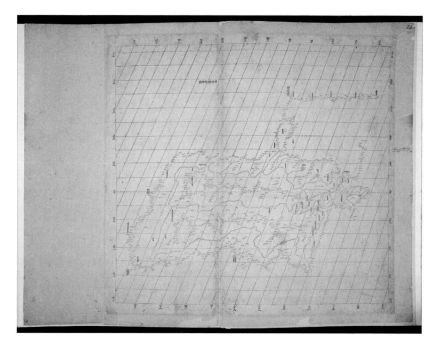

Figure 12.2 Kangxi Map Atlas (*Huangyu quanlan tu*) 1721 (© The British Library Board).

description of the natural world through verifiable methods. On his grand tour to Western Europe in 1697 to 1698, Peter visited shipyards in the Netherlands incognito in order to obtain a first-hand understanding of the craft, even working there as a carpenter under the name of Peter, de timmerman van Zaandam. He would later make several return trips to Western Europe, where in 1717 he met the young Louis XV in Paris. On this same trip, his early interest in mapping was heightened and he determined to commission an atlas of the Russian Empire, which would eventually be completed in 1745 by Joseph Nicholas Delisle, who worked in Russia from 1726 to 1747. Peter I was also keen on disseminating scientific knowledge and had a vision for training a core group of individuals schooled in modern methods to assist in building the empire. He gave the order for the founding of the Russian Academy of Sciences, which was established in 1725 shortly after his death.

The Kangxi emperor also had a great thirst for and interest in knowledge about the natural world and in science as a means to gaining a better understanding of it. He expressed scepticism over blind adherence to received book learning not verified by experience and direct observation, and believed in the importance of careful planning. On hunting expeditions to the north, he himself determined the group's location according to astronomical calculations. He also calibrated the measure of the Chinese *li* (exactly 0.5 kilometers) to correlate precisely with astronomical measurements. Like Peter I, he too traveled extensively, making six trips south to the richest and culturally elitist Jiangnan region of the empire, where he personally inspected waterworks along the Yangzi River. While not international in their scope, in some ways these trips parallel Peter's visits to the cultural and economic centers of Europe.

The confluence in these contemporary monarchs' outlooks and interests is remarkable, but perhaps not coincidental. Both were following the impera- tives necessary to successful statecraft in the early modern period using an array of methods and technologies available to them both domestically and internationally. As each prioritized the growth and integration of his own empire, they faced similar sets of challenges to which they responded in similar ways. Their legitimacy depended on fostering imperial growth and grandeur through a flourishing of the arts and sciences and a relative openness towards technologies from the outside world for purposes of empire building at home. In a sense, it is hardly remarkable that advances in scientific mapping were made simultaneously under their reigns.[15]

Mapping the globe, and different imperial spaces within it, was of necessity a cooperative global endeavor, yet the necessity and desirability of cooper- ation was also always tempered by the competition between imperial centers. The extent of cooperation versus competition fluctuated at different times according to a variety of circumstances. A certain measure of openness was essential to laying claim to territories mapped and to asserting one's expertise. The surveying and cartographical work was greatly facilitated through international cooperation and communication between the scholars in centers of learning such as Paris, Beijing and Muscovy who carried out the work and who were often members of the Academies of Sciences of more than one country. There was also formal exchange of information between the various courts. The Kangxi emperor sent a copy of his recently completed atlas to Peter the Great in 1721. A few years later, a Russian embassy to Beijing

---

[15] For an argument that Peter's interest in cartography was not only a question of importing European technology, but also grew also out of more long-term indigenous cartographic traditions that had themselves emerged out of the demands of statecraft, see Denis J. B. Shaw, "Mapmaking, Science and State Building in Russia before Peter the Great," *Journal of Historical Geography* 31 (2005), 409–29.

offered as a gift a 1725 atlas by Johann Homann that had been printed at Nuremberg and included maps of the Caspian Sea as well as of Kamchatka—an area of particular interest to the Qing court. The Kangxi maps were also sent to Paris for engraving, from whence they circulated quite widely throughout Europe in various forms.

Yet, at other times, secrecy and mistrust were the order of the day. Sino-European relations began to founder over disputes concerning the practice of Catholicism in China and what kind of foreign supervision European missionaries in China should be working under.[16] The Qing court had been eager to employ European missionary scientists as free agents, but was not receptive when foreign entities wanted representation in China, whether in the form of papal supervision of missionaries, or requests for rights of diplomatic residency. After 1706, the Kangxi emperor required all Jesuits remaining in China to sign an agreement stating that they would not return to Europe without imperial permission. Mapping activity continued in the context of these tensions, but gradually increasing amounts of secrecy surrounded these endeavors; under the reigns of the Yongzheng (1722 to 1735) and Qianlong emperors (1735 to 1796), Jesuits at court would still be given a role in map-making, but it would be more limited, and access to geographic information more tightly constrained.

Antoine Gaubil was a Jesuit missionary who arrived in Beijing shortly after the death of the Kangxi emperor. He was soon pressed into cartographic service under the Yongzheng emperor. His collected letters provide a marvelous source for information on the Qing court, particularly with regard to its relations with Europe and the ongoing collection of geographic knowledge. He was especially interested in regions to the north of China where Russian exploration was also occurring. A letter he penned in the autumn of 1726 mentions receiving two maps made by M. Delisle,[17] and further asserts that the correction made by him with regard to the lake to the east of the Caspian Sea accorded well with the findings of the Jesuits in China. He further reports that another of the Jesuits at the court in Beijing would forward to Paris what he had learned in the palace regarding the Kalmuk Tartars.[18]

---

[16] The Russian Orthodox Church in Beijing operated under separate arrangements.

[17] From the context it is not clear whether he is referring to Guillaume Delisle in Paris, or his brother, Joseph Nicholas, who moved to Russia in the same year. Gaubil would correspond extensively with Joseph Nicholas in Russia in the coming years.

[18] Antoine Gaubil, *Correspondance de Pékin, 1722–1759* (Geneva: Libraire Droz, 1970) pp. 116–17. Translation from French by the author.

It seems that preparations for the Treaty of Kiakhta (ratified in 1728) spurred further geographical interest and preparations at the Qing court. Gaubil relates that in January 1727 a group of Jesuits was called to the palace, where they were quizzed on their geographical knowledge. Having apparently measured up, they were then brought to another location where they were presented with an assortment of atlases with maps of the four major continents and further questioned. They were then given the commission to make a map of the countries situated between the Amur River, the North Sea and the Eastern Sea. In the course of the commission, they had the opportunity to examine a variety of maps held in the palace and to interview travelers who had been to the areas in question. The commission accounts at least in part for Gaubil's eagerness for cartographic information on Russia, whether in correspondence with fellow Jesuits in France, or with Joseph Nicholas Delisle in Russia.

The preparations for the treaty negotiations also involved additional diplomatic activity. In 1725, Moscow sent another embassy to Beijing. The visit occasioned a great number of questions on the part of the Qing court to the Jesuits in Peking. They were particularly interested in knowing what questions had been put to the Jesuits by members of the embassy, whether in respect of religion or other topics. Unsatisfied with the answer that the Russians had asked about the Dutch activities in Batavia, the questioner is said to have replied that the ambassador "M. Sava, is a European with more than fifty Europeans in his entourage. I doubt that these people are coming here for commerce; they come to inform themselves on the state of things."[19] In other words, those at court doubted that the embassy was inspired only by an interest in trade, but believed it had further intelligence designs as well. Gaubil, in his response, took the opportunity to describe Russian patronage of arts and sciences, perhaps in the dual hope of inspiring respect for Imperial Russian scientific and artistic achievements and spurring the Qing court to compete in this realm. More specifically, he wrote:

> I took the floor and made common ground regarding the protection that the Russians were giving to the arts, which had attracted many European workers that were quite well paid. I spoke of the observatory that they are considering building in St. Petersburg, and of the great estimation in which the scholars of Europe are currently held in Russia, I also added that I knew of two capable astronomers who had recently journeyed from France to St. Petersburg, invited by the Tsarina.

[19] Gaubil, *Correspondance de Pékin*, p. 173.

Later in the same letter, he added that "the Russian embassy gave no pleasure to the emperor, and we had occasion to believe that the Prince would report everything he learned through us about Russia to the emperor."[20] From these accounts, it is clear that competition between the empires was intense, and mistrust was growing.

Competition with Russia formed the topic of other letters written in the same year. In his annual letter to Father Gaillard, Gaubil relates that on 16 March he had been able to meet with representatives from the Russian ambassador, and that he personally preferred to keep a certain distance in relation to the negotiations at Kiakhta. More specifically, Gaubil did not want to travel with the ambassador's retinue, nor did he want any other Jesuits from the court to make the return trip to Russia with the group.

Yet, Gaubil was keen to learn what he could about Russian activities in the border regions. He was especially interested in information regarding Kamchatka, or Jesso as the French called it, and divulges what he had learned about Russian plans for the first Kamchatka expedition—namely, that: "The Tsarina has given the order to equip vessels on the coast of Jesso that are to reconnoiter and prowl the coasts of Japan, Korea, and China." And that "sailors, pilots, carpenters, geographers, and officers had already arrived at Erguskoy [Irkutsk] with the items necessary for the expedition."[21] In a later letter, he asserted:

> It will be up to the Muscovites to instruct us on whether large ships will be able to navigate the strait that separates Jesso from Tartary. It is also by them that we may be able to be instructed on geographical points regarding the northern, western and eastern coasts of Jesso, and on navigation from the gulf and the Kamchatka sea to the lands of Jesso, Japan, Korea and China. If Russian establishments are able to construct the vessels and have the other things necessary for navigation, it would be easy for them to come to the ports of China by the strait between Jesso and Tartary if they can get through, and if not, they could easily come to China via the east of Jesso in passing by the Ryukyu islands.[22]

The fact that Gaubil could not get information from the Chinese side made him especially eager for whatever he could learn about Russia whether from contacts in France, or directly from Russia. The Qing court was also eager for this information, and pressed the Jesuits for what they could learn.

---

[20] Gaubil, *Correspondance de Pékin*.   [21] Gaubil, *Correspondance de Pékin*, p. 176.
[22] Gaubil, *Correspondance de Pékin*, pp. 222–3.

Demands on the Jesuits for information about Russia and its neighboring countries grew especially intense in 1729 during the preparations for a Chinese embassy to Russia. Gaubil was asked to map out Russia's borders with all of its neighboring lands and stated specifically that anything to do with Russia was of the utmost importance. The court was also interested in revolution in Persia, in connections between the Turks and Russia, the war with Sweden (by then over), "the great number of Europeans in the Russian army, and those who went there in pursuit of the arts and sciences, but above all relations between Muscovites and other Europeans." Other questions ranged from Russia's ancient history to information on a possible route to China from Europe via the Arctic Sea and of course the route from Beijing to Moscow. Later in the same letter, Gaubil relates that there were those in China who wished that Persia and Turkey, or even Sweden, would make war against Russia, no doubt to keep its great power in check.[23]

Meanwhile, cartographic activity continued apace in both countries. In 1717, Peter I had commissioned scaled maps of the entire empire, based on the coordinate system using latitude and longitude. Peter's imperially sponsored maps would first appear in 1734 in an atlas published by I. K. Kirilov, and more officially in 1745 in the *Atlas Russicus*, over which Joseph Nicolas Delisle presided.[24] Meanwhile, the survey maps commissioned by the Yongzheng emperor that covered territory including not only all of China, but also extending north to include all of the Russian Empire and west to the Mediterranean, would be completed by circa 1735. A letter by Gaubil to J. N. Delisle dated 1732 asking for precise coordinates of several locations within Russia—Archangel, Astrakhan, Tobolsk, Lake Baikal, the mouth of the Lena and Kamchatka—ideally together with a map, indicates that work on the Yongzheng map was ongoing at that point.[25] Unlike Delisle's *Atlas Russicus*, however, the information in the Yongzheng map would remain guarded within the court and did not circulate through publication.

Exploration and expansion in the Russian Empire

Cartographic activity was, of course, closely related to exploration itself. A multifaceted literature of exploration also burgeoned in each empire

---

[23] Gaubil, *Correspondance de Pékin*, p. 235.
[24] Shortly before the resultant maps appeared, maps made by Philipp Johann von Strahlenberg, who had been a Swedish prisoner of war in Russia from 1709 to 1721, were also published.
[25] Gaubil, *Correspondance de Pékin*, p. 306.

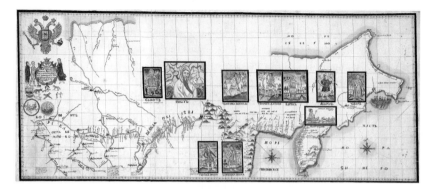

Figure 12.3 "Karte des Reisewegs der 1. Kamtschatkaexpedition von Tobolsk bis nach Kamtschatka mit ethnographischen Darstellungen." (1729) by Pjotr Awraamowitsch Tschaplin (Peter Chaplin). (Cod. Ms. Asch 246, Lower Saxonian State and University Library, Göttingen).

during the eighteenth century. The embassies themselves collected and recorded information regarding the regions through which they traveled. Eberhard Ysbrand-Ides and Adam Brand both published travelogues based on the journeys they undertook as part of the 1692–94 Russian embassy to Beijing. These illustrated accounts are not confined to routes and topographical features, but also show an interest in the peoples of Siberia and their livelihood. Only a few years after this embassy, in 1697, a group of Cossacks explored Kamchatka, and in 1711 an exploratory mission visited the Kurile Islands. 1719 would see another voyage to Kamchatka, allowing progress in mapping the Kurile Islands. However, not all Russian geographical attention was focused on Siberia. In the 1710s, effort was also expended towards finding a viable sea route to India.

With the establishment of the Academy of Sciences in 1725, the infrastructure was in place to support more systematic and extensive exploration both by land and by sea. Under its auspices, Russia would make two more major expeditions to Kamchatka and the Kurile Islands. The first, alluded to in Gaubil's letter above, occurred from 1725 to 1730. It was led by Captain Vitus Bering. A route map made by Peter Chaplin in 1729 on a Mercator projection details: the route taken; geographical features encountered, including both rivers and settlements; coastlines; ethnographic sketches of peoples encountered; and even a somewhat cartoonish depiction of the explorers themselves at the farthest extent of their voyage in a boat off the far coast (Figure 12.3). The international interest in the findings of this expedition is demonstrated by inclusion of maps of Bering's explorations from Tobolsk to Kamchatka in D'Anville's 1737 *Nouvelle Atlas de la Chine*.

As the first Kamchatka expedition was unable to determine whether Northeast Asia and North America were connected by land, a second expedition was proposed. The second, also led by Bering, was a full decade in duration, lasting from 1733 to 1743. More ambitious than the first, it had three main goals, each to be carried out by a different subset of the expedition party. One goal was to explore and map the coast of Siberia; a second was to search for a passage by sea from Okhotsk to the Kuril Islands and to Japan; the third was to attempt an actual voyage to the coast of North America. In addition, the expedition included a contingent of scholars from the Academy of Sciences charged with studying the peoples, natural environment and history of Siberia. The fruits of the expedition included extensive studies in botany, natural history, ethnography and of course cartography. The land expedition, led by Gerhard Friedrich Müller and Johann Georg Gmelin, surveyed Siberia's geography, its plant and animal life, and also its inhabitants. This information, together with documents collected from local archives, would form the basis for Müller's *Description of the Siberian Kingdom*, published in Russian in 1750, and his *Sammulung Russischer Geschichte* (*Collection of Russian History*), published in 1759, as well as two four-volume works by Gmelin: *Reise durch Siberien* (*Travels through Siberia*), which first appeared in 1751 to 1752, and *Flora Siberica*, which appeared between 1749 and 1769. Other scholars in this contingent of the second expedition included Stepan Krasheninnikov (1711 to 1755) and Georg Wilhelm Steller (1709 to 1746).

Under Catherine II (1762 to 1796), many more expeditions were sponsored through the Academy of Sciences. Generally speaking, these expeditions were designed to survey the empire more thoroughly in ways that would both add to knowledge and facilitate the exploitation of natural resources. During the 1760s and 1770s, no fewer than five major expeditions were made. These included an Orenburg expedition, whose leadership included Peter Simon Pallas, and an Astrakan expedition, whose leadership included Samuel Gottlieb Gmelin (nephew to Georg Gmelin). Pallas was especially prolific. His reports appeared in Russian, German, French and English editions under the general title *Journey through Various Provinces of the Russian Empire* (1771 to 1776). He also published on botany (*Flora Rossica*, 1784 to 1788) and, at Catherine's behest, compiled a dictionary of all languages, which included almost as many languages (200) as words (273). Gmelin's expedition mainly explored the Caspian and Caucasus. He did not leave the same kind of prolific record as Pallas, for he died captive in a prison in Ak-Mechet.

The Academy expeditions also gave rise to a series of ethnographic surveys. Johann Gottlieb Georgi, who took part in Pallas's Orenburg expedition, published a four-volume work that included descriptions of the inhabitants of Siberia based both on his own observations and those of others. The title, in direct translation from the German, reads: *Description of All the Nationalities of the Russian Empire*. It was published in Russian, German, French and eventually English. Its subtitle, *Their Way of Life, Religion, Customs, Dwellings, Clothing and Other Characteristics*, again in direct translation from the German, gives one a sense of the range of the contents. Heavily illustrated, this work has been called "the first ethnographic survey of the Russian empire."[26] The work has also been described as Linnean in its efforts to categorize the peoples of the Russian Empire. And indeed, Georgi did engage in personal correspondence with the Dutch taxonomist. While remarkable in its scope, Georgi's work was by no means unique in the interest it took in the peoples of the Russian Empire and the effort it made to depict them. A number of additional exploratory missions would be undertaken in the 1780s and 1790s, and more scholarly works of a similar nature would derive from them. Among these later expeditions was another by Pallas in 1793 to 1794. Afterwards, Pallas published an account in two volumes illustrated by Christian Gottfried Heinrich Geissler, who accompanied him on the trip. The illustrations include ethnographic images of peoples of various ethnicities, animals, landscapes and maps. Geissler also published a series of additional ethnographically-oriented albums based on his time in Russia in the 1790s.[27]

Generally speaking, the Academy expeditions were designed to facilitate a better command of knowledge of the lands, peoples and other resources of the Russian Empire. The fruits of the research carried out in conjunction with the Academy expeditions sponsored by Catherine II were so prolific that they caused Willam Coxe, author of *Travels into Poland, Russia, Sweden, and Denmark*, to remark in print that "perhaps no country can boast, within the space of so few years, such a number of excellent publications on its internal state, on its natural productions, on its topography, geography, and history; on the manners, customs, and languages of the different people."[28]

---

[26] Richard Wortman, "Texts of Exploration and Russia's European Identity" in Cynthia Hyla Whittaker (ed.), *Russia Engages the World, 1453–1825* (Cambridge, MA: Harvard University Press, 2003), p. 99.

[27] The illustrated 1803 German edition of this book is available online through the HathiTrust digital library at: http://catalog.hathitrust.org/Record/008633798.

[28] Elena V. Barkhatova, "Visual Russia: Catherine II's Russia through the Eyes of Foreign Graphic Artists" in Whittaker, *Russia Engages the World*, p. 84.

There would have been no reason for Coxe to have been aware of the Qing dynasty's contemporaneous production of both pictorial ethnographic works and increasingly detailed and extensive maps. Yet, around 1750, the Qianlong emperor commissioned an illustrated compendium describing over 300 of its frontier peoples and tributaries. This work was in many ways a more comprehensive empire-wide version of the provincial "Miao Albums" made to assist administrators in governing areas heavily populated by cultur- ally non-Chinese peoples in remote regions. The *Qing Imperially Commis- sioned Illustrations of Tributary Peoples* (*Huang Qing zhigong tu*) represented Qing power at the height of its territorial reach. It included Central Asian tribes on the border with Russia who submitted to the Qing in the wake of the Zunghar conquests, which were completed in 1759, as well as the Torghuts, who voluntary returned to Qing territory and rule from the region of the Volga River basin where they had migrated several generations earlier. At the same time, the Qianlong emperor also sponsored additional mapping projects that encompassed not only the Qing dynasty, but also the entire Russian Empire, reaching north to the Arctic Sea, west to the Caspian and east to Kamchatka. These maps, although not widely distributed, would form the basis of Julius von Klaproth's nineteenth-century maps of Central Asia. Knowledge of frontier areas, especially in Xinjiang—the "New Territories"— was furthered by highly educated Chinese exiled to the region for political reasons. Their scholarship played an important part in making the area and its local conditions accessible to a broader audience. In short, knowledge of new territories and the management of peoples of a variety of ethnicities were central to the growth and maintenance of both the Qing and Russian Empires during this period of intense mutual imperial expansion.

Patronage of art and literature

The final way in which the Russian and Qing Empires both competed to build legitimacy and create lasting legacies was through the patronage of arts and the creation of a distinctive literature. Art and literature were powerful ways to represent an empire both at home and abroad. Official histories, as well as other types of literature and works of art and architecture, all played a hand in projecting an image of empire whether Russian or Qing—or French or Ottoman for that matter—during the early modern period. The first actual histories of Russia appeared during the reign of Catherine the Great, and a major dictionary of the Russian language was also begun. Similarly, the Qianlong emperor commissioned special histories of the Manchu people, as well as multilingual dictionaries. All of these fostered a sense of imperial grandeur and identity and accrued legitimacy for the rulers who patronized their compilation.

Conclusion

During the early modern period, maintenance of viable imperial formations required the allegiance of a variety of peoples, access to the finest objects in the realm, the best scholarship that the known world had to offer, and the ability to demonstrate command over all of these things by incorporating them into one's own imperial milieu. As we have seen in the specific instances of Russia and China, this also called for successful tribute relationships and sponsorship of the most up-to-date science and technology. Imperial legitimacy also called for a thriving art and architecture as well as the development of a distinctive literature and a history that one could claim as one's own. Successful empires, or at least their leaders, were cognizant of the achievements of their competitors. Their success was always based at least in part on patronage of and cooperation from individuals of various origins. Early modern empires drew on the talents of various peoples, their ethnic or national origin being relatively unimportant in and of itself.

Yet, at the same time that imperial courts called on the service of experts of a wide variety of international backgrounds, managing difference *within* their expanding empires became a central preoccupation of rule. Especially in frontier areas, where the peoples they governed were from a variety of linguistic and cultural backgrounds, a tension existed in both Russia and China between the urge to "civilize"—i.e. to make the other like us with regard to manners, customs and values—and to perpetuate distinctions between those who governed and those who were governed. Was political unity throughout the empire best achieved through cultural sameness, or could political unity—and even greater imperial glory—be better achieved through the allowance of cultural difference? The answer to the question was debated. This evident tension may have also served to mask an equally important cultural shift in which the ruling houses embraced an epistemological shift in what constituted knowledge—one that privileged the role of science and measurement—in order to bolster their own power and legitimacy.

The management of difference was also complicated by a desire to preserve the special position of those in power vis-à-vis the larger population. This latter imperative produced pressure to perpetuate difference in a way that would guarantee continuing privilege for the elite in the future—to somehow fix it indefinitely. This shift would allow those who successfully wielded tools of technology for state building, or their descendants, to see their own success as a product of who they were rather than what they had achieved through scholarship, collaboration and imperial sponsorship at a given historical moment. One way to perpetuate elite privilege was to link it with descent. Perpetuating privilege through the accumulation of wealth handed down through family lines was an age-old strategy. However, growing emphasis and awareness of ethnic difference introduced a new twist, one that would rigidify into concepts of racial difference in the nineteenth century. Manchu privilege, for example, hardened under the Qianlong emperor when the Han banners, formed of Chinese who had pledged loyalty to the Qing before the conquest, were dissolved due to financial constraints. Those Han Chinese who had been supported by the state as bannermen became "free" to earn a living in other ways, while Manchu bannermen retained privileges inherited with their position. In Russia, too, discourses of difference shifted during the eighteenth century in ways that gave increasing attention to ethnic identity.

In Europe, the rise of national consciousness played out differently. Political legitimacy was tightly connected to an ideology of sameness within the nation-state. Yet, a dynamic of difference similar to that found in the imperial context contributed to the European construction of itself vis-à-vis non-European "others" during the same period. Even as nations within Europe came to be constituted (at least ideologically) on the basis of majority nationalities, Europe itself came to be at least partially defined in relationship to its own perceived others. In the face of its own internal ethnic, linguistic and other national differences, Europe was also held together by the geographic proximity of its countries and by certain commonalities in terms of shared experience. More specifically, the kinds of changes that European countries went through beginning in the eighteenth century—while not unlike those that would occur elsewhere—were so pivotal and thorough-going that they became in and of themselves essential to Europe's self-definition, thus contributing to its creation and coherence as a supra-national entity. This dynamic has obscured the fact that Qing China and Imperial Russia also underwent similar changes in terms of the technologies of rule at more or less the same time as other early modern powers, including many leading European countries.

In much of the scholarly literature on Russian history, the "Greats," Peter and Catherine, have come to be characterized as Europeanizers. However, a world-historical perspective that encompasses a comparative view with the Qing court, which strategically deployed these same strategies, helps us to see that it was not European culture per se that allowed Russia to become the important empire it was. Rather, successful patronage and mastery of early modern technologies and tools of empire allowed both empires to thrive and to successfully compete with one another during the early modern period. Viewed in this way, it is not surprising that individuals of Germanic, Scottish, Danish and other origins were involved in exploring and documenting the Russian Empire. Nor is it surprising that Manchus used European Jesuit labor in mapping the Qing Empire. Peter the Great, the Kangxi emperor, Catherine the Great and, to an extent, the Qianlong emperor, recognized that fluency in the emergent idioms of empire would be crucial to the success of their reigns and their fluency in the currency of early modern empire allowed them to compete successfully in this arena throughout the early modern period.

Yet, ethnic nationalisms, born at least partly through imperial cataloging and deployment of difference, would in due course come to play havoc with the imperial visions of both Qing China and Russia. In China, rising Han nationalism confronted Manchu privilege, while in the Russian Empire a Slavic backlash pushed against the reforms of the eighteenth century. In this context, leaders in both empires would feel obliged to cater to internal nationalisms to maintain their own positions. As a result, each would need to weigh the use of technologies perceived as foreign against their own survival as imperial formations by appearing to patronize important internal majority constituencies. Thus, the documentation, and thereby the creation, of ethnic difference undertaken under empire proved to be a double-edged sword.

FURTHER READING

Breyfogle, Nicholas, Abby Schrader and Willard Sunderland (eds.), *Peopling the Russian Periphery: Borderland Colonization in Eurasian History* (New York: Routledge, 2007).
Burbank, Jane and Frederick Cooper (eds.), *Empires in World History: Power and the Politics of Difference* (Princeton University Press, 2010).
Crossley, Pamela Kyle, "Manzhou Yuanliu Kao and the Formalization of the Manchu Heritage," *Journal of Asian Studies* 46 (1987), 761–90.
 A Translucent Mirror: History and Identity in Qing Imperial Ideology (Berkeley, CA: University of California Press, 1999).
Deal, David M. and Laura Hostetler, *The Art of Ethnography: A Chinese "Miao Album"* (Seattle, WA: University of Washington Press, 2006).

Dmytryshyn, Basil, E. A. P. Crownhart-Vaughan and Thomas Vaughan (eds.), *Russia's Conquest of Siberia 1558–1700: A Documentary Record* (Portland, OR: Oregon Historical Society, 1985), vol. 1.

Donnert, Erich, *Russia in the Age of Enlightenment* (Leipzig: Edition Leipzig, 1986).

Fletcher, Joseph, "Sino-Russian Relation, 1800–62" in John King Fairbank (ed.), *The Cambridge History of China* (Cambridge University Press, 1978), vol. x, pt 1.

Glebov, Sergey, "Siberian Middle Ground: Languages of Rule and Accommodation of the Siberian Frontier" in Ilya Gerasimov, Jan Kusber and Alexander Semyonov (eds.), *Empire Speaks Out Languages of Rationalization and Self-Description in the Russian Empire* (Leiden: Brill, 2009), pp. 121–51.

Grumbach, Lutz, Heike Heklau and Thomas Nikol, *Terra incognita Sibirien: die Anfänge der wissenschaftlichen Erforschung Sibiriens unter Mitwirkung deutscher Wissenschaftler im 18. Jahrhundert ; eine Ausstellung der Frankeschen Stiftungen zu Halle in Zusammenarbeit mit dem Archiv der Russischen Akademie der Wissenschaften St. Petersburg* (Halle: Verl. der Franckeschen Stiftungen, 1999).

Hempel, Friedrich and Christian Gottfried Heinrich Geißler, *Abbildung und Beschreibung Der Völkerstämme und Völker Unter Des Russischen Kaisers Alexander Menschenfreundlichen Regierung. Oder Charakter Dieser Völker Aus Der Lage und Beschaffenheit Ihrer Wohnplätze Entwickelt und in Ihren Sitten, Gebräuchen und Beschäftigungen Nach Den Angegebenen Werken Der in-und Ausländischen Litteratur* (Leipzig: Industrie-Comptoir, 1803).

Hostetler, Laura, "Contending Cartographic Claims? The Qing Empire in Manchu, Chinese, and European Maps" in James R. Akerman (ed.), *The Imperial Map: Cartography and the Mastery of Empire* (University of Chicago Press, 2009), pp. 92–132.

"Early Modern Mapping at the Qing Court: Survey Maps from the Kangxi, Yongzheng, and Qianlong Reign Periods" in Yongtao Du and Jeff Kyong-McClain (eds.), *Chinese History in Geographical Perspective* (Lanham, MD: Lexington Books, 2013).

Qing Colonial Enterprise: Ethnography and Cartography in Early Modern China (University of Chicago Press, 2001).

Hughes, Lindsey, *Russia in the Age of Peter the Great* (New Haven, CT: Yale University Press, 1998).

Kao, Ting Tsz, *The Chinese Frontiers* (Palatine, IL: Chinese Scholarly Publishing Company, 1980).

Khodarkovsky, Michael, *Russia's Steppe Frontier: The Making of a Colonial Empire, 1500–1800* (Bloomington, IN: Indiana University Press, 2002).

Where Two Worlds Met: The Russian State and the Kalmyk Nomads, 1600–1771 (Ithaca, NY: Cornell University Press, 1992).

Kivelson, Valerie A., *Cartographies of Tsardom: The Land and Its Meanings in Seventeenth-Century Russia* (Ithaca, NY: Cornell University Press, 2006).

Mancall, Mark, *Russia and China: Their Diplomatic Relations to 1728* (Cambridge, MA: Harvard University Press, 1971).

Millward, James A., "Qing Inner Asian Empire and the Return of the Torghuts" in James A. Millward, Ruth W. Dunnell, Mark C. Elliott and Philippe Forêt (eds.), *New Qing Imperial History: The Making of Inner Asian Empire at Qing Chengdu* (New York: RoutledgeCurzon, 2004), pp. 91–105.

Perdue, Peter C., "Boundaries, Maps, and Movement: Chinese, Russian, and Mongolian Empires in Early Modern Central Eurasia," *International History Review* 20 (1998), 263–86.

  China Marches West: The Qing Conquest of Central Eurasia (Cambridge, MA: Belknap Press of Harvard University Press, 2005).

Quested, R. K. I., *Sino-Russian Relations: A Short History* (Sydney: Allen & Unwin, 1984).

Schimmelpenninck van der Oye, David, *Russian Orientalism: Asia in the Russian Mind from Peter the Great to the Emigration* (New Haven, CT: Yale University Press, 2010).

Shaw, Denis J. B., "Mapmaking, Science, and State Building in Russia before Peter the Great," *Journal of Historical Geography* 31 (2005), 409–29.

Sunderland, Willard, "Imperial Space: Territorial Thought and Practice in the Eighteenth Century" in Jane Burbank, Mark Von Hagen and Anatolyi Remnev (eds.), *Russian Empire: Space, People, Power, 1700–1930* (Bloomington, IN: Indiana University Press, 2008), pp. 33–66.

  Taming the Wild Field: Colonization and Empire on the Russian Steppe (Ithaca, NY: Cornell University Press, 2006).

Tulišen, *Narrative of the Chinese Embassy to the Khan of the Tourgouth Tartars, in the Years 1712, 13, 14, & 15* (Arlington, VA: University Publications of America, 1976).

Waley-Cohen, Joanna, *Exile in Mid-Qing China: Banishment to Xinjiang, 1758–1820* (New Haven, CT: Yale University Press, 1991).

Whittaker, Cynthia Hyla, *Russia Engages the World, 1453–1825* (Cambridge, MA: Harvard University Press, 2003).

13

The Islamic empires of the early modern world

GIANCARLO CASALE

In March 1591, a great battle took place at Tondibi, an important trading center just upstream from Timbuktu on the Niger River. On one side of the battlefield stood the rested and well-provisioned army of the Songhay ruler Askia Ishaq II, who had assembled a force of at least 10,000 troops—and by some accounts many times that number—to defend his kingdom from foreign invasion. On the opposing side was a Moroccan expeditionary force of no more than 2,500 men. Led by Juwdar Pasha, a household slave of the Moroccan Sultan Ahmed al-Mansur (r. 1578 to 1603), this company of adventurers reached Tondibi after an excruciating three-month trek across the Sahara, during which their members had fallen to thirst, hunger and exposure to the elements at the terrifying rate of one death per mile.

Thus, to any independent observer, the odds must have seemed to heavily favor the Songhay as the Battle of Tondibi commenced. And yet, like so many equally lopsided encounters from the history of European imperial expansion, it was not the native Songhay but the Moroccan invaders who were destined to emerge victorious. For although they found themselves outnumbered, exhausted and in unfamiliar territory, Juwdar Pasha's men also arrived at Tondibi with an important advantage: large quantities of gunpowder weapons, including muskets, mortars and even a battery of English artillery. Against an opposing army brandishing cudgels, arrows and poisoned-tipped javelins, the outcome of the battle was hardly ever in doubt.

The decisive role of gunpowder was not the only similarity between this Moroccan expedition and the contemporary imperial ventures of the Spanish and Portuguese, Dutch and English. Like them, the Moroccan campaign involved the conquest of a remote and previously inaccessible part of the world (in this instance, accomplished by crossing the desert rather than the sea). Also like them, the Moroccans' ultimate goal was to seize control of a distant source of precious metals (in this case, the elusive gold mines of West

Africa). And perhaps most surprisingly, the Moroccan campaign was undertaken by many of the *very same people* as the overseas expeditions of contemporary European states. At the Battle of Tondibi, the ranks of the Moroccan army included Spanish and Portuguese captives, renegades from England and the Low Countries, and slave solders from throughout Europe—all fighting side by side with Ottoman mercenaries and Iberian *Moriscos*. Fittingly, even the commander of this polyglot force, Juwdar Pasha, had begun life as a Christian Spaniard.

So why, then, is the history of the Moroccan conquest of Niger nowhere to be found in standard narratives of early modern imperial expansion? Tempting as it may be to blame "Eurocentrism," this explanation does not do justice to the depth of the problem. For, if anything, specialists of Islamic history have proven even less likely to take the Battle of Tondibi into account. Instead, following a long-established scholarly convention, their overwhelming focus has been on the accomplishments of the three early modern Muslim states traditionally deemed worthy of the label "empire": the Mughals (or Timurids) of India, the Safavids of Iran and the Ottomans of the eastern Mediterranean.

When speaking of the Islamic empires, we are therefore faced with two basic quandaries that the example of Morocco helps to bring into stark relief. First, by too closely associating the history of the entire early modern Muslim world with the historical experience of only three "empires," we risk oversimplifying a story that is in fact a good deal more geographically extensive, culturally diverse and politically dynamic than might otherwise be imagined. Second, by defining these three empires as first and foremost "Islamic," we risk exaggerating the extent to which they should be considered, in certain fundamental or predictable ways, distinct from other early modern empires that were not Islamic. With these two important caveats in mind, let us now gingerly step into the world of the Islamic empires, all the while remaining mindful that our ultimate goal is not to cordon them off from the rest of history, but to insert them into the larger narrative of political and economic integration that defines early modernity on a global scale.

Chronology, geography and demography

For all its limitations, one of the most compelling arguments in favor of Islamic empires as a category is that the early modern centuries as a whole are very much defined by the process of imperial expansion. At the beginning of the period, say around the year 1450, an imaginary traveler making the overland voyage from Europe to China would necessarily have passed through a bewildering number of small and parochially defined states—to such an extent that it was extremely unusual for someone to even attempt such a voyage. But by the year 1600, the entire middle belt of the globe (including, by this point, the New World) had been encompassed by just a handful of very large empires, all aware of each others' rival claims to imperial status and, to a greater or lesser extent, in direct contact with one another.

Within the confines of Western history, the turn of the sixteenth century is considered the moment in which this "Age of Empires" began, its origins heralded by the earliest Spanish conquests in the New World and simultaneous Portuguese colonization of the Indian Ocean. Less often noted, however, is the fact that these same years marked a moment of remarkable political transformation across the Muslim world as well, during which virtually all of the leading states of the early modern period first took shape.

In Iran, for example, the history of the Safavid Empire began with the enthronement of the teenaged Shah Ismail in 1501. Just three years later, the Mughal state was born with Babur's conquest of Kabul in 1504. Still further afield, the Shaybanid Khanate of Central Asia, the Saʿadi dynasty in Morocco, the Sultanate of Aceh in insular Southeast Asia, and even the remote but formidable Kanem-Bornu Sultanate in Africa's Lake Chad region all owe their genesis to the same handful of decades clustered around the year 1500. Only the Ottoman state has a somewhat older history, tracing its origins to the beginning of the fourteenth century. But even here, a strong case can be made that it was not until the conquests of Selim "the Grim," a contemporary of both Shah Ismail and Babur, that the Ottoman state was transformed into a bona fide empire.

Thus, the early modern period should be considered an Age of Empires in a truly global sense, as political life across both the Old and New Worlds was redefined by the emergence of a dynamic and interactive system of competing trans-regional states. And far from lying at the political margins of this process, the lands of Islam found themselves at the vital center of this imperializing world. With the possible exception of Spain (and, by some criteria, Muscovy), the states that witnessed the most impressive territorial and demographic expansion, at least through the mid-seventeenth century, were not the empires of Europe, but rather the Islamic empires of the Ottomans, Mughals and Safavids.

At the same time, however, there existed such disparities in territory and demography among these three states that one wonders whether they can all

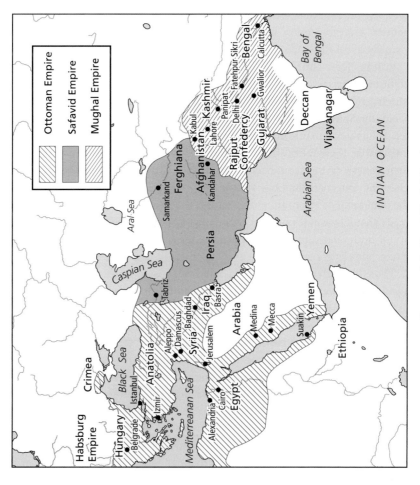

13.1 Ottoman, Safavid and Mughal Empires

be meaningfully included in the same category. In the Mughal Empire, population estimates from the early seventeenth century run well upwards of 100 million people, comprising nearly a fifth of the world's total and placing Mughal India on a par with Ming China as early modern humanity's most populous state. But the Ottoman Empire, while encompassing a roughly equivalent geographical area, was much more sparsely settled, with at most 25 to 30 million inhabitants. And Safavid Iran, at the opposite extreme, was not only considerably smaller territorially, but even more sparsely populated, with between 5 and 7 million inhabitants in all. Demographically, Iran was thus a full order of magnitude smaller than Mughal India, more comparable to minor Muslim states like Morocco or the Khanate of Samarqand (or, for that matter, the diminutive Kingdom of England).

These disparities are matched by another area of marked demographic divergence: the percentage of these empires' subjects who were actually Muslims. In the ostensibly Islamic state of Mughal India, for example, Muslims were never more than a sizeable minority, living together with a heterogeneous population of which the diverse group termed "Hindus" were the most numerous. In the Ottoman lands, Muslims probably remained a minority until some point in the sixteenth century, when a combination of conversion and territorial expansion tipped the overall demographic balance in their favor, although Orthodox and Armenian Christians continued as the majority in many parts of the empire. Safavid Iran is once again an outlier, the only one of the three states with a large Muslim majority from the beginning. But even the Safavids ruled, throughout their history, over significant minorities of Jews, Zoroastrians and Armenian Christians.

Finally, what of the many Muslims who lived outside of these three states? Here, population figures range from speculative to non-existent. But allowing for such uncertainty, it still seems likely that the population of Muslims in sub-Saharan Africa, Central Asia, China and particularly Southeast Asia were in the aggregate equal to or possibly larger than the total Muslim population of the Mughal, Ottoman and Safavid states. In other words, even at the period of their greatest extent, most of the world's Muslims probably lived outside of the three Islamic empires, just as most of the people who lived inside these empires, when counted in the aggregate, were not Muslim.

Thus, rather than Islam per se, it is the ability of these empires to accommodate and in some instances even to encourage confessional diversity under Islam's banner that stands as a hallmark of their rule. This confessional diversity is also perhaps their most striking contrast with the states of early modern Europe and their colonies in America.

Land tenure, state revenues and imperial elites

If there is one key to explaining these empires' success in maintaining their rule over such diverse populations, it can be found in their unique system of land tenure, an area in which—in contrast to the realms of demography and geography—all three empires display a high degree of cohesiveness. This system fundamentally shaped the ways in which both political and economic power were organized across their territories. But in order to understand how, we must first temporarily lay aside our own modern expectations—and terminologies—about what constitutes "ownership" and "property."

Unlike the norms governing ownership of agricultural land most common in the early modern West, the Ottomans, Mughals and Safavids all employed a land tenure system that might be described as a three-leveled "layer cake," according to which legal title to the land, the right to collect rent and the right to actually use the land were intentionally kept separate. At the top of this layer cake was the state itself, to which many categories of agricultural land were deemed to exclusively belong. Ironically, however, this exclusive form of titular ownership deprived the state of one of the most important privileges normally associated with owning land: the right to sell it to someone else. Meanwhile, at the bottom layer were the peasants who actually occupied the land. Since they were often not owners of their plots in a legal sense, they too were deprived of the ability to buy and sell them. But what they did enjoy were usufruct rights to work the soil and, in most cases, to pass their plots on to their descendants in perpetuity. So they too, in their own way, could claim a certain "inalienable" right to the land.

Finally, between these two layers lay the class with the most tenuous claims to landed property: the rent collectors, who enjoyed the privilege, but not the right, of extracting a pre-established surplus (either in cash or in kind) from a given tract. In some ways, their position was not so different from that of the landlord of a modern rent-controlled apartment. But unlike a landlord, they had no actual title to any property, and their claims to revenue were neither permanent nor inheritable. Instead, their revenue assignments were granted—and could be altered, augmented or revoked—at the ruler's pleasure. Even life-term appointments, while by no means uncommon, were rendered null and void upon the death of a sovereign unless reconfirmed by his successor.

For obvious reasons, this system provided central governments with an unusual amount of control over the distribution of revenues from agriculture, far and away the largest and most productive sector of the economy in each of the three empires. And it is therefore no surprise that agricultural revenue assignments became the primary mechanism used by the Ottomans, Mughals and Safavids to pay their soldiers, staff their bureaucracies and otherwise finance their imperial infrastructures.

In the Ottoman case, the best documented of the three, the basic unit of land assignment was known as a *timar*, and was put to work in the following way: at the initial conquest of a given territory, a cadastral survey would be carefully conducted and the land divided up, with each *timar* receiving a particular designation, based on its size, which corresponded to a specific pay grade in the Ottoman hierarchy. These would then be assigned to various individuals according to their rank, with good performance and seniority resulting in reassignment to a new *timar* with a higher pay grade, and poor performance resulting in the reverse. Collectively, the class of people who made their living in this way were known as the *'askeri* or "military class," but included those in the court system, the chancellery and other professions that hardly qualified as "military" in the strict sense. Everyone else, expected to pay taxes rather than to benefit from government largesse, belonged to the *re'aya*, or the "flock" of protected subjects.

We find almost exactly the same institution at work in the Mughal Empire, but expressed through a different terminology: *timars* were instead known as *jagirs* (and associated with a comparatively more intricate hierarchy of ranks), their holders were known as *jagirdars*, and the people under their protection were once again referred to as "the flock." Similarly, in the Safavid state, the basic unit of assigned land was known as an *iqta'*. Here, however, while the basic distinction between "the military class" and "the flock" still held, the rankings and pay grades were less elaborately organized, and the system as a whole less comprehensively implemented.

Regardless of its variant forms, the basic goal of this system was everywhere the same: to ensure that the richest agricultural lands eventually reverted back to state control, thereby preventing the emergence of either a hereditary landed gentry or an independent agricultural bourgeoisie. To this end, the central governments of each empire made quite self-conscious efforts to regularly circulate to different parts of their realm the revenue assignments of their most powerful underlings, in order to prevent them from developing regional power bases, hereditary claims or independent estates that might be used to challenge the authority of the sovereign. But in doing so, they also provided the material basis for the formation of truly "imperial" elites, who became deracinated by this system from the ethnic, regional and tribal affiliations of their birth, and developed a sense of self wholly dependent on their place in an evolving imperial hierarchy.

To a considerable extent, this unique structure of land tenure was therefore the glue that held together these large and heterogeneous states, which otherwise might have been easily pulled apart by the powerful centripetal forces of linguistic and confessional diversity. As a measure of the system's flexibility, ethnic minorities, non-Muslims, foreigners and (as we shall discuss in more detail below) even slaves were routinely integrated into the imperial elite through these revenue assignments—frequently receiving preferential treatment and rapid promotion not despite, but *because* of, their lack of any base of support beyond the ruler's largesse.

Equally surprising, such policies seem to have been accepted as a matter of course by even the most established insiders, among whom it was exceedingly rare to hear complaints about the concentration of ownership in the hands of the state or the deracination of local elites that this entailed. If anything, political theorists, jurists and other elite commentators of the day were prone to denounce *departures* from this system as instances of tyranny, and to portray the monopoly of redistributive power by the sovereign as the epitome of "just rule."

In fact, this collective enthusiasm on the part of the three empires' elite literati presents its own set of interpretive challenges, by providing an idealized picture that, if taken at face value, can lead us to overstate both the extent to which state ownership was actually instituted and its uniformity. In reality, there were any number of ways that, either formally or informally, land could pass out of state control. Ordinarily, for example, state rights extended only to tilled fields of grain, not to residential dwellings, commercial real estate or land with significant capital improvements (including orchards and vineyards) that were considered private property. And even tilled fields could be permanently alienated from state control by means of the Islamic institution of the *waqf* or permanent pious endowment— commonly used as a sort of tax shelter by the well heeled (including powerful female landholders) in all three empires.

Beyond these legal means, sovereigns routinely entered into more informal arrangements with vassals, erstwhile antagonists and powerful underlings, along the way granting autonomy or unofficial hereditary landholding rights of various kinds as opportunity or necessity dictated. This was especially prevalent in areas controlled by tribes of pastoral nomads, since these lands— as pasturage rather than cultivated fields—in any case fell outside the purview of "state land."

Finally, even in areas under the most direct state control, there was a tendency over the centuries to experiment with alternative forms of land tenure, including new ways of monetizing the agricultural economy. By the seventeenth century, for example, it became standard practice in the Ottoman Empire to simply auction off *timars* as tax farms, and then to use the proceeds of these auctions to pay soldiers and other state servants directly in cash. Thus, as in so many other aspects of Ottoman, Safavid and Mughal history, the success of the land tenure system lay in its pragmatism and flexibility, rather than any rigorous adherence to abstract principles of state ownership.

Islamic law, slave elites and "Oriental Despotism"

Once upon a time, not so very long ago, the specter of "Oriental Despotism" lurked behind virtually every serious discussion of the political, social and economic histories of the early modern Islamic empires. According to this venerable paradigm, especially cherished by students of Marx and Weber, the Ottomans, Mughals and Safavids stood as archetypes of a political and economic system defined by the unadulterated exercise of sovereign author-ity. Unrestrained by an independent judiciary, the institutions of civil society or any other check on their executive power, the rulers of these empires were thought capable of depriving subjects of their property, their liberty and even their lives on any pretext, thereby reducing them to a wretched status equivalent to slavery. Among other more immediately distasteful consequences, this despotic form of government was thought, in the long run, to have made impossible the accumulation of private wealth and the development of institutions necessary for a modern "rational" state, dooming their economies to stagnation and eventual collapse.

While continuing to play a powerful role in the popular imagination of the Islamic empires, "Oriental Despotism" has in recent years fallen some-what out of favor among scholars. Instead, attention has increasingly turned to the *shari'a*, or Islamic law, as the key to understanding the basic patterns of social and economic life in these empires—and the reasons for their perceived divergence from the road to modern Western capitalism. According to this newly resurgent view, the *shari'a* could—and did—provide a convenient legal cover for a ruler's arbitrary exercise of power (the system of "Islamic land tenure" providing a case in point). But as a divinely sanctioned legal system immutable to change, the *shari'a* also thwarted development in more gentle but still insidious ways, by preserving a series of outmoded rules, customs and practices that were inimical to the emergence of a free-market economy and a modern bureaucracy. These included, to name just three of the most commonly cited examples, a prohibition on collecting interest, a refusal to recognize the legal personhood of corporations and an enforcement of strict inheritance laws that required family patrimonies to be broken apart.

Without discounting such arguments out of hand—some of which we will have occasion to return to in a subsequent section—we must carefully guard against the temptation to describe the *shari'a* as a legal system inherently hostile to either property rights or economic exchange, much less as one that sanctioned despotic rule as a matter of course. Quite to the contrary, virtually all canonical interpretations of *shari'a* from the early modern period emphatically prohibited a just ruler from seizing the property of his subjects (be they Muslim or non-Muslim). They also severely circumscribed the ruler's ability to impose taxes on his subjects' income, to restrict the flow of either domestic or international trade, or to levy import or transit tariffs at anything other than a fixed rate established by the *shari'a* itself. Even in the realm of criminal law, the limitations on sovereign power were extreme: capital punishment, for example, was strictly forbidden for all but a handful of narrowly defined offenses (mainly limited to the categories of apostasy, adultery and sedition).

On the whole, then, the *shari'a* provided subjects of the early modern Islamic empires with a range of legal protections to their lives and livelihoods that were, in many respects, decidedly more comprehensive than those enjoyed by their contemporaries in either Western Europe or East Asia. In fact, rather than giving free rein to despotic rule, the considerable set of legal restrictions imposed by the *shari'a* required Muslim rulers who wished to circumvent them to resort to an institution that is among the most disorienting from the modern perspective: slave elites.

For all its counterintuitive qualities, the basic principle behind elite slavery is relatively simple. Since slaves were not afforded the same legal guarantees as their free-born compatriots, those who belonged to the ruler were completely subject to his authority. Unlike free men and women, slaves could not marry or produce legitimate offspring without the sovereign's permission, could be punished or even summarily executed at his pleasure and, unless emancipated, could expect all of their property to revert to his possession upon their death.

But crucially, this lack of legal rights did not imply the kind of degraded social standing that one would normally associate with slavery. Instead, as individuals who "belonged," in the most literal sense of the word, to the household of the ruling dynasty (including, importantly, the women of the imperial harem), royal slaves enjoyed a uniquely intimate relationship with power that, unmediated by legal restrictions, translated into an elevated status *superior* to that of ordinary men. In this sense, the Marxist-Weberian paradigm of the Oriental Despot, with all of its concomitant implications about the lack of individual rights or the absence of the rule of law, can be said to derive from a basic misunderstanding of the role of slavery in early modern Islamic states.

Because of the way in which this "peculiar institution" was articulated through the *shari'a*, royal slavery also dovetailed with the system of Islamic land tenure in a crucial way: by providing a legal justification for the general tendency, already alluded to above, to target foreigners and other political outsiders for incorporation into the imperial elites. Specifically, the Qur'an itself unambiguously forbids the enslavement of any Muslim, as well as any non-Muslim who lives as the subject of a Muslim ruler. This meant, in theory, that slave elites had to be continually replenished from stocks of able-bodied and culturally adaptable non-Muslims who hailed from beyond the borders of the Muslim world. Juwdar Pasha, the Spanish-born slave who led the Moroccan army to victory at the Battle of Tondibi, provides us with a perfect illustration of the life trajectory of just this type of individual.

All too often, however, the need for royal slaves outstripped this inherently limited and unpredictable pool of recruits. As a result, rulers inevitably turned to alternative strategies to ensure a stable supply of slaves to run their empires—strategies that, in one of history's great ironies, were often themselves illegal by the standards of the *shari'a*.

Perhaps the most famous example of just this type of extralegal practice is the Ottoman *devşirme* (literally "collection"). Beginning as early as the fourteenth century, the Ottoman state began to designate certain Christian villages of the empire, predominantly in the Balkans, as being subject to a periodic levy of young boys. These were selected according to pre-established standards of mental and physical fitness, and they were separated from their families and forcibly converted to Islam. Most were then sent to live in agricultural areas of Anatolia, where they were hardened by farm work, taught to speak Turkish and then went on to become Janissaries (literally "new troops"), the Ottomans' elite military corps of slave infantry. But for the best and the brightest, a different future awaited. After another round of selection, these lucky few were sent to the Sultan's palace, where they were raised in his household, trained in the palace academy and then began a *cursus honorum* leading to the upper echelons of the Ottoman imperial establishment.

For nearly 200 years, from the mid-fifteenth until the early seventeenth centuries, the overwhelming majority of the Ottoman Empire's viziers, generals, naval commanders and even its architects, engineers and master artisans were products of this system, as the state systematically passed over free-born Muslims for these positions in favor of its slaves. And yet, from a strictly legal standpoint, the *devşirme* stood in flagrant violation of two of the most basic and inviolable Qur'anic precepts: the injunction against the enslavement of a ruler's protected non-Muslim subjects; and the prohibition against the forcible conversion of non-Muslims.

Even so, the *devşirme* is known to have been originally instituted—and wholeheartedly endorsed—by ranking members of the Ottoman religious elite or *'ulema*, and to have continued for generations without any serious legal challenges being raised within the empire. Furthermore, when the *devşirme* was eventually phased out, it was replaced by a new convention equally at odds with canonical understandings of the *shari'a*: beginning in the seventeenth century, Ottoman administrators began to classify all members of the "military class" (composed, by this time, predominantly of native Muslims) as "slaves" (*kul*) simply by virtue of their service to the state. In a manner quite distinct from the original intent of the *devşirme*, this enabled the formation of a new, hereditary and self-reproducing class of free-born Muslims who came to monopolize the Ottoman bureaucratic and military establishment—but who, in exchange for these privileges, became subject to confiscation and to summary execution at the Sultan's will.

Fascinatingly, we find service to the state being used in almost exactly the same way to justify the dispossession and summary execution of *jagirdars* and other members of the elite in the contemporary Mughal Empire. But in the Mughal case, while it was equally common for elites to celebrate their devotion and total subjection to the ruler in terms of "slavery," they seem to have done so only in a metaphoric sense, without ever feeling the need to rationalize their system with explicit reference to the *shari'a*. Just how this was possible in an avowedly Islamic state is a subject that we are now ready to explore in somewhat more detail.

Power, sovereignty and orthodoxy

As the above discussion has hopefully made clear, it is inherently misleading to think of the *shari'a* as a legal system that, through its unyielding conservatism, dependably served as a buttress for authoritarian rule. At the times and places in which it did serve this function, it did so only by means of a considerable amount of flexibility and creativity on the part of its practitioners. And because it could just as easily be turned against sovereigns to impose limitations on their autonomy, rulers had every incentive to look for alternative bases for their legitimacy—and to fall back on the *shari'a* only when these proved inadequate.

Of these alternatives, the first in importance can be labeled "Messianism," with the proviso that the Messiah of early modern Islam was associated with divinely inspired leadership in this world (in the model of the Prophet Muhammad) rather than eternal salvation in the next world (in the model of Christ). The resulting possibilities for messianic politics were therefore wide ranging, and are particularly well illustrated in the rise to power of Shah Ismail I, the scion of a distinguished line of Sufi mystics before he became the founder of the Safavid dynasty. Ismail's political career, in fact, began early in life when he was hailed by followers as the *Mahdi* or "rightly guided one," a messianic figure sent by God to restore justice and, through his divinely inspired rule, usher in a new and everlasting age of peace and prosperity. This extraordinary status allowed Ismail, at least for a time, to claim a kind of transcendent authority that rendered the *shari'a*—a legal system designed for a world of imperfect men and equally imperfect rulers—obsolete.

By its very nature, Messianism provided a powerful but volatile basis for legitimacy, heavily dependent on individual charisma and difficult to maintain across generations (or even over the lifetime of an individual ruler). This volatility naturally led sovereigns to consider a second alternative, which offered the promise of greater permanence and stability. This option, at some risk of anachronism, might be defined as "Secularism," and counted among its earliest adopters the Ottoman Sultan Mehmed "the Conqueror." Following his conquest of Constantinople in 1453, Mehmed began to style himself "Roman Emperor" (*Kayser-i Rum*) as well as "Great Khan" (*Kha-Khan* or *Khaqan*), thereby bringing together in his own personage the most important pre-Muslim imperial traditions of both the Mediterranean and the Central Asian steppe. From this basis, he then began to legislate through the *Kanun*, a secular legal code of his own creation drawn from a combination of dynastic custom and royal prerogative. Like the millenarian claims of Shah Ismail, this provided him with a way of transcending the limitations on executive power embodied in the *shari'a*. But rather than simply abrogating Islamic law through his own (potentially fleeting) messianic charisma, the

Kanun offered Mehmed a way to permanently formalize his rule according to a completely separate set of codified legal principles.

Of course, Messianism and Secularism were by no means mutually exclusive foundations of sovereignty. Both provided paths around *shari'a* that, with a bit of creativity, could reinforce one another. And by making appeals to universal justice or to the great imperial traditions of the pre-Islamic past, both could also serve a legitimizing function—in a way that the *shari'a* alone never could—in the eyes of subjects (and foreign rulers) who belonged to faiths other than Islam. For this reason, it is in the Mughal Empire, with by far the most confessionally diverse population of any early modern state, where we find the most comprehensive and enduring combination of both Messianism and Secularism.

In this Mughal synthesis, fully elaborated during the reign of Akbar "the Great" (r. 1556 to 1605), a good part of the apparatus of state was reconfigured along the lines of a devotional mystical order. Many members of the elite—of all faiths—were understood to be not merely servants of the ruler, but his spiritual disciples, pursuing a path towards mystical enlightenment through their service to his divinely inspired person. In this way, Akbar assumed a status akin to a messianic ruler, whose authority closely approximated that of Shah Ismail in Iran. But at the same time, Akbar's millenarian charisma was consolidated and bureaucratized through an elaborate set of rituals, regulations and rankings, all formalized and preserved in a massive compendium known as the *A'in-i Akbari* or "Regulations of Akbar." In this respect, Akbar followed in the footsteps of Mehmed the Conqueror rather than Shah Ismail, by formulating an alternative legal basis for Mughal rule analogous to the Ottoman *Kanun*.

Due to the unusual success and longevity of this Mughal synthesis, Akbar and his descendants today enjoy a reputation for syncretism and heterodoxy, while their Ottoman and Safavid contemporaries are imagined to have been staunch defenders of Sunni and Shiite "orthodoxy." But in reality, the confessional path of all three empires was equally winding and unpredictable, only to be straitened and sanitized in retrospect. It was through just such an act of selective memory and wishful thinking, for example, that later generations of *shari'a*-minded intellectuals in the Safavid Empire portrayed the antinomian millenarianism of Shah Ismail as "Shiite"—just as they would paper over the fact that, a half century later, Ismail's grandson and namesake, Shah Ismail II, actually embraced Sunnism during his brief reign in the 1570s. In a similar vein, the earliest Ottoman sultans, who ruled before their empire's long and polarizing conflict with the Safavids, are known to have openly endorsed a whole range of messianic myths and ritual practices that their own religious establishment would later denounce as "Shiite heresy." And like both the Mughals and the Safavids, the Ottomans too, as they bobbed and weaved around the constraints of the *shari'a*, rarely hesitated to draw from the language and ritual of Sufi mysticism.

In consequence, rather than imagining these empires as defined from their inception by Sunnism, Shiism or syncretism, these categories should be understood as the *outcome* rather than the starting point of a shared process of inter- and intra-state legitimation—in much the same way that the distinction between "Catholic" and "Protestant" emerged, during exactly the same centuries, out of the competitive state system of the early modern West. In each of the three Islamic empires, in fact, we can identify a strikingly parallel historical trajectory, as the heterodoxy and experimentation of early periods gradually gave way to an emphasis on conservatism and uniformity in later years.

Thus, in Safavid Iran, the ecstatic millenarianism of Shah Ismail was eventually transformed into the legalistic and bureaucratic Shiism of Shah Abbas—turning Iran, in the process, into a predominantly Shiite society for the first time in its history. In the Ottoman Empire, the eclectic "secularism" of Mehmed the Conqueror gradually gave way to an ideology in which enforcing the *shari'a*—and defending it from the pernicious influence of Shiism—became the essential raison d'être of the Ottoman state. And in Mughal India, the famously ecumenical and charismatic rule of Akbar would eventually succumb, during the second half of the seventeenth century, to the comparatively austere and *shari'a*-minded Sunni legalism of his great-grandson Aurangzeb.

It would be difficult to overemphasize the long-term consequences of this shared path to state-sponsored orthodoxy, which permanently redefined the terms of Muslim religious and political identity in ways that are rarely acknowledged today. Far from being a primordial aspect of Muslim society— or, for that matter, a recent construct of colonial Western modernity—it was in the early modern Islamic empires in which the all-encompassing, overtly politicized and oppositional dichotomy between Sunnis and Shiites was first given modern form.

Gunpowder empires and the military revolution

Alongside Islamic land tenure, Oriental Despotism and Islamic law, there are few subjects more closely associated with the early modern Islamic empires than gunpowder. Indeed, for a previous generation of historians, these three states' technical mastery of gunpowder weapons was considered their signature achievement, explaining their collective success to such an extent that they were frequently referred to as the "gunpowder empires." More recently, scholars have raised doubts about these weapons' singular importance, emphasizing instead the three empires' continued reliance on more traditional military units (such as heavy cavalry), as well as their highly developed competence in the more prosaic realms of logistics and supply. Even so, there is little room to dispute that the Mughals, Ottomans and Safavids all proved early and enthusiastic adopters of gunpowder weapons, inevitably reshaping both the nature of their own power and their relationship with the world beyond their respective borders.

As the most precocious of the three empires, it is hardly a surprise that the Ottomans were at the vanguard in embracing this new technology. There is firm evidence that the Ottomans' famed Janissary corps began making regular use of matchlocks by the early fifteenth century, thereby boasting pride of place as the first firearm-wielding standing infantry unit of any early modern state—Muslim or otherwise. This went hand-in-hand with the Ottomans' systematic adoption of siege artillery in the decades that followed, allowing them not only to breach the walls of Constantinople in 1453, but of dozens of other fortresses throughout the Balkans and Anatolia theretofore considered "impregnable." By the turn of the sixteenth century, the Ottomans had also added field artillery to their arsenal, using it to devastating effect in their victory over the Safavids at Çaldiran (1514) and their subsequent conquest of Mamluk Egypt (1517).

Once introduced by these campaigns to the Ottomans' eastern neighbors, it is astonishing how quickly these weapons, and even the basic tactics with which they were deployed, spread to the farthest corners of the Islamic world. During the mid-fifteenth century, for example, the Hungarian field commander John Hunyadi had famously foiled the Ottomans' cavalry charges by deploying field guns behind a circle of fortified wagons (a tactic Hunyadi had himself adopted from teams of Austrian gunners). A half century later, at the Battle of Çaldiran, the Ottomans themselves successfully adopted this same formation to rout the Safavid cavalry. But a mere decade after Çaldiran, at the Battle of Panipat in 1526, Babur used exactly the same tactic in his decisive victory over Ibrahim Lodi, thereby consolidating Mughal rule in north India.

By this time, gunpowder weapons had become widespread enough—and desirable enough—to serve as the engine for an entirely new kind of internationalized "gunpowder diplomacy." After their defeat at Çaldiran, for instance, the Safavids began to rapidly acquire their own arsenal, initially relying on renegades from the Ottoman army and later seeking help from Portugal and Venice. Their success prompted their rivals to the north, the Uzbeks or Shaybanids of Central Asia, to respond in kind, by seeking their own source of firearms through a direct alliance with Istanbul. And this, in turn, prompted a further escalation on the Safavid side, as Iran expanded its relations with foreign powers in a relentless search for more reliable and affordable sources of weapons and expertise. By the reign of Shah Abbas, these had grown to include Spain, England, Russia and even the Papacy.

Meanwhile, in the Indian Ocean, a similar dynamic took shape, as petty rulers throughout the region, in response to the novel threat posed by the seaborne firepower of the Portuguese, forged ties with ever-more distant powers to guarantee a continuous supply of guns and those skilled in their use. Thus, in the horn of Africa, the Emir of Zeyla became a tributary of the Ottoman sultan as early as the 1530s, thereby securing a unit of Ottoman musketeers for his ongoing war with the Negus of Ethiopia. At the opposite extreme of the Indian Ocean, the Sultan of Aceh followed the same strategy, using teams of Ottoman gunners in an attack on Portuguese Melaka in 1567. Even more dramatically, in the 1570s, an embassy appeared in Istanbul from the Kanem-Borno Sultanate on Lake Chad, leading to the introduction of gunpowder weapons in Africa's central Sahel by the following decade—an area where no gun-toting Europeans would dare to tread until the nineteenth century.

In each of these cases, gunpowder acted as the catalyst for an entirely new web of international relationships that simply had no precedent in earlier periods of history. Never before had a ruler in Southeast Asia or sub-Saharan Africa been in regular contact with Istanbul, just as no ruler of Iran had ever before sought direct military assistance from England or Spain. Against this background, gunpowder weapons must be accorded an importance as agents of global integration that far outweighed their usefulness on the battlefield. To return to the example with which we began this chapter, guns not only handed victory to the Moroccans at the Battle of Tondibi in 1591, but helped to create the world that brought them to Tondibi to begin with.

Islamic empires and the global economy

Because of its many military applications, and the consequent attention paid to it by the machinery of government, gunpowder provides an unusually clear illustration of the ways in which Islamic empires engaged with, and were in turn influenced by, the emerging global economy of the early modern period. But gunpowder was by no means the only new product to take the lands of Islam by storm during these centuries, and the widespread adoption of many of its less combustible counterparts was to have equally profound economic and social consequences—both for the Muslim world itself, and for the larger global history of early modernity.

Maize, for example, unknown outside of the Americas before the sixteenth century, was in the Old World first cultivated as a large-scale commercial crop in Egypt, such that it became known in most European languages as "Turkish Grain." Tobacco, another New World commodity, grew equally deep roots in the Islamic world from an early date, to the extent that, five centuries later, a leading brand of American cigarettes continues to sport a "Turkish" dromedary as its inimitable trademark. Opium, despite a much older history of cultivation in India and the Middle East, reached equally unprecedented levels of popularity in the early modern period, where it could be smoked in the same new-fangled contraptions—and in the same disreputable establishments—that catered to users of tobacco. And coffee, originally brewed by medieval Sufis of the southern Red Sea to enhance their mystical rites, was similarly transformed into a product of mass consumption in the sixteenth century, spreading from Cairo and Istanbul to the far corners of the Ottoman Empire (and from there to Iran and points farther east) in a matter of just a few decades. By contrast, coffee did not make the jump to Paris and London (and points farther west) until well over a century later.

As elsewhere in the early modern world, the introduction of so many novel sources of nourishment, pleasure and profit shook the foundations of the established order in all of the Islamic empires. In the countryside, the cultivation of new crops dramatically changed the rhythms of agricultural life. In the marketplace, the demand for new products overturned the traditional hierarchies of merchant elites. And in cities, the growing appetite for stimulants, narcotics and exotic foods led to the proliferation of coffee-houses and other venues for their public consumption.

Inevitably, these novel habits and the new modes of sociability they engendered led to sweeping re-evaluations of the standards of propriety, legality and ethical conduct inherited from the pre-modern past. Physicians, legal scholars and religious authorities were drawn into heated and surprisingly public debates on these issues, remarkable both for their diversity and for their pervasiveness across the Muslim world. Rulers, too, were by no means aloof from these concerns, anxious as they were about the implications of such rapid changes for their own grip on power. Sometimes, in fact, they took extravagant measures to root them out at the source: for a brief period in the mid-seventeenth century, the Ottoman Sultan Murad IV even went so far as to declare coffee drinking a capital offense.

But just as often, rulers found themselves attracted rather than repulsed by the dynamism of early modern commerce, and pioneered new strategies of state entrepreneurship that were typically of the age both in their reach and in their rationale. In the Indian Ocean, largely in response to the aggressive Portuguese ventures "in search of Christians and spices," the Ottomans developed a rival commercial and military presence to protect Muslim pilgrimage routes and, in the process, secure a steady supply of spices for state-owned pepper galleys. Members of the Mughal dynasty, once they had secured their own outlets onto the Indian Ocean, invested even more directly in maritime trading ventures from their bustling port-city of Surat. And in Morocco, in reaction to the burgeoning international market for sugar, the ruling Sa'adian dynasty declared a state monopoly over sugar exports, and aggressively expanded its cultivation throughout the sixteenth century. By the eve of the Battle of Tondibi, no less than 600,000 pounds of sugar were exported annually from Morocco to England alone—much of it exchanged directly for English artillery.

Ironically, however, the very openness that characterized the economies of the early modern Muslim world could also present systemic obstacles when it came to experimentation in at least some matters of commercial policy. In contrast to Europe (and, to a certain extent, Ming China or Tokugawa Japan), where political and economic space had long been defined more parochially, the cosmopolitan commercial traditions of the lands of Islam—often directly reflected in the language of the *shari'a*—made it difficult for Muslim sovereigns to legally discriminate in favor of "their" merchants and "their" markets. Instead, since a basic measure of a ruler's efficacy was precisely his ability to ensure the free and unobstructed flow of trade across borders, a whole array of policies that became standard practice in the emerging mercantilist economies of Europe, ranging from protective tariffs and "staple rights" to the imposition of medical quarantines, tended to be viewed very differently in the Islamic empires: as gross violations of the compact between ruler and subject, rather than as normal expressions of sovereign or national prerogative.

Tellingly, the instance where we see the most systematic departure from this principle of open borders is found in the one Islamic empire that, at least for a time, defined itself as juridically and confessionally distinct from its

Muslim neighbors: the Shiite state of Safavid Iran. Here, particularly during the reign of Shah Abbas I (r. 1587 to 1629), the Safavids adopted policies surprisingly reminiscent of European mercantilism, including a ban on the export of precious metals, the imposition of targeted tariffs to protect local products, a comprehensive reorganization of the silk trade as a state monopoly and, when politically expedient, a strict embargo on exports to the Ottoman Empire. By no means coincidentally, this aggressive European-style assertion of economic sovereignty was also accompanied by tumultuous social policies equally characteristic of early modern Europe, including the dispossession of religious minorities, forced conversions, heresy trials and other measures designed to enhance state power through the creation of a confessionally homogenous population.

Historians continue to debate the impact of these policies on Iran's long-term economic development—a debate complicated by the fact that they were comprehensively instituted for only a very short time. What is clear, however, is that Shah Abbas's economic strategy was in many ways *sui generis*, and probably only possible because of his regime's unique self-consciousness as a Shiite state surrounded and besieged by Sunni rivals. By contrast, the same period saw the Ottoman Empire's relations with Western Europe defined by the so-called "capitulations," a series of agreements designed to ensure peaceful intercourse and the steady inflow of products by granting friendly Western nations the right to trade at a *lower* rate of taxation than was paid even by the Sultan's own subjects.

How to explain such laissez-faire confidence in the virtue of open borders, maintained long after the resulting cost to the economies of the lands of Islam were apparent for all to see? For historians of the twentieth century, their assumptions shaped by an age of nation-states and protected national economies, such insouciance seemed inexplicably naïve, and pointed inevitably to the conclusion that the Islamic empires, locked into the outmoded economic mindset of an earlier "agrarian" age, were incapable of adapting to the realities of a new world dominated by commerce.

But today, as the age of national economies itself passes into history, it is difficult not to have more sympathy for early modern Islam's cosmopolitan quandary. For we too, much like the Islamic empires at the end of the early modern period, live in an age in which the world's most developed economies—married to their own "orthodox" beliefs about the virtue of open borders and unobstructed commerce—watch with bemusement as their wealth and productive capacity flow relentlessly elsewhere. As the twenty-first century continues to unfold, it therefore seems likely that both the successes, and the failures, of the Ottomans, Mughals and Safavids may look a good deal more modern to historians of future generations than they did to those of even the recent past.

FURTHER READING

Abisaab, Rula Jurdi, *Converting Persia: Religion and Power in the Safavid Empire* (London: I. B. Tauris, 2004).

Alam, Muzaffar and Sanjay Subrahmanyam (eds.), *The Mughal State: 1526–1750* (Oxford University Press, 1998).

Asher, Catherine B. and Cynthia Talbot, *India before Europe* (Cambridge University Press, 2006).

Babaie, Sussan, Kathryn Babayan, Ina Baghdiantz McCage and Massumeh Farhad, *Slaves of the Shah: New Elites of Safavid Iran* (London: I. B. Tauris, 2004).

Babayan, Kathryn, *Mystics, Monarchs and Messiahs: Cultural Landscapes of Early Modern Iran* (Cambridge, MA: Harvard Middle Eastern Monographs, 2003).

Casale, Giancarlo, *The Ottoman Age of Exploration* (Oxford University Press, 2011).

Dale, Stephen, *The Muslim Empires of the Ottomans, Safavids, and Mughals* (Cambridge University Press, 2010).

Das Gupta, Ashin, *The World of the Indian Ocean Merchant 1500–1800* (Oxford University Press, 2001).

Eaton, Richard, *A Social History of the Deccan, 1300–1761: Eight Indian Lives* (Cambridge University Press, 2008).

Floor, Willem and Edmund Herzig (eds.), *Iran and the World in the Safavid Age* (London: I. B. Tauris, 2012).

Goffman, Daniel, *The Ottomans and Early Modern Europe* (Cambridge University Press, 2002).

Gommans, J. J. L., *Mughal Warfare: Indian Frontiers and High Roads to Empire* (London: Routledge, 2002).

Hanna, Nelly, *Making Big Money in 1600: The Life and Times of Isma'il Abu Taqiyya, Egyptian Merchant* (Syracuse University Press, 1997).

Hattox, Ralph, *Coffee and Coffeehouses: The Origins of a Social Beverage in the Medieval Near East* (Seattle, WA: University of Washington Press, 1985).

Inalcik, Halil and Donald Quataert, *An Economic and Social History of the Ottoman Empire* (Cambridge University Press, 1994).

Koch, Ebba, *Mughal Art and Imperial Ideology: Collected Essays* (Oxford University Press, 2001).

Matar, Nabil, *Turks, Moors and Englishmen in the Age of Discovery* (New York: Columbia University Press, 2000).

Matthee, Rudolph, *The Politics of Trade in Safavid Iran: Silk for Silver, 1600–1730* (Cambridge University Press, 2003).

Moin, Azfar, *The Millennial Sovereign: Sacred Kingship and Sainthood in Islam* (New York: Columbia University Press, 2012).

Murphey, Rhoads, *Ottoman Warfare, 1500–1700* (New Brunswick, NJ: Rutgers University Press, 1999).

Newman, Andrew, *Safavid Iran: Rebirth of a Persian Empire* (London: I. B. Tauris, 2008).

Reid, Anthony, *Southeast Asia in the Age of Commerce, 1450–1680*, 2 vols. (New Haven, CT: Yale University Press, 1988–95).

Richards, John, *The Mughal Empire* (Cambridge University Press, 1996).

Risso, Patricia, *Merchants and Faith: Muslim Commerce and Culture in the Indian Ocean* (Boulder, CO: Westview Press, 1995).

Smith, Richard, *Ahmad al-Mansur: Islamic Visionary* (London: Longman, 2005).

Streusand, Douglas, *Islamic Gunpowder Empires: Ottomans, Safavids and Mughals* (Boulder, CO: Westview Press, 2010).

Subrahmanyam, Sanjay, *Explorations in Connected History: From the Tagus to the Ganges* (Oxford University Press, 2005).

Tezcan, Baki, *The Second Ottoman Empire: Political and Social Transformation in the Early Modern World* (Cambridge University Press, 2010).

PART FOUR

★

CROSSROADS REGIONS

14

Crossroads region: Central Asia

MORRIS ROSSABI

Central Asia had been vital in contacts between East and West long before 1400. During the Mongol Empire of the thirteenth and fourteenth centuries, it was the crossroads through which merchants, scientists and envoys traveled, generally without hindrance, from one part of the Mongol domain to another, and then to other lands. Chinggis Khan's son Chaghadai had become the ruler of Central Asia after his father's death in 1227. His descendants and successors lacked Chaghadai's abilities, and by the late thirteenth century, non-entities filled the position of Khan, while military commanders or leaders with powerful armies actually governed. Unity proved elusive in Central Asia until a charismatic and brilliant commander arose in the latter third of the fourteenth century. Temür (who became known in English as Tamerlane) came to power around 1369 and initiated military campaigns to unite Central Asia and to incorporate more territories into his domains.[1]

Central Asia was difficult to unify, partly owing to the diversity of its landscapes and peoples. A landlocked region, it stretched from the Gansu corridor in China to the borders of Iran, and included the oases and cities that lay between the Amu Darya and Syr Darya Rivers, as well as much of modern Afghanistan. Its different environments dictated a variety of different economic adaptations. Aridity plagued most of the region except for Ili in northern sections of the modern Xinjiang Uyghur Autonomous Region and Kazakhstan, areas suitable for a nomadic pastoral economy. A second type of economy was based in the oases and towns, which were fortuitously located along the major East–West trade routes. Merchants, artisans and ordinary laborers dominated these venues. Most of these towns developed a self-sufficient agriculture, often supported by carefully husbanded irrigation works, with water from melting snows of the region's lofty mountains.

---

[1] On Temür, see Beatrice Forbes Manz, *The Rise and Rule of Tamerlane* (Cambridge University Press, 1989).

The same diversity characterized the various Central Asian groups in the late fourteenth and early fifteenth centuries. The Timurid Empire, which descended from Temür, was predominantly Turkic and dominated much of Central Asia with capitals in Samarkand and Herat. The Timurids relied on Iranian officials to assist in ruling their vast domains, stretching from Central Asia to Iran and West Asia. Because Iranians had experience in governing empires, they proved invaluable to the Timurids. The Ottoman Turks, whose original homeland was also in Central Asia, had moved farther west and would soon detach much of West Asia from Timurid control and destroy the Byzantine Empire and Egypt's Mamluk dynasty. The Uzbeks, descended from the Mongol Khan Özbeg of the Golden Horde in Russia, were uniting and would soon play a significant role in Central Asia. The Chinese had traditionally been highly involved in the regions neighboring them to the west. Although the Mongol Empire had waned, Mongols still inhabited specific areas in Central Asia. Indians and Russians were poised to involve themselves in the region. This astonishing array of peoples continued to play a role in the region's history through 1800.

Central Asia had traditionally been a cradle for or transmitter of an extraordinary variety of religions, including Hinduism, Buddhism, Nestorian Christianity, Zoroastrianism, Judaism and Islam. By 1400, Buddhism and Islam, of different sects and orders, dominated.

In 1400, indigenous rulers governed Central Asia. The states and Khanates in the region were independent and were not bound to a foreign empire, Khanate or kingdom. By 1800, Qing dynasty China had encroached upon eastern Central Asia, overwhelming mostly Turkic Muslim peoples and bringing them within its empire. At the same time, Tsarist Russia had gradually gained influence in western Central Asia and was in a strong position to incorporate the region within its domains. Part of the explanation for the expansion of China and Russia in the region lies in what Victor Lieberman has described as a general pattern of growing consolidation and centralization of political units in the early modern and modern worlds, but these changes were also caused by the decline of the Central Asian states.[2]

Ming and Central Asia

After the collapse of Mongol rule in China in 1368, the Ming, an indigenous dynasty, took power. Having endured Mongol domination for almost a

---

[2] Victor Lieberman, *Strange Parallels: Southeast Asia in Global Context, c. 800–1830* (Cambridge University Press, 2009), vol. II, pp. 9–11.

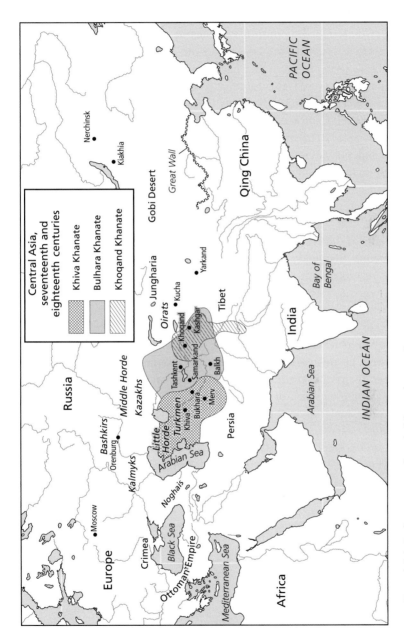

14.1 Central Asia in the seventeenth and eighteenth centuries

Central Asia,
seventeenth and
eighteenth centuries

Khiva Khanate

Bulhara Khanate

Khoqand Khanate

Europe

Russia

Moscow

Crimea

Black Sea

Ottoman Empire

Mediterranean Sea

Africa

Bashkirs

Orenburg

Kalmyks

Noghais

Arabian Sea

Little
Horde

Middle Horde

Kazakhs

Tashkent

Turkmen

Khiva

Bukhara

Merv

Samarkand

Khoqand

Balkh

Kashgar

Yarkand

Persia

India

Arabian Sea

INDIAN OCEAN

Bay of
Bengal

Oirats

Jungharia

Kucha

Tibet

Gobi Desert

Great Wall

Qing China

Nerchinsk

Kiakhta

PACIFIC
OCEAN

349

century in South China and for 130 years in North China, China sought to limit contact with foreigners to avert another invasion. The first Ming Emperor determined the number of foreign trade and tribute missions permitted to enter China. Despite this generally isolationist policy, the Ming court was determined to control such nearby oases as Turfan and Hami, which it often described as gateways to the Western Regions. Moreover, court officials recognized that they needed to trade for horses for China's self-defense, and they were well aware that some Chinese subjects profited from commerce with China's neighbors to the northwest as well as with more distant regions in Central Asia. The Ming court would not sanction free trade or the Mongol Yuan dynasty's robust support for the Silk Roads, but its realpolitik policies mandated that it allow Central Asian trade and tribute, although under carefully regulated circumstances. It specified the frequency of foreign embassies, the number of men on each embassy, the types of banquets each would receive (which would depend upon a Chinese evaluation of the states', Khanates' or towns' power and prestige) and the value of official gifts to the envoys.

Realpolitik frequently subverted the Confucian ideology that underlay Chinese relations with Central Asia. This ideology proposed that Chinese culture was superior to other cultures and that the emperor, as the Son of Heaven, embodied the correct principles for governance and was superior to all other rulers. As one Chinese historian has noted: "The emperor, or the court in general, was the arbiter of what was appropriate behavior by any person or polity."[3] Because China and its court and emperors had developed the proper paths for civilization, foreign rulers and envoys ought to follow Chinese models or seek to become sinicized. Other societies should learn from China, while the Chinese did not need to know much about foreigners.[4] Chinese officials professed to have scant interest in Central Asian culture and society. They also claimed to be economically self-sufficient and asserted that the Central Asian goods presented in tribute or trade were meaningless to China. It turned out that these views had to be modified,

---

[3] Geoffrey Wade, "Some Topoi in Southern Border Historiography During the Ming (and Their Modern Relevance)" in Sabine Dabringhaus and Roderich Ptak (eds.), *China and Her Neighbours* (Wiesbaden: Harrassowitz Verlag, 1997), p. 139.

[4] See Morris Rossabi, "Introduction" in Morris Rossabi (ed.), *China among Equals* (Berkeley, CA: University of California Press, 1983), pp. 1–4 for an elucidation of this so-called tribute system of foreign relations; and David C. Kang, *East Asia Before the West: Five Centuries of Trade and Tribute* (New York: Columbia University Press, 2010), pp. 161–71 for an attempt to interpret China's current foreign policy based on the recent critiques of the tribute system theory.

if not abandoned, however, especially in perilous times. Actual policies often deviated from Chinese rhetoric.

The Yongle emperor (r. 1403 to 1424), the dynasty's third emperor, was the first ruler to restore China's domination over the region centered on the Hami oasis.[5] In 1405, he helped to enthrone Toghto, a reliable Mongol, as the *Zhongshun wang* (Loyal and Obedient Prince) of Hami. Having been educated at the Chinese court, Toghto was not suited to rule nomadic pastoralists or oasis-dwelling merchants, the two prominent groups in Hami. The indigenous population, composed principally of Uyghurs and some Hui (or Chinese Muslims), reacted adversely to the installation of Toghto, but his death in 1410 afforded the Yongle emperor an opportunity to enthrone Toghto's more capable cousin Mianli Temür as *Zhongyi wang* (Loyal and Righteous Prince), which made still another Mongol the new governor.[6] This more experienced and more stable ruler ushered in a period of good relations, which translated into close commercial contact. Within fourteen years, thirty official embassies and no doubt individual commercial missions arrived in Beijing from Hami.[7] The Ming court generally received such valuable and essential products as horses or sable and squirrel pelts, all of which it could use. It provided in return silk and other textiles, which China possessed in abundance and the dynasty could easily afford to offer in exchange. These relationships became ever closer, and the Ming court even tried to protect Hami from the attacks of the Oyirad Mongol leader Esen in the 1440s. Yet, this campaign rebounded against the court, as the expedition went awry. Esen captured the Ming emperor in 1449, deflating the dynasty's prestige and initiating difficulties between China and Hami.[8]

Turfan, eventually the center of power in the region, originally established a peaceful relationship with China, but ultimately also came into conflict with the Ming. In the early fifteenth century, Buddhists and Muslims coexisted in the town, and indeed Buddhist monks led so-called tribute missions

---

[5] On this fascinating emperor, see Shih-san Henry Tsai, *Perpetual Happiness: The Ming Emperor Yongle* (Seattle, WA: University of Washington Press, 2001).

[6] *Ming shilu (Guoli zhongyang tushuguan)*, Taizong, 54, 5b–6a; 74, 2a–2b; and 114, 2b.

[7] Ma Wensheng, *Xingfu Hamizhi* in the *Zhilu huibian*, 1b, and *Ming shilu*, Taizong, 216, 3a.

[8] Frederick W. Mote, "The T'u-mu Incident of 1449" in Frank A. Kierman Jr., and John K. Fairbank (eds.), *Chinese Ways in Warfare* (Cambridge, MA: Harvard University Press, 1974), pp. 251–8; Ph. De Heer, *Care-Taker Emperor: Aspects of the Imperial Institution in Fifteenth-Century China as Reflected in the Political History of the Reign of Chu Ch'i-yü* (Leiden: Brill, 1986), p. 16; and *Ming shilu*, Yingzong, 120, 7b.

to the court. They offered horses, invaluable for China, and received silk and paper money that they could use to purchase other products. An envoy from western Central Asia who passed through Turfan observed that the town "had large idol-temples of superb beauty inside which there were many idols, some of them having been made newly and others old. In foreground of the platform there was a big image which was asserted by them to be the statue of Sakyamuni."[9]

Relations with both Hami and Turfan began to sour after the capture of the Ming emperor in 1449. The rulers of Turfan adopted a more strident policy towards the Ming and sought to annex Hami and additional territories in eastern Central Asia. Their and their subjects' conversions to Islam may have also contributed to their unwillingness to accept a tributary status to China. The Ming army had clearly deteriorated, the court faced revenue shortfalls and powerful eunuchs, on occasion, dominated the government. The rulers of Turfan recognized these problems, all of which facilitated Turfan's challenge to Chinese hegemony. Commercial disputes first ensnarled relations, as the Ming complained about the quality of horses sent by Turfan and the large number of men on each so-called tribute mission, all of whose expenses in China were borne by the court. Similar commercial disputes bedeviled relations with Hami. Ming authorities repeatedly criticized Hami's overly frequent embassies and its tribute items of poor quality jade and weak, if not emaciated, horses. Their response to what they perceived to be abuses was to restrict the number of tribute and trade missions, enraging Turfan and Hami.[10]

Capitalizing on China's declining influence in neighboring areas and antagonized by the Ming court's limits on tribute and commerce, Turfan adopted an increasingly bellicose policy. In 1473, its ruler Sultan ʿAlī occupied Hami, and almost a decade elapsed before the Ming liberated this gateway to the so-called Western Regions.[11] For the next three decades, Turfan and China vied for control over Hami. In 1482, the Ming court supported a Uyghur leader to recapture Hami, but seven years later, Sultan ʿAlī's son Ahmad killed the Uyghur governor and reoccupied Hami. The Ming court retaliated by denying entry to Turfan's trade and tribute missions. Ahmad

[9] Hafiz-i Abru, *A Persian Embassy to China Being an Extract from Zubdatu't Tawarikh of Hafiz Abru*, K. M. Maitra (trans.) (New York: Paragon Book Corp., 1970), p. 13.
[10] Morris Rossabi, "Ming China and Turfan, 1406–1517," *Central Asiatic Journal* 16 (1972), 214.
[11] Fu Weilin (ed.), *Ming shu* (Shanghai, 1928), p. 3294

responded by submitting and withdrawing his troops from Hami. This initial Ming success was, in large part, based upon the development and recruitment of a coterie of foreign experts who recognized that commerce was vital for Turfan. Ma Wensheng, the Minister of War, had been stationed as an official in northwest China and was the principal proponent of the policy of rejecting trade with Turfan as a means of undermining what the Chinese conceived of as belligerence.[12] Xu Jin, who was governor of Gansu province and had spent most of his career in northwest China, led a campaign to oust Turfan from Hami and neighboring oases.[13] As early as the Yongle reign, the court had established a College of Interpreters and a College of Translators to train interpreters and translators in languages spoken in nearby regions. Although both agencies were flawed, they provided the court with a few qualified men who knew foreign languages.[14]

Despite such expertise, the Ming dynasty ultimately did not have the resources to protect Hami and to deter challenges. It received a brief respite when Ahmad responded to a plea from his brother, who governed the western regions of their domains, to defend his lands against the expansionist Uzbek Turks. In 1505, Ahmad traveled westward to assist his brother, but shortly thereafter he was captured and died in captivity. His son Mansūr was not to be deterred.[15] In 1513, he conquered Hami, and this time the Ming could not mount a campaign to oust Turfan.[16] Four years later, Mansūr occupied Shazhou, an oasis even closer to China. At this point, the Ming relented and allowed Turfan to dispatch trade and tribute embassies to China. A steady flow of such missions, which were intent on trade rather than diplomacy, reached the court throughout the sixteenth century, and commerce along the frontiers persisted.[17] The Ming dynasty had become, in Wang Gungwu's words, a "lesser empire" in eastern Central Asia, unable to enforce its will on its neighbors to the northwest.[18]

---

[12] Zhang Tingyü, Ming shih (Taipei, 1962–63), 329, p. 3785.
[13] Ma Wensheng, Xingfu Hamizhi, 4b–5a. See the translation of Xu Jin's report in Ruby Lam, "Memoir on the Campaign Against Turfan," Journal of Asian History 24 (1990), 111.
[14] Pamela Crossley, "Structure and Symbol in the Role of the Ming-Qing Foreign Translation Bureau (siyi guan)," Central and Inner Asian Studies 5 (1991), 38–70; and Paul Pelliot, "Le Sseu-yi-kouan et le Houei-t'ong-kouan" in Paul Pelliot, Le Hôja et le Sayyid Husain de l'Histoire des Ming, T'oung Pao 38 (Leiden: Brill, 1948), pp. 2–5 and 207–90.
[15] On some of these events, see also Wheeler Thackston (ed. and trans.), Mirza Haidar Dughlat's Tarikh-i-Rashidi: A History of the Khans of Moghulistan (Cambridge, MA: Harvard University, 1996).
[16] Ming shi, p. 3792.   [17] Ming shi, p. 3826.
[18] See Wang Gung-wu, "The Rhetoric of a Lesser Empire" in Rossabi, China among Equals, pp. 47–65.

Timurids in Central Asia

Farther away from China but lying at the center of the Timurid Empire was western Central Asia. In the last third of the fourteenth century, Temür had occupied a vast domain, including western Central Asia, Iran, parts of West Asia, northern India and the Caucasus, and had established his capital in Samarkand, the heart of Central Asia. He actually conquered more territory than Chinggis Khan had, but never assumed the title "Khan" because he was not directly descended from Chinggis. In the last decade of the fourteenth century, he received Chinese embassies with letters from the Chinese emperor that addressed him as a vassal. Taking umbrage at such disrespect and having heard rumors that the Ming mistreated the Muslims in China, he determined to avenge his Islamic brothers and planned a military campaign against China.[19] While heading towards China, he died of natural causes in February 1405. His death was a blessing for China, as the Ming dynasty had not made any preparations to defend its realm. Indeed, the Chinese scarcely knew about Temür and were unaware that he planned to invade China.

Temür's death generated the same succession struggles that plagued many states with a nomadic and decentralized origin. He had based his power, in part, on the personal loyalty of leaders throughout his domains. His appointment of his own sons and grandsons as rulers of his lands further assured him of stable control. However, his death released these individuals from their obligations and permitted some of them to fight to replace him. Four years of intermittent conflict elapsed before Shah Rukh, one of Temür's sons, vanquished his opponents and became the new ruler. Although Shah Rukh emerged victorious, he governed a diminished empire. Many local governors had capitalized on the chaos attending the succession to assert their autonomy. The Timurid Empire had been weakened. Shah Rukh's father had assigned him to rule Khurasan from Herat, and after his victory, he ruled from there and placed Ulugh Beg, his own son, in charge of Samarkand, Temür's capital. Although he tried to recover some of the territories that had been lost, he was unable to restore control over key areas, including Azerbaijan and Iraq. He maintained jurisdiction principally in Central Asia and Iran. Like his father, he recruited Iranian officials to assist him in ruling,

---

[19] Joseph Fletcher, "China and Central Asia, 1368–1884" in John Fairbank (ed.), *The Chinese World Order: Traditional China's Foreign Relations* (Cambridge, MA: Harvard University Press, 1968), pp. 209–10.

but relied mostly on Turkic peoples for his military forces. For a time, this reliance on the Turco-Mongolian system of *jasagh* law and the Iranian *shari'a* law worked out, but this dichotomy eventually proved to be troublesome because it created a split between the Iranians, who associated with sedentary civilizations and Islamic law, and the Turks, who identified with the traditional nomadic culture, values and law.[20] Individual rivalries among governors compelled Shah Rukh to engage in military campaigns to pacify opponents, which actually weakened his state. Lacking his father's military talents, he turned to diplomacy, occasionally with great success. For example, he abandoned his father's Eastern campaign and instead established a stable relationship with Ming China. The Chinese sent an official named Chen Cheng to improve relations, and Chen produced an excellent account of fifteenth-century Herat.[21] In turn, Shah Rukh's envoy to China wrote a lengthy description of the Ming at its height.[22] These exchanges led to a resumption of trade between the two empires through the early sixteenth century.

Despite the political infighting and progressively unstable political situation, Shah Rukh in Herat and Ulugh Beg in Samarkand fostered a cultural and artistic renaissance in the Timurid domains. Even earlier, Temür and his family had constructed imposing buildings, often related to their Islamic faith, in Samarkand. His sisters built mausolea with exquisite tile mosaics, but the most renowned structure was the unique ribbed dome Gur-I Mir, with tombs for Temür himself and his grandson Ulugh Beg. Temür's construction of the Mosque of Bibi Khanum was another indication of his devotion to Islam. Gauhar Shad, Shah Rukh's wife, was a patron of architecture in his capital at Herat. A mosque, a madrassah, a shrine and her own mausoleum, adorned with spectacular tile work, attest to her patronage[23].

---

[20] Beatrice Manz, "Temür and the early Timurids to c. 1450" in Nicola Di Cosmo, Allen Frank and Peter Golden (eds.), *The Cambridge History of Inner Asia: The Chinggisid Era* (Cambridge University Press, 2009), pp. 194–6.

[21] Bruno Richtsfeld, *Die Aufzeichnungen des Ch'en Ch'eng und Li Hsien über ihre Gesandtschafts-reise nach Herat: Ein chinesischer Beitrag zur Kenntnis Mittelasiens im 15. Jahrhundert* (Magisterarbeit: Universität München, 1985); and Felicia Hecker, "A Fifteenth-Century Chinese Diplomat in Herat," *Journal of the Royal Asiatic Society* 3 (1993), 85–98 offers a translation of Chen's report on Herat.

[22] See K. M. Maitra, *A Persian Embassy to China* (New York: Paragon Book Reprint Corp., 1970). See also Kanda Kiichrō, "Chin Sei no *Shi saiiki ki ni tsuite*" ["Concerning Chen Cheng's *Shi xiyü zi*"]. A history of this text can be found in Morris Rossabi, "Two Ming Envoys to Inner Asia," *T'oung Pao* 42 (1976), 19.

[23] Manz, "Temür and the early Timurids to c. 1450" in Di Cosmo, Frank and Golden, *Cambridge History of Inner Asia*, pp. 80 and 90.

Few Timurid carpets have survived, although some specialists believe that several types of carpets currently attributed to a later period date from the fifteenth century.

The Timurid rulers and the merchants who prospered from the continuance of trade also subsidized a variety of other arts and crafts.[24] The Herat school of artists was famous for its miniatures for manuscripts. Shah Rukh commissioned Hafiz-i Abru to continue Rashid al-Din's great universal history, and the resulting work offered numerous images. The *Khalila wa Dimna*,[25] a book consisting of animal fables, was another illustrated text, and the Herat school continued to produce outstanding miniatures throughout the Timurid reign. The Timurids also supported metalwork and showed a fondness for Chinese porcelains, commissioning potters who attempted to provide acceptable copies. Trade with China led to the development of a considerable collection of Ming dynasty blue-and-white porcelains, some of which wound up in Ardebil in Iran.[26] Religious objects such as prayer stands for the Koran, as well as other artifacts, also received considerable patronage. Husain Baiqara (r. 1470 to 1506), a Timurid descendant based in Herat, was a patron of the literary arts.[27] Poetry, sometimes imbued with Sufi mystical connotations, blossomed during his reign. 'Abd al-Rahman Jami (1414 to 1492) was a particularly renowned Iranian poet of that era. Husain Baiqara supported the construction of such spectacular architectural monuments as madrassahs, mosques, caravanserais and hospitals. Similarly, historians and biographers, sometimes of religious figures, also received patronage.

Shah Rukh retained power, escaping an attempt at assassination in 1427, and maintained a semblance of order until the end of his reign in 1447. Like so many nomadic-based empires, succession to leadership was often a problem. Shah Rukh's son Ulugh Beg initially appeared to be victorious after

---

[24] See Thomas W. Lentz and Glenn D. Lowry, *Timur and the Princely Vision: Persian Art and Culture in the Fifteenth Century* (Los Angeles County Museum of Art, 1989); Lisa Golombek and Maria Subtelny (eds.), *Timurid Art and Culture in Iran and Central Asia in the Fifteenth Century* (Leiden: Brill, 1992); and Wheeler Thackston, *A Century of Princes: Sources on Timurid History and Art* (Cambridge, MA: The Aga Khan Program for Islamic Architecture, 1989).

[25] See the translation by Jill Sanchia Cowen (trans.), *Khalila wa Dimna: An Animal Allegory of the Mongol Court: The Istanbul University Album* (Oxford University Press, 1989), but see also the reviews of this work by Sheila Blair in *Iranian Studies* 22 (1989), 133–5 and by Sheila Canby in *Speculum* 68 (1993), 488.

[26] See John A. Pope, *Chinese Porcelains from the Ardebil Shrine* (Washington, DC: Freer Gallery of Art, Smithsonian Institution, 1956).

[27] Stephen Dale, "The Later Timurids c. 1450–1526" in Di Cosmo, Frank and Golden, *Cambridge History of Inner Asia*, pp. 207–11.

his father's death, but he faced opposition.[28] His own son defected, defeated his father's forces and had him killed in 1449. In his four decades as a governor, Ulugh Beg contributed to cultural efflorescence in Samarkand. Like his grandfather Temür, he added to the city's architectural splendor. His fame rests on his construction of an observatory, as well as his own writings on astronomy. His political and military skills lagged behind, however, preventing him from gaining control over and unifying his ancestors' domains.

His death unleashed still another struggle for succession, with two rulers coming to power and each being killed. Finally, in 1451, Abu Said, Temür's great grandson, took power for almost two decades, but he governed over a much lesser empire. Many of the West Asian domains subjugated by Temür, including western Iran, had broken away. Abu Said faced opposition within his own princely family and also from Türkmen and Uzbek leaders in the region, and in 1469 succumbed to one of his Türkmen enemies.[29] Subsequent Timurid leaders continued to lose ground, especially to the Uzbeks, until the accession of Babur (b. 1483).[30] Later the founder of the Mughal dynasty of India, Babur tried to retain his ancestors' territory, especially the Timurid capital of Samarkand, but a defeat to the Uzbeks in Herat in 1506 compelled him eventually to migrate. The Uzbek leader Muhammad Shaibani allowed Babur to depart for Kabul. Although Babur tried, for a time, to reclaim his ancestral lands, he eventually abandoned his efforts, and in 1526 decisively changed course by attacking and occupying Delhi.

Instability gave rise to considerable religious fervor, as Sufism, in particular, gained adherents. Its mysticism appealed initially to the lower classes, who often bore the brunt of the violence and destruction that characterized the turbulence of some of the Timurid reigns. The poor turned to sheikhs, who offered the promise of inner spiritual peace, to cope with chaotic conditions. Veneration of saints, asceticism, fear of God, vocalization of prayers and whirling movements that could lead to union with the divine were all means of achieving a calmer state. People of all classes came to seek solace via Sufism. Merchants, in particular, became effective vehicles for transmitting the Sufi message throughout Central Asia.

---

[28] On him, see the somewhat dated but useful biography by Vasilii V. Barthold, *Four Studies on the History of Central Asia: Ulugh Beg*, V. Minorsky and T. Minorsky (trans.) (Leiden: E. J. Brill, 1956–1962), vol. II.

[29] Dale, "The later Timurids c. 1450–1526" in Di Cosmo, Frank and Golden, *Cambridge History of Inner Asia*, pp. 201–2.

[30] See his renowned work *Baburnama: Memoirs of Babur*, Wheeler Thackston (trans.) (New York: Random House, 2002).

Like the Mongols, Temür and his descendants have been portrayed as barbaric devastators of the economies and cultures of the regions they subjugated. This chapter has already challenged such perceptions by pointing to their contributions to the arts, architecture and sciences. The concept of economic devastation also needs to be questioned. The original conquests in Central Asia and Iran proved damaging, but the Timurids quickly initiated policies to ensure the recovery of these domains. They fostered commerce by constructing roads, rebuilding sections of cities that had been damaged and offering reductions in taxes to merchants. Although the pace of commercial activity diminished from the halcyon days of the Mongol Empire, trade persisted with areas as far away as China in the east and Anatolia in the west.[31] The Timurids moved expeditiously to restore agriculture near the oases and towns, in particular repairing the complicated and essential irrigation systems that had been damaged during the warfare. Political and military instability, succession disputes and conflicts with the Türkmen and Uzbeks vitiated these remarkable economic achievements, weakening the Timurids and making them vulnerable to the previously nomadic Uzbeks, who became the dominant force in Central Asia from the sixteenth to the early nineteenth century.

Uzbek dominance

Allegedly descended from Özbeg Khan (r. 1313 to 1341), a ruler of the Golden Horde who had converted to Islam, the Uzbeks resided in the Central Asian grasslands and pursued a nomadic pastoral economy in the late fourteenth and early fifteenth centuries. Abul Khayr Khan united the disparate Uzbek groups, composed of ninety-two tribes, between 1428 and 1468. His attempts at expansion resulted in conflicts with the Timurids, the Golden Horde, Iran and the Western or Oyirad Mongols. Yet, such conflicts contributed to a growing identity of the Uzbeks as a distinct group. Although the Uzbeks were often divided by internal struggles and wars, they persisted in perceiving themselves to be of the same origin.

Muhammad Shaibani (1451 to 1510), Abul Khayr Khan's grandson, led the Uzbeks into greater territorial expansion. Reared in the steppelands rather than in the Central Asian cities, he developed a profound attachment to his

---

[31] Morris Rossabi, "The 'Decline' of the Central Asian Caravan Trade" in James Tracy (ed.), *The Rise of Merchant Empires* (Cambridge University Press, 1990), pp. 351–71.

beautiful land and its flora and fauna.[32] He also benefited from a stay in Bukhara, where he was exposed to learned Sufis and became a devotee of the arts. Despite these religious and cultural interests, he was also a strong military leader, whose ventures led to the destruction of the Timurids and annexation of their lands in Central Asia. By the end of the first decade of the sixteenth century, he had overrun the Timurid domains and became the most important ruler in Central Asia. Despite his victory, however, the break-up of the Timurids led to the independence and establishment of the Safavid dynasty in Iran and its support for Shiite Islam. Religious disputes, as well as diplomatic and political rivalry, caused a rift between these two areas that had been part of the Timurid domains.

The Uzbeks began to settle in cities and to engage in trade and self-sufficient farming, but were plagued by internal conflicts. Shaibani's descendants established a capital city in Bukhara, later known as an emirate, and fostered commerce. Trade along the traditional Silk Roads, which centered on China and Iran, diminished, and new trading partners developed. Tsarist Russia and Mughal India would generally replace Iran and China as the Uzbeks' principal foreign relationships. Yet, despite their commercial successes, the Uzbeks' internal fragmentation permitted the Ashtarkhanids (1599 to 1785), supported by Sufi leaders, to overwhelm the Shaibanids, and then similarly the Manghits (1753 to 1920) defeated the Ashtarkhanids after an Iranian invasion had weakened them. Other Uzbek groups broke away and founded Khanates in Khiva (1511 to the late seventeenth century and 1770 to 1920) and Khoqand (1798 to 1876).

Uzbek political instability did not undermine trade, often the lifeblood of Central Asian history. The ruling dynasties were not averse to commerce, even with such former enemies as the Timurids, whose descendants ruled as India's Mughal dynasty.[33] Uzbeks had expelled the Timurids from Central Asia in the early sixteenth century, but within several decades had developed a thriving trading relationship with the Mughals. Their common religion of Islam facilitated a renewal of contacts, but it was often Indian Hindus who promoted and served as middlemen in this commerce. The mostly Muslim population did not perceive the Hindus favorably, but recognized that they

---

[32] Edward Allworth, *The Modern Uzbeks: From the Fourteenth Century to the Present: A Cultural History* (Stanford, CA: Hoover Institution Press, Stanford University, 1990), pp. 47–53.

[33] According to Richard Foltz, *Mughal India and Central Asia* (Karachi: Oxford University Press, 1998), the Mughals themselves continued to maintain strong bonds with Central Asia.

fostered trade, offered loans to Uzbek merchants, and supported the government in its efforts to devise and collect taxes in cash. Hindu merchants transported cotton textiles, slaves, sugar, spices, herbs and jewelry, among other products, to the Uzbeks and obtained horses, furs and slaves.[34]

Safavid-Uzbek hostilities, especially over northeast Iran or Khurasan, persisted, but India now began to play an important role in Central Asia. Nonetheless, commerce persisted in western Central Asia in the seventeenth and early eighteenth centuries, but with new partners, India and then Russia—not China.

The last Mongol Empire

In eastern Central Asia, although the Silk Roads had declined after the mid-sixteenth century, a new commercial interchange with China developed in the seventeenth century. Before its restoration, however, threats arose from the nomadic Kazakh and Kyrgyz peoples to the oases and towns of the Tarim River basin. In the seventeenth century, a new movement around the Sufi Naqshbandi order, which approved of political involvement, gained control over the region and finally supplanted the descendants of the Chaghadai rulers.[35] Shortly thereafter, the Naqshbandi leadership split into a White Mountain group and a Black Mountain group and became embroiled in violent battles, making them vulnerable to Galdan Khan, who unified the Zunghar or western Mongols and swept into the Tarim basin in 1678 to 1680. After their withdrawal from China in 1368, the Mongols had been unable to achieve unity, despite the bonds created by their conversion to Tibetan Buddhism in the late sixteenth and early seventeenth centuries. Galdan, with the Dalai Lama's implicit support, initiated the last Mongol effort to create a nomadic empire.

Earlier, Galdan had been studying in Tibet when he learned of a coup and the assassination of his brother, the leader of the Zunghars. Returning

---

[34] Scott Levi, *The Indian Diaspora in Central Asia and Its Trade, 1550–1900* (Leiden: Brill, 2002), pp. 54–82.

[35] See several works on these Khojas: Joseph Fletcher, "Confrontations between Muslim Missionaries and Nomad Unbelievers in the Late Sixteenth Century" in W. Heissig (ed.), *Tractata Altaica* (Wiesbaden: Otto Harrassowitz, 1976), pp. 167–70; Joseph Fletcher, "Central Asian Sufism and Ma Ming-hsin's New Teaching" in Ch'en Chieh-hsin (ed.), *Proceedings of the Fourth East Asian Altaistic Conference* (Taipei: National Taiwan University, 1975), pp. 75–96; and Joseph Fletcher, "The Naqshbandiyya and the Dhikr-I Arra," *Journal of Turkish Studies* 1 (1987), 113–19.

to Mongolia in 1671, he defeated his rivals and continued to build up the Zunghars' power.[36] A few of these Mongols had begun to farm, others started to mine natural resources, and still others made their own weapons and manufactured articles. Zaya Pandita, a renowned advocate of Tibetan Buddhism, developed a new written script. Seeking to capitalize on these economic and cultural advances, Galdan began to challenge the Manchu-led Qing dynasty of China, which had ousted the Ming dynasty in 1644. Earlier, in 1640 and 1660, representatives of the leading Mongol groups had met to create a coalition, but unity had proven elusive. Neither the Khalkha, or Eastern Mongols, nor the Bogd Gegen, the spiritual heads of the Mongolian Buddhists, joined Galdan, and the Khalkha themselves were divided into at least four warring Khanates. Galdan took the bold and decisive step of attacking one of the Khanates, but was unable to secure much support from the others. Without Mongol unity, Galdan could not be assured of success against the Qing.[37] The conflict between him and the Qing revolved around commercial disputes, and his occupation of the Tarim River basin in 1678 to 1680 derived, in part, from these conflicts.

This struggle shortly became global. Russia, which had crossed the Ural Mountains and colonized Siberia, began to encroach upon the Qing's northeastern frontiers in the middle of the seventeenth century. Diplomacy did not initially resolve their differing territorial claims, leading to a potential Russian-Zunghar alliance. From the early seventeenth century, the Russians and the Zunghars had exchanged diplomatic and commercial missions.[38] But the Qing and the Tsarist courts pulled back from a confrontation because they had complementary interests. Russia wished to trade for Chinese tea, silk, porcelain and rhubarb, and the Qing wanted the Russians to withdraw from China's frontier areas and to devise a boundary that favored China's interests. The Sino-Russian Treaty of Nerchinsk of 1689 contained such provisions, ending the dispute between the two great empires. Russia was permitted to send trade caravans to Beijing, and the border demarcation suited China.[39] Bereft of allies and surrounded by the two empires, Galdan

---

[36] Zhao Erxün et al. (eds.), Qing shi (Taibei: Guofang yanjiu yüan, 1961), p. 5637.
[37] See Morris Rossabi, "Ch'ing Conquest of Inner Asia" in Willard Peterson (ed.), The Cambridge History of China: Early Ch'ing (forthcoming), vol. ix, pt 2.
[38] Mark Mancall, Russia and China: Their Diplomatic Relations to 1728 (Cambridge, MA: Harvard University Press, 1971), pp. 87–8 and 104–6; Vincent Chen, Sino-Russian Relations in the Seventeenth Century (The Hague: Martinus Nijhoff, 1966), pp. 59–62; and Gaston Cahen, History of the Relations of Russia and China under Peter the Great, 1689–1730, W. Sheldon Ridge (trans.) (Bangor: University Print Reprints, 1914).
[39] Mancall, Russia and China, pp. 156–8.

could no longer avoid a conflict with the Qing by fleeing into the steppes or Siberia. In 1691, the Khalkha Mongols further bolstered the Qing by accepting its sovereignty, ending Galdan's hopes for a Mongolian confederation under his leadership. In 1696, Qing armies caught up with and defeated Galdan. His nephew Tsewang Rabdan, who had earlier rebelled against his uncle, managed to escape and headed for the Tarim River basin, where he posed a threat to the oases and towns of eastern Central Asia. In 1717, he even conceived of a greater enterprise and dispatched an army on a successful foray to occupy Tibet. However, in 1720, the Qing, still concerned about a Mongol force not far away, sent a force that overcame logistical and transport problems to expel the Zunghars from that Himalayan country and to impose its own rule. Although it faced resistance from a variety of different Tibetan and Mongolian groups, it established a precarious peace in Tibet by the late 1720s.[40]

Meanwhile, Qing commanders still sought to drive the Zunghars out of eastern Central Asia. A campaign in the northwest required a supply line and proper logistics. The Qing learned this via an abortive effort against the Zunghars in the area in 1731. Its forces lost, in large part, because the oases had meager supplies for a substantial army. When the Qianlong emperor took power in 1736, no decision had been made about a campaign towards eastern Central Asia, but divisions among the Zunghars, a common problem among the nomadic pastoral empires, gave the Qing an opening. The Qing authorities started by demanding funds, considerable supplies and recruits from the Khalkha Mongols, while the Zunghars sought assistance from Russia and the nomadic Kazakhs. Under great pressure, the Khalkha provided help, but the tremendous burdens imposed upon them provoked a violent outbreak led by Chingünjav, a descendant of Chinggis Khan, in 1756. Qing troops quickly crushed his forces and accused the Bogd Gegen, the Buddhist religious leader, of supporting Chingünjav. The Qing court, fearful of a nationalist alliance between a Mongol secular commander and the Buddhist leader, now mandated that all future Bogd Gegens be Tibetan. Once the court had suppressed Chingünjav's rebellion, it could rely on some Mongols to assist in its most difficult and dramatic campaign, the defeat of the Zunghars in the northwest.[41]

[40] Luciano Petech, *China and Tibet in the Early 18th Century* (Leiden: Brill, 1950), pp. 108–25, and Hugh Richardson (ed.), *Tibet and Its History* (Boulder, CO: Shambhala, 1984), pp. 50–2.

[41] Charles Bawden, "The Mongol Rebellion of 1756–1757," *Journal of Asian History* 2 (1968), 22–6; and Morris Rossabi, "The Development of Mongol Identity in the Seventeenth and Eighteenth Centuries" in Leonard Blussé and Felipe Fernández-Armesto (eds.),

In the 1750s, Qing commanders added to the territories under the dynasty's control. In 1755, they crushed one Zunghar leader, but then faced Amursana, still another adversary, for another couple of years. Amursana gained support from the Kazakhs, but could not unite his own Zunghar people. Unaware of his difficulties in building up a powerful force, the Qing court ordered its commanders to show no mercy in wiping out the Zunghars. Such instructions emboldened the Qing military, leading both sides to engage in horrific massacres. Amursana himself successfully evaded the Qing, but eventually succumbed instead to smallpox while seeking Russian support. The Zunghars then disappeared as a group from historical accounts. Many were killed in battle, and some died of smallpox or other diseases. Yet, some also eluded the enemy, crossed into Russian territory and intermarried with Mongol groups who had moved there previously. They assumed the identities of the groups to which they became linked. Thus, the conception that the Qing massacred all of the Zunghars needs to be modified.[42]

Qing occupation of eastern Central Asia

Once the Zunghars had been ousted from the northwest, the Qing still needed to overwhelm the Muslim communities to gain control of the region. Khojas, the religious leaders, posed a threat because of their desire to return to a form of Islam untainted by foreign influences. In effect, their views dictated autonomy or independence. Qing troops who had reached this distant region were determined to occupy the oases in the northwest. By 1760, they had pacified the principal oases of what eventually came to be called Xinjiang. By venturing into the northwest and subjugating and seeking to occupy a vast territory inhabited by a non-Chinese population, the Qing controverted traditional Chinese foreign policy and the advice of many emperors of the past. This new policy aroused considerable opposition from Chinese officials at the court who feared the consequences of such an occupation. They regarded these new lands, which consisted of sizeable deserts and barren terrain, as economically unproductive and as a burden

---

Shifting Communities and Identity Formation in Early Modern Asia (Leiden: Research School of Asian, African, and Amerindian Studies, Universiteit Leiden, 2003), pp. 56–60.

[42] The most important work on this struggle between the Qing and the Zunghars is Peter Perdue, *China Marches West: The Qing Conquest of Central Eurasia* (Cambridge, MA: Harvard University Press, 2005). For a different approach, see L. I. Duman, "The Qing Conquest of Junggariye and Eastern Turkestan" in S. L. Tikhvinsky (ed.), *Manzhou Rule in China*, David Skvirsky (trans.) (Moscow: Progress Publishers, 1983), pp. 237–9.

on the army that was required to secure a region with a mostly non-Chinese population. Many of the non-Chinese were restive and strongly opposed to Qing rule, which had to maintain a military force along the frontiers.

The stationing of troops so far from China's center necessitated vast expenditures unless other practices or policies were developed. The Qing turned to the traditional system of military colonies (*tuntian*) to defray expenses. The colonists were expected to support themselves while maintaining their military skills. However, they inhabited marginal agrarian lands in the northwest and could not always be self-sufficient.[43] As an occupation force, they were vulnerable to attacks. The court also planned to encourage them to help sinicize the local peoples, another burden on them. Still another obligation was the taxes on the surpluses they produced. Disgraced officials, exiled criminals, and other Chinese and Manchus in the northwest did not prove to be effective cultivators of the land, especially under the difficult conditions in the region.[44] The Manchu armies had so-called Banners, administrative divisions of soldiers that were each represented by a different color. Banner soldiers stationed in the northwest were not required to farm, and yet they had to be supplied. The Qing court also moved Muslim inhabitants from southern Xinjiang to the north to cultivate the land. All of these efforts prevented famine, but supplying the military and local residents was burdensome. The court's attempts to develop an iron industry to fashion agricultural implements for the farmers were only partially successful, and corruption further ensnarled its policies in the northwest.

Despite these difficulties, the court continued to claim domination over Xinjiang. It commissioned the production of maps, the creation and erection of stelae, and the writing of official histories to back up these claims. It used these tangible artifacts to legitimize its claims to control over Xinjiang.

Governance remained in the hands of the local rulers as long as they provided the required taxes and other services. The native leaders, especially those who had cooperated with the Qing, were granted responsibility for security, collection of taxes and legal affairs, while under the supervision of Manchu *ambans* or governors. Known as *begs*, these Muslim leaders had considerable autonomy if they submitted taxes to the court and maintained

---

[43] James Millward, *Eurasian Crossroads: A History of Xinjiang* (New York: Columbia University Press, 2007), pp. 103–5.
[44] On the exiled population and its influence, see Joanna Waley-Cohen, *Exile in Mid-Qing China: Banishment to Xinjiang, 1758–1820* (New Haven, CT: Yale University Press, 1991).

the peace.[45] The Qing allowed the local authorities wide latitude and did not impose Chinese law on them. The *begs* and *qadis*, or jurists, used *shar'ia* law to resolve disputes and to punish criminals. The Qing also did not seek to promote Confucianism or Buddhism in the region. In short, it did not attempt to sinicize the local inhabitants by compelling the use of Chinese language or other practices of Chinese civilization. The Manchu and Mongol Banner troops, who were stationed in northern Xinjiang and had abundant grass for their animals, abided by military rules. The Chinese in the area and some of the most reliable native inhabitants were considered to be part of the regular government structure, basically a province.

The court sought to promote economic development in these new territories, but the native inhabitants may not have gained as much as outsiders, specifically Chinese merchants and entrepreneurs. The government's central motivation in its efforts to foster economic growth was to supply the military forces meant to maintain Qing control over the region. Because of its inability to provide enough resources for its troops, it had to transmit considerable quantities of silver to meet the military's basic needs. In attempting to reduce expenses, Qing officials tapped the region's natural resources, collected fine quality jade from the traditional center of Khotan, set up shops, transported tea to Xinjiang and facilitated the travels of merchants, mostly Chinese but with a sprinkling of Indians and Muslims, to this relatively remote region.[46] Profits from these economic policies frequently accrued to Chinese merchants, who also "rewarded" officials, and to the *begs* and a few leaders in the Muslim communities. The native peoples did not gain as much from this economic growth, and as a result the Chinese and Muslim elites earned their wrath and enmity. Moreover, even these dramatic policies did not secure sufficient funds to subsidize the military stationed in Xinjiang.

The colonial occupation, the anti-Muslim policies of some Qing officials, the Chinese merchants' exploitation of the native inhabitants and the frequently poor quality of officials generated hostility towards the occupiers. An area that had been autonomous had now fallen under foreign and, in particular, non-Muslim outsider control. Muslim orders such as the

---

[45] *Hamizhi* (Taibei: Xusheng shuju, 1967), p. 25 on its military organization. See also James A. Millward and Laura J. Newby, "The Qing and Islam on the Western Frontier" in Pamela Kyle Crossley, Helen F. Siu and Donald S. Sutton (eds.), *Empire at the Margins: Culture, Ethnicity and Frontier in Early Modern China* (Berkeley, CA: University of California Press, 2006), pp. 113–33.

[46] Millward, *Eurasian Crossroads*, pp. 102–4.

Naqshbandiyya, a Sufi mystical group that emphasized a silent remembrance of God (*dhkir*) and sought to revert to the original form of Islam, arose in opposition to Qing rule. Foreign control was unacceptable for an order that did not wish to be polluted by foreign practices and beliefs. A few exchanges with Muslim religious leaders in West and Central Asia further stimulated these orders and their Khojas to break away from China. Promulgating a so-called New Teaching (*xinjiao*) version of Islam, the Naqshbanddiya leaders who took an active role in secular life fostered growing dissatisfaction with Qing domination.[47]

Their responses would ultimately lead to violence, although animosity developed slowly. Economic, ethnic and religious factors contributed to these conflicts. Some years elapsed before these fissures translated into violent outbreak that would wrack the Qing Empire. Nonetheless, a rebellion erupted in 1765, and Ma Mingxin, a Muslim leader who had studied in West Asia, led a revolt from 1781 to 1784. The Qing rapidly crushed these rebellions. Yet, the stage was set for further confrontations. As the Qing declined in the nineteenth century and faced even greater threats from Western countries along its east coast, dissidents in the northwest would capitalize on China's weakness to gain independence. But China's problems would also prompt Western countries to challenge its domination in the northwest. Great Britain and especially Russia would be the main threats to Qing hegemony in Xinjiang.

Tsarist court and Central Asia

Tensions and disputes involving Britain and Russia did not simply involve Xinjiang, but all of Central Asia in a competition for supremacy that became known in the nineteenth century as the Great Game. Great Britain sought to protect its base in India and, for that matter, its economic interests in China, while Russia attempted to annex additional Central Asian territories adjacent to its Siberian domains. The two powers had diametrically opposed interests, and their initiatives and policies would return Central Asia to the seminal role it had played when the Silk Roads were at their height of importance. Developments in the seventeenth and eighteenth centuries in Central Asia set the stage for its re-emergence as a vital area in global interactions.

Even before the onset of full-scale Russo-British rivalry, the Tsarist court had started to secure leverage over neighboring Central Asian regions.

---

[47] Joseph Fletcher, "The Naqshbandiyya in Northwest China" in Joseph Fletcher, *Studies on Chinese and Islamic Central Asia* (Aldershot: Variorum, 1995), pp. 1–4.

It focused first on the pastoral nomads, whose mobility posed obstacles in controlling them. Yet, these leaders of the Kazakh peoples were not as numerous as the dwellers in the Central Asian towns and cities, and they were divided into three confederations. Because these Kazakhs lacked unity, they were more vulnerable to Russian pressure. By the sixteenth century, they had overwhelmed the remaining Chinggisid rulers and had converted to Islam, incorporating the Khojas and their Sufi rituals around saints' tombs and shrines. At the same time, in the sixteenth and early seventeenth centuries, the Kazakhs had fought against the Uzbeks, a struggle that weakened both sides. The Junior Kazakhs, one of three confederations, had suffered to such an extent that they sought Russian protection and submitted to the Tsarist court in 1730.[48] Their leaders retained the title "Khan" until 1824, when the Russians became totally dominant and eliminated the designation. The Middle Kazakhs were more independent and only after the death of Ablay Khan, a strong and charismatic ruler, in 1782 did the Tsarist court gain control over the group. The Senior Kazakhs remained independent until the middle of the nineteenth century, when a Russian military campaign caused them to fall to the Tsarist court.

Once it exerted its power over two of the three Kazakh confederations, the Tsarist court moved expeditiously to govern these regions. It first limited the herders' migrations, commanding them to use specific lands in their movements. By restricting mobility, Russia would, in theory, be able more readily to supervise the Kazakhs. The Tsarist court also supported Islam as a means of control. Mosques, madrassas and saints' tombs would be constructed in towns or cities, contributing further to efforts to settle the Kazakhs in a permanent location rather than having them roam around the grasslands. The court then fostered trade with the Kazakhs, with the Russians offering grain and manufactured articles in return for horses, sheep, goats and animal products. Such commerce would foster greater integration into Russia, the court's principal objective. Finally, Tsarist officials both coerced and encouraged Cossacks, Muslims from other regions and Russians to settle in the Kazakh lands, an additional attempt to bring these territories into the Russian fold.[49]

The instability of the sedentary Uzbek Khanates also provided opportunities for the Tsarist court. By the early seventeenth century, Uzbek rulers had

---

[48] Allen Frank, "The Qazaqs and Russia" in Di Cosmo, Frank and Golden, *Cambridge History of Inner Asia*, p. 368.

[49] Allen Frank, "The Qazaqs" in Di Cosmo, Frank and Golden, *Cambridge History of Inner Asia*, pp. 372–5; see also, for more detail, Martha Olcott, *Kazakhs* (Stanford, CA: Hoover Institution Press, Stanford University, 1995), pp. 28–53.

established Khanates in Khiva and Bukhara, and Bukharan merchants, who served as intermediaries in trade with India, Russia and China, had prospered from their vital positions along the major Asian trade routes. Despite these commercial successes, however, the two Khanates were politically vulnerable, partly due to foreign enemies and partly due to their own lack of unity and to conflicts about proper succession to rulership. Assassinations of Khans, invasions by foreign countries and attacks from steppe nomads contributed to the weaknesses of the Khanates and ultimately facilitated Russian conquest in the nineteenth century.

The steady deterioration of the Khanates' power began in the early eighteenth century. Khiva, the first to face chaotic conditions, was plagued by Turkmen and Kazakh attacks, and even disaffected and principally nomadic Uzbeks raided their ethnic brothers' lands in the town. Such repeated violence undermined Khiva's stability. Bukhara confronted similar difficulties. Nomadic Turkmen and Kazakhs repeatedly attacked Bukhara or the adjacent territories controlled by it, and its ruling families themselves harmed the town by assassinations and struggles for power. As a result of this violence, Bukhara became vulnerable, culminating in the Iranian Safavid ruler Nadir Shah's invasion and occupation in 1740. Khiva also fell to the Safavids, and both towns were compelled to provide tribute of grain and fodder and to contribute soldiers to Nadir Shah's forces. Iran had some influence over the two towns until the Safavids themselves were beset by turmoil. Nadir Shah chose members of the Manghit tribe of the Uzbeks to rule Khiva and Bukhara, and offered them considerable autonomy. However, in 1747, Nadir Shah was assassinated, leading to further turbulence among the Safavids. At the same time, his death allowed dissident Uzbeks who resented Iranian influence to challenge what had become the Manghit dynasty. Warring Uzbek forces continued to threaten the dynasty in Bukhara throughout the eighteenth century. The Mangits engaged in wars and raids against Merv in Iran and Afghan territories. Although the Mangits maintained support of Islam, including construction of mosques and patronage of *waqfs*, or pious endowments, the repeated defensive and offensive military campaigns sapped the dynasty's strength and made it vulnerable to Russian expansion in the nineteenth century.[50]

The Mangit dynasty in Khiva encountered similar instability. Turkmen, Kazakh and Uzbek groups repeatedly challenged the dynasty's control, and a Kazakh Khan briefly occupied the town from 1753 to 1758. Assassinations,

---

[50] Levi, *Indian Diaspora*, pp. 238–41.

oppressive rule and squabbles among the Mangit rulers harmed efforts to establish a stable government. By the early nineteenth century, political chaos had a devastating impact, once again permitting the Russians to gain leverage and then control over the town.

In the late eighteenth century, the Uzbeks founded the Kokand Khanate, the last of these Central Asian states in this era. Based in the fertile Ferghana valley, it had optimal conditions for a prosperous society. Yet, after the reign of Norbuti Biy (1770 to 1798), it fragmented into the same disunity that had characterized Bukhara and Khiva. Unity proved elusive.[51] Part of the difficulties faced by the Khanates arose from increasing dependence on Russia for trade. After the sixteenth century, they had limited contact with China, and by the late eighteenth century commerce with India also decreased. Such major towns as Bukhara, Samarkand and Tashkent, which had flourished in the past through trade and had been centers of astronomy, mathematics and the arts, now engaged in less commerce, produced fewer cultural and scientific innovations, and began to decline. Their militaries did not develop the weapons available to the Russians in the late eighteenth and early nineteenth centuries. Their lack of unity and their inferior weapons were no match for Russia.

Conclusions

Although Central Asia appeared to be less central to global history from 1400 to 1800, it continued to be a crossroads, with links to numerous states across all of Asia. After Tamerlane's death and the eventual accession of his son Shahrukh in 1409, the Timurid Empire resumed relations with China. Oases neighboring China such as Turfan and Hami permitted the conduct of trade with the Ming dynasty. In western Central Asia, the Timurids in the fifteenth century and the Uzbek Khanate from the sixteenth century onwards enjoyed extensive trade relations with India and, subsequently, Russia. The Moghuls of India, descendants of the Timurids, and their Hindu subjects had Central Asian roots and maintained a trade in horses, grain and manufactured articles with the Uzbeks. After crossing the Urals in the late sixteenth century, Russia became an Asian power. The Tsarist court began to trade for wild rhubarb found in northwest China and eastern Central Asia. At the same time, its merchants sought to obtain products from the Kazakhs, Turkmen and Uzbeks in western Central Asia.

---

[51] See Laura J. Newby, *The Empire and the Khanate: A Political History of Qing Relations with Khoqand, c. 1760–1860* (Leiden: Brill, 2005) for Khoqand's relations with China.

However, by the eighteenth century, Central Asian powers had weakened as a result of their disunity. The local Turkic leaders resented the Zunghars, who had moved into eastern Central Asia and did not unite with them against China's dynasty when it sent forces to crush the Mongols. Facing a weak opposition, the Qing incorporated eastern Central Asia as part of its domains. Similarly, western Central Asia, consisting of a variety of peoples, including the Kazakhs, Turkmen and Kazakhs, lacked unity. In fact, they often fought amongst each other. By the end of the eighteenth century, two of the three Kazakh groups had become virtual dependencies of Russia, and the three Uzbek Khanates were in disarray. As the nineteenth century wore on, the Khanates fell to Russian onslaughts. The obvious desire of the Tsarist and Qing courts to annex different areas of Central Asia, and the considerable resources they expended in these efforts, confirm the region's value and significance. Through its links with Russia and China, Central Asia remained part of global history.

The growing Islamization of Central Asia during this era also contributed to its importance. Eastern Central Asia still had Buddhist monasteries in the fifteenth century. Within a hundred years, a vast majority of the population was Muslim. In western Central Asia, Sufi Khojas played increasingly significant secular and religious roles. The Uzbeks in the west followed the same trajectory as in the east, as they gradually converted to Islam over several centuries from 1500 to 1800. The Uzbek Khanates constructed mosques and madrassas and established *waqfs*, which ultimately contributed to increased urbanization. The Kazakhs turned to Islam even more slowly, as conversions of pastoral nomads were not as rapid as those of town dwellers. Nonetheless, by 1800, most of the Kazakh herders identified with Islam. The conversions of most Central Asians to Islam put them in touch with the world's Muslim community, especially in West Asia and the Indian subcontinent. These connections were another way in which Central Asia was linked into larger patterns of global history.

FURTHER READING

Abru, Hafiz-I, *A Persian Embassy to China, Being an Extract from Zubdatu't Tawarikh of Hafiz Abru*, K. M. Maitra (trans.) (New York: Paragon Book Company, 1970).
Allen, Terry, *Timurid Herat* (Wiesbaden: Reichert, 1983).
Allworth, Edward, *The Modern Uzbeks From the 14th Century to the Present: A Cultural History* (Stanford, CA: Hoover Institution Press, Stanford University, 1990).
Barthold, Vasilli V., *Four Studies on the History of Central Asia*, V. Minorsky and T. Minorsky (trans.), 4 vols. (Leiden: Brill, 1956–62).
Bawden, Charles, *The Modern History of Mongolia* (New York: Frederic Praeger, 1968).

Burton, Audrey, *The Bukharans: A Dynastic, Diplomatic, and Commercial History, 1550–1702* (New York: St. Martin's Press, 1997).

Cosmo, Nicola Di, Allen Frank and Peter Golden (eds.), *The Cambridge History of Inner Asia: The Chinggisid Era* (Cambridge University Press, 2009).

Dabringhaus, Sabine and Roderick Ptak (eds.), *China and Her Neighbours* (Wiesbaden: Harrassowitz Verlag, 1997).

Dale, Stephen, *Indian Merchants and Eurasian Trade, 1600–1750* (Cambridge University Press, 1994).

Elverskog, Johan, *Our Great Qing: The Mongols, Buddhism, and the State in Late Imperial China* (Honolulu: University of Hawaii Press, 2006).

Foltz, Richard, *Mughal India and Central Asia* (New Delhi: Oxford University Press, 1998).

Gommans, Jos, *The Rise of the Indo-Afghan Empire, c. 1710–1780* (Leiden: Brill, 1995).

Hambly, Gavin, *Central Asia* (London: Weidenfeld and Nicolson, 1969).

Kauz, Ralph, *Politik und Handel zwischen Ming und Timuriden: China, Iran, and Zentralasien im Spätmittelalter* (Wiesbaden: Reichert, 2005).

Khodarkovsky, Michael, *Russia's Steppe Frontier: The Making of a Colonial Empire, 1500–1800* (Bloomington, IN: Indiana University Press, 2002).

Lentz, Thomas W. and Glenn D. Lowry, *Temür and the Princely Vision: Persian Art and Culture in the 15th Century* (Los Angeles County Museum of Art, 1989).

Levi, Scott, *The Indian Diaspora in Central Asia and Its Trade, 1550–1900* (Leiden: Brill, 2002).

Mancall, Mark, *China and Russia: Their Diplomatic Relations to 1728* (Cambridge, MA: Harvard University Press, 1971).

Manz, Beatrice Forbes, *Power, Politics, and Religion in Timurid Iran* (Cambridge University Press, 2007).

The Rise and Rule of Tamerlane (Cambridge University Press, 1989).

McChesney, Robert, *Waqf in Central Asia: Four Hundred Years in the History of a Muslim Shrine, 1480–1889* (Princeton University Press, 1991).

Millward, James, *Eurasian Crossroads: A History of Xinjiang* (New York: Columbia University Press, 2007).

Olcott, Martha, *The Kazakhs* (Stanford, CA: Hoover Institution Press, Stanford University, 1987).

Ostrowski, Donald, *Muscovy and the Mongols: Cross-Cultural Influences on the Steppe Frontier, 1304–1589* (Cambridge University Press, 1998).

Perdue, Peter, *China Marches West: The Qing Conquest of Central Eurasia* (Cambridge, MA: Harvard University Press, 2005).

Rossabi, Morris, *China and Inner Asia* (New York: Thames and Hudson, Ltd., 1975).

"The Decline of the Central Asian Caravan Trade" in James Tracy (ed.), *The Rise of Merchant Empires* (Cambridge University Press, 1990), pp. 351–71.

Thackston, Wheeler (trans.), *Baburnama: Memoirs of Babur* (New York: Random House, 2002).

Mirza Haidar Dughlat's Tarikh-i-Rashidi: A History of the Khans of Moghulistan (Cambridge, MA: Harvard University Press, 1996).

Watt, James C. Y. and Anne E. Wardwell (eds.), *When Silk Was Gold: Central Asian and Chinese Textiles* (New York: Metropolitan Museum of Art, 1997).

15

Crossroads region: Southeast Asia

MICHAEL LAFFAN

Southeast Asia is home to a diverse array of peoples whose livelihoods once revolved around combinations of shifting swidden cultivation in highland areas, wet rice production on the lowland plains, and the harvesting of rare forest and sea products – many of which were destined for the world market. By the opening of the fifteenth century, many Southeast Asian peoples – from the Tibeto-Burman, Tai, Vietnamese and Mon-Khmer speakers of the mainland, to the Austronesians of the archipelago – had long been involved with a vibrant inter-regional trade that networked their polities together. This trade furthermore established them as key waypoints between the ports ruled by the successive Chinese empires and the constellation of entrepots that made up the Indian Ocean World.

Such globally networked transactions, necessitated by the prevailing monsoonal systems that forced traders to break their journeys between oceanic zones, engaged Southeast Asians as much beyond their home world as within it. They moreover empowered numerous dynasties – both agrarian and trade-focused – such as those based around the central plains of Pagan in Burma, Angkor in Cambodia and the Mekong Delta, the volcanic heartland of Java and even the coastal polities of Champa in what is now Central Vietnam.

Islam and Buddhism between China and India

All the aforementioned kingdoms and their many subordinates and potential rivals, which were often located within relatively easy reach of the region's permeable estuarine and coastal systems, had long prided themselves on offering a standing welcome to sojourners bringing not only goods, but expertise and prestige. For in a world that was far less populated than today, the comparative ability to attract or (as was often the case) capture people through warfare marked polities as successes. In the process, too, the visitations and peregrinations of key foreigners generated and then reinforced a commitment to the religious traditions of the subcontinent. Such was symbolized most powerfully by the impressive monuments of the charter states, many of which, such as Angkor Wat and Borobudur, were consecrated for Hindu or Mahayana Buddhist purposes, although Theravadan Buddhism, long identified with Sri Lanka, was also present in Burma.

But even if these states demonstrated their ideological commitments to Indic modes of governance, scriptures and scripts (usually of some form derived from the Pallava script of Southeastern India), it was long recognized that the greatest source of political power lay to the north. Indeed, it appears that early Buddhist and, later, Muslim trading networks were actively facilitated by the opportunities afforded by the successive dynasties of China. Certainly, Chinese patronage was often sought by the states that contested the Southeast Asian mainland and archipelagic regions.

This is not to say that such relations were unproblematic, or yet that Southeast Asian states could only profit from their position as mediators between east and west. While some parts of what is now Southeast Asia were claimed at times as fractious "tributaries" of China, others, such as the Red River basin of northern Vietnam, were deemed integral to it and treated accordingly. And from the West, too, the Chola rulers of Southern India and Sri Lanka (at their peak between the ninth and thirteenth centuries) even staked a claim to the route to China in the first quarter of the eleventh century by sacking numerous ports along the coasts of Sumatra and the Malay Peninsula.

Even so, the Tamil incursions of the eleventh century were an exception, as the major political impulses continued to flow south. The extension of Mongol (Yuan) rule and ambitions in the thirteenth and fourteenth centuries, followed by the establishment of Ming authority in 1368, would herald major changes in the interconnected insular and mainland worlds. On the mainland, a new set of states would coalesce in the southern reaches of the major river basins, enjoying access to significant arable land and forest resources, and links both upriver to Yunnan and downstream to the Indian Ocean. It was these polities, dominated at the end of the sixteenth century by the aggressive rival states of Toungoo Burma and Tai-dominated Ayudhya, which would increasingly identify with a revived Theravadan Buddhism sourced to the coastal states of Sri Lanka.

This turbulent period moreover saw significant shifts in the island world away from older Hinduized state religious practices. But rather than embracing Theravadan Buddhism in the manner of the Burmese and Tai dynasties, by the end of the thirteenth century the rulers of the interlinked ports of northern Sumatra had begun to adopt another faith whose exponents had global ambitions. For Islam had by now become the majoritarian faith of much of the Middle East, where many of island Southeast Asia's products – particularly its spices, aloes and aromatics – had long found a market. Indeed, seen from a global perspective, Islam had also become the dominant state faith of the coasts from East Africa to northern India, much as it had emerged as a ubiquitous presence in the southern littoral of the subcontinent.

Islam also had its representatives in China, and Marco Polo, sailing from ports long familiar with that faith, made reference to communities of Muslim merchants in northern Sumatra when returning from Yuan China in the 1290s. Some fifty years later, the Tangiers-born Ibn Battuta (1304 to 1369) would also attest to the presence in the same area of scholars from Central Asia and Iran. Certainly, Southeast Asia was becoming more familiar to Arab traders based in Yemen by this time, given the increasing mention in their sources of the toponymic term *Jawa* (used as a coverall for all of Southeast Asia), with the added sense of there no longer being merely *Jawi* products, such as camphor, but (sometimes Muslim) *Jawi* peoples.

In short, by the fifteenth century, Southeast Asia was in the process of affirming a majoritarian commitment to two key traditions that would ultimately define much of its mainland and insular zones: Theravadan Buddhism and Sunni Islam. Yet, the region can hardly be said to have consisted merely of two distinct spheres during this time, as would be apparent to the chroniclers of the Ming Voyages led by Zheng He (1371 to 1433), whose overlords ordered the re-annexation of the heavily Sinified territory of Annam after some four centuries of independence. Moreover, with the direct entrance of the Iberians into the region in the sixteenth century, this interlocking inheritance of Buddhist, Muslim and Sinic cultures would be further complicated by European engagements and Christianity.

Ming impacts, archipelagic Islamization, mainland Buddhist consolidations

Perhaps the greatest single external impact on Southeast Asia in the fifteenth century was the series of armadas dispatched by the Ming state between 1405 and 1433. While hardly the first case of intensive sojourning to Southern Asia by the Chinese – bearing in mind that Marco Polo and Ibn Battuta had both reported Chinese junks on their travels – the account derived from three of Admiral Zheng He's missions to the region gives a sense of a maritime world that was at once filled with similarities and profound differences. Cataloguing the findings of these missions, Ma Huan (1380 to 1460) referred to many shared Austronesian practices and beliefs (such as that of vampiric spirits or an aversion to the touching of another's head), the chewing of betel, and a general distinction between apparently cosmopolitan, if small, port polities and their often-forested hinterlands that were believed to be teeming with cannibals. Certainly, a tone of condescension, and even revulsion, pervaded such accounts when they turned to the indigenous populations of the coasts, while being little aware of the major states further upriver. For example, Ma Huan mocked the kingly pretensions of some Malay rulers, and claimed that the Javanese were dirty and ate all manner of things deemed unclean to the Muslim minority living among them. For their part, these Muslims were described as 'foreigners' coming from all corners of the world, although this designation was applied as much to the many Chinese said to have migrated or fled to the region in previous eras.

It is thus clear that Islamic and Chinese sojourners were already an integral part of the fabric of maritime Southeast Asia. Given that Zheng He and many of his officers, including Ma Huan, were themselves Muslims, it makes sense to see some synergy in terms of Islamicate and Sinic civilizations. It is conceivable that the foundation and subsequent development of the entrepot of Malacca may well have been spurred on by this very relationship, with a Hindu prince from Palembang adopting Islam at the moment when the Ming were eager to re-establish the older tributary relationships, and perhaps even customs collection points, at either end of the crucial strait. Clearly, the Ming were happy to reach out to other newly Islamized polities such as Brunei, on the great island of Borneo, much as there is favourable reference in the Ming Annals to the Indic ports of Champa being host to Muslims too.

It also appears that communities of these Muslims in what is now central Vietnam had dealings of some sort with the then Islamizing towns of the northeast salient of Java. And, after the absorption of their territories by the Vietnamese in the 1470s, many Muslim Chams would go on to play a role in the establishment of the north Sumatran state of Aceh, in addition to making their naval expertise available to the hegemonic Tai state of Ayudhya, which had come to dominate the southern sections of the Chaophraya River.

The strongly Islamic tinge to the global conjuncture of the first half of the fifteenth century is also in evidence in the stele that Zheng He ordered to be erected at the Sri Lankan port of Galle in 1411, given that a third of its face was covered by a statement in Persian. At the same time, however, one still need not claim Islam as the hegemonic faith, for the Galle stone gave as much space to Tamil and Chinese declarations; all of which detailed the offerings made by Zheng He to whichever deity might grant protection and favour. This repertoire of recognizably transcendent languages of power might readily be compared to the previous colocation of Chinese and Persian statements with Tai and Khmer analogues on Wat Ratchaburana, a Buddhist temple constructed at Ayudhya soon after 1424. Ayudhya would enjoy fame among Persian traders, although ever since the foundation of their city in the mid-fourteenth century, the multi-ethnic rulers of that polity had directed their mercantilist ambitions towards China and the approval of its resolutely non-Muslim rulers.

Ming activities in Southeast Asia were hardly intended to expedite the process of Islamization, even if one curious legend from Cirebon, on Java, makes this very claim, and goes well beyond the normal legends of a linkage between a Muslim Cham princess and a Javanese sovereign. Rather, the Ming state sought both direct rule and the renewal of older patron ties, whether in enforcing regime change in the port kingdoms of South Sumatra and Sri Lanka, or by occupying Annam in 1407.

Whereas the Lê dynasty would eject their Ming occupiers in 1428 and reassert Vietnamese independence under the name of Đại Việt, they would nevertheless remain enthusiastic emulators of Sinic models of kingship and Confucian bureaucracy as they expanded their own influence over the Chamic central plains and the Khmer-speaking Mekong Delta – seeding the Chamic diaspora referred to above. Equally, the moribund kingdom of Angkor would provide the model, and then the physical space, for the expansion of Ayudhyan (and other Tai) influence beyond the Chaophraya basin, with the former jostling with Java's rulers for influence over the straits.

Being strategically placed between the Siamese and Javanese spheres of influence, Muslim Melaka would emerge at any rate as the primary trading node of the region. Even if the Malay chronicles retrospectively depicted Melaka as the military equal to Java and Ayudhya, the city was as dependent on the trade of the Sino-Muslim ports of the former and the supply of rice from the latter as it was on Chinese approval and the regular visits of Gujarati, Tamil, Peguan (Burmese) and other merchants.

Abetted by such recognition and connections, by the end of the fifteenth century the rulers of Melaka could even claim territory, or at least the fealty, of many of the predecessor Muslim ports of Sumatra. Melaka's foundational myths would ultimately enfold those of the port of Pasai, on north Sumatra, which spoke of dream communications between an ancestor king and the Prophet, as well as the visits of Arab and southern Indian teachers. Once

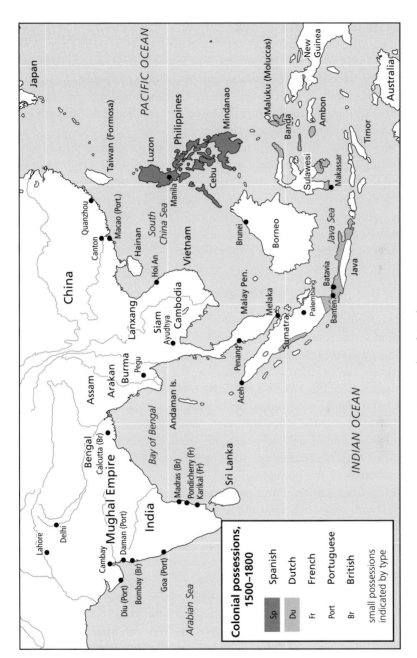

15.1 South and Southeast Asia

Colonial possessions, 1500–1800

Sp	Spanish
Du	Dutch
Fr	French
Port	Portuguese
Br	British

small possessions
indicated by type

Japan

China

PACIFIC OCEAN

Taiwan (Formosa)

Quanzhou

Canton

Macao (Port.)

Hainan

South
China Sea

Luzon

Philippines

Manila

Cebu

Mindanao

Maluku (Moluccas)

Banda

Ambon

Sulawesi

Makassar

New
Guinea

Australia

Timor

Brunei

Borneo

Java Sea

Batavia

Java

Banten

Palembang

Melaka

Sumatra

Malay Pen.

Penang

Aceh

Hoi An

Vietnam

Cambodia

Lanxang

Siam
Ayudhya

Burma

Pegu

Arakan

Assam

Andaman Is.

Bay of Bengal

Bengal

Calcutta (Br)

Madras (Br)

Pondicherry (Fr)
Karikal (Fr)

Sri Lanka

INDIAN OCEAN

Mughal Empire

India

Delhi

Lahore

Cambay

Daman (Port)

Diu (Port)

Bombay (Br)

Goa (Port)

Arabian Sea

again, though, it is worth emphasizing that Islam in Southeast Asia was not monopolized by any one ethnic community, nor yet did it dominate. At its height, Melaka attracted the regular attentions of peoples from all across maritime Afro-Asia, including Abyssinia and the Ryukyuan archipelago. And much as Arabic sources could now speak of a zone known as *Jawa*, Persians, such as the fifteenth-century ambassador Abd al-Razzaq Samarqandi, could speak in 1442 both of *Jawi* people abroad in Bengal and a region known as *Zirbad*, seemingly a calque from the Malay term for Southeast Asia as a set of lands 'below the wind' (*bawah angin*).

With time, the coasts of these lands below the winds, accessed through the Malay language – now rendered in Arabic rather than Indic script – would expand to include the restive north coast ports of Java, which were linked in turn to the freshly Islamizing polities of the Moluccas; the source of many of the costly spices still sought after by Chinese and Western traders alike. It was these ports, above all, whose Muslim captains would slowly erode the authority of the lingering Indic power of Java.

The spice wars

Much as medieval Arab geographers and chroniclers had begun to pay closer attention to the sources of a great array of Southeast Asian products, from the fragrant aloes of the mainland to the highly valued spices of the Moluccas (principally cloves, mace and nutmegs), by the end of the fifteenth century the Iberians would seek out a more direct route to the wealth of Asia, whose cities were simply more unreachable than mysterious. While hardly the 'Arab Lake' that some historians have chosen to see as a precursor to the later 'British' one of the late nineteenth century, the Indian Ocean's well-connected Muslim communities were perhaps the ones to suffer most from the incursions of the Portuguese. Still, it is worth noting that some local Muslim polities saw the Portuguese as forces to be used through alliance rather than feared. Such were the respective experiences of the rival ports of East Africa, which either cooperated with or resisted the advances of such captains as Pedro Álvares Cabral and Vasco da Gama, who infamously put a boatload of pilgrims to the torch off the coast of Kannur, in southern India.

Equally, after initial encounters in 1512, the rulers of the volcanic island of Ternate, one of the principal sultanates of the far-removed Moluccas, would form an alliance with the Portuguese, expecting not domination, but material aid in their long-standing rivalry with the neighbouring (and equally Muslim) polity of Tidore. The Tidorese, for their part, tried to enlist the support of the Spanish after a small party of survivors of the Magellan expedition washed up on their shores in 1521.

Playing such oppositional politics was not, however, an option open to Melaka, which had been swiftly identified by the Portuguese in 1509 as a key site of acquisition. Despite its capture in 1511, however, the port faded in importance as the many traders who had once thronged there, and especially the Gujaratis and southern Indians, headed for rival, and even more avowedly Islamicate ports. Of these, the most prominent were Aceh, at the northern entrance to the Malacca Strait, and, soon after, Banten, on the western end of Java. Aceh in particular seems to have reached out, by way of Gujarat and Egypt, for the expanding imperium in the West, being well aware of the recent Ottoman conquest of Cairo and its dependencies in 1517, as well as the rise of Turkic power in Gujarat itself.

The old contest of Cross and Crescent seems to have played out afresh in the sixteenth century, although it is worth bearing in mind that some Muslim polities, including such peninsular successors to Melaka as Johor, could be allied at times with the Iberians rather than their co-religionists. This was especially the case when the Acehnese, under such rulers as Ala al-Din Riayat Shah (r. 1537 to 1571) and Iskandar Muda (r. 1607 to 1636), would martial their war galleys in the hope of securing regional hegemony at the expense of Melaka and Johor alike.

The western archipelago was not the only site of contestation. With their foothold in Ternate, and a more tenuous presence in the tiny Banda archipelago further to the south, the Portuguese laid claim to some of the richest sources of wealth in their day, even as they struggled to enforce any monopoly over the extraction and export of those riches in ships other than their own. Theirs was also a claim that was contested in Europe, given that the 1494 Treaty of Tordesillas was unclear as to where Portuguese and Castilian claims met on the other side of the globe. Further to the north, the insular region we now know as the Philippines was increasingly the site of Spanish incursions stemming from Mexico, with an abortive attempt made to colonize the area in the 1540s. This eventually led to the foundation of a post in the bounds of the then Muslim-ruled bay of Manila in 1571, a post subsequently declared as the capital of a new colony and increasingly fortified thereafter, with its main gate even being dedicated to St James 'the Moor killer'.

Despite the union of Spain and Portugal in 1580, the eastern islands of Southeast Asia can hardly be said to have fallen completely under the sway of Habsburg authority. Still, with the aid of such mendicant orders of friars as the Augustinians, Dominicans and Franciscans, the lowland regions of the Philippines were marked out for campaigns of proselytization and incorporation, while Manila served as a crucial way station for the galleon trade between China and the New World. In many senses, the exploitation of Manila and its environs, which offered few of the mercantile benefits of the Moluccas, was long seen as a subsidiary project to an engagement with China and the long-dreamed conversion of its population. But while St Francis Xavier (1506 to 1552) had once enjoyed some successes in the Moluccas in 1546 to 1547, and then briefly in Japan thereafter, lasting conversions to Christianity would really only take place in Southeast Asia, and often among the mestizo Chinese. There, they continued to form the key mercantile community that arguably sustained the European presence, though not without friction, as the 1603 massacre of Chinese within the walls of Manila portended.

Further complicating matters in the island world, and following on from its final conquest by the north coast sultanate of Demak in 1527, central Java had begun to revive under the now Islamic dynasty of Mataram, while the eastern Muslim ports of Giri and Tuban would make renewed efforts both to secure the share of the spice trade and encourage the Islamization of the many islands and communities that surrounded the Portuguese. Once again, this is not to say that this heralded a moment of pan-Islamic unity in the archipelago. Mataram's rulers would look to subdue the north coast port polities and engage more directly in regional power struggles. And among its most important rivals into the seventeenth century was another product of Demak's expansion – the leading west Javanese port of Banten. Captured and Islamized in 1526, and thus foiling Portuguese plans for a factory (much as Aceh's capture of Pasai had scotched similar plans in 1524), Banten attracted southern Indian, Peguan and Chinese traders to its harbour, laying the basis for one of the more powerful sultanates of the region by the century's end.

It could be argued that by the close of the sixteenth century, the Christian presence in Southeast Asia was a marginal one, being confined to Melaka, Timor and the eastern spice islands, and governed from Goa far to the West. By contrast, many Islamic polities were ascendant and making good use of vital connections with the now Ottoman- and Mughal-dominated west to ship high-value spices, especially pepper, and to increase their treasuries and arm themselves for further expansion at the expense of their non-Muslim hinterlands and their Muslim neighbours alike. Aceh's rulers, for example, were particularly aggressive in taking over the mantle of Pasai and Malacca, raiding their Batak interior and inviting an array of foreign experts to their

Malay-speaking court, be they gunners, sappers or religious scholars from Egypt and Arabia to Abyssinia and Anatolia.

Such was the world that the mariners dispatched from the rising Protestant states of England and the Netherlands would encounter by the end of the sixteenth century. Sir Walter Raleigh (1554 to 1618) would sail to the Moluccas soon after the ruler of Ternate, Babullah (r. 1570 to 1583), had made use of Turkic and Abyssinan auxiliaries to expel the Portuguese in 1575, causing them to regroup in Ambon. Equally, the first Dutch expeditions to Aceh and Banten would be met with a mix of suspicion and hostility, made all the more potent by the intemperate acts of commanders like Cornelis de Houtman (1565 to 1599), who committed outrages of similar ferocity to Cabral and Gama nearly a century beforehand.

VOC arrival and engagement

Even with early failures at Aceh and Banten – where the Dutch met with unexpectedly high prices and detentions – the wealth brought back to the West was far too great to ignore, especially after the so-called 'second voyage' of 1598 to 1600 under Jacob Corneliszoon van Neck (1564 to 1638) brought the Dutch to the Moluccas, where they were even welcomed by a local Turkish trader. By 1602, and echoing efforts made in London in 1600, Dutch mercantilists would form the 'United East India Company' or VOC, a joint-stock company whose emissaries were empowered to act under the Dutch flag to establish forts and raise armies in Asia. And this they did with alacrity, targeting and then displacing the Portuguese in the key island of Ambon in 1605. Equally, they directed their attention to making exclusive treaties with the region's sovereigns, and especially at the cost of rival English factors in the ports of Banten, Ambon and Banda.

By 1619, the Dutch fort of Batavia, located at the former Bantenese port of Jayakarta, would become the capital of VOC operations, with the Dutch having bested their Atlantic rivals for control of the estuary. In 1621, and in the wake of their daring to continue trading with rival parties, Dutch Governor Jan Pieterszoon Coen (1587 to 1629) would order the wholesale massacre and deportation of the population of Banda, a process carried out by the VOC's force of Japanese mercenaries. Then, in 1623, nervous Dutch merchants in Ambon would execute Japanese and English merchants alike for fear of a conspiracy against themselves.

The Amboyna Massacre, as it was known, was a major cause of hostility between the English and the Dutch, although the former were arguably bested in the seventeenth century by their continental rivals. This is not to say that all went easily for the Dutch at Batavia, who had to weather two major sieges of their new capital by Mataram's Sultan Agung (1613 to 1645) in 1628 and 1629. Still, Agung was really turning his attention to the Dutch somewhat belatedly, having suppressed the north coast ports, culminating in the sack of Surabaya in 1625. In time, he was compelled to leave the Dutch in place as something of a buffer, emulating his Bantenese rivals by sending missions to Mecca in the quest of legitimacy granted by the descendants of the Prophet.

None of this is to say that in sending their delegates and scholars to Mecca, the rulers of Mataram, Banten or Aceh, for that matter, ever imagined themselves as anything less than the equals to the rulers of 'Rome' (as the Ottoman Empire was termed) and China. Moreover, as scholars have demonstrated, the undeniably Islamic court of Mataram would foster a synthetic understanding of Javanese texts, seeing mystical value in its Indic-infused literary inheritance, and situating Sultan Agung as the harmonizer of the external and internal worlds. Naturally, such perspectives were not always embraced, nor were the north coast *ulama* necessarily enamoured of their overlords, with their recalcitrance being infamously rewarded when Agung's successor, Amangkurat (r. 1646 to 1677), had several hundred massacred in 1647.

The Dutch, meanwhile, would face major challenges from the very active rulers of Gowa (Makassar), on Sulawesi, who had adopted Islam at the opening of the seventeenth century, and then suppressed and forcibly converted their local Bugis rivals. To add to their challenges, the Dutch were forced in 1662 to surrender their principal fortress on Taiwan to the Sino-Japanese Ming loyalist Koxinga (Zheng Chenggong, 1624 to 1662), whose expanding sphere of influence even caused the Spanish to worry about the fate of the Philippines. Yet, despite the loss of Taiwan and their apparent inability to stem the tide of Islamization, VOC fortunes were on the rise globally, with the Dutch company boasting a chain of possessions from the Cape of Good Hope to Sri Lanka, Java and Japan. And with the final conquest of Gowa and the conclusion of a treaty with its rulers in 1669, the Dutch had seemingly bested the last of their archipelagic rivals, although such actions would seed the region with small bands of Bugis fighting men, who would become crucial players in the Malay courts to the west, and even deep into the mainland.

Mainland ambitions

While the story of Christian–Muslim confrontation tinged by Chinese or greater Eurasian influence is one that is readily told for the island world, the increasingly Theravadan mainland would itself be the site of globally imbricated intrigues and contestations. There would be attempts by Spanish missionaries, Muslim traders and even Japanese mercenaries to influence or overthrow the kings of Cambodia in the sixteenth and seventeenth centuries, yet it was arguably an aggressive Ayudhya to the west and the fast-expanding Sino-Vietnamese presence in the Mekong Delta that was spelling the final demise of the ancient line of Angkor, whose capital of Lovek, founded in 1431, was taken by the Siamese in 1594.

This is not to say that the Siamese had enjoyed unbroken hegemony since the foundation of Ayudhya in the mid-fourteenth century. Its rise as the premier disseminator of metropolitan Tai-ness in the sixteenth century was a role won as much through the domestication of Portuguese military expertise against rival Tai centres such as Lan Na from the 1530s as by the trade-supported religious patronage that had already led to the creation, between 1500 and 1503, of the largest-cast standing Buddha ever known. Even so, after clashing repeatedly with the northern Tai polities that sought Burmese aid, and then conceding territory and several royal hostages to the Burmese in the mid-1550s, Ayudhya would itself fall in 1569 to its western Theravadan rival. More particularly, it would fall into the direct orbit of King Bayin-naung (r. 1551 to 1581), the paramount ruler of Pegu, whose campaigns, launched in the name of the restoration of Sinhalese religion, led to major Burmese territorial gains – first within what is now Burma, and then across the mainland.

At his death, Bayin-naung, whose victory had depended in no small measure on the efforts of his Tai allies, could claim the allegiance of sovereigns inhabiting the Muslim coastal polity of Arakan, in the Bay of Bengal, to the Lao highlands bordering Vietnam. His was thus a reign of truly regional, and perhaps even greater, pretentions. After the siege of Ayudhya, Bayin-naung's armies had made sure both to kill the recently arrived Dominican missionaries sent from the Philippines in 1567, and to remove regalia and statuary captured from Angkor by the Siamese in the fifteenth century. Perhaps the most enduring legacy of Bayin-naung, though, was the (final) incorporation of the Tai-speaking Shan principalities that had alternately thwarted and aided Burmese and Siamese ambitions as they sought to maintain their independence in the teak- and gemstone-rich hills. At the same time, the presence of so many Tai captives, including artisans and royal performers, ensured that Burma would itself become thoroughly steeped in Tai culture.

Bayin-naung's hold over Southeast Asia would not endure long after his death and Ayudhya's rulers, from Naresuan (r. 1590 to 1605), would long be engaged in fierce contest with their erstwhile overlords for suzerainty over the environs of Tavoy. Born in 1555, Naresuan had been taken to Burma in 1564, although he was returned in 1571 in exchange for his sister's marriage to Bayin-naung. The rulers of Pegu named him as heir-apparent in Ayudhya, and he was careful to pay his respects to them, but he nonetheless sought a new seal of office from China in 1575. Relations between Pegu and Ayudhya deteriorated in the 1580s and Naresuan refused to appear at court in Pegu, leading to Burma's sending of several punitive missions. These culminated in the key battle at Nong Sarai in January 1593, at which the heir to the Burmese throne, Bayin-naung's grandson, was killed.

Having previously offered aid to China against Japan, Naresuan safely turned his attentions to the Khmers in 1594, and used his Cham-infused navy to range widely, confirming treaties with Ryukyu and the Spanish in the Philippines and Cambodia in 1598. Even so, the Dominicans would lose their mainland base at Phnom Penh in 1599, when local Cambodians made common cause with Malayo-Muslim mercenaries in a coup attempt, after which time the Siamese began to make western Cambodia a Tai protectorate.

While the western edge of Siam itself quieted after the death of Burma's King Nanda-bayin in 1599, the Isthmus of Kra would be a site of ongoing contestation. For here the situation was further complicated by the fact that the local Muslim sultanates (linked as they were to the archipelagic trade) would, like the Tai polities of the north, seek some form of autonomy from their looming neighbours, whose rule was justified with reference to Buddhist codes and voluble support for Theravadan monasticism.

With the benefit of recognition from the Qing dynasty and visits from traders from across the region, the rejuvenated Siamese capital continued to gain the upper hand into the seventeenth century and became a focus for the attentions of an even broader range of players. By the 1680s, Ayudhya even had a Greek prime minister, Constantine Gerakis (1647 to 1688). Born in Ottoman territory, he had found his way to Mergui aboard an East India Company ship in 1675. That said, Gerakis had plans for Siam that would have pleased neither Atlantic traders nor Islamicate adventurers, as he encouraged the attentions of French missionaries and the French state alike, which sent a large-scale mission up the Chaophraya in 1688 expecting to gain exclusive trading privileges and the final conversion of the seemingly curious King Narai (r. 1656 to 1688).

Indeed, Narai, who had come to the throne at the expense of his uncle in a coup involving local Persian and Japanese merchants, had long been able to domesticate global forces. For their part, the French had been given to expect much, given that there had been successful Siamese embassies to Paris, and the previous year had seen the Siamese expel various privateers from Mergui and install a French governor, leading to war with England. What the French rather found in 1688, however, was a kingdom in crisis, for the Anglo-Siamese War had damaged Gerakis and the now ailing sovereign, after having also faced down an uprising by the substantial Muslim Cham and Bugis community in 1686.

Siam was not, then, for turning to Christianity or yet Islam, a fact noted with some disappointment by one disdainful Persian emissary, who had waxed lyrically about Narai's seeming proclivity towards Persian food and dress. Indeed, the Persians had been a key community marginalized by the rise of Gerakis, and they were thus more than happy to see their traditional role facilitating trade and governance restored once the French had sailed away empty-handed and a fresh coup brought Phra Phetracha to the throne. Moreover, the ascent of Phra Phetracha saw a return to the more traditional Chinese trading linkages that would sustain his successors until the cataclysmic Burmese invasions of 1766 to 1767.

The fast shifting Will of Heaven

Just as what might be called the Tai world was riven by the great power rivalries of Ayudhya and Burma, which both shaped and shared Theravadan state culture on the mainland, the long expanse of increasingly Vietnamese territory was the site of constant contestation between rival clans (the Trinh and the Nguyễn) that upheld Confucian models and the Will of Heaven. Both moreover claimed, particularly in the case of the Trinh, to represent the Lê Dynasty ensconced in Hanoi (1533 to 1789): first against the Mạc clan and then, after the defeat of the latter in 1592, against each other. With the conclusion of hostilities in 1672, after over four decades of war, the eastern coast of mainland Southeast Asia could be said to have crystallized as two kingdoms. The more Sinophilic Trinh, still committed to a Confucian examination system like that of China, ruled over the northern environs down towards present-day Huế, while the Nguyễn expanded both into the central highlands and the Mekong Delta, and their territory was additionally marked by the presence of many adherents of Mahayana Buddhism.

Arguably the key to ongoing Nguyễn expansion lay, as for the rulers of Ayudhya, in their greater contact with, and domestication of, outside forces. Such domestication could take the form of Portuguese gunners and engineers, or one could point to the inflows of wealth coming into the port of

Hội An (Faifo), a major destination to the south of Đà Nẵng that would see significant trade with Chinese and Japanese shippers deep into the eighteenth century.

However, while the Southeast Asian mainland powers – now ever-more clearly Burmese, Siamese and Vietnamese – would experience a period of relative confidence and consolidation for much of the first half of the eighteenth century – whether serviced by relationships with a diverse array of foreign partners, and most especially the Chinese shippers and English country traders – the once hegemonic archipelagic states of Aceh, Banten and Mataram would fall into a more exclusive relationship with the VOC (and its unofficial Chinese partners). But while the VOC depended in no small measure on the labours of Chinese mercantilists, millers and sharecroppers, especially in the private estates that surrounded Batavia, and much as many of the smaller sultanates of the archipelago encouraged Chinese tillers and miners to enrich their treasuries, the relationship was increasingly uneasy.

By 1740, the Chinese had come to vastly outnumber their anxious European hosts in Batavia and the rumour took hold that the VOC had plans to expel, and perhaps even murder, large numbers of them. Hence, when the Chinese community began to arm in anxious preparation, the Europeans and their clients panicked in their turn, unleashing nearly two weeks of violence that October and reducing some of the wealthiest parts of the city to ashes. This wholesale slaughter of the Chinese population within and around the walls of Batavia – estimated by some to have been around 10,000 prior to the massacre – was only the beginning of what was in many senses a major tipping point in Javanese history. During the ensuing conflict that erupted from the other north coast ports over the next two years, starting with anti-Chinese pogroms in Semarang, Surabaya and Gresik, the inland court of Mataram under Pakubuwana II (r. 1726 to 1749) opted to side with the Chinese, seeing the opportunity to take up arms with the particular encouragement of a clique of key figures with connections to an emerging network of Sufi activists.

As scholars have shown, there had been increasing debate in courtly circles concerning the mystic synthesis that had emerged over the previous century, and Pakubuwana would gamble on the teachings of the mystics with connections to a wider Indian Ocean network of scholars and emissaries. Even if the aftermath of the war saw the political defeat of the Chinese and Pakubuwana's mystical allies, one can say that the eighteenth century would continue to witness the rising influence of Sufi-inspired reformism across island Southeast Asia. Now, whether supported by pepper sold at the rising sultanate of Palembang in Sumatra, or yet by the tax-free gleanings of an expanding network of religious schools on Java (where coffee was often grown to help finance their activities), a new cadre of scholars would return to preach against the perhaps too-liberal practice of Islam in the region. Hence, from the still vital courts of coastal Sumatra to those of the Malay Peninsula, Sulawesi and Banjarmasin on Borneo, greater attention would be focused on emulating the traditions and practices of the western Muslim world. But even if the particular teachings of Sufi orders seem to have been embraced by the elite, there was hardly one united programme, nor were the calls of recent returnees from Arabia taken up without contestation.

Such new modes continued to be of interest among the expanding body of religious schools in a more politically fractured Java. And while such rising Islamic influence was not exactly akin to a new spirit of anti-colonialism, nor yet nationalism, it was increasingly a success story to be contrasted with the relative failure of Christianization, even within VOC-ruled enclaves. For despite official proscription, the environs of Batavia sheltered sites of prayer for the significant population of Muslims and the many Chinese who had returned to service the colonial economy alongside so many locals, enslaved or free, whose fate was still determined by the VOC.

Still, like the by now disease-ridden canals of Batavia, the VOC was hardly a fit master. Having invested in a series of interventions in Java's numerous wars of succession (1704 to 1708, 1719 to 1723 and 1747 to 1757), in addition to fighting a losing battle against the English, then rising to supremacy in Bengal, the VOC was in decline. The once priceless spices were now found elsewhere, and the passage home of key Dutch cargoes – principally coffee and sugar – was often interrupted by war with the English. By the 1790s, a French invasion of the Netherlands and the installation of a new republican regime would spell the end of the company and the commencement of a new mode of metropolitan rule, or at least the aspiration for it. Equally, the Bourbons of Spain would try to implement reforms to open the Philippines to more direct metropolitan control, although with little success in the face of entrenched opposition from the friar estates run by the mendicant orders, long used to governing for the Church. An attempt to establish a Spanish joint-stock company in 1785 for trade in Asia that was analogous to the Atlantic East India companies would also fall victim to the vicissitudes of the Napoleonic era. The time of trading corporations other than the British East India Company was at an end, and new states were rising to face the challenge of metropolitan colonial ambitions in the nineteenth century.

Taksin, the birth of the Chakri dynasty
and the cession of Penang

While initial attempts to establish an enduring presence had failed at Mergui in the seventeenth century, the East India Company and their country trader kin would enjoy greater success at the end of the eighteenth century, and in the shadow of turmoil between the Siamese and their southern Malay vassals. For its part, the Siamese state was commencing a new phase of consolidation after enduring the total destruction of Ayudhya at the hands of Burma's newly established Kon-baung dynasty in 1767.

After relative peace in the 1750s, which had even seen the interior Kingdom of Kandy, in Sri Lanka, send missions to Ayudhya to gain aid in restoring Buddhism among the Sinhalese, conflict flared between the Burmese and the Siamese over the control of the Tenasserim Coast, of which Mergui was a key port. And while the Burmese would not long remain in the Chaophraya basin, facing a Chinese invasion during the very months in which they had besieged the Siamese capital, 1767 marked the final victory of the Burmese down to the Isthmian coast and their lasting ascendancy over the Mon minority population.

In the wake of the Burmese withdrawal, there were several factions duelling for control of Siam. During three ensuing years of chaos, it was a Sino-Thai general, Taksin (r. 1767 to 1782), who was able to vanquish the other contenders for the throne and establish a new capital at Thonburi, at the opening of the Chaophraya across from the fort of Bangkok. As a ruler, Taksin not only restored Siamese prestige, but he actively extended Siamese claims on Lao and Cambodian territory. But while he was initially popular, opening the treasury to the population during the post-invasion famine of 1767 to 1778 and restoring order, his tenure was increasingly unstable – he even insisted on the obeisance of the monkhood in an inversion of established practice that had traditionally seen Siamese kings defer to the monastic clergy (*sangha*). By 1781, the elite had determined that Taksin had to be removed. Hence, with his forces actively engaged in Cambodia, Taksin was killed, clearing the way for the ascension of General Chakri, who, as Rama I (r. 1782 to 1809), inaugurated the dynasty that remains on the throne of modern Thailand.

Whereas Rama I took off where Taksin had left off – emphasizing trading and diplomatic relations with China and encouraging the immigration of Chinese (especially ethnic Teochiu) into his realm – the capital was moved across the estuary to Bangkok and deliberately enlarged with boatloads of material from the ruins of Ayudhya. Further, after a full coronation in 1785 and his successful repulsing of a Burmese invasion, Rama I restored the ceremonial linkage between royalty and the monkhood, and in 1788 to 1789 established a grand council to establish the definitive Pali text of the Tripitaka.

Having lost access to Mergui, the new state was naturally in need of access to the Bay of Bengal through other vassals. To that end, the Malay polities of the south were encouraged to offer tribute and allegiance with practical business handled by Chinese intermediaries. In the face of such challenges, Sultan Abdullah Mukarram Shah of Kedah (r. 1778 to 1797) sought to hedge his bets by reaching out in 1786 to the English in Bengal, represented locally by Francis Light (1740 to 1794). The sultan would be sorely disappointed by the results of this deal, and watched as his new English tenants smiled on the Chinese mercantilists and sought good relations with Bangkok, while their trade ate into his own earnings. Indeed, the East India Company even repulsed the Malays in 1791 when they attempted to regain possession of the island, and compelled their erstwhile hosts to renounce all claim on the slip of land that Light had renamed Prince of Wales Island.

The Tây Sơn period, 1771 to 1802

The instability born of the Burmese invasions and Taksin's subsequent incursions into Cambodia had direct repercussions on the Nguyễn rulers of Cochin China, who were themselves actively engaged on Khmer soil. Indeed, the Nguyễn polity was by this time overextended, and the constant levying of troops, coupled with corruption and rampant devaluation of the currency in circulation, hit many sectors of the economy and laid the ground for the emergence, in 1771, of a new force stemming from the hamlet of Tây Sơn, near the old Cham heartland of central Vietnam.

Led by three siblings with connections to the Nguyễn court and the betel trade, the Tây Sơn 'revolt' would eventually unify the highly diverse territory of Vietnam. Certainly, the famous 'hissing armies', which initially attained something of a Robin Hood-like reputation for robbing the rich and leaving the poor unmolested, claimed to act in the name of Heaven. Initially, they claimed to act in the name of their Nguyễn enemies, seeking to marry into the elite and even to make use of one prince, Nguyễn Anh, who later fled to Siam.

The Tây Sơn brothers also enjoyed the support of Chinese traders and the Cham minority, whose surviving royalty they courted with the aim of making use of their sacred regalia, in addition to making the old Cham city of Vijaya their capital. Yet, civil war was the main result of Tây Sơn depredations, and the Chinese would be alienated by such acts as the massacre of the Han population (and much of the Nguyễn royal family) following the siege of Gia Định in 1776. Indeed, the brothers often disagreed on the treatment of ethnic minorities and the many southerners who had by this time converted to Catholicism. Over the following decade, the Tây Sơn would reinforce their control over the south, continuing to fend off the Siamese and then facing invasion from the Trinh in 1774 to 1775. Hindered by disease and the monsoons, by 1786 the Trinh were themselves invaded, having lost the services of a key general.

Despite being offered positions of rank by the Trinh, the Tây Sơn were determined to defeat their northern rivals, which was achieved by 1787, leading to a punitive expedition from China in 1788. That attack would also founder, and the Qing opted to recognize the most active Tây Sơn brother, Nguyễn Huệ (1753 to 1792), as a vassal ruler who now claimed the empire of Đại Việt in his name. For his part, Nguyễn Huệ, who took the regnal name Quang Trung, had ambitions on southern Chinese territory, but his aims would remain unrealized at his death in 1792. Divided as they were over the territorial extent of their territory, the heirs of the Tây Sơn brothers (who were all dead by the end of 1793) presided over a much weakened expanse of territory that would eventually be conquered by Nguyễn Anh when he returned with more determined Siamese aid in 1802 and established the dynasty that would remain in place until the abdication of Bảo Đại in 1945.

Conclusion

Seen from a *longue durée* perspective, the four centuries after 1400 saw the lasting bifurcation of Southeast Asia into its island and mainland components, and away from a once shared commitment to Buddhism and/or Hindu models of kingship. This bifurcation was especially marked by the adoption of explicitly Sinhalese-style Theravadan Buddhism in many of the polities above the Isthmus of Kra and monotheism below and to the east of it. While the presence of Christianity in the archipelago was clearly a result of the interventions of Western states, or their clerical agents whose presence served as a counterpoint to the increasing numbers of Muslim sojourners and returning pilgrims, the ongoing role of Southeast Asian dynasties in directing or encouraging particular doctrines is not to be disregarded in the face of seeming Iberian and then VOC dominance.

And there were other constants, too, with the continual presence of Asian (particularly Chinese) sojourners, the export of key spices and, increasingly, cash crops destined for the world market. Such engagement, coupled with the rise of larger, more hegemonic states, also helped to feed the expansion of populations with less and less recourse to flight into under-populated spaces, whether claimed by traditional Southeast Asian rulers or their Western rivals and sometime patrons. In short, Southeast Asia was a far busier and much more contested space by 1800. Certainly, the mainland bore special witness to ever-more violent and absolutist claims made by Burmese, Tai and Vietnamese sovereigns who made effective use of a wide variety of outsiders and universal doctrines in the quest for enduring hegemony.

Still, one must bear in mind that universal claims were as yet unmatched by ethnic homogeneity. Kon-baung Burma continued to rule over Shans, Mons and Muslims, much as the Siamese state engaged with Laos, Malays and Khmers, and Vietnam struggled with Khmers, Laos and Cham. Even Java included non-Muslim populations whose cultural horizons stretched to still Hindu-ized Bali, while Sumatra's hinterlands remained occupied by swidden farmers and gatherers with little desire to be absorbed by the lowland kingdoms, whose peoples remained anxious about tales of cannibals and wild animals lurking in the forests.

FURTHER READING

Andaya, Leonard Y., *The World of Maluku: Eastern Indonesia in the Early Modern Period* (Honolulu: University of Hawaii Press, 1993).

Andrade, Tonio, *Lost Colony: The Untold Story of China's First Great Victory over the West* (Princeton University Press, 2011).

Aung-Thwin, Michael, *Pagan: The Origins of Modern Burma* (Honolulu: University of Hawaii Press, 1985).

Blussé, Leonard, *Visible Cities: Canton, Nagasaki, and Batavia and the Coming of the Americans* (Cambridge, MA: Harvard University Press, 2008).

Brown, C. C. (trans.), 'Sějarah Mělayu or "Malay Annals": A Translation of Raffles MS 18', *Journal of the Malayan Branch of the Royal Asiatic Society* 25 (1952), pts 2 and 3.

Dutton, George, *The Tây Sơn Uprising: Society and Rebellion in Eighteenth-Century Vietnam* (Honolulu: University of Hawaii, 2006).

Lieberman, Victor, *Strange Parallels: Southeast Asia in Global Context, c. 800–1830* (Cambridge University Press, 2003).

Ma Huan, *Ying-yai sheng-lan: 'The Overall Survey of the Ocean's Shores' [1433]*, Feng Ch'eng-Chün (ed.), J. V. G. Mills (trans.) (Cambridge University Press for the Hakluyt Society, 1970).

O'Kane, John (ed. and trans.), *The Ship of Sulaiman* (New York: Columbia University Press, 1972).

Pires, Tomé, *The Suma Oriental of Tomé Pires*, Armando Cortesão (ed. and trans.) (London: The Hakluyt Society, 1944).

Reid, Anthony, *Southeast Asia in the Age of Commerce*, 2 vols (New Haven, CT: Yale University Press, 1987–93).

Remmelink, Willem G. J., *The Chinese War and the Collapse of the Javanese State, 1725–1743* (Leiden: KITLV Press, 1994).

Ricklefs, M. C., *The Seen and Unseen Worlds in Java 1726–1749: History, Literature and Islam in the Court of Pakubuwana II* (St Leonards: Allen & Unwin, 1998).

Subrahmanyam, Sanjay, *The Career and Legend of Vasco da Gama* (Cambridge University Press, 1998).

Wyatt, David, *Thailand: A Short History* (New Haven, CT: Yale University Press, 2000).

16

The Caribbean region: crucible for modern world history

ALAN L. KARRAS

> In fourteen hundred and ninety two,
> Columbus sailed the Ocean Blue.
> He had three ships and left from Spain;
> he sailed through sunshine, wind, and rain.

This familiar childhood poem, of unknown authorship, eventually mentions the Bahamas, the site of the first European landing in the Americas. It also references the Arawak Amerindians whom the Spanish sailors encountered, though not much more than to mention that "they were very nice" and "gave the sailors food and spice." Its anodyne qualities belie the violence and collisions that characterize the Caribbean region's development and integration into the world historical narrative. Indeed, the Caribbean should be seen as a harbinger of world historical developments that would take place centuries later.

Because the Caribbean region was the first area of the Americas that Europeans encountered and therefore the first region of the "New World" to connect with the "Old World," it ought to be considered a crucible for understanding many of the modern world's historical processes. These processes, at least through the years covered by this volume, include implantation and colonization, global migration, enslavement, extraction, economic transformation and integration, as well as (very briefly) revolution and state building. Although the Caribbean region faced these problems first, many world historians overlook it, preferring instead to study more populous areas in Africa and Asia. Within the field of global history, then, there is much more knowledge about connections within the "Old World" than there is familiarity with the same kinds of connections that existed in the "New World." This is true despite the fact that, though known to Europeans much longer than places in the Americas, Asian and African societies were not fully integrated into the growing European-dominated global economy until relatively late in the eighteenth century, just as relations between the American colonies—including those in the Caribbean—and their various European powers had begun to deteriorate.

Making matters worse, scholars of the mainland Americas, North and South, rarely consider the Caribbean region at all. Such neglect can be easily explained: islands are not continents. Their finite geographies limited their ability to expand their frontiers and, with the exception of the Greater Antilles (Hispaniola, Cuba, Puerto Rico and Jamaica), they quickly ran out of land as more and more territory was placed into cultivation. Moreover, the islands' economic contributions to European empires, which were strongly bound to sugar monoculture, deteriorated in the nineteenth century as new luxury products from Asia became more accessible to European consumers and the Caribbean islands failed to diversify, instead doubling down on increasing sugar production.

It certainly did not help, either historically or historiographically, that the region never developed a singular national, regional or even linguistic identity. Instead, the Caribbean archipelago remained politically and linguistically fragmented, with different European powers involved in each island's government and economy—often creating negative consequences for all of those who lived there, whether black or white. Although there were certain policies and practices, such as sugar price supports within various European empires, which benefited at least the elite in their colonies, in general policies were designed in Europe to benefit those in Europe. As the centuries progressed, the ire of many who resided in the Caribbean grew. This ire was caused not so much by the lack of political representation, as happened elsewhere, but by economic regulations that made no sense for Caribbean consumers. The lack of a single regional identity allowed much of the Caribbean to remain under colonial rule through the nineteenth and twentieth centuries, and it diluted the colonial voice, as local concerns across the region did not frequently get connected and amplified.

Although Columbus's voyages began the process of communication between the New and the Old Worlds, this nascent global integration never resulted in either a clear regional Caribbean identity or a historical view of the region's contributions to rising globalization over the *longue durée*. This is extremely unfortunate, as the region has much to offer historians of the global past. Although the Caribbean islands did not develop their own national histories until after independence, and were generally excluded from the much larger national histories of places like Mexico and the United States, the colonization and economic growth of all these areas were part of the same historical processes at the same historical moment. The national histories of Mexico and the United States would have looked very different had the Spanish not forayed into the Caribbean region as they sought trade routes to Asia. (We can leave aside the question of historical accident for the moment, as Columbus did not realize that he had not managed to reach the outskirts of Asia.) It therefore becomes important to place the Caribbean region into an integrated world history, one that better reflects the prominent position held by the region at the start of the "modern world."

One solution to this neglect might appear to be the new scholarly emphasis on the Atlantic World, which linked the four continents that bordered the ocean: Europe, Africa, and North and South America. The Caribbean straddles North and South America, so is clearly included in the Atlantic World. Taking this approach, however, is now fraught with peril. Scholars of the United States—which has a very clear national narrative—have colonized Atlantic History as a field and are gradually finding ways to insert the creation of the United States into international history. In one sense, this is a positive development as it tackles the persistent problem of American exceptionalism that has in many ways deeply permeated scholarship about the Western Hemisphere. But in other ways it compounds the issues faced by the Caribbean in being admitted to the world history club. By focusing on the mainland North American colonies as part of a larger Atlantic World, some scholars have again relegated the Caribbean colonies to a bit part—this time because they did not join in the American War for Independence, the modern world's first anti-colonial revolt. Wealthy Caribbean planters and those who worked for them saw their fates much more closely tied to the imperial enterprises that created protected markets for their products and provided them in return with food. Thus, ignoring the Caribbean skews the story of the Atlantic World, and it says nothing about non-British colonies in the Caribbean, which had long before forged accommodations with their European capitals. Moreover, such scholarship generally ignores the fundamental fact that until the late eighteenth century, all Caribbean colonies were surely much more profitable and therefore desirable than the mainland North American colonies—at least from a European perspective.

The Caribbean colonies were, and ought to remain, central—not just to scholars of the Western Hemisphere in the early modern world, but also to world historians who can see in this region a microcosm of encounters and exchange that would be replicated time and time again over the next several centuries. The Caribbean must surely be considered a crucible in the laboratory of historical examination.

Colonization and violence

After Columbus's voyages both symbolically and historically opened up the Caribbean area to European exploration and settlement, Spanish settlers crossed the ocean and occupied the Greater Antilles. They established forts, built small-scale cities and developed staging areas that ultimately supported those who went on to colonize mainland Spanish America. These bases came at the expense of the indigenous Amerindian populations, which consisted of several groups: the Arawaks (including the Taino and Lucayans) in the north and west of the region, and the Caribs, in the south and east. In virtually all of the islands, native peoples quickly died off as they encountered the arriving bands of European sailors and soldiers. Either they succumbed to Old World diseases, such as smallpox, which overran their New World immune systems, or they were victims of weapons that were unknown in the isolated world of the Americas before the Iberians' arrival. By the middle of the sixteenth century, the region's population had dramatically declined to the point that the Spanish began to shift their focus from the Caribbean to the mainland—which had much larger Amerindian populations and thus more plentiful labor, even after being ravaged by conquest, disease and warfare.

In the islands, the indigenous populations generally did not recover, although the Spanish did try to move Amerindians from one island to another, first as slaves and then, when the government and church in Spain frowned upon this practice and encouraged greater indigenous evangelization, as (poorly) compensated workers. The Spanish further shifted their attentions to the mainland, which had the effect of opening up the rest of the Caribbean region—an area over 2,000 miles across—for other European interlopers to claim territory that was officially Spanish, but did not have sufficient military protection to prevent its capture. It was then up to those from England, France, the Netherlands and even Denmark to figure out what to do with their newly acquired territories. All of them eventually turned to African slavery, which came to characterize the region and is discussed in greater detail below.

Because Spain was always more focused on the larger islands in the western part of the Caribbean (and on conquering the powerful expansionist empires on the mainland), it never spent much time or energy ensuring that the smaller, often volcanic, islands of the eastern Caribbean (the Lesser Antilles) were brought under strict control. Especially after 1550, this allowed predators from elsewhere in Europe to enter the area and find ways to harass Spanish shipping and interrupt the gigantic flow of silver bullion that was leaving the Americas in convoy and making its way to Spain. Before 1550, Northern Europeans generally came to the Caribbean with the hope of trading with Spanish residents there. The trade was, of course, contraband as Spain did not allow trade with nationals of other countries, but it was nevertheless profitable, encouraging more entrepreneurs to brave the Atlantic crossing with the hopes of striking it rich. Traders from Northern Europe were also not above resorting to violence, robbing those who would not willingly engage in commerce with them, which gave the region a reputation as a place where almost anything could happen.[1]

Violence certainly became part of the popular perception of the Caribbean region in many European metropoles. Residents came to see the region as a place in which quick wealth could be accumulated, though also as a place where there was an ever-present risk of a quick death. Northern European rulers tacitly encouraged migration, especially as a way to increase their own treasuries. Moreover, they licensed men like Sir Francis Drake, and their ships, to harass Spanish shipping, and capture wealth that would otherwise find its way into the Spanish treasury. Such captains' initial successes at diverting bullion from Spain encouraged other young men, who were not generally licensed by their states, to set off for the Caribbean in search of their own fortunes. By the beginning of the seventeenth century, these "get rich quick" schemes caused a further change in the Caribbean region's geopolitics. Pirates, for that is what these young men were, became non-state actors whose redistribution of wealth through robbery on the high seas propelled the region into the popular imagination, and caused its reputation as a place where anything could happen and where one's personal safety could not be guaranteed. And this was assuming that pale Europeans were able to survive the hot and humid days for which tropical climates are known.

Pirate raids on the Spanish treasure fleet cost Spain enormously—both in its treasury and in its prestige relative to its Old World rivals. After all, the Spanish state was unable to prevent piracy from getting off the ground, nor was it especially successful at slowing or eradicating its continued growth. (Because the Spanish treasure fleet sailed in convoy at precise moments in the year, and because the ocean currents and winds made only two routes possible, the *flota* was an easy, yet a moving, target.)

---

[1] Anne Pérotin-Dumon, "French, English, and Dutch in the Lesser Antilles: From Privateering to Planting, c. 1550 to c. 1650" in UNESCO, *General History of the Caribbean* (London: UNESCO, 1997–2011), vol. 2, pp. 116–17.

If there is anything that persistently occupies the popular imagination about the Caribbean, it is pirates. Most people know very little about the Caribbean region and its early history, except of course that there were pirates. Whether from the rides in Disney theme parks around the world, or the eponymous movie series, many people strongly associate the region with pirates, who were (allegedly) ready at a moment's notice to plunder passing treasure ships or burn small cities to the ground if the residents failed to hand over their valuables on command. In some ways, this is not an unreasonable picture, as there is some truth in these images. There *were* quite a number of pirates in the region during this period; many came from across Northern Europe (and, later, North America) hoping to strike it rich and taking advantage of Spain's extremely loose border enforcement. Drawn mostly from the lower social orders across Europe, pirates saw robbery on the high seas as an escape from the grinding poverty that they had experienced for much of their lives. Their lives were not at all easy, but if they survived they at least had the potential to amass fortunes that would otherwise have been beyond their grasp if they had instead remained at home in Europe.

Many people now romanticize the region's pirates as rebels against a system that bred inequality. Because many ships had a pirate code of conduct, voted on some aspects of the way in which their ships would operate, developed schemes for dividing up "booty" and provided compensation for permanent injury (such as the loss of a limb), some have suggested that pirates were nascent democrats whose contributions to early modern politics illuminate democratic tendencies in a manifestly undemocratic age. This can be a problematic reading, and one the victims of the pirates would no doubt dispute. Pirates heavily relied on the use (or threat) of force in order to extract riches from those who happened to be in the wrong (or right) place at the wrong (or right) time. Initially welcomed by the surviving Amerindian populations of the smaller islands—because they were not Spanish and indeed had the express purpose of robbing the Spanish—they soon overstayed their welcome. They did so by effectively occupying some of the smaller islands, and creating zones of control. Successful pirates had money to spend, which caused those willing to take their money, usually in exchange for drink, lodging and sex, to migrate to the Caribbean in order to serve this *nouveau riche* clientele. As a result, some of the smaller Caribbean islands began to be developed, further reducing the Amerindian population and causing more Europeans to migrate, either to turn pirate or to serve those whose adventures resulted in pecuniary gain. To focus on romanticized rebellion masks the essentially mercantilist, or at least financial, motives of pirates. They represented the logical outcome of mercantilism run amok.

Through colonialism and violence, what was once a densely populated and geographically isolated region became incorporated into the Afro-Eurasian economy—making it truly global. The price was millions of Amerindian lives. The islands' decentralized political structures, especially in comparison to those on the mainland, were left decentralized, even though most islands were incorporated into the European empires emerging at the time. The source of law was always at some distance from the place that it was to be carried out, making consistent legal enforcement an issue. This diffused power and authority came to characterize the region, as it would later characterize other empires in other places.

Spain consistently maintained that it had a right to control the region, and demanded that other European states, such as the English, French and Dutch, police those of their subjects who had become pirates in the Caribbean. Such demands did not go down especially well in London, Paris and Amsterdam. Although the Spanish and Portuguese had divided any newly discovered territories in the Americas between them in the Treaty of Tordesillas (1494), other European powers generally ignored this treaty. This left it to the Iberians to police their own territories and the terms of the treaty itself. This was not an easy task: the Americas were vast, but the small size of the Caribbean islands (along with the large sea that created their borders) made them hard to monitor, especially given that those who most needed prolonged police observation generally had no fixed address. To make matters worse, those charged with enforcing the legal regime frequently had inadequate resources to accomplish their tasks. The Europeans had inadequate resources to run and consistently monitor their empires.

The European occupation, and later settlement, of the Caribbean islands illustrates the ways in which Europeans gained control over areas of the world that they sought to dominate. In the case of the Caribbean, the job became easier than it ought to have been—and that it would prove to be in other areas of the world—because of the region's massive population loss. Nevertheless, the colonization process across the Caribbean foretold what would happen elsewhere around the globe several centuries later. At first, a few Europeans showed up, wanting to trade with the local populations—either for luxury products or for bullion that they could use to purchase luxury products somewhere else. Limited trade generally followed, and the Europeans eventually ended up controlling the commercial and exchange processes. For a variety of reasons, Asian and African populations did not anticipate the degree to which many European traders would relentlessly pursue their own mercantilist agendas. This frequently caused Europeans to change tactics and terms and frustrated their trading partners, politically weakening some of them along the way. The African slave trade is one such example; the opium trade between India and China yet another. From the Caribbean to Canton, Europeans succeeded in dominating the economic systems that they encountered. This process happened first in the Americas, and especially in the Caribbean, simply because Europeans went to the Americas and were able to take over the hemisphere relatively quickly.

Another, and perhaps more useful, way to think about this would be to consider these early points of contact between colonizer and colonized as part of an *implantation* process that accompanies all colonial activity. Examining the Caribbean region when it first became known to Europeans and was integrated into the pre-existing "Old World" networks of exchange generates a kind of rough model to understand global interactions in subsequent centuries. During this process, colonizers—European and otherwise—implant themselves along with their ideas, values and cultural practices, into the place and society that will be colonized. Typically, the colonial power develops points of entry that result in their being able to take over places and spaces, running them to the colonial power's advantage. In the Caribbean region, this process took some time, despite being aided by the rapid depopulation that took place when the Old and New World peoples encountered each other. There are several main explanations for the slow speed at which implantation happened: (1) the Caribbean region is geographically spread out; (2) there were actually very few Europeans who were involved in conquest; (3) the political systems of the indigenous people were relatively diffuse; (4) there were several European state actors, in many ways working against each other; (5) indigenous depopulation made it more difficult to have a reliable and docile labor force; and (6) the European colonizers did not have a clear idea of what they wanted to achieve, because they were never really intending to "discover" a new continent. Mercantilist competition among European states no doubt fueled the desire to find new routes to Asia, and to colonize the Caribbean as a substitute; at the same time, islands that had been brought under European authority needed something that would simultaneously attract new settlers *and* generate some sort of economic reward for their efforts. The islands were not teeming with spices, or luxuries, or even bullion; thus, Europeans in the Caribbean sought an alternative source of treasure to make the journeys worth their while. To put it another way, they needed to put something in their crucible that would sell in a global—and mercantile—world, while using the region's comparative advantages.

That something would be sugar, a luxury product in sixteenth-century Europe, both rare and expensive. The introduction of sugar took time, however. Although it had been introduced to Hispaniola as early as the late 1520s, sugar mills there remained rather small. It took several generations before the crop went into widespread production around the Caribbean, resulting in it becoming more easily available. By the middle of the seventeenth century, many of the Caribbean islands produced vast quantities of sugar—production that would only continue to grow. The English, French and Dutch (along with the Danes) found ways to *trade* sugar produced with coerced African labor for Spanish bullion. This effort at trade eventually and generally made piracy unnecessary, and reshaped the whole of the region's economy, environment and population. As mainland America had done with mining of precious gold and silver (and as other colonial societies and polities did later), the Caribbean made a dramatic turn, and moved towards resource extraction. That process of resource extraction defined the Caribbean for centuries to come.

Sugar and slavery

Just as pirates dominate modern popular consciousness about the Caribbean region, the association between sugar and slavery dominates the work of historians. They have largely focused their energies on this association. Indeed, it is hard to find much Caribbean history that does not deal with either sugar or slavery—even in history that focuses on the era after slavery was abolished in the nineteenth century. More often, historical scholarship has mined the many connections between sugar monoculture and the slaves who worked in this industry, or who supported it with their labors elsewhere on the plantations.

Scholarship on the Caribbean region has tried to achieve what might be called a holistic study of sugar and slavery across the region, but there are still linguistic barriers that make this difficult. Although sugar itself regularly crossed borders, historians of one linguistic zone rarely consider what happened in another linguistic zone. This is not surprising, given the language skills required to work in the many languages in which documents appear in Caribbean archives. Geographical divisions are ever-present in this literature: few studies look at more than a few (if that) countries, and fewer

Colonial spheres in the
Caribbean region, 1800

SP	Spanish
BR	British
FR	French
DU	Dutch

ATLANTIC OCEAN

Gulf of Mexico

U.S.A.

Mexico

British Honduras

Bay Is. **BR**

Guatemala

Honduras

El Salvador

Nicaragua

Costa Rica

PACIFIC OCEAN

Colombia

Venezuela

Guiana

Caribbean Sea

Cuba

Cayman Is. **BR**

Swan Is.

Providence I. **BR**

San Andrés I. **BR**

Corn I. **BR.**

Jamaica **BR**

Bahamas Is. **BR**

Turks and Caicos **BR**

Dominican
Republic

Haiti

Puerto Rico **SP**

St. Croix (**Danish**)

Guadeloupe **FR**

Dominica **BR**

St. Lucia **BR**

St. Vincent **BR**

Grenada **BR**

DU

DU/FR
St. Martin

Antigua **BR**

Martinique **FR**

Barbados **BR**

Tobago **BR**

Trinidad **SP**

16.1 The Caribbean in 1800

402

still have worked on comparing what happened in, for instance, the Leeward islands with what happened in Cuba, or Suriname. Research fields are largely defined by European language groups, and follow European colonial patterns. This is not necessarily bad, but it does suggest an area for future exploration. Slavery was not established in all of these places at the same time, nor did it end in all of these places at the same time. But it was practiced simultaneously in many countries across the region, and sugar was the dominant crop in virtually all of the larger colonies.

Despite this common pattern, people other than historians generally have only a vague sense of just how tightly sugar and slavery were connected in the seventeenth and eighteenth centuries. This is problematic for several reasons. First, it ignores a major shift in consumption. The history of a crop whose consumption grew from 4 lbs. per capita per year in 1700 to 13 lbs. per capita per year in 1800 has to be by definition significant. (It has also been estimated that by 1933 per capita consumption of sugar in the United Kingdom and United States reached nearly 100 lbs. per person and has remained close to that level ever since; these high rates of consumption were made possible by the development of more efficient ways of extracting sugar, combined with industrial food processing in which sugar and sugar products such as corn syrup were used in many, many products.[2]) Second, it separates production from consumption, a pattern that continues today. Most people in the developed world rarely—if ever—think about the origins of products they consume, whether foodstuffs, clothing or something else altogether. A factory collapse in Bangladesh may raise awareness of such connections, but after a few days of righteous indignation, consumers go back to consuming, not thinking about those who produce what they consume. So it was earlier—European consumers were rarely reminded that Africans, who had been forced to migrate across the Atlantic and faced very poor prospects when it came to life expectancy, produced the addictive sugar that they craved. The ocean allowed European consumers to be intellectually divorced from the global economy, or to participate in it only in a sanitized way. This extended the lifespan of the sugar economy, while shortening those of its laborers. The removal of slaves from European sight also extended slavery, which continued even after it may not have been the most economical system that could have been used to produce sugar. By

---

[2] Noel Deerr, *The History of Sugar* (London: Chapman & Hall, 1949–50), vol. 2, p. 532. See also www.businessinsider.com/chart-american-sugar-consumption-2012-2.

then, of course, slavery had become an ingrained cultural practice—something important to the maintenance of social order.

Moreover, the Africans who had been imported specifically to labor on producing this crop not only sacrificed their lives, as death rates remained lamentably high almost everywhere through the eighteenth century, but also greatly contributed to the New World's profits. This was often at the African continent's expense. Although eventually the African population recovered, it is hard to see how exporting 12 million people could not have had an impact on the productivity of those African societies that sent slaves. The mortality rate of Caribbean slaves improved in most places in the early nineteenth century, but for much of the seventeenth and eighteenth centuries, it proved to be cheaper to buy a new slave, mistreat him or her, and then buy another, than to buy a slave and make sure that he or she was well cared for and could live to reproduce. The wanton disregard of human feeling (fellow-feeling, as Adam Smith would later say) resulted in asymmetrical social orders that would appear elsewhere in the colonial worlds of the nineteenth and twentieth centuries.[3]

The growing production of sugar, coupled with the dramatically rising slave importation into virtually all of the Caribbean colonies, best characterizes the mature colonial Caribbean world. At the same time, connections between the Caribbean colonies and the European metropoles strengthened, as transoceanic communication became more regular and as sugar fostered economic growth and increased profits, at least for slave-owners. The earliest sugar planters made vast sums of money and retired to extremely large houses in their native European countries. Few wanted to stay in the islands, finding slavery distasteful and the climate unpleasant. Other young men followed them, hoping to replicate their successes and themselves become absentee estate owners—or at least move up in the world. But opportunities to do so diminished, as the geographical boundaries of island societies limited the amount of land that could be placed into cultivation and sugar prices declined as production increased. Many island economies also developed small middle or managerial classes, which consisted of professionals—doctors, lawyers, accountants, managers—and skilled craftsmen—carpenters and coopers—who came to the region to make their fortunes

---

[3] The best general discussion of slave mortality is found in Stanley L. Engerman and B. W. Higman, "The Demographic Structure of the Caribbean Slave Societies in the Eighteenth and Nineteenth Centuries" in UNESCO, *General History of the Caribbean*, vol. 3, pp. 45–104.

while practicing trades.[4] Although all were upwardly mobile, few achieved their goals of earning quick fortunes, and, like pirates, they were enmeshed in a system of violence-driven mercantalism. Even so, their presence created at least the semblance of a European rank-ordered society that would have been somewhat familiar to them, despite their location in exotic locations surrounded, and outnumbered, by African slaves.

Many, if not most, Caribbean societies did not open schools until the late eighteenth or early nineteenth centuries, requiring parents who wanted their sons (and, occasionally, their daughters) to be educated to send them back to Europe. This provided a constant stream of migration back and forth across the Atlantic between Europe and the Caribbean. The colonies were seen as transitory opportunities for advancement, much as Europeans in those nineteenth-century states with empires envisioned prospects for themselves around the globe as temporary, almost a rite of passage. Indeed, in the British colonies at least, many of the same families that migrated to and from the Caribbean later had relatives migrating to and from India, as well as other places in the imperial world. The movement of people to fill "white" jobs, combined with the movement of African (and creole) slaves, provided the framework for a kind of European-centered social hierarchy, one that would be used elsewhere in the world, though with indigenous workers filling many jobs. After slavery had been universally abolished, Asian contract workers were shipped around the globe to perform work that was deemed to be beneath European workers. (The Caribbean received its share of Chinese and Indian "coolies," but they did not arrive until the mid-nineteenth century.)

The creation of new social hierarchies that took place in the Caribbean presaged developments in later colonies around the world, and was inevitably entwined with racial stratification. This stratification resulted not from any kind of indigenous hierarchy, as the indigenes had been eliminated, but rather from the Caribbean's demographic imbalance, combined with the huge power imbalances in Caribbean plantation societies. More African men than African women went to most areas of the Caribbean, which meant that African women had a difficult time starting (or raising) families with male slaves. If they labored on the plantations, their fecundity and life expectancy

---

[4] A. L. Karras, *Sojourners in the Sun: Scots Migration to Jamaica and the Chesapeake, 1740–1820* (Ithaca, NY: Cornell University Press, 1992); and Heather Cateau, "Beyond Planters and Plantership" in H. Cateau and R. Pemberton (eds.), *Beyond Tradition: Reinterpreting the Caribbean Historical Experience* (Kingston: Ian Randle Publishers, 2006), pp. 3–21.

were low. The preponderance of European migrants consisted of young men, and in general blacks outnumbered whites by as much as 10:1.[5] With relatively few white women from which to choose a sexual partner, many men took slave mistresses, either with or without their consent, often from among the African women who worked in their households.

There were restrictions against this mixing or that limited the social position of the mixed race progeny in a number of Caribbean islands, which suggests that laws were created *ex post facto* in an attempt to prevent something that was already widely happening. Despite legal limitations on their social mobility, the resulting progeny held elevated status when compared with those of purely African descent, and could take on menial, frequently non-agricultural jobs or, in the eighteenth century, certain artisanal or craft-worker jobs. The limits of the positions that those of mixed race could achieve were generally precisely defined in law, but this was not always enforceable. In most Caribbean societies, there was a clear hierarchy of color. At least in general, the lighter one's skin, the higher one's social status; the opposite was also true, for dark skin generally brought low status. Being born in the colony, a creole, generally meant higher status than being a slave newly arrived from Africa. Skin color did not always match parentage, however, so what was supposed to be a strict hierarchy was often much more fluid and malleable, especially when compared to places in North America.

There has been insufficient attention paid to the ways in which interracial sex provided an essential buffer for many of Caribbean slavery's harshest conditions. By creating a group of people that stood between Africans and Europeans, interracial sexual liaisons also generated a way for the wealthiest whites to maintain order.

Slavery is one half of the combination that so dominated Caribbean history in the seventeenth and, especially, the eighteenth centuries. Sugar, of course, is the other half; it was the crop that required large quantities of labor to produce and it was the crop that powered the Caribbean economy to profitability. Extracting this resource allowed Northern Europeans to compete with the Spanish, who were extracting precious metal with cheap Amerindian labor. The Northern Europeans won, especially because sugar was so cheaply produced and because it was addictive, which helped to increase demand. Even the Spanish were willing

---

[5] Engerman and Higman, "Demographic Structure," pp. 48–9.

to part with their bullion in exchange for sugar (along with tobacco, another addictive New World product).

It would be impossible to consider the Caribbean as a crucible for world history without some discussion of the general principles of resource extraction, which came to characterize colonial economies throughout the modern world. The standard description of this in the nineteenth and twentieth centuries suggests that colonies extracted the raw materials for industrializing (and industrial) European societies, which then turned around and provided cheaply produced industrial products, such as cotton textiles, to their colonies. Such cheaply made goods increased consumption in the colonies, but also changed the nature of local economies, as indigenous artisans—say, weavers in India—confronted diminished demand for their wares. As a flood of mass-produced goods arrived in Africa and Asia, the colonies became more dependent on the metropoles for life's basic necessities. In this particular example, cotton producers thus became cotton consumers. Societal independence vanished as empires took root.

While this argument makes sense in imperialism's nineteenth- and twentieth-century contexts, it is difficult to make a direct analogy with the pre-industrial Caribbean. Indeed, it is possible to make the opposite case. Few in the colonies could afford European-produced luxury products; they remained an aspiration for most whites, and for slaves they were out of the question. Some whites would go into debt to acquire them, mortgaging their plantations and future crops in order to buy goods on credit. Caribbean slaves, through their labor in a monoculture economy, generated profits for their owners, which were expressed in merchant house account books. In turn, these credits allowed European residents (and absentee owners) to consume simply by borrowing against their credit.

Moreover, the price of sugar, which was often protected, generated enough profit from European consumers for the merchants either to spend their money consuming luxury goods (which transferred wealth to other merchants) or to invest in Europe's nascent industrial economy, whether directly or indirectly. In this way, Caribbean slavery, with its cheap labor, fueled European economic development by allowing extra European capital that could have been used for wage labor in the Caribbean to enter other areas of the economy, including, indirectly, European factories, which would later mass-produce goods for both European and colonial markets. In this particular example, Caribbean producers enabled European consumers to increase their consumption, growing the economy and transforming it. Although sugar was the main resource being produced with slave labor in

the Caribbean islands, coffee, cocoa, cattle and timber—as well as a smatter-
ing of other products, such as cotton, tobacco and indigo—were also being
produced.[6] In no case did Europeans or those of mixed race do much more
than supervise the agricultural labor performed by the slaves. Food was
generally imported in these economies, although a number of Caribbean
islands found that allowing slaves time to produce their own food diminished
the likelihood of revolt and increased the likelihood that slaves would
live more than a few years. Although these actions certainly helped improve
local conditions for the slaves, they did not challenge the slave system in
any meaningful way, allowing it to continue through the mature phase
of Caribbean colonialism. But these actions did provide a useful model for
subsequent colonists in other places around the world who needed a relatively docile labor force to extract what European colonists came to demand.

Sugar production with slave labor provides the main way that most
scholars understand the Caribbean's mature colonialism. It is an accurate
depiction of virtually all of the colonies, regardless of which European power
controlled the island. Colonies that did not grow much sugar were certainly
involved in exporting it to Europe; places like Dutch St. Eustatius were little
more than transshipment ports. Caribbean sugar was not consumed by
its producers; rather, it was shipped across the Atlantic Ocean and purchased
by Europeans, who increased the demand for the crop, causing the number
of slaves in the Caribbean islands to rise in order to increase production
to meet demand. This cycle continued into the nineteenth century.

Rising consumption on one side of the Atlantic required more than
just increased production on the other. It also required a regular distribution
network, which of course the Caribbean had. Throughout the period
of mature colonialism, trading practices were at once extremely restrictive
and clearly defined in law. All of the European powers, with the exception
of the Dutch, limited trade and proscribed certain activities. In general, trade
between Europe and the Americas had to be carried out in ships that
belonged to the mother country and that were manned with crews consisting
of a certain percentage of that country's nationals. In Spain and France, for
example, only certain ports had been authorized to receive the colonial trade.
Prohibitive tariffs were introduced in order to dissuade foreign produce
and manufactures from entering either the colonies or the metropoles. And
in many places, price supports guaranteed European merchants a minimum

---

[6] See Verene A. Shepherd (ed.), *Slavery Without Sugar: Diversity in Caribbean Economy since
the Seventeenth Century* (Gainesville, FL: University of Florida Press, 2002).

return on their investments. Caribbean sugar magnates had precious little choice about where to sell their sugar legally.

Although these restrictions were widespread throughout the Atlantic World, they were also regularly ignored or challenged. European colonists in the Americas realized that the commercial policies under which they lived had been designed to benefit European traders, by creating for them (or actually a subgroup of them) a monopoly on trade with their country's colonies. The resulting policies were not well regarded by those actually living in the Caribbean. Island residents rightly argued that the trading restrictions took money out of their pockets, requiring them to buy both provisions and consumer goods from the mother country that were either more expensive than or inferior to things they could get closer to home. Moreover, they had to wait until ships from the mother country arrived to buy anything, despite having unmet needs and shortages on a regular basis. (On occasion, and especially during wartime, some colonies opened their ports to anyone, in order to get enough provisions to feed the slaves.) Although commercial policy ensured a regular system of trade across the Atlantic, the very same merchant houses that argued to keep commercial restrictions in place also regularly and repeatedly violated them.

Smuggling therefore became endemic to the region. And everything was smuggled, from slaves who had been brought from a neighboring island, to sugar from one country's colony to be exported as sugar from the colony into which it was smuggled, to fancy clothing that would otherwise not have been available, to food from North America. All of this was done in plain view of imperial authorities, from customs collectors to governors, from sailors to admirals. Local government officials knew that challenging smuggling activities risked upsetting the populations who were smuggling, which had a potential negative side effect. Those populations had the ability to make the colony ungovernable, by raising complaints to those in Europe actually tasked with running the empire. They could also resort to bad local behavior, by throwing up challenges to whatever policies the governor intended to implement. There were no shortage of conflicts between local governors and the planter elite over how vigorously to enforce commercial restrictions or when to open the ports to foreign trade because a food shortage was developing. Local planters could also cause the governor to be recalled to Europe, and be forced to explain himself, which had the discrete advantage of removing a potential rule enforcer from the island and not enforcing unpopular laws and policies. What becomes clear from all of this is that trading policy was created for the convenience of the metropole, and not for those who were actual producers. This sadly also proved to be the case in Europe's subsequent colonies, again suggesting that examining the Caribbean, and considering it as a crucible, will provide valuable insight for world historians looking at later European expansion into Africa and Asia. Or to put it another way, rather than starting their examinations of imperialism with what happened after industrialization or the American Revolution, it behooves scholars to consider looking to the Caribbean—looking backwards to find a large number of historical antecedents.

Although commerce between the Caribbean and Europe largely helps to define the mature colonial period, it does not tell the whole of the story. Over the course of the seventeenth and eighteenth centuries, Europeans fought many wars with each other. Those wars were also fought in the Caribbean, as the colonies were dragged into the parent countries' conflicts. As a result, colonies could sometimes change from being Spanish to British or from French to British (and vice versa). While this created problems for some colonists, in general, such transitions happened relatively gracefully. But ways around new commercial regulations were almost always continued, even if it meant slightly adapting them to the behavior of the new country's legal regime and its enforcers. The colonists looked after themselves and their slaves—by consistently trying to get waivers of policy that would allow food importation from neighboring islands and from North America. The ways in which colonies changed hands and became involved in European wars also suggests that the Caribbean region offers fertile comparisons—historical antecedents—to those who are interested in more recent empires, where world wars involved conscripting subjugated populations.

Rebellion and decolonization

The Caribbean region generally disappears from world history after the plantation economy reaches full speed and the last pirates are eradicated, sometime in the first half of the eighteenth century. In a way, this makes perfect sense, as global forces had begun to move on. The Caribbean does appear again at two other moments, which happen to be related—although a century and a half chronologically separates them. The first is the creation of the state of Haiti. This began as a slave rebellion in 1792, and was deeply influenced by both the American and French Revolutions. It was, in fact, a protracted series of battles, with the stated political positions of the sides changing on a very regular basis. The French revolutionaries who wound up controlling the colonies did not quite know what to do about granting equality to anyone in their very profitable sugar colony, Saint Domingue, despite demand from the *gens de couleur* for equality and furious resistance to this from the island's white population.

At some moments, the French were prepared to grant independence, and at other moments, they contemplated re-conquering the island and re-imposing slavery. The Haitian Revolution (as it is popularly called, although Haiti did not exist at the start of the war) went on for several phases and for over a decade, but it is nevertheless significant for being the most successful slave revolt in modern world history. It demonstrates to historians, as it did to slave-holders, just how violent slave populations could be when pushed to the brink. Since it resulted in France being forced to give up its colony, it is also properly classified as decolonization, which generally happened much later for the rest of the Caribbean. What happened in Haiti set a pattern for later developments. The way in which the other European colonial powers rallied around France when it was kicked out of the colony, even trying to help it retake Haiti, provides an early example of the ways in which colonial powers would coordinate to try to figure out how best to decolonize, or avoid decolonizing, their colonies. France was also indemnified for its loss, setting a pattern for later examples of other colonial powers being compensated when they lost their colonies.

The second moment when the Caribbean region sometimes enters into general world historical discussion is decolonization. This movement generally took place around the Caribbean in the twentieth century, after World War II. Many scholars consider the Cuban Revolution led by Fidel Castro to be the most significant event to take place within this historical process. Like Haiti, the Cuban Revolution was a violent mutiny against those in power. Unlike Haiti, however, the colonial power, Spain, had given up on Cuba decades before, after some violent uprisings and belated efforts to have it successfully join the plantation complex. This allowed the United States to fill the gap, becoming an unofficial (some might say neo-) colonial power. Because the Cuban Revolution took place at the height of the Cold War, it is not at all surprising that the period's competing ideologies of capitalism and Communism came to center stage in the debate over what Castro's Cuba ought to look like. Cuba then became a case study for the Cold War in the Americas and the proxy battles that took place with some frequency between Moscow and Washington.

Apart from these two moments, the Caribbean's general position in the nineteenth and twentieth centuries remains somewhat peripheral to the field of world history; it had already gone through what the rest of the world was dealing with as it integrated into or resisted the European global order. This is extremely unfortunate, as societies in Africa and Asia, to say nothing of New Zealand and Oceania, might have been able to glean something of some value from studying the history of global connections that emanated from the Caribbean several generations earlier. Despite this lack of attention, Caribbean societies were hardly stagnant, as there were continued ways to resist the increasing poverty of the (now-emancipated) population as Afro-Caribbeans worked to find new economic approaches that the largely white plantocracy could not accept. Moreover, as empires expanded globally, those whites who held political office generally sought to bring in new ethnic groups, especially Indians and Chinese, to serve as buffers between free black populations and the planters. All of this begs the question of why the Caribbean colonies did not find a way out of colonization.

There were generally two things that prevented the eighteenth-century Caribbean colonies from declaring their independence and opting to go it alone. First, the colonies generated enough profit, or at least enough credit, for enough (white) people that ending the colonial system's restricted, but protected, trade never became a high priority. It is quite possible that full national independence could have produced better results, but the risk was not something that those in power in the Caribbean could easily tolerate. So they stuck with what they—and their ancestors—knew. Second and more important was the problem of slavery. The United States had a much smaller slave population, as a proportion of total population, at its independence than did the Caribbean during the same period. The latter region's white minority could not envision a world without slavery or a world with slavery, for that matter, without a large army provided by the colonial state to prevent and extinguish uprisings. It is possible that the colonists could have raised their own militaries, or otherwise paid for protection, but given the frequent complaints of Caribbean governors that the planters did not like to pay for their island's defenses, this would not have been easy. So, instead, the plantocracy doubled down on slavery—seeking to find ways to remain profitable within a slave system that coincidentally allowed them to remain in power.

The subject of decolonization is more properly the subject of another essay; suffice it to say here that the established planter classes at the turn of the nineteenth century did not generally choose to make demands of their European governments. The slaves found other ways to gain control over their lives and, eventually, after they had been emancipated by the mid-century, cobbled together livelihoods as free men and women. Perhaps such small improvements were all that the residents of small societies could have expected, given that they were now on the periphery of the European empire, yet they had once been at the core of it. There is surely a model in here for world historians. Gazing into the crucible of Caribbean history could easily reveal it to them.

FURTHER READING

Beckles, Hilary and Verene Shepherd (eds.), *Caribbean Slave Society: A Student Reader* (Kingston: Ian Randle Publishers, 1991).

Blackburn, Robin, *The Making of New World Slavery, From the Baroque to the Modern: 1492–1800* (London: Verso, 1997).

The Overthrow of Colonial Slavery, 1776–1848 (London: Verso, 1988).

Cateau, Heather and Rita Pemberton (eds.), *Beyond Tradition: Reinterpreting the Caribbean Historical Experience* (Kingston: Ian Randle Publishers, 2006).

Columbus, Christopher, *The Four Voyages*, J. M. Cohen (trans.) (New York: Penguin Classics, 1992).

Crosby, Alfred W., *The Columbian Exchange: Biological and Cultural Consequences of 1492* (Westport, CT: Greenwood Press, 1972).

Curtin, Philip, *The Atlantic Slave Trade: A Census* (Madison, WI: University of Wisconsin Press, 1970).

The Rise and Fall of the Plantation Complex: Essays in Atlantic History (Cambridge University Press, 1990).

Deerr, Noel, *The History of Sugar* (London: Chapman & Hall, 1949–50).

Dubois, Laurent, *Avengers of the New World: The Story of the Haitian Revolution* (Cambridge, MA: Belknap Press, 2004).

Dunn, Richard S., *Sugar and Slaves: The Rise of the Planter Class in the English West Indies, 1624–1713* (Chapel Hill, NC: University of North Carolina Press, 1972).

Emmer, P. C., *The Dutch in the Atlantic Economy, 1580–1880: Trade, Slavery and Emancipation* (Aldershot: Ashgate, 1998).

Exquemelin, A. O., *The Buccaneers of America* (New York: DigiReads, 2010).

Higman, B. W., *A Concise History of the Caribbean* (Cambridge University Press, 2011).

Karras, Alan L., *Smuggling: Contraband and Corruption in World History* (Lanham, MD: Rowman & Littlefield, 2010).

Sojourners in the Sun: Scots Migration to Jamaica and the Chesapeake, 1740–1820 (Ithaca, NY: Cornell University Press, 1992).

Knight, Franklin, *The Caribbean: The Genesis of a Fragmented Nationalism* (Oxford University Press, 1978).

McNeill, J. R., *Mosquito Empires: Ecology and War in the Greater Caribbean, 1620–1914* (Cambridge University Press, 2010).

Palmié, Stephan and Francisco Scarano (eds.), *The Caribbean: A History of the Region and Its Peoples* (University of Chicago Press, 2011).

Rediker, Marcus, *Between the Devil and the Deep Blue Sea: Merchant Seamen, Pirates, and the Anglo-American Maritime World* (Cambridge University Press, 1987).

Richardson, Bonham, *The Caribbean in the Wider World, 1492–1992: A Regional Geography* (Cambridge University Press, 1992).

Shepherd, Verene, *Slavery without Sugar: Diversity in Caribbean Economy and Society since the Seventeenth Century* (Gainesville, FL: University of Florida Press, 2002).

Shepherd, Verene, Bridget Brereton and Barbara Bailey (eds.), *Engendering History: Caribbean Women in Historical Perspective* (London: Palgrave McMillan, 1995).

Sheridan, Richard, *Sugar and Slavery: An Economic History of the British West Indies, 1623–1775* (Baltimore, MD: Johns Hopkins University Press, 1974).

Stinchcombe, Arthur, *Sugar Island Slavery in the Age of Enlightenment: The Political Economy of the Caribbean World* (Princeton University Press, 1995).

Tarrade, Jean, *Le Commerce Colonial de la France á la fin de l'Ancien Régime* (Paris: Presses Universitaires de France, 1972).

UNESCO, *General History of the Caribbean*, 6 vols. (London: UNESCO, 1997–2011).

Williams, Eric, *Capitalism and Slavery* (Chapel Hill, NC: University of North Carolina Press, 1994).

From Columbus to Castro: A History of the Caribbean, 1492–1969 (New York: Vintage, 1984).

17

Crossroads region: the Mediterranean

FILIPPO DE VIVO

In the summer of 1499, disastrous news reached Venice, provoking panic on the market and ruining several companies and banks. In previous years, the Ottomans had seized many of the republic's outposts on the Greek mainland. Now, in their first serious victory at sea, they crushed the Venetian fleet in the Southern Adriatic, and incidentally captured a small port in the Gulf of Corinth, Lepanto, that would later become the focal point of the Christian states' most famous counteroffensive against the sultan. In the same charged months of 1499, Venetian merchants, who had been ordered to devote all their great galleys to the war effort and away from trade, heard that the Portuguese had reached India by circumnavigating Africa. One of them, who initially believed the exploration to have been conducted by Christopher Columbus, annotated in disbelief: 'these news and their consequences are huge, if they are true'.[1] As we know, it was the first of a series of ventures that would soon enable Lisbon to redirect much of the spice trade away from its traditional routes.

War and discovery, then, determined – or were long considered to determine – a symbolic turning point, epitomising the decline not just of Venice, but of the Mediterranean as a whole. Following the rise of the Ottomans in the east and the first oceanic discoveries in the west, what had once been the cradle of civilization turned into a battlefield between fanatically opposed blocks, an embattled frontline that, moreover, became increasingly irrelevant as new powers came to dominate the world, and new routes to bypass the old sea.

Closer consideration leads to a different interpretation. The Venetians, who first heard of the Portuguese feat from commercial agents based in Egypt, quickly dispatched envoys to Lisbon in order to assess the extent of

---

[1] Girolamo Priuli, *I diarii*, 3 vols. (Bologna: Zanichelli, 1912–41), vol. I, p. 153.

the challenge; they later offered themselves as intermediaries for the spices' further transportation to Antwerp. Meanwhile, the Mamluk sultan asked Venice for aid in building a fleet to fight the Portuguese, and the Venetians went as far as making projects for cutting the Suez isthmus. Within two years, moreover, Venice and Istanbul were again at peace. The deal was brokered by Andrea Gritti, a Venetian merchant who had lived for twenty years in Istanbul, and acted as an informal representative when diplomatic communication failed. In the following decades, the Ottomans went on to capture Egypt and unify the Red Sea, before turning against the Portuguese in a global war that extended through India to Sumatra. These developments reveal not fracture, but interconnectedness, not decline caused by provincialisation, but resilience resulting from global knowledge and contacts.

How, then, are we to interpret this crisis and the long period in which it took place? Was this a time of stiffening frontiers or of increasing connections, both between the shores of the Mediterranean and between it and the world beyond? Historians who focus on political and military events have long underlined the emergence of opposite blocks, and described the power struggle as a clash of civilisations. By contrast, the most influential twentieth-century historian of the early modern Mediterranean, Fernand Braudel, insisted that deep geographical structures and long-term economic conjunctures made for a fundamental unity of the region, transcending political and religious boundaries. More recently, anthropologically trained cultural historians have underlined less the unity of the sea than the high degree of connections among the diverse societies that thrived on its shores since ancient times, on both the macro-scale of long-distance trade and the micro-level of local life. Economic historians have concerned themselves with the social and cultural preconditions that made regular long-distance trade possible, while historians of so-called high culture – ideas, art, architecture – have underlined cross-pollination, whether in the form of attentive study or deforming stereotype. As part of these shifts in scholarly attitudes and agendas, we can now also benefit from far wider research on the Ottoman Empire and North Africa than could Braudel's generation, and these areas can finally be integrated into our understanding of the region as a whole.

Emerging frontiers

In order to understand the true significance of the contacts that, as we shall see, so many people and institutions were willing to institute across boundaries, we first need to take into account the massive rifts that divided the sea. They were cultural and political more than geographical. A narrow space dotted with reprovisioning points that made navigation relatively easy, the Mediterranean was since ancient times a region marked by a high degree of intense exchanges. Historians now agree that both the fall of the Roman Empire and the Arabic conquests had changed, but not ended, these strong traditions. Since the Norman conquest of Sicily and the Crusades in the eleventh century, Christians controlled most crucial islands and peninsulas. What changed in the fifteenth century was that this long Western domination gave way to polarisation, breaking the sea into hostile spheres of influence.

The rise of Muslim powers brought substantial aggregation and consolidation to the eastern basin. Following the death of Temür in 1405, the last remnants of the Byzantine Empire and a host of Muslim and Christian statelets in Anatolia and the Aegean fell first to the Mamluk rulers or Egypt and then to the Ottomans, a Turkic tribe originating from Central Asia. The Ottomans' new imperial expansion climaxed with the highly symbolic capture of Constantinople in 1453. In the following decades, they also expanded their dominions in the Balkans (which they had entered in the previous century), annexed Albania, permanently secured a foothold on the eastern coast of the Adriatic, and also briefly captured a number of towns on the heel of the Italian peninsula. In their seemingly unstoppable advance, they defeated the Mamluks in 1517 and went on to subdue the caliphates of North Africa. Meanwhile, the new Saadian dynasty unified Morocco and in 1578 crushed the Portuguese. Thus, the entire coastline from the Balkans through Anatolia and the Maghreb to the Atlantic was in Muslim hands.

The rise of Muslim sea power was due in part to the Ottomans' vassals on the Barbary coast, who operated the pirate centres of Algiers and Tunis in the west, but above all to solid control of the coasts and effective patrolling in the eastern basin. Traumatic as this might have been for Christian powers and churchmen, it brought about a security not seen since late antiquity to the vast area stretching from the Bosphorus to Egypt, where Christian raids had until then been a regular feature. This made it possible to protect both traditional trading routes connecting the Mediterranean to Asia, via the Black Sea, and to the Indian Ocean, via the Red Sea. In due course, the Ottomans also captured the last large islands that were still in Christian hands in the east: Rhodes (1522), Cyprus (1573) and Crete (1669).

Meanwhile, the western basin fell under Christian control. The Aragonese, who ruled over Catalonia and the Balearic islands, captured Sicily in 1392 and completed the subjection of Sardinia in 1409. Under Alfonso the

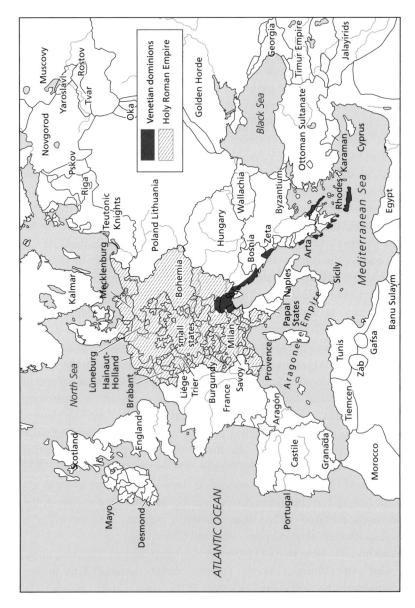

17.1 Europe and the Mediterranean c. 1400

Magnanimous (1416 to 1458), they defeated the Genoese, secured a stronghold in Corsica and annexed the kingdom of Naples, including the whole of southern Italy. In parallel fashion to the Ottomans, but building on solid nautical traditions, they thus put together an impressive 'thalassocracy', a far-flung state united by systematic and frequent navigation, and benefiting the great ports of Barcelona and Valencia. As the Portuguese captured Ceuta in 1415 and the Castilians Gibraltar in 1462, the Western Mediterranean became an overwhelmingly Christian area, with the consequent decline of once flourishing Muslim ports such as Malaga, Almería and Ceuta itself. In contrast to the eastern basin, however, the west saw competition between different powers, especially Spain and France, which both at this time emerged from protracted periods of division and internal war. In 1442, Alfonso expelled from Naples the Florentines who had dominated trade under the Angevin crown, in favour of Catalan merchants; from 1494 onwards, France and Spain were locked in a long military struggle for the control of the rich industries and ports of the Italian peninsula.

The clash between Muslim, mainly Ottoman, power in the east, and Christian, mainly Spanish, power in the west developed along a double frontier. One ran between north and south in the western basin, opposing Italian and Aragonese, later Spanish, fleets to those of the Ottomans and of their allies and dependents in North Africa. The other separated the western from the eastern basins. It is no coincidence that some of the greatest and most protracted clashes of the whole period took place along that border, as in the contest for Tripoli (1510 to 1551) and Tunis (1534 to 1574), the siege of Malta (1565), and the great naval battles of Prevesa (1538) and Lepanto (1571). The latter especially was a great symbol of Christian recovery, but, by that time, a stalemate was reached that was to last substantially until the end of the early modern period, as the Ottomans refrained from pursuing domination in the west and even Spain opened diplomatic negotiations with the Porte.

Between violence and adaptation

War had a serious impact on the ways in which people lived and related to one another on all shores of the Mediterranean, not least because they provoked displacement on a scale rarely seen before this period. In the fifteenth century, faced with the Ottoman invaders, scores of Greek-speaking Christian subjects of the old Byzantine emperors escaped west, while the completion of the Reconquista paved the way for the expulsion of Jews and

17.2 Europe and the Mediterranean c. 1750

Venetian dominions
Holy Roman Empire

Muscovy-Rus

Georgia
Persia

Black Sea

Ottoman Empire

Poland-Lithuania

Baltic Sea

Sweden

Denmark

Mecklenburg

Bavaria

Habsburg Lands

Venice

Mediterranean Sea

Ottoman Empire

North Sea

Denmark

Hanover

Netherlands

England

Scotland

Saxony

Switz.

Trier

France

Savoy

Tuscany

Corsica

Sardinia

Kingdom of the Two Sicilies

Malta

Bay of Biscay

Spain

Portugal

Fez-Morocco

ATLANTIC OCEAN

Muslims, who in huge numbers moved east and south. War did not dominate Mediterranean life in this period, however, and in fact was relatively rare. The Ottoman envoy bringing the declaration of war that would lead to the War of Cyprus and the Battle of Lepanto in 1571 knew as much: 'with a pale face and trembling voice, he said [to the doge]: "Your Serenity rest well, this war will not last forever, and then we shall again make peace"'.[2]

Especially since the end of the sixteenth century, open war gave way to more endemic violence, occasionally masked by the rhetoric of religious fervour, but in fact operated by mixed crews against co-religionists as much as infidels. Piracy increased to an extent not seen since the Saracens in the tenth century, as practised more or less systematically by groups of all religions, causing insecurity among merchants and wreaking terror on coastal villages and towns. Southern Italians feared the incursions of Barbary corsairs operating from their bases in North Africa, especially Algiers, Tripoli and Tunis, just as the Arabs feared the slave-raids of the Christian Knights of St John, operating a sort of permanent crusade first from Rhodes and, after 1530, from Malta.[3]

It would be wrong to divide pirates too neatly along religious lines, however, as they also included Orthodox Greek subjects of the Ottomans, Latin-Christian pirates based on small remnants of Aegean fiefs gained during the crusades, and Uskok Croatians and Slavs operating from the dominions of the Austrian Habsburgs, as well as Dutch and English Protestants who found employment with the Barbary corsairs. Unsurprisingly, Neapolitan officials complained with equal strength about the 'Affricani' and the French, whom they regarded as supporting pirates.[4] The response against such piratical activities equally crossed confessional lines in occasionally surprising ways. In 1464, the Knights of Rhodes stopped two Venetian galleys on the way from Alexandria to Tunis and seized all Muslim and Jewish passengers despite the protests of the commanders. Anxious to protect its trade with Egypt, the Venetian Senate sent the war fleet – then supposed to engage in war against the Ottomans – to Rhodes, where it ravaged the island until all prisoners were handed back.[5]

---

[2] Venice, Archivio di Stato, *Collegio, Esposizioni Principi*, register 2, fol. 3r.

[3] Michel Fontenay, *La Méditerranée entre la croix et le croissant: navigation, commerce, course et piraterie (XVIe-XIXe siècle)* (Paris: Classiques Garnier, 2010).

[4] Rossella Cancila, 'Introduzione. Il Mediterraneo assediato', in Rossella Cancila, (ed.), *Mediterraneo in armi (secc. XV–XVIII)*, 2 vols. (Palermo: Mediterranea, 2007), vol. 1, p. 64.

[5] Frederic C. Lane, *Venice: A Maritime Republic* (Baltimore, MD: Johns Hopkins University Press, 1973), pp. 349–50.

As these episodes suggest, if some states chose war, others preferred pragmatic adaptation. As intra-confessional rivalries trumped hostility to the infidel, new and unprecedented diplomatic contacts became possible between fellow rivals of a common enemy. In the 1480s and 1490s, Venice was prepared to make more or less secret deals with the Ottomans against the Aragonese in the Adriatic. In the 1520s, Francis I of France made deals first with the Barbary corsairs and then with the Ottoman sultan himself, urging him to attack the Spanish possessions in Italy. In 1543, a Franco-Ottoman fleet captured Nice (part of the dominions of the duke of Savoy, Spanish ally and imperial subject), after which the Turkish fleet wintered in Toulon and for six months turned the city's cathedral into a mosque.[6] Joint operations continued into the 1550s against the Balearic Islands and the Neapolitan coastline. Both sides regarded these alliances as temporary measures barely permissible under Christian or Islamic ideology – yet they renewed their agreements time and again. Meanwhile, on the other side of both the sea and the religious divide, the Hafsid dynasty of Algiers tried to stop the Ottoman advance through an alliance with Spain itself.

By the early seventeenth century, such contacts extended Mediterranean diplomatic networks beyond the Mediterranean itself, as several enemies of the Ottoman Empire, including the papacy, cultivated contacts with Persia. In 1600, the sultan of Morocco sent an envoy to the Queen of England to foster an anti-Spanish alliance, while England and the United Provinces pursued similar goals by establishing permanent diplomatic relations with the Porte itself in 1582 and 1615. By the 1750s, even Vienna–Istanbul alliances became conceivable, as a way of countering the common Russian enemy. For their part, in order to create buffers against the Habsburgs, the Ottomans were ready to rule through Christian dependencies, such as Transylvania and Walachia, and they tolerated the vassalage of Dubrovnik, a Catholic republic whose rulers had in Istanbul the same recognition as the North African *beys*.

The evolving framework of exchange

Meanwhile, a series of disparate developments facilitated mobility and trade even in the face of war and piracy. Some of them consolidated earlier advances in commercial techniques that helped to meet the burgeoning costs deriving from the permanent danger of armed encounter. Different forms of contracts

---

[6] Christine Isom-Verhaaren, *Allies with the Infidel: The Ottoman and French Alliance in the Sixteenth Century* (London: I. B. Tauris, 2011), pp. 114–40.

made it possible to collect investments from associates and so contain the costs for each investor, whether with agreements relating to single voyages or with more long-lasting partnerships. The maritime insurance business also helped to spread the risks deriving from insecure navigation – although skyrocketing premiums occasionally indicated real difficulties.[7]

Foreseeing dangers and exploiting business opportunities required information, which in this age travelled along markedly improved channels to reach unprecedented levels of distribution. Medieval networks of merchants exchanged regular letters with detailed news, but in the fifteenth century, the practice grew more systematic and could avail itself of better communication systems; later, the model of the merchant letter led to the diffusion of manuscript newsletters – *avvisi, avisos* – prepared by professionals for customers paying a subscription. From the seventeenth century onwards, printed newspapers kept people abreast of developments on both sides of the sea, while travel literature became a popular genre. One should not exaggerate the progressive, unifying effect of the press – gazettes also served to inspire hatred for the enemy, and travel accounts popularised received stereotypes as much as they spread accurate knowledge. But one way or another, the availability of information was a product of increased communication across the sea that also permitted greater mobility. While economic historians focus on the exchange of goods, historians of information have shown that news influenced the social and professional behaviour even of people who had little exposure to the luxury items that were a staple of Mediterranean trade; as we saw at the start, the arrival of news determined the price of commodities and shaped the performance of markets.[8] Systematic knowledge was a prerequisite of long-distance credit relations and trade cooperation.

A series of nautical innovations also helped because they facilitated long-distance sailing. Here, it is important to remember that the notion of dominion of the sea only really applied to coastal waters. As the Venetians found out on even as narrow a space as the Adriatic, enemy navigation could only effectively be prevented close to land, detecting and attacking ships or denying them access to ports. From the fifteenth century onwards, more

---

[7] Alberto Tenenti, *Naufrages, Corsaires et Assurances maritimes à Venise, 1592–1609* (Paris: SEVPEN, 1959).

[8] Filippo de Vivo, *Information and Communication in Venice: Rethinking Early Modern Politics* (Oxford University Press, 2007); and John-Paul Ghobrial, *The Whispers of Cities: Information Flows in Istanbul, London, and Paris in the Age of William Trumbull* (Oxford University Press, 2013).

sailors could steer longer courses, thanks to the diffusion of portolan charts, first introduced in the previous century, and to the improvement of astronomic navigation. Most importantly, ships grew larger and less dependent on oar-power, therefore requiring smaller crews and, so, fewer calls in ports.[9] From about 1400, there was a steady increase in the size of the square-rigged round ship, or cog, recently introduced from Northern Europe, but perfected with the addition of a second mast and of sails derived from the autochthonous tradition of the lateen. Their manoeuvring required fewer crewmen, and they carried larger quantities of cargo and could defend themselves with heavier cannons. In Venice, the number of ships trading with the east did not substantially alter in the period 1448 to 1558, but the overall tonnage increased by more than a third.[10] By the end of the century, they completely displaced the galley for commerce, although more manoeuvrable light galleys, which could add oar-power to wind propulsion, were still the backbone of navies at Lepanto. Naval construction did not essentially change in the rest of the period, but ships grew even larger, with the appearance of carracks and galleons, and later of frigates and ships-of-the-line. With multiple decks and three or four masts rigged with more numerous and smaller sails, they could navigate closer to the wind and stay at sea longer than any of their predecessors.

The development of heavy artillery was another technological innovation that had far-reaching consequences including, paradoxically, making life in Mediterranean ports more rather than less secure. Gunpowder was originally imported from China, and in the fifteenth century applied to ever larger cannons, first in continental Europe and then in the Ottoman Empire. In the very same year, 1453, the Ottomans made large-scale use of artillery to knock down the ancient walls of Constantinople, and the French to achieve the victory which put an end to the Hundred Years War. Artillery made naval attacks on ports more difficult. Once defended by well-placed cannons, no harbour could be stormed, as had previously happened frequently, such as the pillaging of Beirut and Alexandria in 1422, by two Catalan ships unhindered by local archers.[11] Of course, cities could be subject to devastating bombardments, as Genoa was to find out at the hands of Louis XIV's fleet in 1684. But even the French could not force their way into the harbour.

---

[9] Richard W. Unger (ed.), *Shipping and Economic Growth, 1350–1850* (Leiden: Brill, 2011).

[10] Frederic C. Lane, *Venetian Ships and Shipbuilders of the Renaissance* (Baltimore, MD: Johns Hopkins University Press, 1992).

[11] Eliyahu Ashtor, *Levant Trade in the Later Middle Ages* (Princeton University Press, 1983), p. 287.

A final point relates to the institutional framework of cross-cultural contacts and trade. In rejecting Braudel's idea of the unity of the Mediterranean, political historians have rightly shown that he neglected the agency of states, but they have focused exclusively on the aggressive role of states in foreign politics. However, states also, and increasingly, created the infrastructure for economic exchange. For example, they granted foreign merchants concessions, protected quarters and legal security; they included clauses for the respect of merchant shipping in their diplomatic treaties; they established and maintained networks of consular representatives, in agreement with merchants and often drawn from the merchants themselves. Non-state actors sometimes did this as well, including pirates such as the Knights of Malta, who issued safe-conducts, until the French monarchy intervened to rein in their pirateering. With encouragement came regulation: this was the great age of bureaucracy, ranging from health checks to customs and borders control, to the issuing of travelling documents.[12]

Routes old and new

Such developments made it possible for traders to exploit commercial opportunities that were expanding as a result of growing demand for distant products. Between 1400 and 1800, the population recovered from the crisis of the Black Death and went on to increase massively on all Mediterranean shores. In the sixteenth century, the Ottoman Empire grew according to some from some 12 to perhaps 35 million.[13] Europe grew from about 80 million in 1500 to 104 million in 1600, then slowed down, reaching 115 million in 1700, but picked up again in the eighteenth century, reaching more than 150 million by 1800. As the period was also marked by increasing urbanization, the result was greater demand for agricultural products to feed and clothe increasingly large populations living far away from the fields.

A huge number of trading routes continued to tie together distant regions on either side of the borders described above. Of course, some declined, and the goods they once transported had to be sourced elsewhere. This is the case of alum – a crucial material for tanning and wool production, which the Genoese had long been trading from Anatolian mines through their base in Chios to the west. The Ottoman expansion led to a steep increase in taxes

---

[12] Claudia Moatti, (ed.), *La Mobilité des personnes en Méditerranée de l'Anqtiquité à l'époque moderne: procédures de controle et documents d'identification* (Rome: École française de Rome, 2004).

[13] Halil Inalcik and Donald Quataert, *An Economic and Social History of the Ottoman Empire, 1300–1914* (Cambridge University Press, 1994), p. 28.

and a drop in export. But Roman miners – helped by an expert who had long lived in Constantinople – discovered new sources in Latium, a feat which Pope Pius II described as 'a victory against the Turks', and this went on to feed a thriving commerce from Italy to France, England and Flanders.[14]

More often, conquest changed rather than stopped patterns of exchange, as new merchants took over old routes and built on the networks established by their predecessors. For example, it is true that Mehmed the Conqueror closed the Black Sea to Christian merchants, just as Byzantine emperors had done to non-Byzantine subjects until 1204. But the Ottomans put their monopoly at the service of profitable trade, first in Bursa and later in Istanbul. The latter grew to become a commercial centre for eastern–western exchange in a way that Constantinople had not been for a long time: crucial in the export of ceramics, cotton and foodstuffs, and in the mediation of long-distance commerce in silk, spices and porcelain from China and India. Historians no longer regard the Ottoman Empire as a 'warfare state' uninterested by commerce, and have recently underlined how the governing apparatus was keen to increase customs and the income generated by the rental of khans and covered markets. The Ottomans attracted foreign merchants with special privileges, and brought security to the crucial Istanbul–Alexandria route, which was the one most used at sea by their own subjects – in 1645, they unleashed war on Crete precisely in order to protect that route from unrelenting piracy.

The Venetians continued to play a solid role as intermediaries, especially as their traditional competitors, the Genoese, turned away from commerce to finance. In the fifteenth century, they sent regular convoys of merchant galleys (*mude*), protected by the state, along five regulated routes: Constantinople; Cyprus and Syria; Alexandria; Languedoc ('Aque morte') and Catalonia; England and Flanders. At the beginning of the sixteenth century, they added two more to North Africa. In the meantime, they also established fortified ports along the entire coast of the Adriatic, and so secured the movement of their galleys. The *mude* later shrank and eventually ended in 1564, but historians now agree that this should not be seen as a sign of absolute commercial decline. In fact, regulated convoys always only constituted a small proportion of Venetian trade, which between the late fifteenth and late sixteenth centuries made increasing use of large cogs and other round ships that required less state protection and regulation.[15]

---

[14] Jean Delumeau, *L'Alun de Rome, XVe–XIXe siècle* (Paris: SEVPEN, 1962), p. 21.
[15] Claire Judde de Larivière, *Naviguer, commercer, gouverner. Économie maritime et pouvoirs à Venise (XVe–XVIe siècles)* (Leiden: Brill, 2008).

Thereafter, Venice turned from a long-distance to a regional centre, loading goods originating from all outlying regions and then operating as a port of call for large foreign ships that knew they could quickly load and unload their cargoes there. But the Venetians also had to face unexpected competition – for example, from the collaboration between the papal city of Ancona and Dubrovnik, where merchants encouraged a new route across the Balkans. When Venice responded by investing in the coastal city of Split, further to the north, this in fact reinforced the new land route, which acquired considerable importance throughout the period, especially as it could be used through all seasons, compared to sailing, which was still restricted to some nine months of the year.

In the seventeenth century, French traders, who had long been over-shadowed by Catalan competitors, emerged as serious and later dominant players in east–west commerce, partly thanks to French cooperation with the Ottomans from the late sixteenth century onwards. In the seventeenth and eighteenth centuries, they organised large convoys – known as *caravanes* – to Syrian ports, where they met land traders who brought goods from further east. Even Muslims, including both merchants and pilgrims, made use of French ships in order to escape Maltese pirates. In the eighteenth century, French shipowners had to face increasing competition from Greek orthodox ones, who established themselves as the principal carriers on the sea routes of the eastern Mediterranean, whether on their own or on Muslim-owned ships.[16] But French merchants still dominated the north–south trade in the western Mediterranean, particularly between Marseilles, Algiers and Tunis.[17]

Expanding horizons

Long-established as well as recently introduced routes, then, undermined the frontiers that were emerging inside the Mediterranean. From the fifteenth century onward, such routes started intersecting with, and extending into, new ones, which expanded the horizons of the sea far from its close geographical boundaries. Thanks to the silk roads, European and Arabic merchants had long traded with China and India; but in the sixteenth century, the global framework in which they acted expanded massively as they were joined by explorers, soldiers, missionaries and permanent settlers.

---

[16] Molly Greene, *Catholic Corsairs and Greek Merchants: A Maritime History of the Mediterranean, 1450–1700* (Princeton University Press, 2010).

[17] Daniel Panzac, *La caravane maritime: marins européens et marchands ottomans en Méditerranée, 1680–1830* (Paris: CNRS, 2004).

The traditional historical consensus is that the European expansion across the Atlantic and in the Indian Ocean turned the Mediterranean from the centre of the medieval economy into a periphery of economic empires.[18] This Euro-centric perspective of one-way, westerly displacement is now giving way to one that highlights growing interconnections between all coasts of the sea *and* the rest of the world.

First, it was not just Christian European states that experienced an age of imperial expansion. In the course of the sixteenth and seventeenth centuries, the Ottomans also made gains that had profound effects on the Mediterranean's political and commercial relations with the outside world. To the south, they permanently secured the Red Sea and so eliminated the high taxes paid to the different emirs ruling its coastline; they established their control over the holy sites of Islam, and tried to assert themselves as protectors of Muslim pilgrims from three continents; and they seized large stretches of the Persian Gulf, which emerged as an alternative route in the spice trade, especially once the conquest of Baghdad in 1534 facilitated movement across Mesopotamia to Aleppo and Beirut. To the north, the Ottomans extended their influence over the Tatar Khanate and the Black Sea region. Meanwhile, they also asserted themselves as a global sea power, and from their new arsenal at Suez – provisioned with timber from Lebanon, sailcloth from Anatolia and gunners from Istanbul – they mustered a succession of daring campaigns in the Indian Ocean with expeditions as far as Sumatra. While fighting the Safavids in Persia, they also cultivated good relations with other Muslim powers in Gujarat and the Horn of Africa.[19] Meanwhile, at the other end of Africa, the Saadian sultan of Morocco captured the Songhay Empire in Mali in 1590 to 1591, the first time that a Mediterranean power established a permanent stronghold south of the Sahara desert. Throughout the period, moreover, Muslim merchants travelled on the backs of camels from North to Central Africa in search of gold, ivory and slaves destined for Mediterranean trade.

Second, the oceanic expansion of the sixteenth century resulted not so much in provincialisation, but in new opportunities for political, economic and cultural transactions with distant regions on a totally unprecedented scale. As is well known, the exploration of the New World drew from the experience of Mediterranean sailors and captains. But a city like Genoa did

---

[18] Immanuel Wallerstein, *The Modern World System*, 3 vols. (New York: Academic Press, 1974–80).
[19] Giancarlo Casale, *The Ottoman Age of Exploration* (Oxford University Press, 2010).

not just give birth to Columbus; it also financed Spain's Atlantic expeditions and participated in the profits. Regular advances of money from Genoa to Spain, earned in Mediterranean commerce, served in the wars of the Netherlands, and were repaid through an easterly flow of American silver from Spain through Italy to, eventually, the Levant.[20] In fact, it may be argued that the reason why the Ottoman Empire was interested in trading with Western Europe was because of America. Largely self-sufficient in terms of basic raw materials and foodstuffs, the empire had no substantial gold or silver mines, so it exported to European states in exchange for the bullion which the latter drew, directly or indirectly, from Mexico and Peru. It was partly through Istanbul that the impact of America's precious metals seriously expanded on a global scale, as Ottoman merchants used bullion to buy coffee, spices and silk from (respectively) Yemen, India and China.[21] Some Mediterranean cities availed themselves of growing colonial connections to act as intermediaries. Thus, in the period 1729 to 1788, Marseilles, a port that was central in intra-Mediterranean transport, saw its imports from the French Caribbean rise more than twelvefold.[22]

Just as with the new frontiers emerging inside the Mediterranean, so the expansion of the sea's horizons outside resulted in some changes to traditional patterns of exchange. Some routes declined, but others emerged. Thus, the Mediterranean spice trade lost importance compared to the routes south of Africa – especially when the latter became dominated not by the Portuguese, but, later, by the Dutch. Sugar cane, first imported from India, was successfully refined in warm islands such as Sicily, Crete and Cyprus in the fifteenth century; at that time it was also planted in the Azores and brought to the Caribbean. By 1600, Brazil became Europe's largest source of sugar.[23] But other products gained ground too, such as coffee. Cultivated in Yemen and first brewed along the Red Sea, it became a product of widespread consumption throughout Ottoman coffeehouses in the sixteenth century and, later, a staple of European (and American) drinking habits: from the Arabian Peninsula through the Mediterranean, coffee conquered

---

[20] Aurelio Musi, *Mercanti genovesi nel regno di Napoli* (Naples: Edizioni scientifiche italiane, 1996).

[21] Suraiya Faroqhi, *The Ottoman Empire and the World Around It* (London: I. B. Tauris, 2004), pp. 137–60.

[22] Pierre Goubert and Daniel Roche, *Les Français et l'Ancien Régime*, 2 vols. (Paris: Colin, 1984), vol. I, p. 326.

[23] Sidney Wilfred Mintz, *Sweetness and Power: The Place of Sugar in Modern History* (Harmondsworth: Penguin, 1985).

the world.[24] In reverse, some crops were imported from America but successfully commercialised to become mass commodities from their Mediterranean fields. Maize was cultivated in Egypt and is still known in Italy not under its Mesoamerican name, but as 'granturco' or 'Turkish grain'. For its part, tobacco, for a time known as 'bortugal' in Arabia, was imported to Anatolia and extensively cultivated there and in Egypt to feed the market both at home and in the rest of the Mediterranean.[25]

The late sixteenth century also saw an intensification in the contacts between Northern Europe and the Mediterranean, as English and Dutch traders increasingly came to compete directly with local merchants for trade. For a long time, for example, Venice had prevented Greek islanders from selling their highly valued currants directly to English merchants, but by the early seventeenth century this proved impossible.[26] Some historians have described this as a 'northern invasion', but this characterisation requires revision. Dutch and English ships were more active in long-distance voyages than in the regional networks, which remained in the hands of locals. In the eastern Mediterranean, the northerners never really displaced Greek Ottoman merchants who, in fact, launched their own 'eastern invasion' of the Atlantic.[27] Also, increased competition was not necessarily a bad thing. Favouring the local monopoly of traffic in and out of harbours such as Venice and Genoa had pushed up the price of shipping. By the late sixteenth century, freight charges began diminishing: what was a net loss for well-established investors constituted an opportunity for the more numerous smaller traders.

Many merchants, moreover, began enlisting the services of the shipbuilding industry in Northern Europe in order to tackle the decrease in timber from Mediterranean forests depleted by centuries of exploitation. In this sense, connections between distant regions helped to overcome a regional deficiency. The same goes for the trade in basic foodstuffs, as Mediterranean Europe saw a drop in the productivity of wheat, and so began to import it from the north and the east of the continent, especially from the

---

[24] Ralph S. Hattox, *Coffee and Coffeehouses: The Origins of a Social Beverage in the Medieval Near East* (Seattle, WA: University of Washington Press, 1985).

[25] Relli Shechter, *Smoking, Culture and Economy in the Middle East: The Egyptian Tobacco Market 1850–2000* (London: I. B. Tauris, 2006), pp. 15–26.

[26] Maria Fusaro, *Uva passa. Una guerra commerciale tra Venezia e l'Inghilterra (1540–1640)* (Venice: Il Cardo, 1996).

[27] Gelina Harlaftis, 'The "Eastern Invasion:" Greeks in Mediterranean Trade and Shipping in the Eighteenth and Early Nineteenth Centuries', in Maria Fusaro, Colin Heywood and Mohamed-Salah Omri (eds), *Trade and Cultural Exchange in the Early Modern Mediterranean* (London: I. B. Tauris, 2010), pp. 223–52.

Baltic area where, one after the other, the main Italian states established consular representations in the seventeenth century. Here, increasing reliance on non-Mediterranean products originated not from the impoverishment, but rather from the enrichment, of Mediterranean countries. For example, the renewed growth of Istanbul following centuries of contraction under the last Byzantine emperors meant that the city absorbed much of the grain produced in the Black Sea.

Rather than the provincialisation of the Mediterranean, the centuries between 1400 and 1800 saw the diversification of its trade into a new global framework bringing distant cultures and economies into regular contact. The export of manufactured goods from the Old to the New World shaped consumer habits in the Americas just as the ability to turn exotic luxuries into products for mass consumption lay at the heart of a consumer revolution in the Mediterranean.

Crossroads centres

Where did roads actually cross? The geography of the Mediterranean, with its numerous islands and peninsulas, together with the simultaneous presence of different political entities and cultural groups, created a particularly large number of places where the possibilities for economic and cultural exchange were especially thick, including regions, cities and, as we shall see, even smaller places.

On the edge of empires, large areas were defined as frontiers not so much by the presence of boundaries as by the long tradition of exchange between different religious, linguistic and ethnic groups on either side of those boundaries.[28] The spirit of jihad or crusade incited empires to conquest, but they showed markedly different attitudes to religious minorities in their midst. The Ottomans wished to protect Muslims – particularly pilgrims on alien roads – from the infidel, but they preferred to tolerate religious minorities (and occasionally majorities) in their own territories. They recognised and protected Orthodox and Armenian Christians, and Jews, in exchange for special taxes, and even granted official honours to their religious leaders, notably the Greek Orthodox patriarch and the chief rabbi. By contrast, Christian states enacted increasing repression of minorities in this period, perhaps because, divided by rivalry and competition, each ruler

---

[28] Peter Sahlins, *Boundaries: The Making of France and Spain in the Pyrenees* (Berkeley, CA: University of California Press, 1989).

had to reinforce the conformity of his subjects. Even relatively tolerant Christian cities such as Venice would have seemed hostile to non-Christian subjects of the sultan, in comparison with the freedom and coexistence back home. That Christians were prepared to live in the Muslim Mediterranean, while no openly Muslim group could be found in Western Europe, has to do with the difference in the treatment of minorities, not with the often-cited Islamic law that forbade Muslims to live in non-Muslim countries, a rule that had not prevented large Muslim communities from living under non-Muslim rule in Africa and Indonesia.

The Iberian kings, who had already allowed widespread violence against the Jews since the 1390s, forced them to convert or leave Iberia immediately after the capture of Granada in 1492. In the sixteenth century, a similar fate was reserved for Muslims even in regions that had long been 're-conquered' already, such as Valencia, where Muslims made up perhaps one-third of the population. Those who wished to retain their faith were expelled in 1502 from Castile and in 1525 from Aragon and Valencia. For some time, a degree of coexistence continued, as large communities of Moriscos went on living and working with little more than outward conformity to Christianity. But as enforcement stiffened, violence broke out, culminating in the Alpujarras rebellion of 1568 to 1571 followed by the traumatic deportation of some 300,000 Moriscos to North Africa forty years later.

And yet military conquests could not change culture overnight. Even in Valencia, the Spanish crown accepted the request of local Morisco leaders in 1528 that after conversion they would be free for two generations from any prosecution by the Inquisition: the authorities recognised that people could not shed all their customs at once.[29]

If, in the long run, all forms of religious dissent were repressed in Spain, other regions went through different developments. Crete, Venice's largest overseas territory, was long a crucial station on the trade routes between east and west; as an agriculturally prosperous island, it exported wine to Europe and olive oil to the Ottoman Empire. The different communities living on the island – Latin and Greek Christians as well as Muslims – were united by a high degree of conversion and intermarriage, and the main religious conflict was not between Christians and Muslims, but between Catholics and Orthodox, as the former – in control under Venice – hindered the latter's clergy, disestablished their bishopric and allowed no ties with the

---

[29] Tullio Halperín Donghi, 'Recouvrements de civilisation: les Morisques du royaume de Valencia au XVIe siècle', *Annales. Économies, Sociétés, Civilisations* 11 (1956), 168–9.

patriarch in Constantinople. Unsurprisingly, after the Ottoman conquest in 1669, the religiously Latin (but linguistically Greek) Christian elite left for Venice, but the Orthodox population was happy to stay and benefit from the large Ottoman trading network. The conversion rate was so high that soon the Ottoman military presence on the island was assured by formerly Christian soldiers, and most merchants became Muslims.[30]

In addition to old traditions of coexistence, the economy of trade brought familiarity with other cultures to entire regions. Long-distance routes passed through even landlocked regions, and in the process identified those valleys and passes as contact areas. Thus, in Bosnia – itself an area of mixed religion and culture populated by Orthodox, Catholics and Muslims, as well as Jews, Greeks, Vlachs, Roms and Armenians – the traders who moved between Istanbul, Split and Dubrovnik (and later Triest) became a regular presence that hugely benefited the local economy.[31] Other areas thrived on supplying goods and labour to important ports, which then redeployed both in long-distance commerce, as Catalonia did for Barcelona and Liguria for Genoa. Entire stretches of coast could thrive on commerce, especially in the earlier part of the period, when most maritime travelling consisted of short trips in sight of land. As shown in contemporary portolan maps, a huge number of ports dotted coastlines on all sides. At each stop, merchants and sailors exchanged part of their merchandise and information for local products which they either consumed on board or sold elsewhere. As long-distance exchange functioned through networks of small-scale interactions, the global and the local were tied together at all sorts of levels, and even small centres could develop strong connections with the rest of the world.

Where roads crossed, cities grew, and in turn they fuelled trade because they could muster investments, technologies and far-flung connections. We have already seen that this was a period of increasing urbanisation, leading to the formation of veritable metropolises. Around 1600, Istanbul had some 300,000 inhabitants (some estimate even more) and Cairo was beginning to emerge as a significant rival with some 200,000; Naples had as many as 400,000. The late sixteenth century also saw the creation of free ports, such as Livorno in Italy and Izmir in Anatolia, followed in the eighteenth century by papal Ancona and Habsburg Fiume and, especially, Triest. They thrived on their 'freedom', in the double sense that they attracted long-distant traders

---

[30] Molly Greene, *A Shared World: Christians and Muslims in the Early Modern Mediterranean* (Princeton University Press, 2000).

[31] Noel Malcolm, *Bosnia: A Short History* (London: Macmillan, 1994), pp. 43–118.

by granting customs reductions or exceptions, and because they allowed a degree of peaceful coexistence between different religious and ethnic communities. Livorno was home to the second largest Jewish community in the West after Amsterdam, at 10 per cent of the total population.[32] Izmir saw increasing numbers of English, Dutch and, to a lesser extent, French, shipping, while the city also attracted Sephardic Jews from Spain who contributed to the diffusion in Anatolia of a form of Spanish known as Ladino, still spoken today in some communities of modern Turkey.[33]

Some cities were special intermediaries on a number of levels. Thus, Dubrovnik, from 1472 a vassal of the sultan, benefited from this status to maintain rights of trade in the Black Sea; it enjoyed close relations to the north, with Venice, but traded in the west with Spanish Apulia and in the east with the Ottoman Balkans. It mediated not just in commodities, but also as a centre of information for the Spaniards and the popes about the Ottomans and, vice versa, about European powers in Istanbul. As neutral ground, it was also frequently chosen as a site for the exchange of prisoners.[34]

On a smaller scale, specific neighbourhoods can be described as global villages where patterns of exchange combined with the daily experience of mutual knowledge. In the Istanbul neighbourhood of Galata, for example, across the Golden Horn from the sultan's Topkapi palace, Latin and Orthodox Christians, Armenians, Jews and Turks lived side by side in a microcosm that at once represented all the different communities of the Mediterranean as a whole and also made it possible to overcome its macro conflicts. The Venetian ghetto at once enclosed the Jews of Venice, but also made it possible for them to live in the city; not only were there daily encounters between Jews and Christians, but also between Jews of different origins: Levantines, Ponentines, Germans and Italians.

Single buildings provided shelter for the encounters between foreigners and between foreigners and locals. On the other side of Venice's Grand Canal from the Ghetto, Ottoman merchants, including Muslims, found accommodation and storage space at the 'fondaco dei Turchi', whose rooms were

---

[32] Francesca Trivellato, *The Familiarity of Strangers: The Sephardic Diaspora, Livorno, and Cross-Cultural Trade in the Early Modern Period* (New Haven, CT: Yale University Press, 2009).

[33] Daniel Goffman, *Izmir and the Levantine World 1550–1650* (Seattle, WA: University of Washington Press, 1990).

[34] Bariša Krekić, *Dubrovnik: A Mediterranean Urban Society, 1300–1600* (Aldershot: Ashgate Variorum, 1997); and Nicolaas H. Biegman, *The Turco-Ragusan Relationship According to the Firmans of Murad III (1575–1595) Extant in the State Archives of Dubrovnik* (The Hague: Mouton, 1967); pp. 130–1.

formally assigned to two groups: 'Asiatic and Constantinopolans', and 'Bosnian and Albanians'. The word – which also applied to other hostelries, including the large German *fondaco* near Rialto – came from the Arabic, and was used in Middle Eastern cities too, where there were plentiful Venetian, Genoese, French and English *funduqs*.[35]

Crossroads areas were not just fixed points in space. Thousands of ships were mobile meeting places between people of different social and ethnic origins, and between them and the inhabitants of the ports they visited. As well as the sailors, officers and merchants, they embarked chaplains (who also served as notaries), doctors, barbers, diplomats, pilgrims and other paying passengers. Large Venetian galleys were also required to carry small groups of noblemen with the explicit purpose of furthering their mercantile education; from 1559, they had to employ pauper children as cabin boys. A Venetian commander advocated making place on his galley for an Orthodox priest because the Catholic one could not take the confessions of the largely Greek crews. On most ships, even the lowliest mariners were to some extent active participants in trade, because each had a right to collect and carry, freight-free, a small amount of goods that increased over time from 10 to 20 ducats for each galley oarsman. Aboard the more capacious carracks, the value was even greater, as the crews of between fifty and seventy could carry variable amounts, from half a ton for the deck hands to one and a half for craftsmen such as carpenters.[36] As ships entered a harbour, they were surrounded by swarms of small craft peddling a variety of foods and merchandise, while pilgrims describe *galeotti* going ashore and setting up booths to trade their wares at every stop.

Crossroads people

This brings us from the spaces to the human protagonists of encounters: the people for whom it was normal or necessary to travel along the routes we have seen so far, moving between different crossroads centres, or mediating between different groups in particular places. What was it like to live at the crossroads, in places where a large part of life was dominated by the coexistence between diverse languages, religions, ethnicities, dietary habits and dress?

---

[35] Olivia Remie Constable, *Housing the Stranger in the Mediterranean World: Lodging, Trade, and Travel in Late Antiquity and the Middle Ages* (Cambridge University Press, 2003).
[36] Lane, *Venice: A Maritime Republic*, pp. 356 and 382.

Some acquired spectacular expertise in crossing boundaries, like Hasan Al-Wazzan, known in the west as Ioannes Leo Africanus (1486 to 1554).[37] Born in Granada, in 1492 he took refuge with his family in Fez, was trained as a legal scholar and travelled as a diplomat to Songhay Mali and Mamluk Egypt (at the time of the Ottomans' conquest). Captured by Spanish pirates in 1518, he was given as a slave to Pope Leo X and baptised. He spent the next ten years in Rome writing, amongst other things, an Arabic grammar, possibly a bilingual translation of the Qur'an, and a description of Africa which was later translated into many European languages. He escaped probably during the sack of Rome and returned to Morocco. As an exile and later a captive, but also as a professional emissary and a man who spread great knowledge about distant lands, his life symbolises the capacity to adapt to events he could not control, by moving between different worlds.[38]

Many others chose to spend much of their lives travelling, and systematically turned the expertise gained into a source of recognition at home and abroad. Samuel Pallache (1550 to 1616),[39] a Jewish merchant from Fez, worked for the sultan of Morocco as an agent in the Netherlands, informed the Spanish, the Dutch and the Moroccans about one another, and was an active privateer.[40] Pietro della Valle (1586 to 1652) was a Roman scholar who acquired huge knowledge of Oriental cultures and languages. Having set out on a pilgrimage to the Holy Land in 1614, he visited Egypt, Anatolia, Persia and India, and finally returned in 1626; his Syrian Nestorian wife also travelled with him for five years, although she died at Hormuz on the way back. Conversely, others sought abroad the status they were denied at home, as in the case of Mulay Alal Merin, Marinid pretender to the throne of Fez, who in 1570 fled Morocco and travelled in search of military support, was baptised and, as Don Gaspar Beninmarin, fought for the King of Spain, then settled down and married in Naples.[41]

These individuals may have been special, but they were not isolated, as travel and mobility often involved entire kin-groups. Many Venetians had second lives and families in Istanbul, like Andrea Gritti, the merchant

[37] These dates are conjectural.
[38] Natalie Zemon Davis, *Trickster Travels: A Sixteenth-Century Muslim between Worlds* (London: Faber, 2007).
[39] Note that his birth date is uncertain.
[40] Mercedes García-Arenal and Gerard Wiegers, *A Man of Three Worlds: Samuel Pallache, a Moroccan Jew in Catholic and Protestant Europe* (Baltimore, MD: Johns Hopkins University Press, 2003).
[41] Gennaro Varriale, 'La media luna al revés: don Gaspar Benimerín en la Nápoles de los virreyes', forthcoming.

and diplomat who brokered peace with the Ottomans in 1502. As well as a son and two grand-daughters in Venice, he had four children with a Greek woman and lived with them for twenty years in his house in the district of Pera. In late life, he became doge of the republic; when Venice entered a war against the Ottomans, under his rule but against his judgment, one of his sons moved back to Istanbul – another one, Alvise, had stayed behind, risen as favourite of the grand visir and died while leading Ottoman troops in Transylvania.[42] Men had more opportunities than women for travelling, but women, too, could cross borders. Kin strategies meant that women in the Ottoman world could move to Istanbul from the provinces, and then cultivate family networks back home from inside the sultan's or a pasha's harem. Conversely, border-crossing was a choice for other women wishing to escape overbearing families and husbands, as shown for example by Beatrice Michiel, who fled from Venice to Istanbul where she adopted the name Fatima Hatun, and by the three Muslim sisters of Milos who moved to Corfu and converted to Christianity to escape the neglectful husband of one of them. But in such cases, women had no way back, in contrast to men, who could shuttle back and forth.[43]

If some travellers were extraordinary, travelling itself was beginning to turn into a habit. Pilgrimage had long been a relatively normal moment in life, for Christians and especially for Muslims. Both benefited from networks of institutions – hospitals, religious houses, caravanserais – which contributed to helping the faithful to cross the Mediterranean or to reach it from more distant parts of the world.[44] Christian pilgrimages, long associated with the era of the crusades, continued under the Mamluks and then began to increase in the eighteenth century. Since the seventeenth century, rich Northern Europeans began considering it normal to spend part of their education on a 'grand tour' of Mediterranean countries, including initially mostly Italy, but then looking further south, to Morocco and the Middle East.[45] It was an elite occupation that then contributed to spreading distant knowledge, however slanted by the Orientalist stereotypes of the travellers, among wider social strata. We know more about Western travellers to the

---

[42] Heinrich Kretschmayr, 'Ludovico Gritti. Eine Monographie', *Archiv für österreichische Geschichte* 83 (1897), 1–104.

[43] Eric Dursteler, *Renegade Women: Gender, Identity, and Boundaries in the Early Modern Mediterranean* (Baltimore, MD: Johns Hopkins University Press, 2011).

[44] Suraiya Faroqhi, *Pilgrims and Sultans: The Hajj under the Ottomans 1517–1683* (London: I. B. Tauris, 1994); and Michael Prior and William Taylor (eds), *Christians in the Holy Land* (London: World of Islam Festival Trust, 1994).

[45] Antoni Maczak, *Travel in Early Modern Europe* (Cambridge: Polity, 1995).

east than about eastern ones in the west, but this is not because, as was once thought, Muslims had no interest in the outside world. It is true that educated Ottomans tended to have greater familiarity with the world further east, the Arabic peninsula and North Africa – knowledge of Persian and Arabic was common in Istanbul's elite. But there are exceptions, such as the traveller and travel writer Evliya Çelebi (1611 to 1685).[46,47]

Some of these apparently extraordinary individuals belonged to professional groups with regular and stable patterns of exchange, such as the merchants who occasionally settled overseas in new-style diasporas with their own representatives (the consuls), decision-making institutions (the nations) and (as we have seen already) collective stores or storage places. By definition, merchants thrived on the ability to move away from home and to make home in more than one place, like the English 'pashas' of the Levant Company in Aleppo. Even when they did not personally move, merchants required knowledge and familiarity with distant agents in alien communities; cultivating far-flung connections, whether through family or contractual engagement, was a key to success in long-distance trade for the Christian and Jewish mercantile elite of eighteenth-century Anatolian harbours, who were honorary citizens of France and other European commercial powers, or for Anatolian Armenians and Livorno Jews, who both relied on networks of agents to trade as far as the Indian Ocean on one side and the Netherlands on the other.[48] Without wishing to exaggerate the internal coherence of these groups, it is important to bear in mind the opportunities afforded by their connections and accumulated experience in combining local with global knowledge.

Lower down the economic scale, artisans too migrated, both short and long distances, leading to the diffusion of skills and technologies. Most famously, highly mobile German craftsmen spread printing from the Rhineland throughout Europe, but some of their Ottoman and Venetian colleagues moved in the opposite direction to disseminate knowledge of glass and porcelain and of silk production. In Istanbul, artisans' guilds included foreigners from Iran and the West.[49] Mercenaries constituted a special case of professional migration: Scottish and Irish Catholics in the service of Spain;

---

[46] Note that his date of death is uncertain.

[47] Robert Dankoff, *An Ottoman Mentality: The World of Evliya Çelebi* (Leiden: Brill, 2004).

[48] Michel Aghassian and Kéram Kévonian, 'The Armenian Merchant Network: Overall Autonomy and Local Integration' in Sushil Chaudhury and Michel Morineau (eds), *Merchants, Companies and Trade, Europe and Asia in the Early Modern Era* (Cambridge University Press, 1999), pp. 74–94; and Trivellato, *Familiarity of Strangers*.

[49] Suraiya Faroqhi, *Artisans of Empire: Crafts and Craftspeople under the Ottomans* (London: I. B. Tauris, 2009), pp. 83–4.

Bosnians deployed in Hungary and Eastern Anatolia; Christian privateers embarked on Barbary ships every time a peace treaty back home endangered their activities; Dutch and English Protestants who fought for Venice against the Habsburgs and provoked fears (and hopes) of religious schism inside Italy; and Albanians who served on both sides of the Ottoman–Venetian front. It is well known that the military revolution of the long sixteenth century was also the golden age of mercenaries, but more attention should be given to their role as cultural intermediaries.[50]

As we have seen already, migration did not take place only in the name of pleasure or profit, but also resulted from captivity. Slave-raiders operated on both sides of the Mediterranean: Muslim Circassians were brought from the Black Sea to Italy, and Berbers from North Africa to Spain; Greek subjects of the Venetians and southern Italian subjects of the King of Spain were sold in the Ottoman Empire and North Africa. Slaves, both male and female, were objects of exploitation – mental, economic and physical.[51] But some were fortunate enough to turn the experience into a spur for great achievements. Uruj Khaireddin Barbarossa, the pirate 'king' of Algiers, was a Calabrian who had been captured and sold as a galley slave in his youth, a fate that had also befallen Jean de la Valette, the Grand Master of the Knights of Malta who oversaw the defence of the island against the Ottoman fleet. A special case of forced migration was the *devşirme* (literally 'collection') of Christian boys levied from the Balkans, separated from their families, forcibly converted to Islam, and trained for the Ottomans' infantry or, for the most gifted, for the imperial service. Until the early seventeenth century, the great majority of the Ottoman ruling apparatus was selected in this way, although later the Turkish elites managed to obtain the best posts for themselves.

Behind mobile individuals and groups, entire communities lived permanently as minorities. Some were displaced by wars, as the Croatian Uskoks (literally 'refugees'), who lived on piracy perpetrated against both Ottoman traders and Venetian ships, or the Greek Orthodox who resettled as peasants in southern Italy. Others were left behind by moving frontiers, as in the case of the Almogataces, a socio-professional class of Muslim informers, guides and auxiliaries who played especially important roles in helping the

---

[50] David Parrott, *The Business of War: Military Enterprise and Military Revolution in Early Modern Europe* (Cambridge University Press, 2012).

[51] Robert C. Davis, *Christian Slaves, Muslim Masters: White Slavery in the Mediterranean, the Barbary Coast, and Italy, 1500–1800* (Basingstoke: Palgrave, 2003); and Wolfgang Kaiser (ed.), *Le commerce des captifs. Les intermédiaires dans l'échange et le rachat des prisonniers en Méditerranée, XVe–XVIIe siècle* (Rome: École française de Rome, 2008).

Spanish conquerors of Oran, particularly as intermediaries with the population in and outside the city.[52] Similarly, in the fifteenth century, the Genoese
established a colony at Tabarka, in Tunisia, which continued well into the
eighteenth; only then did they move to the island of San Pietro in Sardinia,
where they brought their Genoese language and mixed eating habits, including both *pesto* and *couscous*. Others migrated to escape hardship, particularly
from mountains – Braudel's 'reserves of labour' – to lowlands, first in small
numbers and later followed by larger groups: in 1562, on his way to Constantinople (to promote French-Ottoman cooperation against the Genoese rule
in Corsica), Sampiero Corso visited Algiers and there found a thriving
community of Corsican immigrants (estimated at 6,000), while Bergamasco
quarters could be found in many Italian cities throughout this period.[53]

Conclusion

The different societies that lived in the Mediterranean crossroads were accustomed to a great many contacts and exchanges both with one another and,
increasingly, with people further away. Coexistence did not preclude conflict,
but even conflict could result in the diffusion of knowledge, as in the case of
the Byzantine refugees who taught Italian humanists eager to learn Greek in
the fifteenth century, or the Spanish Jews who set up printing workshops that
published books in Greek, Latin, Italian, Spanish and Hebrew in the Ottoman
Empire in the sixteenth.[54] The reception of new knowledge was rarely neutral.
At one end of the spectrum was adaptation and even syncretism, as in the art
and architecture of some centres, like the moresque pottery of Christian
Spain, the oriental arches of Venetian buildings, and the increasingly realistic
portraiture of Istanbul miniaturists. At the other end, the distant other inspired
fear and condemnation, as witnessed in the negative representations of the
Turks in Western iconography, historiography and civic ceremonials.[55] They
amounted to an obsession whose force was related to an imagined danger as

---

[52] Felipe Maíllo Salgado, 'The Almogataces: A Historical Perspective', *Mediterranean Historical Review* 6 (1991), 86–101.

[53] Fernand Braudel, *The Mediterranean and the Mediterranean World in the Age of Philip II* (London: Harper Collins, 1992), pp. 46 and 159.

[54] Avigdor Levy, *The Sephardim in the Ottoman Empire* (Princeton, NJ: Darwin Press, 1992), pp. 26 and 37–9.

[55] Bronwen Wilson, *The World in Venice: Print, the City, and Early Modern Identity* (University of Toronto Press, 2005); Margaret Meserve, *Empires of Islam in Renaissance Historical Thought* (Cambridge, MA: Harvard University Press, 2007); and Iain Fenlon, *The Ceremonial City: History, Memory and Myth in Renaissance Venice* (New Haven, CT: Yale University Press, 2007).

much as to the real threat posed by the Ottomans, as it emerged in places that were far from the frontier, like Renaissance Ferrara.[56]

In between conscious choices ranging from borrowing to rejection, the experience of encounter marked everyone's culture. Language, as is so often the case, bears powerful testimony of the effects of continuous interaction. The juxtaposition of different languages was a fact of everyday life in many crossroad centres. Venice was only one of many polyglot cities, where various Italian and European vernaculars could be heard alongside the Yiddish and Ladino of the Jews, Slavic languages, Turkish and Arabic. Even more remarkably, languages mixed following the contacts between populations, from the Italian and Greek nautical vocabulary used by the Turks to Arabic words used by Italians and French to describe customs control. Meanwhile, in North Africa, corsairs and diplomats were equally familiar with *lingua franca* – Frankish, or free, tongue – a fluid mixture that was essential in everyday transactions.[57] For most people, a degree of adaptation to this multifaceted linguistic landscape was a normal fact of everyday life, as for the Cretan Jew Abraham Balanzas. Descended from Spain and the son and father of rabbis, in 1626 he recorded his will, ending with the desire to end his life in Jerusalem, in favour of his daughter Parigoría (the Greek translation of the Spanish name Consolación) before two Greek Orthodox witnesses. He declared that he knew only Hebrew writing and signed in Hebrew, but dictated the will in a Cretan Greek full of Italian words, all of which the Venetian notary wrote down in the Latin alphabet.[58]

For most of the period we have considered, conflict was inescapable, but in the full knowledge that no one side could seriously or protractedly claim dominance over the others. In the eighteenth century, things began to change. International commerce experienced a new boom after the slump of the previous century, powered by renewed and unprecedented demographic growth, and fuelled by the increase in the output of agriculture and manufactures. But the new economy was to a large extent dominated by Western traders. The Dutch, English and French wrested concessions from the Ottoman Empire that were increasingly damaging both to the Ottomans

---

[56] Giovanni Ricci, *Ossessione turca. In una retrovia cristiana dell'Europa moderna* (Bologna: Il Mulino, 2002).

[57] Jocelyne Dakhlia, *Lingua Franca – Histoire d'une langue métisse en Méditerranée* (Arles: Actes Sud, 2008).

[58] Chryssa A. Maltezou, 'From Crete to Jerusalem: The Will of a Cretan Jew (1626)' in Benjamin Arbel (ed.), *Intercultural Contacts in the Medieval Mediterranean* (London: Frank Cass, 1996), pp. 189–201.

and to other competitors. This era also saw the emergence of increasingly aggressive states. The French navy supported French traders unleashing war against both Maltese and Barbary pirates. France obtained an agreement from the knights that they abstain from attacking French ships, but it allowed them to continue harassing merchants of other nations. Unsurprisingly, by the end of the period, many Venetian ships sailing west carried a French 'convenience' flag to hoist when sailing near North Africa.[59]

Thus, the decline of piracy did not open an era of peace. Instead, the Mediterranean became a battleground for European powers, especially France and Britain, who fought over it just as they did over North America and the Caribbean. In the 1680s, the French bombarded Algiers and Genoa and sailed close to Venice to give a similar message; in 1768, they purchased Corsica from Genoa and, in 1785, they obtained a monopoly of trade over the Suez isthmus. Napoleon's invasion of Egypt in 1798 (which in the process ended the rule of the Knights of St John in Malta) was not just the dream of an ambitious general, but the culmination of French policy over more than a century. For its part, Britain became a serious contender for Mediterranean supremacy on gaining Gibraltar and Menorca from Spain in 1713; in the period before 1750, it stationed more soldiers in the Mediterranean than in North America, and soon it would capture Malta, too.[60] Britain also pursued a systematic policy of expanding influence, for example by supplying – and controlling – the navy of the newly independent Kingdom of Naples (and Sicily), and by brokering deals with the Ottomans in North Africa.

New powers also entered the scene. Russia gained a foothold in the Balkans in 1699, and in 1768 to 1774 humiliated the Ottoman Empire in a war, with which it won not only free access to the Black Sea – thereby ending the Ottoman monopoly over its trade which, as we have seen, had been established at the time of Mehmed the Conqueror – but also the right to trade in the rest of the Mediterranean through the Bosphorus. The damages inflicted by Russia, in particular, together with the Russian claim of influence over Orthodox Christians, facilitated the rise of quasi-autonomous provincial overlords in the Ottoman Empire and helped the rise of incipient national movements in its territories, from the Balkans to the Maghreb. In the following decades, one after the other, the North African *beys* obtained various degrees of autonomy from Istanbul, while the decline of shipyards and the construction of numerous

---

[59] Greene, *Catholic Corsairs and Greek Merchants*.
[60] Linda Colley, *Captives: Britain, Empire and the World, 1600–1850* (London: Jonathan Cape, 2002), p. 70.

fortresses reflected the new defensive outlook of the Ottomans. Here lay the foundations for a new age of Mediterranean relations, dominated by national independence movements and colonial expansion.

FURTHER READING

General introductions and discussions

Abulafia, David, *The Great Sea: A Human History of the Mediterranean* (Harmondsworth: Penguin, 2011).

Braudel, Fernand, *The Mediterranean and the Mediterranean World in the Age of Philip II* (London: Harper Collins, 1992).

Horden, Peregrine and Nicholas Purcell, *The Corrupting Sea: A Study of Mediterranean History* (Oxford University Press, 2000).

MacLean, Gerald (ed.), *Re-orienting the Renaissance: Cultural Exchanges with the East* (New York: Palgrave Macmillan, 2005).

Marino, John A., *Early Modern History and the Social Sciences: Testing the Limits of Braudel's Mediterranean* (Kirksville, MO: Truman State University Press, 2002).

Said, Edward W., *Orientalism* (London: Routledge and Kegan Paul, 1978).

Wallerstein, Immanuel, *The Modern World System*, 3 vols (New York: Academic Press, 1974–80).

War and peace

Earle, Peter, *Corsairs of Malta and Barbary* (London: Sidgwick and Jackson, 1970).

Goffman, Daniel, *The Ottoman Empire and Early Modern Europe* (Cambridge University Press, 2002).

Greene, Molly, *Catholic Corsairs and Greek Merchants: A Maritime History of the Mediterranean, 1450–1700* (Princeton University Press, 2010).

Guilmartin, John Francis, *Gunpowder and Galleys: Changing Technology and Mediterranean Warfare at Sea in the Sixteenth Century* (Cambridge University Press, 1974).

Hess, Andrew C., *The Forgotten Frontier: A History of the Sixteenth-Century Ibero-African Frontier* (Chicago University Press, 1978).

Isom-Verhaaren, Christine, *Allies with the Infidel: The Ottoman and French Alliance in the Sixteenth Century* (London: I. B. Tauris, 2011).

Panzac, Daniel, *La marine ottomane: de l'apogée à la chute de l'Empire, 1572–1923* (Paris: CNRS, 2009).

Schwoebel, Robert, *The Shadow of the Crescent: The Renaissance Image of the Turk, 1453–1517* (Nieuwkoop: B. de Graaf, 1967).

Tenenti, Alberto, *Piracy and the Decline of Venice* (London: Longmans, 1967).

Trade and trade routes

Ashtor, Eliyahu, *Levant Trade in the Later Middle Ages* (Princeton University Press, 1983).

Casale, Giancarlo, *The Ottoman Age of Exploration* (Oxford University Press, 2010).

Chaudhury, Sushil and Michel Morineau (eds), *Merchants, Companies and Trade: Europe and Asia in the Early Modern Era* (Cambridge University Press, 1999).

Faroqhi, Suraiya, *The Ottoman Empire and the World Around It* (London: I. B. Tauris, 2004).

Fleet, Kate, *European and Islamic Trade in the Early Ottoman State: The Merchants of Genoa and Turkey* (Cambridge University Press, 1999).

Pujades, Ramon, *Les cartes portolanes: la representació medieval d'una mar solcada* (Barcelona: Institut d'Estudis Catalans, 2007).

Tabak, Faruk, *The Waning of the Mediterranean 1550–1870: A Geohistorical Approach* (Baltimore, MD: Johns Hopkins University Press, 2008).

Trivellato, Francesca, *The Familiarity of Strangers: The Sephardic Diaspora, Livorno, and Cross-Cultural Trade in the Early Modern Period* (New Haven, CT: Yale University Press, 2009).

Crossroads centres, crossroads people

Ben-Zaken, Avner, *Cross-Cultural Scientific Exchanges in the Eastern Mediterranean, 1560–1660* (Baltimore, MD: Johns Hopkins University Press, 2010).

Burnett, Charles and Anna Contadini (eds), *Islam and the Italian Renaissance* (London: Warburg Institute, 1999).

Davis, Natalie Zemon, *Trickster Travels: A Sixteenth-Century Muslim between Worlds* (London: Faber, 2007).

Davis, Robert C., *Christian Slaves, Muslim Masters: White Slavery in the Mediterranean, the Barbary Coast, and Italy, 1500–1800* (Basingstoke: Palgrave, 2003).

Dursteler, Eric R., *Renegade Women: Gender, Identity, and Boundaries in the Early Modern Mediterranean* (Baltimore, MD: Johns Hopkins University Press, 2011).

Venetians in Constantinople: Nation, Identity, and Coexistence in the Early Modern Mediterranean (Baltimore, MD: Johns Hopkins University Press, 2006).

Earle, T. F. and K. J. P. Lowe (eds), *Black Africans in Renaissance Europe* (Cambridge University Press, 2005).

Eldem, Edhem, Daniel Goffman and Bruce Alan Masters, *The Ottoman City between East and West: Aleppo, Izmir, and Istanbul* (Cambridge University Press, 1999).

Faroqhi, Suraiya, *Pilgrims and Sultans: The Hajj under the Ottomans 1517–1683* (London: I. B. Tauris, 1994).

Goffman, Daniel, *Izmir and the Levantine World 1550–1650* (Seattle, WA: University of Washington Press, 1990).

Husain, Adnan Ahmed and K. E. Fleming (eds), *A Faithful Sea: The Religious Cultures of the Mediterranean, 1200–1700* (Oxford: Oneworld, 2007).

Levy, Avigdor, *The Sephardim in the Ottoman Empire* (Princeton, NJ: Darwin Press, 1992).

Krekić, Bariša, *Dubrovnik: A Mediterranean Urban Society, 1300–1600* (Aldershot: Ashgate Variorum, 1997).

Maczak, Antoni, *Travel in Early Modern Europe* (Cambridge: Polity, 1995).

Prior, Michael and William Taylor (eds), *Christians in the Holy Land* (London: World of Islam Festival Trust, 1994).

Sahlins, Peter, *Boundaries: The Making of France and Spain in the Pyrenees* (Berkeley, CA: University of California Press, 1989).

PART FIVE

★

OVERVIEW

18

Political trajectories compared

JACK A. GOLDSTONE

The rise of modern states in a globalizing world

If you travel internationally, you have a passport that identifies you as the citizen of a particular state. Some people have more than one, and refugees forced to flee across borders may have none. Nonetheless, the universal expectation in the twenty-first century is that everyone is a citizen of some country, and that country is ruled by a bureaucratic government according to man-made laws that apply to all within its boundaries, with a chief executive and state officials (with the exception of ceremonial heads of state) who owe their positions to electoral, military, administrative or other success—but not to hereditary rights or ownership of their positions.

Yet, the rise of such modern states is a relatively recent development. By 1800, the process of creating such states was still new and incomplete; Japan became a modern state only after 1868, China after 1911, Russia after 1917, Turkey after 1923 and India after 1947. Even in Western Europe, the process was uneven: Great Britain still has a very pre-modern House of Lords (mostly appointed, but still with nearly 100 hereditary members) as a component of its government; France invented many characteristics of the modern state in its First Republic (1792 to 1804), yet reverted to various kinds of monarchies and empire up to 1870; and although Prussia adopted many modernizing state reforms after 1815, it did not develop into the modern state of Germany until 1871. Nor is this process complete even in 2014: from the Sultanate of Brunei and the monarchies of Saudi Arabia, Jordan, Morocco and the Persian Gulf to the European principality of Monaco, there remain states where hereditary rulers still actively rule, and in some of them sacred texts (the Qur'an) rather than modern rational legal codes still form the basis for civil or criminal laws.

From 1400 to 1800, global trends led to the rise of the modern state. In the thirteenth and fourteenth centuries, several events had disrupted older states and empires all across Eurasia. First, tribes of Mongol nomadic warriors who usually spent their energies quarrelling with each other were united by Genghis Khan, who honed their tactics of rapidly advancing and highly maneuverable cavalry archers into an unstoppable force. Spreading both east and west from Central Asia, the Mongols overwhelmed states from Poland to China. Second was climate change; the Medieval Warm Period ended around 1300, followed by the first phase of the "Little Ice Age" which lasted for the next two centuries,[1] affecting crop yields all across the northern temperate zone. Third, bubonic plague (better known as the "Black Death") became a global pandemic, inflicting a swift but painful death on from one-third to one-half of the populations of states from England to Egypt, and from Persia to China. The world thus entered the 1400s depleted and distressed; it took another century of war, disorder and political chaos before new, stable states would emerge.

In the fourteenth century, most people did not think of themselves as being ruled from the central capital city of large territorial states. Rather, people saw themselves as being ruled mainly by *local* authorities, who had only a loose allegiance to those who claimed to be kings or emperors. These local authorities were virtually unchallenged rulers within their local domains, whether as independent feudal-type lords or as appointed or hereditary governors or officials ruling in the name of a great imperial or royal overlord. Even for the great lords and officials, kinship and allegiance to dynastic families, often in the framework of household or personal service, took priority over any abstract idea of "the state." With the exception of a few Italian city republics, people were never citizens of a state, but rather lords or subjects relative to those above or below them in the political, religious and social hierarchies.

Political domains were loosely organized entities with fuzzy boundaries, very far from exercising what the great German sociologist Max Weber identified as the key criteria of a modern state, namely a "monopoly of legitimate use of force" within a clearly marked territory.[2] In many areas, religious officials had as much authority as political leaders, or themselves held critical political positions or had resources and authority beyond the reach of state control. In some cases, religious groups (bishops, popes and

---

[1] Jan Oosthoek, Environmental History Resources website, www.eh-resources.org/timeline/timeline_lia.html
[2] Max Weber, 'Politics as a Vocation', 1919 lecture, www.sscnet.ucla.edu/polisci/ethos/Weber-vocation.pdf

religious orders in the West, more commonly monastic groups or Islamic sects in the East) raised their own armies and fought against state rulers or founded states themselves.

Moreover, in the fourteenth century, the world map showed a wide scattering of states large and small. Many of the most successful were city-states, such as Florence, Venice and Genoa in Italy, or federations of city-states, such as the Hanseatic League. At the same time, large areas of the Eurasian steppes, the deserts of the Middle East and North Africa, and America's Great Plains were dominated by nomadic warrior and trading groups, rather than states.

Over the centuries from 1400 to 1800, kings and emperors sought to recover and expand their authority, gradually gaining control over larger and better defined territories and over local officials and landlords. They also greatly increased the regularity and size of their tax collection and their military establishments (these two trends being closely interrelated); raised the size, professionalism and uniformity of their official administrations; adopted contemporary vernaculars as their languages of administration and education in place of classical or sacred tongues;[3] and supported scientific, commercial, cultural and welfare endeavors designed to increase the wealth of their territories.

Some of the states that took root after 1400 were empires ruling diverse peoples of different ethnicities, religions and cultures: the Russian Empire, the Habsburg Empire, the Ottoman Empire, the Chinese Empire and the Mughal Empire. Others were based on the idea of building a single nation, with a common shared identity based on a constitutional, linguistic or religious heritage that would be the core of that identity: Germany, the United States and Sweden, but also Iran, Thailand, Vietnam, Japan and Korea. There were also incipient national states that had seized (and in 1800 still held) large overseas empires: Britain, France, the Netherlands, Spain and Portugal. All of these larger states proceeded to squeeze out or absorb the minor principalities and nomadic regions, until the global map was dominated by large, centrally run territorial states.

While growth in the size, professionalization and power of these territories and their administration laid the basis for the modern state, these trends coexisted with older, traditional structures of authority. The sociologist of

---

[3] China was an exception in that while regional spoken Chinese vernaculars (dialects) had long been distinct from classical written Chinese, a literary form modeled on the latter remained the language of administration and literature throughout the Imperial era.

empires Karen Barkey speaks of "the layering of old and new institutions" to describe this process.[4] Hereditary military officers and officials, and nearly independent local authorities, continued to exist alongside officials appointed for merit. Religious authorities and canonical classic texts continued to influence state policy despite efforts to create more rational state policies and administration. And, notwithstanding increased efforts by state administrations to provide security and welfare services, and rights to petition officials and use state-supported courts, the great mass of people usually experienced states passively as subjects. They were "subject" to military recruitment, taxation and other forms of service to local lords and to the state, but had no escape from their prescribed place in the social order.

It thus took many centuries for the fully realized modern state—based on uniform legal codes and free of hereditary rule or privileged local authorities—to emerge, often violently, from the shell of these multi-layered political regimes.

The culmination of this trend can be seen in the French Revolution of 1789 at the very end of this period. The French Revolutionary state burst forth from the French monarchy by abolishing every traditional and feudal element of political administration, including the monarchy itself. The Revolutionary state wholly subordinated the Catholic Church in France and all its properties, making clerics into state employees; ended all feudal privileges that had previously protected self-sufficient local and provincial authorities; obliterated all older administrative regions and categories and ranks, creating a new administrative map, new courts and jurisdictions, and even a new calendar; and assumed central control over virtually all educational, welfare and administrative functions. The Revolutionary state also built up larger armies than any previously seen in Europe, supported scientific expeditions and created a new uniform legal code, and aimed to treat all free French men (though not yet women) as equal citizens under direct authority of, and owing their highest loyalty to, the state itself.

While the French Revolutionary state was an extreme example, almost all states throughout the world were moving in roughly the same directions, trying to make rulers more powerful versus local and hereditary officials, make state administrations and laws more rational, raise the size and firepower of their armies and navies, make tax collections more effective and efficient, and promote the wealth (and thus the tax base) of their territories.

[4] Karen Barkey, *Empire of Difference: The Ottomans in Comparative Perspective* (Cambridge University Press, 2008), p. 1.

Yet, we should not think that all states pursuing these goals had a similar character. They varied widely in the relationship between the state and religious authorities, their degree of centralization, the manner in which they recruited military and civil officials, the extent to which they had any institutionalized representative bodies, and their involvement in various welfare, scientific and educational efforts. They also varied considerably in the way in which they related to other states in their neighborhood, with great implications for the conduct of war and diplomacy and the pursuit of military technology. The basis and organization of their economies also differed, again with great implications for social and financial arrangements that in turn affected state operations.

We also must bear in mind that progress from the loose, highly localized and internally variegated administrations that characterized states c. 1400 to the larger, more centralized, more territorially focused, actively administered, militarily effective and economically progressive states that were increasingly typical by 1800 was *not* a smooth and continuous process. In almost every state there were cycles of progress and regress, unexpected periods of political crisis and collapse, and issues of problem-solving that states managed in different ways, some more successfully than others. Over these centuries, we almost invariably find that the very strongest states from the beginning of this period—the Aztecs in Mexico, the Holy Roman Empire in Central Europe, the Delhi Sultanate and Vijayanagara Empire in India, the Ming Empire in China and the Mongol Empires in Central Asia—had disappeared by around 1800, replaced by more powerful states.

Finally, we must bear in mind that states in this globalizing era did not shape their trajectories independently. An overarching trend across these centuries is that Europe, which in 1500 was a relatively uninfluential and isolated area, divided into many hundreds of constantly warring city-states, bishoprics, dukedoms, monarchies, electorates and small empires, with very weak central governments, especially compared to the larger, more centralized, and richer Ottoman and Chinese states, had by 1800 come to politically and militarily (although not yet economically) dominate the rest of the world. It had conquered and colonized all of the Americas and Australia, most of India and Indonesia, and penetrated deeply into Africa, from which it exported human cargo as slaves on an immense scale. How European states came to dominate the global political scene by 1800 is also a key part of the political trajectories of this era.

Yet, it would be a great mistake to simply see the political trajectories of 1400 to 1800 as a story of the "Rise of the West." Although the Western states did emerge from this period relatively stronger than they had been at the beginning, the development of states was initially further advanced in the Middle East, South Asia and the Far East, and Western states borrowed a great deal of their technology and administrative innovations from Eastern states. As late as the eighteenth century, Voltaire was promoting the Chinese model of officials chosen by examinations as a basis for reform in France, and Britain—which only adopted civil service examinations to select officials in the mid-nineteenth century—still calls its higher civil servants "mandarins," from the name given by China to its top officials.

Moreover, the development of the modern state in the West was in many ways shaped by interactions with Eastern states, through both direct military competition and economic exchange. Finally, while the West was the first region to realize the development of fully modern states, the modern state model quickly transcended the West, and after 1850 new forms of modern states, including military and party-states, were adapted and further developed in Asia, Latin America and Africa, as well as in Europe. The rise of the modern state, both from 1400 to 1800 and afterwards, was an inherently global process, and indeed would likely not have occurred without the globalization of the world in the fifteenth through eighteenth centuries.

Many patterns, many states

The fifteenth century was a period of violent disorder and incipient state building all across the world. Population remained at low levels, as new rounds of the Black Death periodically returned and warfare wracked the continents. This century saw the height of the Hundred Years War between England and France and the conclusion of the Christian re-conquest of Spain in Europe, and the rise of the Ottoman Empire in the Middle East, including the final collapse of the Byzantine Empire and the fall of Constantinople. Further east, the 1400s began with Tamerlane's destruction of Damascus and Baghdad, and the sacking of Angkor Wat in Cambodia. Iran (Persia) was ruled by a succession of Turko-Mongol dynasties, and India was divided into a number of warring states. In China, the new Ming dynasty was extending its authority and moving its capital from Nanjing in the south to its new northern capital, Beijing, while Japan was suffering through the Onin War. In the Americas, the Incas were just founding and conquering their empire on the northwest coast of South America, while the Mexica in the Valley of Mexico were asserting themselves over other Mesoamerican societies and building the Aztec Empire.

By the early 1500s, in the Old World much of this open warfare had devolved into border conflict among more established states. The adoption of firearms—both muskets and artillery—put a premium on the ability to raise vast funds to equip armies and navies. The heavily armed knights and marching archers of the Middle Ages gave way to armies organized around three main branches: the infantry, increasingly armed with muskets as well as swords; cavalry for scouting and flanking and charges armed with lances, swords and pistols; and artillery to break down fortifications and shatter enemy lines. Navies, especially in Western Europe, increasingly armed their ships with artillery as well. Supporting these armies and navies, and building the complex fortifications to resist them, required resources on an enormous scale. So rulers sought to make their domains more productive, and to increase their ability to raise resources from those domains.

The sociologist Charles Tilly has argued that there were two main routes by which states in this period raised the resources for wars.[5] One was to focus on capital-intensive activities—aggressively expanding manufacturing and trade—and to levy taxes on the movement and consumption of goods. This approach was particularly favorable for maritime countries with many ports and with valuable products to trade. Prosperous city-states as well as larger states could follow this route, using their profits to hire mercenary armies and build powerful navies. The other route was to conquer ever-larger territories and coerce ever-larger amounts of taxation out of the peasantry— sometimes by direct collection, and sometimes by selling the rights to squeeze the peasants to intermediaries ("tax-farming"). This approach was favoured by kings and emperors who commanded large and expanding territories, such as the rulers of France, Austria-Hungary, Russia, the Ottoman Empire, Persia, the Mughal Empire and China. But this description is too simple; aside from the fact that most rulers sought to follow both methods insofar as they could, there were yet more ways for rulers to acquire wealth. Moreover, this approach omits the fact that not all regions of the world fought wars to the same degree or in the same way, so that international relations were also critical.

By the early to mid-1500s, relatively stable states and empires had emerged in almost all the major areas of the world. In the Americas, in 1500, the Inca and Aztec Empires were near their height. In Europe, the Tudors in England, the Valois in France and the Habsburgs in Spain and

---

[5] Charles Tilly, *Coercion, Capital, and European States AD 990–1992* (Oxford: Blackwell, 1992).

Central Europe had created Renaissance monarchies with highly educated officials and increasingly centralized control of their territories. In
the Middle East and North Africa, the Ottomans had built the largest
empire (in size) since ancient Rome, with a sophisticated bureaucracy
and nearly unstoppable army. In Russia, the tsars from the time of Ivan
the Terrible had thrown off their Mongol overlords and were building
their own empire. In Persia, the Safavids had established control and
expanded the Persian Empire to its greatest extent since the time of
Mohammed; and in India the Mughals had begun to unify most of the
subcontinent under their rule. China was united under the flourishing
Ming dynasty, while Japan was becoming unified thanks to the victories
of Oda Nabunaga and Toyotomi Hideyoshi, and developed a stable
central state after 1603 under the Tokugawa shogunate. Even on the
mainland of Southeast Asia, the rulers of Siam, Burma and Vietnam
were similarly creating larger, more administratively effective and unified
states. The main exceptions to this pattern were in Africa, where pre-
literate states grew but were unable to adopt Eurasian-style military
technologies on a large scale, and therefore were raided by slave-seeking
traders from Europe and Asia; and in the islands of Southeast Asia,
where fragmented island states in Indonesia and the Philippines became
targets for colonial control by Europeans.

Yet, these varied states coexisted in very different patterns of relations in
different parts of the world. In Europe, by 1600, the prevailing pattern was
one of near-constant land and naval conflict among relatively compact
kingdoms, with territorial states, including Denmark, Sweden and Russia in
the north, and the Duchies of Milan and Tuscany, the Papal States, and the
Kingdom of Naples and Sicily in the south, gradually weakening the formerly
independent city-states of the Hanseatic League and Italy. The commercial
city-states of Genoa and Venice persisted, but became marginal. From 1500 to
1650, European wars mainly pitted kingdoms—usually of different religions
(Protestant or Catholic), but not always—against each other for control of
territory or naval domination. Yet, despite the constant struggles, no clear
winner emerged; Europe settled into a permanent fragmentation among
different states, each with their own dominant religion (Catholicism,
Anglicanism, Calvinism, Lutheranism) and their own dynastic claims to
territory. Unable to wholly defeat each other, and limited in their territorial
gains by the persistence of other states, Europeans turned outward, and
developed a different way to raise resources: the conquest and colonization
of overseas states.

The Spanish and Portuguese initially dominated this approach. By the mid-1500s, the Spaniards had used their advantages in steel and gunpowder to conquer the Aztec and Inca Empires, appropriating their accumulated wealth and setting up massive mining operations to continue the flow of treasure to their coffers. The Portuguese acquired Brazil, as well as establishing fortified trading centers on the coasts of East and West Africa, India and southern China. They were soon followed by the Dutch, who first dominated access to Indonesia and later conquered it, placed settlers in southern Africa and on Manhattan island ("New Amsterdam") in North America, and established trading relations with Japan at the port of Nagasaki. But this was not the end. By the early 1600s, the British, who established a foothold in northeast India, had placed even more settlers in southern Africa, and colonized the east coast of North America. The French, too, pushed into both North America and Asia, and all of these countries now fought naval and territorial wars against each other over their colonies as well as over their European lands.

The development of Atlantic empires by Europeans led to continual combat at sea over access to treasure, and control of Atlantic trade routes. From roughly 1450 to 1700, naval warfare involving Spain, Portugal, Britain, France, the Netherlands and also substantial forces of pirates (some of the latter deployed by states as "privateers") produced a rapid development of vessels, armaments and tactics designed for oceanic warfare. Naval gunnery developed lighter and faster-firing broadside cannon; naval architecture strengthened the naval platforms for gunnery and the resistance of ships to shelling; and sails and tactics developed for pursuit, attack and combat for taking enemy ships or destroying enemy fleets. While similar goals had motivated naval development of galleys in the Mediterranean, which grew heavier and better armed, naval combat in the Atlantic Ocean was something altogether different, requiring ships and crews that could remain at sea for weeks or months, and able to haul and defend huge loads of treasure between continents. By the seventeenth century, the Atlantic states of Europe had developed heavily armed ships unlike those anywhere else in the world.

A different pattern prevailed in East Asia. Not only did the Ming dynasty unite all of China, it also worked out a symbolic integration with its major neighbors. In previous centuries, Korea, Japan and Vietnam had all borrowed their writing systems, religions and systems of administration, with officials recruited by examination on the Confucian classics, from China. These states thus looked to China as the source of many of their key traditions. They did fight wars among themselves: China invaded Vietnam in 1409 and Japan invaded Korea in 1592 to 1598, but in contrast to Europe these conflicts were extremely rare and were separated by centuries of peace.

This is because China developed the "tribute system" during the Han dynasty (206 BC to 220 AD). Under this system, states wishing to trade with the Chinese Empire would pay tribute and acknowledge the central role of the Chinese emperor; the emperor would then give the tributary nation trading rights at designated ports. Even more important, this largely symbolic action bestowed recognition and legitimacy on the Confucian elites of the tribute states, who thus gained prestige and the freedom to manage their domestic affairs without any anxiety about Chinese aggression. Tributary states included Nepal and Burma, in addition to others. There were dynastic wars within Korea, and Vietnam often attacked its neighbors in Southeast Asia; but major wars between China and its main neighbors were largely avoided.[6]

China did continue to fight wars, but these were almost entirely against the nomadic groups on its northern and western frontiers. For the most part, China's task was to prevent and repel the nomads' raids on Chinese territory. These wars did not involve set battles between comparable forces, and artillery and massed musket-bearing infantry were of limited use against mounted nomads who would strike and retreat to the steppes. Thus, unlike Europe, China did not have the incentives to continually develop and improve its military technology to keep pace with equal competitors. Rather, China developed the administrative tools (including merchant finance and paper money) to keep large forces of farmer-soldiers settled and supplied in frontier areas to repel raids. The Ming also rebuilt and extended the Great Wall as a barrier. This was asymmetric warfare, often expensive and demanding large numbers of troops, but of a different nature from what was routine in the European states system.

In the Middle East, Central Asia and India, the Ottoman, Safavid and Mughal Empires adopted firearms so enthusiastically that they are often referred to as "gunpowder empires." As a group, they were so successful that they filled up the entire space of Eurasia below the steppes (see Map 13.1). Throughout the 1500s, these were arguably the most successful states in the world. The Ottomans spread across North Africa, the Middle East and the Balkans, pushing Europeans back to the walls of Vienna; the Safavids expanded their empire into Armenia, Afghanistan and Central Asia; and the

---

[6] David C. Kang, *China before the West: Five Centuries of Trade and Tribute* (New York: Columbia University Press, 2010).

Mughals pushed their control from the Arabian Sea to the Bay of Bengal and from the Himalayan mountains to the deserts of the Deccan.

From the New World to the Old, the 1500s was thus a century of great empire-building. It was also a century of relative prosperity. A warm interval from roughly 1500 to 1590 interrupted the "Little Ice Age." New crops from the Americas—potatoes, sweet potatoes, maize and peanuts—proved highly adaptable to the Old World, even in difficult soils, providing expanded nourishment. With the growth of centralized administrations to provide security, trade flourished more than at any time previously in world history, and new circuits of trade arose. Within China, the rebuilding of the Grand Canal to link northern and southern China, the expansion of cotton farming in the north and cotton spinning and weaving in the south, and of rice production up the Yangzi river basin and silk production in the delta, tied China together into a great continental trading system. Not only rice and textiles, but lacquer, ceramics, tropical woods, tea, paper, books, soy, fertilizers and luxuries such as ivory flowed through the coastal ports and river arteries. China adopted silver as its main form of tax payments and copper for its currency, leading to vast imports of these metals from European traders and from Japan.

Europe used its New World colonies to obtain bullion, which was sent to China across the Pacific by way of Manila and to both China and India across the Atlantic and Indian Oceans as well. Europe was the "underdeveloped nation" in global trade in the 1500s and 1600s, exporting raw materials, mainly bullion, to India in exchange for cotton cloth, which India produced in the greatest volume and quality for trade of any country in the world,[7] and to China for silk, cotton and ceramics. Indian cotton was also used in huge volumes by Europeans to purchase slaves in Africa, who were sent to the New World to harvest sugar and work in the mines. European nations had a few fine manufactured specialties to export, such as heavy wool textiles, muskets and cannon, furs and glass (especially Venetian production). Yet, until the early 1800s, India and China led the world in manufactured exports, and European countries financed their trade deficits with Asia mainly by exports of bullion.

Although the Ottomans, Safavids and Mughals rapidly deployed muskets and artillery in their armies, in contrast to Europeans, they did not do the same at sea. Whereas most European countries were modest in size, so their

---

[7] Giorgio Riello, *Cotton: The Fabric that Made the Modern World* (Cambridge University Press, 2013).

rulers were eager to gain and protect trade to augment their state's revenues, this was not the case to the East. European merchant ships hauled precious cargoes of bullion, gems and spices across the Atlantic or from Asia all the way around Africa. They needed to defend these precious cargoes against pirates, and to protect their ports and sources of wealth against other nations' privateers, hence their development of heavily armed vessels. Because of the costs and risks involved, Europeans' oceanic trade was usually carried out by state-sponsored expeditions (as with the Spanish and Portuguese), or by state-chartered corporations (such as the English and Dutch East India Companies), which could handle the required investments. The Ottomans, Safavids and Mughals, with their huge and rich land empires, instead relied mainly on tax revenues from their own territories to support their states' operations. Their rulers valued trade mainly as a way of bringing in locally scarce but necessary materials (especially silver), but let private merchants manage maritime trade, rather than invest in it themselves.

Asians were certainly capable of building large ocean-going vessels: Chinese ships had enjoyed features such as multiple water-tight compartments and stern-post rudders from the beginning of the first millennium that Europeans would not adopt until centuries later. In the 1600s, the Mughals built large ships to take tribute to the Holy City of Mecca, some armed with dozens of cannon and crews of several hundred. In the early fifteenth century, the Chinese built fleets of huge "treasure ships" much larger than anything produced by Europeans, which sailed all the way from China to the east coast of Africa. Yet, these voyages were commercial failures and hence discontinued; unlike Spanish expeditions to the New World that found rich stores of gold and silver to plunder and lands to colonize, the Chinese found mainly densely settled lands with few resources they did not already produce themselves, or which Arab and Indian merchants had not already eagerly brought to China at their own expense. Facing no major threats from the sea, and focused on the challenge of controlling the steppe frontier, later Ming emperors dismantled the oceanic fleet and ceased to invest in long-distance voyages.

From the late fourteenth to the early seventeenth centuries, Asian empires developed their own counterpart to the Atlantic trading system, but along very different lines. Taking advantage of the prevailing monsoon winds, which produced steady but seasonal support for sailing, merchants developed a rough division of labor among themselves guided by nature.[8] In the Far

---

[8] See Jos Gommans's chapter in this volume, "Continuity and change in the Indian Ocean basin."

Eastern seas, Chinese merchant junks dominated trade with Japan, the Philippines and Taiwan, mainly bringing Japanese silver and copper to China in exchange for cotton and silk; the junks would go as far as the Malacca Straits, where Malacca served as an entrepot for goods in transit from the Bay of Bengal to the South China Sea. In the Bay of Bengal and the Indian Ocean, Indian merchants would take over the coastal trade, moving goods between the Malay/Indonesia region and the east and west coasts of India. India's coasts would market goods produced inland, from pepper and dyes to its most famed products—finely woven and exquisitely dyed cottons. Other spices, medicinal herbs and manufactured goods would come from Indonesia, Sri Lanka and Southeast Asia. Then between India's west coast and the Middle East and East Africa, Arab and Muslim merchants would take over, moving slaves, ivory and gold from Africa, and coffee and carpets from the Middle East, to India in exchange for South and East Asian products. Cambay and Surat, in Gujarat on the Indian coast, became the primary entrepots for this trade, their merchants amassing fortunes of millions of silver rupees. Further west, the port of Aden was a flourishing gateway for Asian goods to reach the Middle East, from which they would flow to the Ottoman lands and thence via the Mediterranean to Europe. This natural division meant that states did not engage in naval struggles to control particular routes. Rather, with a population several times larger than that of Europe, and a much more diverse range of ecologies, climates and products to trade, the merchants of the Indian Ocean/China Seas maritime routes prospered through volume and diversification.[9]

By the early 1600s, the entire globe was girdled by trade flows, mostly oceanic and riverine, but also across the Mediterranean and the Sahara and Persian caravan routes, moving wool, silk and cotton textiles; ceramics (Ming porcelain was especially prized in Europe and the Middle East); sugar, spices, coffee, tea, glassware, metal goods, wood (ranging from tropical woods to whole trees for ships' masts), dried fish, ivory, gems, pearls, horses, camels, elephants, slaves, gold, silver, tobacco, saltpetre, guns, and a host of processed foods, dyes and other manufactured goods. For overseas and trans-continental trade, cargoes with a high value-to-weight ratio were essential, such as spices, sugar, ivory, gems and textiles, as well as precious

---

[9] After Europeans entered the region, Chinese pirates equipped their ships with cannon, but the Chinese state responded by banning settlements along the coast to deny the pirates plunder, rather than build its own armed fleets to attack them.

metals. But for internal river and coastal trade, even bulk goods—grains, coal, fertilizers—would travel long distances.

Warmer weather, increased trade, new foodstuffs and relative peace naturally led to rapid overall population growth and urbanization. From 1500 to 1650, the population in most European and Asian societies at least doubled; and cities such as London, Beijing, Edo, Istanbul and Delhi, as well as thousands of smaller towns, grew even faster. The urban expansion and commercial growth fuelled the rise of commercial groups—bankers, merchants, ship-builders and manufacturers, and the lawyers, notaries and insurers who served them, but also commercial farmers producing crops for sale. State expansion also meant a growth in the ranks of officials, as well as the printers and booksellers, proprietors of shops and cafes, and artisans who served the burgeoning commercial and official classes. This was as true in China, India and Anatolia as in Europe and the New World.

Not every place flourished. Africa was increasingly torn by fighting—not only with Europeans and Arabs seeking slaves, but with Africans fighting each other to be the groups offering slaves for sale rather than being the enslaved. The natives of North and South America were nearly completely destroyed by the diseases and disregard of their lives brought by European conquerors and colonists. Still, across Eurasia, compared to 1400, by 1600 the world had become a much more populated, more urbanized, centrally ruled and administered place, with vastly expanded local, regional and international trade fuelling the desire for goods and stimulating new ideas.

Yet, as so often in history, just when things seemed to be going well, it was all about to come crashing down.

The crisis of the seventeenth century: strain and recovery

The larger, more populous, more urban, more commercialized, more centralized states that had been built up in the 1500s and 1600s were complex organizations, and diverse flows of people and resources had to be maintained to keep them flourishing. Towns had to be supplied with food; taxes had to be collected to pay for much larger and better equipped armies and navies; peasants had to have sufficient land to feed their families and pay rents and taxes; and the economic, military and administrative elites had to be paid, kept loyal, and efficiently recruited and replaced. The rapidly expanding commercial and trading classes had to find their place in society alongside the privileged aristocratic and bureaucratic elites, and yet provided with the money, credit and security to keep trade flourishing; and intellectual and religious elites had to continue to find reason to inspire the masses and lead the elites in support of the social order and the regime. In the course of the seventeenth century, many of these requirements ceased to be met; both material circuits of supply and social circuits of recruitment became over-loaded and states suffered increasingly severe financial and social strains. The result was a global crisis of political and religious authority that undermined states all across Eurasia.

The warmer interlude that had begun in 1500 faded by the 1590s, and the rigors of the Little Ice Age were felt again all across the world—freezing winters, torrential downpours and floods, disruptions of the monsoon rains, late springs and short summers.[10] As prior generations of population growth pressed on harvests that no longer increased, prices for grains and basic foodstuffs rose everywhere; prices for fuel rose even faster. However, prices for other goods—including bullion, the wages of labor and manufactured goods—rose much more slowly. Population growth had reduced family landholdings and sent more workers to the cities; but as rents rose and real wages fell, both peasants and workers had less to spend on manufactured goods. Merchants and guild workers sought to increase output to compensate for declining relative prices, but found it hard to fight against lower demand, weaker prices for manufactured goods and rising costs of raw materials.

Whether in European kingdoms, the Ottoman Empire or China, landlords resisted the increasing demands of the state, seeking to keep as much revenue as possible in their own hands; yet, rulers faced rapidly expanding expenses from larger armies and administrations and the rising costs of basic foodstuffs. Some landlords were themselves in trouble, unable to keep their own incomes rising in pace with rising prices, but others were able to increase their wealth by buying up the lands of peasants or less fortunate elites, lending money to the state or profiting from the sale of commodities produced on their lands. Officials and aristocrats of older lineages also sought to fend off the social challenge from rising commercial and financial elites.

The difficulties of states in paying their militaries led to desertions, and deserters with guns usually became bandits. In China and the Ottoman Empire, banditry grew to such a scale that leaders emerged to head armies recruited from bandits and attack government forces. In China, one such

---

[10] Geoffrey Parker, *Global Crisis: War, Climate Change, and Catastrophe in the Seventeenth Century* (New Haven, CT: Yale University Press, 2013).

bandit army reached Beijing, where defeat led the last Ming emperor to hang himself as his capital fell. In the Ottoman lands, the bandit leaders negotiated with the sultan to gain grants of land, titles and official positions, morphing into provincial governors and bureaucrats. The sultans also faced uprisings of their own infantry, angry over inflation and the declining value of their pay, sometimes leading to the deposition or even assassination of the sultan.

In Europe, fiscally weakened rulers were unable to keep the balance between the older aristocrats and newly created meritocratic officials, and between older landed and new commercial elites. They also faced urban or peasant uprisings and religious revolts. By the middle of the century, Britain was wracked by revolts in Scotland and Ireland and a civil war between different factions of the elite; France similarly was torn by elite factions and nobles who raised their own armies against the Crown; Spain faced uprisings in Portugal, Catalonia, southern Italy and Sicily; the German lands were devastated by the Thirty Years War (1618 to 1648); and in Russia the 1600s opened with one of the worst famines in its history and a decade of uprisings, invasions and civil wars that led to the replacement of the Rurik dynasty of tsars by the Romanovs.

Global trade continued, and a few areas that had staked their fortunes on trade, such as Holland, which was the leading center of international commerce in the West, and the Mughal Empire, which was Asia's main exporter of cotton and pepper and importer of silver, continued to prosper. Both enjoyed "Golden Ages" of wealth and artistic achievement in the first three-quarters of the seventeenth century. India, situated more to the south than the rest of Eurasia, also seems to have been spared the worst effects of the Little Ice Age. But even in India, by the end of the century the Mughal ruler Aurangzeb found his resources exhausted by the Maratha wars and demands from his followers for state positions, and thus had to restructure his administration.

The theme of restructuring became common after the crises of the early and mid-seventeenth century. The major states were able to recover, and by making adjustments were able to resume the process of increasing their incomes and building their armies and administrations, emerging stronger than before. From 1650 to 1730, population growth stagnated almost everywhere in Europe and Asia; but this was often a benefit to rulers. The breakneck pace of urbanization slowed; food supplies grew relative to population and prices stabilized or declined. Social mobility slowed as well, and rulers were able to restructure their tax systems and administrations without racing against constantly rising prices or rapidly expanding numbers of elites competing for positions.

In England, shortly after the civil war, the Stuart dynasty was restored to the throne, and under James II set about further centralizing royal control over the country and increasing its revenues. James became embroiled in a religious dispute with his own elites, who invited the Dutch leader William of Orange to enter England and challenge James; after James fled, Parliament offered William and his wife Mary the crown. Yet, despite this brief conflict, known as the "Glorious Revolution" of 1688, over the next seventy-five years Britain's navy only grew stronger, its colonies more extensive, and its revenues and credit dramatically increased.

The French monarchy put down the mid-seventeenth century revolt known as the Fronde, and under Louis XVI created a massively powerful absolutist state that became the model for all European monarchs to emulate. Louis XVI appointed new professional administrators to manage the provinces, and reduced the independence of aristocratic lords by forcing them to take up expensive positions in his court, much like the policy that Tokugawa shoguns used to similarly domesticate their regional lords. Spain lost control of Portugal, but reasserted its authority over its other territories and by exploiting new mines in Mexico continued to pump ever-larger volumes of bullion out of its American possessions. In Central and Eastern Europe, the Peace of Westphalia ended the Thirty Years War, allowing Austria-Hungary, Poland and Russia to rebuild their finances and militaries so that they could focus on containing the Ottomans.

Although the Ottoman sultans in the early seventeenth century were certainly weakened by the crisis, with Sultan Ibrahim strangled in 1648 and women of the harem exercising influence over sultans who were often minors, in the second half of the seventeenth century the empire made a significant recovery. Under a series of strong Grand Veziers (chief ministers), the army and navy were strengthened and tax collections greatly increased by selling tax-farming rights to local notables. During this period, the Ottomans were self-sufficient in manufacturing a wide variety of firearms and cannon of quality equal to those of other European powers,[11] and enjoyed a run of military victories, retaking Crete from Venice and expanding their territories in North Africa, Romania and southern Poland. Their fortunes were certainly mixed; although their armies pushed to the

---

[11] Gábor Ágoston, *Guns for the Sultan: Military Power and the Weapons Industry in the Ottoman Empire* (Cambridge University Press 2005).

walls of Vienna in 1683, they were unable to take the city, as a relief force organized by Poland and the Habsburgs came upon them while much of their army was still engaged in siege operations, and the Ottomans' allies from the Crimean Khanate refused to fight. Nonetheless, the Ottomans remained formidable, fighting a see-saw war with the Habsburgs over the next thirty years in which the Ottomans retained most of their Balkan territories, and winning a major battle against Russia in 1710. While the period after 1650 was once described as a long Ottoman decline, this view is no longer tenable. From 1650 to 1870, during a period when Europeans were conquering the rest of the world, the Ottoman Empire kept control of almost all of its territories, continually refashioning itself to keep up its military and administrative effectiveness.

In China, as bandit armies were menacing Beijing, elite officials sought to prevent total disaster by inviting a neighboring ruler to come to their aid. To the north of China proper, in Manchuria, a series of ambitious Manchu rulers had been adopting some of the methods of Chinese statecraft to build a standing army and central administration in place of looser tribal structures. In 1618, the Manchus declared their own Qing dynasty and started to move south against the Ming. A few decades later, Ming generals asked the Qing to send their armies to help them repel the bandit forces. In 1644, after Qing forces had destroyed the bandit army threatening the capital, the Qing declared themselves the successor of the Ming as rulers of China.

The Qing rulers had to fight for decades to subdue all of China, and in the process had to restructure the state to strengthen their authority. Although they adopted the Confucian system of civil administration by officials recruited through competitive examinations, they developed a distinctive banner system to organize the military. They also passed legislation to force large landowners to pay their taxes, and to restore land to the peasantry, because in the late Ming landlords in the fertile Yangzi regions had often forced thousands of poor peasants into virtual bondage on their estates. After subduing the whole of China, the Qing also pushed deeply into Central Asia, defeating the remaining Mongol chiefdoms and firming up their authority over Tibet.

Not all states emerged stronger; the Safavids entered a terminal decline after 1666, and were destroyed by Afghan forces in 1722. The island states of Southeast Asia fell to the Dutch; and the remnants of Mongol Hordes were suppressed by Russia and China. Nonetheless, the world map of 1700, like that of 1600, was dominated by large empires: the Spanish, Portuguese, English and French in the Americas; the Ottomans in North Africa, the

Balkans and the Middle East; the Safavids hanging on in Central Asia; the Mughals dominating India; and Russia and China controlling northern and eastern Asia (see Map 18.1). There were new ruling dynasties in Britain and in China, and all states had worked to reverse the growing threat from over-powerful local lords and to improve their revenues and militaries. But in the aftermath of the crisis of the seventeenth century, restructuring and recovery had prevailed.

Cultural retrenchment

So far, we have spoken of states mainly in terms of their material and organizational basis—raising taxes, recruiting and training administrative elites, deploying military forces, managing trade and administering territor-ies. Yet, no states were able to maintain elite loyalty and keep order over vast and diverse territories simply by force of arms. States also relied on carefully supported ideologies and religious beliefs to maintain support, and on intellectual and religious elites to promulgate them. Of course, every society also had its schisms, sects and heterodox beliefs that challenged the prevailing order; but rulers worked diligently to keep these within bounds and to maintain an ideological framework that supported their power.

As religious faith was a major source of legitimacy everywhere, reactions to the economic and political disorders of the seventeenth century frequently took the form of religious critiques.

In China in the early 1600s, scholars associated with private academies were sharply critical of the regime. Some claimed that the regime had lost the "mandate of heaven" by abandoning proper Confucian conduct of governance. Others, inspired by the early-sixteenth-century official and scholar Wang Yangming, argued for a more innovative and practical approach to current problems, rather than relying entirely on the Confucian classics. In the mid-century, as disorder increased, in parts of China the peasants who had been reduced to serf-like bondage on large estates rebelled and "sharpened their hoes into swords and took to themselves the title of 'Levelling Kings,' declaring that they were levelling the distinction between masters and serfs, titled and mean, rich and poor. The tenants ... would ... say 'We are all of us equally men. What right had you to call us serfs?'"[12]

---

[12] Mark Elvin, *The Pattern of the Chinese Past* (Stanford University Press, 1973).

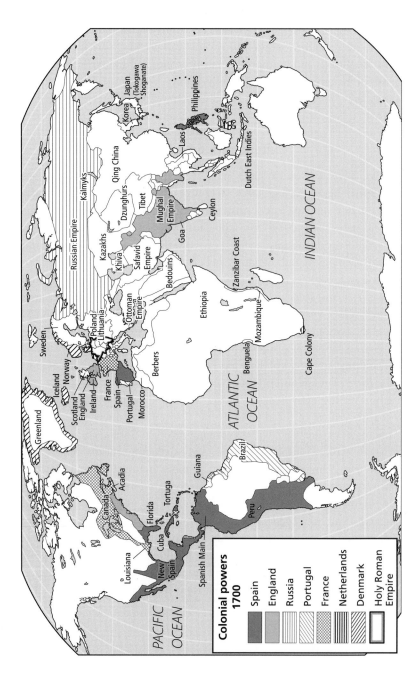

18.1 The world in 1700

Colonial powers 1700

- Spain
- England
- Russia
- Portugal
- France
- Netherlands
- Denmark
- Holy Roman Empire

PACIFIC OCEAN

ATLANTIC OCEAN

INDIAN OCEAN

Greenland

Iceland
Norway
Sweden
Scotland
England
Ireland
France
Spain
Portugal
Morocco

Louisiana
New Spain
Cuba
Florida
Tortuga
Acadia
Canada
Spanish Main
Peru
Guiana
Brazil

Berbers
Ottoman Empire
Bedouins
Ethiopia
Benguela
Mozambique
Zanzibar Coast
Cape Colony

Poland
Lithuania
Russian Empire
Kalmyks
Kazakhs
Khiva
Safavid Empire
Mughal Empire
Goa
Dzunghurs
Tibet
Qing China
Ceylon
Laos
Korea
Japan (Tokogawa Shoganate)
Philippines
Dutch East Indies

In the Ottoman Empire, the bandit rebellions of the early seventeenth century were accompanied by the rise of the deeply conservative Kadizadeli religious movement, advocating a return to pure Sunni Islam, the destruction of heterodox groups and the submission of non-Muslims. Kadizadeli preachers gained a following in the main cities of the empire, and among officials as well.

This fundamentalism was not dissimilar from that of two movements in Europe, which began in the late sixteenth century and came to power in the seventeenth: the Puritans in England and the Jesuits in the Catholic Church. The Puritans attacked the Church of England for being too "popish" in its policies and practices, and wanted to "purify" it. Its opposite number in many ways was the Jesuit movement, "warriors for the Church" who sought to restore the influence of Rome and adherence to Catholic ritual and doctrine as defined by the Pope. Like China, Europe too had its "Levellers," a group of religious dissenters in England who advocated equality and denied the authority of kings and noble lords. In the Islamic lands, Sufi orders also sometimes advocated a socially unsettling equality, saying the Qur'an promoted the equality of men *and women* in the eyes of God.

Throughout the seventeenth century, religious wars added to the general disorder: Confucian Ming Loyalists fought against the shamanist and Buddhist Manchus; Sunni rulers fought against followers of Shi'ism, and sometimes against Sufis; Puritans fought against supporters of the Church of England; and all across Europe Protestants fought against Catholics in conflicts that were international, civil and sometimes both. Thus, one of the imperatives for rulers in the latter half of the seventeenth century was a cultural retrenchment to re-establish their legitimacy and the loyalty of their officials and subjects.

Having no deep understanding of climate change, demography or modern economics, seventeenth-century intellectuals usually blamed rulers' tolerance of diversity, syncretism and deviations from orthodoxy as having been responsible for the disorders of the age. (In Western Europe, religious and political authorities sometimes even blamed witches for catastrophic weather events.) Thus, cultural retrenchment took the path of tightening up enforcement of orthodox beliefs, often accompanied by a strengthening of religious establishments and the suppression of dissent. As the best-established and most legitimate sources of ideology were the classic texts at the core of each civilization's belief system, the orthodoxies that were enforced were generally based on the Bible, the Qur'an and the Confucian classics.

In Europe, the Thirty Years War ended with an agreement that rulers could determine religious practice in the boundaries of their states, and that other rulers should recognize and respect their sovereignty in this regard. The Austrian Habsburgs joined the Spanish in making Roman Catholicism the official religion in their realms; the Scandinavians opted for Lutheran church establishments, and even the Dutch Reformed Church sought to exclude other faiths. In France, Louis XIV decided to enforce Catholicism in his kingdom, forcing French Protestants to flee to Britain, the Netherlands and Prussia, where Protestant rulers took them in.

A few smaller kingdoms—Britain, Prussia, Denmark—which did not have such large populations that they could enjoy the luxury of expelling portions of their population for religious reasons, remained islands of relative pluralism and limited toleration. But most of Europe settled into state-enforced orthodoxy within national borders. The most striking change was in Poland, where the Jesuits had their greatest success. The pluralism that had been maintained in the sixteenth century ended, and by the close of the seventeenth century Poland's Christian population was converted almost entirely to Roman Catholicism, and its Jewish population—the largest and most culturally important in Europe—was the target of riots and violence.

In both the Ottoman and Mughal Empires, the relative tolerance of diverse groups that prevailed in the fifteenth and sixteenth centuries gave way to a more rigid enforcement of Sunni orthodoxy. Ottoman Sultan Mehmed IV (r. 1648 to 1687) embraced the Kadizadeli fundamentalists, and "the renewed project of Islamization . . . was touted as a solution to enhance the somewhat battered legitimacy of the Ottoman state."[13] Christians, Jews and Sufis all came under harsh and unprecedented attacks. Although attacks on minorities faded after 1700, the Sunni preachers (*'ulema*) grew in strength, and in the eighteenth century conservative readings of religious texts formed the basis for an increasingly orthodox Sunni identity of the empire.

In the Mughal Empire, a tightening of Sunni orthodoxy also occurred, similar to but not as severe as that in the Ottoman lands. Emperor Aurangzeb (r. 1656 to 1707), facing rebellions from the Marathas and the Sikhs, restored discriminatory taxation on Hindus and ordered the destruction of Hindu and Sikh temples that were associated with rebellions. Aurangzeb gave greater authority to the *'ulema* to enforce Islamic law, and encouraged non-Muslims to convert. Aurangzeb was personally devout, but did not encourage or

---

[13] Barkey, *Empire of Difference*, p. 188.

undertake attacks against non-Sunni subjects, as occurred in the Ottoman lands. Nor did he exclude non-Muslims from his state administration, as did the Ottomans, and indeed most European monarchs who rarely appointed officials who were not adherents of the state religion. Nonetheless, Aurangzeb's policies encouraged a closer identification of the empire with adherence to orthodox Sunni beliefs.

The Safavid Empire employed the most extreme religious policy of any of the gunpowder empires. Having determined to build a distinctive Iranian, Shi'a identity for their empire, the Safavids forced the conversion of all Muslims in their territory to Shi'ism. Much as Spain had given its non-Catholic population the choice of conversion, exile or death in 1492 to 1526, the Safavids forced all of its Muslim population to convert to Shi'ism or die. When the empire expanded to Iraq and Azerbaijan, these areas were enjoined to adopt Shi'ism as well.

In China, the conquering Manchus decided that the best way to legitimate themselves with the Chinese elite was to become even more Confucian than their predecessors. Scholars and officials were co-opted by prodigious support for efforts to study, purify and reconstitute the original meaning of the classical sacred Confucian texts, using a new scientific philology based on historical studies. The Qianlong Emperor (r. 1736 to 1795) sponsored an enormous project to collect corrected editions of all the classic texts of China's Confucian tradition, in the "Complete Imperial Library in the Four Branches of Literature." This project employed hundreds of scholars for nearly a quarter century and the final product, published in almost 80,000 volumes, was reproduced for distribution in all the major centres of the empire. However, the process was combined with harsh censorship; any books critical of the Manchus or deemed as too heterodox were banned and destroyed.

Thus, by 1700, in addition to the world being dominated by major empires—European states with their Atlantic possessions, the Islamic gunpowder empires, Russia and China—intellectual life within those empires was increasingly dominated by a focus on restoring allegiance to orthodox beliefs founded on their core classical texts. Science and scholarship continued at high levels, as long as they did not come into conflict with those core texts; and military, agricultural and manufacturing technology continued to move forward. In the late seventeenth and early eighteenth centuries, global trade rebounded, as the Atlantic exchange in slaves, sugar, tobacco, bullion and other items surged to new levels, and Asian output of cotton and silk, tea and coffee, and spices and ceramics boomed.

In 1500, the population of Asia was approximately three times that of Europe; by 1700, it was three and a half times as large. Real wages of urban workers in Beijing and Constantinople were virtually the same as those in Paris or Florence. There was nothing obvious to indicate that in a century and a half, Europeans would humiliate China and take over India; detach the Balkans from Ottoman control; and become considerably richer per head than Asians, while (with the exception of Russia) living in constitutionally limited national states. Certainly, Europeans had secured some small footholds on the coasts of East Asia and conquered a few Pacific islands; but as of 1700, after two centuries of activity in the Indian Ocean, they had not penetrated beyond the coasts of Africa or Asia, and had to follow the dictates of the Mughal, Chinese and Japanese rulers who regulated their activities.

In 1689, when representatives of the British East India Company refused to negotiate with the Mughal Emperor Aurangzeb, a Mughal fleet attacked the company's trading post at Bombay. After a year of resistance, the EIC surrendered, and in 1690 the company sent envoys to Aurangzeb's camp to plead for a pardon. The company's envoys had to prostrate themselves before the emperor, pay a large indemnity and promise better behavior in the future.

So what changed in the following 150 years?

The Western exception: falling out of love with ancient wisdom

Since the West first became aware of its sudden leap forward relative to the rest of world around 1850, scholars have sought to explain it. Naturally, they found the answer in some form of European superiority or early lead, such as a lead in weapons, or science, or productivity, or the virtues of Christianity, or Roman law, or the philosophy of the Ancient Greeks. The problem with this approach, however, is that if history proves anything, it is that an early lead in almost any kind of technology or skill means nothing in the long run.

Chinese and Indians had early leads in naval technology over Europeans, but it was the European fleets that eventually controlled the seas. Indian mathematicians and Arab scientists had a considerable lead over medieval European scholars with regard to advanced arithmetic, chemistry, optics and astronomy, so much so that almost all of modern and medieval European physics build directly on Arab commentaries and translations; yet, it was Europeans who first moved on to develop calculus, natural logarithms, laws of motion and the periodic table. India had a huge lead over Europe in cotton textile production, with regard to both productivity and quality of products. Yet, Britain came to dominate global cotton markets and industrialize production. China had roughly a 700-year lead over Britain in the production of cast iron and smelting with coke (coal) instead of charcoal; yet, it was Britain that developed coal and iron-based industry. Even within Europe, the seventeenth-century Dutch held the lead in shipping, energy production (from peat and windmills), fine textile production, agricultural productivity, finance, warehousing, artistic production and military drill; yet, by the eighteenth century, Holland's textile output collapsed, its military and naval strength deteriorated, and it was quickly overtaken by Britain as Europe's leading maritime and manufacturing power.

What we see time and time again is European nations, and especially Britain, vaulting from the back of the pack to take the lead in one field after another after 1700. Let me therefore suggest that what enabled Britain to take the global lead was not any early superiority or advantage, but rather benefits from relative backwardness. I would highlight three distinct forms of backwardness that, quite accidentally, turned into remarkable resources for future gains.

First, compared to all major Asian civilizations, Europe was incredibly isolated after about 700 AD. China, India and the Middle East, even Persia and North Africa, were part of a vast Eurasian cosmopolis.[14] The spread of Islam created an Arabic-literate community that stretched from Spain across Northern Africa into the Indian Ocean and as far as today's Malaysia; and throughout the Middle Ages that Islamic community was in constant trading contact with the other societies around the Indian Ocean and China Seas. By contrast, Europeans prior to 1500 were boxed in on every side, blocked by the Atlantic to the west, polar seas to the north, and the Mongols and Islamic empires to the east and south. Except for the rare merchant/traveller (such as Marco Polo, and even his stories were not widely believed), Europeans had little direct contact with any areas outside the Mediterranean or east of Jerusalem until the late 1400s.

Second, again compared to other civilizations, Europe had been exceptionally cut off from its own classical texts. After the final withdrawal of Byzantine power from Italy, much of the classical literature of Europe, in both Greek and Latin, was lost to Western Europe for centuries. It was only in the tenth century, when the Christian re-conquest of Spain got underway,

---

[14] See Gommans, "Indian Ocean," in this volume.

that Europe gained access to large numbers of classical texts, albeit often in Arabic translations. Certainly, after 500 AD scholarship, science and mathematics had continued within the Church, as scholars could draw on the surviving Latin translations by Boethius of Greek mathematical and philosophical texts, and manuscripts from monastic collections. Yet, many of the major works of Plato, Aristotle and others were not available until the eleventh century or later. The great atomist poem by Lucretius, *On the Nature of Things*, was only rediscovered in 1417. Nothing comparable, not even the Mongol invasions, created the same degree of loss and distance between medieval Chinese and their ancient classics, or Indians and their Sanskrit Vedas, or Muslims and Persian classical literature.

Third, the barbarian invasions had also left Western states administratively backwards compared to Asian empires. Ming China, the Ottomans and the Mughals had all inherited a centuries-old legacy of imperial statecraft and administration, in China from the Tang and Song dynasties, during which the examination system was initiated and developed, in the Islamic empires from Persia and the Baghdad caliphate, where the sultan/vezier model and administrative slaves had developed. These practices were designed to enable rulers to control large empires, and provided an early achievement in absolutist and bureaucratic administration.

In Europe, medieval kings still ruled with institutions inherited from barbarian chiefs, rather than the advanced statecraft of Imperial Rome. The codices of Roman law, like other classical texts, were only recovered in the tenth century. Even once scholars began to study Roman administrative law, and develop it for European states, it did not entirely displace customary feudal practices. Significantly, European states retained councils of nobles as high appeals courts and advisors to the king. These took various forms, including the Parliament in Britain, *parlements* in France, *cortes* in Spain, and provincial and national estates in many kingdoms. All of these bodies had various rights to share in framing royal edicts, advising on fiscal and military matters, and preserved principles of representation and election in the political realm. They also upheld feudal principles that kings' rights over their vassals were limited by agreement and by law (the Magna Carta in England being an early and famous example of such agreements).

Of course, such interference from assemblies of hereditary notables would have been intolerable in the more sophisticated official bureaucratic administrations of great empires—and European rulers, as soon as they became acquainted with Imperial Roman law, worked to replace these bodies with rule through appointed ministers and officials. Yet, Europeans had a late start, and as late as the seventeenth century, while some rulers had succeeded in drastically weakening these troublesome bodies, many others had not.

The result of all these modes of relative backwardness was that Europe underwent an exceptional evolution over the centuries from 1400 to 1800, which led it where no other major civilization went: to a repudiation of its own classical heritage and a search for fundamentally new modes of knowledge-seeking and political administration.

In both China and the Islamic world, the Middle Ages were a glorious period of scholarship; but the result was to reinforce, rather than alter or repudiate, their classical texts. In China, these were the Confucian-era classics. In the twelfth century, Zhu Xi and other Song scholars assembled and codified the key texts of the Confucian tradition into the "Four Books and Five Classics" that became the basis for the imperial exam system, and served as the core legitimatizing texts of imperial rule throughout the Ming and Qing eras. It was a remarkable achievement, but represented a distillation of ancient texts rather than a major departure or new synthesis.

In Islam, scholars had access to the libraries of Christian lands (in Greek and Latin) that they conquered from the Byzantines in the Middle East, Egypt and North Africa, together with the native speakers and scholars who lived there. The intersection of Islamic and Christian thought (which included Greek mathematical, medical, botanical and literary works, as well as philosophy) stimulated Arab mathematicians, astronomers, chemists and philosophers to do experiments, push the boundaries of Greek knowledge and develop their own advances.

The results were enormously impressive, but not revolutionary. Muslim scientists and astronomers improved on Ptolemy's astronomical models and made original advances in optics, mathematics, chemistry, medicine and calendrical accuracy. Yet, they never overturned the fundamental cosmology behind Ptolemy's and Aristotle's work: the belief that all things have a natural motion, and that for heavenly bodies that motion is circular. They also found the profusion of diverse Greek philosophical schools—Aristotelian, Platonic, atomist, Stoic, Sceptic—frustrating, and difficult to reconcile with the authority of the Qur'an. Eventually, one of Islam's most distinguished scholars, al-Ghazali, wrote a damning critique of Greek philosophy, urging scholars to leave it aside and instead focus on the many strands of Islam's own *shari'a* and Sufi traditions. Al-Ghazali was influential but not decisive, as other Arab scholars continued to study and comment on Aristotle, most notably Averroes in Spain. Nonetheless, especially after the destruction of the Baghdad libraries by the Mongols, as in China, Islamic scholarship concentrated on empirical science, especially medicine, astronomy and mathematics, and on studying works in the Persian and Islamic tradition rather than wrestling with the fundamental principles of Greek beliefs. Thus, Greek philosophy, despite its intense study, never became integral to Islamic cultural traditions or its legitimation of authority.

Both Islamic society and China thus emerged from their medieval period with a cosmopolitan world view and a strengthened set of classical texts that could be used to bolster state authority for centuries to come. Even when Europeans arrived in China, and even when they told of a new continent from which they brought silver to trade in Asia, nothing was particularly alarming about this news; the Chinese simply sought to add Europeans as one more foreign group subject to the tribute/trading relationships they had with other regions. Similarly, Islamic societies, having absorbed what they could from Western classical works, and having achieved substantial leads over medieval Europeans in calendrical calculations, navigation, chemistry and other areas, could be fairly complacent about the entry of Europeans into the global circuits of trade. Still expanding their own empires into Europe at the time, they saw no reason to doubt the superiority of their political and intellectual heritage.

By contrast, in Europe, medieval scholars were introduced to their own classical literature in a process of rapid discovery of the unknown. As Europeans pushed into Muslim Spain, and gained direct contact with the Byzantines through the Crusades, they brought back manuscripts of classical texts that had not been seen in the West for centuries. From Spain, many of these texts came with expert commentaries by Islamic scholars that further helped spur interest. The recovery and study of Roman law began in Bologna, whose law school developed into the West's first university. Soon, Oxford and Paris and a dozen other centers had communities of scholars poring over the newly recovered classical texts.

Yet, by now, Western Europe had been a thoroughly Christian society for almost a thousand years, and the clear imperative for scholars was to somehow reconcile the flood of new texts from classical authorities with Biblical revelation and Christian doctrine. This task was undertaken by generations of scholars, culminating in the masterwork of St. Thomas Aquinas, the *Summa Theologica*, in the late thirteenth century.

Medieval scholars were by no means slavish with regard to the Greek classics, picking up where Arab scholars had left off in making marked improvements in such areas as the study of motion and optics, and using observational evidence as well as logic to arrive at an accurate understanding of nature. Still, the ideas gained from the classics had great prestige as ancient and globally recognized wisdom, while at the same time their novelty to medieval scholars was thrilling. Weaving together classical wisdom and Christian doctrine in ways that were complementary and mutually supportive created a powerful new intellectual edifice.

The Renaissance led to further recoveries of classical knowledge, especially regarding sculpture and architectural technique, philology (recovery of the grammar, syntax and style of classical languages), law and statecraft. By 1500, Europe's Renaissance monarchs, like their Mughal, Safavid, Ottoman and Chinese counterparts, had finally begun to gain access to a classical corpus that would provide elegantly schooled bureaucratic administrators, a supportive legal code, and sophisticated religious and philosophical grounds for their absolute authority.

However, just as this seemed to be coming together in Europe, a bewildering set of observations started to tear this new synthesis apart. University curricula which had come to depend on Greek masters such as Ptolemy for geography and astronomy, Aristotle for cosmology and Galen for medicine were soon shown to be inaccurate or incomplete.

This process began with the voyages of discovery. Seeking to break out of their isolated position and enter directly into the Indian Ocean trade circuits, Portuguese and then Spanish expeditions sailed into the Atlantic. First exploring the coast of Africa, then reaching the New World and finally circumnavigating the globe, Europeans came into direct contact with a bewildering variety of peoples, cultures, plants, animals and even continents.

The last was the most perplexing. Once it was clear, by around 1530, that the New World was neither the fabled East Indies (India, Indonesia, China), nor the fabulous lost island of Atlantis, but a previously unknown continent stretching almost from pole to pole, it was unavoidable to recognize that Ptolemy's authoritative geography had been wholly unaware of it. This was the first crack in the authority of ancient texts.

The discovery of new plants and animals unknown to ancient botany and zoology was a similar blow. In 1543, the anatomical research of Vesalius, supported by exquisitely detailed illustrations, showed that Galen had also made fundamental errors. The sixteenth century saw a mania develop in Europe for collections and observations of natural phenomena, as more and more novelties were reported. In 1572 and 1604, supernovae appeared in the skies above Europe. While Chinese and Arab astronomers had recorded the appearance of such "guest stars" for centuries, these too were something new for Europeans. Moreover, they were radically unexpected, as the cosmology of Aristotle had stated that the heavens were perfect and unchanging. Tycho Brahe and Johannes Kepler published studies of these new stars, and Brahe also published an analysis of the trajectory of the comet of 1577; this showed that the comet's path was well above the orbit of the moon and would have smashed through the crystalline spheres that Aristotle claimed carried the heavenly bodies around the Earth.

Even the very centrality and immobility of the Earth—precepts fundamental to Biblical cosmology as interpreted by the Church and supported by Aristotle—came under challenge. As early as 1543, Copernicus had offered a mathematical system to plot planetary orbits with the Earth and all other planets revolving around the sun. This could be accepted or viewed with scepticism as simply a powerful hypothesis. But spurred on by the new observations of Kepler and Brahe and the desire for more, a number of Europeans began to combine multiple lenses—which had been produced for eyeglasses since the thirteenth century—to build telescopes to better observe the heavens. In 1608 and 1609, Thomas Harriott in England and Galileo in Italy recorded their telescopic observations of the moon, which when magnified had features very much like the Earth—another assault on the radical classical distinction between "perfect" heavenly bodies and Earth. Observations of sunspots amplified this point further. Also in 1609, Johannes Kepler showed that the orbital path of Mars, which had always troubled astronomers, was troubling because it was a perfect ellipse, not a circle as Ptolemy and Aristotle had insisted.

The following year, Galileo went on to use the telescope to record moon-like phases of Venus, proving that it indeed revolved around the sun, and to identify additional bodies rotating around Jupiter, thus providing empirical proof that Earth was not the centre of all heavenly motions. Galileo began teaching that Copernicus's system of a moving Earth and sun-centered solar system was physically correct; but this was too much for the Catholic Church, which urged him to refrain from teaching this as doctrine, and proscribed heliocentric views.

The accumulation of so much powerful and novel evidence that contradicted the teachings of ancient scholars led philosophers such as Francis Bacon and René Descartes to argue that a whole new approach to understanding nature was required. For Bacon, that approach had to be based on the further accumulation and collation of empirical observations; for Descartes it had to be based on a reformulation of philosophy that discarded all prior approaches and began fresh from mathematical and logical reasoning. By the late 1500s, many Europeans were increasingly looking at all of nature—from bodies to continents to the heavens—as a set of mechanisms that needed to be carefully examined, deconstructed and explained.

In fact, Bacon, Descartes and other sixteenth- and seventeenth-century philosophers were in many ways taking up where medieval scholars had left off, restating and building on many of the latter's advances and critiques of ancient texts. But the new empirical findings forced them to go further, questioning the value and accuracy of classical understandings of nature in their entirety. In the context of the 1600s, these steps were revolutionary. European rulers had been working to reinforce the legitimacy of growing royal power with the authority of scripture and classical learning in one neat, well-integrated package. To claim that ancient texts were full of fundamental errors and could not be trusted was a threat to this package. Moreover, this threat arose at the same time that Protestantism, on wholly different grounds of critiquing the Church for selfishness, corruption and sinful behaviour, had also urged the denial of papal authority and raised the flag of rebellion against Catholic rulers. Other civilizations at this time also had to deal with rebellions and heterodoxy, but only in Europe were these combined with a continent-wide research program whose results were providing empirical proofs of the falsity of revered classical texts.

The disorders of the seventeenth century, including the plague, forced a young Isaac Newton to leave Cambridge, but from the 1600s onwards progress continued in many fields. In 1614, John Napier published the first extensive tables of logarithms, while in 1628, William Harvey demonstrated that blood circulated continuously in the body, not just through in-and-out pulses as specified by Galen. In 1638, Galileo published his work on relative motion, which—in another repudiation of Aristotle—showed that projectiles travel in parabolic trajectories. This not only was a profound finding; it also improved mathematical approaches to gunnery, with practical consequences for the more accurate aiming and firing of artillery.

Also in the early seventeenth century, Dutch and Swedish military innovators developed and perfected military drill, breaking down the movements of musket-loading and firing to a series of discrete and repeatable steps that musketeers could be trained to follow with precise coordination. Such drill greatly increased the effectiveness of armed infantry. Still, the matchlock firing mechanism of muskets remained clumsy and slow; but when the safer and faster flintlock firing mechanism was invented and widely adopted after 1700, and combined with the precision of European drill, infantry volleys became far more deadly and gave European arms a considerable advantage in the field over armies with less proficient drill and older muskets. This combination proved particularly effective for the British when fighting in India in the eighteenth century.

To return to advances in the pure sciences, in the 1640s, Blaise Pascal and Evangelista Torricelli had developed the barometer and used it to prove the existence of atmospheric pressure. Pascal also wrote on the vacuum, refuting Aristotle's belief that vacuums could not exist in nature, while also developing the first calculating machines and advancing probability theory. Elsewhere in Europe, by the 1660s, Otto von Guericke and Robert Boyle were doing experiments with vacuums, while Anton Van Leeuwenhoek and Robert Hooke were making new discoveries with microscopes. Leibniz and Newton were at work on the invention of the calculus, which enabled them to overcome the limits of classical approaches to the study of motion.

These seventeenth-century advances were crowned by Isaac Newton's *Mathematical Principles of Natural Philosophy*, published in 1687. In that volume, Newton presented a comprehensive theory of motion under the force of gravity, explaining phenomena as varied as the shape of the spinning Earth, the speed and shape of planetary orbits, the movements of falling bodies and projections, and the patterns of the tides. Although Newton had to assume a mysterious gravitational force that acted across space without direct contact between bodies, in Newton's mechanics the motions of all bodies in the universe seemed to be precisely explained without recourse to miracles or a privileged position for the Earth. To some, the absence of divine intervention and the mysterious nature of gravity were distressing. But to others, Newton's universe was a beautiful mechanism that operated regularly and indefinitely according to precise rules, like exquisite clockwork.

I mention all of these items (and I could cite many more) to illustrate how, in the century and a half following 1500, Europe experienced a veritable explosion of scientific discovery and practical invention, spurred on at first by the flood of new and unexpected information that flowed from the voyages of discovery, and then by investigations with new scientific instruments (telescopes, microscopes, barometers) which rapidly unmoored European thought from its classical foundations. Eventually, these advances would lead European technology to become the most productive in the world. But long before steam engines and railways would reshape Europe's economy, these profound changes in thinking would impact the shape of European states.

The Enlightenment and the model
of the modern state

In the late seventeenth century, all major states were restructuring in the wake of the seventeenth-century crisis. The usual pattern, as we have seen, was to further strengthen state authority by resting even more heavily on orthodox readings of classical texts.

European states initially followed the same approach. Catholic and Protestant states alike sought to suppress some of the new scientific findings and philosophical approaches of the seventeenth century. Catholic states sought to suppress the Newtonian view of the solar system; the Jesuits instead promoted an alternative developed by Tycho Brahe that retained the centrality and stationary nature of the Earth, with the sun moving around the Earth and carrying all the other planets with it. Even in Protestant Holland, Cartesian philosophy was condemned at the University of Utrecht in 1643, and by the early eighteenth century Newtonian science was rarely taught there. James II of England sought to place Catholics in key posts in the major universities, which he thought were producing dangerous ideas, although his efforts were resisted by Newton and Protestant elites. Elsewhere in Europe, the mathematical sciences, including the study of projectile motion, hydraulics and probability, continued and were too useful to suppress. But physical theories that conflicted with the teachings of the Church were resisted wherever possible.

Yet, it was not possible to suppress all the consequences of this intellectual shift. At the same time that philosophers of nature were envisioning new sciences, philosophers of society were taking a similar approach. In the seventeenth century, Thomas Hobbes and John Locke started reasoning from first principles, using logic to identify what they felt were natural laws to guide the formation and operation of state authority. In Locke's *Two Treatises of Government* (1690), he first uses logic to demolish the idea that Biblical texts provide support for a divine right of kings; then goes on to argue that civil society exists only to protect the security and property of citizens, so that if a ruler acts arbitrarily to threaten such security and property, the citizens have an obligation to rise against that ruler's authority. Locke knew that these views were dangerous, and he published the *Treatises* anonymously. They were so extreme that they were hardly cited in the next half century, becoming widely acclaimed only after 1760. Yet, they are important for indicating where pure reason, applied to political thought, could lead.

The eighteenth century saw further efforts to treat the science of government in the same fashion as the science of nature: to reason critically, eschew
models based on tradition or sacred texts, and try to develop models based
on natural principles and mechanisms of balancing forces.

After the disorders of the seventeenth century, thinkers focused their
efforts on developing a science of liberty, trying to discern how best to
structure a government to protect the security of its people.

In this, Europeans started from a very different place from Asian societies.
In Islamic societies and China, it was of course expected that for peasants to
farm and merchants to trade they needed to be secure in their persons and
property. It was thus up to the state to protect the weak from the strong and
to enforce justice by passing and administering laws according to Qur'anic or
Confucian principles which embodied justice. But the authority of the state
was embodied in that of the sultan or emperor. It was their responsibility to
provide justice for their subjects by creating appropriate laws and ensuring
their fair enforcement. Advisors, officials and judges aided them, interpreting
classical and sacred texts and developing laws, but the authority of sultans
and emperors was in theory unassailable and unlimited.

Europe, however, had a variety of traditions that pointed to a different
understanding of the relationship between authority and justice. The medieval institutions of vassalage, parliaments and estates were based on the idea
that kings ruled in partnership with their chief and noblest subjects, had
reciprocal obligations to them that must be honoured, and that passing laws
and collecting taxes could only be undertaken with those subjects' consent.
Medieval philosophers spoke of the virtues of "mixed" government which
included kings and their parliaments, and William of Occam and Nicholas of
Cusa wrote that people could not be expected to obey the commands of
kings if those commands were contrary to justice.

There were also republican traditions, which originated in the Greek city-
states and the Roman Republic, handed down in the writings of Aristotle,
Cicero, Herodotus and other classical writers, and revived in the experience
of medieval and Renaissance Italian city-states, which developed the ideas of
citizenship, democracy and republican rule. According to these traditions,
free adult males were citizens who had a right to choose their leaders, and
those leaders' authority was temporary, bestowed and bound by the laws of
the republic and checked by the actions of citizen assemblies. Classical Greek
thought had distinguished between rulers who obeyed the laws and tyrants
who did not. Whereas in Asian polities, the power of laws came from the
power of the ruler, and were unchecked by anything except regard for the

ideas of justice and morality as presented in classical texts, in the republican tradition the power of the ruler came from the laws, and popular assemblies acted to ensure that the ruler acted according to law.

By the seventeenth century, most European rulers had leaned on different traditions, drawing on the divine right of kings, ideas of the "Great Chain of Being" that handed authority directly from God to kings to watch over their people like shepherds over their flocks, and elements of later Roman law, all of which reinforced their absolute authority. They sought to get around parliaments and estates as much as possible, not calling them to meet or appointing officials that took over their responsibilities, and seeking revenue sources not dependent on parliamentary grants. They sought to gain control of judges, using special courts to enforce royal decrees. (In Russia, which drew more on Byzantine traditions, the idea of limits on the ruler's authority were much weaker or absent.) By this time, many of the Italian city-states that had once functioned as republics had been swallowed up by dukes and converted to monarchies; those that remained were regarded as minor exceptions with institutions not suitable for great territorial states.

Yet, when European states were weakened by the crisis of the seventeenth century, the focus of elite opposition was often through the remaining parliaments, and the elites' battle cry in resisting the demands of states for more resources was not just one of injustice, but claims that the liberties of the people were being infringed by tyrannical rulers. Indeed, through the entire period from 1500 to 1650, when states around the world were extending their bureaucracy, authority and resources, resistance in Europe had taken the form of a revival of republican thought.[15] Europe's medieval parliamentary institutions, and its republican intellectual traditions, were reinforced by the sixteenth- and seventeenth-century discoveries and inventions, in which the power of reason was overcoming claims of both ancient and divine authority.

It was an odd mixture, to be sure—scepticism about divine rights based on scientific refutation of scripture and ancient texts, medieval institutions of mixed rule, and long-unused notions of democracy, republicanism and citizenship. Moreover, in the seventeenth century, European rulers for the most part succeeded in overcoming challenges, restoring their authority, and even further reducing the power of nobles, estates and parliaments and

---

[15] J.G.A. Pocock, *The Machiavellian Moment: Florentine Political Thought and the Atlantic Republican Tradition* (Princeton University Press, 1975).

expanding the Crown's bureaucracy and resources. Yet, it proved a potent, even explosive, mixture in the following century.

Philosophical works on government written in the eighteenth century, a period commonly known as the Enlightenment, are quite diverse. They include the work of Montesquieu, whose *Spirit of the Laws* (1748) argued for the separation of political powers among an executive, legislature and judiciary. They also include the Scottish political economy school, including Adam Smith, who sought a science of trade and wealth. Other major authors include Voltaire, who attacked the authority of the Catholic Church and was a passionate advocate of Newtonian science, and Jean-Jacques Rousseau, who attacked all the traditional inequalities of the social order. What they all had in common, however, was an effort to develop an ideal of political organization based on reason, rather than religious belief or traditions, which would be effective in protecting the security and property of people from arbitrary and oppressive actions by the state.

There is an extensive debate on whether these works had any real impact on political change—certainly, most people were more moved by scurrilous tales of royal debauchery or direct threats to their livelihood than abstract philosophical arguments. Yet, there is no doubt that Montesquieu and Locke had a crucial impact on the framers of the American Constitution, whose design for a new kind of republic was one of the most important steps in developing the modern state.

Montesquieu's *The Spirit of the Laws* combined medieval ideas about mixed forms of government with republican goals of averting tyrannical rule. He argued that a government having separate executive, legislative and judicial bodies, each exercising their own power, was the best way to check unjust authority and ensure that people retained their liberty through the protection of the laws.

Montesquieu's theory drew on the practice of Britain, where, exceptionally in Europe, a strong and active Parliament had taken the lead in both 1640 and 1689 in resisting kings whose religious and fiscal policies were seen as oppressing British liberties. The survival of a strong Parliament in England was not inevitable. For much of the sixty years preceding 1689, British rulers had tried to get by without Parliaments, to subordinate them or to pack them with supporters to reduce their independence. It was only the fact that England's Catholic King James II had so deeply lost the trust of Protestant leaders that they conspired to replace him with a Protestant king, and that an Act of Parliament was the necessary vehicle to do this, which resulted in the preservation of Parliament's power in Britain, and elevated that body to a role unmatched by any other representative body in Europe. Britain's revolution of 1688 was thus a pivotal event in the European and global history of state-making, giving substance to traditions of limited royal authority and mixed government that were fading or absent elsewhere.[16]

Montesquieu is frequently cited in the *Federalist Papers*, the publication in which the chief drafters of the US Constitution describe and defend their work. Even more telling is that the *Federalist* on a dozen occasions refers to the "science" of government or politics. *Federalist* 31 compares the principles of the science of government to those of mathematics, noting that while the latter posits "THE INFINITE DIVISIBILITY of matter ... even to the minutest atom," a principle that is widely accepted even if difficult to grasp, the "principles of moral and political knowledge" should be given similar acceptance. At another point, *Federalist* 9 describes the problem of creating a republican form of government in a large territory as "ENLARGEMENT of the ORBIT within which such systems are to revolve."[17] Such language borrowed from Newtonian science is not merely coincidence: Thomas Jefferson once identified Francis Bacon, John Locke and Isaac Newton as "the three greatest men that have ever lived, without any exception."[18]

It was not inevitable that the British colonies would seek to detach themselves from the British state. But it was almost inevitable that when they decided to do so, they would justify their actions in terms of recent works on the science of politics and society that, echoing the works of the scientific revolution, analyzed the authority of kings and the rights of men in terms of natural principles and analytical reasoning, and would find it easy to dismiss claims of divine royal authority.

The Declaration of Independence opens with a statement that "the Laws of Nature" entitle the colonies to claim an equal status to other countries, and recounts the acts of tyranny that King George III had committed against them. The Declaration, the *Federalist Papers* and the Constitution all provide the basis for a large territory to govern itself as a republic, with elected and separate branches of government, a limited executive and laws according to reason.

Yet, these documents are also redolent of the particular history and position of the colonies and of Great Britain. It was only with the more

---

[16] Steven Pincus, *1688: The First Modern Revolution* (New Haven, CT: Yale University Press, 2011).

[17] Emphasis in the original in both instances.

[18] For a fuller exposition of the argument that advances in scientific thought were essential to American political development, see Timothy Ferris, *The Science of Liberty: Democracy, Reason, and the Laws of Nature* (New York: Harper, 2011).

radical statement of Thomas Paine's *Common Sense* (1776) that the hereditary claims of all kings and nobles to power and position are condemned as contrary to reason. Nonetheless, the world viewed the American Revolution as an exceptional event, perhaps a natural experiment, to see if such a thing—a large diverse territory without a king, without a national religion and dominated by an elected legislature—was possible.

What followed were greater changes than anyone could have imagined. The very same year that the United States passed its Constitution, in 1787, a council of French notables was meeting to consider changes to the French monarchy's system of taxation. Having run up large debts in its European wars (including, ironically, fighting against Britain to aid the American colonies to achieve their independence), the French monarchy found it necessary to increase state revenues. However, direct taxation of the peasantry had reached its limits, as population growth, which had resumed in 1730, and rising rents had reduced the land and resources remaining in peasant hands. The richest sectors of late eighteenth-century French society were the commercial, urban, landowning and office-holding classes, who had historically enjoyed a variety of protections and privileges as regards taxation. Moreover, not all the regions of France were taxed equally, as customary rights and distinctions had impeded uniform taxation. The notables informed the Crown that they saw what needed to be done, but they could not change the regional and class-based provisions for tax relief, which were considered "property" attached to various kinds of ownership, without assaulting the liberty of those persons. Frustrated, the king called on the *parlement* of Paris to register tax reforms, but received the same reply. After a fruitless year of trying to pressure, bypass or restructure the *parlement* to gain their assent, and with the treasury empty and loans drying up, the king's ministers decided their only course was to call a meeting of the Estates-General. The Estates, which had not been called since 1614, had the virtue of representing the nobility, the Church and the common people of France, and thus would have the authority to guide the king on changing the laws of taxation and property without trampling on liberty. The date for their meeting was set for 1789.

Thus was put into motion a train of events that would eventually lead to debates over the role of nobility versus commoners in the Estates, and over the power of the Estates as a National Assembly to pass legislation without the consent of the king. Riots in Paris, civil and international war, the trial and execution of the king and queen and the creation of a republic all followed within five years. Although many predicted disaster, France not only moved ahead with the revolution, its armies—filled by mass conscription of citizens fighting for their rights and led by officers chosen for merit, not wealth or social rank—surged victorious across all of Europe. Led by General Napoleon Bonaparte, who in imitation of Roman models became first consul, then emperor, the Revolutionary regime established new legal codes, destroyed feudal and hereditary privileges, and spread the ideals of government by law and natural reason across Europe, with the *Declaration of the Rights of Man and Citizen* sounding refutations of principles of political authority that had prevailed around the world for thousands of years:

1. Men are born and remain free and equal in rights . . .

6. Law is the expression of the general will. Every citizen has a right to participate personally, or through his representative, in its foundation.

Certainly, such radical principles were not readily digested and did not immediately prevail. After French armies were decimated by a winter campaign in Russia and defeated by a grand coalition of British, Prussian and Russian forces, the Revolution was turned back and a monarch was restored to the French throne.

Yet, the French Revolution had unleashed forces that could not be contained. In order to provide the most competitive, efficient administrations and military officers, all Western powers had to reduce or eliminate hereditary rights to office and choose their officials on the basis of merit (although in this they were simply catching up to best practices that had been standard elsewhere in the world for centuries). The authority of the Catholic Church continued to be weakened by claims to individual freedom of conscience and the spread of Protestant congregations, as well as the proliferation of scientific advances. In 1830 and 1848, revolutions burst out across Europe demanding legislatures, citizenship rights and checks on state power. Although not successful in holding power, these revolutions further weakened the claims of absolutist rulers to legitimacy without popular consent, and by the end of the century, most European states had established legislatures and sought legitimacy by winning the support of their people.

In the Americas, the example of the United States was also powerful. When the French Revolutionary wars weakened Spain, the colonies of Mexico and South America rose in revolution to seek their independence, with most states achieving it by the 1820s.

By 1800, the combination of institutional backwardness (hold-over medieval parliaments and estates), the revival of republican ideals and stunning scientific discoveries that had undermined ancient authority had combined to spread in Europe and its American colonies an ideology of government based on natural laws and reason, designed to limit executive authority and protect individual liberty. Over the next two centuries, this ideal would transform state structures around the world.

Postscript: modern states, modern problems

The great empires of the Ottomans and China, and Japan, were at first only slightly affected by the momentous political changes in America and Europe. India did fall under British control in the late eighteenth century, but this was mainly because the Mughal Empire had already been profoundly weakened by the Maratha wars at the end of the seventeenth century. From that point on, the British were able to gain allies and financial support from states seeking to resist the Mughals, and pick at parts of the empire one at a time, starting in Bengal. With superior naval capacity, and local infantry trained to use European drill and flintlock muskets, the British were able to overcome the forces that any individual local Indian lord or ruler set against them, and the fragmenting Mughal territories quickly fell under their control.

The Ottomans, Chinese and Japanese, however, remained aloof. The latter two continued to restrict trade and contact with Europeans to a few specified trading ports. Even though Jesuit and Protestant missionaries brought information on Western astronomical, mathematical and scientific advances, these did not motivate the Asian elites to change their fundamental views on authority, statecraft or even the pursuit of knowledge. After all, Asian societies had their own sophisticated systems of medicine, engineering (for canals and roads), shipbuilding and manufacturing that were, up until the early nineteenth century, as good or better than anything offered by Europe.

The Ottomans were closer to Europe and were more deeply affected. In the early 1800s, ideals of liberty and national sovereignty began to penetrate into their Balkan possessions, setting off rebellions that eventually led to Greek independence in 1832. Also in the early 1800s, the Ottoman governor of Egypt, Muhammad Ali, set about building a more modern army and industrial base, and was able to expand his territory at the expense of the Ottoman sultan (although officially still recognizing the sultan's overlordship, it was nominal only). Eventually, as the sultans sought to incorporate more modernizing reforms in banking, industry, transport and training from Europe, military officers realized that the future of Turkey lay in building a modern, secular, Turkish national state, an ambition that was only realized after World War I.

The story of this chapter, which ends at 1800, is a story of pre-industrial state-building. For most of the period 1400 to 1800, it is a story of strengthening national states and cultural orthodoxy; yet, it ends with the small and once-isolated peninsula of Western Europe developing novel forms of state organization that would eventually overturn and replace that of much larger empires which had been successful for many centuries.

Most of that story of overturn and replacement, however, occurs after 1800, and is a story of state-building and resistance in an industrializing world. Steam and coal, factories, railways and iron gunships transformed state power, while new ideas of communism and capitalism, emerging from the experience of industrialization, changed the terms of state competition and debate. Slavery, women's rights and the shape of constitutional regimes remained difficult issues. New innovations in government, such as the party-state, provided new options for modern state-building, and twists on older ideas, such as the modernizing military-led regime, provided still others. In the industrial era, wars grew astonishingly more destructive, and international competition more intense. Traditional regimes modernized, embracing and adapting Western modes of finance, military, industrial, scientific, educational and diplomatic organization, or perished. The process is not yet entirely complete. But as of 2014, the great multinational empires led by hereditary rulers and elites have vanished; almost all nations claim legitimacy from national sovereignty and some form of democracy (however near or far they are from that ideal in practice), and we live in a world of territorial nation-states.

FURTHER READING

Ágoston, Gábor, *Guns for the Sultan: Military Power and the Weapons Industry in the Ottoman Empire* (Cambridge University Press, 2005).
Asher, Catherine B., *India before Europe* (Cambridge University Press, 2006).
Barkey, Karen, *Empire of Difference: The Ottomans in Comparative Perspective* (Cambridge University Press, 2008).
De Vries, Jan, *European Urbanization 1500–1800* (Cambridge, MA: Harvard University Press, 1984).
Eisenstadt, Shmuel N., "Multiple Modernities," *Daedalus* 129(1) (2000), 1–30.
Elman, Benjamin, *From Philosophy to Philology: Intellectual and Social Aspects of Change in Late Imperial China* (Los Angeles, CA: UCLA Asia Institute, 2001).
  On their Own Terms: Science in China, 1550–1900 (Cambridge, MA: Harvard University Press, 2005).
Elvin, Mark, *The Pattern of the Chinese Past* (Stanford University Press, 1973).
  The Retreat of the Elephants: An Environmental History of China (New Haven, CT: Yale University Press, 2004).

Ferris, Timothy, *The Science of Liberty: Democracy, Reason, and the Laws of Nature* (New York: Harper, 2011).

Goldstone, Jack A., "Efflorescences and Economic Growth in World History: Rethinking the 'Rise of the West' and the British Industrial Revolution," *Journal of World History* 13(2002), 323–89.

"The Problem of the 'Early Modern' World," *Journal of the Economic and Social History of the Orient* 41(1998), 249–84.

Revolution and Rebellion in the Early Modern World (Berkeley, CA: University of California Press, 1991).

Harkness, Deborah E., *The Jewel House: Elizabethan London and the Scientific Revolution* (New Haven, CT: Yale University Press, 2007).

Henry, John, *The Scientific Revolution and the Origins of Modern Science* (Houndmills, Basingstoke, UK: Palgrave-Macmillan, 2002).

Inalcik, Halil, Suraiya Faroqhi, Bruce McGowan, Donald Quataert and Sevket Pamuk, *An Economic and Social History of the Ottoman Empire, 1300–1914*, 2 vols. (Cambridge University Press, 1997).

Israel, Jonathan I., *Radical Enlightenment: Philosophy and the Making of Modernity 1650–1750* (New York: Oxford University Press, 2001).

Kang, David, *China before the West: Five Centuries of Trade and Tribute* (New York: Columbia University Press, 2010).

Lee, James Z. and Wang Feng, *One Quarter of Humanity: Malthusian Mythology and Chinese Reality 1700–2000* (Cambridge, MA: Harvard University Press, 2009).

Lieberman, Victor, *Strange Parallels: Southeast Asia in Global Context c. 800–1830*, 2 vols. (Cambridge University Press, 2003/09).

Lindberg, David C., *The Beginnings of Western Science*, 2nd edn. (University of Chicago Press, 2007).

Livi-Bacci, Massimo, *The Population of Europe* (Oxford: Blackwell, 2000).

McCloskey, Deidre, *The Bourgeois Virtues* (University of Chicago Press, 2007).

Mokyr, Joel, *The Enlightened Economy* (New Haven, CT: Yale University Press, 2009).

Parker, Geoffrey, *Global Crisis: War, Climate Change, and Catastrophe in the Seventeenth Century* (New Haven, CT: Yale University Press, 2013).

Perdue, Peter, *China Marches West: The Qing Conquest of Central Eurasia* (Cambridge, MA: Harvard University Press, 2005).

Pincus, Steven, *1688: The First Modern Revolution* (New Haven, CT: Yale University Press, 2011).

Pocock, J. G. A., *The Machiavellian Moment: Florentine Political Thought and the Atlantic Republican Tradition* (Princeton University Press, 1975).

Pomeranz, Kenneth, *The Great Divergence: China, Europe, and the Making of the Modern World Economy* (Princeton University Press, 2000).

Rawski, Evelyn, *The Last Emperors: A Social History of Qing Imperial Institutions* (Berkeley, CA: University of California Press, 2001).

Richards, J. F., *The Mughal Empire* (Cambridge University Press, 1995).

Riello, Giorgio, *Cotton: The Fabric that Made the Modern World* (Cambridge University Press, 2013).

Robertson, John, *The Case for Enlightenment: Scotland and Naples 1680–1760* (Cambridge University Press, 2005).

Saliba, George, *Islamic Science and the Making of the European Renaissance* (Cambridge, MA: MIT Press, 2007).

Shapin, Steven, *The Scientific Revolution* (University of Chicago Press, 1998).

Subrahmanyan, Sanjay, *Merchant Networks in the Modern World* (Aldershot: Variorum, 1996).

Subrahmanyan, Sanjay and Muzaffar Alam (eds.), *The Mughal State 1526–1750* (Delhi: Oxford University Press, 1998).

Tilly, Charles, *Coercion, Capital, and European States AD 990–1992* (Oxford: Blackwell, 1992).

Wong, R. Bin, *China Transformed* (Ithaca, NY: Cornell University Press, 1997).

Zagorin, Perez, *How the Idea of Religious Toleration Came to the West* (Princeton University Press, 2005).

Index